IDEALS AND IDEOLOGIES

A READER

PRAISE FOR THE TENTH EDITION

An anthology of classic readings, *Ideals and Ideologies* has itself become a classic. This is a textbook, but it is also a deep reflection on and of our political world. Introducing students to the powerful ideas that have mobilized and inspired political actors and causes across the contemporary landscape, it is a wonderful teaching tool and useful reference guide. Chosen for accessibility as well as significance, and updated with important and timely new voices, each reading is expertly introduced by the editors. This latest edition maintains the high standards one has come to expect from Ball, Dagger, and O'Neill.

Simone Chambers, *University of California-Irvine, USA*

This comprehensive, up-to-date, judicious selection of sources reveals alternative ideologies in their contexts and especially as practically applied in American discourse and policy. An important collection with concise introductions, edited by some of the most informed American teachers and scholars of political theory and political thought, it is well-suited for student use and for anyone seeking to make sense of the evolution of conflicting worldviews and their consequences.

Janet Coleman, *London School of Economics, UK*

The leading introductory textbook in political theory for good reason, *Ideals and Ideologies* continues to provide the accessibility and clarity demanded by students without sacrificing the richness and rigor desired by faculty. The tenth edition maintains the hallmarks of the previous versions: a comprehensive yet manageable collection, featuring classic statements alongside less orthodox voices and visions, all updated with new "-isms" and thinkers for the contemporary reader, who will appreciate the insightful introductions, helpful annotations, and modernized translations.

Robert W.T. Martin, *Hamilton College, USA*

This long-essential reader continues to demonstrate the relevance of political ideologies for the present. Combining classic texts in the history of political thought with decisive declarations and manifestos, the most recent edition invites study of new texts from Krugman, Sanders, hooks, and Pope Francis as well as the Manhattan Declaration and ISIS's Declaration of a Caliphate.

Michaelle L. Browers, *Wake Forest University, USA*

IDEALS AND IDEOLOGIES

A READER

TENTH EDITION

TERENCE BALL

Arizona State University

RICHARD DAGGER

University of Richmond

DANIEL I. O'NEILL

University of Florida

Routledge
Taylor & Francis Group

NEW YORK AND LONDON

Tenth edition published 2017
by Routledge
711 Third Avenue, New York, NY 10017

and by Routledge
2 Park Square, Milton Park, Abingdon, Oxon, OX14 4RN

Routledge is an imprint of the Taylor & Francis Group, an informa business

Seventh edition published by Pearson Education, Inc., 2009
Eighth edition published by Pearson Education, Inc., 2011
Ninth edition published by Pearson Education, Inc. 2014, and Routledge, 2016

Library of Congress Cataloging in Publication Data
Names: Ball, Terence, editor. | Dagger, Richard, editor. | O'Neill, Daniel L, editor.
Title: Ideals and ideologies : a reader / editors, Terence Ball, Arizona State University, Richard Dagger, University of Richmond, Daniel L. O'Neill, University of Florida.
Description: Tenth edition. | New York, NY : Routledge is an imprint of the Taylor & Francis Group, an Informa Business, [2017]
Identifiers: LCCN 2016008737| ISBN 9781138650022 (hardback) | ISBN 9781138650039 (pbk.) | ISBN 9781315625546 (ebook)
Subjects: LCSH: Political science--History. | Ideology. | Right and left (Political science)
Classification: LCC JA81 .I34 2017 | DDC 320.5--dc23
LC record available at https://lccn.loc.gov/2016008737

ISBN: 978-1-138-65002-2 (hbk)
ISBN: 978-1-138-65003-9 (pbk)
ISBN: 978-1-315-62554-6 (ebk)

Typeset in Galliard
by Saxon Graphics Ltd, Derby

To

Jonathan and Stephen Ball

and

Emily and Elizabeth Dagger

and

Cassidy and Jackson O'Neill

CONTENTS

Part 4   Conservatism 187

Part 5   Socialism and Communism: From More to Marx 247

PREFACE TO THE TENTH EDITION

More than twenty-five years ago we decided to collect readings from primary sources into an anthology for courses in political ideologies and modern political thought. We knew that we faced difficult choices—what to put in, what to leave out—but we believed that we could compile a set of readings that would be comprehensive and rigorous enough to meet instructors' standards while satisfying students' desires for a readable and reasonably accessible "reader." The fact that we are now issuing a tenth edition of this book suggests that our belief was not ill-founded. Since the sociopolitical world keeps changing, the thrust and contents of this anthology must change, too, and this tenth edition is no exception to that rule.

NEW TO THIS EDITION

The tenth edition includes the following additions:

- Paul Krugman, "The Conscience of a Liberal" (A distinguished Nobel Laureate's defense of liberalism as a kind of rational conservatism, inasmuch as it seeks to conserve the gains and reforms of the New Deal and the Great Society—Social Security, Medicare, minority voting rights, environmental protection, and more.)

- Robert George, et al., "Manhattan Declaration: A Call of Christian Conscience" (The authors and signers of this 2009 declaration contend that the secularizing of America has gone too far and that Christians must work to reverse this trend.)

- Bernie Sanders, "On Democratic Socialism in the United States" (The fiery candidate for the 2016 Democratic presidential nomination, who calls himself a "democratic socialist," offers an unapologetic defense of his creed.)

- bell hooks, "Feminism is for Everybody" (A distinguished feminist theorist and author argues that feminism isn't only for or about women, but benefits everyone.)

- Val Plumwood, "Feminism and the Mastery of Nature" (An eminent Australian ecofeminist emphasizes what feminists bring to the debate over human beings' role in and relationship with nature.)

- Vine Deloria, Jr., "On Liberation" (A prominent Native American author and thinker outlines his vision of native peoples liberation.)
- Pope Francis, "*Laudato Si*": On Care for our Common Home" (The current Pope's pleas for Christians and others to address climate change and other environmental issues.)
- Abu Bakr al-Baghdadi, "Declaration of a Caliphate" (The radical Islamist leader or *caliph* of Islamic State [ISIS] announces the creation of a spiritual and geographic home for all "true" Muslims.)

FEATURES

As in the previous editions, we have been guided by our sense that an ideal anthology for this subject would combine four features. First, it would present a wide range of alternative ideological visions: right, left, middle, and unorthodox. Second, it would include a generous sampling of key thinkers in the different ideological traditions, old and new alike. Third, an ideal anthology would, when necessary, modernize the prose of thinkers long dead. Fourth, and finally, it would supply the student with some sense of the intellectual and political context within which these thinkers thought and wrote.

In this tenth edition of *Ideals and Ideologies* we have tried once again to satisfy these four criteria. First, we have attempted to cover the broad canvas of contemporary political ideologies, from the standard categories of liberalism-conservatism-fascism-socialism to a broader range of newly emerging ideological alternatives. Among these are the "liberation" ideologies, including indigenous or native peoples' liberation, an ecological or "green" ideology, and the ideology of radical Islamism. Second, we have tried to supply a fairly generous and reasonably representative sample of alternative ideological views, including those not represented in any other anthology. Third, we have, wherever possible, simplified the prose of older thinkers—in several instances providing our own translations of works not written in English. And finally, we have provided brief introductions and added explanatory notes to place these selections and their authors in their political and historical contexts.

We have tried, in short, to supply the student with an accessible and readable anthology of original sources. The end result does not necessarily make for easy reading. But, as we remind our students, the old adage "No pain, no gain" applies to the building not only of muscles, but also of minds. We have merely attempted to remove some of the unnecessary strain from a profitable, if sometimes taxing, exercise.

The present volume is paired with the new tenth edition of our *Political Ideologies and the Democratic Ideal*, also published by Routledge. Although each book stands alone, each complements and can be used in combination with the other.

We should note, finally, that many of the readings included here easily fall under more than one heading. For example, Franklin D. Roosevelt's 1932 Commonwealth Club Address could as easily fit into Part 2 (The Democratic Ideal) as under Part 3 (Liberalism). And black liberation theologian James H. Cone's

"Whose Earth Is It, Anyway?" could as well be included in Part 8 (Liberation Ideologies) as in Part 9 (Green Politics). There are, in short, many combinations, and many ways to use this book. But whatever the preferred combination may be, the aim is always the same: to convey to the student-citizen a vivid sense of the centrality and ongoing importance of ideas, ideals, and ideologies in modern politics.

This text is available in a variety of formats—digital and print. To learn more about Routledge programs, pricing options, and customization, visit www.routledge.com.

ACKNOWLEDGMENTS

In preparing this new edition, we had the benefit of detailed and thoughtful reviews from the following scholars, whom we wish to thank here: Dilshod Achilov, East Tennessee State University; Robert Brem, College of Alameda and CSU—East Bay; Ralph Carter, Texas Christian University; Nicholas Damask, Scottsdale Community College; Gretchen Knudson Gee, Northern Arizona University; and Patrizia Longo, St. Mary's College of California. We would also like to give special thanks to Zhipei Chi (Renmin University Beijing), Anna Brailovsky (University of Minnesota), and Lina Benabdallah (University of Florida) for their new translations of works by Mao Zedong, V. I. Lenin, and Sayyid Qutb, respectively.

ABOUT THE EDITORS

TERENCE BALL received his Ph.D. from the University of California at Berkeley and is Emeritus Professor of Political Science and Philosophy at Arizona State University. He taught previously at the University of Minnesota and has held visiting professorships at Oxford University, Cambridge University, and the University of California, San Diego. His books include *Transforming Political Discourse* (Blackwell, 1988), *Reappraising Political Theory* (Oxford University Press, 1995), and a mystery novel, *Rousseau's Ghost* (SUNY Press, 1998). He has also edited *The Federalist* (Cambridge University Press, 2003), *James Madison* (Ashgate, 2008), *Abraham Lincoln: Political Writings and Speeches* (Cambridge University Press, 2013), and coedited *The Cambridge History of Twentieth-Century Political Thought* (Cambridge University Press, 2003).

RICHARD DAGGER earned his Ph.D. from the University of Minnesota and has taught at Arizona State University and Rhodes College, and the University of Richmond, where he is currently the E. Claiborne Robins Distinguished Chair in the Liberal Arts. He is the author of many publications in political and legal philosophy, including *Civic Virtues: Rights, Citizenship, and Republican Liberalism* (Oxford University Press, 1997), and the forthcoming *Playing Fair: Political Obligation and the Problem of Punishment* (Oxford University Press).

DANIEL I. O'NEILL received his Ph.D. from the University of California, Los Angeles, and is currently associate professor of political science at the University of Florida. He is the author of *The Burke-Wollstonecraft Debate: Savagery, Civilization, and Democracy* (Penn State University Press, 2007), coeditor of *Illusion of Consent: Engaging with Carole Pateman* (Penn State University Press, 2008), and author, most recently, of *Edmund Burke and the Conservative Logic of Empire* (University of California Press, 2016).

INTRODUCTION

The world in which we live continues to be shaped and scarred by political ideologies. Indeed, the truth of the old saying "ideas have consequences" must now be evident to everyone. And the most consequential are those embedded in those systems of ideas called *ideologies*. It was, in reality, ideas that toppled the Twin Towers in New York City and brought down two other hijacked airliners on September 11, 2001; the terrorists were merely the carriers or agents of the ideas—the ideology—that motivated them. The same is true of the Boston Marathon bombings in 2013, the Russian airliner bombed by ISIS in 2015, the deadly terrorist attacks in Paris and Mali and California in 2015, and many others elsewhere. The Great Recession that began in 2007 exposed and deepened divisions between those who believe that government has a duty to regulate the economy and those who hold that government "interference" in markets is dangerous and counterproductive. For better or for worse, the twenty-first century, like the one that preceded it, is a century of ideas—and particularly of those clusters or systems of ideas called "ideologies." These ideologies have raised hopes, inspired fear, and drawn blood from millions of human beings. To study political ideologies, then, is not to undertake a merely "academic" study. It is to dissect and analyze the tissue of our times.

During the second decade of the twenty-first century, some ideologies, such as the Marxist-Leninist version of socialism, are clearly in eclipse, while others—such as radical Islamism and a newly emerging ecological or "green" ideology—appear to be gaining in influence and importance. Yet, despite their differences, these ideologies are similar in at least one respect: they all have their histories. All, that is, have emerged out of particular historical contexts and have changed in response to changing conditions and circumstances. And all have been formed from the ideas of thinkers old and new. As the economist John Maynard Keynes observed in the 1930s, when Benito Mussolini, Adolf Hitler, and Joseph Stalin all held power, "madmen in authority, who hear voices in the air, are distilling their frenzy from some academic scribbler of a few years back."

This book is about, and by, those "academic scribblers"—and a number of those "madmen in authority" as well. Their ideas have formed the ideologies and fueled the conflicts that shaped and reshaped the political landscape of the twentieth—and now the twenty-first—century. We live in the shadow, and under the influence, of these scribblers and madmen. To be ignorant of their influence is not to escape it. By tracing modern ideologies back to their original sources, we can see more clearly how our own outlooks—and those of our enemies—have been shaped by earlier thinkers. To return to and read these authors is to gain some insight into the shaping of the modern political mind—or rather minds, plural, since ideological disagreement continues unabated.

Some modern commentators have claimed—wrongly, we believe—that ideological disagreements are at last coming to an end. The age of ideology, they say, is over. As evidence, they cite the end of the Cold War, the emancipation of Eastern Europe, the collapse of the Soviet Union, and the democratizing of former dictatorships. Important as they are, however, these events do not presage "the end of ideology." Rather, they suggest that ours is an age of important ideological realignments. Marxism–Leninism may be dead in Eastern Europe and the former Soviet Union, but other versions of it linger on in the politics of China, Vietnam, North Korea, and Cuba. Radical Islamism is increasingly influential in the Middle East, Southeast Asia, and elsewhere. And, of course, ideological conflict persists as conservatives, liberals, and socialists continue to disagree with one another, animal liberationists fight for animal rights, gays for gay rights, and Greens campaign to protect the environment. The worldwide financial crisis that began in 2007 cast grave doubt on the deregulation of markets championed by libertarians and modern conservatives whose movements are, for the moment at least, in partial eclipse. Other movements, motivated by other ideologies, are poised to challenge and perhaps replace them.

Like it or not, in short, ours is likely to remain an age of ideological diversity and disagreement. Anyone who hopes to understand this diversity and disagreement will benefit, we believe, from a careful reading of the selections that follow, which provide a generous sampling of some of the writings that have helped to form the ideologically varied political terrain of the small planet on which we dwell together, if not always, alas, in peace and harmony.

Terence Ball
Richard Dagger
Daniel I. O'Neill

PART 1

THE CONCEPT OF IDEOLOGY

That ideologies and ideological conflict have persisted throughout modern history should come as no surprise to anyone. Ideologies are born of crisis and feed on conflict. People need help to comprehend and cope with turbulent times and confusing circumstances, and—for better or worse—ideologies provide this help. An ideology does this by performing four important and perhaps indispensable functions for those who subscribe to it. First, it *explains* political phenomena that would otherwise remain mysterious or puzzling. Why are there wars and rumors of war? Why are there conflicts between nations, between classes, and between races? What causes depressions? The answer that one gives to these, and to many other, questions depends to some degree on one's ideology. A Marxian socialist will answer one way, a fascist another, and a feminist yet another.

Second, an ideology provides its adherents with criteria and standards of *evaluation*—of deciding what is right and wrong, good and bad. Are class differences and vast disparities of wealth good or bad things? Is interracial harmony possible, and, if so, is it desirable? Is censorship permissible, and, if so, under what conditions? Again, the answers one gives will depend on which ideology one subscribes to.

Third, an ideology *orients* its adherents, giving them a sense of who they are and where they belong—a social and cultural compass with which to define and affirm their individual and collective identity. Fascists, for example, will typically think of themselves as members of a superior nation or race. Communists will see themselves as people who defend the working class against capitalist oppression and exploitation. Animal liberationists will identify themselves as defenders of animals that are unable to protect themselves against human abuse and exploitation.

Fourth and finally, an ideology supplies its adherents with a rudimentary political *program*. This program provides an answer to the question posed by the Russian revolutionary Lenin, among many others: What is to be done? And, no less important: Who is to do it? With what means? A Marxist-Leninist, for instance, will answer these questions as follows: The working class must be emancipated from capitalist exploitation by means of a revolution led by a vanguard party. Fascists, feminists, Greens, liberals, conservatives, and others will, of course, propose other—and very different—programs of political action.

To summarize, a political ideology is a more or less systematic set of ideas that performs four functions for those who hold it: the explanatory, the evaluative, the orientative, and the programmatic functions. By performing these functions, an ideology serves as a guide and compass through the thicket of political life.

There are, as we shall see, many different political ideologies in the modern world. But what of democracy? Is it an ideology? In our view, democracy is not an ideology but an *ideal* that different ideologies interpret in different ways. For the ancient Greeks, who coined the word, democracy [*demos-kratein*] meant rule by, and in the interest of, the common people. In the modern world, some Marxists have insisted that a "people's democracy" in which the leaders of a revolutionary party rule in the name of the masses is the best way to serve the interests of the common people. For liberals, however, democracy means "liberal democracy"—that is, majority rule, but with ample provision for the protection of minority rights. For most modern environmentally oriented Greens, democracy means decentralized "participatory" or "grassroots" democracy. Other ideologies interpret the democratic ideal in other ways. Democracy, then, is an ideal that most ideologies claim to strive for, but it is an ideal whose meaning they vigorously contest.

As with "democracy," so too with "freedom." What "freedom" means for liberals is something quite different from what it means for fascists, for example. We can see this more clearly by thinking of freedom (or liberty) as a triadic or three-sided relation among an *agent*, a *goal*, and any *obstacle* standing between the agent and the goal that he, she, or they seek to achieve. We represent this relationship in the following diagram (Figure 1.1).

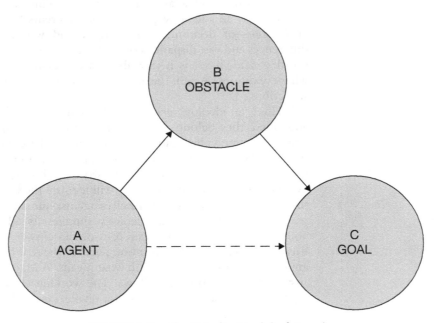

FIGURE 1.1 The Triadic Model of Freedom

Every ideology identifies the three elements of the triad in its own way. A liberal will typically identify the agent as an individual, the goal as the satisfaction of an individual's own preferences or desires, and the obstacle as any unreasonable restraint or restriction on such "want satisfaction." A Marxist, by contrast, will characteristically identify the agent as an entire class—the working class or "proletariat"—that struggles to overcome capitalist exploitation in order to achieve a classless communist society. A fascist will conceive of the agent as a whole nation or race attempting to overcome so-called "inferior" nations or races in a collective search for racial or national supremacy and purity. And other ideologies conceive of freedom in still other ways. Understanding how they conceive of freedom is, in fact, one of the best ways to understand the differences that separate any political ideology from its ideological rivals.

Ideology:
The Career of a Concept

TERRELL CARVER*

The concept of ideology has undergone dramatic changes in meaning since the term *ideologie* was first coined in late eighteenth-century France. In the following essay, the Anglo-American political theorist Terrell Carver (1946–) traces these changes, concluding with a critical consideration of the ways in which the term "ideology" is used today.

---

* *Source*: This essay was written expressly for *Ideals and Ideologies*.

IDEOLOGY: THE CAREER OF A CONCEPT

As a coined word, the term "ideology" has a precise origin in the era of the French Revolution. The decisive shifts in its meaning, moreover, have been associated with some of the most colorful and influential figures in modern history—Napoleon Bonaparte (1769–1821), Karl Marx (1818–1883), Friedrich Engels (1820–1895), and V. I. Lenin (1870–1924). From its very inception, in fact, ideology has been associated with highly abstract philosophy and forceful, even brutal, political repression.

Behind the term "ideology" are the familiar features of politics—ideas and power. Philosophers have not been conspicuous for their participation in politics, but through the actions of others they have been influential at times. Improving the connection between philosopher and politician to extend this influence was one of the main concerns of Antoine Louis Claude Destutt, Comte de Tracy (1754–1836), one of the Enlightenment *philosophes*. De Tracy coined the term "ideology" during the wild revolutionary decade in France when ideas inspired many thousands to test their powers in politics and to put their immediate material interests, even lives, at risk. Although the substance of de Tracy's thought drew on the specific philosophies of Étienne Bonnot de Condillac (1715–1780) and John Locke (1632–1704), among others, his work was explicitly directed toward political action. He assumed that criteria for the truth and falsity of ideas could be established and definitively employed, and that there was a point to doing so. That point was overtly political.

De Tracy and his colleagues aimed to promote progress in all areas of human endeavor, theoretical and practical, by reforming elite and middle-class opinion. Their Institut de France was established by the Convention in 1795 to disseminate higher learning as the *savants* of the revolution defined it. Their work began with three assumptions: that progress in social life is desirable; that progress comes only from correct ideas; and that incorrect ideas must be resisted, especially in the schools. In opposition to the traditions of the Catholic Church and to the personal authority of anointed monarchs, de Tracy and his colleagues in the Institut favored the ideals of the new science associated with Francis Bacon (1561–1626), Galileo Galilei (1564–1642), Réne Descartes (1596–1650), and other thinkers who espoused rational inquiry into the natural and social world. The rationalism of the Institut was especially hostile to religious thought if conceived mystically.

In 1796 a British commentator reported that de Tracy had read a paper at the Institut in which he proposed to call the philosophy of mind "ideology." Five years later, in his *Elements of Ideology* (1801; translated into English by Thomas Jefferson for an edition of 1817), de Tracy summarized the results of his logic within a "plan of the elements of ideology ... to give a complete knowledge of our intellectual faculties, and to deduce from that knowledge the first principles of all other branches of our knowledge." Without these first principles "our knowledge" could "never be founded on any other solid base."[1] With correct ideas would come a correct psychology or theory of human behavior, and with that the justification for such political prescriptions as intellectuals might devise and enlightened politicians might enforce.

De Tracy's system, while sweeping, was disarmingly simplistic, dismissive of skepticism, and surprisingly concise. Even at the time it must have raised some strong doubts among philosophers. Indeed, the association of ideology with intellectual shortcuts, oversimplification, and distortion seems inherent in de Tracy's original conception. That de Tracy also associated his ideology with a political program and authoritarian politics provides further clues to the way the concept has functioned since his day.

There are three important features of de Tracy's conception of ideology: (1) the explicit linkage between logic, psychology, and politics, set down in a "table" of simple propositions and backed up with more extensive observations; (2) the assumption that intellectuals discover the truth and that well-advised political authorities implement policies to match; and (3) the claim that logic, psychology, and politics, as linked, are coincident with science and history, properly understood.

In 1797 Napoleon Bonaparte, the leading general of the revolutionary army, became an honorary member of the Institut, and his fellow "ideologues" supported the *coup d'état* by which he seized power in 1799. With their boundless faith in reason, the "ideologues," de Tracy amongst them, expected to achieve the same success in psychology, morality, social and economic relations, and politics that the new "natural philosophers" had achieved in studying planetary and terrestrial motion, optics, and mathematics. Such was their certainty that they committed themselves to an administrative structure to promote their ideas and to discourage what they termed prejudices—and with that they necessarily engaged in politics. As their concept of truth presupposed the authority of the intellectual (validated by the "correct" assumptions and methods), so their politics created no great obstacles to authoritarian rule—provided, of course, that the authority had proper intellectual guidance. There was little in the doctrines of the "ideologues" to favor the unenlightened intellect or to afford it any great role in decision making. Because politics was supposed to be subject to the new science, democracy with its popular decision making would have little to recommend itself to the Enlightenment intellectual unless it were properly guided. Tutoring rulers was obviously the easier and more immediately efficacious task. With Napoleon a member of the Institut, furthermore, the "ideologues" could expect enlightenment and progress to spread all the more quickly throughout France and beyond its borders. The forces of reaction were to be swept away by the enlightened use of political power as the resources of the state were made available to the intellectual elite.

The crucial event in the development of the concept of ideology came when Napoleon turned against the "ideologues" and decisively reversed their interpretation of the proper relationship between intellectuals and rulers, philosophers and politicians. Around 1812 he dismissed de Tracy's work and the work of the Institut de France as "ideology, that sinister metaphysics." This hostility to the "ideologues" apparently reflected a shift in Napoleon's political tactics—from alliance with the rationalists of the Institut against religion and the Church, to the reverse. Eradicating what the "ideologues" saw as prejudice was politically costly, and Napoleon sought to increase his personal power by making peace with the Church and allying himself with other conservative forces.[2]

About thirty years later the German Communist Karl Marx seized on "ideology" as a term of abuse. He criticized German intellectuals whose philosophy and politics displeased him by dismissing them as "ideologists," proponents of "the German ideology." He and Friedrich Engels coauthored a manuscript of that name which remained unpublished as a whole until 1932, though sections of the large work appeared in excerpts from 1903 onward.[3] In other published works that circulated during his lifetime and in his private correspondence, Marx used the term "ideology" in ways that drew on the more extensive airing he had given the concept in *The German Ideology*.

Ideologies and ideologists arise in class-divided societies, according to Marx. In particular, "the class which has the means of material production at its disposal consequently also controls the means of mental production." Thinkers are "producers of ideas," in other words, while ruling classes regulate "the production and distribution of the ideas of their age." Thus "the ideas of the ruling class are in every epoch the ruling ideas: i.e., the class which is the ruling *material* force of society is at the same time its ruling *intellectual* force." Within the ruling class the division of labor divides mental from material tasks, so that:

> Inside this class one part appears as the thinkers of the class (its active, conceptualizing ideologists, who make the formation of the illusions of the class about itself their chief source of livelihood), while the other's attitude to these ideas and illusions is more passive and receptive, because they are in reality the active members of this class and have less time to make up illusions and ideas about themselves.[4]

The German ideology was to be explained, Marx argued, "from its connection with the illusion of ideologists in general, e.g., the illusions of the jurists, politicians (including practical statesmen), from the dogmatic dreamings and distortions of these fellows." All those illusions and distortions were "explained perfectly easily from their practical position in life, their job, and the division of labour."[5] In this realm of jobs and economic activity Marx introduced a notion of material interest which made illusions demonstrably functional for some individuals and classes in societies as they pursued economic advantages for themselves at others' expense. Some of these useful illusions were dressed up as claims about nature or God—for example, "some people are slaves by nature," "God made woman to serve man"—and some were more elaborately cloaked in a universalism that Marx dismissed as spurious. He argued, for example, that the "rights of man and the citizen" proclaimed in the French Revolution ultimately worked for the benefit of owners of private property at the expense of workers, who had no property to sell but their own labor. Thus in Marx's analysis an ideology came to mean not just a body of ideas that conformed to certain formal characteristics, such as those of de Tracy's system, but any ideas, however unsophisticated, that gave apparent validity and assumed authority to the claims that members of different classes might make when they pursued their various interests. Those who characteristically made such claims were deemed "ideologists"; others merely repeated in their speech or reflected in their behavior an "ideology."

In Marx's view ideologies could be reactionary, conservative, reformist, or revolutionary, depending on the way that material interests (typically the use and control of resources, goods, and services) were pursued by individuals and then protected socially and politically. In keeping with his depiction of history as the history of class struggles—now hidden, now open, Marx defined ideologies as the "legal, political, religious, aesthetic or philosophic—in short, ideological—forms" in which people become conscious of class conflict "and fight it out."[6] In that way, "the existence of revolutionary ideas in a particular period," he wrote, "presupposes the existence of a revolutionary class."[7]

Marx thus extended de Tracy's term "ideology" to cover ideas that reflected, and were somehow useful in pursuing, the material interests of classes. But his own work was supposed to identify, explain, and promote working-class interests in current political struggles. It might seem, therefore, to be ideological itself. Marx did not refer to his work in those terms, however, or to the pursuit of working-class politics as requiring an ideology. He identified the working class as a revolutionary class, but one distinguished from previous revolutionary classes in that it was becoming a majority and already expressed "the dissolution of all classes, nationalities etc., within present society."[8] A revolutionary class was to overthrow a ruling class, as had already happened many times, but with the *proletarian* revolution would come the abolition of class society altogether. This could happen, Marx said, because the interest of the proletariat coincides with the interests of all individuals "as individuals."[9]

Marx's arguments for the proletariat's abolition of class-divided society are sketchy and unconvincing, but they are quite distinct from the views he described as ideological. His communism, and the theory behind it, were not ideologies on his definition, because the formal properties and political reference were profoundly different. Instead, Marx considered his work to be scientific, taking due regard for the historical character of the social phenomena under investigation. It was also supposed to have political significance in the struggle for socialism. But it was not formally identical to the pattern for an "ideology" established by de Tracy because there was no Marxian logic and psychology from which his politics were deduced. Rather he worked from a less comprehensive conception, that of economic activity ("so-called material interests"), toward prescriptions that could be useful, so he argued, in proletarian politics.[10] The role of the theoretically informed individual or group was said, in the *Communist Manifesto* and elsewhere, to be advisory, not authoritative. Marx contemptuously dismissed sects and other ways in which ideals were supposed to be imposed on people so that reality could be created, in a sense, by ideas. Communism, he claimed, was a "real movement" already in existence, to which his science was intended to contribute.[11]

Friedrich Engels was the architect of a Marxism that fitted the formal requirements of an ideology, though he himself dismissed ideology all too simplistically as mere "false consciousness," a phrase not used by Marx.[12] While he did not term Marx's work an ideology, but a science—namely, "scientific socialism"—Engels elaborated a view that Marx's science had specified fundamental laws of dialectics in the realm of "thought" (presumably a protopsychology), in the development of human behavior in history, and in the matter-in-motion of the universe itself. Engels's widely circulated *Anti-Dühring* (1878) advertised those pretensions, producing extended discussions of historical and contemporary economic development that were supposed to substantiate his claims for a materialistic dialectic in logic. These were repeated in his later *Ludwig Feuerbach and the End of Classical German*

Philosophy (1888) and the posthumously published *Dialectics of Nature* (1925), edited from notebooks largely contemporary with *Anti-Dühring*.

Whether Marx shared Engels's views is a matter of controversy.[13] There is no explicit endorsement of them in his works. Indeed, as I am arguing here, the way that Marx identified such logico-deductive constructions as "ideological" suggests that he could not have agreed with Engels's views without major inconsistency.

Thus Marx's followers did their best to make his ideas fit the formal and political definitions of ideology that Marx himself had applied to other systems of ideas. In doing so his followers seemed to undermine the pejorative connotations of the term. This introduced an obvious contradiction between Marx's own consistently pejorative usage with respect to German ideologists and other apologists for the ruling classes, on the one hand, and his followers' use of the term in an approving sense, on the other, to identify his work as a comprehensive system that promoted the interests of one particular class in society—the working class. This working-class or proletarian "ideology" was a science, Marx's followers said, precisely because it was a body of thought reflecting proletarian interests. As a result we have Marxism identified by Soviet philosophers and many others as a "scientific ideology"—a contradiction in terms from Marx's own point of view.

The Russian revolutionary Lenin (pseudonym for Vladimir Ilyich Ulyanov) followed Engels in identifying Marxism as a comprehensive science derived from an abstract logic, thus accepting it formally as an ideology. While this identification was merely tacit in Engels's case, Lenin made it specific and went one stage further in his highly influential *What Is to Be Done?* (1902). Citing Engels on the necessity for political, economic, and theoretical struggle in pursuing working-class interests, Lenin concluded very generally and with particular reference to Russia that "without revolutionary theory there can be no revolutionary practice." "Modern socialist consciousness," he wrote, "can only arise on the basis of profound scientific knowledge."[14]

Lenin identified this science as "socialist ideology" and claimed that the only political choice available in his time was between the bourgeois ideology and the socialist one. He thus defined ideologies as doctrines reflecting class interests that were in some sense products of theoretical thinking, not the commonplace consciousness of class members themselves. For the working class this was crucial in Lenin's eyes, because he viewed them as likely victims of bourgeois ideology (or unwitting servants of it via "trade union consciousness"), unless socialist intellectuals and party workers, using the "socialist ideology," awakened the workers to the "irreconcilable antagonism of their interests to the whole of the modern political and social system."[15] On this view it was a matter of fact that science served proletarian interests because it revealed the true character of class antagonism in capitalist society, the very truth that bourgeois ideology had veiled in illusions, such as "self-help," "parliamentary democracy," "market forces," and so on.

Presumably Lenin's use of "ideology" to include science, as well as the interest-serving mystifications Marx had loosely identified as ideologies, was a kind of shorthand. Lenin conceived of a "scientific ideology" opposed to unscientific ones, all serving different class interests. In that political sense—ideology as ideas serving class interests—Lenin made Marxism ideological. By the early twentieth century, then, ideology had wandered in meaning from a science of ideas, to a sinister metaphysics, to class-serving illusions, to false consciousness as opposed to scientific socialism, to scientific socialism as one ideology competing with others.

The "science" within the socialism of Engels and Lenin was very vulnerable to criticism, as the first principles of their dialectical materialism were incomplete and unconvincing. But the insight, derived ultimately from Marx, that ideas serve the interests of individuals, groups, and classes, and that individuals, groups, and classes often generate and defend the ideas that do this, has made a systematic sociology of consciousness possible. This project was set out by the German sociologist Karl Mannheim (1893–1947), who explained that the principal thesis of his "sociology of knowledge" is that there are modes of thought which cannot be adequately understood as long as their social origins are obscured. In his view the study of these "ideologies" involves unmasking the more or less conscious deceptions and disguises of interest groups, particularly those of political parties.[16] For Mannheim "ideology" was a name for two related conceptions which he distinguished as "particular" and "total":

> The particular conception of ideology is implied when the term denotes that we are skeptical of the ideas and representations advanced by our opponent. They are regarded as more or less conscious disguises of the real nature of a situation, the true recognition of which would not be in accord with his interests.

"This conception of ideology," wrote Mannheim, "has only gradually become differentiated from the commonsense notion of the lie." It was "particular" by comparison with the more inclusive "total" conception of ideology: "Here we refer to the ideology of an age or of a concrete historico-social group, e.g., of a class, when we are concerned with the characteristics and composition of the total structure of the mind of this epoch or of this group."[17]

Mannheim argued that this total conception of ideology raised the problem of "false consciousness" as "the totally distorted mind which falsified everything." The possibility that our whole conception of reality might be systematically distorted and continuously distorting had "a special significance and relevance for the understanding of our social life." From the awareness of this possibility arose a "profound disquietude" which Mannheim felt very deeply.[18]

De Tracy confidently described his ideology, a general grammar and logic, as a science, about whose methods, truth, and timelessness he had no doubts. Since the time of the *philosophes* confidence has given way to skepticism, and the term "ideology" has reflected this exactly. When there was certainty about truth and science, a new word, "ideology," was coined. This fell victim to a vengeful politics when Napoleon dismissed it as "sinister metaphysics," and the term came to stand for illusion as opposed to science. Because of Marx's attacks on the elitism of the philosopher-politicians and his pithy theorizing on the origins of ideas in class-divided societies, the concept has almost become synonymous with ax-grinding. Engels's "scientific socialism" and Lenin's "proletarian ideology" reincarnate de Tracy's confidence, but to less than universal satisfaction, as modern skepticism about truth admits no conclusive grounds for the judgments that those doctrines claim to justify. Ideology has thus been moved from denoting the elements of a comprehensive, programmatic politics to functioning as an element in a supremely doubtful academic taxonomy. It is confused to the point of babel, as it variously signifies unambiguous truth, myth or illusion, false consciousness, scientific socialism, and ideas that distort and conceal a dynamically changing social reality.

This has not stopped contemporary writers from trying to extract order from chaos. Recently Malcolm B. Hamilton has formulated no fewer than 27 "definitional elements" of the concept from no less than 85 sources. His own selective synthesis is as follows: "An ideology is a system of collectively held normative and reputedly factual ideas and beliefs and attitudes advocating a particular pattern of social relationships and arrangements, and/or aimed at justifying a particular pattern of conduct, which its proponents seek to promote, realize, pursue or maintain."[19]

Hamilton recommends this definition for purposes of "empirical application and research," and so excludes some of the "definitional elements" that have historically been important to participants in and theorists of political action. Hence the association of ideology with class interest that has been so important to Marxist politics is rejected, as is the whole question of the relationship between ideology and science. Indeed, a number of other issues that have been famously explored in discussions about what ideology is and what are examples of it are rather flippantly discarded, as if specialists in epistemology or philosophy of science were the only ones competent to "settle" such questions. These include the way that ideas are determined in society, the distinction between descriptive and explanatory claims, the relationship between political advocacy and social science, and the way in which ideas are or are not "functional." In justifying his exclusions Hamilton appeals to a realm of "reason, logic or ... evidence" that he believes is independent of the interests of the human beings who use such concepts.[20] One can argue, however, that this claim is not only impossible to sustain, but that it lays the author open to the very kind of scrutiny in which the term "ideology" has figured. What exactly are the interests of social scientists? Are these not reflected in their concept of an "empirical fact"? Can they escape their own social and political context so easily by modeling themselves on what they take to be the natural sciences? Can they appeal so conveniently to what philosophers term reason and logic?

Ideology, in sum, is not a concept that denotes some particular phenomenon in the world. It is not a template against which something is or is not an ideology; nor is it a recipe stating how to make an ideology correctly. Rather it is an agenda of things to discuss, questions to ask, hypotheses to make. We should be able to use it when considering the interaction between ideas and politics, especially systems of ideas that make claims, whether justificatory or hortatory. Cutting the concept off from its history, even if historically it has been used in contradictory ways, is no service. Political theory is not an exercise in grave-digging so that inconvenient problems can "disappear." Instead, it provides a wealth of critical perspective, if only we are prepared to use it.

NOTES

1   Count Destutt de Tracy, *A Treatise on Political Economy; to Which Is Prefixed a Supplement to a Preceding Work on the Understanding, or Elements of Ideology; with an Analytical Table, and an Introduction on the Faculty of the Will,* translated by Thomas Jefferson, in John M. Dorsey, *Psychology of Political Science* (Detroit: Center for Health Education, 1973), "Advertisement," p. ix.
2   George Lichtheim, *The Concept of Ideology and Other Essays* (New York: Random House, 1967), pp. 4–5.
3   Karl Marx and Friedrich Engels, *Collected Works,* vol. 5 (London: Lawrence and Wishart, 1976), pp. 586–587.
4   Ibid., pp. 59–60.
5   Ibid., p. 62.
6   Karl Marx and Friedrich Engels, *Selected Works in One Volume* (London: Lawrence and Wishart, 1984), p. 183.
7   Marx and Engels, *Collected Works,* vol. 5, p. 60.
8   Ibid., p. 52.
9   Ibid., p. 80.
10 Marx and Engels, *Selected Works in One Volume,* p. 181.
11 Marx and Engels, *Collected Works,* vol. 5, p. 49.
12 Terrell Carver, *Marx's Social Theory* (Oxford: Oxford University Press, 1982), p. 44.
13 See Terrell Carver, *Marx and Engels: The Intellectual Relationship* (Brighton: Wheatsheaf Books, 1983), *passim.*
14 V. I. Lenin, *Collected Works,* vol. 5, translated by Joe Fineberg and George Hanna, ed. Victor Jerome (Moscow: Progress Publishers, 1973), pp. 369, 370, 383–384.
15 Ibid., pp. 375, 383–384.
16 Karl Mannheim, *Ideology and Utopia,* translated by Louis Wirth and Edward Shils (London: Routledge and Kegan Paul, 1948), pp. 2, 238.
17 Ibid., pp. 49–50.
18 Ibid., p. 62.
19 Malcolm B. Hamilton, "The Elements of the Concept of Ideology," *Political Studies* 35 (1987), p. 38.
20 Ibid., p. 32.

PART 2

THE DEMOCRATIC IDEAL: HISTORICAL AND PHILOSOPHICAL FOUNDATIONS

Some politicians, scholars, and journalists speak of democracy as if it were an ideology, distinct from and in opposition to other ideologies—especially communism and fascism. But this is mistaken. Democracy is not itself an ideology but an *ideal* that different ideologies define and pursue (or reject) in different ways and for different reasons. Everyone agrees that "democracy" means "rule by the people," of course, but what *is* rule by the people? Who are *the people*, and *how* are they to rule? On these points there is little agreement because each ideology answers these questions in its own way. With the exception of fascism, Nazism, and radical Islamism, however, all major or mainstream ideologies now agree that democracy is certainly the most desirable form of government—an ideal toward which all societies should strive.

The popularity of democracy in our time is extraordinary not only because so many people of such different views claim to be democrats but also because democracy was long regarded as a bad or corrupt form of government. The word "democracy" itself first came into use in ancient Greece, where a conflict developed between those who favored democracy—rule by the *demos* or the common people—and those who preferred aristocracy—literally, "rule by the best." In Athens in the fifth century BCE, the *demos* found a leader in Pericles, whose famous "Funeral Oration" was one of the first defenses of democracy as a way of life. The Athenian democracy was short-lived, however, and philosophers such as Plato (c. 428–348 BCE) and Aristotle (384–322 BCE) concluded that democracy is inherently unstable. The common people, Plato argued, are simply too shortsighted and too unruly to govern wisely. Democracy will soon descend into anarchy, a lawless condition that will lead the people to call for a strong leader to restore law and order. But that strong leader will be a despot who subjects everyone else to slavery. From democracy, according to Plato, it is but a short step to tyranny, the worst of all forms of government.

Like Plato, his pupil Aristotle regarded democracy as a selfish or corrupt form of government. Democracy is "rule by the many" in the selfish interest of the common people as a distinct class, he said, not rule in the interest of the community as a whole. But Aristotle also noted that democracy has some desirable features, and he went further to argue that rule by many in the interests of the whole community is not only possible but probably the best of all forms of government.

Aristotle called this best form of government a polity, but it later became better known by the Roman name of "republic," from the Latin *res publica* (meaning "public thing" or "public business"). The republican idea was that the forms of government must be mixed in such a way that some power is in the hands of the common people, some in the hands of the aristocratic few, and some in the hands of a single person. Because each element of society would have some power, but not enough to rule without the cooperation of the other two elements, a system of checks and balances would lead to a government that ruled in the common interest. It would then be a popular government because the people (*populus*) would have a significant voice, but it would not be a democracy. In a republic the power of the people would be tempered and guided by the wisdom of the few.

For centuries, the republic, and not democracy, was considered the ideal form of popular government. Its supporters included Niccolò Machiavelli (1469–1527) and John Adams (1735–1826), the second president of the United States. But in the late eighteenth and early nineteenth centuries sentiment began to shift in favor of democracy. Exactly why this happened is not clear. But with the growth of cities and industry came increasing literacy and improved means of communications, and the nineteenth century soon came to be known as the age of "the common man." In the United States this change was associated with Jacksonian democracy, as the period of Andrew Jackson's presidency (1829–1837) was called. Democracy was taken to be a means of expression or self-government for the common man, as well as a device by which he could protect his rights and interests. But "rule by the people" did not include women and members of other groups, such as slaves in the United States, who were not yet counted among "the people."

Some observers saw the rise of democracy as a mixed blessing. Alexis de Tocqueville (1805–1859), a French aristocrat who traveled throughout the United States in the 1830s, welcomed the increased opportunities that democracy brought to the common people. In his *Democracy in America*, Tocqueville particularly praised the opportunities for participation in local government that democracy made possible. But he also worried that democracy placed so much emphasis on equality that a new form of tyranny would emerge—the "tyranny of the majority." The emphasis on equality will lead to the pressure to conform, Tocqueville feared, so that people will be afraid to think and act for themselves. In England, John Stuart Mill (1806–1873) reached much the same conclusion. The old days of tyrannical rule by kings and emperors were vanishing, he wrote in *On Liberty*, but now the individual's ability to think and live freely was subject to "the moral coercion of public opinion" (see the selection from Mill's *On Liberty* in Part 3). Like Tocqueville, Mill welcomed the increased opportunities for political participation that democracy opened, for he saw participation as a way of educating and improving men and women. But he also suggested that it might be prudent, at least temporarily, to give the wiser, better-informed, and more responsible members of society more votes than the common person.

Despite these concerns, democracy became more widespread throughout the nineteenth century. Voting rights were extended to almost all adult males in the industrialized countries of Europe and North America by the end of the century, and then extended to women in the early or middle years of the twentieth century. Fascism reacted against this democratic trend in the years following World War I, but the defeat of Germany, Italy, and Japan in World War II seems, for a time, to have crushed fascism as a significant antidemocratic force. Now, throughout most of the world, democracy is recognized rhetorically—if not always in practice—as the best of all forms of government.

But "democracy" means different things to different people. In particular, three conceptions of democracy competed with one another in the twentieth century. The most familiar in the English-speaking world is *liberal democracy*. For liberals like Mill, democracy is indeed government by the people, but the people must be willing to respect the rights and liberties of the individuals who compose society. In liberal democracy, then, the chief concern is to prevent majority rule from becoming majority tyranny. The advocates of *social democracy* accept the need to protect individual rights, but they argue that some of these rights—especially the right to own and dispose of property—may be used to frustrate true democracy. That is why social democrats typically take the socialist point of view that property ought to be controlled more or less directly for the public good, not for the private benefit of individuals. Property and wealth are forms of power, they say, and no society can be truly democratic when some people have considerably more power than others. Social democrats thus stress the importance of equality for democracy, with equality understood as a roughly equal chance to influence the decisions that govern one's society. A not-so-distant echo of this theme is often heard in debates over campaign financing, in which critics complain that the campaign contributions of wealthy citizens and special-interest groups buy them political influence that ordinary or poor citizens can never achieve.

The third conception of democracy that vied for acceptance in the twentieth century—but with little success in recent years—is *people's democracy*. This view is linked most closely with communism, or Marxism-Leninism. In this view, democracy is rule by, or *in the interests of*, the common people, which means that it is possible for a single group, such as the Communist party, to wield power democratically so long as it acts to promote the interests of the working class or proletariat. Democracy and dictatorship are compatible with each other, in other words, as the Chinese leader Mao Zedong (1893–1976) insisted in his essay "On the People's Democratic Dictatorship" (in Part 6 of this book).

As we enter the second decade of the twenty-first century, the idea of "people's democracy" seems to have few adherents outside the ranks of the Chinese Communist party and Communist parties in Cuba, North Korea, and Vietnam. But democracy in general is more popular than ever, and the question we now face is whether liberals and socialists will continue to quarrel over the proper definition of democracy, or whether they will find enough common ground to satisfy—and perhaps unite—the two groups.

Democracy and Despotism

*EURIPIDES**

Greeks of fifth and fourth centuries BCE Athens took pride in a form of government that they had invented—democracy (from *demos*, meaning "people" or "common people," and *kratein*, meaning "rule"). While other peoples chafed under the rule of despots, the Athenians ruled themselves. In his play *The Suppliants*, first performed in 422 BCE, Euripides (c. 485–407 BCE) contrasts democratic and despotic government, celebrating the former while condemning the latter. The occasion of the following exchange is the arrival in Athens of an envoy from Thebes, which was then ruled by the tyrant Creon. The envoy cannot quite believe that the people are capable of ruling themselves. The Athenian leader Theseus replies with a resounding defense of democracy.

---

* *Source*: Euripides, *The Suppliants*, lines 394–465. Translated by Terence Ball.

THE SUPPLIANTS

Theban Messenger:	Who is the tyrant who rules this land? To whom must I deliver my message from Creon, ruler of Thebes?
Theseus:	Esteemed visitor, your speech proceeds from a false premise. No tyrant rules here, for this city is free. Here the people rule, each taking his turn without respect of wealth or poverty.
Theban Messenger:	Surely you jest. The city from which I come is ruled not by the gullible multitude but by one man only. No one there uses high-sounding words to pander to the crowd, manipulating them for his own advantage while cloaking his crimes and failures in fair-sounding phrases. So I ask you: Since the common people [*demos*] are such poor judges of everything, how can they possibly govern the city? They have neither the time nor the talent to understand the intricacies of politics. Even if he had been educated, a poor working stiff would have no time or energy left over from his labors to learn about political affairs. Besides, wiser and better people would recoil from a system in which such a man might, through his own way with words, fool the people and rise from being a nobody to occupy a position of political prominence.
Theseus:	You yourself have a way with words and would, if you could, fool us with your kit of clever verbal tricks. But since you have chosen to play this game of words, permit me to take my turn while you listen. Nothing is worse for a city than a tyrant. Wherever he rules, the law does not. In his hands there is no law that rules over all alike. But where the laws [*nomoi*] rule, all— rich and poor, powerful and weak—are equal before them. There the poor are able to speak the same language as the strong—the language of law and justice. If his cause be just, the poor man can prevail against a wealthy adversary. The hallmark of freedom is this: Anyone having good advice to give to the city should be heard, and anyone with nothing to say may choose to remain silent. What greater equality [*isonomia*] can exist in a city? Where all the citizens rule, they take pride in their young people. But where a tyrant rules, he fears them, and, seeing the most talented among them as a threat to his own power, he puts them to the sword. How can the city survive and prosper, where its ruler stifles all initiative and uses his sword like a scythe, cutting down its youths like the flowers of spring? Why work and save for the sake of your children, only to have the tyrant take it all away? Why raise your daughters to be virtuous, when they can be ravished at whim by a lustful tyrant while their tearful parents are powerless to prevent it? I would rather die than have my children be subjected to such arbitrary power!

This thunderbolt I hurl in answer to your words ... If you weren't a messenger and therefore under the protection of the law, you would pay dearly for your outrageous remarks. It is the messenger's duty to deliver one message and to return with another. So take this reply back to Creon: Next time, send to our city a messenger who talks less foolishly than this one.

Funeral Oration

*PERICLES**

After defeating the numerically larger forces of the despotic Persian Empire in 480 BCE, democratic Athens assumed a preeminent position among the city-states of Greece. But other Greek city-states grew wary of Athens's power and angry at its arrogance. Led by Athens's chief rival, Sparta, they waged war—the Peloponnesian War—against Athens. In his famous Funeral Oration (430 BCE), Pericles (c. 495–429 BCE) commemorates the sacrifice of the Athenians who died in battle in the first years of the war and celebrates the ideals of Athenian democracy.

* *Source*: Thucydides, *The Peloponnesian War*, 2nd ed., revised, vol. 1, translated by Benjamin Jowett (Oxford: Clarendon Press, 1900), pp. 126–135. The editors have altered the translation slightly for purposes of clarity.

FUNERAL ORATION

Most of those who have spoken here before me have commended the lawgiver who added this oration to our other funeral customs; it seemed to them a worthy thing that such an honor should be given at their burial to the dead who have fallen on the field of battle. But I should have preferred that, when men's deeds have been brave, they should be honored in deed only, and with such an honor as this public funeral, which you are now witnessing. Then the reputation of many would not have been imperiled on the eloquence or want of eloquence of one, and their virtues believed or not as he spoke well or ill. For it is difficult to say neither too little nor too much; and even moderation is apt not to give the impression of truthfulness. The friend of the dead who knows the facts is likely to think that the words of the speaker fall short of his knowledge and of his wishes; another who is not so well informed, when he hears of anything which surpasses his own powers, will be envious and will suspect exaggeration. Mankind are tolerant of the praises of others so long as each hearer thinks that he can do as well or nearly as well himself, but, when the speaker rises above him, jealousy is aroused and he begins to be incredulous. However, since our ancestors have set the seal of their approval upon the practice, I must obey, and to the utmost of my power shall endeavor to satisfy the wishes and beliefs of all who hear me.

… But before I praise the dead, I should like to point out by what principles of action we rose to power, and under what institutions and through what manner of life our empire became great. For I conceive that such thoughts are not unsuited to the occasion, and that this numerous assembly of citizens and strangers may profitably listen to them.

Our form of government does not enter into rivalry with the institutions of others. We do not copy our neighbors, but are an example to them. It is true that we are called a democracy, for the administration is in the hands of the many and not of the few. But while the law secures equal justice to all alike in their private disputes, the claim of excellence is also recognized; and when a citizen is in any way distinguished, he is preferred to the public service, not as a matter of privilege, but as the reward of merit. Neither is poverty a bar, but a man may benefit his country whatever be the obscurity of his condition. There is no exclusiveness in our public life, and in our private intercourse we are not suspicious of one another, nor angry with our neighbor if he does what he likes; we do not put on sour looks at him which, though harmless, are not pleasant. While we are thus unconstrained in our private intercourse, a spirit of reverence pervades our public acts; we are prevented from doing wrong by respect for the authorities and for the laws, having an especial regard to those which are ordained for the protection of the injured as well as to those unwritten laws which bring upon the transgressor of them the reprobation of the general sentiment.

And we have not forgotten to provide for our weary spirits many relaxations from toil; we have regular games and sacrifices throughout the year; our homes are beautiful and elegant; and the delight which we daily feel in all these things helps to banish melancholy. Because of the greatness of our city the fruits of the whole earth flow in upon us; so that we enjoy the goods of other countries as freely as of our own.

Then, again, our military training is in many respects superior to that of our adversaries. Our city is thrown open to the world, and we never expel a foreigner or prevent him from seeing or learning anything of which the secret if revealed to an enemy might profit him. We rely not upon management or trickery, but upon our own hearts and hands. And in the matter of education, whereas they from early youth are always undergoing laborious exercises which are to make them brave, we live at ease, and yet are equally ready to face the perils which they face. And here is the proof. The Lacedaemonians [i.e., Spartans] come into Attica [i.e., Athenian territory] not by themselves, but with their whole confederacy following; we go alone into a neighbor's country; and although our opponents are fighting for their homes and we on a foreign soil, we have seldom any difficulty in overcoming them. Our enemies have never yet felt our united strength; the care of a navy divides our attention, and on land we are obliged to send our own citizens everywhere. But they, if they meet and defeat a part of our army, are as proud as if they had routed us all, and when defeated they pretend to have been vanquished by us all.

If then we prefer to meet danger with a light heart but without laborious training, and with a courage which is gained by habit and not enforced by law, are we not greatly the gainers?

… For we are lovers of the beautiful, yet simple in our tastes, and we cultivate the mind without loss of manliness. Wealth we employ, not for talk and ostentation, but when there is a real use for it. To avow poverty with us is no disgrace; the true disgrace is in doing nothing to avoid it. An Athenian citizen does not neglect the state because he takes care of his own household; and even those of us who are engaged in business have a very fair idea of politics. We alone regard a man who takes no interest in public affairs, not as a harmless, but as a useless character; and if few of us are originators, we are all sound judges of a policy. The great impediment to action is, in our opinion, not discussion, but the want of that knowledge which is gained by discussion preparatory to action. For we have a peculiar power of thinking before we act and of acting too, whereas other men are courageous from ignorance but hesitate upon reflection. And they are surely to be esteemed the bravest spirits who, having the clearest sense both of the pains and pleasures of life, do not on that account shrink from danger. In doing good, again, we are unlike others; we make our friends by conferring, not by receiving, favors. Now he who confers a favor is the firmer friend, because he would fain by kindness keep alive the memory of an obligation; but the recipient is colder in his feelings, because he knows that in requiting another's generosity he will not be winning gratitude but only paying a debt. We alone do good to our neighbors not upon a calculation of interest, but in the confidence of freedom and in a frank and fearless spirit. To sum up: I say that Athens is the school of Hellas [i.e., Greece], and that the individual Athenian in his own person seems to have the power of adapting himself to the most varied forms of action with the utmost versatility and grace. This is no passing and idle word, but truth and fact; and the assertion is verified by the position to which these qualities have raised the state. For in the hour of trial Athens alone among her contemporaries is superior to the report of her. No enemy who comes against her is indignant at the reverses which he sustains at the hands of such a city; no subject complains that his masters are unworthy of him. And we shall assuredly not be without witnesses; there are mighty monuments of our power which will make us the wonder of this and of succeeding ages; we shall not need the praises of Homer or of any other panegyrist whose poetry may please for the moment, although his representation of the facts will not bear the light of day. For we have compelled every land and every sea to open a path for our valor, and have everywhere planted eternal memorials of our friendship and of our enmity. Such is the city for whose sake these men nobly fought and died; they could not bear the thought that she might be taken from them; and every one of us who survive should gladly toil on her behalf.

I have dwelt upon the greatness of Athens because I want to show you that we are contending for a higher prize than those who enjoy none of these privileges, and to establish by manifest proof the merit of these men whom I am now commemorating. Their loftiest praise has been already spoken. For in magnifying the city I have magnified them, and men like them whose virtues made her glorious. And of how few Hellenes [i.e., Greeks] can it be said as of them, that their deeds when weighed in the balance have been found equal to their fame! I believe that a death such as theirs has been given the true measure of a man's worth; it may be the first revelation of his virtues, but is at any rate their final seal. For even those who come short in other ways may justly plead the valor with which they have fought for their country; they have blotted out the evil with the good, and have benefited the state more by their public services than they have injured her by their private actions. None of these men were weakened by wealth or hesitated to forgo the pleasures of life; none of them put off the evil day in the hope, natural to poverty, that a man, though poor, may one day become rich. But, deeming that the punishment of their enemies was sweeter than any of these things, and that they could fall in no nobler cause, they determined at the hazard of their lives to be honorably avenged, and to leave the rest. They resigned to hope their unknown chance of happiness; but in the face of death they resolved to rely upon themselves alone. And when the moment came they were minded to resist and suffer, rather than to flee and save their lives; they ran away from the word of dishonor, but on the battle-field their feet stood fast, and in an instant, at the height of their fortune, they passed away from the scene, not of their fear, but of their glory.

Such was the end of these men; they were worthy of Athens, and the living need not desire to have a more heroic spirit, although they may pray for a less fatal result. The value of such a spirit is not to be expressed in words. Any one can talk to you forever about the advantages of a brave defense, which you know already. But instead of listening to him I would have you day by day fix your eyes upon the greatness of Athens, until you become filled with the love of her; and when you are impressed by the spectacle of her glory, reflect that this empire has been acquired by men who knew their duty and had the courage to do it, who in the hour of conflict had the fear of dishonor always present to them, and who, if ever they failed in an enterprise, would not allow their virtues to be lost to their country, but freely gave their lives to her as the fairest offering which they could present at her feast. The sacrifice which they collectively made was individually repaid to them; for they received again each one for himself a praise which grows not old, and the noblest of all sepulchers—I speak not of that in which their remains are laid, but of that in which their glory survives, and is proclaimed always and on every fitting occasion both in word and deed. For the whole earth is the sepulcher of famous men; not only are they commemorated by columns and inscriptions in their own country, but in foreign lands there dwells also an unwritten memorial of them, graven not on stone but in the hearts of men. Make them your examples, and, esteeming courage to be freedom and freedom to be happiness, do not weigh too nicely the perils of war. The unfortunate who has no hope of a change for the better has less reason to throw away his life than the prosperous who, if he survives, is always liable to a change for the worse, and to whom any accidental fall makes the most serious difference. To a man of spirit, cowardice and disaster coming together are far more bitter than death striking him unperceived at a time when he is full of courage and animated by the general hope.

Wherefore I do not now commiserate the parents of the dead who stand here; I would rather comfort them. You know that your life has been passed amid many great changes; and that they may be deemed fortunate who have gained most honor, whether an honorable death like theirs, or an honorable sorrow like yours, and whose days have been so ordered that the term of their happiness is likewise the term of their life. I know how hard it is to make you feel this, when the good fortune of others will too often remind you of the gladness which once lightened your hearts. And sorrow is felt at the want of those blessings, not which a man never knew, but which were a part of his life before they were taken from him. Some of you are of an age at which they may hope to have other children, and they ought to bear their sorrow better; not only will the children who may hereafter be born make them forget their own lost ones, but the city will be doubly a gainer. She will not be left desolate, and she will be safer. For a man's counsel cannot have equal weight or worth, when he alone has no children to risk in the general danger. To those of you who have passed their prime, I say: "Congratulate yourselves that you have been happy during the greater part of your days; remember that your life of sorrow will not last long, and be comforted by the glory of those who are gone. For the love of honor alone is ever young, and not riches, as some say, but honor is the delight of men when they are old and useless."

To you who are the sons and brothers of the departed, I see that the struggle to emulate them will be an arduous one. For all men praise the dead, and, however preeminent your virtue may be, hardly will you be thought, I do not say to equal, but even to approach them. The living have their rivals and detractors, but when a man is out of the way, the honor and good which he receives is unalloyed. And, if I am to speak of womanly virtues to those of you who will henceforth be widows, let me sum them up in one short admonition: To a woman not to show more weakness than is natural to her sex is a great glory, and not to be talked about for good or for evil among men.

I have paid the required tribute, in obedience to the law, making use of such fitting words as I had. The tribute of deeds has been paid in part; for the dead have been honorably buried, and it remains only that their children should be maintained at the public charge until they are grown up: This is the solid prize with which, as with a wreath, Athens crowns her sons living and dead, after a struggle like theirs. For where the rewards of virtue are greatest, there the noblest citizens are enlisted in the service of the state. And now, when you have duly lamented, every one his own dead, you may depart.

Democratic Judgment and the "Middling" Constitution

*ARISTOTLE**

Although critical of democracy as a form of government, the Greek philosopher Aristotle (384–322 BCE) nevertheless recognized the democratic principle that "many heads are better than one." Just as a feast to which many people contribute is richer, more varied, and more nourishing than a meal prepared by one or a few, so a government that makes use of many talents and perspectives is wiser than one that does not. That is Aristotle's argument in Book III, Chapter 11, of his *Politics*. But the best form of government, as he goes on to say in Book IV, Chapter 11, is not democracy but "polity," that is, rule by the many in the interest of all. Aristotle thus anticipates the kind of popular self-rule that came to be called "republican." On the republican form of government, see selections 2.5 and 2.6.

* *Source*: Aristotle, *The Politics*, translated by Benjamin Jowett (Oxford: Clarendon Press, 1885). The editors have altered the translation slightly for the sake of clarity.

THE POLITICS: BOOK III
Chapter 11

... The principle that the multitude ought to be supreme rather than the few best is one that is maintained, and, though not free from difficulty, yet seems to contain an element of truth. For the many, of whom each individual is but an ordinary person, when they meet together may very likely be better than the few good, if regarded not individually but collectively, just as a feast to which many contribute is better than a dinner provided out of a single purse. For each individual among the many has a share of virtue and prudence, and when they meet together, they become in a manner of speaking one man, who has many feet, and hands, and senses ... Hence the many are better judges than a single man of music and poetry; for some understand one part, and some another, and among them they understand the whole. There is a similar combination of qualities in good men, who differ from any individual of the many, as the beautiful are said to differ from those who are not beautiful, and works of art from realities, because in them the scattered elements are combined, although, if taken separately, the eye of one person or some other feature in another person would be fairer than in the picture. Whether this principle can apply to every democracy, and to all bodies of men, is not clear. Or rather, by heaven, in some cases it is impossible of application; for the argument would equally hold about animals; and wherein, it will be asked, do some men differ from animals? But there may be bodies of men about whom our statement is nevertheless true. And if so, the difficulty which has been already raised, and also another which is akin to it—viz. what power should be assigned to the mass of freemen and citizens, who are not rich and have no personal merit—are both solved. There is still a danger in allowing them to share the great offices of state, for their folly will lead them into error, and their dishonesty into crime. But there is a danger also in not letting them share, for a state in which many poor men are excluded from office will necessarily be full of enemies. The only way of escape is to assign to them some deliberative and judicial functions. For this reason Solon and certain other legislators[1] give them the power of electing to offices, and of calling the magistrates to account, but they do not allow them to hold office singly. When they meet together their perceptions are quite good enough, and combined with the better class they are useful to the state (just as impure food when mixed with what is pure sometimes makes the entire mass more wholesome than a small quantity of the pure would be), but each individual, left to himself, forms an imperfect judgment. On the other hand, government by the people involves certain difficulties. In the first place, it might be objected that he who can judge of the healing of a sick man would be one who could himself heal his disease, and make him whole—that is, in other words, the physician; and so in all professions and arts. As, then, the physician ought to be called to account by physicians, so ought men in general to be called to account by their peers. But physicians are of three kinds: there is the ordinary practitioner, and there is the physician of the higher class, and thirdly the intelligent man who has studied the art: in all arts there is such a class; and we attribute the power of judging to them quite as much as to professors of the art. Secondly, does not the same principle apply to elections? For a right election can only be made by those who have knowledge; those who know geometry, for example, will choose a geometrician rightly, and those who know how to steer, a pilot; and, even if there be some occupations and arts in which private persons share in the ability to choose, they certainly cannot choose better than those who know. So that, according to this argument, neither the election of magistrates, nor the calling of them to account, should be entrusted to the many. Yet possibly these objections are to a great extent met by our old answer, that if the people are not utterly degraded, although individually they may be worse judges than those who have special knowledge: as a body they are as good or better. Moreover, there are some arts whose products are not judged of solely, or best, by the artists themselves, namely those arts whose products are recognized even by those who do not possess the art; for example, the knowledge of the house is not limited to the builder only; the user, or, in other words, the master, of the house will be even a better judge than the carpenter, just as the pilot will be a better judge of a rudder than the boat-builder, and the guest will be a better judge of a feast than the cook.

This difficulty seems now to be sufficiently answered, but there is another akin to it. That inferior persons should have authority in greater matters than the good would appear to be a strange thing, yet the election and calling to account of the magistrates is the greatest of all. And these, as I was saying, are functions which in some states are assigned to the people, for the assembly is supreme in all such matters. Yet persons of any age, and having but a small property qualification, sit in the assembly and deliberate and judge, although for the great officers of state, such as treasurers and generals, a high qualification is required. This difficulty may be solved in the same manner as the preceding, and the present practice of democracies may be really defensible. For the power does not reside in the juror, or senator, or assemblyman, but in the court, and the senate, and the assembly, of which individual senators, or assemblymen or jurors, are only parts or members. And for this reason the many may claim to have a higher authority than the few; for the people, and the senate, and the courts consist of many persons, and their property collectively is greater than the property of one or of a few individuals holding great offices. But enough of this.

The discussion of the first question shows nothing so clearly as that laws, when good, should be supreme; and that the magistrate or magistrates should regulate those matters only on which the laws are unable to speak with precision owing to the difficulty of any general principle embracing all particulars. But what are good laws has not yet been clearly explained; the old difficulty remains. The goodness or badness, justice or injustice, of laws varies of necessity with the constitutions of states. This, however, is clear, that the laws must be adapted to the constitutions. But if so, true forms of government will of necessity have just laws, and perverted forms of government will have unjust laws.

Chapter 12

In all sciences and arts the aim or end [*telos*] is a good, and the greatest good and in the highest degree a good is the most authoritative of all—this is the political science of which the good is justice, in other words, the common interest. All men think justice to be a sort of equality; and to a certain extent they agree in the philosophical distinctions which have been laid down by us about Ethics.[2] For they admit that justice is a thing and has a relation to persons, and that equals ought to have equality.

THE POLITICS: BOOK IV
Chapter 11

We have now to inquire what is the best constitution for most states, and the best life for most men, neither assuming a standard of virtue which is above ordinary persons, nor an education which is exceptionally favored by nature and circumstances, nor yet an ideal state which is an aspiration only, but having regard to the life in which the majority are able to share, and to the form of government which states in general can attain. As to those aristocracies, as they are called, of which we were just now speaking, they either lie beyond the possibilities of the greater number of states, or they approximate to the so-called constitutional government [or polity], and therefore need no separate discussion. And in fact the conclusion at which we arrive respecting all these forms rests upon the same grounds. For if what was said in the *Ethics* is true, that the happy life is the life according to virtue lived without impediment, and that virtue is a mean between extremes, then the life which is in a mean, and in a mean attainable by every one, must be the best. And the same principles of virtue and vice are characteristic of cities and of constitutions; for the constitution is in a figure of speech the life of the city.

Now in all states there are three elements: one class is very rich, another very poor, and a third is a mean between those extremes. It is admitted that moderation and the mean are best, and therefore it will clearly be best to possess the gifts of fortune in moderation; for in that condition of life men are most ready to follow rational principle. But he who greatly excels in beauty, strength, birth, or wealth, or on the other hand who is very poor, or very weak, or very much disgraced, finds it difficult to follow rational principle. Of these two the one sort grow into violent and infamous criminals, the others into rogues and petty rascals. And two sorts of offences correspond to them, the one committed from violence, the other from roguery. Again, the middle class is least likely to shrink from rule, or to be overambitious for it; both of which are injuries to the state. Again, those who have too much of the goods of fortune, strength, wealth, friends, and the like, are neither willing nor able to submit to authority. The evil begins at home; for when they are boys, by reason of the luxury in which they are brought up, they never learn, even at school, the habit of obedience. On the other hand, the very poor, who are in the opposite extreme, are too degraded. So that the one class cannot obey, and can only rule despotically; the other knows not how to command and must be ruled like slaves. Thus arises a city, not of freemen, but of masters and slaves, the one despising, the other envying; and nothing can be more fatal to friendship [*philia*] and good fellowship in states than this: for good fellowship springs from friendship; when men are at enmity with one another, they would rather not even share the same path. But a city ought to be composed, as far as possible, of equals and similars; and these are generally the middle classes. Wherefore the city which is composed of middle-class citizens is necessarily best constituted in respect of the elements of which we say the fabric of the state naturally consists. And this is the class of citizens which is most secure in a state, for they do not, like the poor, covet their neighbors' goods; nor do others covet theirs, as the poor covet the goods of the rich; and as they neither plot against others, nor are themselves plotted against, they pass through life safely. Wisely then did [the poet] Phocylides pray—"Many things are best in the mean; I desire to belong to the middle class in my city."

Thus it is manifest that the best political community is formed by citizens of the middle class, and that those states are likely to be well-administered, in which the middle class is large, and stronger if possible than both the other classes, or at any rate than either singly; for the addition of the middle class tips the scale, and prevents either of the extremes from being dominant. Great then is the good fortune of a state in which the citizens have a moderate and sufficient property; for where some possess much, and the others nothing, there may arise an extreme democracy, or a pure oligarchy; or a tyranny may grow out of either extreme— either out of the most rampant democracy, or out of an oligarchy; but it is much less likely to arise out of the middle constitutions and those akin to them. I will explain the reason of this hereafter, when I speak of the revolutions of states. The mean condition of states is clearly best, for no other is free from faction; and where the middle class is large, there are least likely to be factions and dissensions. For a similar reason large states are less liable to faction than small ones, because in them the middle class is large; whereas in small states it is easy to divide all the citizens into two classes who are either rich or poor, and to leave nothing in the middle. And democracies are safer and more permanent than oligarchies, because they have a middle class which is more numerous and has a greater share in the government; for when there is no middle class, and the poor greatly exceed the rich in number, troubles arise, and the state soon comes to an end. A proof of the superiority of the middle class is that the best legislators have been of a middle condition; for example, Solon, as his own verses testify; and Lycurgus, for he was not a king; and Charondas, and almost all legislators.[3]

These considerations will help us to understand why most governments are either democratic or oligarchic. The reason is that the middle class is seldom numerous in them, and whichever party, whether the rich or the common people, transgresses the mean and predominates, draws the constitution its own way, and thus arises either oligarchy or democracy. There is another reason—the poor and the rich quarrel with one another, and whichever side gets the better, instead of establishing a just or popular government, regards political supremacy as the prize of victory, and the party of the poor sets up a democracy and the party of the rich establishes an oligarchy. Further, both the parties which had the supremacy in Hellas [Greece] looked only to the interest of their own form of government, and established in states, the one, democracies, and the other, oligarchies; they thought of their own class' advantage, of the public not at all. For these reasons the middle form of government has rarely, if ever, existed, and among a very few only. One man alone of all who ever ruled in Hellas was induced to give this middle constitution to states. But it has now become a habit among the citizens of states, not even to care about equality [*isonomia*]; all men are seeking for dominion, or, if conquered, are willing to submit.

What then is the best form of government, and what makes it the best, is now clear; and of other constitutions, since we say that there are many kinds of democracy and many of oligarchy, it is not difficult to see which has the first and which the second or any other place in the order of excellence, now that we have determined which is the best. For that which is nearest to the best must of necessity be better, and that which is furthest from it worse, if we are judging absolutely and not relative to given conditions: I say "relative to given conditions," since a particular form of government may be preferable for some people, but another form may be better for others.

NOTES

1 Solon (c. 638–559 BCE) was the "legislator" or "lawgiver" who drafted the fundamental laws, or constitution, of Athens.—Eds.
2 Here Aristotle refers to his *Nicomachean Ethics* (especially Book V, Chapter 3).—Eds.
3 Like Solon in Athens, Lycurgus and Charondas were "legislators" who drafted the fundamental laws of their city-states: in Lycurgus's case, Sparta; in Charondas's, Catana, a Greek colony in what is now Sicily.—Eds.

What's Wrong with Princely Rule?

NICCOLÒ MACHIAVELLI*

The Italian Renaissance of the fourteenth and fifteenth centuries saw the rebirth of many of the ideals of classical Greece and Rome, including the ideal of self-government. Among those who celebrated the rebirth of "republican" government was Niccolò Machiavelli (1469–1527). Machiavelli is best known as the author of *The Prince*, a short book in which he apparently advocates rule by a single person who should not hesitate to use cruelty and deceit to stay in power. In his longer book, *The Discourses*, however, he takes a very different position. In the following excerpt from *The Discourses*, Machiavelli criticizes the claim that the people, acting collectively, are less wise than a single king or prince.

---

* *Source*: Niccolò Machiavelli, *The Discourses*, translated by Christian Detmold (Boston: James R. Osgood and Co., 1882) chap. 58, pp. 214–219.

THE PEOPLE ARE WISER AND MORE CONSTANT THAN PRINCES

Titus Livius [or Livy][1] as well as all other historians affirm that nothing is more uncertain and inconstant than the multitude; for it appears from what he relates of the actions of men, that in many instances the multitude, after having condemned a man to death, bitterly lamented it, and most earnestly wished him back. This was the case with the Roman people and Manlius Capitolinus, whom they had condemned to death and afterwards most earnestly desired him back, as our author [i.e., Livy] says in the following words: "No sooner had they found out that they had nothing to fear from him, than they began to regret and to wish him back." And elsewhere, when he relates the events that occurred in Syracuse after the death of Hieronymus, nephew of Hiero, he says: "It is the nature of the multitude either humbly to serve or insolently to dominate." I know not whether, in undertaking to defend a cause against the accusations of all writers, I do not assume a task so hard and so beset with difficulties as to oblige me to abandon it with shame, or to go on with it at the risk of being weighed down by it. Be that as it may, however, I think, and ever shall think, that it cannot be wrong to defend one's opinions with arguments founded upon reason, without employing force or authority.

I say, then, that individual men, and especially princes, may be charged with the same defects of which writers accuse the people; for whoever is not controlled by laws will commit the same errors as an unbridled multitude. This may easily be verified, for there have been and still are plenty of princes, and a few good and wise ones, such, I mean, as needed not the curb that controlled them. Amongst these, however, are not to be counted either the kings that lived in Egypt at that ancient period when that country was governed by laws, or those that arose in Sparta; neither such as are born in our day in France, for that country is more thoroughly regulated by laws than any other of which we have any knowledge in modern times. And those kings that arise under such constitutions are not to be classed amongst the number of those whose individual nature we have to consider, and see whether it resembles that of the people; but they should be compared with a people equally controlled by law as those kings were, and then we shall find in that multitude the same good qualities as in those kings, and we shall see that such a people neither obey with servility nor command with insolence. Such were the people of Rome, who, so long as that republic remained uncorrupted, neither obeyed basely nor ruled insolently, but rather held its rank honorably, supporting the laws and their magistrates …

Therefore, the character of the people is not to be blamed any more than that of princes, for both alike are liable to err when they are without any control. Besides the examples already given, I could adduce numerous others from amongst the Roman Emperors and other tyrants and princes, who have displayed as much inconstancy and recklessness as any populace ever did. Contrary to the general opinion, then, which maintains that the people, when they govern, are inconsistent, unstable, and ungrateful, I conclude and affirm that these defects are not more natural to the people than they are to princes. To charge the people and princes equally with them may be the truth, but to except princes from them would be a great mistake. For a people that governs and is well regulated by laws will be stable, prudent, and grateful, as much so, and even more, according to my opinion, than a prince, although he be esteemed wise; and, on the other hand, a prince, freed from the restraints of the law, will be more ungrateful, inconstant, and imprudent than a people similarly situated. The difference in their conduct is not due to any difference in their nature (for that is the same, and if there be any difference for good, it is on the side of the people); but to the greater or less respect they have for the laws under which they respectively live. And whoever studies the Roman people will see that for four hundred years they have been haters of royalty, and lovers of the glory and common good of their country; and he will find any number of examples that will prove both the one and the other ... But as regards prudence and stability, I say that the people are more prudent and stable, and have better judgment than a prince; and it is not without good reason that it is said, "The voice of the people is the voice of God"; for we see popular opinion prognosticate events in such a wonderful manner that it would almost seem as if the people had some occult virtue, which enables them to foresee the good and the evil. As to the people's capacity of judging of things, it is exceedingly rare that, when they hear two orators of equal talents advocate different measures, they do not decide in favor of the best of the two; which proves their ability to discern the truth of what they hear. And if occasionally they are misled in matters involving questions of courage or seeming utility (as has been said above), so is a prince also many times misled by his own passions, which are much greater than those of the people. We also see that in the election of their magistrates they make far better choices than princes; and no people will ever be persuaded to elect a man of infamous character and corrupt habits to any post of dignity, to which a prince is easily influenced in a thousand different ways. When we see a people take an aversion to anything, they persist in it for many centuries, which we never find to be the case with princes. Upon both these points the Roman people shall serve me as a proof, who in the many elections of Consuls and Tribunes had to regret only four times the choice they had made. The Roman people held the name of king in such detestation, as we have said, that no extent of services rendered by any of its citizens who attempted to usurp that title could save him from his merited punishment. We furthermore see the cities where the people are masters make the greatest progress in the least possible time, and much greater than such as have always been governed by princes; as was the case with Rome after the expulsion of the kings, and with Athens after they rid themselves of Pisistratus;[2] and this can be attributed to no other cause than that the governments of the people are better than those of princes.

It would be useless to object to my opinion by referring to what our historian [i.e., Livy] has said in the passages quoted above, and elsewhere; for if we compare the faults of a people with those of princes, as well as their respective good qualities, we shall find the people vastly superior in all that is good and glorious. And if princes show themselves superior in the making of laws, and in the forming of civil institutions and new statutes and ordinances, the people are superior in maintaining those institutions, laws, and ordinances, which certainly places them on par with those who established them.

And finally to sum up this matter, I say that both governments of princes and of the people have lasted a long time, but both required to be regulated by laws. For a prince who knows no other control but his own will is like a madman, and a people that can do as it pleases will hardly be wise. If now we compare a prince who is controlled by laws, and a people that is restricted by them, we shall find more virtue in the people than in the prince; and if we compare them when both are freed from such control, we shall see that the people are guilty of fewer excesses than the prince, and that the errors of the people are of less importance, and therefore more easily remedied. For a licentious and mutinous people may easily be brought back to good conduct by the influence and persuasion of a good man, but an evil-minded prince is not amenable to such influences, and therefore there is no other remedy against him but cold steel. We may judge then from this of the relative defects of the one and the other; if words suffice to correct those of the people, whilst those of the prince can only be remedied by violence, no one can fail to see that where the greater remedy is required, there also the defects must be greater. The follies which a people commits at the moment of its greatest license are not what is most to be feared; it is not the immediate evil that may result from them that inspires apprehension, but the fact that such general confusion might afford the opportunity for a tyrant to seize the government. But with evil-disposed princes the contrary is the case; it is the immediate present that causes fear, and there is hope only in the future; for men will persuade themselves that the termination of his wicked life may give them a chance of liberty. Thus we see the difference between the one and the other to be, that the one touches the present and the other the future. The excesses of the people are directed against those whom they suspect of interfering with the public good; whilst those of princes are against apprehended interference with their individual interests. The general prejudice against the people results from the fact that everybody can freely and fearlessly speak ill of them in mass, even whilst they are at the height of their power; but a prince can only be spoken of with the greatest circumspection and apprehension.

NOTES

1   Titus Livius (59 BCE–CE 17), or Livy, was a Roman historian. Machiavelli's *Discourses* is, in part, a commentary on the first ten books of Livy's *History of Rome.*—Eds.
2   Pisistratus (?–527 BCE) was notorious for his long, tyrannical rule of Athens.—Eds.

What Is a Republic?

JOHN ADAMS*

The ideal of republican self-rule played an important part in the political struggles and debates of eighteenth-century America. Thomas Paine and Thomas Jefferson used republican arguments during the American Revolution to justify independence from Great Britain, and the Founding Fathers drafted a republican constitution in 1787. In 1776, when he was a member of the Continental Congress, John Adams (1735–1826) wrote the following selection, *Thoughts on Government*, in which he expounds and defends the principles of republican government.

---

* *Source*: *The Works of John Adams*, C. F. Adams, ed., vol. 4 (Boston: Little, Brown, 1856), pp. 193–200.

THOUGHTS ON GOVERNMENT

My Dear Sir,—If I was equal to the task of forming a plan for the government of a colony, I should be flattered with your request, and very happy to comply with it; because, as the divine science of politics is the science of social happiness, and the blessings of society depend entirely on the constitutions of government, which are generally institutions that last for many generations, there can be no employment more agreeable to a benevolent mind than a research after the best.

Pope[1] flattered tyrants too much when he said,

> For forms of government let fools contest, That which is best administered is best.

Nothing can be more fallacious than this. But poets read history to collect flowers, not fruits; they attend to fanciful images, not the effects of social institutions. Nothing is more certain, from the history of nations and nature of man, than that some forms of government are better fitted for being well administered than others.

We ought to consider what is the end of government, before we determine which is the best form. Upon this point all speculative politicians will agree, that the happiness of society is the end of government, as all divines and moral philosophers will agree that the happiness of the individual is the end of man. From this principle it will follow, that the form of government which communicates ease, comfort, security, or, in one word, happiness, to the greatest number of persons, and in the greatest degree, is the best.

All sober inquirers after truth, ancient and modern, pagan and Christian, have declared that the happiness of man, as well as his dignity, consists in virtue. Confucius, Zoroaster, Socrates, Mahomet [i.e., Mohammed], not to mention authorities really sacred, have agreed in this.

If there is a form of government, then, whose principle and foundation is virtue, will not every sober man acknowledge it better calculated to promote the general happiness than any other form?

Fear is the foundation of most governments; but it is so sordid and brutal a passion, and renders men in whose breasts it predominates so stupid and miserable, that Americans will not be likely to approve of any political institution which is founded on it.

Honor is truly sacred, but holds a lower rank in the scale of moral excellence than virtue. Indeed, the former is but a part of the latter, and consequently has not equal pretensions to support a frame of government productive of human happiness.

The foundation of every government is some principle or passion in the minds of the people. The noblest principles and most generous affections in our nature, then, have the fairest chance to support the noblest and most generous models of government.

A man must be indifferent to the sneers of modern Englishmen, to mention in their company the names of Sidney, Harrington, Locke, Milton, Nedham, Neville, Burnet, and Hoadly.[2] No small fortitude is necessary to confess that one has read them. The wretched condition of this country, however, for ten or fifteen years past, has frequently reminded me of their principles and reasonings. They will convince any candid mind, that there is no good government but what is republican. That the only valuable part of the British constitution is so; because the very definition of a republic is "an empire of laws, and not of men." That, as a republic is the best of governments, so that particular arrangement of the powers of society, or, in other words, that form of government which is best contrived to secure an impartial and exact execution of the laws, is the best of republics.

Of republics there is an inexhaustible variety, because the possible combinations of the powers of society are capable of innumerable variations.

As good government is an empire of laws, how shall your laws be made? In a large society, inhabiting an extensive country, it is impossible that the whole should assemble to make laws. The first necessary step, then, is to depute power from the many to a few of the most wise and good. But by what rules shall you choose your representatives? Agree upon the number and qualifications of persons who shall have the benefit of choosing, or annex this privilege to the inhabitants of a certain extent of ground.

The principal difficulty lies, and the greatest care should be employed, in constituting this representative assembly. It should be in miniature an exact portrait of the people at large. It should think, feel, reason, and act like them. That it may be the interest of this assembly to do strict justice at all times, it should be an equal representation, or, in other words, equal interests among the people should have equal interests in it. Great care should be taken to effect this, and to prevent unfair, partial, and corrupt elections. Such regulations, however, may be better made in times of greater tranquillity than the present; and they will spring up themselves naturally, when all the powers of government come to be in the hands of the people's friends. At present, it will be safest to proceed in all established modes, to which the people have been familiarized by habit.

A representation of the people in one assembly being obtained, a question arises, whether all the powers of government, legislative, executive, and judicial, shall be left in this body? I think a people cannot be long free, nor ever happy, whose government is in one assembly. My reasons for this opinion are as follows:

1 A single assembly is liable to all the vices, follies, and frailties of an individual; subject to fits of humor, starts of passion, flights of enthusiasm, partialities, or prejudice, and consequently productive of hasty results and absurd judgments. And all these errors ought to be corrected and defects supplied by some controlling power.

2 A single assembly is apt to be avaricious, and in time will not scruple to exempt itself from burdens, which it will lay, without compunction, on its constituents.

3 A single assembly is apt to grow ambitious, and after a time will not hesitate to vote itself perpetual. This was one fault of the Long Parliament;[3] but more remarkably of Holland, whose assembly first voted themselves from annual to septennial, then for life, and after a course of years, that all vacancies happening by death or otherwise, should be filled by themselves, without any application to constituents at all.

4 A representative assembly, although extremely well qualified, and absolutely necessary, as a branch of the legislative, is unfit to exercise the executive power, for want of two essential properties, secrecy and despatch.

5   A representative assembly is still less qualified for the judicial power, because it is too numerous, too slow, and too little skilled in the laws.

6   Because a single assembly, possessed of all the powers of government, would make arbitrary laws for their own interest, execute all laws arbitrarily for their own interest, and adjudge all controversies in their own favor.

But shall the whole power of legislation rest in one assembly? Most of the foregoing reasons apply equally to prove that the legislative power ought to be more complex; to which we may add, that if the legislative power is wholly in one assembly, and the executive in another, or in a single person, these two powers will oppose and encroach upon each other, until the contest shall end in war, and the whole power, legislative and executive, be usurped by the strongest.

The judicial power, in such case, could not mediate, or hold the balance between the two contending powers, because the legislative would undermine it. And this shows the necessity, too, of giving the executive power a negative upon the legislative, otherwise this will be continually encroaching upon that.

To avoid these dangers, let a distinct assembly be constituted, as a mediator between the two extreme branches of the legislature, that which represents the people, and that which is vested with the executive power.

Let the representative assembly then elect by ballot, from among themselves or their constituents, or both, a distinct assembly, which, for the sake of perspicuity, we will call a council. It may consist of any number you please, say twenty or thirty, and should have a free and independent exercise of its judgment, and consequently a negative voice in the legislature.

These two bodies, thus constituted, and made integral parts of the legislature, let them unite, and by joint ballot choose a governor, who, after being stripped of most of those badges of domination, called prerogatives, should have a free and independent exercise of his judgment, and be made also an integral part of the legislature. This, I know, is liable to objections; and, if you please, you may make him only president of the council, as in Connecticut. But as the governor is to be invested with the executive power, with consent of council, I think he ought to have a negative upon the legislative. If he is annually elective, as he ought to be, he will always have so much reverence and affection for the people, their representatives and counsellors, that, although you give him an independent exercise of his judgment, he will seldom use it in opposition to the two houses, except in cases the public utility of which would be conspicuous; and some such cases would happen.

In the present exigency of American affairs, when, by an act of Parliament, we are put out of the royal protection, and consequently discharged from our allegiance, and it has become necessary to assume government for our immediate security, the governor, lieutenant-governor, secretary, treasurer, commissary, attorney-general, should be chosen by joint ballot of both houses. And these and all other elections, especially of representatives and counsellors, should be annual, there not being in the whole circle of the sciences a maxim more infallible than this, "where annual elections end, there slavery begins."

These great men, in this respect, should be, once a year,

> Like bubbles on the sea of matter borne,
> They rise, they break, and to that sea return.

This will teach them the great political virtues of humility, patience, and moderation, without which every man in power becomes a ravenous beast of prey.

This mode of constituting the great offices of state will answer very well for the present; but if by experiment it should be found inconvenient, the legislature may, at its leisure, devise other methods of creating them, by elections of the people at large, as in Connecticut, or it may enlarge the term for which they shall be chosen to seven years, or three years, or for life, or make any other alterations which the society shall find productive of its ease, its safety, its freedom, or, in one word, its happiness.

A rotation of all offices, as well as of representatives and counsellors, has many advocates, and is contended for with many plausible arguments. It would be attended, no doubt, with many advantages; and if the society has a sufficient number of suitable characters to supply the great number of vacancies which would be made by such a rotation, I can see no objection to it. These persons may be allowed to serve for three years, and then be excluded three years, or for any longer or shorter term.

Any seven or nine of the legislative council may be made a quorum, for doing business as a privy council, to advise the governor in the exercise of the executive branch of power, and in all acts of state.

The governor should have the command of the militia and of all your armies. The power of pardons should be with the governor and council.

Judges, justices, and all other officers, civil and military, should be nominated and appointed by the governor, with the advice and consent of council, unless you choose to have a government more popular; if you do, all officers, civil and military, may be chosen by joint ballot of both houses; or, in order to preserve the independence and importance of each house, by ballot of one house, concurred in by the other. Sheriffs should be chosen by the freeholders of counties; so should registers of deeds and clerks of counties.

All officers should have commissions, under the hand of the governor and seal of the colony.

The dignity and stability of government in all its branches, the morals of the people, and every blessing of society depend so much upon an upright and skillful administration of justice, that the judicial power ought to be distinct from both the legislative and executive, and independent upon both, that so it may be a check upon both, as both should be checks upon that. The judges, therefore, should be always men of learning and experience in the laws, of exemplary morals, great patience, calmness, coolness, and attention. Their minds should not be distracted with jarring interests; they should not be dependent upon any man, or body of men. To these ends, they should hold estate for life in their offices; or, in other words, their commission should be during good behavior, and their salaries ascertained and established by law. For misbehavior, the grand inquest of the colony, the house of representatives, should impeach them before the governor and council, where they should have time and opportunity to make their defence; but, if convicted, shall be removed from their offices, and subjected to such other punishment as shall be thought proper.

A militia law, requiring all men, or with very few exceptions besides cases of conscience, to be provided with arms and ammunition, to be trained at certain seasons; and requiring counties, towns, or other small districts, to be provided with public stocks of ammunition and intrenching utensils, and with some settled plans for transporting provisions after the militia, when marched to defend their country against sudden invasions; and requiring certain districts to be provided with field-pieces, companies of matrosses [i.e., gunners], and perhaps some regiments of light-horse, is always a wise institution, and, in the present circumstances of our country, indispensable.

Laws for the liberal education of youth, especially of the lower class of people, are so extremely wise and useful, that, to a humane and generous mind, no expense for this purpose would be thought extravagant.

The very mention of sumptuary laws [i.e., taxes on or prohibitions of luxury goods] will excite a smile. Whether our countrymen have wisdom and virtue enough to submit to them, I know not; but the happiness of the people might be greatly promoted by them, and a revenue saved sufficient to carry on this war [i.e., the Revolutionary War] forever. Frugality is a great revenue, besides curing us of vanities, levities, and fopperies, which are real antidotes to all great, manly, and war-like virtues.

But must not all commissions run in the name of a king? No. Why may they not as well run thus, "The colony of ... to A. B. greeting," and be tested by the governor?

Why may not writs, instead of running in the name of the king, run thus, "The colony of ... to the sheriff," etc., and be tested by the chief justice?

Why may not indictments conclude, "against the peace of the colony of ... and the dignity of the same?"

A constitution founded on these principles introduces knowledge among the people, and inspires them with a conscious dignity becoming freemen; a general emulation takes place, which causes good humor, sociability, good manners, and good morals to be general. That elevation of sentiment inspired by such a government, makes the common people brave and enterprising. That ambition which is inspired by it makes them sober, industrious, and frugal. You will find among them some elegance, perhaps, but more solidity; a little pleasure, but a great deal of business; some politeness, but more civility. If you compare such a country with the regions of domination, whether monarchical or aristocratical, you will fancy yourself in Arcadia or Elysium.[4]

If the colonies should assume governments separately, they should be left entirely to their own choice of the forms; and if a continental constitution should be formed, it should be a congress, containing a fair and adequate representation of the colonies, and its authority should sacredly be confined to these cases, namely, war, trade, disputes between colony and colony, the post-office, and the unappropriated lands of the crown, as they used to be called.

These colonies, under such forms of government, and in such a union, would be unconquerable by all the monarchies of Europe.

You and I, my dear friend, have been sent into life at a time when the greatest lawgivers of antiquity would have wished to live. How few of the human race have ever enjoyed an opportunity of making an election of government, more than of air, soil, or climate, for themselves or their children! When, before the present epoch, had three millions of people full power and a fair opportunity to form and establish the wisest and happiest government that human wisdom can contrive? I hope you will avail yourself and your country of that extensive learning and indefatigable industry which you possess, to assist her in the formation of the happiest governments and the best character of a great people. For myself, I must beg you to keep my name out of sight; for this feeble attempt, if it should be known to be mine, would oblige me to apply to myself those lines of the immortal John Milton, in one of his sonnets:—

> I did but prompt the age to quit their clogs By the known rules of ancient liberty, When straight a barbarous noise
> environs me
> Of owls and cuckoos, asses, apes, and dogs.

NOTES

1   Alexander Pope (1688–1744), English poet and author of *An Essay on Man* (1734), from which Adams quotes here and below.—Eds.
2   Algernon Sidney, James Harrington, John Locke, John Milton, Marchamont Nedham, Henry Neville, Gilbert Burnet, and Benjamin Hoadley were English republican or "commonwealth" writers of the seventeenth and early eighteenth centuries.—Eds.
3   So called because the members of the British House of Commons who convened in 1640 enacted a law that denied the king the power to dissolve Parliament.—Eds.
4   Arcadia was a region of ancient Greece renowned for its simple, rural pleasures; in Greek mythology, Elysium was where the blessed dwelled after death.—Eds.

Bill of Rights of the United States

One of the central tensions within the democratic tradition concerns the conflict between majority rule and minority rights. How can the one be reconciled with the other? The men who drafted the U.S. Constitution thought that the separation of governmental powers and the system of checks and balances incorporated into the Constitution would protect the rights and interests of individuals from the power of the majority, but many others believed that a list of specific limits on government authority was needed to guarantee individual rights. When the first Congress met, it moved to add the following ten amendments to the Constitution. These amendments, known as the Bill of Rights, took effect on November 3, 1791.

UNITED STATES CONSTITUTION

Articles in addition to, and Amendment of the Constitution of the United States of America, proposed by Congress, and ratified by the Legislatures of the several States, pursuant to the fifth Article of the original Constitution.

Art. I

Congress shall make no law respecting an establishment of religion, or prohibiting the free exercise thereof; or abridging the freedom of speech, or of the press; or the right of the people peaceably to assemble, and to petition the government for a redress of grievances.

Art. II

A well regulated Militia, being necessary to the security of a free State, the right of the people to keep and bear Arms, shall not be infringed.

Art. III

No Soldier shall, in time of peace be quartered in any house, without the consent of the Owner, nor in time of war, but in a manner to be prescribed by law.

Art. IV

The right of the people to be secure in their persons, houses, papers, and effects, against unreasonable searches and seizures, shall not be violated, and no Warrants shall issue, but upon probable cause, supported by Oath or affirmation, and particularly describing the place to be searched, and the persons or things to be seized.

Art. V

No person shall be held to answer for a capital, or otherwise infamous crime, unless on a presentment or indictment of a Grand Jury, except in cases arising in the land or naval forces, or in the Militia, when in actual service in time of War or public danger; nor shall any person be subject for the same offence to be twice put in jeopardy of life or limb; nor shall be compelled in any criminal case to be a witness against himself, nor be deprived of life, liberty, or property, without due process of law; nor shall private property be taken for public use, without just compensation.

Art. VI

In all criminal prosecutions, the accused shall enjoy the right to a speedy and public trial, by an impartial jury of the State and district wherein the crime shall have been committed, which district shall have been previously ascertained by law, and to be informed of the nature and cause of the accusation; to be confronted with the witnesses against him; to have compulsory process for obtaining witnesses in his favor, and to have the Assistance of Counsel for his defence.

Art. VII

In Suits at common law, where the value in controversy shall exceed twenty dollars, the right of trial by jury shall be preserved, and no fact tried by a jury, shall be otherwise re-examined in any Court of the United States, than according to the rules of the common law.

Art. VIII

Excessive bail shall not be required, nor excessive fines imposed, nor cruel and unusual punishments inflicted.

Art. IX

The enumeration in the Constitution, of certain rights, shall not be construed to deny or disparage others retained by the people.

Art. X

The powers not delegated to the United States by the Constitution, nor prohibited by it to the States, are reserved to the States respectively, or to the people.

Democracy and Equality

ALEXIS DE TOCQUEVILLE*

One of the key features of democracy is its emphasis on equality. Among the first to trace the implications of this theme was the French writer and statesman Alexis de Tocqueville (1805–1859). After visiting the United States in 1831–1832, Tocqueville wrote *Democracy in America*, one of the first—and, some say, still the greatest—explorations of the American democratic experience. When Tocqueville analyzed American democracy, moreover, he did so with an eye to the implications of democracy for Europe as well.

---

* *Source*: Alexis de Tocqueville, *Democracy in America*, vol. 1, translated by Henry Reeve (New York: Henry G. Langley, 1845), pp. 1–13.

DEMOCRACY IN AMERICA: INTRODUCTION

Among the novel objects that attracted my attention during my stay in the United States, nothing struck me more forcibly than the general equality of conditions. I readily discovered the prodigious influence which this primary fact exercises on the whole course of society, by giving a certain direction to public opinion, and a certain tenor to the laws; by imparting new maxims to the governing powers, and peculiar habits to the governed.

I speedily perceived that the influence of this fact extends far beyond the political character and the laws of the country, and that it has no less empire over civil society than over the government; it creates opinions, engenders sentiments, suggests the ordinary practices of life, and modifies whatever it does not produce.

The more I advanced in the study of American society, the more I perceived that the equality of conditions is the fundamental fact from which all others seem to be derived, and the central point at which all my observations constantly terminated.

I then turned my thoughts to our own hemisphere, where I imagined that I discerned something analogous to the spectacle which the New World presented to me. I observed that the equality of conditions is daily advancing toward those extreme limits which it seems to have reached in the United States; and that the democracy which governs the American communities, appears to be rapidly rising into power in Europe.

I hence conceived the idea of the book which is now before the reader.

It is evident to all alike that a great democratic revolution is going on among us; but there are two opinions as to its nature and consequences. To some it appears to be a novel accident, which as such may still be checked; to others it seems irresistible, because it is the most uniform, the most ancient, and the most permanent tendency which is to be found in history.

Let us recollect the situation of France seven hundred years ago, when the territory was divided among a small number of families, who were the owners of the soil and the rulers of the inhabitants; the right of governing descended with the family inheritance from generation to generation; force was the only means by which man could act on man; and landed property was the sole source of power.

Soon, however, the political power of the clergy was founded, and began to exert itself; the clergy opened its ranks to all classes, to the poor and the rich, the villain and the lord; equality penetrated into the government through the church, and the being who, as a serf, must have vegetated in perpetual bondage, took his place as a priest in the midst of nobles, and not infrequently above the heads of kings.

The different relations of men became more complicated and more numerous, as society gradually became more stable and more civilized. Thence the want of civil laws was felt; and the order of legal functionaries soon rose from the obscurity of the tribunals and their dusty chambers, to appear at the court of the monarch, by the side of the feudal barons in their ermine and their mail.

While the kings were ruining themselves by their great enterprises, and the nobles exhausting their resources by private wars, the lower orders were enriching themselves by commerce. The influence of money began to be perceptible in state affairs. The transactions of business opened a new road to power, and the financier rose to a station of political influence in which he was at once flattered and despised.

Gradually the spread of mental acquirements, and the increasing taste for literature and art, opened chances of success to talent; science became the means of government, intelligence led to social power, and the man of letters took a part in the affairs of the state.

The value attached to the privileges of birth, decreased in the exact proportion in which new paths were struck out to advancement. In the eleventh century nobility was beyond all price; in the thirteenth it might be purchased; it was conferred for the first time in 1270; and equality was thus introduced into the government by the aristocracy itself.

In the course of these seven hundred years, it sometimes happened that, in order to resist the authority of the crown or to diminish the power of their rivals, the nobles granted a certain share of political rights to the people. Or, more frequently, the king permitted the lower orders to enjoy a degree of power, with the intention of repressing the aristocracy.

In France the kings have always been the most active and the most constant of levelers. When they were strong and ambitious, they spared no pains to raise the people to the level of the nobles; when they were temperate or weak, they allowed the people to rise above themselves. Some assisted the democracy by their talents, others by their vices. Louis XI and Louis XIV reduced every rank beneath the throne to the same subjection; Louis XV descended, himself and all his court, into the dust.

As soon as land was held on any other than a feudal tenure, and personal property began in its turn to confer influence and power, every improvement which was introduced in commerce or manufacture, was a fresh element of the equality of conditions. Henceforward every new discovery, every new want which it engendered, and every new desire which craved satisfaction, was a step toward the universal level. The taste for luxury, the love of war, the sway of fashion, the most superficial, as well as the deepest passions of the human heart, co-operated to enrich the poor and to impoverish the rich.

From the time when the exercise of the intellect became the source of strength and of wealth, it is impossible not to consider every addition to science, every fresh truth, and every new idea, as a germ of power placed within the reach of the people. Poetry, eloquence, and memory, the grace of wit, the glow of imagination, the depth of thought, and all the gifts which are bestowed by Providence with an equal hand, turned to the advantage of the democracy; and even when they were in the possession of its adversaries, they still served its cause by throwing into relief the natural greatness of man; its conquests spread, therefore, with those of civilization and knowledge; and literature became an arsenal, where the poorest and weakest could always find weapons to their hand.

In perusing the pages of our history, we shall scarcely meet with a single great event, in the lapse of seven hundred years, which has not turned to the advantage of equality.

The crusades and the wars of the English decimated the nobles, and divided their possessions; the erection of communes introduced an element of democratic liberty into the bosom of feudal monarchy; the invention of firearms equalized the villain and the noble on the field of battle; printing opened the same resources to the minds of all classes; the post was organized so as to bring the same information to the door of the poor man's cottage and to the gate of the palace; and Protestantism proclaimed that all men are alike able to find the road to heaven. The discovery of America offered a thousand new paths to fortune, and placed riches and power within the reach of the adventurous and the obscure.

If we examine what has happened in France at intervals of fifty years, beginning with the eleventh century, we shall invariably perceive that a twofold revolution has taken place in the state of society. The noble has gone down on the social ladder, and the commoner has gone up; the one descends as the other rises. Every half-century brings them nearer to each other, and they will very shortly meet.

Nor is this phenomenon at all peculiar to France. Whithersoever we turn our eyes, we shall discover the same continual revolution throughout the whole of Christendom.

The various occurrences of national existence have everywhere turned to the advantage of democracy; all men have aided it by their exertions: those who have intentionally labored in its cause, and those who have served it unwittingly—those who have fought for it, and those who have declared themselves its opponents—have all been driven along in the same track, have all labored to one end, some ignorantly, and some unwillingly; all have been blind instruments in the hands of God.

The gradual development of the equality of conditions is, therefore, a providential fact, and it possesses all the characteristics of a divine decree: it is universal, it is durable, it constantly eludes all human interference, and all events as well as all men contribute to its progress.

Would it, then, be wise to imagine that a social impulse which dates from so far back, can be checked by the efforts of a generation? Is it credible that the democracy which has annihilated the feudal system, and vanquished kings, will respect the citizen and the capitalist? Will it stop now that it has grown so strong and its adversaries so weak?

None can say which way we are going, for all terms of comparison are wanting: the equality of conditions is more complete in the Christian countries of the present day, than it has been at any time, or in any part of the world; so that the extent of what already exists prevents us from foreseeing what may be yet to come.

The whole book which is here offered to the public, has been written under the impression of a kind of religious dread, produced in the author's mind by the contemplation of so irresistible a revolution, which has advanced for centuries in spite of such amazing obstacles, and which is still proceeding in the midst of the ruins it has made.

It is not necessary that God himself should speak in order to disclose to us the unquestionable signs of his will; we can discern them in the habitual course of nature, and in the invariable tendency of events; I know, without a special revelation, that the planets move in the orbits traced by the Creator's finger.

If the men of our time were led by attentive observation and by sincere reflection, to acknowledge that the gradual and progressive development of social equality is at once the past and future of their history, this solitary truth would confer the sacred character of a divine decree upon the change. To attempt to check democracy would be in that case to resist the will of God; and the nations would then be constrained to make the best of the social lot awarded to them by Providence.

The Christian nations of our age seem to me to present a most alarming spectacle; the impulse which is bearing them along is so strong that it cannot be stopped, but it is not yet so rapid that it cannot be guided: their fate is in their hands; yet a little while and it may be so no longer.

The first duty which is at this time imposed upon those who direct our affairs is to educate the democracy; to warm its faith, if that be possible; to purify its morals; to direct its energies; to substitute a knowledge of business for its inexperience, and an acquaintance with its true interests for its blind propensities; to adapt its government to time and place, and to modify it in compliance with the occurrences and the actors of the age.

A new science of politics is needed for a new world.

This, however, is what we think of least; launched in the middle of a rapid stream, we obstinately fix our eyes on the ruins which may still be descried upon the shore we have left, while the current sweeps us along, and drives us backward toward the gulf.

In no country in Europe has the great social revolution which I have been describing, made such rapid progress as in France; but it has always been borne on by chance. The heads of the state have never had any forethought for its exigencies, and its victories have been obtained without their consent or without their knowledge. The most powerful, the most intelligent, and the most moral classes of the nation have never attempted to connect themselves with it in order to guide it. The people have consequently been abandoned to its wild propensities, and it has grown up like those outcasts who receive their education in the public streets, and who are unacquainted with aught but the vices and wretchedness of society. The existence of a democracy was seemingly unknown, when, on a sudden, it took possession of the supreme power. Everything was then submitted to its caprices; it was worshipped as the idol of strength; until, when it was enfeebled by its own excesses, the legislator conceived the rash project of annihilating its power, instead of instructing it and correcting its vices; no attempt was made to fit it to govern, but all were bent on excluding it from the government.

The consequence of this has been that the democratic revolution has been effected only in the material parts of society, without that concomitant change in laws, ideas, customs, and manners, which was necessary to render such a revolution beneficial. We have gotten a democracy, but without the conditions which lessen its vices, and render its natural advantages more prominent; and although we already perceive the evils it brings, we are ignorant of the benefits it may confer.

While the power of the crown, supported by the aristocracy, peaceably governed the nations of Europe, society possessed, in the midst of its wretchedness, several different advantages which can now scarcely be appreciated or conceived.

The power of a part of his subjects was an insurmountable barrier to the tyranny of the prince; and the monarch who felt the almost divine character which he enjoyed in the eyes of the multitude, derived a motive for the just use of his power from the respect which he inspired.

High as they were placed above the people, the nobles could not but take that calm and benevolent interest in its fate which the shepherd feels toward his flock;

and without acknowledging the poor as their equals, they watched over the destiny of those whose welfare Providence had entrusted to their care.

The people, never having conceived the idea of a social condition different from its own, and entertaining no expectation of ever ranking with its chiefs, received benefits from them without discussing their rights. It grew attached to them when they were clement and just, but it submitted without resistance or servility to their exactions, as to the inevitable visitations of the arm of God. Custom, and the manners of the time, had moreover created a species of law in the midst of violence, and established certain limits to oppression.

As the noble never suspected that any one would attempt to deprive him of the privileges which he believed to be legitimate, and as the serf looked upon his own inferiority as a consequence of the immutable order of nature, it is easy to imagine that a mutual exchange of good-will took place between two classes so differently gifted by fate. Inequality and wretchedness were then to be found in society; but the souls of neither rank of men were degraded.

Men are not corrupted by the exercise of power or debased by the habit of obedience; but by the exercise of power which they believe to be illegal, and by obedience to a rule which they consider to be usurped and oppressive.

On one side were wealth, strength, and leisure, accompanied by the refinement of luxury, the elegance of taste, the pleasures of wit, and the religion of art. On the other were labor, and a rude ignorance; but in the midst of this coarse and ignorant multitude, it was not uncommon to meet with energetic passions, generous sentiments, profound religious convictions, and independent virtues.

The body of a state thus organized, might boast of its stability, its power, and above all, of its glory.

But the scene is now changed, and gradually the two ranks mingle; the divisions which once severed mankind, are lowered; property is divided, power is held in common, the light of intelligence spreads, and the capacities of all classes are equally cultivated; the state becomes democratic, and the empire of democracy is slowly and peaceably introduced into the institutions and manners of the nation.

I can conceive a society in which all men would profess an equal attachment and respect for the laws of which they are the common authors; in which the authority of the state would be respected as necessary, though not as divine; and the loyalty of the subject to the chief magistrate would not be a passion, but a quiet and rational persuasion. Every individual being in the possession of rights which he is sure to retain, a kind of manly reliance and reciprocal courtesy would arise between all classes, alike removed from pride and meanness.

The people, well acquainted with its true interests, would allow, that in order to profit by the advantages of society, it is necessary to satisfy its demands. In this state of things, the voluntary association of the citizens might supply the individual exertions of the nobles, and the community would be alike protected from anarchy and from oppression.

I admit that in a democratic state thus constituted, society will not be stationary; but the impulses of the social body may be regulated and directed forward; if there be less splendor than in the halls of an aristocracy, the contrast of misery will be less frequent also; the pleasures of enjoyment may be less excessive, but those of comfort will be more general; the sciences may be less perfectly cultivated, but ignorance will be less common; the impetuosity of the feelings will be repressed, and the habits of the nation softened; there will be more vices and fewer crimes.

In the absence of enthusiasm and of an ardent faith, great sacrifices may be obtained from the members of a commonwealth by an appeal to their understandings and their experience: each individual will feel the same necessity for uniting with his fellow-citizens to protect his own weakness; and as he knows that if they are to assist he must co-operate, he will readily perceive that his personal interest is identified with the interest of the community.

The nation, taken as a whole, will be less brilliant, less glorious, and perhaps less strong; but the majority of the citizens will enjoy a greater degree of prosperity, and the people will remain quiet, not because it despairs of melioration, but because it is conscious of the advantages of its condition.

If all the consequences of this state of things were not good or useful, society would at least have appropriated all such as were useful and good; and having once and for ever renounced the social advantages of aristocracy, mankind would enter into possession of all the benefits which democracy can afford.

But here it may be asked what we have adopted in the place of those institutions, those ideas, and those customs of our forefathers which we have abandoned.

The spell of royalty is broken, but it has not been succeeded by the majesty of the laws; the people have learned to despise all authority. But fear now extorts a larger tribute of obedience than that which was formerly paid by reverence and by love.

I perceive that we have destroyed those independent beings which were able to cope with tyranny single-handed; but it is the government that has inherited the privileges of which families, corporations, and individuals, have been deprived; the weakness of the whole community has, therefore, succeeded to that influence of a small body of citizens, which, if it was sometimes oppressive, was often conservative.

The division of property has lessened the distance which separated the rich from the poor; but it would seem that the nearer they draw to each other, the greater is their mutual hatred, and the more vehement the envy and the dread with which they resist each other's claims to power; the notion of right is alike insensible to both classes, and force affords to both the only argument for the present, and the only guarantee for the future.

The poor man retains the prejudices of his forefathers without their faith, and their ignorance without their virtues; he has adopted the doctrine of self-interest as the rule of his actions, without understanding the science which controls it, and his egotism is no less blind than his devotedness was formerly.

If society is tranquil, it is not because it relies upon its strength and its well-being, but because it knows its weakness and its infirmities: a single effort may cost it its life; everybody feels the evil, but no one has courage or energy enough to seek the cure; the desires, the regret, the sorrows, and the joys of the time, produce nothing that is visible or permanent, like the passions of old men which terminate in impotence.

We have, then, abandoned whatever advantages the old state of things afforded, without receiving any compensation from our present condition; having destroyed an aristocracy, we seem inclined to survey its ruins with complacency, and to fix our abode in the midst of them.

The phenomena which the intellectual world presents are not less deplorable. The democracy of France, checked in its course or abandoned to its lawless passions, has overthrown whatever crossed its path, and has shaken all that it has not destroyed. Its control over society has not been gradually introduced, or peaceably established, but it has constantly advanced in the midst of disorder, and the agitation of a conflict. In the heat of the struggle each partisan is hurried beyond the limits of his opinions by the opinions and the excesses of his opponents, until he loses sight of the end of his exertions, and holds a language which disguises his real sentiments or secret instincts. Hence arises the strange confusion which we are beholding.

I cannot recall to my mind a passage in history more worthy of sorrow and of pity than the scenes which are happening under our eyes; it is as if the natural bond which unites the opinions of man to his tastes, and his actions to his principles, was now broken; the sympathy which has always been acknowledged between the feelings and the ideas of mankind, appears to be dissolved, and all the laws of moral analogy to be abolished.

Zealous Christians may be found among us, whose minds are nurtured in the love and knowledge of a future life, and who readily espouse the cause of human liberty, as the source of all moral greatness. Christianity, which has declared that all men are equal in the sight of God, will not refuse to acknowledge that all citizens are equal in the eye of the law. But, by a singular concourse of events, religion is entangled in those institutions which democracy assails, and it is not infrequently brought to reject the equality it loves, and to curse that cause of liberty as a foe, which it might hallow by its alliance.

By the side of these religious men I discern others whose looks are turned to the earth more than to heaven; they are the partisans of liberty, not only as the source of the noblest virtues, but more especially as the root of all solid advantages; and they sincerely desire to extend its sway, and to impart its blessings to mankind. It is natural that they should hasten to invoke the assistance of religion, for they must know that liberty cannot be established without morality, nor morality without faith; but they have seen religion in the ranks of their adversaries, and they inquire no farther; some of them attack it openly, and the remainder are afraid to defend it.

In former ages slavery has been advocated by the venal and slavish-minded, while the independent and the warm-hearted were struggling without hope to save the liberties of mankind. But men of high and generous characters are now to be met with, whose opinions are at variance with their inclinations, and who praise that servility which they have themselves never known. Others, on the contrary, speak in the name of liberty as if they were able to feel its sanctity and its majesty, and loudly claim for humanity those rights which they have always disowned.

There are virtuous and peaceful individuals whose pure morality, quiet habits, affluence, and talents, fit them to be the leaders of the surrounding population; their love of their country is sincere, and they are prepared to make the greatest sacrifices to its welfare, but they confound the abuses of civilization with its benefits, and the idea of evil is inseparable in their minds from that of novelty.

Not far from this class is another party, whose object is to materialize mankind, to hit upon what is expedient without heeding what is just; to acquire knowledge without faith, and prosperity apart from virtue; assuming the title of the champions of modern civilization, and placing themselves in a station which they usurp with insolence, and from which they are driven by their own unworthiness.

Where are we then?

The religionists are the enemies of liberty, and the friends of liberty attack religion; the high-minded and the noble advocate subjection, and the meanest and most servile minds preach independence; honest and enlightened citizens are opposed to all progress, while men without patriotism and without principles, are the apostles of civilization and of intelligence.

Has such been the fate of the centuries which have preceded our own? And has man always inhabited a world, like the present, where nothing is linked together, where virtue is without genius, and genius without honor; where the love of order is confounded with a taste for oppression, and the holy rites of freedom with a contempt of law; where the light thrown by conscience on human actions is dim, and where nothing seems to be any longer forbidden or allowed, honorable or shameful, false or true?

I cannot, however, believe that the Creator made man to leave him in an endless struggle with the intellectual miseries which surround us: God destines a calmer and a more certain future to the communities of Europe; I am unacquainted with his designs, but I shall not cease to believe in them because I cannot fathom them, and I had rather mistrust my own capacity than his justice.

There is a country in the world where the great revolution which I am speaking of seems nearly to have reached its natural limits; it has been effected with ease and simplicity, say rather that this country has attained the consequences of the democratic revolution which we are undergoing, without having experienced the revolution itself.

The emigrants who fixed themselves on the shores of America in the beginning of the seventeenth century, severed the democratic principle from all the principles which repressed it in the old communities of Europe, and transplanted it unalloyed to the New World. It has there been allowed to spread in perfect freedom, and to put forth its consequences in the laws by influencing the manners of the country.

It appears to me beyond a doubt, that sooner or later we shall arrive, like the Americans, at an almost complete equality of conditions. But I do not conclude from this, that we shall ever be necessarily led to draw the same political consequences which the Americans have derived from a similar social organization. I am far from supposing that they have chosen the only form of government which a democracy may adopt; but the identity of the efficient cause of laws and manners in the two countries is sufficient to account for the immense interest we have in becoming acquainted with its effects in each of them.

It is not, then, merely to satisfy a legitimate curiosity that I have examined America; my wish has been to find instruction by which we may ourselves profit. Whoever should imagine that I have intended to write a panegyric would be strangely mistaken, and on reading this book, he will perceive that such was not my design: nor has it been my object to advocate any form of government in particular, for I am of [the] opinion that absolute excellence is rarely to be found in any legislation; I have not even affected to discuss whether the social revolution, which I believe to be irresistible, is advantageous or prejudicial to mankind; I have acknowledged this revolution as a fact already accomplished or on the eve of its accomplishment; and I have selected the nation, from among those which have undergone it, in which its development has been the most peaceful and the most complete, in order to discern its natural consequences, and, if it be possible, to distinguish the means by which it may be rendered profitable. I confess that in America I saw more than America; I sought the image of democracy itself, with its inclinations, its character, its prejudices, and its passions, in order to learn what we have to fear or to hope from its progress.

Democratic Participation and Political Education

JOHN STUART MILL*

As the English philosopher John Stuart Mill (1806–1873) noted, there are several reasons for preferring democracy to other forms of government. One is that it enables individuals to speak up for—and thus protect—their own interests. But, in addition to this "protectionist" argument, there is a second and perhaps more important *educative* argument to be made in favor of democracy: that it educates and improves citizens by providing them with "hands-on" experience of self-rule.

---

* *Source*: John Stuart Mill, *Considerations on Representative Government*, in *Utilitarianism, Liberty, and Representative Government*, A. D. Lindsay, ed. (New York: E. P. Dutton and Co., 1910), chap. 3, pp. 202–205, 207–208, 211–218.

THAT THE IDEALLY BEST FORM OF GOVERNMENT IS REPRESENTATIVE GOVERNMENT

(From *Considerations on Representative Government*)

It has long (perhaps throughout the entire duration of British freedom) been a common saying, that if a good despot could be ensured, despotic monarchy would be the best form of government. I look upon this as a radical and most pernicious misconception of what good government is; which, until it can be got rid of, will fatally vitiate all our speculations on government.

The supposition is, that absolute power, in the hands of an eminent individual, would ensure a virtuous and intelligent performance of all the duties of government. Good laws would be established and enforced, bad laws would be reformed; the best men would be placed in all situations of trust; justice would be as well administered, the public burthens would be as light and as judiciously imposed, every branch of administration would be as purely and as intelligently conducted, as the circumstances of the country and its degree of intellectual and moral cultivation would admit. I am willing, for the sake of the argument, to concede all this: but I must point out how great the concession is; how much more is needed to produce even an approximation to these results, than is conveyed in the simple expression, a good despot. Their realization would in fact imply, not merely a good monarch, but an all-seeing one. He must be at all times informed correctly, in considerable detail, of the conduct and working of every branch of administration, in every district of the country, and must be able, in the twenty-four hours per day which are all that is granted to a king as to the humblest labourer, to give an effective share of attention and superintendence to all parts of this vast field; or he must at least be capable of discerning and choosing out, from among the mass of his subjects, not only a large abundance of honest and able men, fit to conduct every branch of public administration under supervision and control, but also the small number of men of eminent virtues and talents who can be trusted not only to do without that supervision, but to exercise it themselves over others. So extraordinary are the faculties and energies required for performing this task in any supportable manner, that the good despot whom we are supposing can hardly be imagined as consenting to undertake it, unless as a refuge from intolerable evils, and a transitional preparation for something beyond. But the argument can do without even this immense item in the account. Suppose the difficulty vanquished. What should we then have? One man of superhuman mental activity managing the entire affairs of a mentally passive people. Their passivity is implied in the very idea of absolute power. The nation as a whole, and every individual composing it, are without any potential voice in their own destiny. They exercise no will in respect to their collective interests. All is decided for them by a will not their own, which it is legally a crime for them to disobey. What sort of human beings can be formed under such a regimen? What development can either their thinking or their active faculties attain under it? On matters of pure theory they might perhaps be allowed to speculate, so long as their speculations either did not approach politics, or had not the remotest connexion with its practice. On practical affairs they could at most be only suffered to suggest; and even under the most moderate of despots, none but persons of already admitted or reputed superiority could hope that their suggestions would be known to, much less regarded by, those who had the management of affairs. A person must have a very unusual taste for intellectual exercise in and for itself, who will put himself to the trouble of thought when it is to have no outward effect, or qualify himself for functions which he has no chance of being allowed to exercise. The only sufficient incitement to mental exertion, in any but a few minds in a generation, is the prospect of some practical use to be made of its results. It does not follow that the nation will be wholly destitute of intellectual power. The common business of life, which must necessarily be performed by each individual or family for themselves, will call forth some amount of intelligence and practical ability, within a certain narrow range of ideas. There may be a select class of savants [i.e., wise people], who cultivate science with a view to its physical uses, or for the pleasure of the pursuit. There will be a bureaucracy, and persons in training for the bureaucracy, who will be taught at least some empirical maxims of government and public administration. There may be, and often has been, a systematic organization of the best mental power in the country in some special direction (commonly military) to promote the grandeur of the despot. But the public at large remain without information and without interest on all the greater matters of practice; or, if they have any knowledge of them, it is but a dilettante knowledge, like that which people have of the mechanical arts who have never handled a tool. Nor is it only in their intelligence that they suffer. Their moral capacities are equally stunted. Wherever the sphere of action of human beings is artificially circumscribed, their sentiments are narrowed and dwarfed in the same proportion. The food of feeling is action: even domestic affection lives upon voluntary good offices. Let a person have nothing to do for his country, and he will not care for it. It has been said of old, that in a despotism there is at most but one patriot, the despot himself; and the saying rests on a just appreciation of the effects of absolute subjection, even to a good and wise master. Religion remains: and here at least, it may be thought, is an agency that may be relied on for lifting men's eyes and minds above the dust at their feet. But religion, even supposing it to escape perversion for the purposes of despotism, ceases in these circumstances to be a social concern, and narrows into a personal affair between an individual and his Maker, in which the issue at stake is but his private salvation. Religion in this shape is quite consistent with the most selfish and contracted egoism, and identifies the votary as little in feeling with the rest of his kind as sensuality itself.

A good despotism means a government in which, so far as depends on the despot, there is no positive oppression by officers of state, but in which all the collective interests of the people are managed for them, all the thinking that has relation to collective interests done for them, and in which their minds are formed by, and consenting to, this abdication of their own energies. Leaving things to the Government, like leaving them to Providence, is synonymous with caring nothing about them, and accepting their results, when disagreeable, as visitations of Nature. With the exception, therefore, of a few studious men who take an intellectual interest in speculation for its own sake, the intelligence and sentiments of the whole people are given up to the material interests, and when these are provided for, to the amusement and ornamentation, of private life. But to say this is to say, if the whole testimony of history is worth anything, that the era of national decline has arrived: that is, if the nation had ever attained anything to decline from. If it has never risen above the condition of an Oriental people, in that condition it continues to stagnate. But if, like Greece or Rome, it had realized anything higher, through the energy, patriotism, and enlargement of mind, which as national qualities are the fruits solely of freedom, it relapses in a few generations into the Oriental state. And that state does not mean stupid tranquility, with security against change for the worse; it often means being overrun, conquered, and reduced to domestic slavery, either by a stronger despot, or by the nearest barbarous people who retain along with their savage rudeness the energies of freedom.

There is no difficulty in showing that the ideally best form of government is that in which the sovereignty, or supreme controlling power in the last resort, is vested in the entire aggregate of the community; every citizen not only having a voice in the exercise of that ultimate sovereignty, but being, at least occasionally, called on to take an actual part in the government, by the personal discharge of some public function, local or general.

To test this proposition, it has to be examined in reference to the two branches into which ... the inquiry into the goodness of a government conveniently divides itself, namely, how far it promotes the good management of the affairs of society by means of the existing faculties, moral, intellectual, and active, of its various members, and what is its effect in improving or deteriorating those faculties.

The ideally best form of government, it is scarcely necessary to say, does not mean one which is practicable or eligible in all states of civilization, but the one which, in the circumstances in which it is practicable and eligible, is attended with the greatest amount of beneficial consequences, immediate and prospective. A completely popular government is the only polity which can make out any claim to this character. It is pre-eminent in both the departments between which the excellence of a political constitution is divided. It is both more favourable to present good government, and promotes a better and higher form of national character, than any other polity whatsoever.

Its superiority in reference to present wellbeing rests upon two principles, of as universal truth and applicability as any general propositions which can be laid down respecting human affairs. The first is, that the rights and interests of every or any person are only secure from being disregarded, when the person interested is himself able, and habitually disposed, to stand up for them. The second is, that the general prosperity attains a greater height, and is more widely diffused, in proportion to the amount and variety of the personal energies enlisted in promoting it.

Putting these two propositions into a shape more special to their present application; human beings are only secure from evil at the hands of others, in proportion as they have the power of being, and are, self-protecting; and they only achieve a high degree of success in their struggle with Nature, in proportion as they are self-dependent, relying on what they themselves can do, either separately or in concert, rather than on what others do for them ...

If we now pass to the influence of the form of government upon character, we shall find the superiority of popular government over every other to be, if possible, still more decided and indisputable.

This question really depends upon a still more fundamental one—viz., which of two common types of character, for the general good of humanity, it is most desirable should predominate—the active, or the passive type; that which struggles against evils, or that which endures them; that which bends to circumstances, or that which endeavours to make circumstances bend to itself.

The commonplaces of moralists, and the general sympathies of mankind, are in favour of the passive type. Energetic characters may be admired, but the acquiescent and submissive are those which most men personally prefer. The passiveness of our neighbours increases our sense of security, and plays into the hands of our wilfulness. Passive characters, if we do not happen to need their activity, seem an obstruction the less in our own path. A contented character is not a dangerous rival. Yet nothing is more certain, than that improvement in human affairs is wholly the work of the uncontented characters; and, moreover, that it is much easier for an active mind to acquire the virtues of patience, than for a passive one to assume those of energy.

Of the three varieties of mental excellence, intellectual, practical, and moral, there never could be any doubt in regard to the first two, which side had the advantage. All intellectual superiority is the fruit of active effort. Enterprise, the desire to keep moving, to be trying and accomplishing new things for our own benefit or that of others, is the parent even of speculative, and much more of practical, talent. The intellectual culture compatible with the other type is of that feeble and vague description, which belongs to a mind that stops at amusement, or at simple contemplation. The test of real and vigorous thinking, the thinking which ascertains truths instead of dreaming dreams, is successful application to practice. Where that purpose does not exist, to give definiteness, precision, and an intelligible meaning to thought, it generates nothing better than the mystical metaphysics of the Pythagoreans or the Vedas.[1]

With respect to practical improvement, the case is still more evident. The character which improves human life is that which struggles with natural powers and tendencies, not that which gives way to them. The self-benefiting qualities are all on the side of the active and energetic character: and the habits and conduct which promote the advantage of each individual member of the community, must be at least a part of those which conduce most in the end to the advancement of the community as a whole.

But on the point of moral preferability, there seems at first sight to be room for doubt. I am not referring to the religious feeling which has so generally existed in favour of the inactive character, as being more in harmony with the submission due to the divine will. Christianity as well as other religions has fostered this sentiment; but it is the prerogative of Christianity, as regards this and many other perversions, that it is able to throw them off. Abstractedly from religious considerations, a passive character, which yields to obstacles instead of striving to overcome them, may not indeed be very useful to others, no more than to itself, but it might be expected to be at least inoffensive. Contentment is always counted among the moral virtues. But it is a complete error to suppose that contentment is necessarily or naturally attendant on passivity of character; and unless it is, the moral consequences are mischievous. Where there exists a desire for advantages not possessed, the mind which does not potentially possess them by means of its own energies, is apt to look with hatred and malice on those who do. The person bestirring himself with hopeful prospects to improve his circumstances, is the one who feels goodwill towards others engaged in, or who have succeeded in, the same pursuit. And where the majority are so engaged, those who do not attain the object have had the tone given to their feelings by the general habit of the country, and ascribe their failure to want of effort or opportunity, or to their personal ill luck. But those who, while desiring what others possess, put no energy into striving for it, are either incessantly grumbling that fortune does not do for them what they do not attempt to do for themselves, or overflowing with envy and ill-will towards those who possess what they would like to have ...

There are, no doubt, in all countries, really contented characters, who not merely do not seek, but do not desire, what they do not already possess, and these naturally bear no ill-will towards such as have apparently a more favoured lot. But the great mass of seeming contentment is real discontent, combined with indolence or self-indulgence, which, while taking no legitimate means of raising itself, delights in bringing others down to its own level. And if we look narrowly even at the cases of innocent contentment, we perceive that they only win our admiration, when the indifference is solely to improvement in outward circumstances, and there is a striving for perpetual advancement in spiritual worth, or at least a disinterested zeal to benefit others. The contented man, or the contented family, who have no ambition to make any one else happier, to promote the good of their country or their neighbourhood, or to improve themselves in moral excellence, excite in us neither admiration nor approval. We rightly ascribe this sort of contentment to mere unmanliness and want of spirit. The content which we approve, is an ability to do cheerfully without what cannot be had, a just appreciation of the comparative value of different objects of desire, and a willing renunciation of the less when incompatible with the greater. These, however, are excellences more natural to the character, in proportion as it is actively engaged in the attempt to improve its own or some other lot. He who is continually measuring his energy against difficulties, learns what are the difficulties insuperable to him, and what are those which though he might overcome, the success is not worth the cost. He whose thoughts and activities are all needed for, and habitually employed in, practicable and useful enterprises, is the person of all others least likely to let his mind dwell with brooding discontent upon things either not worth attaining, or which are not so to him. Thus the active, self-helping character is not only intrinsically the best, but is the likeliest to acquire all that is really excellent or desirable in the opposite type ...

Now there can be no kind of doubt that the passive type of character is favoured by the government of one or a few, and the active self-helping type by that of the many. Irresponsible rulers need the quiescence of the ruled, more than they need any activity but that which they can compel. Submissiveness to the prescriptions of men as necessities of nature, is the lesson inculcated by all governments upon those who are wholly without participation in them. The will of superiors, and the law as the will of superiors, must be passively yielded to. But no men are mere instruments or materials in the hands of their rulers, who have will or spirit or a spring of internal activity in the rest of their proceedings: and any manifestation of these qualities, instead of receiving encouragement from despots, has to get itself forgiven by them. Even when irresponsible rulers are not sufficiently conscious of danger from the mental activity of their subjects to be desirous of repressing it, the position itself is a repression. Endeavour is even more effectually restrained by the certainty of its impotence, than by any positive discouragement. Between subjection to the will of others, and the virtues of self-help and self-government, there is a natural incompatibility. This is more or less complete, according as the bondage is strained or relaxed. Rulers differ very much in the length to which they carry the control of the free agency of their subjects, or the supersession of it by managing their business for them. But the difference is in degree, not in principle; and the best despots often go the greatest lengths in chaining up the free agency of their subjects. A bad despot, when his own personal indulgences have been provided for, may sometimes be willing to let the people alone; but a good despot insists on doing them good, by making them do their own business in a better way than they themselves know of. The regulations which restricted to fixed processes all the leading branches of French manufacturers, were the work of the great Colbert.[2]

Very different is the state of the human faculties where a human being feels himself under no other external restraint than the necessities of nature, or mandates of society which he has his share in imposing, and which it is open to him, if he thinks them wrong, publicly to dissent from, and exert himself actively to get altered. No doubt, under a government partially popular, this freedom may be exercised even by those who are not partakers in the full privileges of citizenship. But it is a great additional stimulus to any one's self-help and self-reliance when he starts from even ground, and has not to feel that his success depends on the impression he can make upon the sentiments and dispositions of a body of whom he is not one. It is a great discouragement to an individual, and a still greater one to a class, to be left out of the constitution; to be reduced to plead from outside the door to the arbiters of their destiny, not taken into consultation within. The maximum of the invigorating effect of freedom upon the character is only obtained, when the person acted on either is, or is looking forward to becoming, a citizen as fully privileged as any other. What is still more important than even this matter of feeling, is the practical discipline which the character obtains, from the occasional demand made upon the citizens to exercise, for a time and in their turn, some social function. It is not sufficiently considered how little there is in most men's ordinary life to give any largeness either to their conceptions or to their sentiments. Their work is a routine; not a labour of love, but of self-interest in the most elementary form, the satisfaction of daily wants; neither the thing done, nor the process of doing it, introduces the mind to thoughts or feelings extending beyond individuals; if instructive books are within their reach, there is no stimulus to read them; and in most cases the individual has no access to any person of cultivation much superior to his own. Giving him something to do for the public, supplies, in a measure, all these deficiencies. If circumstances allow the amount of public duty assigned him to be considerable, it makes him an educated man. Notwithstanding the defects of the social system and moral ideas of antiquity, the practice of the dicastery [i.e., jury system] and the ecclesia [i.e., assembly] raised the intellectual standard of an average Athenian citizen far beyond anything of which there is yet an example in any other mass of men, ancient or modern. The proofs of this are apparent in every page of our great historian of Greece; but we need scarcely look further than to the high quality of the addresses which their great orators deemed best calculated to act with effect on their understanding and will. A benefit of the same kind, though far less in degree, is produced on Englishmen of the lower middle class by their liability to be placed on juries and to serve parish offices; which, though it does not occur to so many, nor is so continuous, nor introduces them to so great a variety of elevated considerations, as to admit of comparison with the public education which every citizen of Athens obtained from her democratic institutions, must make them nevertheless very different beings, in range of ideas and development of faculties, from those who have done nothing in their lives but drive a quill, or sell goods over a counter. Still more salutary is the moral part of the instruction afforded by the participation of the private citizen, if even rarely, in public functions. He is called upon, while so engaged, to weigh interests not his own; to be guided, in case of conflicting claims, by another rule than his private partialities; to apply, at every turn, principles and maxims which have for their reason of existence the common good: and he usually finds associated with him in the same work minds more familiarized than his own with these ideas and operations, whose study it will be to supply reasons to his understanding, and stimulation to his feeling for the general interest. He is made to feel himself one of the public, and whatever is for their benefit to be for his benefit. Where this school of public spirit does not exist, scarcely any sense is entertained that private persons, in no eminent social situation, owe any duties to society, except to obey the laws and submit to the government. There is no unselfish sentiment of identification with the public. Every thought or feeling, either of interest or of duty, is absorbed in the individual and in the family. The man never thinks of any collective interest, of any objects to be pursued jointly with others, but only in competition with them, and in some measure at their expense. A neighbour, not being an ally or an associate, since he is never engaged in any common undertaking for joint benefit, is therefore only a rival. Thus even private morality suffers, while public is actually extinct. Were this the universal and only possible state of things, the utmost aspirations of the law-giver or the moralist could only stretch to making the bulk of the community a flock of sheep innocently nibbling the grass side by side.

From these accumulated considerations it is evident, that the only government which can fully satisfy all the exigencies of the social state, is one in which the whole people participate; that any participation, even in the smallest public function, is useful; that the participation should everywhere be as great as the general degree of improvement of the community will allow; and that nothing less can be ultimately desirable, than the admission of all to a share in the sovereign power of the state. But since all cannot, in a community exceeding a single small town, participate personally in any but some very minor portions of the public business, it follows that the ideal type of a perfect government must be representative.

NOTES

1   Pythagoreans, or followers of the Greek philosopher and mathematician Pythagoras (d. 497 BCE?), believed in, among other things, the mystical significance of numbers; the Vedas are the earliest Hindu sacred writings.—Eds.

2   Jean-Baptiste Colbert (1619–1683), French minister of finance who oversaw improvements in industry and economic infrastructure.—Eds.

The Strange Career of Voter Suppression

ALEXANDER KEYSSAR*

In the history of democracy the democratic ideal of "one person, one vote" has never been fully realized, only imperfectly approximated. In the following essay the American historian Alexander Keyssar (1947–) chronicles the too-often tawdry history of overt or covert voter suppression in the United States. Keyssar is Professor of History and Social Policy at Harvard University and the author of several books, including *The Right to Vote: The Contested History of Democracy in the United States* (2001).

---

* *Source*: *New York Times*, February 13, 2010. Reprinted by permission of the author, who has made several minor changes to the previously published version.

The 2012 general election campaign is likely to be a fight for every last vote, which means that it will also be a fight over who gets to cast one.

Partisan skirmishing over election procedures has been going on in state legislatures across the country for several years. Republicans have called for cutbacks in early voting, an end to same-day registration, higher hurdles for ex-felons, the presentation of proof-of-citizenship documents, and regulations discouraging registration drives by organizations like the League of Women Voters. The centerpiece of this effort has been a national campaign to require prospective voters to present particular types of photo ID documents like driver's licenses in order to cast their ballots. Characterized as innocuous reforms to preserve the integrity of elections, laws beefing up ID requirements have been passed in more than a dozen states since 2005 (usually on straight party-line votes) and are still being considered in more than twenty others.

Opponents of the new laws—mostly Democrats—claim that they are designed to reduce the participation of the young, of the poor and of minority citizens who are most likely to lack government-issued IDs—and also most likely to vote Democratic. Opponents also note that the type of fraud that would be prevented by strict photo ID requirements—in-person voter impersonation—is rare: very few people show up at the polls claiming to be someone else.

Conflict over the right to vote and the exercise of that right has been a longstanding theme in our history. The over-arching trend, which we celebrate, has been in the direction of greater inclusion: property requirements for voting were dropped in most states by 1850; racial barriers were formally eliminated with the ratification of the 15th Amendment in 1870; women were enfranchised nationally in 1920.

Yet there have always been reversals and counter-trends. While the franchise expanded during some moments and in some places, it contracted in others, depriving Americans of a right they had once held. Between 1790 and 1850, for example—precisely the period when property requirements were being dropped—four northern states, including Pennsylvania, disfranchised African-American voters, and New Jersey called a halt to a twenty-year experiment permitting women to vote. During this same period, laws were passed in nine states excluding from political rights all "paupers"—men who were receiving any form of public relief.

After the Civil War and Reconstruction, both major political parties attempted to constrict the electorate, albeit in different locales. In the South—the only part of this story that is well known—Democratic state legislatures deployed a variety of devices to circumvent the Fifteenth Amendment, including literacy tests, poll taxes, "understanding" clauses and eventually (after the Republican party had been severely weakened) Democratic primaries restricted to whites. As a result, African-Americans—who were politically active for two decades or more after the Civil War—were largely excluded from electoral participation from the 1890s until the 1960s.

In the North, similar, if less draconian, legal changes, generally sponsored by Republicans, targeted (among others) the millions of immigrant workers who were pouring into the country. Literacy tests became common. In 1921, for example, New York State adopted an English-language literacy requirement for voters that remained in force (and was enforced) for decades. Almost invariably, these new limits on the franchise were fueled by partisan interests and ethnic or racial tensions; they were embraced by respectable Americans, like the eminent historian Francis Parkman, who had come to view universal suffrage as a "questionable blessing."

Many of the late-nineteenth and early-twentieth century laws operated not by excluding specific classes of citizens but by erecting procedural obstacles that were justified as measures to prevent fraud or corruption. It was to "preserve the purity of the ballot box" that legislatures passed laws requiring voters to bring their sealed naturalization papers to the polls, or to present written evidence that they had cancelled their registration at any previous address, or to register annually, in person, in their precincts, on one of only two Tuesdays. (In 1908, in New York City, most of the days designated for registration were either Saturdays or Yom Kippur, a problem for many Jewish voters.) The new procedures were widely recognized, by both their advocates and their targets, as having a far greater impact on some groups of voters—immigrants, Jews, blue-collar workers, the poor—than on others, and they often succeeded. In Pittsburgh, in 1906, a personal registration law, sponsored by Republicans, cut the number of registered voters in half.

Episodes of suffrage contraction recurred during the twentieth century. In the 1930s, during the Great Depression, several states invoked their "pauper exclusion" laws to disfranchise jobless men and women who were receiving relief. In 2000, Massachusetts disfranchised prison inmates—who had been legal voters—after they formed an organization to promote inmate rights.

Notably, the targets of exclusionary laws have tended to be similar for more than two centuries: the poor, immigrants, African-Americans, people perceived to be something other than "mainstream" Americans. No state has ever attempted to disfranchise upper-middle-class or wealthy white male citizens.

The current wave of procedural restrictions on voting, including strict photo ID requirements, ought to be understood as the latest chapter in a not always uplifting story: the United States has a long tradition of conflict over access to the ballot box, and Americans of both parties have sometimes rejected democratic values or preferred partisan advantage to fair democratic processes. Acknowledging the realities of our history should lead all of us to be profoundly skeptical of laws that burden, or impede, the exercise of what Lyndon Johnson called "the basic right, without which all others are meaningless." More is at stake here than the outcome of the 2012 election. Even a cursory survey of world events over the last twenty—or 100—years makes plain that democracies are fragile, that formally democratic institutions can be undermined from within. Ours are no exception.

PART 3

LIBERALISM

Like "liberty," the word "liberal" is derived from the Latin *liber*, meaning "free." Liberals see themselves as champions of individual liberty who work to create or preserve an open and tolerant society—a society whose members are free to pursue their own ideas and interests with as little interference as possible. This has been their project since liberalism began as a reaction against two features of medieval society in Europe: religious conformity and ascribed status.

Religious conformity was taken for granted in a society in which the church and the state were supposed to be partners in the defense of "Christendom." Indeed, throughout the Middle Ages there was no clear distinction between church and state. The Christian (i.e., Roman Catholic) Church saw its mission as saving souls for the kingdom of God, which could best be done by teaching and upholding orthodoxy, or "correct belief." Those who took an unorthodox view of Christianity—or rejected it altogether—thus threatened the church's attempts to do what it saw as the will of God. To counter this threat, the church called on the kings, princes, and other rulers of Christendom to use their power to enforce conformity to the church's doctrines.

The other feature of medieval society against which liberalism reacted was ascribed status—the view that a person's social standing rested not on achievement but on the status of his or her parents. One was simply born a nobleman, a free commoner, or a serf—and that, with few exceptions, was all there was to it. People may have been equal in the eyes of God, as the church taught, but men and women of different social ranks were not equals on God's earth or in man's state.

Against this society rooted in ascribed status and religious conformity, liberalism emerged as the first distinctive political ideology. Yet this liberal reaction did not take form until a series of social, economic, and cultural crises shook the medieval order to its foundations. Many of these changes were directly related to the outburst of creativity in the fourteenth and fifteenth centuries known as the Renaissance. Perhaps the most important impetus to the rise of liberalism was the Protestant Reformation of the sixteenth century. When Martin Luther (1483–1546) and other reformers taught that salvation comes through faith alone, they encouraged people to value individual conscience more than the preservation of unity and orthodoxy. Without intending to do so, they prepared the way for liberalism. The step from individual conscience to individual liberty was still radical for the time, but it was a step that liberals began to take in the seventeenth and eighteenth centuries.

The first book of philosophical significance to bear the distinctive stamp of liberalism was Thomas Hobbes's *Leviathan* (1651). All individuals are equal, Hobbes said. Everyone has a natural right to be free, and no one has the right to rule another without that person's consent. From these liberal premises, however, Hobbes reached the distinctly illiberal conclusion that people, for the sake of their security, must voluntarily grant absolute power over themselves to a sovereign ruler.

John Locke (1632–1704) and later writers used similar arguments to reach very different conclusions. Locke argued for a measure of religious liberty in his *Letter Concerning Toleration* (1689), and in the *Second Treatise of Government* (1690) he defended the right of the people to overthrow any government that does not protect their natural rights to life, liberty, and property. The arguments he advanced—the natural equality of men, natural rights, government founded on the consent of the governed—were invoked throughout the eighteenth century. They proved particularly attractive to revolutionaries in the American colonies and in France, where they found lasting expression in the American Declaration of Independence (1776) and the French Declaration of the Rights of Man and of Citizens (1789).

In their efforts to remove obstacles to individual liberty, many liberals argued that economic exchanges are a private matter between persons who ought to be free from government regulation. In France, a group of thinkers called the Physiocrats captured this view in the phrase *laissez faire, laissez passer*—"let it be, leave it alone." This is the core idea of capitalism, which found its most influential defense in Adam Smith's *Wealth of Nations* (1776). Smith argued that an economic policy that would allow individuals to compete freely in the marketplace would be not only the most efficient but also the fairest policy, because it gives everyone an equal opportunity to compete.

Throughout the eighteenth century, then, liberalism was a revolutionary doctrine that reshaped the religious, political, social, and economic relations of people in Europe and North America. In the nineteenth century, liberalism began to take new directions. In particular, the liberal attitude toward democracy and government shifted in the course of the 1800s. Whereas earlier liberals had spoken the language of equality, liberals in the nineteenth century went further and called for expansions of voting rights; and, whereas earlier liberals regarded government as, in Thomas Paine's words, "a necessary evil," some liberals in the nineteenth century came to see it as a necessary ally in the struggle to promote individual liberty. In both cases, John Stuart Mill (1806–1873) played a vital part.

An early supporter of women's rights, Mill argued that all literate adults should have the right to vote. Yet he believed that it would be foolish to entrust the ignorant and uninformed with an equal voice in public decisions. Almost every person should have a vote, he concluded, but those with higher levels of education should have two, three, or more in a system of "weighted voting."

This ambivalence toward democracy follows from Mill's fear of the "tyranny of the majority." Now that government is responsible to the people, he said in *On Liberty* (1859), the majority of voters could conceivably use the government to deny liberty to those whose views they find disagreeable or distasteful. More directly, the "moral coercion of public opinion" can and does stifle freedom of thought and action by making a social outcast of anyone who does not conform to social customs and beliefs. Mill's argument against this new tyranny rests on the claim that not only individuals but society as a whole will benefit if people are encouraged to act and think freely. Progress is possible only where there is open competition among different ideas, opinions, and beliefs—a marketplace of ideas.

With its distinction between private and public matters and its suggestion that individual liberty must be protected from interference by government and society, Mill's defense of liberty took a form familiar to earlier liberals. There was another dimension to Mill's view, however, that marked a shift in many liberals' attitude toward government. Freedom, as Mill conceived it, is largely a matter of being free to develop one's own individual potential. In some of Mill's later work, and especially in the writings of T. H. Green (1836–1882), this conception of freedom suggested that government could and should be something more than a night watchman protecting the life, liberty, and property of its citizens. Instead, government should promote the welfare of its people—and should do so in the name of individual liberty. Only in this way could people overcome some of the obstacles—for example, poverty, illness, ignorance, and prejudice—that prevented them from being truly free.

This way of thinking about government led to a split between those who clung to the older views—the neoclassical liberals—and those who followed Green along the path of "welfare" or "reform" liberalism. In the late 1800s, the most prominent version of neoclassical liberalism was the Social Darwinism of such writers as Herbert Spencer (1820–1903) and William Graham Sumner (1840–1910). As the franchise expanded to include the working class and the welfare state began to emerge, however, neoclassical liberalism began to fade. Welfare liberalism gradually came to be known simply as liberalism.

Yet neoclassical liberalism never entirely disappeared. After President Franklin Delano Roosevelt's New Deal (1933–1944) put welfare liberalism into practice in the United States, some economists (e.g., Friedrich Hayek [1899–1992] and Milton Friedman [1912–2006]) and at least one novelist, Ayn Rand (1905–1982), reasserted the case against active government and the welfare state in their writings. Their ideas and arguments helped to inspire the creation of the Libertarian Party, which advocates what one libertarian—the Harvard philosopher Robert Nozick (1938–2002)—called "the minimal state." Some libertarians, such as Murray Rothbard (1926–1995), have even argued for anarchism on the grounds that government is an entirely *un*necessary evil. The worldwide Great Recession that began in 2007 and continued into the presidency of Barack Obama called into question the free-market ideology of libertarianism, and could conceivably bring about a revival of New Deal liberalism, as exemplified in the passage of the Affordable Care Act (ACA) or "Obamacare," as critics call it.

So the debate within liberalism that began over one hundred years ago continues today. Both groups agree on the end they want to achieve—an open and tolerant society in which every person has an opportunity to live as freely as possible. But what are the best means to achieve this end? Is government the chief obstacle to individual liberty, as the neoclassical liberals claim, or an aid and an ally that is useful in removing other barriers to freedom, as the welfare liberals insist? On this point, welfare and neoclassical liberals continue to disagree, with no resolution in sight. Indeed, the debate has grown more complicated in recent years with the emergence of *communitarians*, who complain that welfare and neoclassical liberals both pay too little attention to what individuals owe to their communities. Liberals are right to stress the importance of individual liberty, according to Philip Selznick (1919–2010) and other communitarians, but they must also recognize that individuals have a duty to help preserve the communities that make individual liberty possible.

The State of Nature and the Basis of Obligation

*THOMAS HOBBES**

Thomas Hobbes (1588–1679) might best be described as a preliberal, or perhaps a protoliberal, thinker. The main features of liberalism are to be found in his *Leviathan* (1651), particularly in the imaginary "state of nature," but his conclusions are seldom considered liberal. In the following excerpts from *Leviathan*, Hobbes invites his readers to imagine a world without laws, police, courts, and prisons—a world of "perfect" liberty and equality—and then goes on to show "scientifically" that such a world would be nothing less than a "war of every man against every man." Thus, he concluded, rational, self-interested people would have every reason to enter into a "social contract" in which they put themselves under the unlimited authority of a sovereign ruler.

* *Source: The English Works of Thomas Hobbes of Malmesbury,* vol. 3, Sir William Molesworth, ed. (London: John Bohn, 1839), pp. 110–130. The editors have modernized the spelling of some words.

OF THE NATURAL CONDITION OF MANKIND AS CONCERNING THEIR FELICITY AND MISERY

(From *Leviathan*, Chapter 13)

Nature has made men so equal, in the faculties of the body, and mind; as that though there be found one man sometimes manifestly stronger in body, or of quicker mind than another; yet when all is reckoned together, the difference between man, and man, is not so considerable, as that one man can thereupon claim to himself any benefit, to which another may not pretend, as well as he. For as to the strength of body, the weakest has strength enough to kill the strongest, either by secret machination, or by confederacy with others, that are in the same danger with himself.

And as to the faculties of the mind, setting aside the arts grounded upon words, and especially that skill of proceeding upon general, and infallible rules, called science; which very few have, and but in few things; as being not a native faculty, born with us; nor attained, as prudence, while we look after somewhat else, I find yet a greater equality amongst men, than that of strength. For prudence, is but experience; which equal time, equally bestows on all men, in those things they equally apply themselves unto. That which may perhaps make such equality incredible, is but a vain conceit of one's own wisdom, which almost all men think they have in a greater degree, than the vulgar; that is, than all men but themselves, and a few others, whom by fame, or for concurring with themselves, they approve. For such is the nature of men, that howsoever they may acknowledge many others to be more witty, or more eloquent, or more learned; yet they will hardly believe there be many so wise as themselves; for they see their own wit at hand, and other men's at a distance. But this proves rather that men are in that point equal, than unequal. For there is not ordinarily a greater sign of the equal distribution of any thing, than that every man is contented with his share.

From this equality of ability, arises equality of hope in the attaining of our ends. And therefore if any two men desire the same thing, which nevertheless they cannot both enjoy, they become enemies; and in the way to their end, which is principally their own conservation, and sometimes their delectation only, endeavour to destroy, or subdue one another. And from hence it comes to pass, that where an invader has no more to fear, than another man's single power; if one plant, sow, build, or possess a convenient seat, others may probably be expected to come prepared with forces united, to dispossess, and deprive him, not only of the fruit of his labour, but also of his life, or liberty. And the invader again is in the like danger of another.

And from this diffidence of one another, there is no way for any man to secure himself, so reasonable, as anticipation; that is, by force, or wiles, to master the persons of all men he can, so long, till he see no other power great enough to endanger him: and this is no more than his own conservation requires, and is generally allowed. Also because there be some, that taking pleasure in contemplating their own power in the acts of conquest, which they pursue farther than their security requires; if others, that otherwise would be glad to be at ease within modest bounds, should not by invasion increase their power, they would not be able, long time, by standing only on their defence, to subsist. And by consequence, such augmentation of dominion over men being necessary to a man's conservation, it ought to be allowed him.

Again, men have no pleasure, but on the contrary a great deal of grief, in keeping company, where there is no power able to over-awe them all. For every man looks that his companion should value him, at the same rate he sets upon himself: and upon all signs of contempt, or undervaluing, naturally endeavours, as far as he dares (which amongst them that have no common power to keep them in quiet, is far enough to make them destroy each other), to extort a greater value from his condemners, by damage; and from others, by the example.

So that in the nature of man, we find three principal causes of quarrel. First, competition; secondly, diffidence; thirdly, glory.

The first, makes men invade for gain; the second, for safety; and the third, for reputation. The first use violence, to make themselves masters of other men's persons, wives, children, and cattle; the second, to defend them; the third, for trifles, as a word, a smile, a different opinion, and any other sign of undervalue, either direct in their persons, or by reflection in their kindred, their friends, their nation, their profession, or their name.

Hereby it is manifest, that during the time men live without a common power to keep them all in awe, they are in that condition which is called war; and such a war, as is of every man, against every man. For WAR, consists not in battle only, or the act of fighting; but in a tract of time, wherein the will to contend by battle is sufficiently known: and therefore the notion of *time*, is to be considered in the nature of war; as it is in the nature of weather. For as the nature of foul weather, lies not in a shower or two of rain; but in an inclination thereto of many days together: so the nature of war, consists not in actual fighting; but in the known disposition thereto, during all the time there is no assurance to the contrary. All other time is PEACE.

Whatsoever therefore is consequent to a time of war, where every man is enemy to every man; the same is consequent to the time, wherein men live without other security, than what their own strength, and their own invention shall furnish them withal. In such condition, there is no place for industry; because the fruit thereof is uncertain: and consequently no culture of the earth; no navigation, nor use of the commodities that may be imported by sea; no commodious building; no instruments of moving, and removing, such things as require much force; no knowledge of the face of the earth; no account of time; no arts; no letters; no society; and which is worst of all, continual fear, and danger of violent death; and the life of man, solitary, poor, nasty, brutish, and short.

It may seem strange to some man, that has not well weighed these things; that nature should thus dissociate, and render men apt to invade, and destroy one another: and he may therefore, not trusting to this inference, made from the passions, desire perhaps to have the same confirmed by experience. Let him therefore consider with himself, when taking a journey, he arms himself, and seeks to go well accompanied; when going to sleep, he locks his doors; when even in his house he locks his chests; and this when he knows there be laws, and public officers, armed, to revenge all injuries shall be done him; what opinion he has of his fellow-subjects, when he rides armed; of his fellow citizens, when he locks his doors; and of his children, and servants, when he locks his chests. Does he not there as much accuse mankind by his actions, as I do by my words? But neither of us accuse man's nature in it. The desires, and other passions of man, are in themselves no sin. No more are the actions, that proceed from those passions, till they know a law that forbids them: which till laws be made they cannot know: nor can any law be made, till they have agreed upon the person that shall make it.

It may peradventure be thought, there was never such a time, nor condition of war as this; and I believe it was never generally so, over all the world: but there are many places, where they live so now. For the savage people in many places, of America, except the government of small families, the concord whereof depends on natural lust, have no government at all; and live at this day in that brutish manner, as I said before. Howsoever, it may be perceived what manner of life there would be, where there were no common power to fear, by the manner of life, which men that have formerly lived under a peaceful government, use to degenerate into, in a civil war.

But though there had never been any time, wherein particular men were in a condition of war one against another; yet in all times, kings, and persons of sovereign authority, because of their independency, are in continual jealousies, and in the state and posture of gladiators; having their weapons pointing, and their eyes fixed on one another; that is, their forts, garrisons, and guns upon the frontiers of their kingdoms; and continual spies upon their neighbours; which is a posture of war. But because they up-hold thereby, the industry of their subjects; there does not follow from it, that misery, which accompanies the liberty of particular men.

To this war of every man, against every man, this also is consequent; that nothing can be unjust. The notions of right and wrong, justice and injustice have there no place. Where there is no common power, there is no law: where no law, no injustice. Force, and fraud, are in war the two cardinal virtues. Justice, and injustice are none of the faculties neither of the body, nor mind. If they were, they might be in a man that were alone in the world, as well as his senses, and passions. They are qualities that relate to men in society, not in solitude. It is consequent also to the same condition, that there be no propriety, no dominion, no *mine* and *thine* distinct; but only that to be every man's, that he can get: and for so long, as he can keep it. And thus much for the ill condition, which man by mere nature is actually placed in; though with a possibility to come out of it, consisting partly in the passions, partly in his reason.

The passions that incline men to peace, are fear of death; desire of such things as are necessary to commodious living; and a hope by their industry to obtain them. And reason suggests convenient articles of peace, upon which men may be drawn to agreement. These articles, are they, which otherwise are called the Laws of Nature: whereof I shall speak more particularly, in ... following chapters.

OF THE FIRST AND SECOND NATURAL LAWS, AND OF CONTRACTS

(From *Leviathan*, Chapter 14)

The right of nature, which writers commonly call *jus naturale*, is the liberty each man has, to use his own power, as he will himself, for the preservation of his own nature; that is to say, of his own life; and consequently, of doing any thing, which in his own judgment, and reason, he shall conceive to be the aptest [most effective] means thereunto.

By liberty, is understood, according to the proper signification of the word, the absence of external impediments: which impediments, may oft take away part of a man's power to do what he would; but cannot hinder him from using the power left him, according as his judgment, and reason shall dictate to him.

A law of nature, *lex naturalis*, is a precept or general rule, found out by reason, by which a man is forbidden to do that, which is destructive of his life, or takes away the means of preserving the same; and to omit that, by which he thinks it may be best preserved. For though they that speak of this subject, use to confound *jus*, and *lex*, *right* and *law*: yet they ought to be distinguished; because RIGHT consists in liberty to do, or to forbear: whereas LAW determines, and binds to one of them: so that law, and right, differ as much, as obligation, and liberty; which in one and the same matter are inconsistent.

And because the condition of man, as has been declared in the precedent chapter, is a condition of war of every one against every one; in which case every one is governed by his own reason; and there is nothing he can make use of, that may not be a help unto him, in preserving his life against his enemies; it follows, that in such a condition, every man has a right to every thing; even to one another's body. And therefore, as long as this natural right of every man to every thing endures, there can be no security to any man, how strong or wise soever he be, of living out the time, which nature ordinarily allows men to live. And consequently it is a precept, or general rule of reason, *that every man, ought to endeavour peace, as far as he has hope of obtaining it; and when he cannot obtain it, that he may seek, and use, all helps, and advantages of war.* The first branch of which rule, contains the first, and fundamental law of nature; which is, *to seek peace, and follow it.* The second, the sum of the right of nature; which is, *by all means we can, to defend ourselves.*

From this fundamental law of nature, by which men are commanded to endeavour peace, is derived this second law; *that a man be willing, when others are so too, as far-forth, as for peace, and defence of himself he shall think it necessary, to lay down this right to all things; and be contented with so much liberty against other men, as he would allow other men against himself.* For as long as every man holds this right, of doing any thing he likes; so long are all men in the condition of war. But if other men will not lay down their right, as well as he; then there is no reason for any one, to divest himself of his: for that were to expose himself to prey, which no man is bound to, rather than to dispose himself to peace. This is that law of the Gospel; whatsoever you require that others should do to you, that do ye to them. And that law of all men, quod tibi fieri non vis, alteri ne feceris [what you don't want done to you, don't do to others].

To *lay down* a man's *right* to any thing, is to *divest* himself of the *liberty*, of hindering another of the benefit of his own right to the same. For he that renounces, or passes away his right, gives not to any other man a right which he had not before; because there is nothing to which every man had not right by nature: but only stands out of his way, that he may enjoy his own original right, without hindrance from him; not without hindrance from another. So that the effect which redounds to one man, by another man's defect of right, is but so much diminution of impediments to the use of his own right original.

Right is laid aside, either by simply renouncing it; or by transferring it to another. By *simply* RENOUNCING; when he cares not to whom the benefit thereof redounds. By TRANSFERRING; when he intends the benefit thereof to some certain person, or persons. And when a man has in either manner abandoned, or granted away his right; then he is said to be OBLIGED, or BOUND, not to hinder those, to whom such right is granted, or abandoned, from the benefit of it: and that he *ought*, and it is his DUTY, not to make void that voluntary act of his own: and that such hindrance is INJUSTICE, and INJURY, as being *sine jure*; the right being before renounced, or transferred. So that *injury*, or *injustice*, in the controversies of the world, is somewhat like to that, which in the disputations of scholars is called *absurdity*. For as it is there called an absurdity, to contradict what one maintained in the beginning: so in the world, it is called injustice, and injury, voluntarily to undo that, which from the beginning he had voluntarily done. The way by which a man either simply renounces, or transfers his right, is a declaration, or signification, by some voluntary and sufficient sign, or signs, that he does so renounce, or transfer; or has so renounced, or transferred the same, to him that accepts it. And these signs are either words only, or actions only; or, as it happens most often, both words, and actions. And the same are the BONDS, by which men are bound, and obliged: bonds, that have their strength, not from their own nature, for nothing is more easily broken than a man's word, but from fear of some evil consequence upon the rupture.

Whensoever a man transfers his right, or renounces it; it is either in consideration of some right reciprocally transferred to himself; or for some other good he hopes for thereby. For it is a voluntary act: and of the voluntary acts of every man, the object is some *good to himself.* And therefore there be some rights, which no man can be understood by any words, or other signs, to have abandoned, or transferred. As first a man cannot lay down the right of resisting them, that assault him by force, to take away his life; because he cannot be understood to aim thereby, at any good to himself. The same may be said of wounds, and chains, and imprisonment; both because there is no benefit consequent to such patience; as there is to the patience of suffering another to be wounded, or imprisoned: as also because a man cannot tell, when he sees men proceed against him by violence, whether they intend his death or not. And lastly the motive, and end for which this renouncing, and transferring of right is introduced, is nothing else but the security of a man's person, in his life, and in the means of so preserving life, as not to be weary of it. And therefore if a man by words, or other signs, seem to despoil himself of the end, for which those signs were intended; he is not to be understood as if he meant it, or that it was his will; but that he was ignorant of how such words and actions were to be interpreted.

The mutual transferring of right, is that which men call CONTRACT.

There is a difference between transferring of right to the thing; and transferring, or tradition, that is delivery of the thing itself. For the thing may be delivered together with the translation of the right; as in buying and selling with ready-money; or exchange of goods, or lands: and it may be delivered some time after.

Again, one of the contractors, may deliver the thing contracted for on his part, and leave the other to perform his part at some determinate time after, and in the mean time be trusted; and then the contract on his part, is called PACT, or COVENANT: or both parts may contract now, to perform hereafter: in which cases, he that is to perform in time to come, being trusted, his performance is called *keeping of promise*, or faith; and the failing of performance, if it be voluntary, *violation of faith*.

When the transferring of right, is not mutual: but one of the parties transfers, in hope to gain thereby friendship, or service from another, or from his friends; or in hope to gain the reputation of charity, or magnanimity; or to deliver his mind from the pain of compassion; or in hope of reward in heaven; this is not contract, but GIFT, FREE-GIFT, GRACE: which words signify one and the same thing.

Signs of contract, are either *express*, or *by inference*. Express, are words spoken with understanding of what they signify: and such words are either of the time *present*, or *past*; as, *I give, I grant, I have given, I have granted, I will that this be yours*: or of the future; as, *I will give, I will grant*: which words of the future are called PROMISE.

Signs by inference, are sometimes the consequence of words; sometimes the consequence of silence; sometimes the consequence of actions; sometimes the consequence of forbearing an action: and generally a sign of inference, of any contract, is whatsoever sufficiently argues the will of the contractor …

In contracts, the right passes, not only where the words are of the time present, or past, but also where they are of the future: because all contract is mutual translation, or change of right; and therefore he that promises only, because he has already received the benefit for which he promises, is to be understood as if he intended the right should pass: for unless he had been content to have his words so understood, the other would not have performed his part first. And for that cause, in buying, and selling, and other acts of contract, a promise is equivalent to a covenant; and therefore obligatory …

If a covenant be made, wherein neither of the parties perform presently, but trust one another; in the condition of mere nature, which is a condition of war of every man against every man, upon any reasonable suspicion, it is void: but if there be a common power set over them both, with right and force sufficient to compel performance, it is not void. For he that performs first, has no assurance the other will perform after; because the bonds of words are too weak to bridle men's ambition, avarice, anger, and other passions, without the fear of some coercive power; which in the condition of mere nature, where all men are equal, and judges of the justness of their own fears, cannot possibly be supposed. And therefore he which performeth first, does but betray himself to his enemy; contrary to the right, he can never abandon, of defending his life, and means of living.

But in a civil estate, where there is a power set up to constrain those that would otherwise violate their faith, that fear is no more reasonable; and for that cause, he which by the covenant is to perform first, is obliged so to do …

Covenants entered into by fear, in the condition of mere nature, are obligatory. For example, if I covenant to pay a ransom, or service for my life, to an enemy; I am bound by it: for it is a contract, wherein one receives the benefit of life; the other is to receive money, or service for it; and consequently, where no other law, as in the condition of mere nature, forbids the performance, the covenant is valid. Therefore prisoners of war, if trusted with the payment of their ransom, are obliged to pay it: and if a weaker prince, make a disadvantageous peace with a stronger, for fear; he is bound to keep it; unless, as hath been said before, there arises some new, and just cause of fear, to renew the war. And even in commonwealths, if I be forced to redeem myself from a thief by promising him money, I am bound to pay it, till the civil law discharge me. For whatsoever I may lawfully do without obligation, the same I may lawfully covenant to do through fear: and what I lawfully covenant, I cannot lawfully break.

A former covenant, makes void a later. For a man that has passed away his right to one man today, has it not to pass tomorrow to another: and therefore the later promise passes no right, but is null.

A covenant not to defend myself from force, by force, is always void. For, as I have showed before, no man can transfer, or lay down his right to save himself from death, wounds, and imprisonment, the avoiding whereof is the only end of laying down any right; and therefore the promise of not resisting force, in no covenant transfers any right; nor is obliging. For though a man may covenant thus, *unless I do so, or so, kill me*; he cannot covenant thus, *unless I do so, or so, I will not resist you, when you come to kill me*. For man by nature chooses the lesser evil, which is danger of death in resisting; rather than the greater, which is certain and present death in not resisting. And this is granted to be true by all men, in that they lead criminals to execution, and prison, with armed men, notwithstanding that such criminals have consented to the law, by which they are condemned.

A covenant to accuse oneself, without assurance of pardon, is likewise invalid. For in the condition of nature, where every man is judge, there is no place for accusation: and in the civil state, the accusation is followed with punishment; which being force, a man is not obliged not to resist.

Toleration and Government

JOHN LOCKE*

Although the word "liberal" was not used to describe a political position until the early 1800s, John Locke (1632–1704) usually is considered the first philosopher to take a clearly liberal perspective on political matters. The power of a political society or "commonwealth," Locke claimed, is limited to the protection of its members' "civil interests." These include life, liberty, and property, but not the private sphere of religious belief—as he argued in *A Letter Concerning Toleration* (1689). In his *Second Treatise of Government*—published in 1690 after the Glorious Revolution of 1688, but written earlier—Locke began from premises quite similar to those of Thomas Hobbes, but arrived at conclusions more recognizably liberal. Everyone has a natural right to life, liberty, and property, Locke said, and no one has authority over us without our consent. Any government that violates our rights releases us from any obligation to obey it and may, indeed, entitle us to overthrow it and establish a new government.

* *Source: The Works of John Locke*, 10 vols. (London: Thomas Tegg; W. Sharpe and Son; G. Offor; G. and J. Robinson; J. Evans and Co., 1823), pp. 9–21 (vol. 6) and 339–347, 352–367, 469–472 (vol. 5).

A LETTER CONCERNING TOLERATION

The commonwealth seems to me to be a society of men constituted only for procuring, preserving, and advancing their own civil interests.

Civil interest I call life, liberty, health, and indolency of body; and the possession of outward things, such as money, lands, houses, furniture, and the like.

It is the duty of the civil magistrate, by the impartial execution of equal laws, to secure unto all the people in general, and to every one of his subjects in particular, the just possession of these things belonging to this life. If any one presume to violate the laws of public justice and equity, established for the preservation of these things, his presumption is to be checked by the fear of punishment, consisting in the deprivation or diminution of those civil interests, or goods, which otherwise he might and ought to enjoy. But seeing no man does willingly suffer himself to be punished by the deprivation of any part of his goods, and much less of his liberty or life, therefore is the magistrate armed with the force and strength of all his subjects, in order to the punishment of those that violate any other man's rights.

Now that the whole jurisdiction of the magistrate reaches only to these civil concernments; and that all civil power, right, and dominion, is bounded and confined to the only care of promoting these things; and that it neither can nor ought in any manner to be extended to the salvation of souls, these following considerations seem unto me abundantly to demonstrate.

First, because the care of souls is not committed to the civil magistrate, any more than to other men. It is not committed unto him, I say, by God; because it appears not that God has ever given any such authority to one man over another, as to compel any one to his religion. Nor can any such power be vested in the magistrate by the consent of the people; because no man can so far abandon the care of his own salvation as blindly to leave it to the choice of any other, whether prince or subject, to prescribe to him what faith or worship he shall embrace. For no man can, if he would, conform his faith to the dictates of another. All the life and power of true religion consists in the inward and full persuasion of the mind; and faith is not faith without believing. Whatever profession we make, to whatever outward worship we conform, if we are not fully satisfied in our own mind that the one is true, and the other well-pleasing unto God, such profession and such practice, far from being any furtherance, are indeed great obstacles to our salvation. For in this manner, instead of expiating other sins by the exercise of religion, I say in offering thus unto God Almighty such a worship as we esteem to be displeasing unto him, we add unto the number of our other sins, those also of hypocrisy, and contempt of his Divine Majesty.

In the second place, The care of souls cannot belong to the civil magistrate, because his power consists only in outward force: but true and saving religion consists in the inward persuasion of the mind, without which nothing can be acceptable to God. And such is the nature of the understanding, that it cannot be compelled to the belief of any thing by outward force. Confiscation of estate, imprisonment, torments, nothing of that nature can have any such efficacy as to make men change the inward judgment that they have framed of things.

It may indeed be alleged that the magistrate may make use of arguments, and thereby draw the heterodox into the way of truth, and procure their salvation.

I grant it; but this is common to him with other men. In teaching, instructing, and redressing the erroneous by reason, he may certainly do what becomes any good man to do. Magistracy does not oblige him to put off either humanity or Christianity. But it is one thing to persuade, another to command; one thing to press with arguments, another with penalties. This the civil power alone has a right to do; to the other, good-will is authority enough. Every man has commission to admonish, exhort, convince another of error, and by reasoning to draw him into truth: but to give laws, receive obedience, and compel with the sword, belongs to none but the magistrate. And upon this ground I affirm, that the magistrate's power extends not to the establishing of any articles of faith, or forms of worship, by the force of his laws. For laws are of no force at all without penalties, and penalties in this case are absolutely impertinent; because they are not proper to convince the mind. Neither the profession of any articles of faith, nor the conformity to any outward form of worship, as has been already said, can be available to the salvation of souls, unless the truth of the one, and the acceptableness of the other unto God, be thoroughly believed by those that so profess and practise. But penalties are no ways capable to produce such belief. It is only light and evidence that can work a change in men's opinions; and that light can in no manner proceed from corporal sufferings, or any other outward penalties.

In the third place, The care of the salvation of men's souls cannot belong to the magistrate; because, though the rigour of laws and the force of penalties were capable to convince and change men's minds, yet would not that help at all to the salvation of their souls. For, there being but one truth, one way to heaven; what hopes is there that more men would be led into it, if they had no other rule to follow but the religion of the court, and were put under a necessity to quit the light of their own reason, to oppose the dictates of their own consciences, and blindly to resign up themselves to the will of their governors, and to the religion, which either ignorance, ambition, or superstition had chanced to establish in the countries where they were born? In the variety and contradiction of opinions in religion, wherein the princes of the world are as much divided as in their secular interests, the narrow way would be much straitened; one country alone would be in the right, and all the rest of the world put under an obligation of following their princes in the ways that lead to destruction: and that which heightens the absurdity, and very ill suits the notion of a Deity, men would owe their eternal happiness or misery to the places of their nativity.

These considerations, to omit many others that might have been urged to the same purpose, seem unto me sufficient to conclude, that all the power of civil government relates only to men's civil interests, is confined to the care of the things of this world, and hath nothing to do with the world to come.

Let us now consider what a church is. A church then I take to be a voluntary society of men, joining themselves together of their own accord, in order to the public worshipping of God, in such a manner as they judge acceptable to him, and effectual to the salvation of their souls.

I say, it is a free and voluntary society. Nobody is born a member of any church; otherwise the religion of parents would descend unto children, by the same right of inheritance as their temporal estates, and every one would hold his faith by the same tenure he does his lands; than which nothing can be imagined more absurd.

Thus therefore that matter stands. No man by nature is bound unto any particular church or sect, but every one joins himself voluntarily to that society in which he believes he has found that profession and worship which is truly acceptable to God. The hopes of salvation, as it was the only cause of his entrance into that communion, so it can be the only reason of his stay there. For if afterwards he discover any thing either erroneous in the doctrine, or incongruous in the worship of that society to which he has joined himself, why should it not be as free for him to go out as it was to enter? No member of a religious society can be tied with any other bonds but what proceed from the certain expectation of eternal life. A church then is a society of members voluntarily uniting to this end.

It follows now that we consider what is the power of this church, and unto what laws it is subject.

Forasmuch as no society, how free soever, or upon whatsoever slight occasion instituted, (whether of philosophers for learning, of merchants for commerce, or of men of leisure for mutual conversation and discourse) no church or company, I say, can in the least subsist and hold together, but will presently dissolve and break to pieces, unless it be regulated by some laws, and the members all consent to observe some order. Place and time of meeting must be agreed on; rules for admitting and excluding members must be established; distinction of officers, and putting things into a regular course, and such like, cannot be omitted. But since the joining together of several members into this church-society, as has already been demonstrated, is absolutely free and spontaneous, it necessarily follows, that the right of making its laws can belong to none but the society itself, or at least, which is the same thing, to those whom the society by common consent has authorized thereunto.

Some perhaps may object, that no such society can be said to be a true church, unless it have in it a bishop, or presbyter, with ruling authority derived from the very apostles, and continued down unto the present time by an uninterrupted succession.

To these I answer: In the first place, Let them show me the edict by which Christ has imposed that law upon his church. And let not any man think me impertinent, if, in a thing of this consequence, I require that the terms of that edict be very express and positive. For the promise he has made us, that "wheresoever two or three are gathered together in his name, he will be in the midst of them," Matth, xviii, 20, seems to imply the contrary. Whether such an assembly want any thing necessary to a true church, pray do you consider. Certain I am, that nothing can be there wanting unto the salvation of souls, which is sufficient for our purpose.

Next, pray observe how great have always been the divisions amongst even those who lay so much stress upon the divine institution, and continued succession of a certain order of rulers in the church. Now their very dissension unavoidably puts us upon a necessity of deliberating, and consequently allows a liberty of choosing that, which upon consideration, we prefer.

And, in the last place, I consent that these men have a ruler of their church, established by such a long series of succession as they judge necessary, provided I may have liberty at the same time to join myself to that society, in which I am persuaded those things are to be found which are necessary to the salvation of my soul. In this manner ecclesiastical liberty will be preserved on all sides, and no man will have a legislator imposed upon him, but whom himself has chosen.

But since men are so solicitous about the true church, I would only ask them here by the way, if it be not more agreeable to the church of Christ to make the conditions of her communion consist in such things, and such things only, as the Holy Spirit has in the holy Scriptures declared, in express words, to be necessary to salvation? I ask, I say, whether this be not more agreeable to the church of Christ, than for men to impose their own inventions and interpretations upon others, as if they were of divine authority; and to establish by ecclesiastical laws, as absolutely necessary to the profession of Christianity such things as the holy Scriptures do either not mention, or at least not expressly command? Whosoever requires those things in order to ecclesiastical communion, which Christ does not require in order to life eternal, he may perhaps indeed constitute a society accommodated to his own opinion, and his own advantage; but how that can be called the church of Christ, which is established upon laws that are not his, and which excludes such persons from its communion as he will one day receive into the kingdom of heaven, I understand not. But this being not a proper place to enquire into the marks of the true church, I will only mind those that contend so earnestly for the decrees of their own society, and that cry out continually the Church, the Church, with as much noise, and perhaps upon the same principle, as the Ephesian silversmiths did for their [goddess] Diana; this, I say, I desire to mind them of, that the Gospel frequently declares, that the true disciples of Christ must suffer persecution; but that the church of Christ should persecute others, and force others by fire and sword to embrace her faith and doctrine, I could never yet find in any of the books of the New Testament.

The end [aim] of a religious society, as has already been said, is the public worship of God, and by means thereof the acquisition of eternal life. All discipline ought therefore to tend to that end, and all ecclesiastical laws to be thereunto confined. Nothing ought, nor can be transacted in this society, relating to the possession of civil and worldly goods. No force is here to be made use of, upon any occasion whatsoever: for force belongs wholly to the civil magistrate, and the possession of all outward goods is subject to his jurisdiction.

But it may be asked, by what means then shall ecclesiastical laws be established, if they must be thus destitute of all compulsive power? I answer they must be established by means suitable to the nature of such things, where of the external profession and observation, if not proceeding from a thorough conviction and approbation of the mind, is altogether useless and unprofitable. The arms by which the members of this society are to be kept within their duty, are exhortations, admonitions, and advice. If by these means the offenders will not be reclaimed, and the erroneous convinced, there remains nothing farther to be done, but that such stubborn and obstinate persons, who give no ground to hope for their reformation, should be cast out and separated from the society. This is the last and utmost force of ecclesiastical authority: no other punishment can thereby be inflicted, than that the relation ceasing between the body and the member which is cut off, the person so condemned ceases to be a part of that church.

These things being thus determined, let us inquire, in the next place, how far the duty of toleration extends, and what is required from every one by it.

And first, I hold, that no church is bound by the duty of toleration to retain any such person in her bosom, as after admonition, continues obstinately to offend against the laws of the society. For these being the condition of communion, and the bond of society, if the breach of them were permitted without any animadversion, the society would immediately be thereby dissolved. But nevertheless, in all such cases care is to be taken that the sentence of excommunication, and the execution thereof, carry with it no rough usage, of word or action, whereby the ejected person may any ways be damnified [i.e., injured] in body or estate. For all force, as has often been said, belongs only to the magistrate, nor ought any private persons, at any time, to use force; unless it be in self-defence against unjust violence. Excommunication neither does nor can deprive the excommunicated person of any of those civil goods that he formerly possessed. All those things belong to the civil government, and are under the magistrate's protection. The whole force of excommunication consists only in this, that the resolution of the society in that respect being declared, the union that was between the body and some member, comes thereby to be dissolved; and that relation ceasing, the participation of some certain things, which the society communicated to its members, and unto which no man has any civil right, comes also to cease. For there is no civil injury done unto the excommunicated person, by the church-minister's refusing him that bread and wine, in the celebration of the Lord's supper, which was not bought with his, but other men's money.

Secondly, No private person has any right in any manner to prejudice another person in his civil enjoyments, because he is of another church or religion. All the rights and franchises that belong to him as a man, or as a denizen, are inviolably to be preserved to him. These are not the business of religion. No violence nor injury is to be offered him, whether he be Christian or pagan. Nay, we must not content ourselves with the narrow measures of bare justice: charity, bounty, and liberality must be added to it. This the Gospel enjoins, this reason directs, and this that natural fellowship we are born into requires of us. If any man err from the right way, it is his own misfortune, no injury to thee: nor therefore art thou to punish him in the things of this life, because thou supposest he will be miserable in that which is to come.

What I say concerning the mutual toleration of private persons differing from one another in religion, I understand also of particular churches; which stand as it were in the same relation to each other as private persons among themselves; nor has any one of them any manner of jurisdiction over any other, no, not even when the civil magistrate, as it sometimes happens, comes to be of this or the other communion. For the civil government can give no new right to the church, nor the church to the civil government. So that whether the magistrate join himself to any church, or separate from it, the church remains always as it was before, a free and voluntary society. It neither acquires the power of the sword by the magistrate's coming to it, nor does it lose the right of instruction and excommunication by his going from it. This is the fundamental and immutable right of a spontaneous society, that it has to remove any of its members who transgress the rules of its institution: but it cannot, by the accession of any new members, acquire any right of jurisdiction over those that are not joined with it. And therefore peace, equity, and friendship, are always mutually to be observed by particular churches, in the same manner as by private persons, without any pretence of superiority or jurisdiction over one another ...

Nobody therefore, in fine, neither single persons, nor churches, nay, nor even commonwealths, have any just title to invade the civil rights and worldly goods of each other, upon pretence of religion. Those that are of another opinion, would do well to consider with themselves how pernicious a seed of discord and war, how powerful a provocation to endless hatreds, rapines, and slaughters, they thereby furnish unto mankind. No peace and security, no, not so much as common friendship, can ever be established or preserved amongst men, so long as this opinion prevails, "that dominion is founded in grace, and that religion is to be propagated by force of arms."

In the third place, Let us see what the duty of toleration requires from those who are distinguished from the rest of mankind, from the laity, as they please to call us, by some ecclesiastical character and office; whether they be bishops, priests, presbyters, ministers, or however else dignified or distinguished. It is not my business to inquire here into the origins of the power or dignity of the clergy. This only I say, that whencesoever [from wherever] their authority be sprung, since it is ecclesiastical, it ought to be confined within the bounds of the church, nor can it in any manner be extended to civil affairs; because the church itself is a thing absolutely separate and distinct from the commonwealth. The boundaries on both sides are fixed and immoveable. He jumbles heaven and earth together, the things most remote and opposite, who mixes these societies, which are, in their origins, end, business, and in every thing, perfectly distinct, and infinitely different from each other. No man therefore, with whatsoever ecclesiastical office he be dignified, can deprive another man, that is not of his church and faith, either of liberty, or of any part of his worldly goods, upon the account of that difference which is between them in religion. For whatsoever is not lawful to the whole church cannot, by any ecclesiastical right, become lawful to any of its members.

SECOND TREATISE OF GOVERNMENT
Of the State of Nature

4. To understand political power right, and derive it from its origins, we must consider what state all men are naturally in, and that is, a state of perfect freedom to order their actions and dispose of their possessions and persons, as they think fit, within the bounds of the law of nature; without asking leave, or depending upon the will of any other man.

A state also of equality, wherein all the power and jurisdiction is reciprocal, no one having more than another; there being nothing more evident than that creatures of the same species and rank, promiscuously born to all the same advantages of nature, and the use of the same faculties, should also be equal one amongst another without subordination or subjection; unless the Lord and Master of them all should, by any manifest declaration of his will, set one above another, and confer on him, by an evident and clear appointment, an undoubted right to dominion and sovereignty ...

6. But though this be a state of liberty, yet it is not a state of licence: though man in that state have an uncontrollable liberty to dispose of his person or possessions, yet he has not liberty to destroy himself, or so much as any creature in his possession, but where some nobler use than its bare preservation calls for it. The state of nature has a law of nature to govern it, which obliges every one: and reason, which is that law, teaches all mankind, who will but consult it, that being all equal and independent, no one ought to harm another in his life, health, liberty, or possessions: for men being all the workmanship of one omnipotent and infinitely wise Maker; all the servants of one sovereign Master, sent into the world by his order, and about his business; they are his property, whose workmanship they are, made to last during his, not another's pleasure: and being furnished with like faculties, sharing all in one community of nature, there cannot be supposed any such subordination among us that may authorize us to destroy another, as if we were made for one another's uses, as the inferior ranks of creatures are for ours. Every one, as he is bound to preserve himself, and not to quit his station willfully, so by the like reason, when his own preservation comes not in competition, ought he, as much as he can, to preserve the rest of mankind, and may not, unless it be to do justice to an offender, take away or impair the life, or what tends to the preservation of life, the liberty, health, limb, or goods of another.

7. And that all men may be restrained from invading others' rights, and from doing hurt to one another, and the law of nature be observed, which willeth the peace and preservation of all mankind, the execution of the law of nature is, in that state, put into every man's hands, whereby every one has a right to punish the transgressors of that law to such a degree as may hinder its violation: for the law of nature would, as all other laws that concern men in this world, be in vain, if there were nobody that in the state of nature had a power to execute that law, and thereby preserve the innocent, and restrain offenders. And if any one in the state of nature may punish another for any evil he has done, every one may do so: for in that state of perfect equality, where naturally there is no superiority or jurisdiction of one over another, what any may do in prosecution of that law every one must needs have a right to do.

8. And thus, in the state of nature, one man comes by a power over another, but yet no absolute or arbitrary power to use a criminal, when he has got him in his hands, according to the passionate heats or boundless extravagancy of his own will; but only to retribute to [i.e., punish] him, so far as calm reason and conscience dictate, what is proportionate to his transgression; which is so much as may serve for reparation and restraint: for these two are the only reasons why one man may lawfully do harm to another, which is that we call punishment. In transgressing the law of nature, the offender declares himself to live by another rule than that of reason and common equity, which is that measure God has set to the actions of men for their mutual security; and so he becomes dangerous to mankind, the tie, which is to secure them from injury and violence, being slighted and broken by him: which being a trespass against the whole species, and the peace and safety of it, provided for by the law of nature; every man upon this score, by the right he hath to preserve mankind in general, may restrain, or, where it is necessary, destroy things noxious to them, and so may bring such evil on any one, who hath transgressed that law, as may make him repent the doing of it, and thereby deter

him, and by his example others, from doing the like mischief. And in this case, and upon this ground, every man hath a right to punish the offender, and be executioner of the law of nature.

9. I doubt not but this will seem a very strange doctrine to some men: but, before they condemn it, I desire them to resolve me by what right any prince or state can put to death or punish an alien for any crime he commits in their country? It is certain their laws, by virtue of any sanction they receive from the promulgated will of the legislative, reach not a stranger: they speak not to him, nor, if they did, is he bound to hearken to them. The legislative authority, by which they are in force over the subjects of that commonwealth, hath no power over him. Those who have the supreme power of making laws in England, France, or Holland, are to an Indian but like the rest of the world, men without authority: and therefore, if by the law of nature every man hath not a power to punish offences against it, as he soberly judges the case to require, I see not how the magistrates of any community can punish an alien of another country; since, in reference to him, they can have no more power than what every man naturally may have over another.

10. Besides the crime which consists in violating the law, and varying from the right rule of reason, whereby a man so far becomes degenerate, and declares himself to quit the principles of human nature, and to be a noxious creature, there is commonly injury done to some person or other, and some other man receives damage by his transgression: in which case he who hath received any damage, has, besides the right of punishment common to him with other men, a particular right to seek reparation from him that has done it: and any other person, who finds it just, may also join with him that is injured, and assist him in recovering from the offender so much as may make satisfaction for the harm he has suffered.

11. From these two distinct rights, the one of punishing the crime for restraint, and preventing the like offence, which right of punishing is in every body; the other of taking reparation, which belongs only to the injured party; comes it to pass that the magistrate, who by being magistrate hath the common right of punishing put into his hands, can often, where the public good demands not the execution of the law, remit the punishment of criminal offences by his own authority, but yet cannot remit the satisfaction due to any private man for the damage he has received. That he who has suffered the damage has a right to demand in his own name, and he alone can remit; the damnified [i.e., injured] person has this power of appropriating to himself the goods or service of the offender, by right of self-preservation, as every man has a power to punish the crime, to prevent its being committed again, by the right he has of preserving all mankind, and doing all reasonable things he can in order to that end: and thus it is that every man, in the state of nature, has a power to kill a murderer, both to deter others from doing the like injury, which no reparation can compensate, by the example of the punishment that attends it from every body; and also to secure men from the attempts of a criminal, who having renounced reason, the common rule and measure God hath given to mankind, hath, by the unjust violence and slaughter he hath committed upon one, declared war against all mankind, and therefore may be destroyed as a lion or a tiger, one of those wild savage beasts with whom men can have no society nor security: and upon this is grounded that great law of nature, "Whoso sheddeth man's blood, by man shall his blood be shed." And Cain was so

fully convinced that every one had a right to destroy such a criminal, that, after the murder of his brother, he cries out, "Every one that findeth me shall slay me," so plain was it writ in the hearts of all mankind.

12. By the same reason may a man in the state of nature punish the lesser breaches of that law. It will perhaps be demanded, with death? I answer, each transgression may be punished to that degree, and with so much severity, as will suffice to make it an ill bargain to the offender, give him cause to repent, and terrify others from doing the like. Every offence that can be committed in the state of nature, may in the state of nature be also punished equally, and as far forth, as it may in a commonwealth: for though it would be beside my present purpose to enter here into the particulars of the law of nature, or its measures of punishment, yet it is certain there is such a law, and that too as intelligible and plain to a rational creature, and a studier of that law, as the positive laws of commonwealths; nay, possibly plainer, as much as reason is easier to be understood than the fancies and intricate contrivances of men, following contrary and hidden interests put into words; for so truly are a great part of the municipal laws of countries, which are only so far right, as they are founded on the law of nature, by which they are to be regulated and interpreted.

13. To this strange doctrine, viz. that in the state of nature every one has the executive power of the law of nature, I doubt not but it will be objected, that it is unreasonable for men to be judges in their own cases, that self-love will make men partial to themselves and their friends: and, on the other side, that ill-nature, passion, and revenge will carry them too far in punishing others; and hence nothing but confusion and disorder will follow: and that therefore God hath certainly appointed government to restrain the partiality and violence of men. I easily grant, that civil government is the proper remedy for the inconveniencies of the state of nature, which must certainly be great, where men may be judges in their own case; since it is easy to be imagined, that he who was so unjust as to do his brother an injury, will scarce be so just as to condemn himself for it: but I shall desire those who make this objection to remember, that absolute monarchs are but men; and if government is to be the remedy of those evils, which necessarily follow from men's being judges in their own cases, and the state of nature is therefore not to be endured; I desire to know what kind of government that is, and how much better it is than the state of nature, where one man, commanding a multitude, has the liberty to be judge in his own case, and may do to all his subjects whatever he pleases, without the least liberty to any one to question or control those who execute his pleasure? and in whatsoever he doth, whether led by reason, mistake, or passion, must be submitted to? Much better it is in the state of nature, wherein men are not bound to submit to the unjust will of another: and if he that judges, judges amiss in his own, or any other case, he is answerable for it to the rest of mankind.

14. It is often asked, as a mighty objection, "where are or ever were there any men in such a state of nature?" To which it may suffice as an answer at present, that since all princes and rulers of independent governments, all through the world, are in a state of nature, it is plain the world never was, nor never will be, without numbers of men in that state. I have named all governors of independent communities, whether they are, or are not, in league with others: for it is not every

compact that puts an end to the state of nature between men, but only this one of agreeing together mutually to enter into one community, and make one body politic; other promises and compacts men may make one with another, and yet still be in the state of nature. The promises and bargains for truck, etc., between the two men in the desert island, mentioned by Garcilasso de la Vega, in his history of Peru; or between a Swiss and an Indian, in the woods of America; are binding to them, though they are perfectly in a state of nature, in reference to one another: for truth and keeping of faith belongs to men as men, and not as members of society.

15. To those that say, there were never any men in the state of nature, I ... affirm, that all men are naturally in that state, and remain so, till by their own consents they make themselves members of some politic society; and I doubt not in the sequel of this discourse to make it very clear ...

Of Property

26. God, who hath given the world to men in common, hath also given them reason to make use of it to the best advantage of life and convenience. The earth, and all that is therein, is given to men for the support and comfort of their being. And though all the fruits it naturally produces, and beasts it feeds, belong to mankind in common, as they are produced by the spontaneous hand of nature; and nobody has originally a private dominion, exclusive of the rest of mankind, in any of them, as they are thus in their natural state: yet being given for the use of men, there must of necessity be a means to appropriate them some way or other before they can be of any use, or at all beneficial to any particular man. The fruit, or venison, which nourishes the wild Indian, who knows no enclosure, and is still a tenant in common, must be his, and so his, *i.e.*, a part of him, that another can no longer have any right to it, before it can do him any good for the support of his life.

27. Though the earth, and all inferior creatures, be common to all men, yet every man has a property in his own person: this nobody has any right to but himself. The labour of his body, and the work of his hands, we may say, are properly his. Whatsoever then, he removes out of the state that nature hath provided, and left it in, he hath mixed his labour with, and joined to it something that is his own, and thereby makes it his property. It being by him removed from the common state nature hath placed it in, it hath by this labour something annexed to it that excludes the common right of other men. For this labour being the unquestionable property of the labourer, no man but he can have a right to what that is once joined to, at least where there is enough, and as good, left in common for others.

28. He that is nourished by the acorns he picked up under an oak, or the apples he gathered from the trees in the wood, has certainly appropriated them to himself. Nobody can deny but the nourishment is his. I ask then, when did they begin to be his? when he digested? or when he ate? or when he boiled? or when he brought them home? or when he picked them up? and it is plain, if the first gathering made them not his, nothing else could. That labour put a distinction between them and common: that added something to them more than nature, the common mother of all, had done; and so they became his private right. And will any one say, he had no right to those acorns or apples he thus appropriated, because he had not the consent of all mankind to make them his? Was it a robbery

thus to assume to himself what belonged to all in common? If such a consent as that was necessary, man had starved, notwithstanding the plenty God had given him. We see in commons, which remain so by compact, that it is the taking any part of what is common, and removing it out of the state nature leaves it in, which begins the property; without which the common is of no use. And the taking of this or that part does not depend on the express consent of all the commoners. Thus the grass my horse has bit; the turfs my servant has cut; and the ore I have digged in any place, where I have a right to them in common with others; become my property, without the assignation or consent of any body. The labour that was mine, removing them out of that common state they were in, hath fixed my property in them.

29. By making an explicit consent of every commoner necessary to any one's appropriating to himself any part of what is given in common, children or servants could not cut the meat, which their father or master had provided for them in common, without assigning to every one his peculiar part. Though the water running in the fountain be every one's, yet who can doubt but that in the pitcher is his only who drew it out? His labour hath taken it out of the hands of nature, where it was common, and belonged equally to all her children, and hath thereby appropriated it to himself.

30. Thus this law of reason makes the deer that Indian's who hath killed it; it is allowed to be his goods who hath bestowed his labour upon it, though before it was the common right of every one. And amongst those who are counted the civilized part of mankind, who have made and multiplied positive laws to determine property, this original law of nature, for the beginning of property, in what was before common, still takes place; and by virtue thereof, what fish any one catches in the ocean, that great and still remaining common of mankind; or what ambergris any one takes up here, is by the labour that removes it out of that common state nature left it in made his property who takes that pains about it. And even amongst us, the hare that any one is hunting is thought his who pursues her during the chase: for being a beast that is still looked upon as common, and no man's private possession; whoever has employed so much labour about any of that kind, as to find and pursue her, has thereby removed her from the state of nature, wherein she was common, and hath begun a property.

31. It will perhaps be objected to this, that "if gathering the acorns, or other fruits of the earth, etc., makes a right to them, then any one may engross as much as he will." To which I answer, Not so. The same law of nature, that does by this means give us property, does also bound that property too. "God has given us all things richly," 1 Tim. vi 17, is the voice of reason confirmed by inspiration. But how far has he given it us? To enjoy. As much as any one can make use of to any advantage of life before it spoils, so much he may by his labour fix a property in: whatever is beyond this, is more than his share, and belongs to others. Nothing was made by God for man to spoil or destroy. And thus, considering the plenty of natural provisions there was a long time in the world, and the few spenders; and to how small a part of that provision the industry of one man could extend itself, and engross it to the prejudice of others; especially keeping within the bounds, set by reason, of what might serve for his use; there could be then little room for quarrels or contentions about property so established.

32. But the chief matter of property being now not the fruits of the earth, and the beasts that subsist on it, but the earth itself; as that which takes in, and carries with it all the rest; I think it is plain, that property in that too is acquired as the former. As much land as a man tills, plants, improves, cultivates, and can use the product of, so much is his property. He by his labour does, as it were, enclose it from the common. Nor will it invalidate his right, to say every body else has an equal title to it, and therefore he cannot appropriate, he cannot enclose, without the consent of all his fellow-commoners, all mankind. God, when he gave the world in common to all mankind, commanded man also to labour, and the penury of his condition required it of him. God and his reason commanded him to subdue the earth, *i.e.*, improve it for the benefit of life, and therein lay out something upon it that was his own, his labour. He that, in obedience to this command of God, subdued, tilled, and sowed any part of it, thereby annexed to it something that was his property, which another had no title to, nor could without injury take from him.

33. Nor was this appropriation of any parcel of land, by improving it, any prejudice to any other man, since there was still enough, and as good left; and more than the yet unprovided could use. So that, in effect, there was never the less left for others because of his enclosure for himself: for he that leaves as much as another can make use of, does as good as take nothing at all. Nobody could think himself injured by the drinking of another man, though he took a good draught, who had a whole river of the same water left him to quench his thirst; and the case of land and water, where there is enough of both, is perfectly the same.

34. God gave the world to men in common; but since he gave it to them for their benefit, and the greatest conveniencies of life they were capable to draw from it, it cannot be supposed he meant it should always remain common and uncultivated. He gave it to the use of the industrious and rational (and labour was to be his title to it), not to the fancy or covetousness of the quarrelsome and contentious. He that had as good left for his improvement as was already taken up, needed not complain, ought not to meddle with what was already improved by another's labour: if he did, it is plain he desired the benefit of another's pains, which he had no right to, and not the ground which God had given him in common with others to labour on, and whereof there was as good left as that already possessed, and more than he knew what to do with, or his industry could reach to.

35. It is true, in land that is common in England, or any other country, where there are plenty of people under government, who have money and commerce, no one can enclose or appropriate any part without the consent of all his fellow-commoners; because this is left common by compact, *i.e.*, by the law of the land, which is not to be violated. And though it be common, in respect of some men, it is not so to all mankind, but is the joint property of this county, or this parish. Besides, the remainder, after such enclosure, would not be as good to the rest of the commoners as the whole was when they could all make use of the whole; whereas in the beginning and first peopling of the great common of the world it was quite otherwise. The law man was under was rather for appropriating. God commanded, and his wants forced him to labour. That was his property which could not be taken from him wherever he had fixed it. And hence subduing or cultivating the earth, and having dominion, we see are joined together. The one

gave title to the other. So that God, by commanding to subdue, gave authority so far to appropriate: and the condition of human life, which requires labour and materials to work on, necessarily introduces private possessions.

36. The measure of property nature has well set by the extent of men's labour and the conveniencies of life: no man's labour could subdue, or appropriate all; nor could his enjoyment consume more than a small part; so that it was impossible for any man, this way, to entrench upon the right of another, or acquire to himself a property, to the prejudice of his neighbour, who would still have room for as good and as large a possession (after the other had taken out his) as before it was appropriated. This measure did confine every man's possession to a very moderate proportion, and such as he might appropriate to himself, without injury to any body, in the first ages of the world, when men were more in danger to be lost, by wandering from their company, in the then vast wilderness of the earth, than to be straitened for want of room to plant in ...

40. It is labour indeed that put the difference of value on every thing; and let any one consider what the difference is between an acre of land planted with tobacco or sugar, sown with wheat or barley, and an acre of the same land lying in common, without any husbandry upon it, and he will find, that the improvement of labour makes the far greater part of the value. I think it will be but a very modest computation to say, that of the products of the earth useful to the life of man, nine-tenths are the effects of labour: nay, if we will rightly estimate things as they come to our use, and cast up the several expenses about them, what in them is purely owing to nature, and what to labour, we shall find, that in most of them ninety-nine hundredths are wholly to be put on the account of labour.

41. There cannot be a clearer demonstration of any thing, than several nations of the Americans are of this, who are rich in land, and poor in all the comforts of life; whom nature having furnished as liberally as any other people with the materials of plenty, *i.e.*, a fruitful soil, apt to produce in abundance; yet, for want of improving it by labour, have not one-hundredth part of the conveniencies we enjoy: and a king of a large and fruitful territory there feeds, lodges, and is clad worse than a day-labourer in England.

42. To make this a little clearer, let us but trace some of the ordinary provisions of life, through their several progresses, before they come to our use, and see how much of their value they receive from human industry. Bread, wine, and cloth, are things of daily use, and great plenty; yet notwithstanding, acorns, water, and leaves, or skins, must be our bread, drink, and clothing, did not labour furnish us with these more useful commodities: for whatever bread is more worth than acorns, wine than water, and cloth or silk than leaves, skins, or moss, that is wholly owing to labour and industry; the one of these being the food and raiment which unassisted nature furnishes us with; the other, provisions which our industry and pains prepare for us; which, how much they exceed the other in value, when any one hath computed, he will then see how much labour makes the far greatest part of the value of things we enjoy in this world: and the ground which produces the materials is scarce to be reckoned in as any, or, at most, but a very small part of it; so little, that even amongst us, land that is left wholly to nature, that hath no improvement of pasturage, tillage, or planting, is called, as indeed it is, waste; and we shall find the benefit of it amount to little more than nothing.

This shows how much numbers of men are to be preferred to largeness of dominions; and that the increase of lands, and the right of employing of them, is the great art of government: and that prince, who shall be so wise and godlike, as by established laws of liberty to secure protection and encouragement to the honest industry of mankind, against the oppression of power and narrowness of party, will quickly be too hard for his neighbours: but this by the by. To return to the argument in hand.

43. An acre of land, that bears here twenty bushels of wheat, and another in America, which, with the same husbandry, would do the like, are, without doubt, of the same natural intrinsic value: but yet the benefit mankind receives from the one in a year is worth 5£. and from the other possibly not worth a penny, if all the profit an Indian received from it were to be valued, and sold here; at least, I may truly say, not one thousandth. It is labour, then, which puts the greatest part of value upon land, without which it would scarcely be worth any thing: it is to that we owe the greatest part of all its useful products; for all that the straw, bran, bread, of that acre of wheat, is more worth than the product of an acre of as good land, which lies waste, is all the effect of labour: for it is not barely the ploughman's pains, the reaper's and thresher's toil, and the baker's sweat, is to be counted into the bread we eat; the labour of those who broke the oxen, who digged and wrought the iron and stones, who felled and framed the timber employed about the plough, mill, oven, or any other utensils, which are a vast number, requisite to this corn, from its being seed to be sown to its being made bread, must all be charged on the account of labour, and received as an effect of that: nature and the earth furnished only the almost worthless materials, as in themselves. It would be a strange catalogue of things, that industry provided and made use of, about every loaf of bread, before it came to our use, if we could trace them; iron, wood, leather, bark, timber, stone, bricks, coals, lime, cloth, dyeing, drugs, pitch, tar, masts, ropes, and all the materials made use of in the ship, that brought any of the commodities used by any of the workmen, to any part of the work, all which it would be almost impossible, at least too long, to reckon up.

44. From all which it is evident, that though the things of nature are given in common, yet man, by being master of himself, and proprietor of his own person, and the actions or labour of it, had still in himself the great foundation of property; and that which made up the greater part of what he applied to the support or comfort of his being, when invention and arts had improved the conveniencies of life, was perfectly his own, and did not belong in common to others.

45. Thus labour, in the beginning, gave a right of property, wherever any one was pleased to employ it, upon what was common, which remained a long while the far greater part, and is yet more than mankind makes use of. Men, at first, for the most part, contented themselves with what unassisted nature offered to their necessities: and though afterwards, in some parts of the world, (where the increase of people and stock, with the use of money, had made land scarce, and so of some value) the several communities settled the bounds of their distinct territories, and by laws within themselves regulated the properties of the private men of their society, and so, by compact and agreement, settled the property which labour and industry began: and the leagues that have been made between

several states and kingdoms, either expressly or tacitly disowning all claim and right to the land in the other's possession, have, by common consent, given up their pretences to their natural common right, which originally they had to those countries, and so have, by positive agreement, settled a property amongst themselves, in distinct parts and parcels of the earth; yet there are still great tracts of ground to be found, which (the inhabitants thereof not having joined with the rest of mankind in the consent of the use of their common money) lie waste, and are more than the people who dwell on it do or can make use of, and so still lie in common; though this can scarce happen amongst that part of mankind that have consented to the use of money.

46. The greatest part of things really useful to the life of man, and such as the necessity of subsisting made the first commoners of the world look after, as it doth the Americans now, are generally things of short duration; such as, if they are not consumed by use, will decay and perish of themselves: gold, silver, and diamonds, are things that fancy or agreement hath put the value on, more than real use, and the necessary support of life. Now of those good things which nature hath provided in common, every one had a right (as hath been said) to as much as he could use, and had property in all that he could effect with his labour; all that his industry could extend to, to alter from the state nature had put it in, was his. He that gathered a hundred bushels of acorns or apples, had thereby a property in them; they were his goods as soon as gathered. He was only to look that he used them before they spoiled, else he took more than his share, and robbed others. And indeed it was a foolish thing, as well as dishonest, to hoard up more than he could make use of. If he gave away a part to any body else, so that it perished not uselessly in his possession, these he also made use of. And if he also bartered away plums, that would have rotted in a week, for nuts that would last good for his eating a whole year, he did no injury; he wasted not the common stock; destroyed no part of the portion of goods that belonged to others, so long as nothing perished uselessly in his hands. Again, if he would give his nuts for a piece of metal, pleased with its colour; or exchange his sheep for shells, or wool for a sparkling pebble or a diamond, and keep those by him all his life, he invaded not the right of others; he might heap as much of these durable things as he pleased; the exceeding of the bounds of his just property not lying in the largeness of his possession, but the perishing of any thing uselessly in it.

47. And thus came in the use of money, some lasting thing that men might keep without spoiling, and that by mutual consent men would take in exchange for the truly useful, but perishable supports of life.

48. And as different degrees of industry were apt to give men possessions in different proportions, so this invention of money gave them the opportunity to continue and enlarge them ...

51. And thus, I think, it is very easy to conceive, how labour could at first begin a title of property in the common things of nature, and how the spending it upon our uses bounded it ... This left no room for controversy about the title, nor for encroachment on the right of others; what portion a man carved to himself was easily seen: and it was useless, as well as dishonest, to carve himself too much, or take more than he needed ...

OF THE DISSOLUTION OF GOVERNMENT

222. The reason why men enter into society is the preservation of their property; and the end why they choose and authorize a legislative is, that there may be laws made, and rules set, as guards and fences to the properties of all the members of the society: to limit the power, and moderate the dominion, of every part and member of the society: for since it can never be supposed to be the will of the society that the legislative should have a power to destroy that which every one designs to secure by entering into society, and for which the people submitted themselves to legislators of their own making; whenever the legislators endeavour to take away and destroy the property of the people, or to reduce them to slavery under arbitrary power, they put themselves into a state of war with the people, who are thereupon absolved from any farther obedience, and are left to the common refuge, which God hath provided for all men, against force and violence. Whensoever therefore the legislative shall transgress this fundamental rule of society; and either by ambition, fear, folly, or corruption, endeavour to grasp themselves, or put into the hands of any other, an absolute power over the lives, liberties, and estates of the people; by this breach of trust they forfeit the power the people had put into their hands for quite contrary ends, and it devolves to the people, who have a right to resume their original liberty, and, by the establishment of a new legislative, (such as they shall think fit), provide for their own safety and security, which is the end for which they are in society. What I have said here, concerning the legislative in general, holds true also concerning the supreme executor, who having a double trust put in him, both to have a part in the legislative, and the supreme execution of the law, acts against both, when he goes about to set up his own arbitrary will as the law of the society. He acts also contrary to his trust, when he either employs the force, treasure, and offices of the society to corrupt the representatives, and gain them to his purposes; or openly pre-engages the electors, and prescribes to their choice, such, whom he has, by solicitations, threats, promises, or otherwise, won to his designs; and employs them to bring in such, who have promised beforehand what to vote, and what to enact. Thus to regulate candidates and electors, and new-model the ways of election, what is it but to cut up the government by the roots, and poison the very fountain of public security? For the people having reserved to themselves the choice of their representatives, as the fence to their properties, could do it for no other end, but that they might always be freely chosen, and so chosen, freely act, and advise, as the necessity of the commonwealth and the public good should, upon examination and mature debate, be judged to require. This, those who give their votes before they hear the debate, and have weighed the reasons on all sides, are not capable of doing. To prepare such an assembly as this, and endeavour to set up the declared abettors of his own will, for the true representatives of the people, and the lawmakers of the society, is certainly as great a breach of trust, and as perfect a declaration of a design to subvert the government, as is possible to be met with. To which if one shall add rewards and punishments visibly employed to the same end, and all the arts of perverted law made use of, to take off and destroy all that stand in the way of such a design, and will not comply and consent to betray the liberties of their country, it will be past doubt what is doing. What power they ought to have in the society, who thus

employ it contrary to the trust that went along with it in its first institution, is easy to determine; and one cannot but see, that he, who has once attempted any such thing as this, cannot any longer be trusted ...

224. The people generally ill-treated, and contrary to right, will be ready upon any occasion to ease themselves of a burden that sits heavy upon them. They will wish, and seek for the opportunity, which in the change, weakness, and accidents of human affairs, seldom delays long to offer itself. He must have lived but a little while in the world, who has not seen examples of this in his time; and he must have read very little, who cannot produce examples of it in all sorts of governments in the world.

225. Such revolutions happen ... not upon every little mismanagement in public affairs. Great mistakes in the ruling part, many wrong and inconvenient laws, and all the slips of human frailty, will be borne by the people without mutiny or murmur. But if a long train of abuses, prevarications, and artifices, all tending the same way, make the design visible to the people, and they cannot but feel what they lie under, and see whither they are going; it is not to be wondered, that they should then rouse themselves, and endeavour to put the rule into such hands which may secure to them the ends for which government was at first erected, and without which, ancient names, and specious forms, are so far from being better, that they are much worse, than the state of nature, or pure anarchy; the inconveniencies, being all as great and as near, but the remedy farther off and more difficult.

Government, Rights, and the Freedom of Generations

THOMAS PAINE*

Although he spent his first thirty-eight years in England, Thomas Paine (1737–1809) is most often associated with the American and French revolutions. Paine moved to Pennsylvania in 1775, and in February of the following year he published a pamphlet, *Common Sense*, that urged the colonists to declare themselves independent of Britain. The beginning of *Common Sense* appears here as the first selection from Paine's writings. He later moved to France, where he actively supported the French Revolution. The second selection is from *The Rights of Man* (1791, 1792), which Paine wrote to defend the revolution against Edmund Burke's *Reflections on the Revolution in France* (see selection 4.28 in this volume).

* Sources: *Common Sense* (1776), from *The Life and Writings of Thomas Paine*, vol. 2. Daniel Edwin Wheeler, ed. (New York: Vincent Parke and Co., 1915), pp. 1–7; and *The Rights of Man: Being an Answer to Mr. Burke's Attack on the French Revolution* (Dublin: G. Burnet, R. Cross, P. Wogan et al., 1791), pp. 8–9.

COMMON SENSE

Some writers have so confounded society with government, as to leave little or no distinction between them; whereas they are not only different, but have different origins. Society is produced by our wants, and government by our wickedness; the former promotes our happiness *positively* by uniting our affections, the latter *negatively* by restraining our vices. The one encourages intercourse, the other creates distinctions. The first is a patron, the last a punisher.

Society in every state is a blessing, but government even in its best state is but a necessary evil; in its worst state an intolerable one; for when we suffer, or are exposed to the same miseries *by a government*, which we might expect in a country *without government*, our calamities are heightened by reflecting that we furnish the means by which we suffer. Government, like dress, is the badge of lost innocence; the palaces of kings are built on the ruins of the bowers of paradise. For were the impulses of conscience clear, uniform, and irresistibly obeyed, man would need no other lawgiver; but that not being the case, he finds it necessary to surrender up a part of his property to furnish means for the protection of the rest; and this he is induced to do by the same prudence which in every other case advises him out of two evils to choose the least. *Wherefore*, security being the true design and end of government, it unanswerably follows that whatever *form* thereof appears most likely to ensure it to us, with the least expense and greatest benefit, is preferable to all others.

In order to gain a clear and just idea of the design and end of government, let us suppose a small number of persons settled in some sequestered part of the earth, unconnected with the rest, they will then represent the first peopling of any country, or of the world. In this state of natural liberty, society will be their first thought. A thousand motives will excite them thereto, the strength of one man is so unequal to his wants, and his mind so unfitted for perpetual solitude, that he is soon obliged to seek assistance and relief of another, who in his turn requires the same. Four or five united would be able to raise a tolerable dwelling in the midst of a wilderness, but *one* man might labour out the common period of life without accomplishing any thing; when he had felled his timber he could not remove it, nor erect it after it was removed; hunger in the mean time would urge him from his work, and every different want call him a different way. Disease, nay even misfortune, would be death, for though neither might be mortal, yet either would disable him from living, and reduce him to a state in which he might rather be said to perish than to die.

Thus necessity, like a gravitating power, would soon form our newly arrived emigrants into society, the reciprocal blessings of which would supersede and render the obligations of law and government unnecessary while they remained perfectly just to each other; but as nothing but heaven is impregnable to vice, it will unavoidably happen, that in proportion as they surmount the first difficulties of emigration, which bound them together in a common cause, they will begin to relax in their duty and attachment to each other; and this remissness, will point out the necessity, of establishing some form of government to supply the defect of moral virtue.

Some convenient tree will afford them a State-House, under the branches of which, the whole colony may assemble to deliberate on public matters. It is more than probable that their first laws will have the title only of REGULANONS, and be enforced by no other penalty than public disesteem. In this first parliament every man, by natural right will have a seat.

But as the colony increases, the public concerns will increase likewise, and the distance at which the members may be separated, will render it too inconvenient for all of them to meet on every occasion as at first, when their number was small, their habitations near, and the public concerns few and trifling. This will point out the convenience of their consenting to leave the legislative part to be managed by a select number chosen from the whole body, who are supposed to have the same concerns at stake which those have who appointed them, and who will act in the same manner as the whole body would act were they present. If the colony continue increasing, it will become necessary to augment the number of the representatives, and that the interest of every part of the colony may be attended to, it will be found best to divide the whole into convenient parts, each part sending its proper number; and that the *elected* might never form to themselves an interest separate from the *electors*, prudence will point out the propriety of having elections often; because as the *elected* might by that means return and mix again with the general body of the *electors* in a few months, their fidelity to the public will be secured by the prudent reflection of not making a rod for themselves. And as this frequent interchange will establish a common interest with every part of the community, they will mutually and naturally support each other, and on this (not on the unmeaning name of king) depends the *strength of government, and the happiness of the governed*.

Here then is the origin and rise of government; namely, a mode rendered necessary by the inability of moral virtue to govern the world; here too is the design and end of government, viz. freedom and security. And however our eyes may be dazzled with snow, or our ears deceived by sound; however prejudice may warp our wills, or interest darken our understanding, the simple voice of nature and of reason will say, it is right.

I draw my idea of the form of government from a principle in nature, which no art can overturn, viz. that the more simple any thing is, the less liable it is to be disordered, and the easier repaired when disordered; and with this maxim in view, I offer a few remarks on the so much boasted constitution of England. That it was noble for the dark and slavish times in which it was erected, is granted. When the world was overrun with tyranny the least remove therefrom was a glorious rescue. But that it is imperfect, subject to convulsions, and incapable of producing what it seems to promise, is easily demonstrated.

Absolute governments (tho' the disgrace of human nature) have this advantage with them, that they are simple; if the people suffer, they know the head from which their suffering springs, know likewise the remedy, and are not bewildered by a variety of causes and cures …

There is something exceedingly ridiculous in the composition of monarchy; it first excludes a man from the means of information, yet empowers him to act in cases where the highest judgement is required. The state of a king shuts him from the world, yet the business of a king requires him to know it thoroughly; wherefore the different parts, unnaturally opposing and destroying each other, prove the whole character to be absurd and useless.

THE RIGHTS OF MAN

Every age and generation must be as free to act for itself, *in all cases*, as the ages and generation which preceded it. The vanity and presumption of governing beyond the grave, is the most ridiculous and insolent of all tyrannies.

Man has no property in man; neither has any generation a property in the generations which are to follow. The Parliament or the people of 1688, or of any other period, had no more right to dispose of the people of the present day, or to bind or to control them *in any shape whatever*, than the Parliament or the people of the present day have to dispose of, bind, or control those who are to live a hundred or a thousand years hence.

Every generation is, and must be, competent to all the purposes which its occasions require. It is the living, and not the dead, that are to be accommodated. When man ceases to be, his power and his wants cease with him; and having no longer any participation in the concerns of this world, he has no longer any authority in directing who shall be its governors, or how its government shall be organized, or how administered.

I am not contending for nor against any form of government, nor for nor against any party here or elsewhere. That which a whole nation chooses to do, it has a right to do. Mr. [Edmund] Burke says, No. Where then *does* the right exist? I am contending for the rights of the *living*, and against their being willed away, and controlled and contracted for, by the manuscript assumed authority of the dead; and Mr. Burke is contending for the authority of the dead over the rights and freedom of the living.

There was a time when kings disposed of their crowns by will upon their death-beds, and consigned the people, like beasts of the field, to whatever successor they appointed. This is now so exploded as scarcely to be remembered, and so monstrous as hardly to be believed. But the parliamentary clauses upon which Mr. Burke builds his political church, are of the same nature.

The laws of every country must be analogous to some common principle. In England, no parent or master, nor all the authority of Parliament, omnipotent as it has called itself, can bind or control the personal freedom even of an individual beyond the age of twenty-one years. On what ground of right, then, could the Parliament of 1688, or any other parliament, bind all posterity for ever?

Those who have quitted the world [i.e., died], and those who are not yet arrived in it, are as remote from each other, as the utmost stretch of moral imagination can conceive. What possible obligation, then, can exist between them; what rule or principle can be laid down, that two nonentities, the one out of existence, and the other not in, and who never can meet in this world, that the one should control the other to the end of time?

Declaration of Independence of the United States

On June 7, 1776, Richard Henry Lee, a representative to the Continental Congress from Virginia, introduced a resolution proclaiming that "these United Colonies are, and of right ought to be, free and independent States." Three days later, Congress appointed a committee to prepare a declaration of independence. One member of the committee, Thomas Jefferson (1743–1826), wrote the initial draft, which the other members of the committee and then the Congress as a whole modified. Jefferson later characterized the Declaration in this way: "Neither aiming at originality of principle or sentiment, nor yet copied from any particular and previous writing, it was intended to be an expression of the American mind."

THE UNANIMOUS DECLARATION OF THE THIRTEEN UNITED STATES OF AMERICA

Locke + Paine

When in the Course of human events, it becomes necessary for one people to dissolve the political bands which have connected them with another, and to assume among the Powers of the earth, the separate and equal station to which the Laws of Nature and of Nature's God entitle them, a decent respect to the opinions of mankind requires that they should declare the causes which impel them to the separation.

Locke + Hobbes Adam Smith

We hold these truths to be self-evident, that all men are created equal, that they are endowed by their Creator with certain unalienable Rights, that among these are Life, Liberty and the pursuit of Happiness. That to secure these rights, Governments are instituted among Men, deriving their just powers from the consent of the governed. That whenever any Form of Government becomes destructive of these ends, it is the Right of the People to alter or to abolish it, and to institute new Government, laying its foundation on such principles and organizing its powers in

Locke

such form, as to them shall seem most likely to effect their Safety and Happiness. Prudence, indeed, will dictate that Governments long established should not be changed for light and transient causes; and accordingly all experience hath shown, that mankind are more disposed to suffer, while evils are sufferable, than to right themselves by abolishing the forms to which they are accustomed. But when a long train of abuses and usurpations, pursuing invariably the same Object evinces a design to reduce them under absolute Despotism, it is their right, it is their duty, to throw off such Government, and to provide new Guards for their future security—Such has been the patient sufferance of these Colonies; and such is now the necessity which constrains them to alter their former Systems of Government. The history of the present King of Great Britain is a history of repeated injuries and usurpations, all having in direct object the establishment of an absolute Tyranny over these States. To prove this, let Facts be submitted to a candid world.

He has refused his Assent to Laws, the most wholesome and necessary for the public good.

He has forbidden his Governors to pass Laws of immediate and pressing importance, unless suspended in their operation till his Assent should be obtained; and when so suspended, he has utterly neglected to attend to them.

He has refused to pass other Laws for the accommodation of large districts of people, unless those people would relinquish the right of Representation in the Legislature, a right inestimable to them and formidable to tyrants only.

He has called together legislative bodies at places unusual, uncomfortable, and distant from the depository of their Public Records, for the sole purpose of fatiguing them into compliance with his measures.

He has dissolved Representative Houses repeatedly, for opposing with manly firmness his invasions on the rights of the people.

He has refused for a long time, after such dissolutions, to cause others to be elected; whereby the Legislative Powers, incapable of Annihilation, have returned to the People at large for their exercise; the State remaining in the mean time exposed to all the dangers of invasion from without, and convulsions within.

He has endeavoured to prevent the population of these States; for that purpose obstructing the Laws of Naturalization of Foreigners; refusing to pass others to encourage their migration hither; and raising the conditions of new Appropriations of Lands.

He has obstructed the Administration of Justice, by refusing his Assent to Laws for establishing Judiciary Powers.

He has made Judges dependent on his Will alone, for the tenure of their offices, and the amount and payment of their salaries.

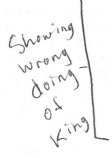
Showing wrong doing of King

He has erected a multitude of New Offices, and sent hither swarms of Officers to harass our People, and eat out their substance.

He has kept among us, in times of peace, Standing Armies without the Consent of our legislatures.

He has affected to render the Military independent of and superior to the Civil Power.

He has combined with others to subject us to a jurisdiction foreign to our constitution, and unacknowledged by our laws; giving his Assent to their acts of pretended legislation:

For quartering large bodies of armed troops among us:

For protecting them, by a mock Trial, from Punishment for any Murders which they should commit on the Inhabitants of these States:

For cutting off our Trade with all parts of the world:

For imposing taxes on us without our Consent:

For depriving us in many cases, of the benefits of Trial by Jury:

For transporting us beyond Seas to be tried for pretended offences:

For abolishing the free System of English Laws in a neighbouring Province, establishing therein an Arbitrary government, and enlarging its Boundaries so as to render it at once an example and fit instrument for introducing the same absolute rule into these Colonies:

For taking away our Charters, abolishing our most valuable Laws, and altering fundamentally the Forms of our Governments:

For suspending our own Legislatures, and declaring themselves invested with Power to legislate for us in all cases whatsoever.

He has abdicated Government here, by declaring us out of his Protection and waging War against us.

He has plundered our seas, ravaged our Coasts, burnt our towns, and destroyed the lives of our people.

He is at this time transporting large armies of foreign mercenaries to compleat the works of death, desolation and tyranny, already begun with circumstances of Cruelty & perfidy scarcely paralleled in the most barbarous ages, and totally unworthy the Head of a civilized nation.

He has constrained our fellow Citizens taken Captive on the high Seas to bear Arms against their Country, to become the executioners of their friends and Brethren, or to fall themselves by their Hands.

He has excited domestic insurrections amongst us, and has endeavoured to bring on the inhabitants of our frontiers, the merciless Indian Savages, whose known rule of warfare, is an undistinguished destruction of all ages, sexes and conditions.

In every stage of these Oppressions We have Petitioned for Redress in the most humble terms: Our repeated Petitions have been answered only by repeated injury. A Prince, whose character is thus marked by every act which may define a Tyrant, is unfit to be the ruler of a free People.

Nor have We been wanting in attention to our British brethren. We have warned them from time to time of attempts by their legislature to extend an unwarrantable jurisdiction over us. We have reminded them of the circumstances of our emigration and settlement here. We have appealed to their native justice and magnanimity, and we have conjured them by the ties of our common kindred to disavow these usurpations, which, would inevitably interrupt our connections and correspondence. They too have been deaf to the voice of justice and of consanguinity. We must, therefore, acquiesce in the necessity, which denounces our Separation, and hold them, as we hold the rest of mankind, Enemies in War, in Peace Friends.

We, therefore, the Representatives of the United States of America, in General Congress, Assembled, appealing to the Supreme Judge of the world for the rectitude of our intentions, do, in the Name, and by Authority of the good People of these Colonies, solemnly publish and declare, That these United Colonies are, and of Right ought to be Free and Independent States; that they are Absolved from all Allegiance to the British Crown, and that all political connection between them and the State of Great Britain, is and ought to be totally dissolved; and that as Free and Independent States, they have full Power to levy War, conclude Peace, contract Alliances, establish Commerce, and to do all other Acts and Things which Independent States may of right do. And for the support of this Declaration, with a firm reliance on the Protection of Divine Providence, we mutually pledge to each other our Lives, our Fortunes, and our sacred Honor.

Declaration of the Rights of Man and of Citizens

In 1788, faced with a financial crisis, King Louis XVI of France called the Estates-General into session for the first time in over 170 years. The traditional representative body of France, the Estates-General consisted of representatives of the church, the nobility, and the people. When the Estates-General convened in 1789, the representatives of the Third Estate (the people) defied the king and declared themselves the National Assembly of France. As one of its first acts, the Assembly approved a declaration of rights that was to serve as the basis of a constitution.

Source: Declaration des Droits de l'Homme et du Citoyen (1789), translated by Thomas Paine and included as an appendix to Paine, *The Rights of Man* (Dublin: G. Burnet et al., 1791).

DECLARATION OF THE RIGHTS OF MAN AND OF CITIZENS
By the National Assembly of France

The representatives of the people of FRANCE, formed into a NATIONAL ASSEMBLY, considering that ignorance, neglect, or contempt of human rights, are the sole causes of public misfortunes and corruptions of government, have resolved to set forth in a solemn declaration, these natural, imprescriptible, and unalienable rights: that this declaration, being constantly present to the minds of the members of the body social, they may be ever kept attentive to their rights and their duties: that the acts of the legislative and executive powers of government, being capable of being every moment compared with the end [aim] of political institutions, may be more respected: and also, that the future claims of the citizens, being directed by simple and incontestable principles, may always tend to the maintenance of the Constitution, and the general happiness.

For these reasons the NATIONAL ASSEMBLY doth recognize and declare, in the presence of the Supreme Being, and with the hope of His blessing and favor, the following *sacred* rights of men and of citizens:

1   Men are born, and always continue, free, and equal in respect of their rights. Civil distinctions, therefore, can be founded only on public utility.

2   The end of all political associations, is, the preservation of the natural and imprescriptible rights of man; and these rights are liberty, property, security, and resistance of oppression.

3   The nation is essentially the source of all sovereignty; nor can any individual, or any body of men, be entitled to any authority which is not expressly derived from it.

4   Political liberty consists in the power of doing whatever does not injure another. The exercise of the natural rights of every man has no other limits than those which are necessary to secure to every *other* man the free exercise of the same rights; and these limits are determinable only by the law.

5   The law ought to prohibit only actions hurtful to society. What is not prohibited by the law, should not be hindered; nor should any one be compelled to that which the law does not require.

6   The law is an expression of the will of the community. All citizens have a right to concur, either personally, or by their representatives, in its formation. It should be the same to all, whether it protects or punishes; and all being equal in its sight, are equally eligible to all honors, places, and employments, according to their different abilities, without any other distinction than that created by their virtues and talents.

7   No man should be accused, arrested, or held in confinement, except in cases determined by the law, and according to the forms which it has prescribed. All who promote, solicit, execute, or cause to be executed, arbitrary orders, ought to be punished; and every citizen called upon or apprehended by virtue of the law, ought immediately to obey, and renders himself culpable by resistance.

8   The law ought to impose no other penalties but such as are absolutely and evidently necessary: and no one ought to be punished, but in virtue of a law promulgated before the offense, and legally applied.

9   Every man being presumed innocent till he has been convicted, whenever his detention becomes indispensable, all rigor to him, more than is necessary to secure his person, ought to be provided against by the law.

10   No man ought to be molested on account of his opinions, not even on account of his *religious* opinions, provided his avowal of them does not disturb the public order established by the law.

11   The unrestrained communication of thoughts and opinions being one of the most precious rights of man, every citizen may speak, write, and publish freely, provided he is responsible for the abuse of this liberty in cases determined by the law.

12   A public force being necessary to give security to the rights of men and of citizens, that force is instituted for the benefit of the community, and not for the particular benefit of the persons with whom it is entrusted.

13   A common contribution being necessary for the support of the public force, and for defraying the other expenses of government, it ought to be divided equally among the members of the community, according to their abilities.

14   Every citizen has a right, either by himself or his representative, to a free voice in determining the necessity of public contributions, the appropriation of them, and their amount, mode of assessment, and duration.

15   Every community has a right to demand of all its agents, an account of their conduct.

16   Every community in which a separation of powers and a security of rights is not provided for, wants a constitution.

17   The rights to property being inviolable and sacred, no one ought to be deprived of it, except in cases of evident public necessity, legally ascertained, and on condition of a previous just indemnity.

Private Profit, Public Good

ADAM SMITH*

Although he was one of the major philosophers of the Scottish Enlightenment, Adam Smith (1723–1790) is today best known for his work in political economy (the forerunner of modern science of economics), notably his *An Inquiry into the Nature and Causes of the Wealth of Nations* (1776), usually abbreviated as *The Wealth of Nations*. Other writers had developed the laissez-faire theory that government should leave people alone in the economic marketplace, but Smith provided the most thorough and influential defense of this doctrine.

---

* *Source*: Adam Smith, *An Inquiry into the Nature and Causes of the Wealth of Nations*, vol. 1 (London: T. Cadell and W. Davies, 1805), pp. 20–27.

OF THE PRINCIPLE WHICH GIVES OCCASION TO THE DIVISION OF LABOR
(From *The Wealth of Nations*, Book I, Chapter 2)

This division of labor, from which so many advantages are derived, is not originally the effect of any human wisdom which foresees and intends that general opulence to which it gives occasion. It is the necessary, though very slow and gradual, consequence of a certain propensity in human nature which has in view no such extensive utility: the propensity to truck, barter, and exchange one thing for another.

Whether this propensity be one of those original principles in human nature, of which no further account can be given; or whether, as seems more probable, it be the necessary consequence of the faculties of reason and speech, it belongs not to our present subject to enquire. It is common to all men, and to be found in no other race of animals, which seem to know neither this nor any other species of contracts. Two greyhounds, in running down the same hare, have sometimes the appearance of acting in some sort of concert. Each turns her toward his companion, or endeavors to intercept her when his companion turns her toward himself. This, however, is not the effect of any contract, but of the accidental concurrence of their passions in the same object at that particular time. Nobody ever saw a dog make a fair and deliberate exchange of one bone for another with another dog. Nobody ever saw one animal by its gestures and natural cries signify to another, this is mine, that yours; I am willing to give this for that. When an animal wants to obtain something either of a man or of another animal, it has no other means of persuasion but to gain the favor of those whose service it requires. A puppy fawns upon its dam, and a spaniel endeavors by a thousand attractions to engage the attention of its master who is at dinner, when it wants to be fed by him. Man sometimes uses the same arts with his brethren, and when he has no other means of engaging them to act according to his inclinations, endeavors by every servile and fawning attention to obtain their good will. He has not time, however, to do this upon every occasion. In civilized society he stands at all times in need of the co-operation and assistance of great multitudes, while his whole life is scarce sufficient to gain the friendship of a few persons. In almost every other race of animals each individual, when it is grown up to maturity, is entirely independent, and in its natural state has occasion for the assistance of no other living creature. But man has almost constant occasion for the help of his brethren, and it is in vain for him to expect it from their benevolence only. He will be more likely to prevail if he can interest their self-love in his favor, and show them that it is for their own advantage to do for him what he requires of them. Whoever offers to another a bargain of any kind, proposes to do this. Give me that which I want, and you shall have this which you want, is the meaning of every such offer; and it is in this manner that we obtain from one another the far greater part of those good offices which we stand in need of. It is not from the benevolence of the butcher, the brewer, or the baker, that we expect our dinner, but from their regard to their own interest. We address ourselves, not to their humanity but to their self-love, and never talk to them of our own necessities but of their advantages. Nobody but a beggar chooses to depend chiefly upon the benevolence of his fellow citizens. Even a beggar does not depend upon it entirely. The charity of well-disposed people, indeed, supplies him with the whole fund of his subsistence. But though this principle ultimately provides him with all the necessaries of life which he has occasion for, it neither does nor can provide him with them as he has occasion for them. The greater part of his occasional wants are supplied in the same manner as those of other people, by treaty, by barter, and by purchase. With the money which one man gives him he purchases food. The old clothes which another bestows upon him he exchanges for other old clothes which suit him better, or for lodging, or for food, or for money, with which he can buy either food, clothes, or lodging, as he has occasion.

As it is by treaty, by barter, and by purchase that we obtain from one another the greater part of those mutual good offices which we stand in need of, so it is this same trucking disposition which originally gives occasion to the division of labor. In a tribe of hunters or shepherds a particular person makes bows and arrows, for example, with more readiness and dexterity than any other. He frequently exchanges them for cattle or for venison with his companions; and he finds at last that he can in this manner get more cattle and venison than if he himself went to the field to catch them. From a regard to his own interest, therefore, the making of bows and arrows grows to be his chief business, and he becomes a sort of armorer. Another excels in making the frames and covers of their little huts or movable houses. He is accustomed to be of use in this way to his neighbors, who reward him in the same manner with cattle and with venison till at last he finds it his interest to dedicate himself entirely to this employment, and to become a sort of house carpenter. In the same manner a third becomes a smith or a brazier; a fourth a tanner or dresser of hides or skins, the principal part of the clothing of savages. And thus the certainty of being able to exchange all that surplus part of the produce of his own labor, which is over and above his own consumption, for such parts of the produce of other men's labor as he may have occasion for, encourages every man to apply himself to a particular occupation, and to cultivate and bring to perfection whatever talent or genius he may possess for that particular species of business.

The difference of natural talents in different men is, in reality, much less than we are aware of; and the very different genius which appears to distinguish men of different professions, when grown up to maturity, is not upon many occasions so much the cause as the effect of the division of labor. The difference between the most dissimilar characters, between a philosopher and a common street porter, for example, seems to arise not so much from nature as from habit, custom, and education. When they came into the world, and for the first six or eight years of their existence, they were, perhaps, very much alike, and neither their parents nor playfellows could perceive any remarkable difference. About that age, or soon after, they come to be employed in very different occupations. The difference of talents comes then to be taken notice of, and widens by degrees, till at last the vanity of the philosopher is willing to acknowledge scarce any resemblance. But without the disposition to truck, barter, and exchange, every man must have procured to himself every necessary and conveniency of life which he wanted. All must have had the same duties to perform, and the same work to do, and there could have been no such difference of employment as could alone give occasion to any great difference of talents.

As it is this disposition which forms that difference of talents so remarkable among men of different professions, so it is this same disposition which renders that difference useful. Many tribes of animals acknowledged to be all of the same species derive from nature a much more remarkable distinction of genius than what, antecedent to custom and education, appears to take place among men. By nature a philosopher is not in genius and disposition half so different from a street porter as a mastiff is from a greyhound, or a greyhound from a spaniel, or this last from a shepherd's dog. Those different tribes of animals, however, though all of the same species, are of scarce any use to one another. The strength of the mastiff is not in the least supported either by the swiftness of the greyhound, or by the sagacity of the spaniel, or by the docility of the shepherd's dog. The effects of those different geniuses and talents, for want of the power or disposition to barter and exchange, cannot be brought into a common stock, and do not in the least contribute to the better accommodation and conveniency of the species. Each animal is still obliged to support and defend itself separately and independently, and derives no sort of advantage from that variety of talents with which nature has distinguished its fellows.

Freedom and Enlightenment

IMMANUEL KANT*

Immanuel Kant (1724–1804), the eminent German philosopher, wrote several influential books, including *The Critique of Pure Reason* (1781) and *Groundwork of the Metaphysics of Morals* (1785). Kant held that autonomy, or self-rule, is the mark of a fully mature and moral person, and he believed that the eighteenth-century intellectual movement known as the Enlightenment embodied that ideal. He wrote the following essay, "What Is Enlightenment?" as a newspaper article in 1784 to describe and defend the ideals of the Enlightenment against some of its critics.

---

* *Source*: "Was Ist Äufklarung?" in Kant's *Sämmtliche Werke* (Leipzig: Leopold Voss, 1838), vol. 7. Translated and abridged by Terence Ball.

WHAT IS ENLIGHTENMENT?

Enlightenment is mankind's leaving behind its self-imposed immaturity. Immaturity is the inability to employ one's own intelligence without being directed by someone else. This immaturity is self-imposed if it results not from lack of intellect but from a lack of willingness and courage to use it without another's guidance. *Sapere Aude!*—"Have the courage to think for yourself!"—that is the motto of the Enlightenment.

Because of laziness and cowardice, many supposedly grown men remain happily immature throughout their lives, readily allowing others to serve as their guardians. After all, it is so easy to remain immature! If I have a book which does my thinking for me, a priest or pastor who serves as my conscience, and a doctor who tells me what to eat, then I need not take the trouble to think for myself. If I have the money to pay them, others will perform that troublesome task for me. The guardians who have so kindly agreed to supervise me will warn me and others like me—including the entire "fair sex"—that any move toward adult maturity is not merely difficult but downright dangerous. Having already made their domestic animals dumb by seeing that these placid creatures remain on a short leash, our guardians likewise warn us of the danger of attempting to stand and walk on our own two feet. In fact, however, the danger is not all that great, since after falling a few times, one finally learns to walk by oneself. Even so, most people are so frightened by the warning that they dare not venture out on their own.

It is no easy task for a lone individual to outgrow the immaturity which has become second nature for him. He has grown fond of his infantile dependency, and is for the moment unable to employ his reason, since no one has previously permitted him to try. Rules and regulations—those mechanical tools of the use, or rather misuse, of his natural talents—are the chains which keep him bound to an endless childhood. Whoever broke these chains would have great difficulty in jumping over the smallest ditch, because he would be unused to moving freely. Thus only a handful of human beings have heretofore succeeded in freeing themselves from their childish dependency on others by cultivating their own minds at their own steady pace.

But it is even more possible that the public can enlighten itself. In fact, such enlightenment is virtually assured under conditions of freedom ... The only thing needed for such enlightenment is freedom, and particularly ... the freedom to make public use of one's reason in every case. And yet I hear people shout from all sides: "Don't argue!" The military commander says: "Don't argue, drill!" The tax collector: "Don't argue, pay!" The priest or pastor: "Don't argue, believe!" ... Everywhere there are restrictions on freedom.

Which of these restrictions hinders enlightenment, and which does not? I answer: The public use of one's reason must always be free, and this by itself can bring about enlightenment among human beings. By contrast, the private use of one's reason may be rather tightly restricted without necessarily impeding the progress of enlightenment. By the public use of one's reason I mean, for example, the way in which a scholar uses reason before the reading public. The private use of reason is the use which one may make of reason in a civil position or office with which he is entrusted. In the latter case, the public interest is served by the office-holder's neutrality and obedience—not by his argument and disagreement, which would be divisive and disruptive. Civil servants should not argue but obey ... A soldier, for example, should not argue with a superior officer who gives him a command ... Nor should a citizen refuse to pay his taxes ... Nor may a priest publicly disagree with the teachings of his church, offering instead his own personal interpretation of the gospel. But in their capacity as scholars, those same people would have the freedom and indeed the duty to criticize the military, the system of taxation, and the teachings of the church ... The scholar, speaking to the world through his writings, has an unrestricted freedom to use his own reason and to speak in his own voice. To insist that the people's spiritual guardians should themselves remain immature children would only perpetuate present-day ignorance.

But should an organization of clergymen be permitted to pledge itself to teach a particular unchanging doctrine, now and forevermore, in order to perpetuate its dominion over its members and their congregations? I say no. Any such agreement which aims to prevent the enlightenment of mankind is null and void. One generation cannot enter into a contract to stifle the intellectual and moral development of a later generation by making it impossible for the latter to expand its knowledge, to expose and eliminate error, and thereby to become ever more enlightened. To do so would be to commit a crime against human nature, whose destiny is to grow and progress. Later generations are utterly justified in ignoring or overturning such an agreement as unjust and illegal ... An individual may for a time hesitate to enlighten himself. But to opt out of such enlightenment entirely, either for oneself or one's descendants, is to ride roughshod over the sacred rights of mankind ... We can now pose the question: Is ours an enlightened age? I answer no: Ours is not an enlightened age, but it *is* an age of enlightenment. Many things continue to prevent people from using their own minds in matters of religion. But there is every indication that even this area is being opened up to critical scrutiny, thereby permitting people to escape from self-imposed immaturity ...

I have stressed the primary point of enlightenment—i.e., of man's release from his self-imposed immaturity—mainly in matters of religion ... because immaturity in this area is the most unfortunate and reprehensible kind. The ruler of a free state recognizes that there is no danger in legislation allowing his people to make public use of their own reason in publicly discussing and criticizing existing or proposed legislation ... A very large degree of civic freedom appears to be beneficial for the freedom of the spirit of a people ... Thus nature has nurtured, inside its tough shell, the embryo of the interest in and need for free thought. This free thought acts slowly but surely upon the mind of the people, permitting them to become ever more able to act freely. Eventually even the government will be influenced by this free thought, and will begin to treat men not as automata but as autonomous and responsible human beings.

Liberty and Individuality

JOHN STUART MILL*

Like Alexis de Tocqueville (see selection 2.8), whose work he admired, John Stuart Mill (1806–1873) feared that the advent of democracy was bringing with it a stifling pressure to conform to the conventional or popular opinion. In Mill's view, no one could live a fully human life unless he—or she, as he made clear in *The Subjection of Women* (1869)— was free to think and act for him- or herself. In the following excerpt from *On Liberty* (1859), Mill proposes "one very simple principle"— sometimes called "the Harm Principle"—for deciding just when society or government may rightfully regulate the individual's conduct and when the individual should be free to do as he or she sees fit.

---

* *Source*: John Stuart Mill, *On Liberty*, in *Utilitarianism, Liberty, and Representative Government*, A. D. Lindsay, ed. (New York: E. P. Dutton and Co., 1910), pp. 72–77, 79, 111–112, 123–128.

ON LIBERTY: INTRODUCTORY

The object of this Essay is to assert one very simple principle, as entitled to govern absolutely the dealings of society with the individual in the way of compulsion and control, whether the means used be physical force in the form of legal penalties, or the moral coercion of public opinion. That principle is, that the sole end for which mankind are warranted, individually or collectively, in interfering with the liberty of action of any of their number, is self-protection. That the only purpose for which power can be rightfully exercised over any member of a civilized community, against his will, is to prevent harm to others. His own good, either physical or moral, is not a sufficient warrant. He cannot rightfully be compelled to do or forbear because it will be better for him to do so, because it will make him happier, because, in the opinions of others, to do so would be wise, or even right. These are good reasons for remonstrating with him, or reasoning with him, or persuading him, or entreating him, but not for compelling him, or visiting him with any evil in case he do otherwise. To justify that, the conduct from which it is desired to deter him, must be calculated to produce evil to some one else. The only part of the conduct of any one, for which he is amenable to society, is that which concerns others. In the part which merely concerns himself, his independence is, of right, absolute. Over himself, over his own body and mind, the individual is sovereign.

It is, perhaps, hardly necessary to say that this doctrine is meant to apply only to human beings in the maturity of their faculties. We are not speaking of children, or of young persons below the age which the law may fix as that of manhood or womanhood. Those who are still in a state to require being taken care of by others, must be protected against their own actions as well as against external injury. For the same reason, we may leave out of consideration those backward states of society in which the race itself may be considered as in its nonage. The early difficulties in the way of spontaneous progress are so great, that there is seldom any choice of means for overcoming them; and a ruler full of the spirit of improvement is warranted in the use of any expedients that will attain an end, perhaps otherwise unattainable. Despotism is a legitimate mode of government in dealing with barbarians, provided the end be their improvement, and the means justified by actually effecting that end. Liberty, as a principle, has no application to any state of things anterior to the time when mankind have become capable of being improved by free and equal discussion. Until then, there is nothing for them but implicit obedience to an Akbar or a Charlemagne, if they are so fortunate as to find one.[1] But as soon as mankind have attained the capacity of being guided to their own improvement by conviction or persuasion (a period long since reached in all nations with whom we need here concern ourselves), compulsion, either in the direct form or in that of pains and penalties for non-compliance, is no longer admissible as a means to their own good, and justifiable only for the security of others.

It is proper to state that I forgo any advantage which could be derived to my argument from the idea of abstract right, as a thing independent of utility.[2] I regard utility as the ultimate appeal on all ethical questions; but it must be utility in the largest sense, grounded on the permanent interests of man as a progressive being. Those interests, I contend, authorize the subjection of individual spontaneity to external control, only in respect to those actions of each, which concern the interest of other people. If any one does an act hurtful to others, there is a *prima facie* case for punishing him, by law, or, where legal penalties are not safely applicable, by general disapprobation. There are also many positive acts for the benefit of others, which he may rightfully be compelled to perform; such as, to give evidence in a court of justice; to bear his fair share in the common defence, or in any other joint work necessary to the interest of the society of which he enjoys the protection; and to perform certain acts of individual beneficence, such as saving a fellow creature's life, or interposing to protect the defenceless against ill-usage [i.e., abuse], things which whenever it is obviously a man's duty to do, he may rightfully be made responsible to society for not doing. A person may cause evil to others not only by his actions but by his inaction, and in either case he is justly accountable to them for the injury. The latter case, it is true, requires a much more cautious exercise of compulsion than the former. To make any one answerable for doing evil to others, is the rule; to make him answerable for not preventing evil, is, comparatively speaking, the exception. Yet there are many cases clear enough and grave enough to justify that exception. In all things which regard the external relations of the individual, he is *de jure* amenable to those whose interests are concerned, and if need be, to society as their protector. There are often good reasons for not holding him to the responsibility; but these reasons must arise from the special expediencies of the case: either because it is a kind of case in which he is on the whole likely to act better, when left to his own discretion, than when controlled in any way in which society have it in their power to control him; or because the attempt to exercise control would produce other evils, greater than those which it would prevent. When such reasons as these preclude the enforcement of responsibility, the conscience of the agent himself should step into the vacant judgement-seat, and protect those interests of others which have no external protection; judging himself all the more rigidly, because the case does not admit of his being made accountable to the judgement of his fellow creatures.

But there is a sphere of action in which society, as distinguished from the individual, has, if any, only an indirect interest; comprehending all that portion of a person's life and conduct which affects only himself, or if it also affects others, only with their free, voluntary, and undeceived consent and participation. When I say only himself, I mean directly, and in the first instance: for whatever affects himself, may affect others through himself; and the objection which may be grounded on this contingency will receive consideration in the sequel. This, then, is the appropriate region of human liberty. It comprises, first, the inward domain of consciousness; demanding liberty of conscience, in the most comprehensive sense; liberty of thought and feeling; absolute freedom of opinion and sentiment on all subjects, practical or speculative, scientific, moral, or theological. The liberty of expressing and publishing opinions may seem to fall under a different principle, since it belongs to that part of the conduct of an individual which concerns other people; but, being almost of as much importance as the liberty of thought itself, and resting in great part on the same reasons, is practically inseparable from it. Secondly, the principle requires liberty of tastes and pursuits; of framing the plan of our life to suit our own character; of doing as we like, subject to such consequences as may follow: without impediment from our fellow creatures, so long as what we do does not harm them, even though they should think our conduct foolish, perverse, or wrong. Thirdly, from this liberty of each individual, follows the liberty, within the same limits, of combination among individuals; freedom to unite, for any purpose not involving harm to others: the persons combining being supposed to be of full age, and not forced or deceived.

No society in which these liberties are not, on the whole, respected, is free, whatever may be its form of government; and none is completely free in which they do not exist absolute and unqualified. The only freedom which deserves the name, is that of pursuing our own good in our own way, so long as we do not attempt to deprive others of theirs, or impede their efforts to obtain it. Each is the proper guardian of his own health, whether bodily, or mental and spiritual. Mankind are greater gainers by suffering each other to live as seems good to themselves, than by compelling each to live as seems good to the rest ...

Apart from the peculiar tenets of individual thinkers, there is also in the world at large an increasing inclination to stretch unduly the powers of society over the individual, both by the force of opinion and even by that of legislation: and as the tendency of all the changes taking place in the world is to strengthen society, and diminish the power of the individual, this encroachment is not one of the evils which tend spontaneously to disappear, but, on the contrary, to grow more and more formidable. The disposition of mankind, whether as rulers or as fellow citizens, to impose their own opinions and inclinations as a rule of conduct on others, is so energetically supported by some of the best and by some of the worst feelings incident to human nature, that it is hardly ever kept under restraint by anything but want of power; and as the power is not declining, but growing, unless a strong barrier of moral conviction can be raised against the mischief, we must expect, in the present circumstances of the world, to see it increase.

OF THE LIBERTY OF THOUGHT AND DISCUSSION
(From *On Liberty*, Chapter 2)

If all mankind minus one, were of one opinion, and only one person were of the contrary opinion, mankind would be no more justified in silencing that one person, than he, if he had the power, would be justified in silencing mankind. Were an opinion a personal possession of no value except to the owner; if to be obstructed in the enjoyment of it were simply a private injury, it would make some difference whether the injury was inflicted only on a few persons or on many. But the peculiar evil of silencing the expression of an opinion is, that it is robbing the human race; posterity as well as the existing generation; those who dissent from the opinion, still more than those who hold it. If the opinion is right, they are deprived of the opportunity of exchanging error for truth: if wrong, they lose, what is almost as great a benefit, the clearer perception and livelier impression of truth, produced by its collision with error.

It is necessary to consider separately these two hypotheses, each of which has a distinct branch of the argument corresponding to it. We can never be sure that the opinion we are endeavouring to stifle is a false opinion; and if we were sure, stifling it would be an evil still ...

We have now recognized the necessity to the mental well-being of mankind (on which all their other well-being depends) of freedom of opinion, and freedom of the expression of opinion, on four distinct grounds; which we will now briefly recapitulate.

First, if any opinion is compelled to silence, that opinion may, for aught we can certainly know, be true. To deny this is to assume our own infallibility.

Secondly, though the silenced opinion be an error, it may, and very commonly does, contain a portion of truth; and since the general or prevailing opinion on any subject is rarely or never the whole truth, it is only by the collision of adverse opinions that the remainder of the truth has any chance of being supplied.

Thirdly, even if the received opinion be not only true, but the whole truth; unless it is suffered to be, and actually is, vigorously and earnestly contested, it will, by most of those who receive it, be held in the manner of a prejudice, with little comprehension or feeling of its rational grounds. And not only this, but, fourthly, the meaning of the doctrine itself will be in danger of being lost, or enfeebled, and deprived of its vital effect on the character and conduct: the dogma becoming a mere formal profession, inefficacious for good, but cumbering the ground, and preventing the growth of any real and heartfelt conviction, from reason or personal experience …

Persons of genius, it is true, are, and are always likely to be, a small minority; but in order to have them, it is necessary to preserve the soil in which they grow. Genius can only breathe freely in an *atmosphere* of freedom. Persons of genius are, *ex vi termini* [from the force of the term], more individual than any other people— less capable, consequently, of fitting themselves, without hurtful compression, into any of the small number of moulds which society provides in order to save its members the trouble of forming their own character. If from timidity they consent to be forced into one of these moulds, and to let all that part of themselves which cannot expand under the pressure remain unexpanded, society will be little the better for their genius. If they are of a strong character, and break their fetters, they become a mark for the society which has not succeeded in reducing them to commonplace, to point at with solemn warning as "wild," "erratic," and the like; much as if one should complain of the Niagara river for not flowing smoothly between its banks like a Dutch canal.

I insist thus emphatically on the importance of genius, and the necessity of allowing it to unfold itself freely both in thought and in practice, being well aware that no one will deny the position in theory, but knowing also that almost every one, in reality, is totally indifferent to it. People think genius a fine thing if it enables a man to write an exciting poem, or paint a picture. But in its true sense, that of originality in thought and action, though no one says that it is not a thing to be admired, nearly all, at heart, think that they can do very well without it. Unhappily this is too natural to be wondered at. Originality is the one thing which unoriginal minds cannot feel the use of. They cannot see what it is to do for them: how should they? If they could see what it would do for them, it would not be originality. The first service which originality has to render them, is that of opening their eyes: which being once fully done, they would have a chance of being themselves original. Meanwhile, recollecting that nothing was ever yet done which some one was not the first to do, and that all good things which exist are the fruits of originality, let them be modest enough to believe that there is something still left for it to accomplish, and assure themselves that they are more in need of originality, the less they are conscious of the want.

In sober truth, whatever homage may be professed, or even paid, to real or supposed mental superiority, the general tendency of things throughout the world is to render mediocrity the ascendant power among mankind. In ancient history, in the middle ages, and in a diminishing degree through the long transition from feudality to the present time, the individual was a power in himself; and if he had either great talents or a high social position, he was a considerable power. At present individuals are lost in the crowd. In politics it is almost a triviality to say that public opinion now rules the world. The only power deserving the name is that of masses, and of governments while they make themselves the organ of the tendencies and instincts of masses. This is as true in the moral and social relations of private life as in public transactions. Those whose opinions go by the name of public opinion, are not always the same sort of public: in America they are the whole white population; in England, chiefly the middle class. But they are always a mass, that is to say, collective mediocrity. And what is a still greater novelty, the mass do not now take their opinions from dignitaries in Church or State, from ostensible leaders, or from books. Their thinking is done for them by men much like themselves, addressing them or speaking in their name, on the spur of the moment, through the newspapers. I am not complaining of all this. I do not assert that anything better is compatible, as a general rule, with the present low state of the human mind. But that does not hinder the government of mediocrity from being mediocre government. No government by a democracy or a numerous aristocracy, either in its political acts or in the opinions, qualities, and tone of mind which it fosters, ever did or could rise above mediocrity, except in so far as the sovereign Many have let themselves be guided (which in their best times they always have done) by the counsels and influence of a more highly gifted and instructed One or Few. The initiation of all wise or noble things, comes and must come from individuals; generally at first from some one individual. The honour and glory of the average man is that he is capable of following that initiative; that he can respond internally to wise and noble things, and be led to them with his eyes open. I am not countenancing the sort of "hero-worship" which applauds the strong man of genius for forcibly seizing on the government of the world and making it do his bidding in spite of itself.[3] All he can claim is, freedom to point out the way. The power of compelling others into it, is not only inconsistent with the freedom and development of all the rest, but corrupting to the strong man himself. It does seem, however, that when the opinions of masses of merely average men are everywhere become or becoming the dominant power, the counterpoise and corrective to that tendency would be, the more and more pronounced individuality of those who stand on the higher eminences of thought. It is in these circumstances most especially, that exceptional individuals, instead of being deterred, should be encouraged in acting differently from the mass. In other times there was no advantage in their doing so, unless they acted not only differently, but better. In this age, the mere example of nonconformity, the mere refusal to bend the knee to custom, is itself a service. Precisely because the tyranny of opinion is such as to make eccentricity a reproach, it is desirable, in order to break through that tyranny, that people should be eccentric. Eccentricity has always abounded when and where strength of character has abounded; and the amount of eccentricity in a society has generally been proportional to the amount of genius, mental vigour, and moral courage which it contained. That so few now dare to be eccentric, marks the chief danger of the time ...

     ... [N]or is it only persons of decided mental superiority who have a just claim to carry on their lives in their own way. There is no reason that all human existence should be constructed on some one or some small number of patterns. If a person possesses any tolerable amount of common sense and experience, his own mode of laying out his existence is the best, not because it is the best in itself, but because it is his own mode. Human beings are not like sheep; and even sheep are not undistinguishably alike. A man cannot get a coat or a pair of boots to fit him, unless they are either made to his measure, or he has a whole warehouseful to choose from: and is it easier to fit him with a life than with a coat, or are human beings more like one another in their whole physical and spiritual conformation than in the shape of their feet? If it were only that people have diversities of taste, that is reason enough for not attempting to shape them all after one model. But different persons also require different conditions for their spiritual development; and can no more exist healthily in the same moral, than all the variety of plants can in the same physical, atmosphere and climate. The same things which are helps to one person towards the cultivation of his higher nature, are hindrances to another. The same mode of life is a healthy excitement to one, keeping all his faculties of action and enjoyment in their best order, while to another it is a distracting burden, which suspends or crushes all internal life. Such are the differences among human beings in their sources of pleasure, their susceptibilities of pain, and the operation on them of different physical and moral agencies, that unless there is a corresponding diversity in their modes of life, they neither obtain their fair share of happiness, nor grow up to the mental, moral, and aesthetic stature of which their nature is capable ...

     There is one characteristic of the present direction of public opinion, peculiarly calculated to make it intolerant of any marked demonstration of individuality. The general average of mankind are not only moderate in intellect, but also moderate in inclinations: they have no tastes or wishes strong enough to incline them to do anything unusual, and they consequently do not understand those who have, and class all such with the wild and intemperate whom they are accustomed to look down upon. Now, in addition to this fact which is general, we have only to suppose that a strong movement has set in towards the improvement of morals, and it is evident what we have to expect. In these days such a movement has set in; much has actually been effected in the way of increased regularity of conduct, and discouragement of excesses; and there is a philanthropic spirit abroad, for the exercise of which there is no more inviting field than the moral and prudential improvement of our fellow creatures. These tendencies of the times cause the public to be more disposed than at most former periods to prescribe general rules of conduct, and endeavour to make every one conform to the approved standard. And that standard, express or tacit, is to desire nothing strongly. Its ideal of character is to be without any marked character; to maim by compression, like a Chinese lady's foot, every part of human nature which stands out prominently, and tends to make the person markedly dissimilar in outline to commonplace humanity ...

The despotism of custom is everywhere the standing hindrance to human advancement, being in unceasing antagonism to that disposition to aim at something better than customary, which is called ... the spirit of liberty ...

The combination of all these causes forms so great a mass of influences hostile to Individuality, that it is not easy to see how it can stand its ground. It will do so with increasing difficulty, unless the intelligent part of the public can be made to feel its value—to see that it is good there should be differences, even though not for the better, even though, as it may appear to them, some should be for the worse. If the claims of Individuality are ever to be asserted, the time is now, while much is still wanting to complete the enforced assimilation. It is only in the earlier stages that any stand can be successfully made against the encroachment. The demand that all other people shall resemble ourselves, grows by what it feeds on. If resistance waits till life is reduced *nearly* to one uniform type, all deviations from that type will come to be considered impious, immoral, even monstrous and contrary to nature. Mankind speedily become unable to conceive diversity, when they have been for some time unaccustomed to seeing it.

NOTES

1   Akbar (1542–1605) was a Mughal (or Mogul) emperor of India; Charlemagne (742–814) was the first emperor of the Holy Roman Empire.—Eds.
2   By "utility" Mill means the principle that all actions, laws, or policies are to be judged according to whether they promote the greatest happiness of the greatest number, or not.—Eds.
3   Here Mill refers to Thomas Carlyle's *On Heroes and Hero-Worship* (1841), which attributes all social progress to the actions of a handful of heroic leaders such as Julius Caesar and Napoleon.—Eds.

According to the Fitness of Things

WILLIAM GRAHAM SUMNER*

Like his English contemporary Herbert Spencer, the American sociologist William Graham Sumner (1840–1910) developed and vigorously defended the theory of Social Darwinism. According to this theory, individual humans are locked in a competition for survival—a life-or-death competition that the strong will win if nature is allowed to take its course. Spencer's and Sumner's adaptations of Darwin's theory of evolution (or, more accurately, natural selection) to human society thus provided some of the first important statements of neoclassical liberalism. As the following excerpts from Sumner's *What Social Classes Owe to Each Other* indicate, the Social Darwinists believed that individuals should be left alone to succeed or to fail in life with no expectation of help from government or society.

---

* *Source*: William Graham Sumner, *What Social Classes Owe to Each Other* (New York: Harper and Brothers, 1883), pp. 112–133.

ON THE VALUE, AS A SOCIOLOGICAL PRINCIPLE, OF THE RULE TO MIND ONE'S OWN BUSINESS
(From *What Social Classes Owe to Each Other*, Chapter 8)

The passion for dealing with social questions is one of the marks of our time. Every man gets some experience of, and makes some observations on social affairs. Except matters of health, probably none have such general interest as matters of society. Except matters of health, none are so much afflicted by dogmatism and crude speculation as those which appertain to society. The amateurs in social science always ask: What shall we do? What shall we do with Neighbor A? What shall we do for Neighbor B? What shall we make Neighbor A do for Neighbor B? It is a fine thing to be planning and discussing broad and general theories of wide application. The amateurs always plan to use the individual for some constructive and inferential social purpose, or to use the society for some constructive and inferential individual purpose. For A to sit down and think, What shall I do? is commonplace; but to think what B ought to do is interesting, romantic, moral, self-flattering, and public-spirited all at once. It satisfies a great number of human weaknesses at once. To go on and plan what a whole class of people ought to do is to feel one's self a power on earth, to win a public position, to clothe one's self in dignity. Hence we have an unlimited supply of reformers, philanthropists, humanitarians, and would-be managers-in-general of society.

Every man and woman in society has one big duty. That is, to take care of his or her own self. This is a social duty. For, fortunately, the matter stands so that the duty of making the best of one's self individually is not a separate thing from the duty of filling one's place in society, but the two are one, and the latter is accomplished when the former is done. The common notion, however, seems to be that one has a duty to society, as a special and separate thing, and that this duty consists in considering and deciding what other people ought to do. Now, the man who can do anything for or about anybody else than himself is fit to be head of a family; and when he becomes head of a family he has duties to his wife and his children, in addition to the former big duty. Then again, any man who can take care of himself and his family is in a very exceptional position, if he does not find in his immediate surroundings people who need his care and have some sort of a personal claim upon him. If, now, he is able to fulfill all this, and to take care of anybody outside his family and his dependents, he must have a surplus of energy, wisdom, and moral virtue beyond what he needs for his own business. No man has this; for a family is a charge which is capable of infinite development, and no man could suffice to the full measure of duty for which a family may draw upon him. Neither can a man give to society so advantageous an employment of his services, whatever they are, in any other way as by spending them on his family. Upon this, however, I will not insist. I recur to the observation that a man who proposes to take care of other people must have himself and his family taken care of, after some sort of a fashion, and must have an as yet unexhausted store of energy.

The danger of minding other people's business is twofold. First, there is the danger that a man may leave his own business unattended to; and, second, there is the danger of an impertinent interference with another's affairs. The "friends of humanity" almost always run into both dangers. I am one of humanity, and I do not want any volunteer friends. I regard friendship as mutual, and I want to have my say about it. I suppose that other components of humanity feel in the same way about it. If so, they must regard any one who assumes the *rôle* of a friend of humanity as impertinent. The reference to the friend of humanity back to his own business is obviously the next step.

Yet we are constantly annoyed, and the legislatures are kept constantly busy, by the people who have made up their minds that it is wise and conducive to happiness to live in a certain way, and who want to compel everybody else to live in their way. Some people have decided to spend Sunday in a certain way, and they want laws passed to make other people spend Sunday in the same way. Some people have resolved to be teetotalers, and they want a law passed to make everybody else a teetotaler. Some people have resolved to eschew luxury, and they want taxes laid to make others eschew luxury. The taxing power is especially something after which the reformer's finger always itches. Sometimes there is an element of self-interest in the proposed reformation, as when a publisher wanted a duty imposed on books, to keep Americans from reading books which would unsettle their Americanisms; and when artists wanted a tax laid on pictures, to save Americans from buying bad paintings ...

The amateur social doctors are like the amateur physicians—they always begin with the question of *remedies*, and they go at this without any diagnosis or any knowledge of the anatomy or physiology of society. They never have any doubt of the efficacy of their remedies. They never take account of any ulterior effects which may be apprehended from the remedy itself. It generally troubles them not a whit that their remedy implies a complete reconstruction of society, or even a reconstitution of human nature. Against all such social quackery the obvious injunction to the quacks is, to mind their own business ...

ON THE CASE OF A CERTAIN MAN WHO IS NEVER THOUGHT OF

(From *What Social Classes Owe to Each Other*, Chapter 9)

The type and formula of most schemes of philanthropy or humanitarianism is this: A and B put their heads together to decide what C shall be made to do for D. The radical vice of all these schemes, from a sociological point of view, is that C is not allowed a voice in the matter, and his position, character, and interests, as well as the ultimate effects on society through C's interests, are entirely overlooked. I call C the Forgotten Man. For once let us look him up and consider his case, for the characteristic of all social doctors is, that they fix their minds on some man or group of men whose case appeals to the sympathies and the imagination, and they plan remedies addressed to the particular trouble; they do not understand that all the parts of society hold together, and that forces which are set in action act and react throughout the whole organism, until an equilibrium is produced by a readjustment of all interests and rights. They therefore ignore entirely the source from which they must draw all the energy which they employ in their remedies, and they ignore all the effects on other members of society than the ones they have in view. They are always under the dominion of the superstition of government, and, forgetting that a government produces nothing at all, they leave out of sight the first fact to be remembered in all social discussion—that the State cannot get a cent for any man without taking it from some other man, and this latter must be a man who has produced and saved it. This latter is the Forgotten Man.

The friends of humanity start out with certain benevolent feelings toward "the poor," "the weak," "the laborers," and others of whom they make pets. They generalize these classes, and render them impersonal, and so constitute the classes into social pets. They turn to other classes and appeal to sympathy and generosity, and to all the other noble sentiments of the human heart. Action in the line proposed consists in a transfer of capital from the better off to the worse off. Capital, however, as we have seen, is the force by which civilization is maintained and carried on. The same piece of capital cannot be used in two ways. Every bit of capital, therefore, which is given to a shiftless and inefficient member of society, who makes no return for it, is diverted from a reproductive use; but if it was put to reproductive use, it would have to be granted in wages to an efficient and productive laborer. Hence the real sufferer by that kind of benevolence which consists in an expenditure of capital to protect the good-for-nothing is the industrious laborer. The latter, however, is never thought of in this connection. It is assumed that he is provided for and out of the account. Such a notion only shows how little true notions of political economy have as yet become popularized. There is an almost invincible prejudice that a man who gives a dollar to a beggar is generous and kind-hearted, but that a man who refuses the beggar and puts the dollar in a savings-bank is stingy and mean. The former is putting capital where it is very sure to be wasted, and where it will be a kind of seed for a long succession of future dollars, which must be wasted to ward off a greater strain on the sympathies than would have been occasioned by a refusal in the first place. Inasmuch as the dollar might have been turned into capital and given to a laborer who, while earning it, would have reproduced it, it must be regarded as taken from the latter. When a millionaire gives a dollar to a beggar the gain of utility to the beggar is enormous, and the loss of utility to the millionaire is insignificant. Generally the discussion is allowed to rest there. But if the millionaire makes capital of the dollar, it must go upon the labor market, as a demand for productive services. Hence there is another party in interest—the person who supplies productive services. There always are two parties. The second one is always the Forgotten Man, and any one who wants to truly understand the matter in question must go and search for the Forgotten Man. He will be found to be worthy, industrious, independent, and self-supporting. He is not, technically, "poor" or "weak"; he minds his own business, and makes no complaint. Consequently the philanthropists never think of him, and trample on him …

Society … maintains police, sheriffs, and various institutions, the object of which is to protect people against themselves—that is, against their own vices. Almost all legislative effort to prevent vice is really protective of vice, because all such legislation saves the vicious man from the penalty of his vice. Nature's remedies against vice are terrible. She removes the victims without pity. A drunkard in the gutter is just where he ought to be, according to the fitness and tendency of things. Nature has set up on him the process of decline and dissolution by which she removes things which have survived their usefulness. Gambling and other less mentionable vices carry their own penalties with them.

Now, we never can annihilate a penalty. We can only divert it from the head of the man who has incurred it to the heads of others who have not incurred it. A vast amount of "social reform" consists in just this operation. The consequence is that those who have gone astray, being relieved from Nature's fierce discipline, go on to worse, and that there is a constantly heavier burden for the others to bear. Who are the others? When we see a drunkard in the gutter we pity him. If a policeman picks him up, we say that society has interfered to save him from perishing. "Society" is a fine word, and it saves us the trouble of thinking. The industrious and sober workman, who is mulcted [i.e., robbed] of a percentage of his day's wages to pay the policeman, is the one who bears the penalty. But he is the Forgotten Man. He passes by and is never noticed, because he has behaved himself, fulfilled his contracts, and asked for nothing.

The fallacy of all prohibitory, sumptuary, and moral legislation is the same. A and B determine to be teetotalers, which is often a wise determination, and sometimes a necessary one. If A and B are moved by considerations which seem to them good, that is enough. But A and B put their heads together to get a law passed which shall force C to be a teetotaler for the sake of D, who is in danger of drinking too much. There is no pressure on A and B. They are having their own way, and they like it. There is rarely any pressure on D. He does not like it, and evades it. The pressure all comes on C. The question then arises, Who is C? He is the man who wants alcoholic liquors for any honest purpose whatsoever, who would use his liberty without abusing it, who would occasion no public question, and trouble nobody at all. He is the Forgotten Man again, and as soon as he is drawn from his obscurity we see that he is just what each one of us ought to be.

Liberalism and Positive Freedom

*T. H. GREEN**

Contrary to the Social Darwinists and other neoclassical liberals, the English philosopher Thomas Hill Green (1836–1882) insisted that liberalism requires an active government to ensure and promote individual liberty. In this excerpt from his speech, "Liberal Legislation and Freedom of Contract" (1880), Green draws a distinction between two kinds of freedom, negative and positive. He then uses this distinction as the basis for his claim that government has a duty to promote the welfare of the people so that they can become free. In this and his other essays and books, Green thus helped to lay the philosophical foundations for modern reform or welfare liberalism.

* *Source: The Works of Thomas Hill Green*, R. L. Nettleship, ed., vol. 3 (London: Longmans, Green and Co., 1888), pp. 370–376.

Liberalism and Positive Freedom

We shall probably all agree that freedom, rightly understood, is the greatest of blessings; that its attainment is the true end of all our efforts as citizens. But when we thus speak of freedom, we should consider carefully what we mean by it. We do not mean merely freedom from restraint or compulsion. We do not mean merely freedom to do as we like irrespectively of what it is that we like. We do not mean a freedom that can be enjoyed by one man or one set of men at the cost of a loss of freedom to others. When we speak of freedom as something to be so highly prized, we mean a positive power or capacity of doing or enjoying something that we do or enjoy in common with others. We mean by it a power which each man exercises through the help or security given him by his fellow-men, and which he in turn helps to secure for them. When we measure the progress of a society by its growth in freedom, we measure it by the increasing development and exercise on the whole of those powers of contributing to social good with which we believe the members of the society to be endowed; in short, by the greater power on the part of the citizens as a body to make the most and best of themselves. Thus, though of course there can be no freedom among men who act not willingly but under compulsion, yet on the other hand the mere removal of compulsion, the mere enabling a man to do as he likes, is in itself no contribution to true freedom. In one sense no man is so well able to do as he likes as the wandering savage. He has no master. There is no one to say him nay. Yet we do not count him really free, because the freedom of savagery is not strength, but weakness. The actual powers of the noblest savage do not admit of comparison with those of the humblest citizen of a law-abiding state. He is not the slave of man, but he is the slave of nature. Of compulsion by natural necessity he has plenty of experience, though of restraint by society none at all. Nor can he deliver himself from that compulsion except by submitting to this restraint. So to submit is the first step in true freedom, because the first step towards the full exercise of the faculties with which man is endowed. But we rightly refuse to recognize the highest development on the part of an exceptional individual or exceptional class, as an advance towards the true freedom of man, if it is founded on a refusal of the same opportunity to other men. The powers of the human mind have probably never attained such force and keenness, the proof of what society can do for the individual has never been so strikingly exhibited, as among the small groups of men who possessed civil privileges in the small republics of antiquity. The whole framework of our political ideas, to say nothing of our philosophy, is derived from them. But in them this extraordinary efflorescence of the privileged class was accompanied by the slavery of the multitude. That slavery was the condition on which it depended, and for that reason it was doomed to decay. There is no clearer ordinance of that supreme reason, often dark to us, which governs the course of men's affairs, than that no body of men should in the long run be able to strengthen itself at the cost of others' weakness. The civilization and freedom of the ancient world were short-lived because they were partial and exceptional. If the ideal of true freedom is the maximum of power for all members of human society alike to make the best of themselves, we are right in refusing to ascribe the glory of freedom to a state in which the apparent elevation of the few is founded on the degradation of the many, and in ranking modern society, founded as it is on free industry, with all its confusion and ignorant licence and waste of effort, above the most splendid of ancient republics.

If I have given a true account of that freedom which forms the goal of social effort, we shall see that freedom of contract, freedom of all the forms of doing what one will with one's own, is valuable only as a means to an end. That end is what I call freedom in the positive sense: in other words, like liberation of the powers of all men equally for contributions to a common good. No one has a right to do what he will with his own in such a way as to contravene this end. It is only through the guarantee which society gives him that he has property at all, or, strictly speaking, any right to his possessions. This guarantee is founded on a sense of common interest. Every one has an interest in securing to every one else the free use and enjoyment and disposal of his possessions, so long as that freedom on the part of one does not interfere with a like freedom on the part of others, because such freedom contributes to that equal development of the faculties of all which is the highest good for all. This is the true and the only justification of rights of property. Rights of property, however, have been and are claimed which cannot thus be justified. We are all now agreed that men cannot rightly be the property of men. The institution of property being only justifiable as a means to the free exercise of the social capabilities of all, there can be no true right to property of a kind which debars one class of men from such free exercise altogether. We condemn slavery no less when it arises out of a voluntary agreement on the part of the enslaved person. A contract by which anyone agreed for a certain consideration to become the slave of another we should reckon a void contract. Here, then, is a limitation upon freedom of contract which we all recognize as rightful. No contract is valid in which human persons, willingly or unwillingly, are dealt with as commodities, because such contracts of necessity defeat the end for which alone society enforces contracts at all.

Are there no other contracts which, less obviously perhaps but really, are open to the same objection? In the first place, let us consider contracts affecting labor. Labor, the economist tells us, is a commodity exchangeable like other commodities. This is in a certain sense true, but it is a commodity which attaches in a peculiar manner to the person of man. Hence restrictions may need to be placed on the sale of this commodity which would be unnecessary in other cases, in order to prevent labor from being sold under conditions which make it impossible for the person selling it ever to become a free contributor to social good in any form. This is most plainly the case when a man bargains to work under conditions fatal to health, in an unventilated factory. Every injury to the health of the individual is, so far as it goes, a public injury. It is an impediment to the general freedom; so much deduction from our power, as members of society, to make the best of ourselves. Society is, therefore, plainly within its right when it limits freedom of contract for the sale of labor, so far as is done by our laws for the sanitary regulations of factories, workshops, and mines. It is equally within its right in prohibiting the labor of women and young persons beyond certain hours. If they work beyond those hours, the result is demonstrably physical deterioration; which, as demonstrably, carries with it a lowering of the moral forces of society. For the sake of that general freedom of its members to make the best of themselves, which it is the object of civil society to secure, a prohibition should be put by law, which is the deliberate voice of society, on all such contracts of service as in a general way yield such a result. The purchase or hire of unwholesome dwellings is properly forbidden on the same principle. Its application to compulsory education may not be quite so obvious, but it will appear on a little reflection. Without a command of certain elementary arts and knowledge, the individual in modern society is as effectually crippled as by the loss of a limb or a broken constitution. He is not free to develop his faculties. With a view to securing such freedom among its members it is as certainly within the province of the state to prevent children from growing up in that kind of ignorance which practically excludes them from a free career in life, as it is within its province to require the sort of building and drainage necessary for public health.

Our modern legislation then with reference to labor, and education, and health, involving as it does manifold interference with freedom of contract, is justified on the ground that it is the business of the state, not indeed directly to promote moral goodness, for that, from the very nature of moral goodness, it cannot do, but to maintain the conditions without which a free exercise of the human faculties is impossible ...

Now, we shall probably all agree that a society in which the public health was duly protected, and necessary education duly provided for, by the spontaneous action of individuals, was in a higher condition than one in which the compulsion of law was needed to secure those ends. But we must take men as we find them. Until such a condition of society is reached, it is the business of the state to make the best security it can for the young citizens' growing up in such health and with so much knowledge as is necessary for their real freedom. In so doing it need not at all interfere with the independence and self-reliance of those whom it requires to do what they would otherwise do for themselves. The man who, of his own right feeling, saves his wife from overwork and sends his children to school, suffers no moral degradation from a law which, if he did not do this for himself, would seek to make him do it. Such a man does not feel the law as constraint at all. To him it is simply a powerful friend. It gives him security for that being done efficiently which, with the best wishes, he might have much trouble in getting done efficiently if left to himself. No doubt it relieves him from some of the responsibility which would otherwise fall to him as head of a family, but, if he is what we are supposing him to be, in proportion as he is relieved of responsibilities in one direction he will assume them in another. The security which the state gives him for the safe housing and sufficient schooling of his family will only make him the more careful for their well-being in other respects, which he is left to look after for himself. We need have no fear, then, of such legislation having an ill-effect on those who, without the law, would have seen to that being done, though probably less efficiently, which the law requires to be done. But it was not their case that the laws we are considering were especially meant to meet. It was the overworked women, the ill-housed and untaught families, for whose benefit they were intended. And the question is whether without these laws the suffering classes could have been delivered quickly or slowly from the condition they were in. Could the enlightened self-interest or benevolence of individuals, working under a system of unlimited freedom of contract, have ever brought them into a state compatible with the free development of the human faculties? No one considering the facts can have any doubt as to the answer to this question. Left to itself, or to the operation of casual benevolence, a degraded population perpetuates and increases itself. Read any of the authorized accounts, given before royal or parliamentary commissions, of the state of the laborers, especially of the women and children, as they were in our great industries before the law was first brought to bear on them, and before freedom of contract was first interfered with in them. Ask yourself what chance there was of a generation, born and bred under such conditions, ever contracting itself out of them. Given a certain standard of moral and material well-being, people may be trusted not to sell their labor, or the labor of their children, on terms which would not allow that standard to be maintained. But with large masses of our population, until the laws we have been considering took effect, there was no such standard. There was nothing on their part, in the way either of self-respect or established demand for comforts, to prevent them from working and living, or from putting their children to work and live, in a way in which no one who is to be a healthy and free citizen can work and live. No doubt there were many high-minded employers who did their best for their work-people before the days of state-interference, but they could not prevent less scrupulous hirers of labor from hiring it on the cheapest terms.

Commonwealth Club Address (1932)

FRANKLIN D. ROOSEVELT*

In the run-up to the American presidential election of 1932, the Democratic candidate, Franklin D. Roosevelt, delivered the following address to California's Commonwealth Club. In it he outlines in broad strokes his plan to end the Great Depression, and offers a historical and philosophical justification for implementing that plan, which he called the New Deal. In so doing, Roosevelt offered a vision of what some call "the new liberalism"—new at least to the United States—that emphasized equality, individual freedom, and greater fairness in American life.

---

* *Source*: Franklin D. Roosevelt, Campaign Speech, San Francisco, September 23, 1932, as reprinted in the *New York Times*, September 24, 1932.

I want to speak not of politics but of government. I want to speak not of parties, but of universal principles. They are not political, except in that larger sense in which a great American once expressed a definition of politics, that nothing in all of human life is foreign to the science of politics …

The issue of government has always been whether individual men and women will have to serve some system of government or economics, or whether a system of government and economics exists to serve individual men and women. This question has persistently dominated the discussion of government for many generations. On questions relating to these things men have differed, and for time immemorial it is probable that honest men will continue to differ.

Can government serve the individual?

The final word belongs to no man; yet we can still believe in change and in progress. Democracy … is a quest, a never-ending seeking for better things, and in the seeking for these things and the striving for better things, and in the seeking for these things and the striving for them, there are many roads to follow. But, if we map the course of these roads, we find that there are only two general directions.

When we look about us, we are likely to forget how hard people have worked to win the privilege of government. The growth of the national governments of Europe was a struggle for the development of a centralized force in the nation, strong enough to impose peace upon ruling barons. In many instances the victory of the central government, the creation of a strong central government, was a haven of refuge to the individual. The people preferred the master far away to the exploitation and cruelty of the smaller master near at hand.

But the creators of national government were perforce ruthless men. They were often cruel in their methods, but they did strive steadily toward something that society needed and very much wanted, a strong central state, able to keep the peace, to stamp out civil war, to put the unruly nobleman in his place, and to permit the bulk of individuals to live safely. The man of ruthless force had his place in developing a pioneer country, just as he did in fixing the power of the central government in the development of nations. Society paid him well for his services and its development. When the development among the nations of Europe, however, has been completed, ambition, and ruthlessness, having served its term tended to overstep their mark.

There came a growing feeling that government was conducted for the benefit of a few who thrived unduly at the expense of all. The people sought a balancing—a limiting force. There came gradually, through town councils, trade guilds, national parliaments, by constitution and by popular participation and control, limitations on arbitrary power. Another factor that tended to limit the power of those who ruled, was the rise of the ethical conception that a ruler bore a responsibility for the welfare of his subjects.

The American colonies were born in this struggle. The American Revolution was a turning point in it. After the revolution the struggle continued and shaped itself in the public life of the country. There were those who because they had seen the confusion which attended the years of war for American independence surrendered to the belief that popular government was essentially dangerous and essentially unworkable. They were honest people, my friends, and we cannot deny that their experience had warranted some measure of fear. The most brilliant, honest and able exponent of this point of view was Hamilton.[1] He was too impatient of slow moving methods. Fundamentally he believed that the safety of the republic lay in the autocratic strength of its government, that the destiny of individuals was to serve that government, and that fundamentally a great and strong group of central institutions, guided by a small group of able and public spirited citizens could best direct all government.

But Mr. Jefferson, in the summer of 1776, after drafting the Declaration of Independence, turned his mind to the same problem and took a different view. He did not deceive himself with outward forms. Government to him was a means to an end, not an end in itself; it might be either a refuge and a help or a threat and a danger, depending on the circumstances. We find him carefully analyzing the society for which he was to organize a government. "We have no paupers. The great mass of our population is of laborers, our rich who cannot live without labor, either manual or professional, being few and of moderate wealth. Most of the laboring class possess property, cultivate their own lands, have families and from the demand for their labor, are enabled to exact from the rich and the competent such prices as enable them to feed abundantly, clothe above mere decency, to labor moderately and raise their families."

These people, he considered, had two sets of rights, those of "personal competency" and those involved in acquiring and possessing property. By "personal competency" he meant the right of free thinking, freedom of forming and expressing opinions, and freedom of personal living, each man according to his own lights. To insure the first set of rights, a government must so order its functions as not to interfere with the individual. But even Jefferson realized that the exercise of the property rights might so interfere with the rights of the individual that the government, without whose assistance the property rights could not exist, must intervene, not to destroy individualism but to protect it.

You are familiar with the great political duel which followed, and how Hamilton, and his friends, building towards a dominant centralized power were at length defeated in the great election of 1800, by Mr. Jefferson's party. Out of that duel came the two parties, Republican and Democratic, as we know them today.

So began, in American political life, the new day, the day of the individual against the system, the day in which individualism was made the great watchword of American life. The happiest of economic conditions made that day long and splendid. On the Western frontier, land was substantially free. No one, who did not shirk the task of earning a living, was entirely without opportunity to do so. Depressions could, and did, come and go; but they could not alter the fundamental fact that most of the people lived partly by selling their labor and partly by extracting their livelihood from the soil, so that starvation and dislocation were practically impossible. At the very worst there was always the possibility of climbing into a covered wagon and moving west where the untilled prairies afforded a haven for men to whom the East did not provide a place. So great were our natural resources that we could offer this relief not only to our own people, but to the distressed of all the world; we could invite immigration from Europe, and welcome it with open arms. Traditionally, when a depression came, a new section of land was opened in the West; and even our temporary misfortune served our manifest destiny.

It was the middle of the 19th century that a new force was released and a new dream created. The force was what is called the industrial revolution, the advance of steam and machinery and the rise of the forerunners of the modern industrial plant. The dream was the dream of an economic machine, able to raise the standard of living for everyone; to bring luxury within the reach of the humblest; to annihilate distance by steam power and later by electricity, and to release everyone from the drudgery of the heaviest manual toil. It was to be expected that this would necessarily affect government. Heretofore, government had merely been called upon to produce conditions within which people could live happily, labor peacefully, and rest secure. Now it was called upon to aid in the consummation of this new dream. There was, however, a shadow over the dream. To be made real, it required use of the talents of men of tremendous will, and tremendous ambition, since by no other force could the problems of financing and engineering and new developments be brought to a consummation.

So manifest were the advantages of the machine age, however, that the United States fearlessly, cheerfully, and, I think, rightly, accepted the bitter with the sweet. It was thought that no price was too high to pay for the advantages which we could draw from a finished industrial system. The history of the last half century is accordingly in large measure a history of a group of financial Titans, whose methods were not scrutinized with too much care, and who were honored in proportion as they produced the results, irrespective of the means they used. The financiers who pushed the railroads to the Pacific were always ruthless, we have them today. It has been estimated that the American investor paid for the American railway system more than three times over in the process; but despite that fact the net advantage was to the United States. As long as we had free land; as long as population was growing by leaps and bounds; as long as our industrial plants were insufficient to supply our needs, society chose to give the ambitious man free play and unlimited reward provided only that he produced the economic plant so much desired.

During this period of expansion, there was equal opportunity for all and the business of government was not to interfere but to assist in the development of industry. This was done at the request of businessmen themselves. The tariff was originally imposed for the purpose of "fostering our infant industry," a phrase I think the older among you will remember as a political issue not so long ago. The railroads were subsidized, sometimes by grants of money, oftener by grants of land; some of the most valuable oil lands in the United States were granted to assist the financing of the railroad which pushed through the Southwest. A nascent merchant marine was assisted by grants of money, or by mail subsidies, so that our steam shipping might ply the seven seas. Some of my friends tell me that they do not want the Government in business. With this I agree; but I wonder whether they realize the implications of the past. For while it has been American doctrine that the government must not go into business in competition with private enterprises, still it has been traditional particularly in Republican administrations for business urgently to ask the government to put at private disposal all kinds of government assistance.

The same man who tells you that he does not want to see the government interfere in business—and he means it, and has plenty of good reasons for saying so—is the first to go to Washington and ask the government for a prohibitory tariff on his product. When things get just bad enough—as they did two years ago—he will go with equal speed to the United States government and ask for a loan; and the Reconstruction Finance Corporation is the outcome of it. Each group has sought protection from the government for its own special interest, without realizing that the function of government must be to favor no small group at the expense of its duty to protect the rights of personal freedom and of private property of all its citizens.

In retrospect we can now see that the turn of the tide came with the turn of the century. We were reaching our last frontier; there was no more free land and our industrial combinations had become great uncontrolled and irresponsible units of power within the state. Clear-sighted men saw with fear the danger that opportunity would no longer be equal; that the growing corporation, like the feudal baron of old, might threaten the economic freedom of individuals to earn a living. In that hour, our antitrust laws were born. The cry was raised against the great corporations. Theodore Roosevelt, the first great Republican progressive, fought a Presidential campaign on the issue of "trust busting" and talked freely about malefactors of great wealth. If the government had a policy it was rather to turn the clock back, to destroy the large combinations and to return to the time when every man owned his individual small business.

This was impossible; Theodore Roosevelt, abandoning the idea of "trust busting," was forced to work out a difference between "good" trusts and "bad" trusts. The Supreme Court set forth the famous "rule of reason" by which it seems to have meant that a concentration of industrial power was permissible if the method by which it got its power, and the use it made of that power, was reasonable.

Woodrow Wilson, elected in 1912, saw the situation more clearly. Where Jefferson had feared the encroachment of political power on the lives of individuals, Wilson knew that the new power was financial. He saw, in the highly centralized economic system, the despot of the twentieth century, on whom great masses of individuals relied for their safety and their livelihood, and whose irresponsibility and greed (if it were not controlled) would reduce them to starvation and penury. The concentration of financial power had not proceeded so far in 1912 as it has today; but it had grown far enough for Mr. Wilson to realize fully its implications. It is interesting, now, to read his speeches. What is called "radical" today (and I have reason to know whereof I speak) is mild compared to the campaign of Mr. Wilson. "No man can deny," he said, "that the lines of endeavor have more and more narrowed and stiffened; no man who knows anything about the development of industry in this country can have failed to observe that the larger kinds of credit are more and more difficult to obtain unless you obtain them upon terms of uniting your efforts with those who already control the industry of the country, and nobody can fail to observe that every man who tries to set himself up in competition with any process of manufacture which has taken place under the control of large combinations of capital will presently find himself either squeezed out or obliged to sell and allow himself to be absorbed."

Had there been no [First] World War—had Mr. Wilson been able to devote eight years to domestic instead of to international affairs—we might have had a wholly different situation at the present time. However, the then distant roar of European cannon, growing ever louder, forced him to abandon the study of this issue. The problem he saw so clearly is left with us as a legacy; and no one of us on either side of the political controversy can deny that it is a matter of grave concern to the government.

A glance at the situation today only too clearly indicates that equality of opportunity as we have know it no longer exists. Our industrial plant is built; the problem just now is whether under existing conditions it is not overbuilt. Our last frontier has long since been reached, and there is practically no more free land. More than half of our people do not live on the farms or on lands and cannot derive a living by cultivating their own property. There is no safety valve in the form of a Western prairie to which those thrown out of work by the Eastern economic machines can go for a new start. We are not able to invite the immigration from Europe to share our endless plenty. We are now providing a drab living for our own people.

Our system of constantly rising tariffs has at last reacted against us to the point of closing our Canadian frontier on the north, our European markets on the east, many of our Latin American markets to the south, and a goodly proportion of our Pacific markets on the west, through the retaliatory tariffs of those countries. It has forced many of our great industrial institutions who exported their surplus production to such countries, to establish plants in such countries within the tariff walls. This has resulted in the reduction of the operation of their American plants, and opportunity for employment.

Just as freedom to farm has ceased, so also the opportunity in business has narrowed. It still is true that men can start small enterprises, trusting to native shrewdness and ability to keep abreast of competitors; but area after area has been preempted altogether by the great corporations, and even in the fields which still have no great concerns, the small man starts with a handicap. The unfeeling statistics of the past three decades show that the independent business man is running a losing race. Perhaps he is forced to the wall; perhaps he cannot command credit; perhaps he is "squeezed out," in Mr. Wilson's words, by highly organized corporate competitors, as your corner grocery man can tell you. Recently a careful study was made of the concentration of business in the United States. It showed that our economic life was dominated by some six hundred odd corporations who controlled two-thirds of American industry.

Ten million small business men divided the other third. More striking still, it appeared that if the process of concentration goes on at the same rate, at the end of another century we shall have all American industry controlled by a dozen corporations, and run by perhaps a hundred men. Put plainly, we are steering a steady course toward economic oligarchy, if we are not there already. Clearly, all this calls for a re-appraisal of values. A mere builder of more industrial plants, a creator of more railroad systems, and organizer of more corporations, is as likely to be a danger as a help. The day of the great promoter or the financial Titan, to whom we granted anything if only he would build, or develop, is over. Our task now is not discovery or exploitation of natural resources, or necessarily producing more goods. It is the soberer, less dramatic business of administering resources and plants already in hand, of seeking to reestablish foreign markets for our surplus production, of meeting the problem of under consumption, of adjusting production to consumption, of distributing wealth and products more equitably, of adapting existing economic organizations to the service of the people. The day of enlightened administration has come.

Just as in older times the central government was first a haven of refuge, and then a threat, so now in a closer economic system the central and ambitious financial unit is no longer a servant of national desire, but a danger. I would draw the parallel one step farther. We did not think because national government had become a threat in the 18th century that therefore we should abandon the principle of national government. Nor today should we abandon the principle of strong economic units called corporations, merely because their power is susceptible of easy abuse. In other times we dealt with the problem of an unduly ambitious central government by modifying it gradually into a constitutional democratic government. So today we are modifying and controlling our economic units.

As I see it, the task of government in its relation to business is to assist the development of an economic declaration of rights, an economic constitutional order. This is the common task of statesman and business man. It is the minimum requirement of a more permanently safe order of things.

Every man has a right to life; and this means that he has also a right to make a comfortable living. He may by sloth or crime decline to exercise that right; but it may not be denied him. We have no actual famine or death; our industrial and agricultural mechanism can produce enough and to spare. Our government formal and informal, political and economic, owes to every one an avenue to possess himself of a portion of that plenty sufficient for his needs, through his own work.

Every man has a right to his own property; which means a right to be assured, to the fullest extent attainable, in the safety of his savings.

By no other means can men carry the burdens of those parts of life which, in the nature of things afford no chance of labor; childhood, sickness, old age. In all thought of property, this right is paramount; all other property rights must yield to it. If, in accord with this principle, we must restrict the operations of the speculator, the manipulator, even the financier, I believe we must accept the restriction as needful, not to hamper individualism but to protect it.

These two requirements must be satisfied, in the main, by the individuals who claim and hold control of the great industrial and financial combinations which dominate so large a part of our industrial life. They have undertaken to be, not business men, but princes—princes of property. I am not prepared to say that the system which produces them is wrong. I am very clear that they must fearlessly and competently assume the responsibility which goes with the power. So many enlightened business men know this that the statement would be little more that a platitude, were it not for an added implication.

This implication is, briefly, that the responsible heads of finance and industry instead of acting each for himself, must work together to achieve the common end. They must, where necessary, sacrifice this or that private advantage; and in reciprocal self-denial must seek a general advantage. It is here that formal government—political government, if you choose, comes in. Whenever in the pursuit of this objective the lone wolf, the unethical competitor, the reckless promoter, the Ishmael[2] or Insull[3] whose hand is against every man's, declines to join in achieving and end recognized as being for the public welfare, and threatens to drag the industry back to a state of anarchy, the government may properly be asked to apply restraint.

Likewise, should the group ever use its collective power contrary to public welfare, the government must be swift to enter and protect the public interest.

The government should assume the function of economic regulation only as a last resort, to be tried only when private initiative, inspired by high responsibility, with such assistance and balance as government can give, has finally failed. As yet there has been no final failure, because there has been no attempt, and I decline to assume that this nation is unable to meet the situation.

The final term of the high contract was for liberty and the pursuit of happiness. We have learnt a great deal of both in the past century. We know that individual liberty and individual happiness mean nothing unless both are ordered in the sense that one man's meat is not another man's poison. We know that the old "rights of personal competency"—the right to read, to think, to speak to choose and live a mode of life, must be respected at all hazards. We know that liberty to do anything which deprives others of those elemental rights is outside the protection of any compact; and that government in this regard is the maintenance of a balance, within which every individual may have a place if he will take it; in which every individual may find safety if he wishes it; in which every individual may attain such power as his ability permits, consistent with his assuming the accompanying responsibility …

Faith in America, faith in our tradition of personal responsibility, faith in our institutions, faith in ourselves demands that we recognize the new terms of the old social contract. We shall fulfill them, as we fulfilled the obligation of the apparent Utopia which Jefferson imagined for us in 1776, and which Jefferson, Roosevelt and Wilson sought to bring to realization. We must do so, lest a rising tide of misery engendered by our common failure, engulf us all. But failure is not an American habit; and in the strength of great hope we must all shoulder our common load.

NOTES

1   Alexander Hamilton (1755–1804), the first Secretary of the Treasury, favored a strong central government, tariffs to protect American manufacturers from foreign competitors, and a National Bank to facilitate commerce.—Eds.

2   According to the Old Testament or Hebrew Bible, Ishmael, the first-born son of Abraham by his handmaid Hagar, was banished from his father's household and made to wander in the desert.—Eds.

3   Samuel Insull (1859–1938) was an American financier and public utilities and railroad magnate renowned for overcharging his customers. His huge and highly leveraged holding company collapsed during the Great Depression, leaving more than half a million investors with nothing to show for their investment. To avoid prosecution, Insull fled to France, where he later died.—Eds.

"To Fulfill These Rights":
Speech at Howard University

LYNDON B. JOHNSON*

Lyndon Baines Johnson, or "LBJ" (1908–1973), was the thirty-sixth President of the United States (1963–1969), assuming the office after the assassination of President John F. Kennedy. Domestically, Johnson pushed through a series of ambitious programs collectively called the "Great Society," which were aimed at addressing poverty and racial injustice. These included passage of the Civil Rights and Voting Rights acts, the "War on Poverty" (which inaugurated the Food Stamp and "Head Start" programs among numerous others), and the creation of Medicare for the elderly and Medicaid for the needy. In this speech, given at Howard University, LBJ provided the rationale for another ambitious program, now known as "affirmative action." In the speech, Johnson hearkens back to Adam Smith's "classical liberal" metaphor of life as a race, but describes African Americans as hobbled by chains, both historical and contemporary, that prevented them from competing on an equal footing in that race without government action to address these impediments. Johnson's speech is a clear example of the ideal of "positive freedom"—not just "freedom from" chains but "freedom to" achieve—the ideal at the heart of the "welfare liberal" vision.

* *Source*: *Public Papers of Presidents of the United States: Lyndon B. Johnson, 1965*, vol. 2 (Washington, D.C.: Government Printing Office, 1966), entry 301, pp. 635–640.

TO FULFILL THESE RIGHTS

… In far too many ways American Negroes have been another nation: deprived of freedom, crippled by hatred, the doors of opportunity closed to hope.

In our time change has come to this Nation, too. The American Negro, acting with impressive restraint, has peacefully protested and marched, entered the courtrooms and the seats of government, demanding a justice that has long been denied. The voice of the Negro was the call to action. But it is a tribute to America that, once aroused, the courts and the Congress, the President and most of the people, have been the allies of progress.

Thus we have seen the high court of the country declare that discrimination based on race was repugnant to the Constitution, and therefore void. We have seen in 1957, and 1960, and again in 1964, the first civil rights legislation in this Nation in almost an entire century.

As majority leader of the United States Senate, I helped to guide two of these bills through the Senate. And, as your President, I was proud to sign the third. And now very soon we will have the fourth—a new law guaranteeing every American the right to vote.

No act of my entire administration will give me greater satisfaction than the day when my signature makes this bill, too, the law of this land.

The voting rights bill will be the latest, and among the most important, in a long series of victories. But this victory—as Winston Churchill said of another triumph for freedom—"is not the end. It is not even the beginning of the end. But it is, perhaps, the end of the beginning."

That beginning is freedom; and the barriers to that freedom are tumbling down. Freedom is the right to share, share fully and equally, in American society—to vote, to hold a job, to enter a public place, to go to school. It is the right to be treated in every part of our national life as a person equal in dignity and promise to all others.

But freedom is not enough. You do not wipe away the scars of centuries by saying: Now you are free to go where you want, and do as you desire, and choose the leaders you please.

You do not take a person who, for years, has been hobbled by chains and liberate him, bring him up to the starting line of a race and then say, "you are free to compete with all the others," and still justly believe that you have been completely fair.

Thus it is not enough just to open the gates of opportunity. All our citizens must have the ability to walk through those gates.

This is the next and the more profound stage of the battle for civil rights. We seek not just freedom but opportunity. We seek not just legal equity but human ability, not just equality as a right and a theory but equality as a fact and equality as a result.

For the task is to give 20 million Negroes the same chance as every other American to learn and grow, to work and share in society, to develop their abilities—physical, mental and spiritual, and to pursue their individual happiness.

To this end equal opportunity is essential, but not enough, not enough. Men and women of all races are born with the same range of abilities. But ability is not just the product of birth. Ability is stretched or stunted by the family that you live with, and the neighborhood you live in—by the school you go to and the poverty or the richness of your surroundings. It is the product of a hundred unseen forces playing upon the little infant, the child, and finally the man.

This graduating class at Howard University is witness to the indomitable determination of the Negro American to win his way in American life.

The number of Negroes in schools of higher learning has almost doubled in 15 years. The number of nonwhite professional workers has more than doubled in 10 years. The median income of Negro college women tonight exceeds that of white college women. And there are also the enormous accomplishments of distinguished individual Negroes—many of them graduates of this institution, and one of them the first lady ambassador in the history of the United States.

These are proud and impressive achievements. But they tell only the story of a growing middle class minority, steadily narrowing the gap between them and their white counterparts.

But for the great majority of Negro Americans—the poor, the unemployed, the uprooted, and the dispossessed—there is a much grimmer story. They still, as we meet here tonight, are another nation. Despite the court orders and the laws, despite the legislative victories and the speeches, for them the walls are rising and the gulf is widening.

Here are some of the facts of this American failure.

Thirty-five years ago the rate of unemployment for Negroes and whites was about the same. Tonight the Negro rate is twice as high.

In 1948 the 8 percent unemployment rate for Negro teenage boys was actually less than that of whites. By last year that rate had grown to 23 percent, as against 13 percent for whites unemployed.

Between 1949 and 1959, the income of Negro men relative to white men declined in every section of this country. From 1952 to 1963 the median income of Negro families compared to white actually dropped from 57 percent to 53 percent.

In the years 1955 through 1957, 22 percent of experienced Negro workers were out of work at some time during the year. In 1961 through 1963 that proportion had soared to 29 percent.

Since 1947 the number of white families living in poverty has decreased 27 percent while the number of poorer nonwhite families decreased only 3 percent.

The infant mortality of nonwhites in 1940 was 70 percent greater than whites. Twenty-two years later it was 90 percent greater.

Moreover, the isolation of Negro from white communities is increasing, rather than decreasing as Negroes crowd into the central cities and become a city within a city.

Of course Negro Americans as well as white Americans have shared in our rising national abundance. But the harsh fact of the matter is that in the battle for true equality too many—far too many—are losing ground every day.

We are not completely sure why this is. We know the causes are complex and subtle. But we do know the two broad basic reasons. And we do know that we have to act.

First, Negroes are trapped—as many whites are trapped—in inherited, gateless poverty. They lack training and skills. They are shut in, in slums, without decent medical care. Private and public poverty combine to cripple their capacities.

We are trying to attack these evils through our poverty program, through our education program, through our medical care and our other health programs, and a dozen more of the Great Society programs that are aimed at the root causes of this poverty.

We will increase, and we will accelerate, and we will broaden this attack in years to come until this most enduring of foes finally yields to our unyielding will.

But there is a second cause—much more difficult to explain, more deeply grounded, more desperate in its force. It is the devastating heritage of long years of slavery; and a century of oppression, hatred, and injustice.

For Negro poverty is not white poverty. Many of its causes and many of its cures are the same. But there are differences—deep, corrosive, obstinate differences—radiating painful roots into the community, and into the family, and the nature of the individual.

These differences are not racial differences. They are solely and simply the consequence of ancient brutality, past injustice, and present prejudice. They are anguishing to observe. For the Negro they are a constant reminder of oppression. For the white they are a constant reminder of guilt. But they must be faced and they must be dealt with and they must be overcome, if we are ever to reach the time when the only difference between Negroes and whites is the color of their skin.

Nor can we find a complete answer in the experience of other American minorities. They made a valiant and a largely successful effort to emerge from poverty and prejudice.

The Negro, like these others, will have to rely mostly upon his own efforts. But he just can not do it alone. For they did not have the heritage of centuries to overcome, and they did not have a cultural tradition which had been twisted and battered by endless years of hatred and hopelessness, nor were they excluded—these others—because of race or color—a feeling whose dark intensity is matched by no other prejudice in our society.

Nor can these differences be understood as isolated infirmities. They are a seamless web. They cause each other. They result from each other. They reinforce each other.

Much of the Negro community is buried under a blanket of history and circumstance. It is not a lasting solution to lift just one corner of that blanket. We must stand on all sides and we must raise the entire cover if we are to liberate our fellow citizens.

One of the differences is the increased concentration of Negroes in our cities. More than 73 percent of all Negroes live in urban areas compared with less than 70 percent of the whites. Most of these Negroes live in slums. Most of these Negroes live together—a separated people.

Men are shaped by their world. When it is a world of decay, ringed by an invisible wall, when escape is arduous and uncertain, and the saving pressures of a more hopeful society are unknown, it can cripple the youth and it can desolate the men.

There is also the burden that a dark skin can add to the search for a productive place in our society. Unemployment strikes most swiftly and broadly at the Negro, and this burden erodes hope. Blighted hope breeds despair. Despair brings indifferences to the learning which offers a way out. And despair, coupled with indifferences, is often the source of destructive rebellion against the fabric of society.

There is also the lacerating hurt of early collision with white hatred or prejudice, distaste or condescension. Other groups have felt similar intolerance. But success and achievement could wipe it away. They do not change the color of a man's skin. I have seen this uncomprehending pain in the eyes of the little, young Mexican-American schoolchildren that I taught many years ago. But it can be overcome. But, for many, the wounds are always open.

Perhaps most important—its influence radiating to every part of life—is the breakdown of the Negro family structure. For this, most of all, white America must accept responsibility. It flows from centuries of oppression and persecution of the Negro man. It flows from the long years of degradation and discrimination, which have attacked his dignity and assaulted his ability to produce for his family.

This, too, is not pleasant to look upon. But it must be faced by those whose serious intent is to improve the life of all Americans.

Only a minority—less than half—of all Negro children reach the age of 18 having lived all their lives with both of their parents. At this moment, tonight, little less than two-thirds are at home with both of their parents. Probably a majority of all Negro children receive federally-aided public assistance sometime during their childhood.

The family is the cornerstone of our society. More than any other force it shapes the attitude, the hopes, the ambitions, and the values of the child. And when the family collapses it is the children that are usually damaged. When it happens on a massive scale the community itself is crippled.

So, unless we work to strengthen the family, to create conditions under which most parents will stay together—all the rest: schools, and playgrounds, and public assistance, and private concern, will never be enough to cut completely the circle of despair and deprivation.

There is no single easy answer to all of these problems.

Jobs are part of the answer. They bring the income which permits a man to provide for his family.

Decent homes in decent surroundings and a chance to learn—an equal chance to learn—are part of the answer.

Welfare and social programs better designed to hold families together are part of the answer. Care for the sick is part of the answer.

An understanding heart by all Americans is another big part of the answer.

And to all of these fronts—and a dozen more—I will dedicate the expanding efforts of the Johnson administration.

But there are other answers that are still to be found. Nor do we fully understand even all of the problems. Therefore, I want to announce tonight that this fall I intend to call a White House conference of scholars, and experts, and outstanding Negro leaders—men of both races—and officials of Government at every level.

This White House conference's theme and title will be "To Fulfill These Rights."

Its object will be to help the American Negro fulfill the rights which, after the long time of injustice, he is finally about to secure.

To move beyond opportunity to achievement.

To shatter forever not only the barriers of law and public practice, but the walls which bound the condition of many by the color of his skin.

To dissolve, as best we can, the antique enmities of the heart which diminish the holder, divide the great democracy, and do wrong—great wrong—to the children of God.

And I pledge you tonight that this will be a chief goal of my administration, and of my program next year, and in the years to come. And I hope, and I pray, and I believe, it will be a part of the program of all America.

For what is justice?

It is to fulfill the fair expectations of man.

Thus, American justice is a very special thing. For, from the first, this has been a land of towering expectations. It was to be a nation where each man could be ruled by the common consent of all—enshrined in law, given life by institutions, guided by men themselves subject to its rule. And all—all of every station and origin—would be touched equally in obligation and in liberty.

Beyond the law lay the land. It was a rich land, glowing with more abundant promise than man had ever seen. Here, unlike any place yet known, all were to share the harvest.

And beyond this was the dignity of man. Each could become whatever his qualities of mind and spirit would permit—to strive, to seek, and, if he could, to find his happiness.

This is American justice. We have pursued it faithfully to the edge of our imperfections, and we have failed to find it for the American Negro.

So, it is the glorious opportunity of this generation to end the one huge wrong of the American Nation and, in so doing, to find America for ourselves, with the same immense thrill of discovery which gripped those who first began to realize that here, at last, was a home for freedom.

All it will take is for all of us to understand what this country is and what this country must become.

The Scripture promises: "I shall light a candle of understanding in thine heart, which shall not be put out."

Together, and with millions more, we can light that candle of understanding in the heart of all America.

And, once lit, it will never again go out.

Speech at Osawatomie, Kansas

BARACK OBAMA*

Barack Obama (1961–) was the forty-fourth president of the United States. In this selection President Obama makes a modern liberal case for government intervention in and partial regulation—and sometimes stimulation—of the economy. This is both necessary and desirable, he contends, because the Great Recession that began during the presidency of his predecessor, George W. Bush, showed all too vividly and tragically what can happen when the federal government forfeits its responsibility to oversee the economy and protect people's jobs, their investments, and their homes and families. President Obama also addresses the issue of increasing inequality of wealth and opportunity in the United States—the greatest gap since the eve of the Great Depression—and says that here, too, the government has an important role to play by way of taxation and other policies.

---

* *Source*: Remarks by the President on the Economy in Osawatomie, Kansas, December 6, 2011, via www.whitehouse.gov.

... As many of you know, I have roots here [in Kansas]. (Applause.) I'm sure you're all familiar with the Obamas of Osawatomie. (Laughter.) Actually, I like to say that I got my name from my father, but I got my accent—and my values—from my mother. (Applause.) She was born in Wichita. (Applause.) Her mother grew up in Augusta. Her father was from El Dorado. So my Kansas roots run deep.

My grandparents served during World War II. He was a soldier in Patton's Army; she was a worker on a bomber assembly line. And together, they shared the optimism of a nation that triumphed over the Great Depression and over fascism. They believed in an America where hard work paid off, and responsibility was rewarded, and anyone could make it if they tried—no matter who you were, no matter where you came from, no matter how you started out. (Applause.)

And these values gave rise to the largest middle class and the strongest economy that the world has ever known. It was here in America that the most productive workers, the most innovative companies turned out the best products on Earth.

And you know what? Every American shared in that pride and in that success— from those in the executive suites to those in middle management to those on the factory floor. (Applause.) So you could have some confidence that if you gave it your all, you'd take enough home to raise your family and send your kids to school and have your health care covered, put a little away for retirement. Today, we're still home to the world's most productive workers. We're still home to the world's most innovative companies. But for most Americans, the basic bargain that made this country great has eroded. Long before the recession hit, hard work stopped paying off for too many people. Fewer and fewer of the folks who contributed to the success of our economy actually benefited from that success. Those at the very top grew wealthier from their incomes and their investments—wealthier than ever before. But everybody else struggled with costs that were growing and paychecks that weren't—and too many families found themselves racking up more and more debt just to keep up. Now, for many years, credit cards and home equity loans papered over this harsh reality. But in 2008, the house of cards collapsed. We all know the story by now: Mortgages sold to people who couldn't afford them, or even sometimes understand them. Banks and investors allowed to keep packaging the risk and selling it off. Huge bets—and huge bonuses—made with other people's money on the line. Regulators who were supposed to warn us about the dangers of all this, but looked the other way or didn't have the authority to look at all.

It was wrong. It combined the breathtaking greed of a few with irresponsibility all across the system. And it plunged our economy and the world into a crisis from which we're still fighting to recover. It claimed the jobs and the homes and the basic security of millions of people—innocent, hardworking Americans who had met their responsibilities but were still left holding the bag.

And ever since, there's been a raging debate over the best way to restore growth and prosperity, restore balance, restore fairness. Throughout the country, it's sparked protests and political movements—from the tea party to the people who've been occupying the streets of New York and other cities. It's left Washington in a near-constant state of gridlock. It's been the topic of heated and sometimes colorful discussion among the men and women running for president. (Laughter.)

But, Osawatomie, this is not just another political debate. This is the defining issue of our time. This is a make-or-break moment for the middle class, and for all those who are fighting to get into the middle class. Because what's at stake is whether this will be a country where working people can earn enough to raise a family, build a modest savings, own a home, secure their retirement.

Now, in the midst of this debate, there are some who seem to be suffering from a kind of collective amnesia. After all that's happened, after the worst economic crisis, the worst financial crisis since the Great Depression, they want to return to the same practices that got us into this mess. In fact, they want to go back to the same policies that stacked the deck against middle-class Americans for way too many years. And their philosophy is simple: We are better off when everybody is left to fend for themselves and play by their own rules. I am here to say they are wrong. (Applause.) I'm here in Kansas to reaffirm my deep conviction that we're greater together than we are on our own. I believe that this country succeeds when everyone gets a fair shot, when everyone does their fair share, when everyone plays by the same rules. (Applause.) These aren't Democratic values or Republican values. These aren't 1 percent values or 99 percent values. They're American values. And we have to reclaim them. (Applause.)

You see, this isn't the first time America has faced this choice. At the turn of the last century, when a nation of farmers was transitioning to become the world's industrial giant, we had to decide: Would we settle for a country where most of the new railroads and factories were being controlled by a few giant monopolies that kept prices high and wages low? Would we allow our citizens and even our children to work ungodly hours in conditions that were unsafe and unsanitary? Would we restrict education to the privileged few? Because there were people who thought massive inequality and exploitation of people was just the price you pay for progress.

Theodore Roosevelt disagreed. He was the Republican son of a wealthy family. He praised what the titans of industry had done to create jobs and grow the economy. He believed then what we know is true today, that the free market is the greatest force for economic progress in human history. It's led to a prosperity and a standard of living unmatched by the rest of the world. But Roosevelt also knew that the free market has never been a free license to take whatever you can from whomever you can. (Applause.) He understood the free market only works when there are rules of the road that ensure competition is fair and open and honest. And so he busted up monopolies, forcing those companies to compete for consumers with better services and better prices. And today, they still must. He fought to make sure businesses couldn't profit by exploiting children or selling food or medicine that wasn't safe. And today, they still can't.

And in 1910, Teddy Roosevelt came here to Osawatomie and he laid out his vision for what he called a New Nationalism. "Our country," he said, "means nothing unless it means the triumph of a real democracy, of an economic system under which each man shall be guaranteed the opportunity to show the best that there is in him." (Applause.)

Now, for this, Roosevelt was called a radical. He was called a socialist— (laughter)—even a communist. But today, we are a richer nation and a stronger democracy because of what he fought for in his last campaign: an eight-hour work day and a minimum wage for women— (Applause.)—insurance for the unemployed and for the elderly, and those with disabilities; political reform and a progressive income tax. (Applause.)

Today, over 100 years later, our economy has gone through another transformation. Over the last few decades, huge advances in technology have allowed businesses to do more with less, and it's made it easier for them to set up shop and hire workers anywhere they want in the world. And many of you know firsthand the painful disruptions this has caused for a lot of Americans. Factories where people thought they would retire suddenly picked up and went overseas, where workers were cheaper. Steel mills that needed 100—or 1,000 employees are now able to do the same work with 100 employees, so layoffs too often became permanent, not just a temporary part of the business cycle. And these changes didn't just affect blue-collar workers. If you were a bank teller or a phone operator or a travel agent, you saw many in your profession replaced by ATMs and the Internet.

Today, even higher-skilled jobs, like accountants and middle management can be out-sourced to countries like China or India. And if you're somebody whose job can be done cheaper by a computer or someone in another country, you don't have a lot of leverage with your employer when it comes to asking for better wages or better benefits, especially since fewer Americans today are part of a union. Now, just as there was in Teddy Roosevelt's time, there is a certain crowd in Washington who, for the last few decades, have said, let's respond to this economic challenge with the same old tune. "The market will take care of everything," they tell us. If we just cut more regulations and cut more taxes—especially for the wealthy—our economy will grow stronger. Sure, they say, there will be winners and losers. But if the winners do really well, then jobs and prosperity will eventually trickle down to everybody else. And, they argue, even if prosperity doesn't trickle down, well, that's the price of liberty. Now, it's a simple theory. And we have to admit, it's one that speaks to our rugged individualism and our healthy skepticism of too much government. That's in America's DNA. And that theory fits well on a bumper sticker. (Laughter.) But here's the problem: It doesn't work. It has never worked. (Applause.) It didn't work when it was tried in the decade before the Great Depression. It's not what led to the incredible postwar booms of the '50s and '60s. And it didn't work when we tried it during the last decade. (Applause.) I mean, understand, it's not as if we haven't tried this theory.

Remember in those years, in 2001 and 2003, Congress passed two of the most expensive tax cuts for the wealthy in history. And what did it get us? The slowest job growth in half a century. Massive deficits that have made it much harder to pay for the investments that built this country and provided the basic security that helped millions of Americans reach and stay in the middle class—things like education and infrastructure, science and technology, Medicare and Social Security.

Remember that in those same years, thanks to some of the same folks who are now running Congress, we had weak regulation, we had little oversight, and what did it get us? Insurance companies that jacked up people's premiums with impunity and denied care to patients who were sick, mortgage lenders that tricked families into buying homes they couldn't afford, a financial sector where irresponsibility and lack of basic oversight nearly destroyed our entire economy.

We simply cannot return to this brand of "you're on your own" economics if we're serious about rebuilding the middle class in this country. (Applause.) We know that it doesn't result in a strong economy. It results in an economy that invests too little in its people and in its future. We know it doesn't result in a prosperity that trickles down. It results in a prosperity that's enjoyed by fewer and fewer of our citizens.

Look at the statistics. In the last few decades, the average income of the top 1 percent has gone up by more than 250 percent to $1.2 million per year. I'm not talking about millionaires, people who have a million dollars. I'm saying people who make a million dollars every single year. For the top one hundredth of 1 percent, the average income is now $27 million per year. The typical CEO who used to earn about 30 times more than his or her worker now earns 110 times more. And yet, over the last decade the incomes of most Americans have actually fallen by about 6 percent.

Now, this kind of inequality—a level that we haven't seen since the Great Depression—hurts us all. When middle-class families can no longer afford to buy the goods and services that businesses are selling, when people are slipping out of the middle class, it drags down the entire economy from top to bottom.

America was built on the idea of broad-based prosperity, of strong consumers all across the country. That's why a CEO like Henry Ford made it his mission to pay his workers enough so that they could buy the cars he made. It's also why a recent study showed that countries with less inequality tend to have stronger and steadier economic growth over the long run.

Inequality also distorts our democracy. It gives an outsized voice to the few who can afford high-priced lobbyists and unlimited campaign contributions, and it runs the risk of selling out our democracy to the highest bidder. (Applause.) It leaves everyone else rightly suspicious that the system in Washington is rigged against them, that our elected representatives aren't looking out for the interests of most Americans.

But there's an even more fundamental issue at stake. This kind of gaping inequality gives lie to the promise that's at the very heart of America: that this is a place where you can make it if you try. We tell people—we tell our kids—that in this country, even if you're born with nothing, work hard and you can get into the middle class. We tell them that your children will have a chance to do even better than you do. That's why immigrants from around the world historically have flocked to our shores.

And yet, over the last few decades, the rungs on the ladder of opportunity have grown farther and farther apart, and the middle class has shrunk. You know, a few years after World War II, a child who was born into poverty had a slightly better than 50-50 chance of becoming middle class as an adult. By 1980, that chance had fallen to around 40 percent. And if the trend of rising inequality over the last few decades continues, it's estimated that a child born today will only have a one-in-three chance of making it to the middle class—33 percent.

It's heartbreaking enough that there are millions of working families in this country who are now forced to take their children to food banks for a decent meal. But the idea that those children might not have a chance to climb out of that situation and back into the middle class, no matter how hard they work? That's inexcusable. It is wrong. (Applause.) It flies in the face of everything that we stand for. (Applause.)

Now, fortunately, that's not a future that we have to accept, because there's another view about how we build a strong middle class in this country—a view that's truer to our history, a vision that's been embraced in the past by people of both parties for more than 200 years.

It's not a view that we should somehow turn back technology or put up walls around America. It's not a view that says we should punish profit or success or pretend that government knows how to fix all of society's problems. It is a view that says in America we are greater together—when everyone engages in fair play and everybody gets a fair shot and everybody does their fair share. (Applause.)

So what does that mean for restoring middle-class security in today's economy? Well, it starts by making sure that everyone in America gets a fair shot at success. The truth is we'll never be able to compete with other countries when it comes to who's best at letting their businesses pay the lowest wages, who's best at busting unions, who's best at letting companies pollute as much as they want. That's a race to the bottom that we can't win, and we shouldn't want to win that race. (Applause.) Those countries don't have a strong middle class. They don't have our standard of living.

The race we want to win, the race we can win is a race to the top—the race for good jobs that pay well and offer middle-class security. Businesses will create those jobs in countries with the highest-skilled, highest-educated workers, the most advanced transportation and communication, the strongest commitment to research and technology.

The world is shifting to an innovation economy and nobody does innovation better than America. Nobody does it better. (Applause.) No one has better colleges. Nobody has better universities. Nobody has a greater diversity of talent and ingenuity. No one's workers or entrepreneurs are more driven or more daring. The things that have always been our strengths match up perfectly with the demands of the moment.

But we need to meet the moment. We've got to up our game. We need to remember that we can only do that together. It starts by making education a national mission—a national mission. (Applause.) Government and businesses, parents and citizens. In this economy, a higher education is the surest route to the middle class. The unemployment rate for Americans with a college degree or more is about half the national average. And their incomes are twice as high as those who don't have a high school diploma. Which means we shouldn't be laying off good teachers right now—we should be hiring them. (Applause.) We shouldn't be expecting less of our schools—we should be demanding more. (Applause.) We shouldn't be making it harder to afford college—we should be a country where everyone has a chance to go and doesn't rack up $100,000 of debt just because they went. (Applause.)

In today's innovation economy, we also need a world-class commitment to science and research, the next generation of high-tech manufacturing. Our factories and our workers shouldn't be idle. We should be giving people the chance to get new skills and training at community colleges so they can learn how to make wind turbines and semiconductors and high-powered batteries. And by the way, if we don't have an economy that's built on bubbles and financial speculation, our best and brightest won't all gravitate towards careers in banking and finance.

(Applause.) Because if we want an economy that's built to last, we need more of those young people in science and engineering. (Applause.) This country should not be known for bad debt and phony profits. We should be known for creating and selling products all around the world that are stamped with three proud words: Made in America. (Applause.)

Today, manufacturers and other companies are setting up shop in the places with the best infrastructure to ship their products, move their workers, communicate with the rest of the world. And that's why the over 1 million construction workers who lost their jobs when the housing market collapsed, they shouldn't be sitting at home with nothing to do. They should be rebuilding our roads and our bridges, laying down faster railroads and broadband, modernizing our schools—(applause)—all the things other countries are already doing to attract good jobs and businesses to their shores.

Yes, business, and not government, will always be the primary generator of good jobs with incomes that lift people into the middle class and keep them there. But as a nation, we've always come together, through our government, to help create the conditions where both workers and businesses can succeed. (Applause.) And historically, that hasn't been a partisan idea. Franklin Roosevelt worked with Democrats and Republicans to give veterans of World War II—including my grandfather, Stanley Dunham—the chance to go to college on the G.I. Bill. It was a Republican President, Dwight Eisenhower, a proud son of Kansas—(applause)— who started the Interstate Highway System, and doubled down on science and research to stay ahead of the Soviets.

Of course, those productive investments cost money. They're not free. And so we've also paid for these investments by asking everybody to do their fair share. Look, if we had unlimited resources, no one would ever have to pay any taxes and we would never have to cut any spending. But we don't have unlimited resources. And so we have to set priorities. If we want a strong middle class, then our tax code must reflect our values. We have to make choices. Today that choice is very clear. To reduce our deficit, I've already signed nearly $1 trillion of spending cuts into law and I've proposed trillions more, including reforms that would lower the cost of Medicare and Medicaid. (Applause.)

But in order to structurally close the deficit, get our fiscal house in order, we have to decide what our priorities are. Now, most immediately, short term, we need to extend a payroll tax cut that's set to expire at the end of this month. (Applause.) If we don't do that, 160 million Americans, including most of the people here, will see their taxes go up by an average of $1,000 starting in January and it would badly weaken our recovery. That's the short term. In the long term, we have to rethink our tax system more fundamentally. We have to ask ourselves: Do we want to make the investments we need in things like education and research and high-tech manufacturing—all those things that helped make us an economic superpower? Or do we want to keep in place the tax breaks for the wealthiest Americans in our country? Because we can't afford to do both. That is not politics. That's just math. (Laughter and applause.) Now, so far, most of my Republican friends in Washington have refused under any circumstance to ask the wealthiest Americans to go to the same tax rate they were paying when Bill Clinton was president. So let's just do a trip down memory lane here.

Keep in mind, when President Clinton first proposed these tax increases, folks in Congress predicted they would kill jobs and lead to another recession. Instead, our economy created nearly 23 million jobs and we eliminated the deficit. (Applause.) Today, the wealthiest Americans are paying the lowest taxes in over half a century. This isn't like in the early '50s, when the top tax rate was over 90 percent. This isn't even like the early '80s, when the top tax rate was about 70 percent. Under President Clinton, the top rate was only about 39 percent. Today, thanks to loopholes and shelters, a quarter of all millionaires now pay lower tax rates than millions of you, millions of middle-class families. Some billionaires have a tax rate as low as 1 percent. One percent.

That is the height of unfairness. It is wrong. (Applause.) It's wrong that in the United States of America, a teacher or a nurse or a construction worker, maybe earns $50,000 a year, should pay a higher tax rate than somebody raking in $50 million. (Applause.) It's wrong for Warren Buffett's secretary to pay a higher tax rate than Warren Buffett. (Applause.) And by the way, Warren Buffett agrees with me. (Laughter.) So do most Americans—Democrats, independents and Republicans. And I know that many of our wealthiest citizens would agree to contribute a little more if it meant reducing the deficit and strengthening the economy that made their success possible.

This isn't about class warfare. This is about the nation's welfare. It's about making choices that benefit not just the people who've done fantastically well over the last few decades, but that benefits the middle class, and those fighting to get into the middle class, and the economy as a whole.

Finally, a strong middle class can only exist in an economy where everyone plays by the same rules, from Wall Street to Main Street. (Applause.) As infuriating as it was for all of us, we rescued our major banks from collapse, not only because a full-blown financial meltdown would have sent us into a second Depression, but because we need a strong, healthy financial sector in this country.

But part of the deal was that we wouldn't go back to business as usual. And that's why last year we put in place new rules of the road that refocus the financial sector on what should be their core purpose: getting capital to the entrepreneurs with the best ideas, and financing millions of families who want to buy a home or send their kids to college.

Now, we're not all the way there yet, and the banks are fighting us every inch of the way. But already, some of these reforms are being implemented. If you're a big bank or risky financial institution, you now have to write out a "living will" that details exactly how you'll pay the bills if you fail, so that taxpayers are never again on the hook for Wall Street's mistakes. (Applause.)

There are also limits on the size of banks and new abilities for regulators to dismantle a firm that is going under. The new law bans banks from making risky bets with their customers' deposits, and it takes away big bonuses and paydays from failed CEOs, while giving shareholders a say on executive salaries.

This is the law that we passed. We are in the process of implementing it now. All of this is being put in place as we speak. Now, unless you're a financial institution whose business model is built on breaking the law, cheating consumers and making risky bets that could damage the entire economy, you should have nothing to fear from these new rules.

Some of you may know, my grandmother worked as a banker for most of her life—worked her way up, started as a secretary, ended up being a vice president of a bank. And I know from her, and I know from all the people that I've come in contact with, that the vast majority of bankers and financial service professionals, they want to do right by their customers. They want to have rules in place that don't put them at a disadvantage for doing the right thing. And yet, Republicans in Congress are fighting as hard as they can to make sure that these rules aren't enforced.

I'll give you a specific example. For the first time in history, the reforms that we passed put in place a consumer watchdog who is charged with protecting everyday Americans from being taken advantage of by mortgage lenders or payday lenders or debt collectors. And the man we nominated for the post, Richard Cordray, is a former attorney general of Ohio who has the support of most attorney generals, both Democrat and Republican, throughout the country. Nobody claims he's not qualified.

But the Republicans in the Senate refuse to confirm him for the job; they refuse to let him do his job. Why? Does anybody here think that the problem that led to our financial crisis was too much oversight of mortgage lenders or debt collectors?

AUDIENCE: No!

THE PRESIDENT: Of course not. Every day we go without a consumer watchdog is another day when a student, or a senior citizen, or a member of our Armed Forces—because they are very vulnerable to some of this stuff—could be tricked into a loan that they can't afford—something that happens all the time. And the fact is that financial institutions have plenty of lobbyists looking out for their interests. Consumers deserve to have someone whose job it is to look out for them. (Applause.) And I intend to make sure they do. (Applause.) And I want you to hear me, Kansas: I will veto any effort to delay or defund or dismantle the new rules that we put in place. (Applause.)

We shouldn't be weakening oversight and accountability. We should be strengthening oversight and accountability. I'll give you another example. Too often, we've seen Wall Street firms violating major anti-fraud laws because the penalties are too weak and there's no price for being a repeat offender. No more. I'll be calling for legislation that makes those penalties count so that firms don't see punishment for breaking the law as just the price of doing business. (Applause.)

The fact is this crisis has left a huge deficit of trust between Main Street and Wall Street. And major banks that were rescued by the taxpayers have an obligation to go the extra mile in helping to close that deficit of trust. At minimum, they should be remedying past mortgage abuses that led to the financial crisis. They should be working to keep responsible homeowners in their home. We're going to keep pushing them to provide more time for unemployed homeowners to look for work without having to worry about immediately losing their house.

The big banks should increase access to refinancing opportunities to borrowers who haven't yet benefited from historically low interest rates. And the big banks should recognize that precisely because these steps are in the interest of middle-class families and the broader economy, it will also be in the banks' own long-term financial interest. What will be good for consumers over the long term will be good for the banks. (Applause.)

Investing in things like education that give everybody a chance to succeed. A tax code that makes sure everybody pays their fair share. And laws that make sure everybody follows the rules. That's what will transform our economy. That's what will grow our middle class again. In the end, rebuilding this economy based on fair play, a fair shot, and a fair share will require all of us to see that we have a stake in each other's success. And it will require all of us to take some responsibility.

It will require parents to get more involved in their children's education. It will require students to study harder. (Applause.) It will require some workers to start studying all over again. It will require greater responsibility from homeowners not to take out mortgages they can't afford. They need to remember that if something seems too good to be true, it probably is.

It will require those of us in public service to make government more efficient and more effective, more consumer-friendly, more responsive to people's needs. That's why we're cutting programs that we don't need to pay for those we do. (Applause.) That's why we've made hundreds of regulatory reforms that will save businesses billions of dollars. That's why we're not just throwing money at education, we're challenging schools to come up with the most innovative reforms and the best results.

And it will require American business leaders to understand that their obligations don't just end with their shareholders. Andy Grove, the legendary former CEO of Intel, put it best. He said, "There is another obligation I feel personally, given that everything I've achieved in my career, and a lot of what Intel has achieved were made possible by a climate of democracy, an economic climate and investment climate provided by the United States."

This broader obligation can take many forms. At a time when the cost of hiring workers in China is rising rapidly, it should mean more CEOs deciding that it's time to bring jobs back to the United States—(applause)—not just because it's good for business, but because it's good for the country that made their business and their personal success possible. (Applause.)

I think about the Big Three auto companies who, during recent negotiations, agreed to create more jobs and cars here in America, and then decided to give bonuses not just to their executives, but to all their employees, so that everyone was invested in the company's success. (Applause.)

I think about a company based in Warroad, Minnesota. It's called Marvin Windows and Doors. During the recession, Marvin's competitors closed dozens of plants, let hundreds of workers go. But Marvin's did not lay off a single one of their 4,000 or so employees—not one. In fact, they've only laid off workers once in over a hundred years. Mr. Marvin's grandfather even kept his eight employees during the Great Depression.

Now, at Marvin's when times get tough, the workers agree to give up some perks and some pay, and so do the owners. As one owner said, "You can't grow if you're cutting your lifeblood—and that's the skills and experience your workforce delivers." (Applause.) For the CEO of Marvin's, it's about the community. He said, "These are people we went to school with. We go to church with them. We see them in the same restaurants. Indeed, a lot of us have married local girls and boys. We could be anywhere, but we are in Warroad."

That's how America was built. That's why we're the greatest nation on Earth. That's what our greatest companies understand. Our success has never just been about survival of the fittest. It's about building a nation where we're all better off. We pull together. We pitch in. We do our part. We believe that hard work will pay off, that responsibility will be rewarded, and that our children will inherit a nation where those values live on. (Applause.) And it is that belief that rallied thousands of Americans to Osawatomie—(applause)—maybe even some of your ancestors— on a rain-soaked day more than a century ago. By train, by wagon, on buggy, bicycle, on foot, they came to hear the vision of a man who loved this country and was determined to perfect it.

"We are all Americans," Teddy Roosevelt told them that day. "Our common interests are as broad as the continent." In the final years of his life, Roosevelt took that same message all across this country, from tiny Osawatomie to the heart of New York City, believing that no matter where he went, no matter who he was talking to, everybody would benefit from a country in which everyone gets a fair chance. (Applause.)

And well into our third century as a nation, we have grown and we've changed in many ways since Roosevelt's time. The world is faster and the playing field is larger and the challenges are more complex. But what hasn't changed—what can never change—are the values that got us this far. We still have a stake in each other's success. We still believe that this should be a place where you can make it if you try. And we still believe, in the words of the man who called for a New Nationalism all those years ago, "The fundamental rule of our national life," he said, "the rule which underlies all others—is that, on the whole, and in the long run, we shall go up or down together." And I believe America is on the way up. (Applause.)

Thank you. God bless you. And God bless the United States of America. (Applause.)

The Conscience of a Liberal

PAUL KRUGMAN*

Paul Krugman (1953–) is a Nobel Prize-winning professor of economics at Princeton and, currently, at the CUNY Graduate Center, and a columnist for the *New York Times*. He is also an unabashed liberal, and in this essay he explains why. Krugman argues that the substantial degree of economic equality that prevailed in the United States for more than a generation after World War II was largely a result of political policies put in place earlier by Franklin Delano Roosevelt, which provided the basis for a broad bipartisan consensus on fundamental economic values between Democrats and Republicans. However, in the 1970s, "movement conservatism" effectively took over the Republican Party, whose leaders subsequently instituted policies that created massive economic inequality, a shrinking middle class, increasing poverty, and the rise of a small class of the super-rich. These policies took root in the Reagan era, and were markedly exacerbated under the presidency of George W. Bush. The moral of this story, according to Krugman, is that political ideologies truly matter, because politics tend to drive economics, not the other way around. Thus if we want greater economic equality, on Krugman's view, we need politicians committed to creating it through appropriate public policy measures. Ironically, Krugman contends, in attempting to reestablish the longstanding historical commitment to a more economically equal society, the "liberals" are the true "conservatives," conserving or protecting past gains from the New Deal and the Great Society—Social Security, Medicare, and other popular programs—while those who call themselves conservatives are, in fact, radicals.

* *Source*: Paul Krugman, *The Conscience of a Liberal* (New York: W.W. Norton & Company, 2007), pp. 3–14. Reprinted by permission of W. W. Norton & Company, Inc.

THE WAY WE WERE

I was born in 1953. Like the rest of my generation, I took the America I grew up in for granted—in fact, like many in my generation, I railed against the very real injustices of our society, marched against the bombing of Cambodia, went door to door for liberal political candidates. It's only in retrospect that the political and economic environment of my youth stands revealed as a paradise lost, an exceptional episode in our nation's history.

Postwar America was, above all, a middle-class society. The great boom in wages that began with World War II had lifted tens of millions of Americans— my parents among them—from urban slums and rural poverty to a life of home ownership and unprecedented comfort. The rich, on the other hand, had lost ground: They were few in number and, relative to the prosperous middle, not all that rich. The poor were more numerous than the rich, but they were still a relatively small minority. As a result, there was a striking sense of economic commonality: Most people in America lived recognizably similar and remarkably decent material lives.

The equability of our economy was matched by moderation in our politics. For most but not all of my youth there was broad consensus between Democrats and Republicans on foreign policy and many aspects of domestic policy. Republicans were no longer trying to undo the achievements of the New Deal; quite a few even supported Medicare. And bipartisanship really meant something. Despite the turmoil over Vietnam and race relations, despite the sinister machinations of Nixon and his henchmen, the American political process was for the most part governed by a bipartisan coalition of men who agreed on fundamental values.

Anyone familiar with history knew that America had not always been thus, that we had once been a nation marked by vast economic inequality and wracked by bitter political partisanship. From the perspective of the postwar years, however, America's past of extreme inequality and harsh partisanship seemed like a passing, immature phase, part of the roughness of a nation in the early stages of industrialization. Now that America was all grown up, we thought, a relatively equal society with a strong middle class and an equable political scene was its normal state.

In the 1980s, however, it gradually became clear that the evolution of America into a middle-class, politically middle-of-the-road nation wasn't the end of the story. Economists began documenting a sharp rise in inequality: A small number of people were pulling far ahead, while most Americans saw little or no economic progress. Political scientists began documenting a rise in political polarization: Politicians were gravitating toward the ends of the left-right scale, and it became increasingly possible to use "Democrat" and "Republican" as synonyms for "liberal" and "conservative." Those trends continue to this day: Income inequality today is as high as it was in the 1920s,[1] and political polarization is as high as it has ever been.

The story of rising political polarization isn't a matter of both parties moving to the extremes. It's hard to make the case that Democrats have moved significantly to the left: On economic issues from welfare to taxes, Bill Clinton arguably governed not just to the right of Jimmy Carter, but to the right of Richard Nixon. On the other side it's obvious that Republicans have moved to the right: Just compare the hard-line conservatism of George W. Bush with the moderation of Gerald Ford. In fact, some of Bush's policies—like his attempt to eliminate the estate [i.e., inheritance] tax—don't just take America back to the way it was before the New Deal. They take us back to the way we were before the Progressive Era.

If we take a longer view, both the beginning and the end of the era of bipartisanship reflected fundamental changes in the Republican Party. The era began when Republicans who had bitterly opposed the New Deal either retired or threw in the towel. After Harry Truman's upset victory in 1948, the leadership of the GOP reconciled itself to the idea that the New Deal was here to stay, and as a matter of political self-preservation stopped trying to turn the clock back to the 1920s. The end of the era of bipartisanship and the coming of a new era of bitter partisanship came when the Republican Party was taken over by a radical new force in American politics, movement conservatism, which will play a large role in this book. Partisanship reached its apogee after the 2004 election, when a triumphant Bush tried to dismantle Social Security, the crown jewel of the New Deal institutions.

There have, then, been two great arcs in modern American history—an economic arc from high inequality to relative equality and back again, and a political arc from extreme polarization to bipartisanship and back again. These two arcs move in parallel: The golden age of economic equality roughly corresponded to the golden age of political bipartisanship. As the political scientists Nolan McCarty, Keith Poole, and Howard Rosenthal put it, history suggests that there is a kind of "dance" in which economic inequality and political polarization move as one.[2] They have used a sophisticated statistical technique to track the political positions of members of Congress. Their data show the Republicans moving left, closer to the Democrats, when income inequality declined, producing the bipartisanship of the fifties and sixties. Then the Republicans moved right, creating today's bitter partisanship, as income inequality rose. But what makes the dancing partners stay together?

One possibility is that inequality takes the lead—that, to change metaphors, the arrow of causation points from economics to politics. In that view the story of the last thirty years would run like this: Impersonal forces such as technological change and globalization caused America's income distribution to become increasingly unequal, with an elite minority pulling away from the rest of the population. The Republican Party chose to cater to the interests of that rising elite, perhaps because what the elite lacked in numbers it made up for in the ability and willingness to make large campaign contributions. And so a gap opened up between the parties, with the Republicans becoming the party of the winners from growing inequality while the Democrats represented those left behind.

That, more or less, is the story I believed when I began working on this book. There's clearly something to it. For example, a close look at the campaign to repeal the estate tax shows that it has largely been financed by a handful of families with huge estates to protect. Forty years ago there weren't many huge estates, and the country's superrich, such as they were, weren't rich enough to finance that kind of campaign. So that's a case in which rising inequality has helped pull Republicans to the right.

Yet I've become increasingly convinced that much of the causation runs the other way—that political change in the form of rising polarization has been a major cause of rising inequality. That is, I'd suggest an alternative story for the last thirty years that runs like this: Over the course of the 1970s, radicals of the right determined to roll back the achievements of the New Deal took over the Republican Party, opening a partisan gap with the Democrats, who became the true conservatives, defenders of the long-standing institutions of equality. The empowerment of the hard right emboldened business to launch an all-out attack on the union movement, drastically reducing workers' bargaining power; freed business executives from the political and social constraints that had previously placed limits on runaway executive paychecks; sharply reduced tax rates on high incomes; and in a variety of other ways promoted rising inequality.

The New Economics of Inequality

Can the political environment really be that decisive in determining economic inequality? It sounds like economic heresy, but a growing body of economic research suggests that it can. I'd emphasize four pieces of evidence.

First, when economists, startled by rising inequality, began looking back at the origins of middle class America, they discovered to their surprise that the transition from the inequality of the Gilded Age to the relative equality of the postwar era wasn't a gradual evolution. Instead, America's postwar middle-class society was *created*, in just the space of a few years, by the policies of the Roosevelt administration—especially through wartime wage controls. The economic historians Claudia Goldin and Robert Margo, who first documented this surprising reality, dubbed it the Great Compression.[3] Now, you might have expected inequality to spring back to its former levels once wartime controls were removed. It turned out, however, that the relatively equal distribution of income created by FDR persisted for more than thirty years. This strongly suggests that institutions, norms, and the political environment matter a lot more for the distribution of income—and that impersonal market forces matter less—than Economics 101 might lead you to believe.

Second, the timing of political and economic change suggests that politics, not economics, was taking the lead. There wasn't a major rise in U.S. inequality until the 1980s—as late as 1983 or 1984 there was still some legitimate argument about whether the data showed a clear break in trend. But the right-wing takeover of the Republican Party took place in the mid-1970s, and the institutions of movement conservatism, which made that takeover possible, largely came into existence in the early 1970s. So the timing strongly suggests that polarizing political change came first, and that rising economic inequality followed.

Third, while most economists used to think that technological change, which supposedly increases the demand for highly educated workers and reduces the demand for less-educated workers, was the principal cause of America's rising inequality, that orthodoxy has been gradually wilting as researchers look more closely at the data. Maybe the most striking observation is that even among highly educated Americans, most haven't seen large income gains. The big winners, instead, have been members of a very narrow elite: the top 1 percent or less of the population. As a result there is a growing sense among researchers that technology isn't the main story. Instead, many have come to believe that an erosion of the social norms and institutions that used to promote equality, ultimately driven by the rightward shift of American politics, has played a crucial role in surging inequality.[4]

Finally, international comparisons provide a sort of controlled test. The sharp rightward shift in U.S. politics is unique among advanced countries; Thatcherite Britain, the closest comparison, was at most a pale reflection. The forces of technological change and globalization, by contrast, affect everyone. If the rise in inequality has political roots, the United States should stand out; if it's mainly due to impersonal market forces, trends in inequality should have been similar across the advanced world. And the fact is that the increase in U.S. inequality has no counterpart anywhere else in the advanced world. During the Thatcher years Britain experienced a sharp rise in income disparities, but not nearly as large as the rise in inequality here, and inequality has risen modestly if at all in continental Europe and Japan.[5]

Political change, then, seems to be at the heart of the story. How did that political change happen?

The Politics of Inequality

The story of how George W. Bush and Dick Cheney ended up running the country goes back half a century, to the years when the *National Review*, edited by a young William F. Buckley, was defending the right of the South to prevent blacks from voting—"the White community is so entitled because it is, for the time being, the advanced race"—and praising Generalissimo Francisco Franco, who overthrew a democratically elected government in the name of church and property, as "an authentic national hero." The small movement then known as the "new conservatism" was, in large part, a backlash against the decision of Dwight Eisenhower and other Republican leaders to make their peace with FDR's legacy.

Over the years this small movement grew into a powerful political force, which both supporters and opponents call "movement conservatism." It's a network of people and institutions that extends far beyond what is normally considered political life: In addition to the Republican Party and Republican politicians, movement conservatism includes media organizations, think tanks, publishing houses and more. People can and do make entire careers within this network, secure in the knowledge that political loyalty will be rewarded no matter what happens. A liberal who botched a war and then violated ethics rules to reward his lover might be worried about his employment prospects; Paul Wolfowitz had a chair waiting for him at the American Enterprise Institute.

There once were a significant number of Republican politicians who weren't movement conservatives, but there are only a few left, largely because life becomes very difficult for those who aren't considered politically reliable. Just ask Lincoln Chafee, the moderate former senator from Rhode Island, who faced a nasty primary challenge from the right in 2006 that helped lead to his defeat in the general election, even though it was clear that the Republicans might well need him to keep control of the Senate.

Money is the glue of movement conservatism, which is largely financed by a handful of extremely wealthy individuals and a number of major corporations, all of whom stand to gain from increased inequality, an end to progressive taxation, and a rollback of the welfare state—in short, from a reversal of the New Deal. And turning the clock back on economic policies that limit inequality is, at its core, what movement conservatism is all about. Grover Norquist, an anti-tax activist who is one of the movement's key figures, once confided that he wants to bring America back to what it was "up until Teddy Roosevelt, when the socialists took over. The income tax, the death tax, regulation, all that."[6]

Because movement conservatism is ultimately about rolling back policies that hurt a narrow, wealthy elite, it's fundamentally antidemocratic. But however much the founders of the movement may have admired the way Generalissimo Franco did things, in America the route to political power runs through elections. There wouldn't be nearly as much money forthcoming if potential donors still believed, as they had every reason to in the aftermath of Barry Goldwater's landslide defeat in 1964, that advocating economic policies that increase inequality is a political nonstarter. Movement conservatism has gone from fringe status to a central role in American politics because it has proved itself able to win elections.

Ronald Reagan, more than anyone else, showed the way. His 1964 speech "A Time for Choosing," which launched his political career, and the speeches he gave during his successful 1966 campaign for governor of California foreshadowed political strategies that would work for him and other movement conservatives for the next forty years. Latter-day hagiographers have portrayed Reagan as a paragon of high-minded conservative principles, but he was nothing of the sort. His early political successes were based on appeals to cultural and sexual anxieties, playing on the fear of communism, and, above all, tacit exploitation of white backlash against the civil rights movement and its consequences.

One key message of this book, which many readers may find uncomfortable, is that race is at the heart of what has happened to the country I grew up in. The legacy of slavery, America's original sin, is the reason we're the only advanced economy that doesn't guarantee health care to our citizens. White backlash against the civil rights movement is the reason America is the only advanced country where a major political party wants to roll back the welfare state. Ronald Reagan began his 1980 campaign with a states' rights speech outside Philadelphia, Mississippi, the town where three civil rights workers were murdered; Newt Gingrich was able to take over Congress entirely because of the great Southern flip, the switch of Southern whites from overwhelming support for Democrats to overwhelming support for Republicans.

A New New Deal

A few months after the 2004 election I was placed under some pressure by journalistic colleagues, who said I should stop spending so much time criticizing the Bush administration and conservatives more generally. "The election settled some things," I was told. In retrospect, however, it's starting to look as if the 2004 election was movement conservatism's last hurrah.

Republicans won a stunning victory in the 2002 mid-term election by exploiting terrorism to the hilt. There's every reason to believe that one reason Bush took us to war with Iraq was his desire to perpetuate war psychology combined with his expectation that victory in a splendid little war would be good for his reelection prospects. Indeed, Iraq probably did win Bush the 2004 election, even though the war was already going badly.

But the war did go badly—and that was not an accident. When Bush moved into the White House, movement conservatism finally found itself in control of all the levers of power—and quickly proved itself unable to govern. The movement's politicization of everything, the way it values political loyalty above all else, creates a culture of cronyism and corruption that has pervaded everything the Bush administration does, from the failed reconstruction of Iraq to the hapless response to Hurricane Katrina. The multiple failures of the Bush administration are what happens when the government is run by a movement that is dedicated to policies that are against most Americans' interests, and must try to compensate for that inherent weakness through deception, distraction, and the distribution of largesse to its supporters. And the nation's rising contempt for Bush and his administration helped Democrats achieve a stunning victory in the 2006 midterm election.

One election does not make a trend. There are, however, deeper forces undermining the political tactics movement conservatives have used since Ronald Reagan ran for governor of California. Crucially, the American electorate is, to put it bluntly, becoming less white. Republican strategists try to draw a distinction between African Americans and the Hispanic and Asian voters who play a gradually growing role in elections—but as the debate over immigration showed, that's not a distinction the white backlash voters the modern GOP depends on are prepared to make. A less crude factor is the progressive shift in Americans' attitudes: Polling suggests that the electorate has moved significantly to the left on domestic issues since the 1990s, and race is a diminishing force in a nation that is, truly, becoming steadily less racist.

Movement conservatism still has money on its side, but that has never been enough in itself. Anything can happen in the 2008 election, but it looks like a reasonable guess that by 2009 America will have a Democratic president and a solidly Democratic Congress. Moreover, this new majority, if it emerges, will be much more ideologically cohesive than the Democratic majority of Bill Clinton's first two years, which was an uneasy alliance between Northern liberals and conservative Southerners.

The question is, what should the new majority do? My answer is that it should, for the nation's sake, pursue an unabashedly liberal program of expanding the social safety net and reducing inequality—a new New Deal. The starting point for that program, the twenty-first-century equivalent of Social Security, should be universal health care, something every other advanced country already has ...

NOTES

1   Much of what we know about long-term trends in inequality comes from the pioneering work of Thomas Piketty and Emmanuel Saez, "Income Inequality in the United States, 1913–1998," *Quarterly Journal of Economics* 118, no. 1 (Feb. 2003), pp. 1–39.

2   Nolan McCarty, Keith Poole, and Howard Rosenthal, *Polarized America: The Dance of Ideology and Unequal Riches* (MIT Press, 2006).

3   Claudia Goldin and Robert Margo, "The Great Compression: The Wage Structure in the United States at Mid-Century," *Quarterly Journal of Economics* 107, no. 1 (1992), pp. 1–34.

4   See, in particular, Ian Dew-Becker and Robert Gordon, "Where Did the Productivity Growth Go? Inflation Dynamics and the Distribution of Income," *Brookings Papers on Economic Activities*, no. 2 (2005), pp. 67–127, and Frank Levy and Peter Temin, "Inequality and Institutions in 20th Century America" (MIT Department of Economics working paper, no. 07-17, June 2007).

5   Thomas Piketty and Emmanuel Saez, "The Evolution of Top Incomes: A Historical and International Perspective" (National Bureau of Economic Research working paper no. 11955, Jan. 2006).

6   William Greider, "Rolling Back the 20th Century," *The Nation* (May 12, 2003).

Paternalism vs. Democracy: A Libertarian View

DONALD ALLEN*

In the last fifty years or so, neoclassical liberalism has enjoyed a remarkable revival in the form of the libertarian movement. In the United States the Libertarian Party regularly nominates and supports candidates for public office, including president, and libertarian scholars are also quite active in academe and in policy "think tanks" such as the Cato Institute. In the following essay, the libertarian writer Donald Allen (1944–) argues that democracy can survive only when individuals are free from government interference to control their own lives.

* *Source*: This essay was written expressly for *Ideals and Ideologies*.

PATERNALISM VS. DEMOCRACY: A LIBERTARIAN VIEW

Paternalism—the doctrine that the state knows better than its citizens what is good for them—is especially insidious in a democracy. As the most morally and intellectually demanding form of government, democracy requires the free flow of information about alternatives and choices. Inasmuch as paternalists propose to dam and channel that flow as they see fit, they are inherently antidemocratic.

Censorship has always been the paternalist's weapon of choice. And it is easy to see why. The paternalist wishes not only to deliver us from evil but to prevent us from even being led into temptation in the first place. By blocking information about attractive but "unacceptable" alternatives, censorship precludes the possibility that some citizens will make the "wrong" choices about what to read, see, say, or smoke.

Now it might be objected that paternalists are good people who have the best of intentions and the interests of others at heart. And so they may be. But in matters moral and political, consequences count for more than intentions. And the consequences of paternalism, whether intended or not, are dangerous to the health of a democratic body politic and the individual citizens who comprise it. If you doubt it, consider the case of Prohibition.

Led by well-intentioned zealots like Carry A. Nation (1846–1911)—who, incidentally, believed that God had given her her name so that she might "carry a nation"—the Prohibitionists singled out for special censure not the consumers who abused alcohol but those who distilled and sold it. The Prohibitionists sincerely believed that their aim was noble and their cause a righteous one, and many Americans apparently agreed. After all, there were drunkards who were killing themselves with Demon Drink. To save such people from themselves the Constitution was amended to outlaw the production, sale, and distribution of intoxicating liquors (18th Amendment, 1920). Like many a well-intentioned scheme, this one went badly awry. The free market in alcohol was replaced by a black market in bootleg whiskey and bathtub gin. The supply of alcohol kept pace with the undiminished demand, even as the quality of the alcohol decreased and the price consumers paid for it (in dollars and in damaged livers) increased. And—not least—politicians and policemen were corrupted and organized crime gained a foothold in America that it has never lost. The harm caused by America's paternalistic experiment with Prohibition is with us even today.

One might think that Americans would have learned by now that paternalism will not and cannot work in a society supposedly blessed with free institutions and free markets. Apparently not, alas. Despite our many virtues, we Americans have, as Alexis de Tocqueville noted in *Democracy in America* more than a century and a half ago, two particularly nasty vices. The first is that we know next to nothing about history. And knowing so little about the past, we are in no position to learn from it, although we are all too apt to repeat its mistakes. We are therefore unable to follow the German Chancellor Bismarck's dictum that "The truly wise man does not learn from his mistakes; he learns from other people's mistakes." Ignorant even of our own recent history, we muddle on, naively trusting a new generation of elected or self-appointed Prohibitionists to tell us which products, ideas, and information we may or may not be exposed to.

Our second vice is one to which democracies may be peculiarly prone. Tocqueville, along with James Madison and John Stuart Mill, observed that in democracies without strong constitutional safeguards, a tyrannical majority can very easily ride roughshod over the rights of unpopular individuals or minorities. That is why a Bill of Rights was added to the U.S. Constitution and why the First Amendment comes first in that list of liberties. And that is why the whole of Mill's magnificent *On Liberty* (1859) is devoted to defending the right of free expression for all citizens, however obnoxious or distasteful others may think their views to be. Mill's essay is also a defense of diversity and a thoroughgoing critique of paternalism. "The only purpose for which power can be rightfully exercised over any member of a civilized community, against his will," wrote Mill, "is to prevent harm to others. His own good, either physical or moral, is not a sufficient warrant. He cannot rightfully be compelled to do or forbear because it will be better for him to do so, because it will make him happier, because, in the opinions of others, to do so would be wise or even right … Over himself, over his own body and mind, the individual is sovereign." It is just this individual sovereignty that the New Prohibitionists find so intolerable.

The New Prohibitionists have in recent years turned their attention not to alcohol but toward drugs, tobacco, and pornography, in particular. To stop the flow of drugs into the United States they propose more laws, stiffer penalties, more police—in short, more state power devoted to preventing people from doing what they like with, and to, their own bodies. It has not worked, and will not work. Exactly the same things that happened during Prohibition are happening all over again. People who want to drink—or take drugs or view pornography or to have sex with another consenting adult—will do so. And if there is no free market in any product or service that is in demand, whether it be drugs or pornography or prostitution, there will inevitably be an illegal or "black" market in that product or service. Because black market goods and services are much more expensive than those sold on the free market, some consumers will pay for them by turning to other illegal, but profitable activities, including prostitution, theft, and the selling of drugs. This of course is exactly what has happened. The result is that our jails and prisons are overflowing, our police officers overworked or corrupted, and our taxes raised in a Canute-like effort to turn back the tide. Once again, well-meaning paternalists, in attempting to solve one "problem," have not only failed to solve it but have created many additional problems as well.

Not content to restrict or outlaw certain kinds of purely private conduct by or between consenting adults, the New Prohibitionists have recently turned their attention to public speech. Their most recent efforts include proposing legislation to restrict or outlaw the production, sale, and distribution of pornography and a ban on the consumption of large sugary drinks and the advertising and public display of tobacco products (cigarettes in particular). The first comes from paternalists on the religious Right, the second from the liberal Left. No matter what their motives, however, their message is essentially the same. Their claim is that certain words, pictures, and products ought to be prohibited by law, lest people be tempted to think, and perchance to act, in ways that the state deems socially unacceptable. And the aim in both cases is to de-diversify a pluralistic society whose strength has traditionally resided in its citizens' diverse and often opposing outlooks, opinions, and tastes. This is, of course, a tall order. It requires nothing less than an assault on our fundamental freedoms, as articulated in the Bill of Rights, and the First Amendment in particular.

Since a full frontal assault on these freedoms would never be tolerated, the New Prohibitionists have turned to other tactics. Scare tactics, for example: some kinds of speech or expression are said to pose too great a danger to our morals or our health to be tolerated or otherwise countenanced. They must therefore be silenced. But, we are assured, this silencing isn't "really" censorship because "free speech" isn't involved. In the case of sexually explicit materials, they say, it isn't words—that is, speech—but morally objectionable pictures that the state should outlaw. The outlawing of tobacco ads is also said not to be censorship, but something else. Casting about for some less loaded euphemism, our Washington wordsmiths have coined the phrase, "ban on advertising." This ban, or whatever it is, is supposed to be highly selective. It is to be aimed only at a small minority whose activities are said to be injurious to the health or morals of the vast majority.

Who in good conscience could object to these or any other measures claiming to promote health or moral decency or any similarly admirable goal?

Answer: I can. And I think that any liberty-loving democrat can, too.

Let me be blunt: I have no particular affection for drug dealers (or users), or for pornographers and their customers, or for tobacco companies or smokers. Nor do I use any of their products. But the fact that they make such tempting targets for the New Prohibitionists should give us pause. It is precisely because there is so little love lost on drug dealers, pornographers, and tobacco producers that those who love liberty had better beware. As Mill warned—and as the history of the twentieth century shows with alarming clarity—scapegoating is always selective at first. Although the members of a particular unpopular minority are always the first to lose their liberty, they are never the last to lose it.

The modern movement toward the all-powerful paternal state has proceeded in a piecemeal way. It is a revolution wrought not by the single great bite but by a long series of small, highly selective nibbles around the unguarded edges of our liberties. For this reason the movement's most fitting symbol would not be the biblical whale Leviathan, as Thomas Hobbes suggested in the seventeenth century, but the humble piranha. The bite of a single piranha, I am told—though I have no wish to test this myself—is neither fatal nor even particularly painful. But the cumulative effect of a series of nibbles by a school of these tiny creatures is dreadful to behold.

So it is with censorship. A tiny bite here, a little nibble there, and we are very soon stripped of our liberties and the life and health of our greater public body—the body politic—is gravely imperiled. However small, however "selective" its target, however carefully it is aimed, the paternalist's favorite weapon must eventually destroy the liberties, and perchance even the lives, of those whose interests it initially purported to protect.

Like it or not, any government restriction on any form of speech—including advertising—amounts to an abridgement of the free speech and expression protected by the First Amendment. If it is to survive and flourish, democracy requires an intelligent and informed citizenry, just as the free market requires intelligent and informed consumers. Because the free society and the free market are alike in requiring the free flow of information in all its forms, a ban on the advertising of any product makes a mockery of both. Censorship—for that is what such restrictions amount to—is nothing less than the constricting of choice through the withholding of ideas and information about alternative ways of thinking and acting and living one's life as one sees fit.

The New Prohibitionists are right in at least one respect. They are correct in casting their crusade against free choice and free speech as a public health issue. The kind of legislation they wish to enact does raise profound questions about health, all right—the health of our democratic body politic. The real issue, in the final analysis, is not whether alcohol, drugs, tobacco, large sugar-laden sodas, or any other product is bad for one's health but whether a democratic polity can survive the ministrations of well-meaning paternalists bent on protecting us from ourselves.

Every well-intentioned proposal to outlaw or restrict any sort of self-regarding or private action and speech in all its forms should be required to carry a label reading "Warning: Paternalism Is Dangerous to the Health of the Body Politic."

Paternalism promises illusory cures for imaginary ailments. In a free society paternalism can never be the remedy for anything. Paternalism is, instead, the disease for which the libertarian philosophy is the cure.

Postscript, 2005

In the late 1980s, when I wrote this essay, I thought that the main threat to liberty in the United States came from the liberal Left. I now believe that the primary threat comes from the conservative Right. The Republican Party, which now controls all three branches of the federal government, is no longer the quasi-libertarian party of Barry Goldwater and Ronald Reagan.[1] That now-defunct party favored fiscal responsibility and small government. The administration of George W. Bush, however, seems bent on bankrupting the country by running record deficits and cutting taxes while fighting an ill-considered and enormously expensive war abroad. Moreover, the government is now using the very real threat of terrorism as a pretext for depriving a gullible American public of their liberties—not by small bites or nibbles but in huge gulps and gobbles by PATRIOT Acts I and II. These misnamed acts give the government *carte blanche* to snoop and spy on Americans in almost every aspect of their lives, from the books they check out of their local library to telephone conversations with family and friends. To make matters even worse, the religious Right promotes legislation to make women's wombs into state property and to persecute gay men and lesbians for exercising their liberty to love whom and how they please. These and other assaults on personal privacy and individual liberty are the baleful result not of small-government conservatism but of large-government activism of the most intrusive, coercive, and paternalistic kind. For all the Bush administration's talk about promoting liberty and democracy abroad, it seems intent on depriving Americans of both at home. Be afraid. Be very afraid.

Postscript, 2013

One of the oldest maxims of economics, going back at least to Adam Smith, is this: Where there is no "white," or legal, market in a good or service for which there is a strong demand, illegal or "black" markets in that good or service will spring up. That was true of bootleg whiskey during Prohibition; it remains true of prostitution; and it is all too painfully and increasingly true of the black markets in labor and drugs. The smuggling of laborers and drugs across the U.S.–Mexican border provides two vivid cases in point.

Labor. There are fewer good jobs in Mexico and most of Central America than in the United States. Mexican and other workers, seeking better lives for themselves and their families, look longingly toward *el norte,* "the north." Beyond that border are better jobs and brighter prospects. Although crossing that border illegally is dangerous and often deadly, tens of thousands of Mexicans and others take their chances each year and cross into the United States. Reduced to its essentials, *illegal immigration is simply another name for a black market in labor.*

This black market can be made "white" by legalizing the importation of workers from Mexico (and elsewhere) through a "guest worker" program or by some other means. But the Congress has so far failed to reform our badly broken immigration system, not out of economic considerations but because of political cowardice. If we put our trust in markets and not in the politics of cowardice, we would solve our immigration problem almost overnight.

Drugs. Mexico is now very nearly a "failed state"—a "narco-state" ruled by rival drug lords and their gangs—and their murderous violence is spreading to the United States. Police forces from Brownsville to El Paso to Tucson to Los Angeles are overwhelmed and outgunned by gangs grown rich from the drug trade. And the explanation is simple. It all has to do with money. There is money—a *lot* of money—to be made from the trade in illegal drugs. These drugs are expensive, and thus very profitable for the dealers, simply because they are illegal.

If we treated drugs such as marijuana and cocaine as we do alcohol—which we regulate the sale of (no sales to minors, for example) and on which government levies taxes (thereby increasing revenues for sorely strapped state services)—the violence would end. Lives would be saved. The surveillance and policing powers of the federal government could be reduced, and on a massive scale. Police, Border Patrol, and DEA and ICE agencies could be scaled back, reducing the federal budget and saving taxpayers' hard-earned dollars. And the monies used by drug lords to corrupt cops and agents would dry up, and corruption would diminish if not disappear altogether. Don't get me wrong: the vast majority of policemen, border patrolmen, and DEA agents are honest; but the temptation to "look the other way" is simply too tempting for some to resist.

The case for legalizing drugs is persuasive, compelling—and more urgent now than ever. Sooner or later we will have to make the "war on drugs" go the way of Prohibition—that is, away, and forever.

Postscript, 2016

Marijuana possession and use is now legalized, or at least decriminalized, in twenty-three states and in the District of Columbia. Details vary from state to state. Some allow its use for medical purposes only, while others permit possession and use for recreational purposes. The rapidity of the public's turnaround on marijuana resembles their widespread about-face on same-sex marriage. Both suggest, to me at least, that America is taking a libertarian turn of late, and that is reason to rejoice.

NOTE

1   In the elections of 2006 the Democratic Party gained control, by narrow margins, of both houses of Congress. In the 2008 elections the Democrats increased their margins in the Congress and won the presidency as well. In 2010 conservative Republicans won the House of Representatives and numerous state legislatures and governorships. In the 2012 elections Democrats retained the presidency and picked up seats in the Senate and House of Representatives. In 2014 the Republicans won a majority of seats in the Senate and still constitute a considerable majority in the House.—Eds.

Libertarian Anarchism

MURRAY ROTHBARD*

One of the best-known libertarian or neoclassical liberal writers, Murray Rothbard (1926–1995) was an American economist who taught at New York Polytechnic Institute and at the University of Nevada, Las Vegas. Rothbard believed not that government should be kept small but that it should be abolished altogether. Rothbard is thus a libertarian anarchist who contends, in the following excerpt from his *For a New Liberty*, that government—far from being a "necessary evil"—is an entirely *un*necessary evil.

* *Source*: Murray Rothbard, *For a New Liberty* (New York: Macmillan, 1973), pp. 8–12, 18–19, 34–35, 40. Reprinted by permission of the Ludwig Von Mises Institute.

LIBERTARIAN ANARCHISM

Throughout the numerous factions and splinters of the movement ... there is agreement on the central core of the libertarian creed. The crucial axiom of that creed is: no man or group of men have the right to aggress against the person or property of anyone else. This might be called the "nonaggression" axiom. "Aggression" is defined as the initiation of the use or threat of physical violence against the person or property of someone else. Aggression is therefore synonymous with "invasion." How this axiom may be arrived at will be discussed below, and the paths toward attaining the axiom vary among different groups of libertarians. But all libertarians agree on nonaggression as the central axiom of their doctrine.

If no man may aggress against—invade—the person or property of another, this means that every man is free to do whatever he wishes, except commit such aggression. The great nineteenth-century libertarian theorist Herbert Spencer formulated a similar axiom: "Law of Equal Liberty." "Freedom" or "liberty" is therefore rigorously defined in such a credo as: the absence of invasion. A man is free when he is not being aggressed against; and all men, or "society," are free when no aggression or invasion is being committed.

If no man may aggress against another; if, in short, everyone has the absolute right to be "free" from aggression, then this at once implies that the libertarian stands foursquare for what are generally known as "civil liberties": the freedom to speak, publish, assemble, and to engage in such "victimless crimes" as pornography, sexual deviation, and prostitution (which the libertarian does not regard as "crimes" at all, since he defines a "crime" as violent invasion of someone else's person or property). Furthermore, he regards conscription as slavery on a massive scale. And since war, especially modern war, entails the mass slaughter of civilians, the libertarian regards such conflicts as mass murder and therefore totally illegitimate.

All of these positions are now considered "leftist" on the contemporary ideological scale. On the other hand, since the libertarian also opposes invasion of the rights of private property, this also means that he just as emphatically opposes government interference with property rights or with the free market economy through controls, regulations, subsidies, or prohibitions. For if every individual has the right to his own property without having to suffer aggressive depredation, then he also has the right to give away his property (bequest and inheritance) and to exchange it for the property of others (free contract and the free market economy) without interference. The libertarian favors the right to unrestricted private property and free-exchange; hence, a system of "laissez-faire capitalism."

In current terminology again, the libertarian position on property and economics would be called "extreme right wing." But the libertarian sees no inconsistency in being "leftist" on some issues and "rightist" on others. On the contrary, he sees his own position as virtually the *only* consistent one, consistent on behalf of the liberty of every individual. For how can the leftist be opposed to the violence of war and conscription while at the same time supporting the violence of taxation and government control? And how can the rightist trumpet his devotion to private property and free enterprise while at the same time favoring war, conscription, and the outlawing of noninvasive activities and practices that he deems immoral? And how can the rightist favor a free market while seeing nothing amiss in the vast subsidies, distortions, and unproductive inefficiencies involved in the military-industrial complex?

While opposing any and all private or group aggression against the rights of person and property, the libertarian sees that throughout history and into the present day, there has been one central, dominant, and overriding aggressor upon all of these rights: the State. In contrast to all other thinkers, left, right, or in-between, the libertarian refuses to give the State the moral sanction to commit actions that almost everyone agrees would be immoral, illegal, and criminal if committed by any person or group in society. The libertarian, in short, insists on applying the general moral law to everyone, and makes no special exemptions for any person or group. But if we look at the State naked, as it were, we see that it is universally allowed, and even encouraged, to commit all the acts which even nonlibertarians concede are reprehensible crimes. The State habitually commits mass murder, which it calls "war," or sometimes "suppression of subversion"; the State engages in enslavement into its military forces, which it calls "conscription"; and it lives and has its being in the practice of forcible theft, which it calls "taxation." The libertarian insists that whether or not such practices are supported by the majority of the population is not germane to their nature: that, regardless of popular sanction, War is Mass Murder, Conscription is Slavery, and Taxation is Robbery. The libertarian, in short, is almost completely the child in the fable, pointing out insistently that the emperor has no clothes.

Throughout the ages, the emperor has had a series of pseudo-clothes provided for him by the nation's intellectual caste. In past centuries, the intellectuals informed the public that the State or its rulers were divine, or at least clothed in divine authority, and therefore what might *look* to the naïve and untutored eye as despotism, mass murder, and theft on a grand scale was only the divine working its benign and mysterious ways in the body politic. In recent decades, as the divine sanction has worn a bit threadbare, the emperor's "court intellectuals" have spun ever more sophisticated apologia: informing the public that what the government does is for the "common good" and the "public welfare," that the process of taxation-and-spending works through the mysterious process of the "multiplier" to keep the economy on an even keel, and that, in any case, a wide variety of governmental "services" could not possibly be performed by citizens acting voluntarily on the market or in society. All of this the libertarian denies: he sees the various apologia as fraudulent means of obtaining public support for the State's rule, and he insists that whatever services the government actually performs could be supplied far more efficiently and far more morally by private and cooperative enterprise.

The libertarian therefore considers one of his prime educational tasks is to spread the demystification and desanctification of the State among its hapless subjects. His task is to demonstrate repeatedly and in depth that not only the emperor but even the "democratic" state has no clothes; that all governments subsist by exploitive rule over the public; and that such rule is the reverse of objective necessity. He strives to show that the very existence of taxation and the State necessarily sets up a class division between the exploiting rulers and the exploited ruled. He seeks to show that the task of the court intellectuals who have always supported the State has ever been to weave mystification in order to induce the public to accept State rule, and that these intellectuals obtain, in return, a share in the power and pelf extracted by the rulers from their deluded subjects.

Take, for example, the institution of taxation, which statists have claimed is in some sense really "voluntary." Anyone who truly believes in the "voluntary" nature of taxation is invited to refuse to pay taxes and to see what then happens to him. If we analyze taxation, we find that, among all the persons and institutions in society, only the government acquires its revenues through coercive violence. Everyone else in society acquires income *either* through voluntary gift (lodge, charitable society, chess club) *or* through the sale of goods or services voluntarily purchased by consumers. If anyone *but* the government proceeded to "tax," this would clearly be considered coercion and thinly disguised banditry. Yet the mystical trappings of "sovereignty" have so veiled the process that only libertarians are prepared to call taxation what it is: legalized and organized theft on a grand scale …

Further, if taxation is robbery, then it becomes clear that a tax or monopoly-coercing government is a robber band, and deserves not reverence but abolition—or, if abolition cannot be achieved, at the least there should be a relentless whittling down of governmental power and activity. Civil disobedience to unjust laws and decrees—including not only the draft but taxation itself—becomes morally legitimate if not always strategically or tactically prudent.

Superpatriotism is at the least very difficult for any anarchist, so the great bulk of anarchocapitalists have abandoned their former rightist devotion to the Cold War and to American foreign policy. Generally, they have adopted an "ultraisolationist" foreign policy as the external corollary to their opposition to domestic statism …

If … land is nature- or God-given then so are the people's talents, health, and beauty. And just as all these attributes are given to specific individuals and not to "society," so then are land and natural resources. All of these resources are given to individuals and not to "society," which is an abstraction that does not actually exist. There is no existing entity called "society": there are only interacting individuals. To say that "society" should own land or any other property in common, then, must mean that a group of oligarchs—in practice, government bureaucrats—should own the property, and at the expense of expropriating the creator or the homesteader who had originally brought this product into existence.

Moreover, no one can produce *anything* without the cooperation of original land, if only as standing room. No man can produce or create anything by his labor alone; he must have the cooperation of land and other natural raw materials.

Man comes into the world with just himself and the world around him—the land and natural resources given him by nature. He takes these resources and transforms them by his labor and mind and energy into goods more useful to man.

Therefore, if an individual cannot own original land, neither can he in the full sense own any of the fruits of his labor. The farmer cannot own his wheat crop if he cannot own the land on which the wheat grows. Now that his labor has been inextricably mixed with the land, he cannot be deprived of one without being deprived of the other.

Moreover, if a producer is *not* entitled to the fruits of his labor, who is? … Land in its original state is unused and unowned. Georgists[1] and other land communalists may claim that the whole world population *really* "owns" it, but if no one has yet used it, it is in the real sense owned and controlled by no one. The pioneer, the homesteader, the first user and transformer of this land, is the man who first brings this simple valueless thing into production and social use. It is difficult to see the morality of depriving him of ownership in favor of people who have never gotten within a thousand miles of the land, and who may not even know of the existence of the property over which they are supposed to have a claim.

The moral, natural rights issue involved here is even clearer if we consider the case of animals. Animals are "economic land," since they are original nature-given resources. Yet will anyone deny full title to a horse to the man who finds and domesticates it—is this any different from the acorns and berries that are generally conceded to the gatherer? Yet in land, too, some homesteader takes the previously "wild," undomesticated land, and "tames" it by putting it to productive use.

The central core of the libertarian creed, then, is to establish the absolute right to private property of every man; first, in his own body, and second, in the previously unused natural resources which he first transforms by his labor. These two axioms, the right of self-ownership and the right to "homestead," establish the complete set of principles of the libertarian system. The entire libertarian doctrine then becomes the spinning out and the application of all the implications of this central doctrine.

NOTE

1   Followers of Henry George (1839–1897), an American economist, whose *Progress and Poverty* (1879) advocated a land-based redistribution of wealth.—Eds.

A Libertarian Utopia

*TERENCE BALL**

Libertarians tend to distrust politics and to trust the unregulated operations of the free market, even in areas traditionally regarded as off-limits to market thinking. The American political theorist Terence Ball invites us to imagine a libertarian utopia or "marketopia" in which every good and service is for sale on the open market. What would such a society look like? How would political, legal, and educational institutions be structured? What would happen when all institutions, goods, and services are privatized and citizens become "consumers" and students "customers"? Would Marketopia be an admirable utopia or a detestable dystopia?

* *Source*: Terence Ball, "Imagining Marketopia," *Dissent* (Summer, 2001): 74–80. Copyright 2001. Reprinted by permission of the University of Pennsylvania Press. The author has made a number of minor revisions.

A LIBERTARIAN UTOPIA

What is the proper place for the market? In the history of social and political thought, this seemingly simple question has elicited many different answers. That the answers vary so widely suggests that the question is not as simple as it seems. Aristotle, and later the Church Fathers, held that the market has a greatly restricted but legitimate place in social life. Bernard de Mandeville and Adam Smith were prepared to give markets a much less restricted role. Karl Marx wanted to abolish the market altogether. Today, however, a school of writers and publicists has emerged that holds that most, if not all, politically imposed limitations on markets are both inefficient and unjust. Liberate the market, they say, and let it work its magic in all spheres of life—education, energy, the environment, health care, crime and punishment, fire and police protection, transportation, and other areas as well.

This libertarian turn is a genuinely new wrinkle in intellectual history, and is hardly confined to the academy. Since the "revolutions" of Margaret Thatcher and Ronald Reagan in the 1980s, this way of thinking has been put into (admittedly selective) practice. "Privatization" and "deregulation" became official watchwords and defining features of public policy. To the question, What is the market's proper place? the answer is: (almost) anywhere and everywhere.

My purpose here is not to ask whether or how well these policies have worked in practice, but to try instead to expose some of the questionable features of market-thinking, especially when applied to spheres of social life traditionally regarded as off-limits to market forces. I'll do this by means of a thought-experiment: the construction of an imaginary society called Marketopia in which the market has taken over every sphere of social life.

I

Imagine a not-so-distant future society called Marketopia. In the middle of its capital city of Nozickia lies Becker Square which can be reached via the city's main thoroughfare, a toll road named Liberty Lane. For a modest admission fee one can enter the square and, for a further fee, gain entry to the mausoleum containing the embalmed body of Gary Becker, national hero and saint. "What Price Immortality?" asks the sign over the glass coffin. And it immediately answers its own question: 243,287 Rothbards (the national currency), raised by the sale of relics—items belonging to or once touched by the late economist and demigod.

In Marketopia everything is for sale. Drugs and sexual services are reasonably priced, of course, but then so are most things because there is a market in every conceivable good and service. There is, for example, a vigorous market in human organs. Organ brokers walk the halls of the private hospitals, keeping close watch on the dying and making deals with family members whose grief is greatly offset by the prospect of profiting from the death of their loved one. Those awaiting organ transplants are prepared to pay the going price for a heart, lung, kidney, or other vital organs. Typically, competing organ brokers play one potential recipient off against the other, thereby raising the price and ensuring that the organ goes to the highest bidder. Most Marketopians opt for a designation on their drivers' license, saying that in event of their death their organs should be sold to the highest bidder.

They shake their heads in disbelief when told that there was a time when human blood and organs were freely donated by community-minded altruists—and then typically ask what the words "community" and "altruist" mean, as these are not in current usage, although they are in their dictionary.

The language spoken in Marketopia bears a close resemblance to English, at least in vocabulary and spelling, though not in the meaning of many words. Marketopian dictionaries are helpful here. Under "society," for example, the entry reads: "Fictitious entity believed by collectivists to be real. See also Public." Under "justice" the entry reads: "Noninterference in market transactions; actions, arrangements and/or decisions conducive to the functioning of free markets." And under "injustice" the obverse: "Interference with and/or regulation of market transactions."

Many Marketopians are quite bright, having been taught to read and calculate from an early age. Children in the private kindergartens learn their ABCs and Marketopian values together. "Now children," the teacher intones in a cheerful voice, "what does A stand for?" To which her eager young charges respond enthusiastically and in unison, "*Assets!*" And so on through the alphabet: B is for Bank, C is for Capital, M is for Market (of course), P is for Privatization, and so on. The teaching of mathematics is even more impressive. By age six most children have mastered decimals and percentages and can calculate compound interest. By age eight they are well-versed in statistics and by ten most have mastered rational-choice theory.

In Marketopia all roads are toll roads, fire and police protection is provided by private companies for a fee, and according to how much protection, delivered how fast, the consumer desires or can afford. If you can't afford, or choose to forgo, fire protection, one or more fire companies will, in the event of a fire at your house, appear with hoses, hooks, and ladders—and the fire captain will engage you in fast-paced negotiations about how much you think his company's services are now worth. These negotiated post-fire fees (as they are called) tend to be very high, often running into the tens or even hundreds of thousands of Rothbards.

If an intruder lurks downstairs you need only phone the private policing company to which you pay a monthly fee and a car and officer will be dispatched. If, however, you don't have a police-protection policy (or a pistol in your nightstand drawer), you can call a company and negotiate a price over the telephone. Uninsured and understandably hysterical consumers typically pay premium prices for post-intrusion police protection. In several instances these hastily negotiated fees have amounted to millions of Rothbards. So, not surprisingly, ads for policing companies emphasize the importance of being fully protected and paid up in advance. Only then can you be assured that your assailant will be apprehended. After being tried in private court before a judge—juries, being slow and inefficient (and unfair to would-be jurors, who are in any event too busy with their own affairs to serve), are never used in Marketopia, even in capital cases—the wrongdoer will be incarcerated in one of the private prisons run by Burglar King, McPrison, and other franchises.

Some activities considered criminal in other societies are quite common and entirely legal in Marketopia. Blackmail, for example, is regarded as a free-market transaction in which one person pays another for the service of remaining silent. The sale of cocaine, heroin, hashish, and other drugs is viewed in a similar light. The only actions punishable by law are transgressions against the person or property of another.

The private prisons of Marketopia have proven to be both profitable and popular. Prisons serve not only to punish criminals but to entertain a vast television audience. One program, called "Con Cam," broadcasts videos of prisoners as they go about their daily business—making homemade knives in the prison workshop, extorting money from weaker prisoners, and buying drugs from the guards (perfectly legal of course). But the most widely watched televised spin-off of the private prison system is the hugely popular "Who Wants to Live?" A month before his or her execution, the condemned prisoner is introduced to the viewing audience, which then submits suggestions for the manner and method of execution— hanging, firing squad, disembowelment, drawing and quartering, and other even more ingenious means. This supplies special incentive to the prisoner and his or her allies in the anti-death penalty movement to raise money for release or at least commutation of the death penalty. The ensuing bidding war is fierce and frenetic. In most instances, the prisoners lose (unless of course they are wealthy enough to outbid their opponents). Two days before the scheduled execution a final vote is taken. The rule is, "One Rothbard, one vote." Some viewers— especially members of the victim's family—are prepared to pay thousands or even millions of Rothbards to ensure the grisliest of deaths for the condemned. And this in turn ensures an even larger viewing audience and therefore increased advertising revenues.

Marketopians love to be entertained and amused. Most television stations do not broadcast depressing programs; there isn't much of a market. This means that reports about floods, famines, airplane crashes, and Middle Eastern politics are not featured on the most widely watched news programs (although they are shown again and again on the Catastrophe Channel). The news and entertainment divisions within broadcasting were merged long ago and the former made a minor part of the latter. To attract viewers, television stations employ such slogans as "News to amuse." One of the most popular news broadcasts is "The Happy News Hour" on PBS, the Private Broadcasting Service.

Although there are lonely people in Marketopia, they needn't remain lonely for long, if they have a desire for company and the means to pay for it. One of Marketopia's more thriving enterprises is Rent-a-Friend. For ten Rothbards an hour one can rent an "acquaintance," for twenty-five a "friend," for fifty a "good friend," and for one-hundred a "best friend." For those who prefer non-human companionship, Rent-a-Pet (a wholly-owned subsidiary of Rent-a-Friend) provides dogs, cats, goldfish, gerbils, pot-bellied pigs, and many other animals for periods ranging from one day to the lifetime of the animal. Renters who tire of or wish to trade their animal companions for another species can do so. Or, for a small additional fee, they can have their rented pets painlessly euthanized.

Other useful services are also available for a fee. For example, from Sycophants, Inc. you can rent a flatterer to follow you around and praise you either in private (for fifty Rothbards per hour) or in public (a hundred per hour). For the athletically inclined, there is Losers, Ltd. From Losers you can rent a partner to play tennis or squash, one-on-one basketball, billiards, darts, and even poker, chess, and other more cerebral and sedentary games. Losers' slogan is "You win, we lose—guaranteed." Rates vary according to the game and other factors, for which there is a rather elaborate rate schedule. White basketball players, for example, pay premium rates to play against very tall black men who cannot jump or shoot accurately. Chess enthusiasts pay more to play against opponents with Russian names and accents to match.

On an even brighter note, love and marriage flourish in Marketopia. The marriage market and the marriage contract are important parts of Marketopian life. Dating services and marriage brokers abound. For the former, one fills out a form on which one lists one's preferences for (say) a non-smoking Caucasian blond meat-eating jogger who is willing to consider having sex on the first date and for a reasonable fee or exchange of services. Marriage is a more serious business, as assets are involved. The marriage contract stipulates what assets each partner will bring to the marriage, which assets they are (or are not) willing to share, how frequently they will engage in sex (and what fee or exchange is involved), how many children they will have (and what the wife will charge the husband for the inconvenience of pregnancy and the pain of childbirth), and so on and on. Some especially wealthy men "upgrade" by exchanging older wives for newer and younger models; wealthy women do the same. The terms on which marriages are to be dissolved, upgraded, or added to (polygamy is perfectly legal) are specified in the marriage contract, which typically runs to forty or more closely printed pages and is periodically renegotiated.

Family values flourish in Marketopia, and children soon learn that the value of being a member of a family can be considerable. For example, a mother might ask her son to "Give Mommy a kiss." To which the son typically replies, "What's it worth to you?" The mother will then say something like, "Two Rothbards." "Four," he says flatly and firmly. She nods, and as he pecks her cheek, she opens her purse and says proudly with a warm maternal smile, "That's my boy. The best bargainer a mother ever had."

Looking through private high school yearbooks reveals that some students are singled out for special meritorious mention as "Most Calculating" or "Shrewdest Negotiator." These youths can be expected to excel at Sumner University.

William Graham Sumner University—a private institution, as are all institutions in Marketopia—is not only "run like a business," it *is* a business, and a very profitable one at that. A grade of "A" can be purchased for the relatively modest sum of five hundred Rothbards, a "B" for four hundred, a "C" for three hundred. Professors—called SPs (short for "service providers")—are eager to teach large undergraduate courses because their salaries are determined by the number of students (called "customers") whose "grade fees" go half to the SP and half to help maintain the institution. Sumner University has no philosophy department, in part because there is insufficient demand, but also because the subjects of ethics and political philosophy are included in the economics curriculum and restricted to works by Robert Nozick, F.A. Hayek, Milton Friedman, and a few other luminaries. There have long been rumors that some students meet secretly to read John Rawls, Karl Marx, Thomas More, and other authors excluded from the curriculum. The rumors appear to be unfounded, however, as acquaintance with these thinkers would hardly advance one's career and would therefore amount to a cost without a corresponding benefit.

All research at Sumner and other centers of higher learning is financed by large corporations. The tobacco industry supports research on smoking and health. Large pharmaceutical firms finance research on drug safety and effectiveness. The chemical industry supports research on the toxicity of herbicides, pesticides, and other chemicals. The mining and timber industries support environmental research. And agribusiness firms are generous in their funding of research on the health and environmental effects of genetically engineered fruits, vegetables, grains, and other crops. Pioneering research at Sumner University has shown that—contrary to a once-popular but now discredited belief—there is no link between smoking and cancers of the lung, throat, and other organs. Nor, as researchers have discovered, are there any adverse effects from any of the commonly used prescription drugs. Their colleagues have also shown scientifically that genetically engineered crops are beneficial both for human health and the natural environment. The same is also true of the new and improved pesticides and herbicides.

Clearly, the people of Marketopia have much to be thankful for. And so, not surprisingly, many Marketopians are religious. There are statues of and shrines to Saint Murray, Saint Milton, Saint Gary—and of course the female saints Ayn and Margaret—and other holy personages. The Austrian saints Ludwig and Friedrich are especially revered. Sacred scripture—found particularly in *The Book of Mammon*—is avidly studied and many Marketopians can quote key scriptures from memory. "What profiteth a person who gaineth his soul but loseth his livelihood?" "It is easier for a rich man to enter the kingdom of heaven." "Do unto others before they do unto you." "Render unto Caesar that which is Caesar's, lest thou not get thy pizza." "The love of money is the root of all good" (this passage is also reprinted on the Rothbard). Especially beloved is the story of Saint Gary's Sermon in the Valley, in which he preached the gospel of self-love while selling day-old loaves and fish fingers. These and other scriptures constitute much of the moral instruction of the young and are a source of solace and comfort for the old.

Last, and certainly least, is politics and citizenship in Marketopia. With the Marketopians' minimal state comes minimal politics. Since most activities and services are privatized, there is little for government to do. Elected officials hurl taunts and insults at one another, and bemused Marketopians view what passes for politics as a form of entertainment closely akin to professional wrestling—which helps explain why professional wrestlers are often elected to public office. Many Marketopians vote for candidates they regard as having the greatest entertainment value. Most, however, sell their votes to the highest bidder in online election-year auctions.[1] Of late there has been much discussion about amending the Marketopian constitution because it does not, at present, allow voters to register the intensity of their preferences at the polls. A proposed amendment would remedy this defect by allowing voters to pay one-hundred Rothbards per vote for as many times as they care to cast a vote.

II

I lack the wit to extend this parable any further. My point in introducing it is to raise three questions. First, why do some (or perhaps all) Marketopian practices make many—perhaps most—of us uneasy or queasy, or worse? Second, what further distortions would the practices I've described introduce into our moral, political, and legal language and thus into our thinking and our practices? And third, are we in several respects already living in Marketopia or at least heading in that direction?

By and large, markets are a good thing—they offer a reasonably efficient means of discerning and satisfying people's preferences, of allocating goods and resources, and rewarding the more enterprising members of a society. The prospect of making a profit is clearly a powerful motive for many people, and the genius of markets is to harness self-interest for purposes that bring general benefits. As Adam Smith famously put it, "It is not from the benevolence of the butcher, the brewer, or the baker that we expect our dinner, but from their regard to their own interest. We address ourselves, not to their humanity but to their self-love, and never talk to them of our own necessities but of their advantages."[2]

So, if markets are such a good thing, why not let them work their magic in any and every sphere of social life? Why not (for example) buy and sell human organs and other things not traded in markets (or rather, in non-black markets)? Why do we balk at extending the sway of the market into these and many other areas?

To these questions modern libertarians and economists of the Chicago School have a ready answer: only blind, unthinking, and irrational prejudice prevents us from making all (or perhaps most) human interactions into market transactions. As Gary Becker argues in *The Economic Approach to Human Behavior*, we not only ought to think and act as self-interested agents but we are already acting (if not yet thinking) in precisely those ways.[3] We are each of us self-interested calculators of our own advantage, however much we might wish to hide that fact from others and even (or perhaps especially) from ourselves. Honesty and candor compel us to own up to that fact and drop the self-serving pretence that we sometimes act altruistically and even against our own interests in hopes of helping our fellow human beings. Even our ostensibly selfless actions are in actuality selfish: if we help others, that is only to help ourselves feel better. Thus there can be, by definition, no selfless acts. Or, if there are, they are, again by definition, irrational. (This is of course an oversimplification bordering on caricature. A good caricature, however, not only contains a grain of truth, but highlights significant features of the object or person it depicts.)

Perhaps it's only an ancient and widespread prejudice that prevents us from turning every good and activity into a marketable commodity. But as Edmund Burke and other traditional conservatives remind us, long-standing prejudices often have rational bases. We overturn certain prejudices at our peril. Such, I believe, are the prejudices against allowing a market in anything and everything. There are very good reasons for our prejudice against, say, auctioning off human organs to the highest bidder or making police protection available only to those who can afford to pay for it or turning executions into televised pay-per-view entertainment. These reasons have to do with our commitment to equality and fairness in the distribution of social goods.

The main shortcoming of Marketopia is its massive and systematic violation of a fundamental sense of fairness. Marketopians who cannot afford health care, education, police protection, and other of life's necessities are denied a fair (or even minimally sufficient) share of social goods. Indeed, they are destitute of every good, excluded from a just share of society's benefits and advantages, pushed to the margins, and rendered invisible (as in my utopian sketch). They are excluded because they lack the resources to purchase goods and services that ought to be theirs by right. Marketopia is not only an unjust society but an indecent one. The argument against Marketopian libertarianism is as much about decency as it is about justice.

The libertarian turn toward free markets is marked by an attempt to alter radically the very vocabulary we use in describing and appraising human action. Martin Heidegger once remarked with uncharacteristic clarity that we do not so much have a language as it has us. James Boyd White makes a similar point. "In important ways," he writes, "we become the language that we use," inasmuch as "the languages we speak, and the cultural practices they at once reflect and make possible, mark or form our minds by habituating them to certain forms of attention, certain ways of seeing and conceiving of oneself and of the world."[4] Who or what do we become, once we begin to speak the language of libertarianism and of free-market economics? For, whatever its status as a science, the discipline of economics has a linguistic or rhetorical dimension.[5] Economics supplies a *language of redescription*—a set of concepts and categories with which one may recast the ways in which we describe and justify our actions, institutions, and practices. And in a capitalist-consumer culture like ours, this discourse appears to have a special authority. To speak and think in its idiom seems straightforward and admirably hard-headed.

By way of illustration, consider what Anthony Downs does in his now-classic contribution to rational-choice theory, *An Economic Theory of Democracy*. Political parties and candidates are redescribed as "entrepreneurs," competing with one another for the votes of "consumers," who will "spend" their votes (and bear the "costs" of voting) for the parties and candidates that they believe will best promote their interests.[6] Such redescriptions are not normatively neutral inasmuch as they can supplant civic discourse, redirecting our attention and reshaping our characters and conduct. Our social and civic world is to a very large degree linguistically or conceptually constituted: as we speak, so do we think, and therefore act. If we redescribe our political actions and institutions in Downs's idiom, we must forgo the older republican language of civic virtue, public service, duties, and obligations. The two discourses are incompatible.[7]

Another example, from my own social sphere: at two American universities with which I have been associated in recent years, the administration (and some faculty) say that the university should become more "entrepreneurial," that it should expand its "customer base" and therefore its "market share" in competition with other institutions. Faculty are "service providers" and students are "customers" for whose patronage departments and programs should compete. This is not merely a way of speaking but of thinking and acting. For example, those departments with the highest number of paying customers should, it is said, be rewarded accordingly, and those with lower enrollments punished, perhaps even by being eliminated altogether. (Under such schemes, needless to say, the business school fares far better than the philosophy department.) Deans and department chairs warn faculty members who teach intellectually demanding courses to "dumb them down" in order to attract more customers. Surveys are conducted to assess "customer satisfaction" with the "product" being delivered. And since the customers tend to be young, inexperienced, and desirous of being entertained while getting good grades, they gravitate toward courses that deliver the goods. The result, unsurprisingly, is not only grade inflation but a dumbing down of the curriculum and therefore, alas, of the "customers" themselves. To redescribe the place of education and the role of the educator in the language of the market is not to speak in a normatively neutral or innocent idiom. It has very real and problematic implications.

This is of course only a small part of a much larger trend toward the increasing marketization of moral, political, and pedagogical discourse. Our changing language may well presage a move toward Marketopia, which we ought to view with alarm. And by "we" I do not mean merely academics who fear being demoted from educators to "service providers." I mean that we as citizens have good grounds for fearing that the language of markets and consumership may be supplanting the language of citizenship and the capacity for critical thinking that it requires and promotes.

We have good grounds for acting while we still have the capacity. For whether our society will resemble Marketopia is a matter of choice—first, of the individual choices that we make as consumers and then, more decisively, of the collective choices that we make as citizens. What is to be the proper place of markets is not itself an economic question but a matter for political deliberation. Markets in their proper place may produce admirable and beneficial results, but markets have limitations as well as virtues—a point persuasively argued by Robert Kuttner in *Everything For Sale* and Thomas Frank in *One Market, Under God*.[8]

Doubts about free-market ideology are spreading. Recent experiences in California, for example, have raised doubts about the wisdom of privatizing electrical power generation and distribution. There is also a growing awareness in the United States and beyond of the downside of unregulated or "free" markets in general, and of neoliberalism in particular. The most spectacular example of the first came in 2007 when largely unregulated big banks and other financial institutions began to fall like dominoes, one after the other, until the federal government injected over a trillion dollars to prop them up and bail them out. As a result of this financial meltdown, millions of Americans lost their jobs, many lost their homes, and some their hope, in the worst financial crisis since the Great Depression. Calls for increased regulation came from liberals and even from some conservatives. Some called for a "new New Deal" to rescue jobless workers, homeowners, investors, and retirees whose pensions were wiped out. And in 2011 the "Occupy Wall Street" movement spread from New York to cities across the country, calling for government to hold corporations, big banks, and other financial institutions accountable for their actions.

That movement, and earlier protests in Seattle and elsewhere against the World Trade Organization and other bastions of neoliberalism could prove to be opening wedges in what promises to be a long and no doubt difficult struggle against the encroachments of the market mentality into non-economic spheres. Revitalized labor unions and a growing Green movement are important allies in this struggle. But so are religious communities—Jewish, Muslim, Buddhist, Catholic, Protestant—which are becoming more vocally critical of consumerism, welfare cuts, environmental degradation, and growing inequality. There may be alliances to be forged among these diverse groups. Politics can still make strange bedfellows.

In a capitalist-consumer society like ours, the discourse of competition and markets seems to be normal, natural, and unexceptionable. Yet this discourse seeps into and influences our understanding of who we are and what we as a society are about. Indeed, this discourse is well-nigh pervasive in our culture. And it is precisely because market-thinking is so central to our capitalist-consumer culture that we should be all the more acutely aware of what it misses, marginalizes, trivializes, or undermines and destroys. As Michael Walzer writes in *Spheres of Justice*, "Market relations are expansive. A radically *laissez-faire* economy would be like a totalitarian state, invading every other sphere, dominating every other distributive process. It would transform every social good into a commodity. This is market imperialism."[9] Walzer goes on to argue that the market's imperialist tendencies can best be tamed and checked by an active and attentive democratic citizenry, wary of the inequalities and injustices—and indecencies— wrought by the free play of market forces.

Why does Marketopia strike most of us as a dystopia? Surely it is because in this context market relations become the totality of human relations. Where everything is for sale, nothing is sacred. Where value is equated with price, nothing is intrinsically valuable. Marketopians (some of them, anyway) may be rich in material ways, but they live impoverished lives.

Postscript 2013

Since this essay was first published in 2001 and revised slightly in 2012 American society seems to have marched ever more steadily toward Marketopia. If you doubt it, you need only read Michael Sandel's deeply disturbing new book, *What Money Can't Buy: The Moral Limits of Markets.*[10] Sandel catalogues a very long list of commercial or market intrusions into everyday life, from baseball games to the school classroom. For example, home runs in professional baseball now have a corporate sponsor, New York Life Insurance. "When the umpire calls a runner safe at home plate," Sandel tells us, "a corporate logo appears on the television screen, and the play-by-play announcer must say, 'Safe at home. Safe and secure. New York Life." It is now commonplace for cash-strapped public schools to sell naming rights to auditoriums, athletic fields, and other school sites. As of 2011 seven states had passed legislation allowing advertisements to appear on the sides of school buses. As more public schools become ever more financially beleaguered we can expect their number to grow steadily if not exponentially. And this is only the thin edge of a much larger wedge.

The problem with such corporate-market encroachments, Sandel says, is that we have gone from being a "market economy" to a "market *society*" in which almost everything is for sale. The result is that market values are crowding out and replacing civic values. And that should be cause for concern for any small-d democrat.

NOTES

1   When I first wrote this I meant it as a parody of a possible world that did not (yet) exist. But in 2000 the *New York Times* reported on a now-defunct website—voteauction. com—where voters could sell their votes to the highest bidders. "The site ... boasts that it is 'bringing capitalism and democracy closer together.' It offers to buy the absentee ballots of undecided voters and then allow organizations and individuals to bid for a block of votes from a state ... [V]ote prices have ranged from $10 to $20 each." (*New York Times*, October 20, 2000, p. A23.)

2   Adam Smith, *The Wealth of Nations* (1776; Oxford: Oxford University Press, 1979), Volume 1, Book I, chapter 2 (pp. 26–27); reprinted in Ball, Dagger, and O'Neill, eds., *Ideals and Ideologies*, 10th edition, selection 3.16.

3   Gary Becker, *The Economic Approach to Human Behavior* (Chicago: University of Chicago Press, 1976).

4   James Boyd White, "Economics and Law: Two Cultures in Tension," *Tennessee Law Review*, 54 (Winter, 1987), pp. 161–202, at p. 166.

5   See Deirdre McCloskey, *The Rhetoric of Economics*, 2nd edition (Madison: University of Wisconsin Press, 1998).

6   Anthony Downs, *An Economic Theory of Democracy* (New York: Addison-Wesley, 1957).

7   See Terence Ball, *Transforming Political Discourse* (Oxford: Blackwell, 1988), Chapter 6, "The Economic Reconstruction of Democratic Discourse."

8   Robert Kuttner, *Everything for Sale: The Virtues and Limits of Markets* (New York: Knopf, 1997); and Thomas Frank, *One Market, Under God* (New York: Doubleday, 2000).

9   Michael Walzer, *Spheres of Justice* (New York: Basic Books, 1983), pp. 119–120.

10 Michael J. Sandel, *What Money Can't Buy: The Moral Limits of Markets* (New York: Farrar, Straus and Giroux, 2012).

PART 4

CONSERVATISM

As the name "conservatism" suggests, conservatives share a desire to *conserve* something—usually the traditions or customary way of life in their societies. Thus, conservatives generally resist change and prefer to cling to the "tried and true" or "time-tested" ways. But different conservatives have different ideas about what is valuable and worth preserving. Besides that, traditions and customs vary widely from one society to another, so a conservative in one society may want to preserve traditions that are at odds with the traditions of another society. Conservatives may all want to conserve something, in other words, but they do not all want to conserve the same things—and that is what makes their ideology so difficult to define in any simple or straightforward way.

For Edmund Burke (1729/30–1797), widely regarded as the father of conservatism, the desire to conserve a traditional way of life is quite clear. The most famous writings of Burke—an Irishman who served for many years as a member of the British Parliament—were directed against the French Revolution, which he saw as a misguided attempt to create an entirely new kind of society based on abstract theory and human reason. The revolutionaries, he charged in *Reflections on the Revolution in France* (1790), are attacking all of the institutions—the king, the aristocracy, the church—that give order and stability to their country. If they succeed, Burke said, they will find themselves and their society adrift in a storm-tossed sea, all sail and no anchor.

Burke, like later conservatives, recognized that change is an inevitable part of life. But he believed that change can occur in either a healthy or a dangerous way. If it is the result of gradual or piecemeal reform, it will promote the health of society. But rapid change and radical innovation are likely to prove disastrous. Revolutionaries who want to transform whole societies overnight are like people who tear down their old house, only to find themselves freezing to death before they can build a new one.

Burke wrote his *Reflections* less out of concern for the future of France than out of fear that the revolution would inspire similar upheaval in England. He did not argue, in any case, that France could and should go back to the way things were before the revolution. But a more extreme group of conservatives reacted in just this way. These "reactionaries," such as Joseph de Maistre (1753–1821), hoped to turn back the clock, returning to a prerevolutionary France guided by "throne and altar," or king and church. Since then, the term "reactionary" has referred to anyone who wants to restore or return to an earlier way of life.

During the first half of the nineteenth century, conservatives generally opposed liberalism and democracy, which they blamed for upsetting the established social order. Liberalism, with its emphasis on the rights and interests of the individual, threatened to tear the delicate fabric of society. A person is not merely an individual, conservatives maintained, but a part of a larger whole who has a duty to other members of the society. When all people are joined together, the society, like the criss-crossing threads of a fabric, is strong and beautiful. When each goes his or her own way, however, the social fabric frays and begins to unravel. Life then becomes dull and drab, especially as capitalism turns the individual's attention to commerce—to "getting and spending" that "lay waste our powers," as the English poet William Wordsworth (1770–1850) put it. Nature, literature, and religion are all reduced in the age of commerce to the lowest common denominator—money.

Many conservatives also regarded democracy as a threat to social order. Like Burke, they believed that human beings are ruled more by their passions than by their reason. If the people govern, who will govern the people? Who or what will keep the common people from destroying their society? At the worst, according to conservatives, democracy will lead to chaos and anarchy because the common people will be too short-sighted to take measures that will restrain their passions and desires. At best, democracy will "level" society by reducing everyone to the same condition. Either way, conservatives warned of the dangers of "mass society"—a warning also sounded in the twentieth century by José Ortega y Gasset (1883–1955) and other writers.

Throughout the twentieth century, an uneasy alliance prevailed between "Burkean" or "classical" conservatives, such as Michael Oakeshott (1901–1990) and Garry Wills (1934–), and modern conservatives, such as British Prime Minister Margaret Thatcher (1925–2013) and U.S. President Ronald Reagan (1911–2004), who declared that government should not "interfere" with individuals competing in the marketplace. The alliance has held together in large part because conservatives of both sorts share a respect for private property, an acceptance (sometimes grudging) of democracy, and a now-fading fear of communism. Now that the communist threat has receded, this conservative alliance is coming under increasing strain.

Whether terrorism will replace communism as a threat that binds conservatives of various kinds together remains to be seen. What is clear, however, is that conservatism now comes in several varieties, including the conservatism of the evangelical Protestants who compose the religious Right in the United States and the conservatism of the increasingly prominent, and controversial, "neoconservatives." As we noted earlier, all conservatives wish to conserve something. But *what* they wish to conserve, and *how* they propose to do it, remain matters of difference and dispute within conservatism.

Society, Reverence, and the "True Natural Aristocracy"

EDMUND BURKE*

When the French Revolution began in 1789, many in England greeted it with enthusiasm. But Edmund Burke (1729/30–1797), an Irishman who moved to England and served for many years in Parliament, saw the revolution as a threat to order and liberty. In his *Reflections on the Revolution in France* (1790), Burke not only criticized the revolutionaries but virtually predicted that the revolution would end in chaos. This and his other speeches and writings—such as the *Appeal from the New to the Old Whigs* (1791), from which the second selection is drawn—have won for Burke the title of father of conservatism.

* *Source*: *The Works of Edmund Burke* (London: George Bell and Sons, 1901), vol. 2, pp. 332–335, 359, 364–369, and vol. 3, pp. 85–87.

REFLECTIONS ON THE REVOLUTION IN FRANCE

Government is not made in virtue of natural rights, which may and do exist in total independence of it; and exist in much greater clearness, and in a much greater degree of abstract perfection: but their abstract perfection is their practical defect. By having a right to every thing they want every thing. Government is a contrivance of human wisdom to provide for human *wants.*[1] Men have a right that these wants should be provided for by this wisdom. Among these wants is to be reckoned the want, out of civil society, of a sufficient restraint upon their passions. Society requires not only that the passions of individuals should be subjected, but that even in the mass and body as well as in the individuals, the inclinations of men should frequently be thwarted, their will controlled, and their passions brought into subjection. This can only be done *by a power out[side] of themselves,* and not, in the exercise of its function, subject to that will and to those passions which it is its office to bridle and subdue. In this sense the restraints on men, as well as their liberties, are to be reckoned among their rights. But as the liberties and the restrictions vary with times and circumstances, and admit of infinite modifications, they cannot be settled upon any abstract rule; and nothing is so foolish as to discuss them upon that principle.

The moment you abate any thing from the full rights of men, each to govern himself, and suffer any artificial positive limitation upon those rights, from that moment the whole organization of government becomes a consideration of convenience. This it is which makes the constitution of a state, and the due distribution of its powers, a matter of the most delicate and complicated skill. It requires a deep knowledge of human nature and human necessities, and of the things which facilitate or obstruct the various ends which are to be pursued by the mechanism of civil institutions. The state is to have recruits to its strength, and remedies to its distempers. What is the use of discussing a man's abstract right to food or to medicine? The question is upon the method of procuring and administering them. In that deliberation I shall always advise to call in the aid of the farmer and the physician, rather than the professor of metaphysics.

The science of constructing a commonwealth, or renovating it, or reforming it, is, like every other experimental science, not to be taught *a priori.* Nor is it a short experience that can instruct us in that practical science; because the real effects of moral causes are not always immediate; but that which in the first instance is prejudicial may be excellent in its remoter operation; and its excellence may arise even … from the ill effects it produces in the beginning. The reverse also happens; and very plausible schemes, with very pleasing commencements, have often shameful and lamentable conclusions. In states there are often some obscure and almost latent causes, things which appear at first view of little moment, on which a very great part of its prosperity or adversity may most essentially depend. The science of government being therefore so practical in itself, and intended for such practical purposes, a matter which requires experience, and even more experience than any person can gain in his whole life, however sagacious and observing he may be, it is with infinite caution that any man ought to venture upon pulling down an edifice which has answered in any tolerable degree for ages the common purposes of society, or on building it up again, without having models and patterns of approved utility before his eyes.

These metaphysic rights entering into common life, like rays of light which pierce into a dense medium, are, by the laws of nature, refracted from their straight line. Indeed in the gross and complicated mass of human passions and concerns, the primitive rights of men undergo such a variety of refractions and reflections, that it becomes absurd to talk of them as if they continued in the simplicity of their original direction. The nature of man is intricate; the objects of society are of the greatest possible complexity; and therefore no simple disposition or direction of power can be suitable either to man's nature, or to the quality of his affairs. When I hear the simplicity of contrivance aimed at and boasted of in any new political constitutions, I am at no loss to decide that the artificers are grossly ignorant of their trade, or totally negligent of their duty. The simple governments are fundamentally defective, to say no worse of them. If you were to contemplate society in but one point of view, all these simple modes of polity are infinitely captivating. In effect each would answer its single end much more perfectly than the more complex is able to attain all its complex purposes. But it is better that the whole should be imperfectly and anomalously answered, than that, while some parts are provided for with great exactness, others might be totally neglected, or perhaps materially injured, by the over-care of a favourite member.

The pretended rights of these theorists are all extremes; and in proportion as they are metaphysically true, they are morally and politically false. The rights of men are in a sort of *middle*, incapable of definition, but not impossible to be discerned. The rights of men in governments are their advantages; and these are often in balances between differences of good; in compromises sometimes between good and evil, and sometimes, between evil and evil. Political reason is a computing principle; adding, subtracting, multiplying, and dividing, morally and not metaphysically or mathematically, true moral denominations.

By these theorists the right of the people is almost always sophistically confounded with their power. The body of the community, whenever it can come to act, can meet with no effectual resistance; but till power and right are the same, the whole body of them has no right inconsistent with virtue, and the first of all virtues, prudence. Men have no right to what is not reasonable, and to what is not for their benefit …

We preserve the whole of our feelings still native and entire, unsophisticated by pedantry and infidelity. We have real hearts of flesh and blood beating in our bosoms. We fear God; we look up with awe to kings; with affection to parliaments; with duty to magistrates; with reverence to priests; and with respect to nobility. Why? Because when such ideas are brought before our minds, it is *natural* to be so affected; because all other feelings are false and spurious, and tend to corrupt our minds, to vitiate our primary morals, to render us unfit for rational liberty; and by teaching us a servile, licentious, and abandoned insolence, to be our low sport for a few holidays to make us perfectly fit for, and justly deserving of slavery, through the whole course of our lives.

You see, Sir, that in this enlightened age I am bold enough to confess, that we are generally men of untaught feelings; that instead of casting away all our old prejudices, we cherish them to a very considerable degree, and, to take more shame to ourselves, we cherish them because they are prejudices;[2] and the longer they have lasted, and the more generally they have prevailed, the more we cherish them. We are afraid to put men to live and trade each on his own private stock of reason; because we suspect that this stock in each man is small, and that the individuals would do better to avail themselves of the general bank and capital of nations, and of ages. Many of our men of speculation, instead of exploding general prejudices, employ their sagacity to discover the latent wisdom which prevails in them. If they find what they seek, and they seldom fail, they think it more wise to continue the prejudice, with the reason involved, than to cast away the coat of prejudice, and to leave nothing but the naked reason; because prejudice, with its reason, has a motive to give action to that reason, and an affection which will give it permanence. Prejudice is of ready application in the emergency; it previously engages the mind in a steady course of wisdom and virtue, and does not leave the man hesitating in the moment of decision, sceptical, puzzled, and unresolved. Prejudice renders a man's virtue his habit; and not a series of unconnected acts. Through just prejudice, his duty becomes a part of his nature ...

The consecration of the state, by a state religious establishment, is necessary also to operate with an wholesome awe upon free citizens; because, in order to secure their freedom, they must enjoy some determinate portion of power. To them therefore a religion connected with the state, and with their duty towards it, becomes even more necessary than in such societies, where the people by the terms of their subjection are confined to private sentiments, and the management of their own family concerns. All persons possessing any portion of power ought to be strongly and awefully impressed with an idea that they act in trust; and that they are to account for their conduct in that trust to the one great master, author and founder of society.

This principle ought even to be more strongly impressed upon the minds of those who compose the collective sovereignty than upon those of single princes. Without instruments, these princes can do nothing. Whoever uses instruments, in finding helps, finds also impediments. Their power is therefore by no means compleat; nor are they safe in extreme abuse. Such persons, however elated by flattery, arrogance, and self-opinion, must be sensible that, whether covered or not by positive law, in some way or other they are accountable even here for the abuse of their trust. If they are not cut off by a rebellion of their people, they may be strangled by the very Janissaries kept for their security against all other rebellion.[3] Thus we have seen the king of France sold by his soldiers for an increase of pay. But where popular authority is absolute and unrestrained, the people have an infinitely greater, because a far better founded, confidence in their own power. They are themselves, in a great measure, their own instruments. They are nearer to their objects. Besides, they are less under responsibility to one of the greatest controlling powers on earth, the sense of fame and estimation. The share of infamy that is likely to fall to the lot of each individual in public acts, is small indeed; the operation of opinion being in the inverse ratio to the number of those who abuse power. Their own approbation of their own acts has to them the appearance of a public judgment in their favour. A perfect democracy is therefore the most shameless thing in the world. As it is the most shameless, it is also the most fearless. No man apprehends in his person he can be made subject to punishment. Certainly the people at large never ought: for as all punishments are for example towards the conservation of the people at large, the people at large can never become the subject of punishment by any human hand. It is therefore of infinite importance that they should not be suffered to imagine that their will, any more than that of kings, is the standard of right and wrong. They ought to be persuaded that they are full as little entitled, and far less qualified, with safety to themselves, to use any arbitrary power whatsoever; that therefore they are not, under a false show of liberty, but, in truth, to exercise an unnatural inverted domination, tyrannically to exact, from those who officiate in the state, not an entire devotion to their interest, which is their right, but an abject submission to their occasional will; extinguishing thereby, in all those who serve them, all moral principle, all sense of dignity, all use of judgment, and all consistency of character, whilst by the very same process they give themselves up a proper, a suitable, but a more contemptible prey to the servile ambition of popular sycophants or courtly flatterers.

When the people have emptied themselves of all the lust of selfish will, which without religion it is utterly impossible they ever should, when they are conscious that they exercise, and exercise perhaps in an higher link of the order of delegation, the power, which to be legitimate must be according to that eternal immutable law, in which will and reason are the same, they will be more careful how they place power in base and incapable hands. In their nomination to office, they will not appoint to the exercise of authority, as to a pitiful job, but as to a holy function; not according to their sordid selfish interest, nor to their wanton caprice, nor to their arbitrary will; but they will confer that power (which any man may well tremble to give or to receive) on those only, in whom they may discern that predominant proportion of active virtue and wisdom, taken together and fitted to the charge, such as in the great and inevitable mixed mass of human imperfections and infirmities, is to be found.

When they are habitually convinced that no evil can be acceptable, either in the act or the permission, to him whose essence is good, they will be better able to extirpate out of the minds of all magistrates, civil, ecclesiastical, or military, any thing that bears the least resemblance to a proud and lawless domination.

But one of the first and most leading principles on which the commonwealth and the laws are consecrated, is lest the temporary possessors and life-renters in it, unmindful of what they have received from their ancestors, or of what is due to their posterity, should act as if they were the entire masters; that they should not think it amongst their rights to cut off the entail, or commit waste on the inheritance, by destroying at their pleasure the whole original fabric of their society; hazarding to leave to those who come after them, a ruin instead of an habitation—and teaching these successors as little to respect their contrivances, as they had themselves respected the institutions of their forefathers. By this unprincipled facility of changing the state as often, and as much, and in as many ways as there are floating fancies or fashions, the whole chain and continuity of the commonwealth would be broken. No one generation could link with the other. Men would become little better than the flies of a summer.

And first of all the science of jurisprudence, the pride of the human intellect, which, with all its defects, redundancies, and errors, is the collected reason of ages, combining the principles of original justice with the infinite variety of human concerns, as a heap of old exploded errors, would be no longer studied. Personal self-sufficiency and arrogance (the certain attendants upon all those who have never experienced a wisdom greater than their own) would usurp the tribunal. Of course, no certain laws, establishing invariable grounds of hope and fear, would keep the actions of men in a certain course, or direct them to a certain end. Nothing stable in the modes of holding property, or exercising function, could form a solid ground on which any parent could speculate in the education of his offspring, or in a choice for their future establishment in the world. No principles would be early worked into the habits. As soon as the most able instructor had completed his laborious course of instruction, instead of sending forth his pupil, accomplished in a virtuous discipline, fitted to procure him attention and respect, in his place in society, he would find every thing altered; and that he had turned out a poor creature to the contempt and derision of the world, ignorant of the true grounds of estimation. Who would insure a tender and delicate sense of honour to beat almost with the first pulses of the heart, when no man could know what would be the test of honour in a nation, continually varying the standard of its coin? No part of life would retain its acquisitions. Barbarism with regard to science and literature, unskilfulness with regard to arts and manufactures, would infallibly succeed to the want of a steady education and settled principle; and thus the commonwealth itself would, in a few generations, crumble away, be disconnected into the dust and powder of individuality, and at length dispersed to all the winds of heaven.

To avoid therefore the evils of inconstancy and versatility, ten thousand times worse than those of obstinacy and the blindest prejudice, we have consecrated the state, that no man should approach to look into its defects or corruptions but with due caution; that he should never dream of beginning its reformation by its subversion; that he should approach to the faults of the state as to the wounds of a father, with pious awe and trembling solicitude. By this wise prejudice we are taught to look with horror on those children of their country who are prompt rashly to hack that aged parent in pieces, and put him into the kettle of magicians, in hopes that by their poisonous weeds, and wild incantations, they may regenerate the paternal constitution, and renovate their father's life.

Society is indeed a contract. Subordinate contracts for objects of mere occasional interest may be dissolved at pleasure—but the state ought not to be considered as nothing better than a partnership agreement in a trade of pepper and coffee, callico or tobacco, or some other such low concern, to be taken up for a little temporary interest, and to be dissolved by the fancy of the parties. It is to be looked on with other reverence; because it is not a partnership in things subservient only to the gross animal existence of a temporary and perishable nature. It is a partnership in all science; a partnership in all art; a partnership in every virtue, and in all perfection. As the ends of such a partnership cannot be obtained in many generations, it becomes a partnership not only between those who are living, but between those who are living, those who are dead, and those who are to be born. Each contract of each particular state is but a clause in the great primeval contract of eternal society, linking the lower with the higher natures, connecting the visible and invisible world, according to a fixed compact sanctioned by the inviolable oath which holds all physical and all moral natures, each in their appointed place.

APPEAL FROM THE NEW TO THE OLD WHIGS

… To enable men to act with the weight and character of a people, and to answer the ends for which they are incorporated into that capacity, we must suppose them (by means immediate or consequential) to be in that state of habitual social discipline in which the wiser, the more expert, and the more opulent conduct, and by conducting enlighten and protect, the weaker, the less knowing, and the less provided with the goods of fortune. When the multitude are not under this discipline, they can scarcely be said to be in civil society …

A true natural aristocracy is not a separate interest in the state, or separable from it. It is an essential integrant part of any large body rightly constituted. It is formed out of a class of legitimate presumptions, which, taken as generalities, must be admitted for actual truths. To be bred in a place of estimation; to see nothing low and sordid from one's infancy; to be taught to respect one's self; to be habituated to the censorial inspection of the public eye; to look early to public opinion; to stand upon such elevated ground as to be enabled to take a large view of the widespread and infinitely diversified combinations of men and affairs in a large society; to have leisure to read, to reflect, to converse; to be enabled to draw the court and attention of the wise and learned, wherever they are to be found; to be habituated in armies to command and to obey; to be taught to despise danger in the pursuit of honor and duty; to be formed to the greatest degree of vigilance, foresight, and circumspection, in a state of things in which no fault is committed with impunity and the slightest mistakes draw on the most ruinous consequences; to be led to a guarded and regulated conduct, from a sense that you are considered as an instructor of your fellow-citizens in their highest concerns, and that you act as a reconciler between God and man; to be employed as an administrator of law and justice, and to be thereby amongst the first benefactors to mankind; to be a professor of high science, or of liberal and ingenuous art; to be amongst rich traders, who from their success are presumed to have sharp and vigorous understandings, and to possess the virtues of diligence, order, constancy, and regularity, and to have cultivated an habitual regard to commutative justice: these are the circumstances of men that form what I should call a *natural* aristocracy, without which there is no nation.

The state of civil society which necessarily generates this aristocracy is a state of Nature,—and much more truly so than a savage and incoherent mode of life. For man is by nature reasonable; and he is never perfectly in his natural state, but when he is placed where reason may be best cultivated and most predominates. Art is man's nature. We are as much, at least, in a state of Nature in formed manhood as in immature and helpless infancy. Men, qualified in the manner I have just described, form in Nature, as she operates in the common modification of society, the leading, guiding, and governing part. It is the soul to the body, without which the man does not exist. To give, therefore, no more importance, in the social order, to such descriptions of men than that of so many units is a horrible usurpation.

When great multitudes act together, under that discipline of Nature, I recognize the PEOPLE. I acknowledge something that perhaps equals, and ought always to guide, the sovereignty of convention. In all things the voice of this grand chorus of national harmony ought to have a mighty and decisive influence. But when you disturb this harmony,—when you break up this beautiful order, this array of truth and Nature, as well as of habit and prejudice,—when you separate the common sort of men from their proper chieftains, so as to form them into an adverse army,—I no longer know that venerable object called the people in such a disbanded race of deserters and vagabonds. For a while they may be terrible, indeed,—but in such a manner as wild beasts are terrible. The mind owes to them no sort of submission. They are, as they have always been reputed, rebels.

NOTES

1   By "wants" Burke does not mean wishes or desires but "defects" or "lacks," as when we might (at the risk of sounding old-fashioned) say that the bicycle cannot be ridden because it wants a wheel.—Eds.

2   As Burke uses the term, "prejudices" are habitual, traditional, and/or unreflective prejudgments or biases. Thus the term does not, for Burke, carry the negative connotations it carries today.—Eds.

3   Janissaries were members of an elite military guard in Turkey.—Eds.

Conservatism as Reaction

JOSEPH DE MAISTRE*

On the European continent, some of the aristocratic opponents of the French Revolution saw it as the logical, if terrible, outcome of the eighteenth-century Enlightenment, with its glorification of human reason. Because they reacted against the revolution, these writers came to be known as the "reactionaries" whose ideas constituted the "Counter-Enlightenment." Perhaps the most important writer who sought to restore the old order of European society—with the church, monarchy, and aristocracy firmly in control—was Joseph de Maistre (1753–1821). The following selections are from Maistre's *Considerations on France* (1796) and *Study on Sovereignty* (first published in 1884).

* *Source: Oeuvres Complètes de Joseph de Maistre* (Lyon: Librairie Générale Catholique et Classique, 1891), vol. 1, pp. 74–75, 343–345, 347–348, 353–355, 376–378, 399–400, 424–426, 449–450. Translated from the French by Terence Ball.

CONSIDERATIONS ON FRANCE

The French constitution of 1795, like its predecessors, was made for *man*. Yet the world contains no such creature as *man*. In my lifetime I have seen Frenchmen, Italians, Russians, etc ... but I swear that I have never ever encountered *man*; if he exists, I have missed him ... A constitution which is made for all nations is made for none; it is a pure abstraction, an academic exercise for the mind, modelled after some imaginary hypothesis, and must therefore be addressed to *man*, in whatever imaginary place he dwells.

What is a constitution? Is it not a solution to the following problem? Taking as given the population, customs and traditions, religion, geographical situation, political relations, wealth, the good and bad features of a particular nation, to find the laws that fit it?

Yet, the problem is not raised at all in the constitution of 1795, which was written only with *man* in mind.

STUDY ON SOVEREIGNTY

The Founders and the Political Constitution

The government of a nation is no more its own creation than is its language. Just as in nature the seeds of countless plants are destined to perish unless some human hand puts them where they can sprout, so, analogously, are there in nations particular qualities and potentials which will remain powerless unless aided by circumstances or by some helping hand.

The founder of a nation [*l'instituteur d'un peuple*] is precisely this helping hand. Blessed with an extraordinary penetration—or, more probably, with an infallible instinct (since individual genius rarely realizes what it is achieving, which makes it different from mere intellect)—he detects those hidden potentials and qualities which form the character of a nation, the means of giving them birth, of putting them into action, and putting them to the best possible use. He is never to be seen writing or debating; his manner of proceeding comes from inspiration; and if he sometimes takes pen in hand, it is not to debate but to issue commands.

One of the great errors of our time is to believe that the political constitution of nations is a purely human creation—that a constitution can be created much as a watchmaker manufactures a watch. Nothing could be more false, except perhaps the claim that a constitution can be created by an assembly of men. God gives a government to a nation in only two ways. In most cases he himself makes it grow, so to speak, slowly and like a plant, through that combination of circumstances that we call fortuitous. But when He wants to establish the foundations of a political edifice in a hurry, He imparts His power to a few truly exceptional men. Appearing only rarely through the centuries, these men rise like towering monuments along time's road, becoming ever rarer as the centuries advance. In order to render their unusual service, God equips them with extraordinary powers, which generally go unrecognized by their contemporaries and perhaps even by themselves ...

No important and genuinely constitutional reform ever establishes anything new; it merely declares and defends rights that already exist—which is why one can never know the constitution of a country simply by reading its written laws, since these laws are made in different epochs to declare rights that have been disputed or forgotten, and since many things are never written down ...

The different forms and degrees of sovereignty have led some to think that peoples have modified sovereignty as they please; nothing could be more false. Each people has the government that is suited to it, and yet none has chosen what they have. Even more remarkable is that, whenever a people (or, more precisely, some portion of a people) tries to give itself a government, they make themselves more miserable than before. For in their deep confusion a people invariably mistake their true interests, pursuing what is not good for them while simultaneously rejecting what is good for them. And we all know how terrible are the mistakes made in this field ...

Human power is not able to create [something from nothing], and everything depends on the primordial aptitude of peoples and individuals ... Men never respect what they themselves have created—which is why an elected ruler never possesses the moral force of an hereditary sovereign, since he is not as *noble*, i.e., does not display the kind of grandeur that is independent of men and that comes only through the work of time ...

In short, the majority of people play no part in politics. Indeed, they respect government only because they had no part in creating it. This sentiment is engraved deeply on their hearts and in their habits. They submit to sovereignty because they sense that it is something sacred that they have neither the power to create nor to destroy. If, through corruption and perfidious influences, this preserving sentiment is erased, if they come to the unhappy conclusion that they are required *en masse* to reform the State, then all is lost. This is why, even in free states, it is infinitely important for the men who govern to be separated from the mass of people by that personal respect that results from birth and wealth. For if opinion does not erect a barrier between itself and authority, if power is not outside its grasp, if the governed multitude think themselves equal to the governing few, then there is government no more. Thus the aristocracy is, in essence, a sovereign or ruling class, and the French Revolution a massive violation of the eternal laws of nature.

The National Soul

All nations ever known have been happy and strong insofar as they have unerringly followed the national soul ... i.e., [a people's] useful prejudices. If everyone relied upon his own reason in religion, you would see at once an emerging anarchy of multiple and conflicting beliefs and the destruction of religious sovereignty. Similarly, were each man to make himself the sole judge of the principles of government, you would soon see the rise of civic anarchy and the complete destruction of political sovereignty. Government, like true religion, has its dogmas, its mysteries, its priests. To subject it to individual analysis would destroy it. It has its life only through the national soul, or political faith, i.e., its creed. Man's main need is that his tendency toward [individual and independent] reason should be restricted in two respects: it should be stifled, and it should submerge itself in the national soul, so that it exchanges its individual existence for an alternative *communal* existence, in much the same way that a river flowing into the sea still exists in the larger body of water, but without being distinct from it.

What is patriotism? It is this national soul of which I speak. It is individual *self-denial*. Faith and patriotism are the two great wonders of the world. Both are divine. They work in miraculous ways. Do not speak in their presence of criticism, choice, or debate, for they will reply that you blaspheme. They know only two words, *surrender* and *belief*, with these two levers they lift the earth. Even their mistakes are sublime. These two children of heaven demonstrate their divine origin by making and maintaining; and if they come together, they jointly take possession of a nation, they raise its stature, render it divine, and multiply its power many times over ...

But you, lowly man—can you ignite this sacred fire that inflames nations? Can you impart a shared soul to millions of men? Can you unite them under laws of your own making? Can you give them a common cause? Can you shape the thoughts of future generations? Can you make them obey you and create those conserving prejudices that father the laws and are more powerful than they? How absurd!

The Same Subject Continued

Without doubt reason is, in one sense, good for nothing. We possess the physical knowledge needed to maintain society. We have made great advances in mathematics and the natural sciences. But, once we get beyond our circle of needs, our knowledge becomes either useless or uncertain. The always-restless human mind produces one theory after another. Theories are born, live, wither, and drop like leaves from a tree ...

In the wider moral and political world, what do we know, and what can we do? We *know* the morality bequeathed to us by our parents, as a set of useful prejudices or dogmas believed by the rational mind. But here we owe nothing to anyone's individual reason. On the contrary, whenever this reason has interfered, it has twisted and subverted morality.

We *know*, in political matters, that we must respect those powers ordained by providence. We *know* that when the passage of time produces abuses that can pervert the basic principle of a government, we then need to remove these abuses, although without affecting the principle itself, through a delicate surgical procedure called reform ...

Monarchy

Men are born for monarchy. Of all forms of government, monarchy is the oldest and most universal ... Monarchical government comes so naturally to men that they unwittingly equate it with sovereignty itself. Men appear to agree that, if there is no king, then there is no real *sovereign* ...

Critics who deny the divine origin of monarchy ... [deny] that the authority of kings comes from God. We need to ask, not about *royalty* in particular, but about *sovereignty* in general. All sovereignty has its source in God. Whatever its form, sovereignty is never the work of man. Sovereignty is in its very nature indivisible, inviolable, and absolute ...

Men must always know about history, which is the one and only teacher in politics. Anyone who says that man is born for liberty has taken leave of his senses.

If some superior being tried to write the *natural history* of man, he would have to look at the factual record. When he found what man is and has always been, what he does now and has always done, he would ... reject the foolish idea that man is not what he should be and that his condition contradicts the laws of creation. The mere statement of this proposition suffices to disprove it.

History is the story of political experiments. And just as, in the physical sciences, entire volumes of speculative theories are falsified by a single experiment, so in political science no theory is credible if it is not the highly probable corollary of verified facts. If we ask, "What government is most natural to man?," history will answer: *monarchy* ...

Man is hungry for power, has infinite desires, and—forever unhappy with what he already has—loves only what he does not have. People decry the despotism of princes; they should instead decry the despotism of *man*. We are all born despots, whether we be an absolute Asian monarch or a child who smothers a bird in his hand for the pleasure of proving that other creatures are weaker than himself. There is no man who does not abuse power, and experience shows the worst despots ... are those who rail against despotism. But God has established limits to the abuse of power. He has decreed that power destroy itself once it exceeds its natural limits. This law He has written everywhere. In the physical as well as the moral world, this law surrounds and speaks to us.

Consider a gun: Up to some point, the longer its barrel, the more effective it will be; but once you exceed its natural limit, the less effective it will be ... This is a crude picture of power. To perpetuate itself, power must restrict itself, always stopping short of that limit beyond which its most extreme expression leads to its own destruction.

To be sure, I do not admire *popular* assemblies; but French folly should not blind us to the truth and wisdom of the happy medium. If there is any undeniable maxim, it is this: In all rebellions and revolutions, *the people always begin by being in the right and always end by being in the wrong.*

On Being Conservative

MICHAEL OAKESHOTT*

One of the leading representatives of traditional or "classical" conservatism in the twentieth century was the British philosopher Michael Oakeshott (1901–1990), who insisted that politics must be rooted in tradition and experience, not abstract reason or principles. As he says in his essay "Political Education," "In political activity ... men sail a boundless and bottomless sea; there is neither harbour for shelter nor floor for anchorage, neither starting-place nor appointed destination. The enterprise is to keep afloat on an even keel; the sea is both friend and enemy; and the seamanship consists in using the resources of a traditional manner of behaviour in order to make a friend of every hostile occasion." Oakeshott develops this theme in the following selection from his essay "On Being Conservative."

* *Source*: Michael Oakeshott, *Rationalism in Politics and Other Essays.* Copyright 1962. Reprinted by permission of Basic Books, a member of Perseus Books, L.L.C.

ON BEING CONSERVATIVE

1

The common belief that it is impossible (or, if not impossible, then so unpromising as to be not worth while attempting) to elicit explanatory general principles from what is recognized to be conservative conduct is not one that I share. It may be true that conservative conduct does not readily provoke articulation in the idiom of general ideas, and that consequently there has been a certain reluctance to undertake this kind of elucidation; but it is not to be presumed that conservative conduct is less eligible than any other for this sort of interpretation, for what it is worth. Nevertheless, this is not the enterprise I propose to engage in here. My theme is not a creed or a doctrine, but a disposition. To be conservative is to be disposed to think and behave in certain manners; it is to prefer certain kinds of conduct and certain conditions of human circumstances to others; it is to be disposed to make certain kinds of choices. And my design here is to construe this disposition as it appears in contemporary character, rather than to transpose it into the idiom of general principles.

The general characteristics of this disposition are not difficult to discern, although they have often been mistaken. They centre upon a propensity to use and to enjoy what is available rather than to wish for or to look for something else; to delight in what is present rather than what was or what may be. Reflection may bring to light an appropriate gratefulness for what is available, and consequently the acknowledgment of a gift or an inheritance from the past; but there is no mere idolizing of what is past and gone. What is esteemed is the present; and it is esteemed not on account of its connections with a remote antiquity, nor because it is recognized to be more admirable than any possible alternative, but on account of its familiarity: not, *Verweile doch, du bist so schön,*[1] but, *Stay with me because I am attached to you.*

If the present is arid, offering little or nothing to be used or enjoyed, then this inclination will be weak or absent; if the present is remarkably unsettled, it will display itself in a search for a firmer foothold and consequently in a recourse to and an exploration of the past; but it asserts itself characteristically when there is much to be enjoyed, and it will be strongest when this is combined with evident risk of loss. In short, it is a disposition appropriate to a man who is acutely aware of having something to lose which he has learned to care for; a man in some degree rich in opportunities for enjoyment, but not so rich that he can afford to be indifferent to loss. It will appear more naturally in the old than in the young, not because the old are more sensitive to loss but because they are apt to be more fully aware of the resources of their world and therefore less likely to find them inadequate. In some people this disposition is weak merely because they are ignorant of what their world has to offer them: the present appears to them only as a residue of inopportunities.

To be conservative, then, is to prefer the familiar to the unknown, to prefer the tried to the untried, fact to mystery, the actual to the possible, the limited to the unbounded, the near to the distant, the sufficient to the superabundant, the convenient to the perfect, present laughter to utopian bliss. Familiar relationships and loyalties will be preferred to the allure of more profitable attachments; to acquire and to enlarge will be less important than to keep, to cultivate and to enjoy; the grief of loss will be more acute than the excitement of novelty or promise. It is to be equal to one's own fortune, to live at the level of one's own means, to be content with the want of greater perfection which belongs alike to oneself and one's circumstances. With some people this is itself a choice; in others it is a disposition which appears, frequently or less frequently, in their preferences and aversions, and is not itself chosen or specifically cultivated.

Now, all this is represented in a certain attitude towards change and innovation; change denoting alterations we have to suffer and innovation those we design and execute.

Changes are circumstances to which we have to accommodate ourselves, and the disposition to be conservative is both the emblem of our difficulty in doing so and our resort in the attempts we make to do so. Changes are without effect only upon those who notice nothing, who are ignorant of what they possess and apathetic to their circumstances; and they can be welcomed indiscriminately only by those who esteem nothing, whose attachments are fleeting and who are strangers to love and affection. The conservative disposition provokes neither of these conditions: the inclination to enjoy what is present and available is the opposite of ignorance and apathy and it breeds attachment and affection. Consequently, it is averse from change, which appears always, in the first place, as deprivation. A storm which sweeps away a copse and transforms a favourite view, the death of friends, the sleep of friendship, the desuetude of customs of behaviour, the retirement of a favourite clown, involuntary exile, reversals of fortune, the loss of abilities enjoyed and their replacement by others—these are changes, none perhaps without its compensations, which the man of conservative temperament unavoidably regrets. But he has difficulty in reconciling himself to them, not because what he has lost in them was intrinsically better than any alternative might have been or was incapable of improvement, nor because what takes its place is inherently incapable of being enjoyed, but because what he has lost was something he actually enjoyed and had learned how to enjoy and what takes its place is something to which he has acquired no attachment. Consequently, he will find small and slow changes more tolerable than large and sudden; and he will value highly every appearance of continuity. Some changes, indeed, will present no difficulty; but, again, this is not because they are manifest improvements but merely because they are easily assimilated: the changes of the seasons are mediated by their recurrence and the growing up of children by its continuousness. And, in general, he will accommodate himself more readily to changes which do not offend expectation than to the destruction of what seems to have no ground of dissolution within itself.

Moreover, to be conservative is not merely to be averse from change (which may be an idiosyncrasy); it is also a manner of accommodating ourselves to changes, an activity imposed upon all men. For, change is a threat to identity, and every change is an emblem of extinction. But a man's identity (or that of a community) is nothing more than an unbroken rehearsal of contingencies, each at the mercy of circumstance and each significant in proportion to its familiarity. It is not a fortress into which we may retire, and the only means we have of defending it (that is, ourselves) against the hostile forces of change is in the open field of our experience; by throwing our weight upon the foot which for the time being is most firmly placed, by cleaving to whatever familiarities are not immediately threatened and thus assimilating what is new without becoming unrecognizable to ourselves. The Masai, when they were moved from their old country to the present Masai reserve in Kenya, took with them the names of their hills and plains and rivers and gave them to the hills and plains and rivers of the new country. And it is by some such subterfuge of conservatism that every man or people compelled to suffer a notable change avoids the shame of extinction.

Changes, then, have to be suffered; and a man of conservative temperament (that is, one strongly disposed to preserve his identity) cannot be indifferent to them. In the main, he judges them by the disturbance they entail and, like everyone else, deploys his resources to meet them. The idea of innovation, on the other hand, is improvement. Nevertheless, a man of this temperament will not himself be an ardent innovator. In the first place, he is not inclined to think that nothing is happening unless great changes are afoot and therefore he is not worried by the absence of innovation: the use and enjoyment of things as they are occupies most of his attention. Further, he is aware that not all innovation is, in fact, improvement; and he will think that to innovate without improving is either designed or inadvertent folly. Moreover, even when an innovation commends itself as a convincing improvement, he will look twice at its claims before accepting them. From his point of view, because every improvement involves change, the disruption entailed has always to be set against the benefit anticipated. But when he has satisfied himself about this, there will be other considerations to be taken into the account. Innovating is always an equivocal enterprise, in which gain and loss (even excluding the loss of familiarity) are so closely interwoven that it is exceedingly difficult to forecast the final up-shot: there is no such thing as an unqualified improvement. For, innovating is an activity which generates not only the "improvement" sought, but a new and complex situation of which this is only one of the components. The total change is always more extensive than the change designed; and the whole of what is entailed can neither be foreseen nor circumscribed. Thus, whenever there is innovation there is the certainty that the change will be greater than was intended, that there will be loss as well as gain and that the loss and the gain will not be equally distributed among the people affected; there is the chance that the benefits derived will be greater than those which were designed; and there is the risk that they will be off-set by changes for the worse.

From all this the man of conservative temperament draws some appropriate conclusions. First, innovation entails certain loss and possible gain, therefore, the onus of proof, to show that the proposed change may be expected to be on the whole beneficial, rests with the would-be innovator. Secondly, he believes that the more closely an innovation resembles growth (that is, the more clearly it is intimated in and not merely imposed upon the situation) the less likely it is to result in a preponderance of loss. Thirdly, he thinks that an innovation which is a response to some specific defect, one designed to redress some specific disequilibrium, is more desirable than one which springs from a notion of a generally improved condition of human circumstances, and is far more desirable than one generated by a vision of perfection. Consequently, he prefers small and limited innovations to large and indefinite. Fourthly, he favours a slow rather than a rapid pace, and pauses to observe current consequences and make appropriate adjustments. And lastly, he believes the occasion to be important; and, other things being equal, he considers the most favourable occasion for innovation to be when the projected change is most likely to be limited to what is intended and least likely to be corrupted by undesired and unmanageable consequences.

The disposition to be conservative is, then, warm and positive in respect of enjoyment, and correspondingly cool and critical in respect of change and innovation: these two inclinations support and elucidate one another. The man of conservative temperament believes that a known good is not lightly to be surrendered for an unknown better. He is not in love with what is dangerous and difficult; he is unadventurous; he has no impulse to sail uncharted seas; for him there is no magic in being lost, bewildered or shipwrecked. If he is forced to navigate the unknown, he sees virtue in heaving the lead every inch of the way. What others plausibly identify as timidity, he recognizes in himself as rational prudence; what others interpret as inactivity, he recognizes as a disposition to enjoy rather than to exploit. He is cautious, and he is disposed to indicate his assent or dissent, not in absolute, but in graduated terms. He eyes the situation in terms of its propensity to disrupt the familiarity of the features of his world.

2

It is commonly believed that this conservative disposition is pretty deeply rooted in what is called "human nature." Change is tiring, innovation calls for effort, and human beings (it is said) are more apt to be lazy than energetic. If they have found a not unsatisfactory way of getting along in the world, they are not disposed to go looking for trouble. They are naturally apprehensive of the unknown and prefer safety to danger. They are reluctant innovators, and they accept change not because they like it but (as Rochefoucauld says they accept death) because it is inescapable. Change generates sadness rather than exhilaration: heaven is the dream of a changeless no less than of a perfect world. Of course, those who read "human nature" in this way agree that this disposition does not stand alone; they merely contend that it is an exceedingly strong, perhaps the strongest, of human propensities. And, so far as it goes, there is something to be said for this belief: human circumstances would certainly be very different from what they are if there were not a large ingredient of conservatism in human preferences. Primitive peoples are said to cling to what is familiar and to be averse from change; ancient myth is full of warnings against innovation; our folklore and proverbial wisdom about the conduct of life abounds in conservative precepts; and how many tears are shed by children in their unwilling accommodation to change. Indeed, wherever a firm identity is felt to be precariously balanced, a conservative disposition is likely to prevail. On the other hand, the disposition of adolescence is often predominantly adventurous and experimental: when we are young, nothing seems more desirable than to take a chance; *pas de risque, pas de plaisir*.[2] And while some peoples, over long stretches of time, appear successfully to have avoided change, the history of others displays periods of intense and intrepid innovation. There is, indeed, not much profit to be had from general speculation about "human nature," which is no steadier than anything else in our acquaintance. What is more to the point is to consider current human nature, to consider ourselves.

With us, I think, the disposition to be conservative is far from being notably strong. Indeed, if he were to judge by our conduct during the last five centuries or so, an unprejudiced stranger might plausibly suppose us to be in love with change, to have an appetite only for innovation and to be either so out of sympathy with ourselves or so careless of our identity as not to be disposed to give it any consideration. In general, the fascination of what is new is felt far more keenly than the comfort of what is familiar. We are disposed to think that nothing important is happening unless great innovations are afoot, and that what is not being improved must be deteriorating. There is a positive prejudice in favour of the yet untried. We readily presume that all change is, somehow, for the better, and we are easily persuaded that all the consequences of our innovating activity are either themselves improvements or at least a reasonable price to pay for getting what we want. While the conservative, if he were forced to gamble, would bet on the field, we are disposed to back our individual fancies with little calculation and no apprehension of loss. We are acquisitive to the point of greed; ready to drop the bone we have for its reflection magnified in the mirror of the future. Nothing is made to outlast probable improvement in a world where everything is undergoing incessant improvement: the expectation of life of everything except human beings themselves continuously declines. Pieties are fleeting, loyalties evanescent, and the pace of change warns us against too deep attachments. We are willing to try anything once, regardless of the consequences. One activity vies with another in being "up-to-date": discarded motorcars and television sets have their counterparts in discarded moral and religious beliefs: the eye is ever on the new model. To see is to imagine what might be in the place of what is; to touch is to transform. Whatever the shape or quality of the world, it is not for long as we want it. And those in the van of movement infect those behind with their energy and enterprise. *Omnes eodem cogemur*:[3] when we are no longer light-footed we find a place for ourselves in the band.[4]

Of course, our character has other ingredients besides this lust for change (we are not devoid of the impulse to cherish and preserve), but there can be little doubt about its pre-eminence. And, in these circumstances, it seems appropriate that a conservative disposition should appear, not as an intelligible (or even plausible) alternative to our mainly "progressive" habit of mind, but either as an unfortunate hindrance to the movement afoot, or as the custodian of the museum in which quaint examples of superseded achievement are preserved for children to gape at, and as the guardian of what from time to time is considered not yet ripe for destruction, which we call (ironically enough) the amenities of life.

Here our account of the disposition to be conservative and its current fortunes might be expected to end, with the man in whom this disposition is strong last seen swimming against the tide, disregarded not because what he has to say is necessarily false but because it has become irrelevant; outmanoeuvred, not on account of any intrinsic demerit but merely by the flow of circumstance; a faded, timid, nostalgic character, provoking pity as an outcast and contempt as a reactionary. Nevertheless, I think there is something more to be said. Even in these circumstances, when a conservative disposition in respect of things in general is unmistakably at a discount, there are occasions when this disposition remains not only appropriate, but supremely so; and there are connections in which we are unavoidably disposed in a conservative direction.

In the first place, there is a certain kind of activity (not yet extinct) which can be engaged in only in virtue of a disposition to be conservative, namely, activities where what is sought is present enjoyment and not a profit, a reward, a prize or a result in addition to the experience itself. And when these activities are recognized as the emblems of this disposition, to be conservative is disclosed, not as prejudiced hostility to a "progressive" attitude capable of embracing the whole range of human conduct, but as a disposition exclusively appropriate in a large and significant field of human activity. And the man in whom this disposition is pre-eminent appears as one who prefers to engage in activities where to be conservative is uniquely appropriate, and not as a man inclined to impose his conservatism indiscriminately upon all human activity. In short, if we find ourselves (as most of us do) inclined to reject conservatism as a disposition appropriate in respect of human conduct in general, there still remains a certain kind of human conduct for which this disposition is not merely appropriate but a necessary condition …

This is so of friendship. Here, attachment springs from an intimation of familiarity and subsists in a mutual sharing of personalities. To go on changing one's butcher until one gets the meat one likes, to go on educating one's agent until he does what is required of him, is conduct not inappropriate to the relationship concerned; but to discard friends because they do not behave as we expected and refuse to be educated to our requirements is the conduct of a man who has altogether mistaken the character of friendship. Friends are not concerned with what might be made of one another, but only with the enjoyment of one another; and the condition of this enjoyment is a ready acceptance of what is and the absence of any desire to change or to improve. A friend is not somebody one trusts to behave in a certain manner, who supplies certain wants, who has certain useful abilities, who possesses certain merely agreeable qualities, or who holds certain acceptable opinions; he is somebody who engages the imagination, who excites contemplation, who provokes interest, sympathy, delight and loyalty simply on account of the relationship entered into. One friend cannot replace another; there is all the difference in the world between the death of a friend and the retirement of one's tailor from business. The relationship of friend to friend is dramatic, not utilitarian; the tie is one of familiarity, not usefulness; the disposition engaged is conservative, not "progressive." And what is true of friendship is not less true of other experiences—of patriotism, for example, and of conversation—each of which demands a conservative disposition as a condition of its enjoyment.

But further, there are activities, not involving human relationships, that may be engaged in, not for a prize, but for the enjoyment they generate, and for which the only appropriate disposition is the disposition to be conservative. Consider fishing. If your project is merely to catch fish it would be foolish to be unduly conservative. You will seek out the best tackle, you will discard practices which prove unsuccessful, you will not be bound by unprofitable attachments to particular localities, pieties will be fleeting, loyalties evanescent; you may even be wise to try anything once in the hope of improvement. But fishing is an activity that may be engaged in, not for the profit of a catch, but for its own sake; and the fisherman may return home in the evening not less content for being empty-handed. Where this is so, the activity has become a ritual and a conservative disposition is appropriate. Why worry about the best gear if you do not care whether or not you make a catch?

What matters is the enjoyment of exercising skill (or, perhaps, merely passing the time), and this is to be had with any tackle, so long as it is familiar and is not grotesquely inappropriate.

All activities, then, where what is sought is enjoyment springing, not from the success of the enterprise but from the familiarity of the engagement, are emblems of the disposition to be conservative …

3

How, then, are we to construe the disposition to be conservative in respect of politics? … [T]o state my view briefly before elaborating it, what makes a conservative disposition in politics intelligible is nothing to do with a natural law or a providential order, nothing to do with morals or religion; it is the observation of our current manner of living combined with the belief (which from our point of view need be regarded as no more than an hypothesis) that governing is a specific and limited activity, namely the provision and custody of general rules of conduct, which are understood, not as plans for imposing substantive activities, but as instruments enabling people to pursue the activities of their own choice with the minimum frustration, and therefore something which it is appropriate to be conservative about …

… [T]he office of government is not to impose other beliefs and activities upon its subjects, not to tutor or to educate them, not to make them better or happier in another way, not to direct them, to galvanize them into action, to lead them or to coordinate their activities so that no occasion of conflict shall occur; the office of government is merely to rule. This is a specific and limited activity, easily corrupted when it is combined with any other, and, in the circumstances, indispensable. The image of the ruler is the umpire whose business is to administer the rules of the game, or the chairman who governs the debate according to known rules but does not himself participate in it.

Now people of this disposition commonly defend their belief that the proper attitude of government towards the current condition of human circumstance is one of acceptance by appealing to certain general ideas. They contend that there is absolute value in the free play of human choice, that private property (the emblem of choice) is a natural right, that it is only in the enjoyment of diversity of opinion and activity that true belief and good conduct can be expected to disclose themselves. But I do not think that this disposition requires these or any similar beliefs in order to make it intelligible. Something much smaller and less pretentious will do: the observation that this condition of human circumstance is, in fact, current, and that we have learned to enjoy it and how to manage it; that we are not children *in statu pupillari*[5] but adults who do not consider themselves under any obligation to justify their preference for making their own choices; and that it is beyond human experience to suppose that those who rule are endowed with a superior wisdom which discloses to them a better range of beliefs and activities and which gives them authority to impose upon their subjects a quite different manner of life. In short, if the man of this disposition is asked: Why ought governments to accept the current diversity of opinion and activity in preference to imposing upon their subjects a dream of their own? it is enough for him to reply: Why not? Their dreams are no different from those of anyone else; and if it is boring to have to listen to dreams of others being recounted, it is insufferable to be forced to re-enact them. We tolerate monomaniacs, it is our habit to do so; but why should we be *ruled* by them? Is it not (the man of conservative disposition asks) an intelligible task for a government to protect its subjects against the nuisance of those who spend their energy and their wealth in the service of some pet indignation, endeavouring to impose it upon everybody, not by suppressing their activities in favour of others of a similar kind, but by setting a limit to the amount of noise anyone may emit?

Nevertheless, if this acceptance is the spring of the conservative's disposition in respect of government, he does not suppose that the office of government is to do nothing. As he understands it, there is work to be done which can be done only in virtue of a genuine acceptance of current beliefs simply because they are current and current activities simply because they are afoot. And, briefly, the office he attributes to government is to resolve some of the collisions which this variety of beliefs and activities generates; to preserve peace, not by placing an interdict upon choice and upon the diversity that springs from the exercise of preference, not by imposing substantive uniformity, but by enforcing general rules of procedure upon all subjects alike.

Government, then, as the conservative in this matter understands it, does not begin with a vision of another, different and better world, but with the observation of the self-government practised even by men of passion in the conduct of their enterprises; it begins in the informal adjustments of interests to one another which are designed to release those who are apt to collide from the mutual frustration of a collision. Sometimes these adjustments are no more than agreements between two parties to keep out of each other's way; sometimes they are of wider application and more durable character, such as the International Rules for the prevention of collisions at sea. In short, the intimations of government are to be found in ritual, not in religion or philosophy; in the enjoyment of orderly and peaceable behaviour, not in the search for truth or perfection …

… Innovation, then, is called for if the rules are to remain appropriate to the activities they govern. But, as the conservative understands it, modification of the rules should always reflect, and never impose, a change in the activities and beliefs of those who are subject to them, and should never on any occasion be so great as to destroy the *ensemble*. Consequently, the conservative will have nothing to do with innovations designed to meet merely hypothetical situations; he will prefer to enforce a rule he has got rather than invent a new one; he will think it appropriate to delay a modification of the rules until it is clear that the change of circumstance it is designed to reflect has come to stay for a while; he will be suspicious of proposals for change in excess of what the situation calls for, of rulers who demand extra-ordinary powers in order to make great changes and whose utterances are tied to generalities like "the public good" or "social justice," and of Saviours of Society who buckle on armour and seek dragons to slay; he will think it proper to consider the occasion of the innovation with care; in short, he will be disposed to regard politics as an activity in which a valuable set of tools is renovated from time to time and kept in trim rather than as an opportunity for perpetual re-equipment …

To some people, "government" appears as a vast reservoir of power which inspires them to dream of what use might be made of it. They have favourite projects, of various dimensions, which they sincerely believe are for the benefit of mankind, and to capture this source of power, if necessary to increase it, and to use it for imposing their favourite projects upon their fellows is what they understand as the adventure of governing men. They are, thus, disposed to recognize government as an instrument of passion; the art of politics is to inflame and direct desire. In short, governing is understood to be just like any other activity—making and selling a brand of soap, exploiting the resources of a locality, or developing a housing estate—only the power here is (for the most part) already mobilized, and the enterprise is remarkable only because it aims at monopoly and because of its promise of success once the source of power has been captured. Of course a private enterprise politician of this sort would get nowhere in these days unless there were people with wants so vague that they can be prompted to ask for what he has to offer, or with wants so servile that they prefer the promise of a provided abundance to the opportunity of choice and activity on their own account. And it is not all as plain sailing as it might appear: often a politician of this sort misjudges the situation; and then, briefly, even in democratic politics, we become aware of what the camel thinks of the camel driver.

Now, the disposition to be conservative in respect of politics reflects a quite different view of the activity of governing. The man of this disposition understands it to be the business of a government not to inflame passion and give it new objects to feed upon, but to inject into the activities of already too passionate men an ingredient of moderation; to restrain, to deflate, to pacify and to reconcile; not to stoke the fires of desire, but to damp them down. And all this, not because passion is vice and moderation virtue, but because moderation is indispensable if passionate men are to escape being locked in an encounter of mutual frustration …

4

Nobody pretends that it is easy to acquire or to sustain the mood of indifference which this manner of politics calls for. To rein-in one's own beliefs and desires, to acknowledge the current shape of things, to feel the balance of things in one's hand, to tolerate what is abominable, to distinguish between crime and sin, to respect formality even when it appears to be leading to error, these are difficult achievements; and they are achievements not to be looked for in the young.

Everybody's young days are a dream, a delightful insanity, a sweet solipsism. Nothing in them has a fixed shape, nothing a fixed price; everything is a possibility, and we live happily on credit. There are no obligations to be observed; there are no accounts to be kept. Nothing is specified in advance; everything is what can be made of it. The world is a mirror in which we seek the reflection of our own desires. The allure of violent emotions is irresistible. When we are young we are not disposed to make concessions to the world; we never feel the balance of a thing in our hands—unless it be a cricket bat. We are not apt to distinguish between our liking and our esteem; urgency is our criterion of importance; and we do not easily understand that what is humdrum need not be despicable. We are impatient of restraint; and we readily believe, like [the poet Percy Bysshe] Shelley, that to have contracted a habit is to have failed. These, in my opinion, are among our virtues when we are young; but how remote they are from the disposition appropriate for participating in the style of government I have been describing. Since life is a dream, we argue (with plausible but erroneous logic) that politics must be an encounter of dreams, in which we hope to impose our own. Some unfortunate people, like Pitt (laughably called "the Younger"), are born old, and are eligible to engage in politics almost in their cradles;[6] others, perhaps more fortunate, belie the saying that one is young only once, they never grow up. But these are exceptions. For most there is what [the novelist Joseph] Conrad called the "shadow line" which, when we pass it, discloses a solid world of things, each with its fixed shape, each with its own point of balance, each with its price; a world of fact, not poetic image, in which what we have spent on one thing we cannot spend on another; a world inhabited by others besides ourselves who cannot be reduced to mere reflections of our own emotions. And coming to be at home in this commonplace world qualifies us (as no knowledge of "political science" can ever qualify us), if we are so inclined and have nothing better to think about, to engage in what the man of conservative disposition understands to be political activity.

NOTES

1   "Stay with me, you are so beautiful."—Eds.
2   "No risk, no pleasure."—Eds.
3   "We are all brought to the same point."—Eds.
4   "Which of us," asks a contemporary (not without some equivocation), "would not settle, at whatever cost in nervous anxiety, for a febrile and creative rather than a static society?"
5   "In the status of pupils."—Eds.
6   The British Statesman William Pitt (1759–1806) became known as "The Younger" because his father was also a prominent political figure named William Pitt (1708–1778).—Eds.

Ten Conservative Principles

RUSSELL KIRK*

Russell Kirk (1918–1994) was a leading American theorist of the mid-twentieth-century conservative revival. His book *The Conservative Mind: From Burke to Santayana* (1953) was a spirited defense of traditional or "Burkean" conservatism. Kirk was also a founding editor of the influential conservative magazine *National Review* (1955–). The following essay from Kirk's *The Politics of Prudence* (1993) provides a succinct summary of the leading principles and precepts of classical or traditional conservatism.

* *Source*: Russell Kirk, "Ten Conservative Principles," from *The Politics of Prudence* (Mecosta, MI: ISI Books, 1993). Reprinted by permission of the Estate of Russell Kirk.

TEN CONSERVATIVE PRINCIPLES

Being neither a religion nor an ideology, the body of opinion termed *conservatism* possesses no Holy Writ and no *Das Kapital* to provide dogmata.[1] So far as it is possible to determine what conservatives believe, the first principles of the conservative persuasion are derived from what leading conservative writers and public men have professed during the past two centuries. After some introductory remarks on this general theme, I will proceed to list ten such conservative principles.

A witty presidential candidate of recent times, Mr. Eugene McCarthy, remarked publicly in 1985 that nowadays he employs the word "liberal" as an adjective merely. That renunciation of "liberal" as a noun of politics, a partisan or ideological tag, is some measure of the triumph of the conservative mentality during the 1980s—including the triumph of the conservative side of Mr. McCarthy's own mind and character.

Perhaps it would be well, most of the time, to use this word "conservative" as an adjective chiefly. For there exists no Model Conservative, and conservatism is the negation of ideology: it is a state of mind, a type of character, a way of looking at the civil social order.

The attitude we call conservatism is sustained by a body of sentiments, rather than by a system of ideological dogmata. It is almost true that a conservative may be defined as a person who thinks himself such. The conservative movement or body of opinion can accommodate a considerable diversity of views on a good many subjects, there being no Test Act or Thirty-Nine Articles of the conservative creed.[2]

In essence, the conservative person is simply one who finds the permanent things more pleasing than Chaos and Old Night.[3] (Yet conservatives know, with Burke, that healthy "change is the means of our preservation.") A people's historic continuity of experience, says the conservative, offers a guide to policy far better than the abstract designs of coffee-house philosophers. But of course there is more to the conservative persuasion than this general attitude.

It is not possible to draw up a neat catalogue of conservatives' convictions; nevertheless, I offer you, summarily, ten general principles; it seems safe to say that most conservatives would subscribe to most of these maxims. In various editions of my book *The Conservative Mind* I have listed certain canons of conservative thought—the list differing somewhat from edition to edition; in my anthology *The Portable Conservative Reader* I offer variations upon this theme. Now I present to you a summary of conservative assumptions differing somewhat from my canons in those two books of mine. In fine, the diversity of ways in which conservative views may find expression is itself proof that conservatism is no fixed ideology. What particular principles conservatives emphasize during any given time will vary with the circumstances and necessities of that era. The following ten articles of belief reflect the emphases of conservatives in America nowadays.

First, the conservative believes that there exists an enduring moral order. That order is made for man, and man is made for it: human nature is a constant, and moral truths are permanent.

This word *order* signifies harmony. There are two aspects or types of order: the inner order of the soul, and the outer order of the commonwealth. Twenty-five centuries ago, Plato taught this doctrine, but even the educated nowadays find it difficult to understand. The problem of order has been a principal concern of conservatives ever since *conservative* became a term of politics.

Our twentieth-century world has experienced the hideous consequences of the collapse of belief in a moral order. Like the atrocities and disasters of Greece in the fifth century before Christ, the ruin of great nations in our century shows us the pit into which fall societies that mistake clever self-interest, or ingenious social controls, for pleasing alternatives to an oldfangled moral order.

It has been said by liberal intellectuals that the conservative believes all social questions, at heart, to be questions of private morality. Properly understood, this statement is quite true. A society in which men and women are governed by belief in an enduring moral order, by a strong sense of right and wrong, by personal convictions about justice and honor, will be a good society—whatever political machinery it may utilize; while a society in which men and women are morally adrift, ignorant of norms, and intent chiefly upon gratification of appetites, will be a bad society—no matter how many people vote and no matter how liberal its formal constitution may be. For confirmation of the latter argument, we have merely to glance at the unhappy District of Columbia.

→ *Second, the conservative adheres to custom, convention, and continuity.* It is old custom that enables people to live together peaceably; the destroyers of custom demolish more than they know or desire. It is through convention—a word much abused in our time—that we contrive to avoid perpetual disputes about rights and duties: law at base is a body of conventions.[4] Continuity is the means of linking generation to generation; it matters as much for society as it does for the individual; without it, life is meaningless. When successful revolutionaries have effaced old customs, derided old conventions, and broken the continuity of social institutions—why, presently they discover the necessity of establishing fresh customs, conventions, and continuity; but that process is painful and slow; and the new social order that eventually emerges may be much inferior to the old order that radicals overthrew in their zeal for the Earthly Paradise.

Conservatives are champions of custom, convention, and continuity because they prefer the devil they know to the devil they don't know. Order and justice and freedom, they believe, are the artificial products of a long social experience, the result of centuries of trial and reflection and sacrifice. Thus the body social is a kind of spiritual corporation, comparable to the church; it may even be called a community of souls. Human society is no machine, to be treated mechanically. The continuity, the lifeblood, of a society must not be interrupted. Burke's reminder of the necessity for prudent change is in the mind of the conservative. But necessary change, conservatives argue, ought to be gradual and discriminatory, never unfixing old interests at once.

→ *Third, conservatives believe in what may be called the principle of prescription.* Conservatives sense that modern people are dwarfs on the shoulders of giants, able to see farther than their ancestors only because of the great stature of those who have preceded us in time. Therefore conservatives very often emphasize the importance of *prescription*—that is, of things established by immemorial usage, so that the mind of man runneth not to the contrary. There exist rights of which the chief sanction is their antiquity—including rights to property, often. Similarly, our morals are prescriptive in great part. Conservatives argue that we are unlikely, we moderns, to make any brave new discoveries in morals or politics or taste. It is perilous to weigh every passing issue on the basis of private judgment and private rationality. The individual is foolish, but the species is wise, Burke declared. In politics we do well to abide by precedent and precept and even prejudice, for the great mysterious incorporation of the human race has acquired a prescriptive wisdom far greater than any man's petty private rationality.

Fourth, conservatives are guided by their principle of prudence. Burke agrees with Plato that in the statesman, prudence is chief among virtues. Any public measure ought to be judged by its probable long-run consequences, not merely by temporary advantage or popularity. Liberals and radicals, the conservative says, are imprudent: for they dash at their objectives without giving much heed to the risk of new abuses worse than the evils they hope to sweep away. As John Randolph of Roanoke put it, Providence moves slowly, but the devil always hurries. Human society being complex, remedies cannot be simple if they are to be efficacious. The conservative declares that he acts only after sufficient reflection, having weighed the consequences. Sudden and slashing reforms are as perilous as sudden and slashing surgery.

Fifth, conservatives pay attention to the principle of variety. They feel affection for the proliferating intricacy of long-established social institutions and modes of life, as distinguished from the narrowing uniformity and deadening egalitarianism of radical systems. For the preservation of a healthy diversity in any civilization, there must survive orders and classes, differences in material condition, and many sorts of inequality. The only true forms of equality are equality at the Last Judgment and equality before a just court of law; all other attempts at levelling must lead, at best, to social stagnation. Society requires honest and able leadership; and if natural and institutional differences are destroyed, presently some tyrant or host of squalid oligarchs will create new forms of inequality.

Sixth, conservatives are chastened by their principle of imperfectibility. Human nature suffers irremediably from certain grave faults, the conservatives know. Man being imperfect, no perfect social order ever can be created. Because of human restlessness, mankind would grow rebellious under any utopian domination, and would break out once more in violent discontent—or else expire of boredom. To seek for utopia is to end in disaster, the conservative says: we are not made for perfect things. All that we reasonably can expect is a tolerably ordered, just, and free society, in which some evils, maladjustments, and suffering will continue to lurk. By proper attention to prudent reform, we may preserve and improve this tolerable order. But if the old institutional and moral safeguards of a nation are neglected, then the anarchic impulse in humankind breaks loose: "the ceremony of innocence is drowned."[5] The ideologues who promise the perfection of man and society have converted a great part of the twentieth-century world into a terrestrial hell.

Seventh, conservatives are persuaded that freedom and property are closely linked. Separate property from private possession, and Leviathan becomes master of all. Upon the foundation of private property, great civilizations are built. The more widespread is the possession of private property, the more stable and productive is a commonwealth. Economic levelling, conservatives maintain, is not economic progress. Getting and spending are not the chief aims of human existence; but a sound economic basis for the person, the family, and the commonwealth is much to be desired.

Sir Henry Maine, in his *Village Communities* [1889], puts strongly the case for private property, as distinguished from communal property: "Nobody is at liberty to attack several property and to say at the same time that he values civilization. The history of the two cannot be disentangled." For the institution of several property—that is, private property—has been a powerful instrument for teaching men and women responsibility, for providing motives to integrity, for supporting general culture, for raising mankind above the level of mere drudgery, for affording leisure to think and freedom to act. To be able to retain the fruits of one's labor; to be able to see one's work made permanent; to be able to bequeath one's property to one's posterity; to be able to rise from the natural condition of grinding poverty to the security of enduring accomplishment; to have something that is really one's own—these are advantages difficult to deny. The conservative acknowledges that the possession of property fixes certain duties upon the possessor; he accepts those moral and legal obligations cheerfully.

⟶ *Eighth, conservatives uphold voluntary community, quite as they oppose involuntary collectivism.* Although Americans have been attached strongly to privacy and private rights, they also have been a people conspicuous for a successful spirit of community. In a genuine community, the decisions most directly affecting the lives of citizens are made locally and voluntarily. Some of these functions are carried out by local political bodies, others by private associations: so long as they are kept local, and are marked by the general agreement of those affected, they constitute healthy community. But when these functions pass by default or usurpation to centralized authority, then community is in serious danger. Whatever is beneficent and prudent in modern democracy is made possible through cooperative volition. If, then, in the name of an abstract Democracy, the functions of community are transferred to distant political direction—why, real government by the consent of the governed gives way to a standardizing process hostile to freedom and human dignity.

For a nation is no stronger than the numerous little communities of which it is composed. A central administration, or a corps of select managers and civil servants, however well intentioned and well trained, cannot confer justice and prosperity and tranquility upon a mass of men and women deprived of their old responsibilities. That experiment has been made before; and it has been disastrous. It is the performance of our duties in community that teaches us prudence and efficiency and charity.

⟶ *Ninth, the conservative perceives the need for prudent restraints upon power and upon human passions.* Politically speaking, power is the ability to do as one likes, regardless of the wills of one's fellows. A state in which an individual or a small group are able to dominate the wills of their fellows without check is a despotism, whether it is called monarchical or aristocratic or democratic. When every person claims to be a power unto himself, then society falls into anarchy. Anarchy never lasts long, being intolerable for everyone, and contrary to the ineluctable fact that some persons are more strong and more clever than their neighbors. To anarchy there succeeds tyranny or oligarchy, in which power is monopolized by a very few.

The conservative endeavors to so limit and balance political power that anarchy or tyranny may not arise. In every age, nevertheless, men and women are tempted to overthrow the limitations upon power, for the sake of some fancied temporary advantage. It is characteristic of the radical that he thinks of power as a force for good—so long as the power falls into his hands. In the name of liberty, the French and Russian revolutionaries abolished the old restraints upon power; but power cannot be abolished; it always finds its way into someone's hands. That power which the revolutionaries had thought oppressive in the hands of the old regime became many times as tyrannical in the hands of the radical new masters of the state.

Knowing human nature for a mixture of good and evil, the conservative does not put his trust in mere benevolence. Constitutional restrictions, political checks and balances, adequate enforcement of the laws, the old intricate web of restraints upon will and appetite—these the conservative approves as instruments of freedom and order. A just government maintains a healthy tension between the claims of authority and the claims of liberty.

Tenth, the thinking conservative understands that permanence and change must be recognized and reconciled in a vigorous society. The conservative is not opposed to social improvement, although he doubts whether there is any such force as a mystical Progress, with a Roman P, at work in the world. When a society is progressing in some respects, usually it is declining in other respects. The conservative knows that any healthy society is influenced by two forces, which Samuel Taylor Coleridge called its Permanence and its Progression. The Permanence of a society is formed by those enduring interests and convictions that gives us stability and continuity; without that Permanence, the fountains of the great deep are broken up, society slipping into anarchy. The Progression in a society is that spirit and that body of talents which urge us on to prudent reform and improvement; without that Progression, a people stagnate.

Therefore the intelligent conservative endeavors to reconcile the claims of Permanence and the claims of Progression. He thinks that the liberal and the radical, blind to the just claims of Permanence, would endanger the heritage bequeathed to us, in an endeavor to hurry us into some dubious Terrestrial Paradise. The conservative, in short, favors reasoned and temperate progress; he is opposed to the cult of Progress, whose votaries believe that everything new necessarily is superior to everything old.

Change is essential to the body social, the conservative reasons, just as it is essential to the human body. A body that has ceased to renew itself has begun to die. But if that body is to be vigorous, the change must occur in a regular manner, harmonizing with the form and nature of that body; otherwise change produces a monstrous growth, a cancer, which devours its host. The conservative takes care that nothing in a society should ever be wholly old, and that nothing should ever be wholly new. This is the means of the conservation of a nation, quite as it is the means of conservation of a living organism. Just how much change a society requires, and what sort of change, depends upon the circumstances of an age and a nation.

Such, then, are ten principles that have loomed large during the two centuries of modern conservative thought. Other principles of equal importance might have been discussed here: the conservative understanding of justice, for one, or the conservative view of education. But such subjects, time running on, I must leave to your private investigation.

Who affirms those ten conservative principles nowadays? In practical politics, commonly a body of general convictions is linked with a body of interests. Marxists argue, indeed, that professed political principle is a mere veil for advancement of the economic interests of a class or faction: that is, no real principle exists—merely ideology. Such is not my view: but we ought to recognize connections between political doctrines and social or economic interest-groups, when such connections exist; they may be innocent enough, or they may make headway at the expense of the general public interest. What interest or group of interests back the conservative element in American politics?

That question is not readily answered. Many rich Americans endorse liberal or radical causes; affluent suburbs frequently vote for liberal men and measures; attachment to conservative sentiments does not follow the line that Marxist analysts of politics expect to find. The owners of small properties, as a class, tend to be more conservative than do the possessors of much property (this latter often in the abstract form of stocks and bonds). One may remark that most conservatives hold religious convictions; yet the officers of mainline Protestant churches, together with church bureaucracies, frequently ally themselves with radical organizations; while some curious political affirmations have been heard recently among the Catholic hierarchy. Half a century ago, it might have been said that most college professors were conservative; that could not be said truthfully today; yet physicians, lawyers, dentists, and other professional people—or most of them—subscribe to conservative journals and generally vote for persons they take to be conservative candidates.

In short, the conservative interest appears to transcend the usual classification of most American voting-blocs according to wealth, age, ethnic origin, religion, occupation, education, and the like. If we may speak of a conservative interest, this appears to be the interest-bloc of people concerned for stability: those citizens who find the pace of change too swift, the loss of continuity and permanence too painful, the break with the American past too brutal, the damage to community dismaying, the designs of innovators imprudent and inhumane. Certain material interests are bound up with this resistance to insensate change: nobody relishes having his savings reduced to insignificance by inflation of the currency. But the moving power behind the renewed conservatism of the American public is not some scheme of personal or corporate aggrandizement; rather, it is the impulse for survival of a culture that wakes to its peril near the end of the twentieth century. We might well call militant conservatives the Party of the Permanent Things.

Perhaps no words have been more abused, both in the popular press and within the Academy, than *conservatism* and *conservative*. *The New York Times*, not without malice prepense, now and again refers to Stalinists within communist states as conservatives. Silly anarchistic tracts, under the label *libertarian*, are represented in some quarters as conservative publications—this in the United States of America, whose Constitution is described by Sir Henry Maine as the most successful conservative device in all history! Even after more than three decades of the renewal of conservative thought in this land, it remains necessary to make it clear to the public that conservatives are not merely folk content with the dominations and powers of the moment; nor anarchists in disguise who would pull down, if they could, both the political and the moral order; nor persons for whom the whole of life is the accumulation of money, like so many [greedy, gold-hoarding king] Midases.

Therefore it is of importance to know whereof one speaks, and not to mistake the American conservative impulse for some narrow and impractical ideology. If the trumpet give an uncertain sound, who shall go forth to battle? For intellectual development, the first necessity is to define one's terms. If we can enlarge the understanding of conservatism's first principles, we will have begun a reinvigoration of the conservative imagination.

The great line of demarcation in modern politics, Eric Voegelin used to point out, is not a division between liberals on one side and totalitarians on the other. No, on one side of that line are all those men and women who fancy that the temporal order is the only order, and that material needs are their only needs, and that they may do as they like with the human patrimony. On the other side of that line are all those people who recognize an enduring moral order in the universe, a constant human nature, and high duties toward the order spiritual and the order temporal.

Conservatives cannot offer America the fancied Terrestrial Paradise that always, in reality, has turned out to be an Earthly Hell. What they can offer is politics as the art of the possible; and an opportunity to stand up for that old lovable human nature; and conscious participation in the defense of order and justice and freedom, Unlike liberals and radicals, conservatives even indulge in prayer, let the Supreme Court say what it may.

This general description of basic assumptions by conservatives I have thrust upon you in the hope of persuading you to think upon these things at your leisure, for the Republic's sake. Conceivably I may have succeeded in rousing some tempers and some hopes. *Pax vobiscum.*[6]

NOTES

1   Kirk refers to Karl Marx's *magnum opus*, *Das Kapital (Capital)*, the first volume of which was published during Marx's lifetime (1867) and the remaining three volumes after his death.—Eds.

2   The Test Act was actually two English laws (1673 and 1678), which were passed to impose religious conformity and orthodoxy. The Thirty-Nine Articles of Religion were issued by the then-new Church of England in 1563 to differentiate itself from Roman Catholicism and from dissenting Protestant sects as well.—Eds.

3   The reference is to John Milton's epic poem *Paradise Lost* (1667): "Sonorous metal blowing martial sounds/At which the universal host up sent/A shout that tore hell's concave, and beyond/Frighted the reign of Chaos and old Night" (Bk. I, lines 540–543).—Eds.

4   I.e., customs, habits, and sentiments.—Eds.

5   From William Butler Yeats's poem, "The Second Coming" (1920), which predicts a coming chaos as political radicals of the right (fascists) and left (communists) took to the streets and gained political power.—Eds.

6   "Peace be with you."—Eds.

Modern American Conservatism

*RONALD REAGAN**

Ronald Reagan (1911–2004) was the fortieth president of the United States. The following selections from three of his presidential addresses—his Inaugural Address (1981), his speech before a convention of evangelical Christians (1983), and his Farewell Address (1989)—provide a compendium of themes that animate and motivate many modern American conservatives. The first theme is fiscal conservatism, low taxation, and minimal government; the second, the importance he attaches to Americans adhering to Christian beliefs and values; the third, a retrospective look at these themes and an added emphasis on what he calls "the new patriotism" praised and prized by him and by many other conservatives.

* *Source*: *The Public Papers of President Ronald W. Reagan*. Ronald Reagan Presidential Library.
https://reaganlibrary.archives.gov/archives/speeches/publicpapers.html

INAUGURAL ADDRESS
January 20, 1981

... These United States are confronted with an economic affliction of great proportions. We suffer from the longest and one of the worst sustained inflations in our national history. It distorts our economic decisions, penalizes thrift, and crushes the struggling young and the fixed-income elderly alike. It threatens to shatter the lives of millions of our people.

Idle industries have cast workers into unemployment, human misery, and personal indignity. Those who do work are denied a fair return for their labor by a tax system which penalizes successful achievement and keeps us from maintaining full productivity.

But great as our tax burden is, it has not kept pace with public spending. For decades we have piled deficit upon deficit, mortgaging our future and our children's future for the temporary convenience of the present. To continue this long trend is to guarantee tremendous social, cultural, political, and economic upheavals.

You and I, as individuals, can, by borrowing, live beyond our means, but for only a limited period of time. Why, then, should we think that collectively, as a nation, we're not bound by that same limitation? We must act today in order to preserve tomorrow. And let there be no misunderstanding: We are going to begin to act, beginning today.

The economic ills we suffer have come upon us over several decades. They will not go away in days, weeks, or months, but they will go away. They will go away because we as Americans have the capacity now, as we've had in the past, to do whatever needs to be done to preserve this last and greatest bastion of freedom.

In this present crisis, government is not the solution to our problem; government is the problem. From time to time we've been tempted to believe that society has become too complex to be managed by self-rule, that government by an elite group is superior to government for, by, and of the people. Well, if no one among us is capable of governing himself, then who among us has the capacity to govern someone else? All of us together, in and out of government, must bear the burden. The solutions we seek must be equitable, with no one group singled out to pay a higher price ...

So, as we begin, let us take inventory. We are a nation that has a government—not the other way around. And this makes us special among the nations of the Earth. Our government has no power except that granted it by the people. It is time to check and reverse the growth of government, which shows signs of having grown beyond the consent of the governed.

It is my intention to curb the size and influence of the Federal establishment and to demand recognition of the distinction between the powers granted to the Federal Government and those reserved to the States or to the people. All of us need to be reminded that the Federal Government did not create the States; the States created the Federal Government ...

If we look to the answer as to why for so many years we achieved so much, prospered as no other people on Earth, it was because here in this land we unleashed the energy and individual genius of man to a greater extent than has ever been done before. Freedom and the dignity of the individual have been more available and assured here than in any other place on Earth. The price for this freedom at times has been high, but we have never been unwilling to pay that price.

It is no coincidence that our present troubles parallel and are proportionate to the intervention and intrusion in our lives that result from unnecessary and excessive growth of government. It is time for us to realize that we're too great a nation to limit ourselves to small dreams. We're not, as some would have us believe, doomed to an inevitable decline. I do not believe in a fate that will fall on us no matter what we do. I do believe in a fate that will fall on us if we do nothing. So, with all the creative energy at our command, let us begin an era of national renewal. Let us renew our determination, our courage, and our strength. And let us renew our faith and our hope ...

In the days ahead I will propose removing the roadblocks that have slowed our economy and reduced productivity. Steps will be taken aimed at restoring the balance between the various levels of government. Progress may be slow, measured in inches and feet, not miles, but we will progress. It is time to reawaken this industrial giant, to get government back within its means, and to lighten our punitive tax burden. And these will be our first priorities, and on these principles there will be no compromise.

On the eve of our struggle for independence a man who might have been one of the greatest among the Founding Fathers, Dr. Joseph Warren, president of the Massachusetts Congress, said to his fellow Americans, "Our country is in danger, but not to be despaired of ... On you depend the fortunes of America. You are to decide the important questions upon which rests the happiness and the liberty of millions yet unborn. Act worthy of yourselves."

Well, I believe we, the Americans of today, are ready to act worthy of ourselves, ready to do what must be done to ensure happiness and liberty for ourselves, our children, and our children's children. And as we renew ourselves here in our own land, we will be seen as having greater strength throughout the world. We will again be the exemplar of freedom and a beacon of hope for those who do not now have freedom.

To those neighbors and allies who share our freedom, we will strengthen our historic ties and assure them of our support and firm commitment. We will match loyalty with loyalty. We will strive for mutually beneficial relations. We will not use our friendship to impose on their sovereignty, for our own sovereignty is not for sale.

As for the enemies of freedom, those who are potential adversaries, they will be reminded that peace is the highest aspiration of the American people. We will negotiate for it, sacrifice for it; we will not surrender for it, now or ever.

Our forbearance should never be misunderstood. Our reluctance for conflict should not be misjudged as a failure of will. When action is required to preserve our national security, we will act. We will maintain sufficient strength to prevail if need be, knowing that if we do so we have the best chance of never having to use that strength.

Above all, we must realize that no arsenal or no weapon in the arsenals of the world is so formidable as the will and moral courage of free men and women. It is a weapon our adversaries in today's world do not have. It is a weapon that we as

Americans do have. Let that be understood by those who practice terrorism and prey upon their neighbors.

I'm told that tens of thousands of prayer meetings are being held on this day, and for that I'm deeply grateful. We are a nation under God, and I believe God intended for us to be free. It would be fitting and good, I think, if on each Inaugural Day in future years it should be declared a day of prayer …

REMARKS AT THE ANNUAL CONVENTION OF THE NATIONAL ASSOCIATION OF EVANGELICALS IN ORLANDO, FLORIDA
March 8, 1983

… I tell you there are a great many God-fearing, dedicated, noble men and women in public life, present company included. And, yes, we need your help to keep us ever mindful of the ideas and the principles that brought us into the public arena in the first place. The basis of those ideals and principles is a commitment to freedom and personal liberty that, itself, is grounded in the much deeper realization that freedom prospers only where the blessings of God are avidly sought and humbly accepted.

The American experiment in democracy rests on this insight. Its discovery was the great triumph of our Founding Fathers, voiced by William Penn when he said: "If we will not be governed by God, we must be governed by tyrants." Explaining the inalienable rights of men, Jefferson said, "The God who gave us life, gave us liberty at the same time." And it was George Washington who said that "of all the dispositions and habits which lead to political prosperity, religion and morality are indispensable supports."

And finally, that shrewdest of all observers of American democracy, Alexis de Tocqueville, put it eloquently after he had gone on a search for the secret of America's greatness and genius—and he said: "Not until I went into the churches of America and heard her pulpits aflame with righteousness did I understand the greatness and the genius of America … America is good. And if America ever ceases to be good, America will cease to be great."

Well, I'm pleased to be here today with you who are keeping America great by keeping her good. Only through your work and prayers and those of millions of others can we hope to survive this perilous century and keep alive this experiment in liberty, this last, best hope of man.

I want you to know that this administration is motivated by a political philosophy that sees the greatness of America in you, her people, and in your families, churches, neighborhoods, communities—the institutions that foster and nourish values like concern for others and respect for the rule of law under God.

Now, I don't have to tell you that this puts us in opposition to, or at least out of step with, a prevailing attitude of many who have turned to a modern-day secularism, discarding the tried and time-tested values upon which our very civilization is based. No matter how well intentioned, their value system is radically different from that of most Americans. And while they proclaim that they're freeing us from superstitions of the past, they've taken upon themselves the job of superintending us by government rule and regulation. Sometimes their voices are louder than ours, but they are not yet a majority …

… Freedom prospers when religion is vibrant and the rule of law under God is acknowledged. When our Founding Fathers passed the first amendment, they sought to protect churches from government interference. They never intended to construct a wall of hostility between government and the concept of religious belief itself.

The evidence of this permeates our history and our government. The Declaration of Independence mentions the Supreme Being no less than four times. "In God We Trust" is engraved on our coinage. The Supreme Court opens its proceedings with a religious invocation. And the Members of Congress open their sessions with a prayer. I just happen to believe the schoolchildren of the United States are entitled to the same privileges as Supreme Court Justices and Congressmen.

Last year, I sent the Congress a constitutional amendment to restore prayer to public schools. Already this session, there's growing bipartisan support for the amendment, and I am calling on the Congress to act speedily to pass it and to let our children pray …

More than a decade ago, a Supreme Court decision literally wiped off the books of 50 States statutes protecting the rights of unborn children. Abortion on demand now takes the lives of up to 1½ million unborn children a year. Human life legislation ending this tragedy will some day pass the Congress, and you and I must never rest until it does. Unless and until it can be proven that the unborn child is not a living entity, then its right to life, liberty, and the pursuit of happiness must be protected.

You may remember that when abortion on demand began, many, and, indeed, I'm sure many of you, warned that the practice would lead to a decline in respect for human life, that the philosophical premises used to justify abortion on demand would ultimately be used to justify other attacks on the sacredness of human life— infanticide or mercy killing. Tragically enough, those warnings proved all too true. Only last year a court permitted the death by starvation of a handicapped infant …

Now, I'm sure that you must get discouraged at times, but you've done better than you know, perhaps. There's a great spiritual awakening in America, a renewal of the traditional values that have been the bedrock of America's goodness and greatness.

One recent survey by a Washington-based research council concluded that Americans were far more religious than the people of other nations; 95 percent of those surveyed expressed a belief in God and a huge majority believed the Ten Commandments had real meaning in their lives. And another study has found that an overwhelming majority of Americans disapprove of adultery, teenage sex, pornography, abortion, and hard drugs. And this same study showed a deep reverence for the importance of family ties and religious belief.

I think the items that we've discussed here today must be a key part of the Nation's political agenda. For the first time the Congress is openly and seriously debating and dealing with the prayer and abortion issues—and that's enormous progress right there. I repeat: America is in the midst of a spiritual awakening and a moral renewal. And with your Biblical keynote, I say today, "Yes, let justice roll on like a river, righteousness like a never-failing stream."

Now, obviously, much of this new political and social consensus I've talked about is based on a positive view of American history, one that takes pride in our country's accomplishments and record. But we must never forget that no government schemes are going to perfect man. We know that living in this world means dealing with what philosophers would call the phenomenology of evil or, as theologians would put it, the doctrine of sin.

There is sin and evil in the world, and we're enjoined by Scripture and the Lord Jesus to oppose it with all our might. Our nation, too, has a legacy of evil with which it must deal. The glory of this land has been its capacity for transcending the moral evils of our past. For example, the long struggle of minority citizens for equal rights, once a source of disunity and civil war, is now a point of pride for all Americans. We must never go back. There is no room for racism, anti-Semitism, or other forms of ethnic and racial hatred in this country …

But whatever sad episodes exist in our past, any objective observer must hold a positive view of American history, a history that has been the story of hopes fulfilled and dreams made into reality. Especially in this century, America has kept alight the torch of freedom, but not just for ourselves but for millions of others around the world.

And this brings me to my final point today. During my first press conference as President, in answer to a direct question, I pointed out that, as good Marxist-Leninists, the Soviet leaders have openly and publicly declared that the only morality they recognize is that which will further their cause, which is world revolution. I think I should point out I was only quoting Lenin, their guiding spirit, who said in 1920 that they repudiate all morality that proceeds from supernatural ideas—that's their name for religion—or ideas that are outside class conceptions. Morality is entirely subordinate to the interests of class war. And everything is moral that is necessary for the annihilation of the old, exploiting social order and for uniting the proletariat.

Well, I think the refusal of many influential people to accept this elementary fact of Soviet doctrine illustrates an historical reluctance to see totalitarian powers for what they are. We saw this phenomenon in the 1930's. We see it too often today.

This doesn't mean we should isolate ourselves and refuse to seek an understanding with them. I intend to do everything I can to persuade them of our peaceful intent, to remind them that it was the West that refused to use its nuclear monopoly in the forties and fifties for territorial gain and which now proposes 50-percent cut in strategic ballistic missiles and the elimination of an entire class of land-based, intermediate-range nuclear missiles.

At the same time, however, they must be made to understand we will never compromise our principles and standards. We will never give away our freedom. We will never abandon our belief in God. And we will never stop searching for a genuine peace. But we can assure none of these things America stands for through the so-called nuclear freeze solutions proposed by some.

The truth is that a freeze now would be a very dangerous fraud, for that is merely the illusion of peace. The reality is that we must find peace through strength …

A number of years ago, I heard a young father, a very prominent young man in the entertainment world, addressing a tremendous gathering in California. It was during the time of the cold war, and communism and our own way of life were very much on people's minds. And he was speaking to that subject. And suddenly, though, I heard him saying, "I love my little girls more than anything —" And I said to myself, "Oh, no, don't. You can't—don't say that." But I had underestimated him. He went on: "I would rather see my little girls die now, still believing in God, than have them grow up under communism and one day die no longer believing in God."

There were thousands of young people in that audience. They came to their feet with shouts of joy. They had instantly recognized the profound truth in what he had said, with regard to the physical body and the soul and what was truly important.

Yes, let us pray for the salvation of all of those who live in that totalitarian darkness—pray they will discover the joy of knowing God. But until they do, let us be aware that while they preach the supremacy of the state, declare its omnipotence over individual man, and predict its eventual domination of all peoples on the Earth, they are the focus of evil in the modern world.

While America's military strength is important, let me add here that I've always maintained that the struggle now going on for the world will never be decided by bombs or rockets, by armies or military might. The real crisis we face today is a spiritual one; at root, it is a test of moral will and faith …

I believe we shall rise to the challenge. I believe that communism is another sad, bizarre chapter in human history whose last pages even now are being written. I believe this because the source of our strength in the quest for human freedom is not material, but spiritual. And because it knows no limitation, it must terrify and ultimately triumph over those who would enslave their fellow man. For in the words of Isaiah: "He giveth power to the faint; and to them that have no might He increased strength … But they that wait upon the Lord shall renew their strength; they shall mount up with wings as eagles; they shall run, and not be weary …"

Yes, change your world. One of our Founding Fathers, Thomas Paine, said, "We have it within our power to begin the world over again. We can do it, doing together what no one church could do by itself."

God bless you, and thank you very much.

FAREWELL ADDRESS TO THE NATION
January 11, 1989

My fellow Americans:

… Well, back in 1980, when I was running for President, it was all so different. Some pundits said our programs would result in catastrophe. Our views on foreign affairs would cause war. Our plans for the economy would cause inflation to soar and bring about economic collapse. I even remember one highly respected economist saying, back in 1982, that "The engines of economic growth have shut down here, and they're likely to stay that way for years to come." Well, he and the other opinion leaders were wrong. The fact is, what they called "radical" was really "right." What they called "dangerous" was just "desperately needed."

And in all of that time I won a nickname, "The Great Communicator." But I never thought it was my style or the words I used that made a difference: it was the content. I wasn't a great communicator, but I communicated great things, and they didn't spring full bloom from my brow, they came from the heart of a great nation—from our experience, our wisdom, and our belief in the principles that have guided us for two centuries. They called it the Reagan revolution. Well, I'll accept that, but for me it always seemed more like the great rediscovery, a rediscovery of our values and our common sense.

Common sense told us that when you put a big tax on something, the people will produce less of it. So, we cut the people's tax rates, and the people produced more than ever before. The economy bloomed like a plant that had been cut back and could now grow quicker and stronger. Our economic program brought about the longest peacetime expansion in our history: real family income up, the poverty rate down, entrepreneurship booming, and an explosion in research and new technology. We're exporting more than ever because American industry became more competitive and at the same time, we summoned the national will to knock down protectionist walls abroad instead of erecting them at home.

Common sense also told us that to preserve the peace, we'd have to become strong again after years of weakness and confusion. So, we rebuilt our defenses, and this New Year we toasted the new peacefulness around the globe. Not only have the superpowers actually begun to reduce their stockpiles of nuclear weapons—and hope for even more progress is bright—but the regional conflicts that rack the globe are also beginning to cease. The Persian Gulf is no longer a war zone. The Soviets are leaving Afghanistan. The Vietnamese are preparing to pull out of Cambodia, and an American-mediated accord will soon send 50,000 Cuban troops home from Angola.

The lesson of all this was, of course, that because we're a great nation, our challenges seem complex. It will always be this way. But as long as we remember our first principles and believe in ourselves, the future will always be ours. And something else we learned: Once you begin a great movement, there's no telling where it will end. We meant to change a nation, and instead, we changed a world.

Countries across the globe are turning to free markets and free speech and turning away from the ideologies of the past. For them, the great rediscovery of the 1980's has been that, lo and behold, the moral way of government is the practical way of government: Democracy, the profoundly good, is also the profoundly productive …

Ours was the first revolution in the history of mankind that truly reversed the course of government, and with three little words: "We the People." "We the People" tell the government what to do; it doesn't tell us. "We the People" are the driver; the government is the car. And we decide where it should go, and by what route, and how fast. Almost all the world's constitutions are documents in which governments tell the people what their privileges are. Our Constitution is a document in which "We the People" tell the government what it is allowed to do. "We the People" are free. This belief has been the underlying basis for everything I've tried to do these past 8 years.

But back in the 1960's, when I began, it seemed to me that we'd begun reversing the order of things—that through more and more rules and regulations and confiscatory taxes, the government was taking more of our money, more of our options, and more of our freedom. I went into politics in part to put up my hand and say, "Stop." I was a citizen politician, and it seemed the right thing for a citizen to do.

I think we have stopped a lot of what needed stopping. And I hope we have once again reminded people that man is not free unless government is limited. There's a clear cause and effect here that is as neat and predictable as a law of physics: As government expands, liberty contracts.

Nothing is less free than pure communism—and yet we have, the past few years, forged a satisfying new closeness with the Soviet Union. I've been asked if this isn't a gamble, and my answer is no because we're basing our actions not on words but deeds. The detente of the 1970's was based not on actions but promises. They'd promise to treat their own people and the people of the world better. But the gulag was still the gulag, and the state was still expansionist, and they still waged proxy wars in Africa, Asia, and Latin America ...

We must keep up our guard, but we must also continue to work together to lessen and eliminate tension and mistrust. My view is that President Gorbachev is different from previous Soviet leaders. I think he knows some of the things wrong with his society and is trying to fix them. We wish him well. And we'll continue to work to make sure that the Soviet Union that eventually emerges from this process is a less threatening one. What it all boils down to is this: I want the new closeness to continue. And it will, as long as we make it clear that we will continue to act in a certain way as long as they continue to act in a helpful manner. If and when they don't, at first pull your punches. If they persist, pull the plug. It's still trust but verify. It's still play, but cut the cards. It's still watch closely. And don't be afraid to see what you see.

I've been asked if I have any regrets. Well, I do. The deficit is one. I've been talking a great deal about that lately, but tonight isn't for arguments, and I'm going to hold my tongue ...

Finally, there is a great tradition of warnings in Presidential farewells, and I've got one that's been on my mind for some time. But oddly enough it starts with one of the things I'm proudest of in the past 8 years: the resurgence of national pride that I called the new patriotism. This national feeling is good, but it won't count for much, and it won't last unless it's grounded in thoughtfulness and knowledge.

An informed patriotism is what we want. And are we doing a good enough job teaching our children what America is and what she represents in the long history of the world? Those of us who are over 35 or so years of age grew up in a different America. We were taught, very directly, what it means to be an American. And we absorbed, almost in the air, a love of country and an appreciation of its institutions. If you didn't get these things from your family you got them from the neighborhood, from the father down the street who fought in Korea or the family who lost someone at Anzio. Or you could get a sense of patriotism from school. And if all else failed you could get a sense of patriotism from the popular culture. The movies celebrated democratic values and implicitly reinforced the idea that America was special. TV was like that, too, through the mid-sixties.

But now, we're about to enter the nineties, and some things have changed. Younger parents aren't sure that an unambivalent appreciation of America is the right thing to teach modern children. And as for those who create the popular culture, well-grounded patriotism is no longer the style. Our spirit is back, but we haven't reinstitutionalized it. We've got to do a better job of getting across that America is [about] freedom—freedom of speech, freedom of religion, freedom of enterprise. And freedom is special and rare. It's fragile; it needs production [sc: protection] ... Let's start with some basics: more attention to American history and a greater emphasis on civic ritual ...

And that's about all I have to say tonight, except for one thing. The past few days when I've been at that window upstairs, I've thought a bit of the "shining city upon a hill." The phrase comes from John Winthrop, who wrote it to describe the America he imagined. What he imagined was important because he was an early Pilgrim, an early freedom man. He journeyed here on what today we'd call a little wooden boat; and like the other Pilgrims, he was looking for a home that would be free.

I've spoken of the shining city all my political life, but I don't know if I ever quite communicated what I saw when I said it. But in my mind it was a tall, proud city built on rocks stronger than oceans, wind-swept, God-blessed, and teeming with people of all kinds living in harmony and peace; a city with free ports that hummed with commerce and creativity. And if there had to be city walls, the walls had doors and the doors were open to anyone with the will and the heart to get here. That's how I saw it, and see it still ...

The Neoconservative Persuasion

IRVING KRISTOL*

Irving Kristol (1920–2009), formerly senior fellow at the American Enterprise Institute, is the author of many books, including *Neoconservatism: The Autobiography of an Idea* (1999). He has served as editor or co-editor of several journals, notably *Commentary* (1947–1952) and *The Public Interest* (1965–2005). Kristol is one of the founders of the neoconservative movement—or, as he prefers to say, "persuasion." In the following essay he outlines the tenets of this persuasion and explains how it differs from other varieties of conservatism.

* *Source*: Irving Kristol, "The Neoconservative Persuasion," *The Weekly Standard*, August 25, 2003. Reprinted by permission of *The Weekly Standard*. http://www.weeklystandard.com.

THE NEOCONSERVATIVE PERSUASION

What exactly is neoconservatism? Journalists, and now even presidential candidates, speak with an enviable confidence on who or what is "neoconservative," and seem to assume the meaning is fully revealed in the name. Those of us who are designated as "neocons" are amused, flattered, or dismissive, depending on the context. It is reasonable to wonder: Is there any "there" there?

Even I, frequently referred to as the "godfather" of all those neocons, have had my moments of wonderment. A few years ago I said (and, alas, wrote) that neoconservatism had had its own distinctive qualities in its early years, but by now had been absorbed into the mainstream of American conservatism. I was wrong, and the reason I was wrong is that, ever since its origin among disillusioned liberal intellectuals in the 1970s, what we call neoconservatism has been one of those intellectual undercurrents that surface only intermittently. It is not a "movement," as the conspiratorial critics would have it. Neoconservatism is what the late historian of Jacksonian America, Marvin Meyers, called a "persuasion," one that manifests itself over time, but erratically, and one whose meaning we clearly glimpse only in retrospect.

Viewed in this way, one can say that the historical task and political purpose of neoconservatism would seem to be this: to convert the Republican party, and American conservatism in general, against their respective wills, into a new kind of conservative politics suitable to governing a modern democracy. That this new conservative politics is distinctly American is beyond doubt. There is nothing like neoconservatism in Europe, and most European conservatives are highly skeptical of its legitimacy. The fact that conservatism in the United States is so much healthier than in Europe, so much more politically effective, surely has something to do with the existence of neoconservatism. But Europeans, who think it absurd to look to the United States for lessons in political innovation, resolutely refuse to consider this possibility.

Neoconservatism is the first variant of American conservatism in the past century that is in the "American grain." It is hopeful, not lugubrious; forward-looking, not nostalgic; and its general tone is cheerful, not grim or dyspeptic. Its 20th-century heroes tend to be TR [Theodore Roosevelt], FDR [Franklin Delano Roosevelt], and Ronald Reagan. Such Republican and conservative worthies as Calvin Coolidge, Herbert Hoover, Dwight Eisenhower, and Barry Goldwater are politely overlooked. Of course, those worthies are in no way overlooked by a large, probably the largest, segment of the Republican party, with the result that most Republican politicians know nothing and could not care less about neoconservatism. Nevertheless, they cannot be blind to the fact that neoconservative policies, reaching out beyond the traditional political and financial base, have helped make the very idea of political conservatism more acceptable to a majority of American voters. Nor has it passed official notice that it is the neoconservative public policies, not the traditional Republican ones, that result in popular Republican presidencies.

One of these policies, most visible and controversial, is cutting tax rates in order to stimulate steady economic growth. This policy was not invented by neocons, and it was not the particularities of tax cuts that interested them, but rather the steady focus on economic growth. Neocons are familiar with intellectual history and aware that it is only in the last two centuries that democracy has become a respectable option among political thinkers. In earlier times, democracy meant an inherently turbulent political regime, with the "have-nots" and the "haves" engaged in a perpetual and utterly destructive class struggle. It was only the prospect of economic growth in which everyone prospered, if not equally or simultaneously, that gave modern democracies their legitimacy and durability.

The cost of this emphasis on economic growth has been an attitude toward public finance that is far less risk averse than is the case among more traditional conservatives. Neocons would prefer not to have large budget deficits, but it is in the nature of democracy—because it seems to be in the nature of human nature—that political demagogy will frequently result in economic recklessness, so that one sometimes must shoulder budgetary deficits as the cost (temporary, one hopes) of pursuing economic growth. It is a basic assumption of neoconservatism that, as a consequence of the spread of affluence among all classes, a property-owning and tax-paying population will, in time, become less vulnerable to egalitarian illusions and demagogic appeals and more sensible about the fundamentals of economic reckoning.

This leads to the issue of the role of the state. Neocons do not like the concentration of services in the welfare state and are happy to study alternative ways of delivering these services. But they are impatient with the Hayekian notion that we are on "the road to serfdom."[1] Neocons do not feel that kind of alarm or anxiety about the growth of the state in the past century, seeing it as natural, indeed inevitable. Because they tend to be more interested in history than economics or sociology, they know that the 19th-century idea, so neatly propounded by Herbert Spencer in his "The Man Versus the State," was a historical eccentricity. People have always preferred strong government to weak government, although they certainly have no liking for anything that smacks of overly intrusive government. Neocons feel at home in today's America to a degree that more traditional conservatives do not. Though they find much to be critical about, they tend to seek intellectual guidance in the democratic wisdom of Tocqueville, rather than in the Tory nostalgia of, say, Russell Kirk.[2]

But it is only to a degree that neocons are comfortable in modern America. The steady decline in our democratic culture, sinking to new levels of vulgarity, does unite neocons with traditional conservatives—though not with those libertarian conservatives who are conservative in economics but unmindful of the culture. The upshot is a quite unexpected alliance between neocons, who include a fair proportion of secular intellectuals, and religious traditionalists. They are united on issues concerning the quality of education, the relations of church and state, the regulation of pornography, and the like, all of which they regard as proper candidates for the government's attention. And since the Republican Party now has a substantial base among the religious, this gives neocons a certain influence and even power. Because religious conservatism is so feeble in Europe, the neoconservative potential there is correspondingly weak.

And then, of course, there is foreign policy, the area of American politics where neoconservatism has recently been the focus of media attention. This is surprising since there is no set of neoconservative beliefs concerning foreign policy, only a set of attitudes derived from historical experience. (The favorite neoconservative text on foreign affairs, thanks to professors Leo Strauss of Chicago and Donald Kagan of Yale, is Thucydides on the Peloponnesian War.) These attitudes can be summarized in the following "theses" (as a Marxist would say): First, patriotism is a natural and healthy sentiment and should be encouraged by both private and public institutions. Precisely because we are a nation of immigrants, this is a powerful American sentiment. Second, world government is a terrible idea since it can lead to world tyranny. International institutions that point to an ultimate world government should be regarded with the deepest suspicion. Third, statesmen should, above all, have the ability to distinguish friends from enemies. This is not as easy as it sounds, as the history of the Cold War revealed. The number of intelligent men who could not count the Soviet Union as an enemy, even though this was its own self-definition, was absolutely astonishing.

Finally, for a great power, the "national interest" is not a geographical term, except for fairly prosaic matters like trade and environmental regulation. A smaller nation might appropriately feel that its national interest begins and ends at its borders, so that its foreign policy is almost always in a defensive mode. A larger nation has more extensive interests. And large nations, whose identity is ideological, like the Soviet Union of yesteryear and the United States of today, inevitably have ideological interests in addition to more material concerns. Barring extraordinary events, the United States will always feel obliged to defend, if possible, a democratic nation under attack from nondemocratic forces, external or internal. That is why it was in our national interest to come to the defense of France and Britain in World War II. That is why we feel it necessary to defend Israel today, when its survival is threatened. No complicated geopolitical calculations of national interest are necessary.

Behind all this is a fact: the incredible military superiority of the United States vis-à-vis the nations of the rest of the world, in any imaginable combination. This superiority was planned by no one, and even today there are many Americans who are in denial. To a large extent, it all happened as a result of our bad luck. During the 50 years after World War II, while Europe was at peace and the Soviet Union largely relied on surrogates to do its fighting, the United States was involved in a whole series of wars: the Korean War, the Vietnam War, the Gulf War, the Kosovo conflict, the Afghan War, and the Iraq War. The result was that our military spending expanded more or less in line with our economic growth, while Europe's democracies cut back their military spending in favor of social welfare programs. The Soviet Union spent profusely but wastefully, so that its military collapsed along with its economy.

Suddenly, after two decades during which "imperial decline" and "imperial overstretch" were the academic and journalistic watchwords, the United States emerged as uniquely powerful. The "magic" of compound interest over half a century had its effect on our military budget, as did the cumulative scientific and technological research of our armed forces. With power come responsibilities, whether sought or not, whether welcome or not. And it is a fact that if you have the kind of power we now have, either you will find opportunities to use it, or the world will discover them for you.

The older, traditional elements in the Republican Party have difficulty coming to terms with this new reality in foreign affairs, just as they cannot reconcile economic conservatism with social and cultural conservatism. But by one of those accidents historians ponder, our current president [George W. Bush] and his administration turn out to be quite at home in this new political environment, although it is clear they did not anticipate this role any more than their party as a whole did. As a result, neoconservatism began enjoying a second life, at a time when its obituaries were still being published.

NOTES

1   Kristol refers here to Friedrich von Hayek, *The Road to Serfdom* (Chicago: University of Chicago Press, 1944).—Eds.
2   Russell Kirk (1918–1994) was an American conservative and author of many books, including the influential *The Conservative Mind* (New York: Avon Books, 1968). See also selection 4.31—Eds.

The Manhattan Declaration

ROBERT GEORGE, ET AL.*

Written in 2009, the *Manhattan Declaration* has since been signed by more than 250 Christian conservative leaders representing a wide variety of religious affiliations across the United States. The document begins with an assertion of the crucial historical and contemporary role played by Christians in such noble causes as fighting against poverty, slavery, political absolutism, and AIDs in Africa; and for women's suffrage and civil rights. However, the *Declaration* goes on to argue that just as Christians have taken political stands on these issues, so too they are morally obliged or "called" by "Christian conscience" to do the same on a number of other controversial contemporary questions as well. Most important among these are the sanctity of human life, the defense of traditional notions of marriage, and the protection of "religious liberty." On the view of the signatories, a religious commitment to any form of Christianity, rightly understood, thereby necessarily entails opposition to abortion and euthanasia, the rejection of all forms of same-sex marriage, and a defense of the rights of Christians to refrain from providing economic goods and services to people whose lifestyles offend their most deeply held beliefs.

---

* *Source*: manhattandeclaration.org

MANHATTAN DECLARATION: A CALL OF CHRISTIAN CONSCIENCE
Released November 20, 2009

Preamble

Christians are heirs of a 2,000-year tradition of proclaiming God's word, seeking justice in our societies, resisting tyranny, and reaching out with compassion to the poor, oppressed and suffering.

While fully acknowledging the imperfections and shortcomings of Christian institutions and communities in all ages, we claim the heritage of those Christians who defended innocent life by rescuing discarded babies from trash heaps in Roman cities and publicly denouncing the Empire's sanctioning of infanticide. We remember with reverence those believers who sacrificed their lives by remaining in Roman cities to tend the sick and dying during the plagues, and who died bravely in the coliseums rather than deny their Lord.

After the barbarian tribes overran Europe, Christian monasteries preserved not only the Bible but also the literature and art of Western culture. It was Christians who combated the evil of slavery: Papal edicts in the 16th and 17th centuries decried the practice of slavery and first excommunicated anyone involved in the slave trade; evangelical Christians in England, led by John Wesley and William Wilberforce, put an end to the slave trade in that country. Christians under Wilberforce's leadership also formed hundreds of societies for helping the poor, the imprisoned, and child laborers chained to machines.

In Europe, Christians challenged the divine claims of kings and successfully fought to establish the rule of law and balance of governmental powers, which made modern democracy possible. And in America, Christian women stood at the vanguard of the suffrage movement. The great civil rights crusades of the 1950s and 60s were led by Christians claiming the Scriptures and asserting the glory of the image of God in every human being regardless of race, religion, age or class.

This same devotion to human dignity has led Christians in recent decades to work to end the dehumanizing scourge of human trafficking and sexual slavery, bring compassionate care to AIDS sufferers in Africa, and assist in a myriad of other human rights causes—from providing clean water in developing nations to providing homes for tens of thousands of children orphaned by war, disease and gender discrimination.

Like those who have gone before us in the faith, Christians today are called to proclaim the Gospel of costly grace, to protect the intrinsic dignity of the human person and to stand for the common good. In being true to its own calling, the call to discipleship, the church through service to others can make a profound contribution to the public good.

Declaration

We, as Orthodox, Catholic, and Evangelical Christians, have gathered, beginning in New York on September 28, 2009, to make the following declaration, which we sign as individuals, not on behalf of our organizations, but speaking to and from our communities. We act together in obedience to the one true God, the triune God of holiness and love, who has laid total claim on our lives and by that claim calls us with believers in all ages and all nations to seek and defend the good of all who bear his image. We set forth this declaration in light of the truth that is grounded in Holy Scripture, in natural human reason (which is itself, in our view, the gift of a beneficent God), and in the very nature of the human person. We call upon all people of goodwill, believers and non-believers alike, to consider carefully and reflect critically on the issues we here address as we, with St. Paul, commend this appeal to everyone's conscience in the sight of God.

While the whole scope of Christian moral concern, including a special concern for the poor and vulnerable, claims our attention, we are especially troubled that in our nation today the lives of the unborn, the disabled, and the elderly are severely threatened; that the institution of marriage, already buffeted by promiscuity, infidelity and divorce, is in jeopardy of being redefined to accommodate fashionable ideologies; that freedom of religion and the rights of conscience are gravely jeopardized by those who would use the instruments of coercion to compel persons of faith to compromise their deepest convictions.

Because the sanctity of human life, the dignity of marriage as a union of husband and wife, and the freedom of conscience and religion are foundational principles of justice and the common good, we are compelled by our Christian faith to speak and act in their defense. In this declaration we affirm: 1) the profound, inherent, and equal dignity of every human being as a creature fashioned in the very image of God, possessing inherent rights of equal dignity and life; 2) marriage as a conjugal union of man and woman, ordained by God from the creation, and historically understood by believers and non-believers alike, to be the most basic institution in society and; 3) religious liberty, which is grounded in the character of God, the example of Christ, and the inherent freedom and dignity of human beings created in the divine image.

We are Christians who have joined together across historic lines of ecclesial differences to affirm our right—and, more importantly, *to embrace our obligation*—to speak and act in defense of these truths. We pledge to each other, and to our fellow believers, that no power on earth, be it cultural or political, will intimidate us into silence or acquiescence. It is our duty to proclaim the Gospel of our Lord and Savior Jesus Christ in its fullness, both in season and out of season. May God help us not to fail in that duty.

Life

So God created man in his own image, in the image of God he created him; male and female he created them.

Genesis 1:27

I have come that they may have life, and have it to the full.

John 10:10

Although public sentiment has moved in a pro-life direction, we note with sadness that pro-abortion ideology prevails today in our government. Many in the present administration want to make abortions legal at any stage of fetal development, and want to provide abortions at taxpayer expense. Majorities in both houses of Congress hold pro-abortion views. The Supreme Court, whose infamous 1973 decision in *Roe v. Wade* stripped the unborn of legal protection, continues to treat elective abortion as a fundamental constitutional right, though it has upheld as constitutionally permissible some limited restrictions on abortion. The President says that he wants to reduce the "need" for abortion—a commendable goal. But he has also pledged to make abortion more easily and widely available by eliminating laws prohibiting government funding, requiring waiting periods for women seeking abortions, and parental notification for abortions performed on minors. The elimination of these important and effective pro-life laws cannot reasonably be expected to do other than significantly increase the number of elective abortions by which the lives of countless children are snuffed out prior to birth. Our commitment to the sanctity of life is not a matter of partisan loyalty, for we recognize that in the thirty-six years since *Roe v. Wade*, elected officials and appointees of both major political parties have been complicit in giving legal sanction to what Pope John Paul II described as "the culture of death." We call on all officials in our country, elected and appointed, to protect and serve every member of our society, including the most marginalized, voiceless, and vulnerable among us.

A culture of death inevitably cheapens life in all its stages and conditions by promoting the belief that lives that are imperfect, immature or inconvenient are discardable. As predicted by many prescient persons, the cheapening of life that began with abortion has now metastasized. For example, human embryo-destructive research and its public funding are promoted in the name of science and in the cause of developing treatments and cures for diseases and injuries. The President and many in Congress favor the expansion of embryo-research to include the taxpayer funding of so-called "therapeutic cloning." This would result in the industrial mass production of human embryos to be killed for the purpose of producing genetically customized stem cell lines and tissues. At the other end of life, an increasingly powerful movement to promote assisted suicide and "voluntary" euthanasia threatens the lives of vulnerable elderly and disabled persons. Eugenic notions such as the doctrine of *lebensunwertes Leben* ("life unworthy of life") were first advanced in the 1920s by intellectuals in the elite salons of America and Europe. Long buried in ignominy after the horrors of the mid-20th century, they have returned from the grave. The only difference is that now the doctrines of the eugenicists are dressed up in the language of "liberty," "autonomy," and "choice."

We will be united and untiring in our efforts to roll back the license to kill that began with the abandonment of the unborn to abortion. We will work, as we have always worked, to bring assistance, comfort, and care to pregnant women in need and to those who have been victimized by abortion, even as we stand resolutely against the corrupt and degrading notion that it can somehow be in the best interests of women to submit to the deliberate killing of their unborn children. Our message is, and ever shall be, that the just, humane, and truly Christian answer to problem pregnancies is for all of us to love and care for mother and child alike.

A truly prophetic Christian witness will insistently call on those who have been entrusted with temporal power to fulfill the first responsibility of government: to protect the weak and vulnerable against violent attack, and to do so with no favoritism, partiality, or discrimination. The Bible enjoins us to defend those who cannot defend themselves, to speak for those who cannot themselves speak. And so we defend and speak for the unborn, the disabled, and the dependent. What the Bible and the light of reason make clear, we must make clear. We must be willing to defend, even at risk and cost to ourselves and our institutions, the lives of our brothers and sisters at every stage of development and in every condition.

Our concern is not confined to our own nation. Around the globe, we are witnessing cases of genocide and "ethnic cleansing," the failure to assist those who are suffering as innocent victims of war, the neglect and abuse of children, the exploitation of vulnerable laborers, the sexual trafficking of girls and young women, the abandonment of the aged, racial oppression and discrimination, the persecution of believers of all faiths, and the failure to take steps necessary to halt the spread of preventable diseases like AIDS. We see these travesties as flowing from the same loss of the sense of the dignity of the human person and the sanctity of human life that drives the abortion industry and the movements for assisted suicide, euthanasia, and human cloning for biomedical research. And so ours is, as it must be, a truly consistent ethic of love and life for all humans in all circumstances.

Marriage

The man said, "This is now bone of my bones and flesh of my flesh; she shall be called woman, for she was taken out of man." For this reason a man will leave his father and mother and be united to his wife, and they will become one flesh.

Genesis 2:23-24

This is a profound mystery—but I am talking about Christ and the church. However, each one of you also must love his wife as he loves himself, and the wife must respect her husband.

Ephesians 5:32-33

In Scripture, the creation of man and woman, and their one-flesh union as husband and wife, is the crowning achievement of God's creation. In the transmission of life and the nurturing of children, men and women joined as spouses are given the great honor of being partners with God Himself. Marriage then, is the first institution of human society—indeed it is the institution on which all other human institutions have their foundation. In the Christian tradition we refer to marriage as "holy matrimony" to signal the fact that it is an institution ordained by God, and blessed by Christ in his participation at a wedding in Cana of Galilee. In the Bible, God Himself blesses and holds marriage in the highest esteem.

Vast human experience confirms that marriage is the original and most important institution for sustaining the health, education, and welfare of all persons in a society. Where marriage is honored, and where there is a flourishing marriage culture, everyone benefits—the spouses themselves, their children, the communities and societies in which they live. Where the marriage culture begins to erode, social pathologies of every sort quickly manifest themselves.

Unfortunately, we have witnessed over the course of the past several decades a serious erosion of the marriage culture in our own country. Perhaps the most telling—and alarming—indicator is the out-of-wedlock birth rate. Less than fifty years ago, it was under 5 percent. Today it is over 40 percent. Our society—and particularly its poorest and most vulnerable sectors, where the out-of-wedlock birth rate is much higher even than the national average—is paying a huge price in delinquency, drug abuse, crime, incarceration, hopelessness, and despair. Other indicators are widespread non-marital sexual cohabitation and a devastatingly high rate of divorce.

We confess with sadness that Christians and our institutions have too often scandalously failed to uphold the institution of marriage and to model for the world the true meaning of marriage. Insofar as we have too easily embraced the culture of divorce and remained silent about social practices that undermine the dignity of marriage we repent, and call upon all Christians to do the same.

To strengthen families, we must stop glamorizing promiscuity and infidelity and restore among our people a sense of the profound beauty, mystery, and holiness of faithful marital love. We must reform ill-advised policies that contribute to the weakening of the institution of marriage, including the discredited idea of unilateral divorce. We must work in the legal, cultural, and religious domains to instill in young people a sound understanding of what marriage is, what it requires, and why it is worth the commitment and sacrifices that faithful spouses make.

The impulse to redefine marriage in order to recognize same-sex and multiple partner relationships is a symptom, rather than the cause, of the erosion of the marriage culture. It reflects a loss of understanding of the meaning of marriage as embodied in our civil and religious law and in the philosophical tradition that contributed to shaping the law. Yet it is critical that the impulse be resisted, for yielding to it would mean abandoning the possibility of restoring a sound understanding of marriage and, with it, the hope of rebuilding a healthy marriage culture. It would lock into place the false and destructive belief that marriage is all about romance and other adult satisfactions, and not, in any intrinsic way, about procreation and the unique character and value of acts and relationships whose meaning is shaped by their aptness for the generation, promotion and protection of life. In spousal communion and the rearing of children (who, as gifts of God, are the fruit of their parents' marital love), we discover the profound reasons for and benefits of the marriage covenant.

We acknowledge that there are those who are disposed towards homosexual and polyamorous conduct and relationships, just as there are those who are disposed towards other forms of immoral conduct. We have compassion for those so disposed; we respect them as human beings possessing profound, inherent, and equal dignity; and we pay tribute to the men and women who strive, often with little assistance, to resist the temptation to yield to desires that they, no less than we, regard as wayward. We stand with them, even when they falter. We, no less than they, are sinners who have fallen short of God's intention for our lives. We, no less than they, are in constant need of God's patience, love and forgiveness. We call on the entire Christian community to resist sexual immorality, and at the same time refrain from disdainful condemnation of those who yield to it. Our rejection of sin, though resolute, must never become the rejection of sinners. For every sinner, regardless of the sin, is loved by God, who seeks not our destruction but rather the conversion of our hearts. Jesus calls all who wander from the path of virtue to "a more excellent way." As his disciples we will reach out in love to assist all who hear the call and wish to answer it.

We further acknowledge that there are sincere people who disagree with us, and with the teaching of the Bible and Christian tradition, on questions of sexual morality and the nature of marriage. Some who enter into same-sex and polyamorous relationships no doubt regard their unions as truly marital. They fail to understand, however, that marriage is made possible by the sexual complementarity of man and woman, and that the comprehensive, multi-level sharing of life that marriage is includes bodily unity of the sort that unites husband and wife biologically as a reproductive unit. This is because the body is no mere extrinsic instrument of the human person, but truly part of the personal reality of the human being. Human beings are not merely centers of consciousness or emotion, or minds, or spirits, inhabiting non-personal bodies. The human person is a dynamic unity of body, mind, and spirit. Marriage is what one man and one woman establish when, forsaking all others and pledging lifelong commitment, they found a sharing of life at every level of being—the biological, the emotional, the dispositional, the rational, the spiritual—on a commitment that is sealed, completed and actualized by loving sexual intercourse in which the spouses become one flesh, not in some merely metaphorical sense, but by fulfilling together the behavioral conditions of procreation. That is why in the Christian tradition, and historically in Western law, consummated marriages are not dissoluble or annullable on the ground of infertility, even though the nature of the marital relationship is shaped and structured by its intrinsic orientation to the great good of procreation.

We understand that many of our fellow citizens, including some Christians, believe that the historic definition of marriage as the union of one man and one woman is a denial of equality or civil rights. They wonder what to say in reply to the argument that asserts that no harm would be done to them or to anyone if the law of the community were to confer upon two men or two women who are living together in a sexual partnership the status of being "married." It would not, after all, affect their own marriages, would it? On inspection, however, the argument that laws governing one kind of marriage will not affect another cannot stand. Were it to prove anything, it would prove far too much: the assumption that the legal status of one set of marriage relationships affects no other would not only argue for same sex partnerships; it could be asserted with equal validity for polyamorous partnerships, polygamous households, even adult brothers, sisters, or brothers and sisters living in incestuous relationships. Should these, as a matter of equality or civil rights, be recognized as lawful marriages, and would they have no effects on other relationships? No. The truth is that marriage is not something abstract or neutral that the law may legitimately define and re-define to please those who are powerful and influential.

No one has a civil right to have a non-marital relationship treated as a marriage. Marriage is an objective reality—a covenantal union of husband and wife—that it is the duty of the law to recognize and support for the sake of justice and the common good. If it fails to do so, genuine social harms follow. First, the religious liberty of those for whom this is a matter of conscience is jeopardized. Second, the rights of parents are abused as family life and sex education programs in schools are used to teach children that an enlightened understanding recognizes as "marriages" sexual partnerships that many parents believe are intrinsically non-marital and immoral. Third, the common good of civil society is damaged when the law itself, in its critical pedagogical function, becomes a tool for eroding a sound understanding of marriage on which the flourishing of the marriage culture in any society vitally depends. Sadly, we are today far from having a thriving marriage culture. But if we are to begin the critically important process of reforming our laws and mores to rebuild such a culture, the last thing we can afford to do is to re-define marriage in such a way as to embody in our laws a false proclamation about what marriage is.

And so it is out of *love* (not "animus") and prudent *concern for the common good* (not "prejudice"), that we pledge to labor ceaselessly to preserve the legal definition of marriage as the union of one man and one woman and to rebuild the marriage culture. How could we, as Christians, do otherwise? The Bible teaches us that marriage is a central part of God's creation covenant. Indeed, the union of husband and wife mirrors the bond between Christ and his church. And so just as Christ was willing, out of love, to give Himself up for the church in a complete sacrifice, we are willing, lovingly, to make whatever sacrifices are required of us for the sake of the inestimable treasure that is marriage.

Religious Liberty

The Spirit of the Sovereign LORD is on me, because the LORD has anointed me to preach good news to the poor. He has sent me to bind up the brokenhearted, to proclaim freedom for the captives and release from darkness for the prisoners.

Isaiah 61:1

Give to Caesar what is Caesar's, and to God what is God's.

Matthew 22:21

The struggle for religious liberty across the centuries has been long and arduous, but it is not a novel idea or recent development. The nature of religious liberty is grounded in the character of God Himself, the God who is most fully known in the life and work of Jesus Christ. Determined to follow Jesus faithfully in life and death, the early Christians appealed to the manner in which the Incarnation had taken place: "Did God send Christ, as some suppose, as a tyrant brandishing fear and terror? Not so, but in gentleness and meekness …, for compulsion is no attribute of God" (Epistle to Diognetus 7.3-4). Thus the right to religious freedom has its foundation in the example of Christ Himself and in the very dignity of the human person created in the image of God—a dignity, as our founders proclaimed, inherent in every human, and knowable by all in the exercise of right reason.

Christians confess that God alone is Lord of the conscience. Immunity from religious coercion is the cornerstone of an unconstrained conscience. No one should be compelled to embrace any religion against his will, nor should persons of faith be forbidden to worship God according to the dictates of conscience or to express freely and publicly their deeply held religious convictions.[1] What is true for individuals applies to religious communities as well.

It is ironic that those who today assert a right to kill the unborn, aged and disabled and also a right to engage in immoral sexual practices, and even a right to have relationships integrated around these practices be recognized and blessed by law—such persons claiming these "rights" are very often in the vanguard of those who would trample upon the freedom of others to express their religious and moral commitments to the sanctity of life and to the dignity of marriage as the conjugal union of husband and wife.

We see this, for example, in the effort to weaken or eliminate conscience clauses, and therefore to compel pro-life institutions (including religiously affiliated hospitals and clinics), and pro-life physicians, surgeons, nurses, and other health care professionals, to refer for abortions and, in certain cases, even to perform or participate in abortions. We see it in the use of antidiscrimination statutes to force religious institutions, businesses, and service providers of various sorts to comply with activities they judge to be deeply immoral or go out of business. After the judicial imposition of "same-sex marriage" in Massachusetts, for example, Catholic Charities chose with great reluctance to end its century-long work of helping to place orphaned children in good homes rather than comply with a legal mandate that it place children in same-sex households in violation of Catholic moral teaching. In New Jersey, after the establishment of a quasi-marital "civil unions" scheme, a Methodist institution was stripped of its tax exempt status when it declined, as a matter of religious conscience, to permit a facility it owned and operated to be used for ceremonies blessing homosexual unions. In Canada and some European nations, Christian clergy have been prosecuted for preaching Biblical norms against the practice of homosexuality. New hate-crime laws in America raise the specter of the same practice here.

In recent decades a growing body of case law has paralleled the decline in respect for religious values in the media, the academy and political leadership, resulting in restrictions on the free exercise of religion. We view this as an ominous development, not only because of its threat to the individual liberty guaranteed to every person, regardless of his or her faith, but because the trend also threatens the common welfare and the culture of freedom on which our system of republican government is founded. Restrictions on the freedom of conscience or the ability to hire people of one's own faith or conscientious moral convictions for religious institutions, for example, undermines the viability of the intermediate structures of society, the essential buffer against the overweening authority of the state, resulting in the soft despotism Tocqueville so prophetically warned of.[1] Disintegration of civil society is a prelude to tyranny.

As Christians, we take seriously the Biblical admonition to respect and obey those in authority. We believe in law and in the rule of law. We recognize the duty to comply with laws whether we happen to like them or not, unless the laws are gravely unjust or require those subject to them to do something unjust or otherwise immoral. The biblical purpose of law is to preserve order and serve justice and the common good; yet laws that are unjust—and especially laws that purport to compel citizens to do what is unjust—undermine the common good, rather than serve it.

Going back to the earliest days of the church, Christians have refused to compromise their proclamation of the gospel. In Acts 4, Peter and John were ordered to stop preaching. Their answer was, "Judge for yourselves whether it is right in God's sight to obey you rather than God. For we cannot help speaking about what we have seen and heard." Through the centuries, Christianity has taught that civil disobedience is not only permitted, but sometimes required. There is no more eloquent defense of the rights and duties of religious conscience than the one offered by Martin Luther King, Jr., in his *Letter from a Birmingham Jail*. Writing from an explicitly Christian perspective, and citing Christian writers such as Augustine and Aquinas, King taught that just laws elevate and ennoble human beings because they are rooted in the moral law whose ultimate source is God Himself. Unjust laws degrade human beings. Inasmuch as they can claim no authority beyond sheer human will, they lack any power to bind in conscience. King's willingness to go to jail, rather than comply with legal injustice, was exemplary and inspiring.

Because we honor justice and the common good, we will not comply with any edict that purports to compel our institutions to participate in abortions, embryo-destructive research, assisted suicide and euthanasia, or any other anti-life act; nor will we bend to any rule purporting to force us to bless immoral sexual partnerships, treat them as marriages or the equivalent, or refrain from proclaiming the truth, as we know it, about morality and immorality and marriage and the family. We will fully and ungrudgingly render to Caesar what is Caesar's. But under no circumstances will we render to Caesar what is God's.

# # #

Drafting Committee: Robert George Professor, McCormick Professor of Jurisprudence, Princeton University; Timothy George Professor, Beeson Divinity School, Samford University; Chuck Colson Founder, the Chuck Colson Center for Christian Worldview (Lansdowne, VA)

NOTE

1   Alexis de Tocqueville, *Democracy in America*, Vol. II, Book 4.

PART 5

SOCIALISM AND COMMUNISM: FROM MORE TO MARX

Socialism and communism, though by no means identical, both belong to a common family of ideologies and spring from a common impulse. Both envision a society in which everyone contributes time, labor, and talent to a common pool and receives in return enough goods to satisfy his or her needs. Both condemn the exploitation of one individual or class by another that occurs, for example, when one profits from another's labor. And both believe that property should be so distributed as to benefit not just the wealthy few but the public at large. Both, therefore, are critical of capitalism as an economic system and of liberalism (or liberal individualism) as an ideology.

But socialism and communism differ in important respects. One crucial difference concerns the means for attaining their ends. Socialists are more apt to favor peaceful and piecemeal reforms as a way of bringing about a socialist society, while communists—at least in the late nineteenth and the twentieth centuries— favored violent revolutionary transformations spearheaded by an elite "vanguard" party. Moreover, the kind of society that each hopes to create differs to some degree. Socialists envision a society in which the major means of production—mines, mills, factories, power plants, and so on—are either publicly owned or at least operated for the public benefit. Modern communists, by contrast, tend to favor public ownership and bureaucratic control of virtually all enterprises, large and small.

Perhaps the best way to understand these differences and the variety of forms socialism and communism have taken is to look back over the long history that socialists of all sorts have shared. As long ago as the fourth century BCE, for example, the Greek philosopher Plato envisioned in his *Republic* an ideal society in which one class, the Guardians, held everything in common, including spouses and children. Many early Christians were communists who shared all their worldly goods with one another—a practice that persists even today in some monasteries and nunneries. This early conception of communism is perhaps most memorably sketched in St. Thomas More's *Utopia* (1516). There, More (1478–1535) imagines a society from which the forces of envy and greed have been banished. Private property and money have been abolished. The Utopians work not for personal profit but for the common good. Although the Utopians are pagans, More maintains that they put "Christian" Europe to shame by behaving selflessly and charitably toward one another.

Later idealistic or "utopian" socialists, such as Charles Fourier (1772–1837) and Robert Owen (1771–1858), provided more secular variations on More's theme. Fourier, for example, imagined an ideal society in which all would work for the common good, even if they did exactly as they pleased. The socialist principle of "harmonism" would harmonize diverse interests or "passions" and would make social cooperation not only possible but pleasant. Owen, a capitalist turned socialist, tried to put his plans for a perfect society into practice. Believing that human labor should be not only productive but morally uplifting, he designed and built factories and adjoining towns to promote these two ideals.

These and other schemes for socialist transformation were derided and condemned by those who thought of themselves as "scientific" socialists. Against the "utopianism" of earlier socialists, Karl Marx (1818–1883) and Friedrich Engels (1820–1895) argued that society is changed not through moral suasion but by understanding the hidden structures and process of material production. The key, they thought, was the "materialist conception of history." Unlike the "idealist" view of history advanced by G. W. F. Hegel (1770–1831), Marx and Engels's "materialist" view made material production and class struggle the primary determinants of social stability and change. All previously existing societies were divided along class lines. On the one side was the dominant or ruling class, the owners of the means of material production; on the other, a subservient class condemned to do the bidding of the ruling class. Who the rulers and the ruled are depends on the type of society or "social formation" one is talking about. In slave society, masters rule over slaves; in feudal society, lords rule over serfs; in capitalist society, the ruling capitalist class or *bourgeoisie* rules over the working class or *proletariat*. These "social relations of production" do not rest on force alone. If a class-divided society is to be stable and long lived, its members must view it as legitimate. The social order, with its inequalities of wealth and opportunity, must be seen as "normal," "natural," "necessary," or "inevitable." This, Marx said, is the function of ideology: to put the stamp of legitimacy on existing social arrangements. The "ruling ideas"—that is, the respectable or mainstream ideas—"are in every society the ideas of the ruling class." Only those ideas that serve the interest of the ruling class by helping it to perpetuate its rule will be disseminated from the pulpit, in the classroom, in the mass media, and elsewhere. All others—especially socialist and communist ideas—will be regarded with suspicion or contempt, or both.

Marx viewed his own theory as *critical*, that is, subversive of the orthodox opinions prevalent in capitalist society. The ideological prop and mainstay of such a society, he held, was political economy—the nineteenth-century term for the "science" of economics—with its "laws" of supply and demand and so on. Marx tried to show that political economy was really a smokescreen to obscure the system of exploitative social relations on which capitalism rested. By exposing the exploitative nature of the system, Marx hoped to enlighten or raise the consciousness of the proletariat, thereby paving the way for a revolution that would free it from the system that oppressed it. Only then, he thought, could the workers begin to bring about a classless communist society that operated according to the principle "From each according to his ability, to each according to his need."

Utopia

THOMAS MORE*

Thomas More (1478–1535) was an important political and literary figure of the "Northern Renaissance" of the early sixteenth century. At one time a close adviser to Britain's King Henry VIII, More fell into disfavor when Henry broke with the Roman Catholic Church to establish the Church of England with himself as head. For refusing to approve Henry's action, More was beheaded. Four centuries later the Roman Catholic Church recognized him as a saint. Before his difficulties with Henry VIII began, More wrote *Utopia* (1516), a book in which he imagined a society from which the evils of envy and poverty had been banished. In the following selection, More's main character, the fictitious explorer Raphael Hythloday, traces the evils of European society to the private ownership of property, which he contrasts to the virtues of the island commonwealth of Utopia, where private property and even money have been abolished.

---

* *Source*: More wrote *Utopia* in Latin. The following selections are from the first English translation, by Ralph Robynson in 1551. We have made numerous changes, including some minor abridgments, to put these passages into a style and language more accessible to modern readers.

UTOPIA[1]

From Book I

"I have no doubt, Master More," said Hythloday, "that wherever men have private property and money is the measure of everything, there it is hardly possible for the commonwealth to be justly governed or to flourish in prosperity. Unless, that is, you think that justice is done when all things are in the hands of evil men, or that prosperity and happiness are found when everything is divided among a few—and even those few do not really thrive—while all the rest live in misery and wretchedness."

"This is so different from the wise and godly ordinances of the Utopians, among whom a few laws are sufficient to keep everything well and happily ordered. In Utopia virtue is greatly esteemed, and even though all things are owned in common, everyone has everything in abundance. Now compare them with the many nations that are always making new, but unsatisfactory, laws. In these countries every man claims that he has his own property, or private goods; but the new laws they make every day are not enough to enable everyone to enjoy or defend those things that he calls his own. This much is made plain by the never-ending legal suits that constantly arise. When I consider these things, then, I have to agree with Plato, and I do not wonder that he made no laws for those who refused to share their wealth equally. For this wise man clearly foresaw that the only way to promote the well-being of the public as a whole is to establish equality of all goods.[2] Such equality can never be found where every man's goods are his private property. For there every man lays claims to as much as he can get. Then, no matter how great the abundance, a few divide all the riches among themselves, leaving the rest in poverty. And for the most part, the poor are more worthy to be happy and prosperous than the others. The rich are covetous, crafty, and really quite useless; the poor, on the other hand, are lowly, simple, and by their daily labor more beneficial to the common welfare than to themselves.

Thus I am fully persuaded that no equitable and just distribution of goods can be made, and that there can be no true well-being in human affairs, unless private property is outlawed and banished. But as long as private property is the rule, the heavy and inevitable burden of poverty and wretchedness will weigh down the largest and best part of mankind. I grant that this burden may be eased, but it cannot be wholly removed while private property reigns. There might be a law that prohibits anyone from possessing more than a certain measure of land, perhaps, or more than a certain sum of money. Or there might be laws preventing the king from being too powerful, or the people from being too proud and unruly. Still other laws might proclaim that public offices must not be obtained by bribes and gifts, or that they cannot be bought or sold. Putting offices up for sale simply encourages the officials to regain the money they spent by defrauding and plundering the public; and if the offices go to those who offer bribes and gifts, the government will be in the hands of the rich, not the wise. By laws such as these, in short, the evils of which I have been speaking can be lightened and mitigated, just as people who are desperately ill and beyond cure can be kept alive with constant care. But these nations will never be completely cured and brought to a healthy condition while every man is master of his own property. You may cure one part, but in doing so you aggravate the illness of another. Helping one person harms another, for nothing can be given to anyone unless it is taken from someone else …"

From Book II (Hythloday's Account of Utopia)

Where money is the standard of everything, many vain and superfluous occupations must be pursued, although they serve only for wanton luxury and false pleasure. If the same multitude that now is occupied in work were divided into the few occupations that the truly necessary work requires, the abundance of goods that would ensue would be so great that the prices would doubtless be too low for the craftsmen to maintain their livelihood. But if all these who are now busy in useless occupations, with the whole flock of those who live idly and slothfully, consuming and wasting every one of them more of those things that come from other men's labor than two of the workers themselves do—if all these, I say, were set to useful occupations, you can easily see how little would be enough, even too much, to supply us with everything we require for the sake of necessity or comfort. Yes, or even for pleasure, as long as the pleasure be true and natural.

This is made plain by the life of Utopia itself. There in each city, including the adjoining countryside, scarcely 500 persons of all those who are neither too old nor too weak to work are excused from labor. Among these are the Syphogrants,[3] who are exempted by law from labor. Yet they do not take advantage of the exemption because they want to set an example by their labor that will encourage others to work. There are also the scholars to whom the people, upon the recommendation of the priest and secret election by the Syphogrants, give an exemption from labor so that they may devote themselves to learning. But if any of the scholars fails to meet the expected standards, he is immediately plucked back to the company of workers. On the other hand, it often happens that a craftsman so earnestly devotes his free time to learning, and so profits by his diligence, that he is taken from his handicraft and promoted to the company of the learned.

From these scholars the ambassadors, priests, and Tranibors[4] are chosen, as is the prince himself, whom they in their old tongue called Barzanes, and now call Ademus.[5] The rest of the people are neither idle nor occupied with useless work, so it may easily be judged how much good work they may do in a few hours. They also have the advantage that in most of the necessary trades they need not work as much as other nations do. First of all, the building or repairing of houses takes everywhere else so many men's time because the careless heir allows the house his father built to fall into decay. So while he might have preserved it at little cost, his successor is now constrained to build it anew at great expense. Many times also one man has so refined and delicate a taste that he sets no value on a house that cost another man much money. As the house is neglected and shortly falls into ruin, the man of refined taste builds another one in another place at no less cost. But among the Utopians, where all things are in good order and the commonwealth is well-regulated, it very seldom happens that they choose a new plot to build a house upon. They not only find quick remedies for existing faults, but also prevent those that are likely to occur. In this way their houses last long with little labor and small repairs—so long that their carpenters and builders sometimes have almost nothing to do, in which case they hew timber at home, and square and trim stones, so that if any work needs to be done, it may be finished even more speedily.

Now note how few workers their clothing requires. First of all, while they are at work they are dressed in simple leather or skins that will last seven years. When they go out they put on a cloak which hides the other homely apparel. These cloaks throughout the island are all the same color, and that is the natural color of the wool. They therefore not only need much less wool than people in other countries, but the wool they do need costs them much less. Linen is made with less labor, so it is used more. But in linen only whiteness is valued, and in wool only cleanliness. As for the fineness of the thread, they don't care. Yet this is why in other places four or five cloth gowns of diverse colors, and as many silk coats, are not enough for one man. Yes, and if he is the fashionable sort, even ten are too few. But in Utopia one garment will serve a man very well for two years. Why should he desire more? If he had them, he would be neither better protected from the cold nor in any way appear better dressed.

Because they are all engaged in useful occupations, there is plenty of everything they need; and because a few workers are enough for each craft, they sometimes bring out great numbers of people to repair the highways, if any need repair. Many times, also, when they have no such work to do, an open proclamation is made that they should devote fewer hours to work. For the authorities do not force the citizens to labor unnecessarily. Why should they? The chief aim of the constitution and government is to spare people as much time as possible from necessary occupations so that they can leave the labor of the body and give time to the freedom and culture of the mind. For this, they suppose, is what makes for a truly happy life ...

The Utopians use gold and silver in such a way as to prevent anyone from placing a greater value on these metals than they naturally deserve. Who does not see that these metals are less valuable than iron? Men can live no better without iron than without fire and water. But nature has given gold and silver no use that we could not do without. It is the folly of men that sets a higher value on them because they are rare. Nature, however, as a tender and loving mother, has placed the best and most necessary things in the open all about us, such as air, water, and the earth itself, and has hidden farthest from us vain and useless things ...

The Utopians have devised, then, a plan that is as consistent with their laws and customs as it is contrary to ours, where gold is so cherished. The plan may even seem incredible, as a result, to those unfamiliar with it. They eat and drink from earthen and glass vessels, which are well and cleverly made, but which have little value. Of gold and silver, however, they make chamber pots and similar containers that serve for the most vile uses, not only in their common halls, but in everyone's private house.[6] Furthermore, they make great chains and fetters of these metals to bind their slaves.[7] Finally, those who commit crimes must wear gold rings on their ears and fingers, gold chains around their necks, and gold crowns around their heads. In this way the Utopians arrange to have gold and silver serve as marks of reproach and infamy. Other peoples grieve if they must do without these metals, as if gold and silver were their own lives. But if they should be taken all at once from the Utopians, no one there would think he had lost as much as a penny.

They gather pearls from the sea and diamonds and rubies from certain rocks. They do not search for them, but if they find them by chance they cut and polish them, then decorate their infants with them. In their early years the children are fond and proud of such ornaments. When they are a little older and wiser, though, they see that only children wear such trifles, and they put them away as shameful, without any bidding from their parents, just as our children cast away their marbles, rattles, and dolls when they grow older. How these laws and customs, so different from other nations, lead to different ideas and desires was made most clear to me by the arrival of the ambassadors of the Anemolians.[8]

These ambassadors came to Amaurot[9] while I was there. Because they came to negotiate great and weighty matters, three representatives from each Utopian city gathered before them. The ambassadors of other countries who had been there before knew the manners of the Utopians, so they knew that no honor was given to sumptuous and costly apparel—silks were condemned, gold considered disgraceful—and they came to Amaurot in plain and simple clothing. But the Anemolians, who lived far away and had little acquaintance with Utopia, decided upon hearing that Utopians all wore the same simple clothing that they must not have the things they did not wear. Being more proud than wise, the Anemolians determined to dress as gorgeously as the gods themselves, and thus to dazzle the eyes of the poor Utopians with their glistening clothes. So in came the three ambassadors with 100 servants dressed in many colors, most of them in silk. The ambassadors themselves, who were noblemen in their own country, wore clothes of gold, with great gold chains, gold hanging from their ears, gold rings on their fingers, brooches and strings of gold glistening with pearls and jewels upon their caps—trimmed and adorned, in short, with all those things which among the Utopians were either the punishment of slaves, the mark of disgrace upon wrong-doers, or trifles for young children's play. It would have done a man good, therefore, to have seen how proudly they displayed their peacock feathers, how much they made of their painted sheaths, and how loftily they advanced themselves when they compared their brilliant apparel with the poor garments of the Utopians, who swarmed into the streets. On the other hand, it was no less pleasant to see how much they were deceived and how far they missed their purpose. For to the eyes of the Utopians, except for the few who had been in other countries, all that gorgeous apparel seemed shameful. In fact, they saluted the lowest and most abject of the Anemolians, mistaking them for the nobles, while they ignored the ambassadors, whom they judged to be slaves because of their golden chains. You should have seen the children who had thrown away their pearls and jewels dig and push when they saw these items on the ambassadors' capes. "Look Mother," they said, "at that big ninny who still wears pearls and jewels like a little child." But the mother would earnestly say, "Hush, Son, I think he is one of the ambassador's fools." Others found fault with the golden chains because they were so small and weak that a slave could easily break them; or so large that he might slip them off and run away.

But when the ambassadors had been there a day or two and saw so much gold so little esteemed, and more gold in the chains of one fugitive slave than in all their costly ornaments, they put away shamefully all that gorgeous array of which they had been so proud. For their part, the Utopians marveled that anyone who may behold the stars or the sun could be so foolish as to delight in the sparkling of a trifling stone, or that any man is so mad as to count himself a better person for the fine quality of the wool he wears. No matter how fine, they say, the same wool was once worn by a sheep, which was nothing but a sheep the whole time she wore it.

They marvel also that gold, so useless in itself, is now valued so highly among all people that man himself is held in less esteem than gold. A lumpish blockhead, with no more wit than an ass, nevertheless shall have many wise and good men at his command simply because he has a great heap of gold. But if the gold should be taken from him and given to the lowest servant in his household either by fortune or by some subtle trick of the law (which no less than fortune raises up the low and pulls down the high), then he as well as his money shall shortly go into the service of his servant ...

I have described to you as truly as I could the form and order of that commonwealth which in my judgment is not only the best, but the only one that can rightly claim the name of a commonwealth or republic. In other places they speak of the common good, but every man procures his private good. Here, where nothing is private, the common affairs are their real concern. In both cases they have good reason to act as they do. For in other countries, no matter how prosperous the country may be, who knows that he will not starve if he makes no special provision for himself? Therefore he is compelled to look out for himself rather than the people—that is, for others. Where all things are owned in common, on the contrary, no one shall lack anything necessary for his private use, so long as the common storehouses and barns are sufficiently stocked. There nothing is distributed in a niggardly way, nor is anyone poor. And though no one owns anything, yet everyone is rich. For what can be richer than to live joyfully, free from worries about making a living? No man is vexed by his wife's importunate complaints, nor dreads poverty for his sons, nor sorrows because he cannot provide a dowry for his daughter. Instead, the Utopians do not worry at all about the livelihood and prosperity of themselves and their kin: their wives, their children, their nephews, their children's children, and all that shall follow in their posterity. Besides this, they provide as much for those who were once laborers, but are now too weak to work, as for those who are still working.

Now I would like to see if anyone is so bold as to compare this with the so-called justice of other nations—among whom, upon my soul, I can find no sign of equity and justice. Is it justice when a rich goldsmith or moneylender, or anyone who either does nothing at all or nothing necessary to the common good, has a pleasant and prosperous life, while poor laborers, carters, ironsmiths, carpenters, and plowmen by great and continual toil are barely able to stay alive? Their work is so necessary that no commonwealth could last a year without it; yet their lives are so wretched and miserable that the condition of the beasts of burden may seem better ... Not only are these wretched workers tormented with hard and unprofitable labor, but they must also suffer the prospect of a penniless old age. For their daily wage is so little that it will not suffice for that day, much less yield any surplus that may be saved for the relief of old age.

Is this not an unjust country?[10] It gives great rewards to so-called gentlemen, goldsmiths, and other idlers and flatterers, or to those who devise useless pleasures, on the one hand; then, on the other, it fails to provide for poor plowmen, coal miners, laborers, carters, ironsmiths, and carpenters, without whom no commonwealth can survive. After it has abused the labors of their lusty and flowering years, it abandons them to a miserable death. Besides this, the rich men every day snatch away from the poor some part of their livelihood, either by private fraud or public law. So to their despicable treatment of the workers whose pains promote the public good, the rich now give the name of justice under law.

Therefore when I consider all these commonwealths which nowadays flourish everywhere, God help me but I perceive nothing but a conspiracy of the rich, who serve their own interests under the name of the common good. They invent all sorts of ways to keep what they have unjustly acquired, as well as ways to employ the labor of the poor for as little money as possible. These devices, the rich declare, must be kept and observed for the sake of the common good—that is, for the welfare also of the poor people—and so they are made laws. But when these most wicked and vicious men have by their insatiable covetousness divided among themselves all those things that would suffice for *all* men, they are still far from enjoying the happiness of the Utopian commonwealth. In Utopia, where the desire for money is banished along with its use, how great a heap of cares is cut away! How great an occasion for wickedness and mischief is pulled up by the roots! Who does not know that fraud, theft, plunder, brawling, quarreling, faction, strife, chiding, contention, murder, treason, and poisoning, which are revenged but not prevented by punishment, die out when money dies? Or that fear, grief, care, toils, and anxiety perish the same moment that money perishes? Yes, poverty itself, which only seemed to be the lack of money, would vanish if money were gone.

That you may perceive this more plainly, consider some barren and unfruitful year in which many thousands of people have starved. I dare to say that at the end of that desperate time enough grain might have been found in the rich men's barns to feed everyone whom famine and pestilence killed. So easily might men make their living if that worthy princess, Lady Money, did not stand in the way. I am sure that the rich understand this. Even they must know that it is better to lack nothing one really needs than to have many unnecessary things—better to be rid of innumerable cares and troubles than to be besieged with great riches. I do not doubt that every man's respect for his private interest, or the authority of our savior Christ (who knew and counselled what is best), would have brought all the world long ago into the ways of the public welfare if it were not for that one beast, the princess and mother of all wrongdoing—pride. Pride measures happiness and prosperity not by her own advantages, but by the miseries and disadvantages of others. She would not be content if there were no wretches to mock and scorn, no one whose misery might bring out her happiness, no one whose poverty she might torment and increase by gorgeously displaying her riches. This hellhound creeps into men's hearts and keeps them from entering the right path of life. Pride is so deeply rooted in men's breasts that she cannot easily be plucked out.

Although I would gladly wish the form of a true commonwealth for all nations, I am glad that it has chanced to fall to the Utopians. They have laid such foundations of their commonwealth as shall endure forever, as far as one can foresee. Because the chief causes of ambition and factions and the other vices have been pulled up by the roots, the Utopians are in no jeopardy of the domestic dissension that has brought to ruin the well fortified and strongly defended wealth and riches of many cities. And as long as perfect concord remains and wholesome laws are enforced at home, the envy of foreign princes will not be able to conquer or shake Utopia, for they have tried many times and always been driven back.

NOTES

1　More coined the word "utopia" as a pun from the Greek *eu-topos*, "good" or "happy place," and *ou-topos*, "no place."—Eds.

2　In the just society Plato envisions in his *Republic*, the rulers, or Guardians, share everything in common, although most of the people are allowed to own private property.—Eds.

3　Hythloday had earlier explained that Utopian cities are divided into groups of thirty households, with each group electing an official called a Syphogrant.—Eds.

4　A Tranibor is an official, elected annually, with authority over ten Syphogrants and the 300 families they represent.—Eds.

5　In classical Greek, *Barzanes* means "Son of Zeus"; *Ademus*, "without people."—Eds.

6　Strictly speaking, houses are not privately owned in Utopia. According to Hythloday's account, moreover, all houses are alike, and every ten years they are redistributed by lottery.—Eds.

7　Most slaves in Utopia are either prisoners of war or people guilty of heinous offenses. There is also a group of what we now would call servants, comprising foreigners who prefer slavery in Utopia to life in their native land.—Eds.

8　*Anemolian* is Greek for "windy people."—Eds.

9　Amaurot is the capital city of Utopia.—Eds.

10　That is, England, and other European countries, and not Utopia.—Eds.

Address to the Inhabitants of New Lanark

ROBERT OWEN*

In 1800, the wealthy industrialist Robert Owen (1771–1858) took control of a cotton mill in New Lanark, Scotland. Unlike other mill owners, Owen took great interest in the living conditions of his workers, providing them with decent housing and schools for their children. New Lanark became a great success, as Owen indicates in this excerpt from his address to his workers, and this success encouraged Owen to engage in other social experiments on a broader scale. One of these was the socialist community of New Harmony, Indiana, which Owen launched in 1824, only to see it collapse at great personal expense within four years.

---

* *Source*: Robert Owen, *A New View of Society and Other Writings*, G. D. H. Cole, ed. (London: J. M. Dent, 1927 [1813]).

ADDRESS TO THE INHABITANTS OF NEW LANARK

Every society which exists at present, as well as every society which history records, has been formed and governed on a belief in the following notions, assumed as *first principles*:

First,—That it is in the power of every individual to form his own character.

Hence the various systems called by the name of religion, codes of law, and punishments. Hence also the angry passions entertained by individuals and nations towards each other.

Second,—That the affections are at the command of the individual.

Hence insincerity and degradation of character. Hence the miseries of domestic life, and more than one-half of all the crimes of mankind.

Third,—That it is necessary that a large portion of mankind should exist in ignorance and poverty, in order to secure to the remaining part such a degree of happiness as they now enjoy.

Hence a system of counteraction in the pursuits of men, a general opposition among individuals to the interests of each other, and the necessary effects of such a system,—ignorance, poverty, and vice.

Facts prove, however—

First,—That character is universally formed *for*, and not *by*, the individual.

Second,—That *any* habits and sentiments may be given to mankind.

Third,—That the affections are *not* under the control of the individual.

Fourth,—That every individual may be trained to produce far more than he can consume, while there is a sufficiency of soil left for him to cultivate.

Fifth,—That nature has provided means by which population may be at all times maintained in the proper state to give the greatest happiness to every individual, without one check of vice or misery.

Sixth,—That any community may be arranged, on a due combination of the foregoing principles, in such a manner, as not only to withdraw vice, poverty, and, in a great degree, misery, from the world, but also to place *every* individual under circumstances in which he shall enjoy more permanent happiness than can be given to *any* individual under the principles which have hitherto regulated society.

Seventh,—That all the assumed fundamental principles on which society has hitherto been founded are erroneous, and may be demonstrated to be contrary to fact. And—

Eighth,—That the change which would follow the abandonment of those erroneous maxims which bring misery into the world, and the adoption of principles of truth, unfolding a system which shall remove and for ever exclude that misery, may be effected without the slightest injury to any human being.

Here is the groundwork,—these are the data, on which society shall ere long be re-arranged; and for this simple reason, that it will be rendered evident that it will be for the immediate and future interest of every one to lend his most active assistance gradually to reform society on this basis. I say *gradually*, for in that word the most important considerations are involved. Any sudden and coercive attempt which may be made to remove even misery from men will prove injurious rather than beneficial. Their minds must be gradually prepared by an essential alteration of the circumstances which surround them, for any great and important change and amelioration in their condition. They must be first convinced of their blindness: this cannot be effected, even among the least unreasonable, or those termed the best part of mankind, in their present state, without creating some degree of irritation. This irritation must then be tranquillized before another step ought to be attempted; and a general conviction must be established of the truth of the principles on which the projected change is to be founded. Their introduction into practice will then become easy,—difficulties will vanish as we approach them,— and, afterwards, the desire to see the whole system carried immediately into effect will exceed the means of putting it into execution.

The principles on which this practical system is founded are not new; separately, or partially united, they have been often recommended by the sages of antiquity, and by modern writers. But it is not known to me that they have ever been thus combined. Yet it can be demonstrated that it is only by their being *all brought into practice together* that they are to be rendered beneficial to mankind; and sure I am that this is the earliest period in the history of man when they could be successfully introduced into practice.

I do not intend to hide from you that the change will be great. "Old things shall pass away, and all shall become new."

But this change will bear no resemblance to any of the revolutions which have hitherto occurred. These have been alone calculated to generate and call forth all the evil passions of hatred and revenge: but that system which is now contemplated will effectually eradicate every feeling of irritation and ill will which exists among mankind. The whole proceedings of those who govern and instruct the world will be reversed. Instead of spending ages in telling mankind what they ought to think and how they ought to act, the instructors and governors of the world will acquire a knowledge that will enable them, in one generation, to apply the means which shall cheerfully induce each of those whom they control and influence, not only to think, but to act in such a manner as shall be best for himself and best for every human being. And yet this extraordinary result will take place without punishment or apparent force.

Under this system, before commands are issued it shall be known whether they can or cannot be obeyed. Men shall not be called upon to assent to doctrines and to dogmas which do not carry conviction to their minds. They shall not be taught that merit can exist in doing, or that demerit can arise from not doing that over which they have no control. They shall not be told, as at present, that they must love that which, by the constitution of their nature, they are compelled to dislike. They shall not be trained in wild imaginary notions, that inevitably make them despise and hate all mankind out of the little narrow circle in which they exist, and then be told that they must heartily and sincerely love all their fellow-men. No, my friends, that system which shall make its way into the heart of every man, is founded upon principles which have not the slightest resemblance to any of those I have alluded to. On the contrary, it is directly opposed to them; and the effects it will produce in practice will differ as much from the practice which history records, and from that which we see around us, as hypocrisy, hatred, envy, revenge, wars, poverty, injustice, oppression, and all their consequent misery, differ from that genuine charity and sincere kindness of which we perpetually hear, but which we have never seen, and which, under the existing systems, we never can see.

That charity and that kindness admit of no exception. They extend to every child of man, however he may have been taught, however he may have been trained. They consider not what country gave him birth, what may be his complexion, what his habits or his sentiments. Genuine charity and true kindness instruct, that whatever these may be, should they prove the very reverse of what we have been taught to think right and best, our conduct towards him, our sentiments with respect to him, should undergo no change; for, when we shall see things as they really are, we shall know that this our fellow-man has undergone the same kind of process and training from infancy which we have experienced; that he has been as effectually taught to deem his sentiments and actions right, as we have been to imagine ours right and his wrong; when perhaps the only difference is, that we were born in one country, and he in another. If this be not true, then indeed are all our prospects hopeless; then fierce contentions, poverty, and vice, must continue for ever. Fortunately, however, there is now a superabundance of facts to remove all doubt from every mind; and the principles may now be fully developed, which will easily explain the source of all the opinions which now perplex and divide the world; and their source being discovered, mankind may withdraw all those which are false and injurious, and prevent any evil from arising in consequence of the varieties of sentiments, or rather of feelings, which may afterwards remain.

In short, my friends, the New System is founded on principles which will enable mankind to *prevent*, in the rising generation, almost all, if not all of the evils and miseries which we and our forefathers have experienced. A correct knowledge of human nature will be acquired; ignorance will be removed; the angry passions will be prevented from gaining any strength; charity and kindness will universally prevail; poverty will not be known; the interest of each individual will be in strict unison with the interest of every individual in the world. There will not be any counteraction of wishes and desires among men. Temperance and simplicity of manners will be the characteristics of every part of society. The natural defects of the few will be amply compensated by the increased attention and kindness towards them of the many. None will have cause to complain; for each will possess, without injury to another, all that can tend to his comfort, his well-being, and his happiness ... Such will be the certain consequences of the introduction into practice of that system for which I have been silently preparing the way for upwards of five-and-twenty years.

The Communist Manifesto

KARL MARX AND FRIEDRICH ENGELS*

Originally written at the request of a small group of radicals known as the Communist League, the *Manifesto of the Communist Party* (1848) has become the most famous, and perhaps the most influential, statement of Karl Marx's views. In other writings Marx (1818–1883) delves more deeply into philosophical, economic, and social issues, but none of these is as comprehensive or as clear as the *Manifesto*. The clarity may be due largely to Friedrich Engels (1820–1895), Marx's longtime friend and collaborator, but the ideas were chiefly Marx's—as Engels himself acknowledged. Beginning with the statement "The history of all hitherto existing society is the history of class struggles," the *Manifesto* sets out Marx's materialist conception of history in bold terms, then draws on this analysis of history and economics to offer a program for radical change. If some of Marx's and Engels's proposals no longer seem radical—"a heavy progressive or graduated income tax," for example, or "free education for all children in public schools"—this is a sign of the changes since 1848. But even by today's standards, some of their proposals—for example, "abolition of property in land" and "equal liability of all to labor"—may seem very radical indeed.

---

* *Source*: The following is an abridged version of the English edition of 1888, translated by Samuel Moore.

MANIFESTO OF THE COMMUNIST PARTY

A specter is haunting Europe—the specter of Communism. All the powers of old Europe have entered into a holy alliance to exorcise this specter: Pope and Czar, Metternich and Guizot, French Radicals and German police-spies.[1]

Where is the party in opposition that has not been decried as Communistic by its opponents in power? Where is the Opposition that has not hurled back the branding reproach of Communism, against the more advanced opposition parties, as well as against its reactionary adversaries?

Two things result from this fact.

1 Communism is already acknowledged by all European Powers to be itself a Power.
2 It is high time that Communists should openly, in the face of the whole world, publish their views, their aims, their tendencies, and meet this nursery tale of the Specter of Communism with a Manifesto of the party itself.

To this end, Communists of various nationalities have assembled in London, and sketched the following Manifesto, to be published in the English, French, German, Italian, Flemish and Danish languages.

I. Bourgeois and Proletarians

The history of all hitherto existing society is the history of class struggles.

Freeman and slave, patrician and plebeian, lord and serf, guild-master and journeyman, in a word, oppressor and oppressed, stood in constant opposition to one another, carried on an uninterrupted, now hidden, now open fight, a fight that each time ended, either in a revolutionary re-constitution of society at large, or in the common ruin of the contending classes.

In the earlier epochs of history, we find almost everywhere a complicated arrangement of society into various orders, a manifold gradation of social rank. In ancient Rome we have patricians, knights, plebeians, slaves; in the Middle Ages, feudal lords, vassals, guild-masters, journeymen, apprentices, serfs; in almost all of these classes, again, subordinate gradations.

The modern bourgeois society that has sprouted from the ruins of feudal society has not done away with class antagonisms. It has but established new classes, new conditions of oppression, new forms of struggle in place of the old ones.

Our epoch, the epoch of the bourgeoisie, possesses, however, this distinctive feature: it has simplified the class antagonisms: Society as a whole is more and more splitting up into two great hostile camps, into two great classes directly facing each other: Bourgeoisie and Proletariat.

From the serfs of the Middle Ages sprang the chartered burghers of the earliest towns. From these burgesses the first elements of the bourgeoisie were developed.

The discovery of America, the rounding of the Cape, opened up fresh ground for the rising bourgeoisie. The East-Indian and Chinese markets, the colonization of America, trade with the colonies, the increase in the means of exchange and in commodities generally, gave to commerce, to navigation, to industry, an impulse never before known, and thereby, to the revolutionary element in the tottering feudal society, a rapid development.

The feudal system of industry, under which industrial production was monopolized by closed guilds, now no longer sufficed for the growing wants of the new markets. The manufacturing system took its place. The guild-masters were pushed on one side by the manufacturing middle class; division of labor between the different corporate guilds vanished in the face of division of labor in each single workshop.

Meantime the markets kept ever growing, the demand ever rising. Even manufacture no longer sufficed. Thereupon, steam and machinery revolutionized industrial production. The place of manufacture was taken by the giant, Modern Industry, the place of the industrial middle class, by industrial millionaires, the leaders of whole industrial armies, the modern bourgeois.

Modern industry has established the world market, for which the discovery of America paved the way. This market has given an immense development to commerce, to navigation, to communication by land. This development has, in its turn, reacted on the extension of industry; and in proportion as industry, commerce, navigation, railways extended, in the same proportion the bourgeoisie developed, increased its capital, and pushed into the background every class handed down from the Middle Ages.

We see, therefore, how the modern bourgeoisie is itself the product of a long course of development, of a series of revolutions in the modes of production and of exchange.

Each step in the development of the bourgeoisie was accompanied by a corresponding political advance of that class. An oppressed class under the sway of the feudal nobility, an armed and self-governing association in the mediaeval commune; here independent urban republic (as in Italy and Germany), there taxable "third estate" of the monarchy (as in France), afterwards, in the period of manufacture proper, serving either the semi-feudal or the absolute monarchy as a counterpoise against the nobility, and, in fact, corner-stone of the great monarchies in general, the bourgeoisie has at last, since the establishment of Modern Industry and of the world-market, conquered for itself, in the modern representative State, exclusive political sway. The executive of the modern State is but a committee for managing the common affairs of the whole bourgeoisie.

The bourgeoisie, historically, has played a most revolutionary part.

The bourgeoisie, wherever it has got the upper hand, has put an end to all feudal, patriarchal, idyllic relations. It has pitilessly torn asunder the motley feudal ties that bound man to his "natural superiors," and has left remaining no other nexus between man and man than naked self-interest, than callous "cash payment." It has drowned the most heavenly ecstasies of religious fervor, of chivalrous enthusiasm, of philistine sentimentalism, in the icy water of egotistical calculation. It has resolved personal worth into exchange value, and in place of the numberless indefeasible chartered freedoms, has set up that single, unconscionable freedom— Free Trade. In one word, for exploitation, veiled by religious and political illusions, it has substituted naked, shameless, direct, brutal exploitation.

The bourgeoisie has stripped of its halo every occupation hitherto honored and looked up to with reverent awe. It has converted the physician, the lawyer, the priest, the poet, the man of science, into its paid wage-laborers.

The bourgeoisie has torn away from the family its sentimental veil, and has reduced the family relation to a mere money relation.

The bourgeoisie has disclosed how it came to pass that the brutal display of vigor in the Middle Ages, which Reactionaries so much admire, found its fitting complement in the most slothful indolence. It has been the first to show what man's activity can bring about. It has accomplished wonders far surpassing Egyptian pyramids, Roman aqueducts, and Gothic cathedrals; it has conducted expeditions that put in the shade all former Exoduses of nations and crusades.

The bourgeoisie cannot exist without constantly revolutionizing the instruments of production, and thereby the relations of production, and with them the whole relations of society. Conservation of the old modes of production in unaltered form was, on the contrary, the first condition of existence for all earlier industrial classes. Constant revolutionizing of production, uninterrupted disturbance of all social conditions, everlasting uncertainty and agitation distinguish the bourgeois epoch from all earlier ones. All fixed, fast-frozen relations, with their train of ancient and venerable prejudices and opinions, are swept away, all new-formed ones become antiquated before they can ossify. All that is solid melts into air, all that is holy is profaned, and man is at last compelled to face with sober senses, his real conditions of life, and his relations with his kind.

The need of a constantly expanding market for its products chases the bourgeoisie over the whole surface of the globe. It must nestle everywhere, settle everywhere, establish connections everywhere.

The bourgeoisie has through its exploitation of the world-market given a cosmopolitan character to production and consumption in every country. To the great chagrin of Reactionaries, it has drawn from under the feet of industry the national ground on which it stood. All old-established national industries have been destroyed or are daily being destroyed. They are dislodged by new industries, whose introduction becomes a life and death question for all civilized nations, by industries that no longer work up indigenous raw material, but raw material drawn from the remotest zones; industries whose products are consumed, not only at home, but in every quarter of the globe. In place of the old wants, satisfied by the productions of the country, we find new wants, requiring for their satisfaction the products of distant lands and climes. In place of the old local and national seclusion and self-sufficiency, we have intercourse in every direction, universal interdependence of nations. And as in material, so also in intellectual production. The intellectual creations of individual nations become common property. National one-sidedness and narrow-mindedness become more and more impossible, and from the numerous national and local literatures, there arises a world literature.

The bourgeoisie, by the rapid improvement of all instruments of production, by the immensely facilitated means of communication, draws all, even the most barbarian, nations into civilization. The cheap prices of its commodities are the heavy artillery with which it batters down all Chinese walls, with which it forces the barbarians' intensely obstinate hatred of foreigners to capitulate. It compels all nations, on pain of extinction, to adopt the bourgeois mode of production; it compels them to introduce what it calls civilization into their midst, *i.e.*, to become bourgeois themselves. In one word, it creates a world after its own image.

The bourgeoisie has subjected the country to the rule of the towns. It has created enormous cities, has greatly increased the urban population as compared with the rural, and has thus rescued a considerable part of the population from the idiocy of rural life. Just as it has made the country dependent on the towns, so it has made barbarian and semi-barbarian countries dependent on the civilized ones, nations of peasants on nations of bourgeois, the East on the West.

The bourgeoisie keeps more and more doing away with the scattered state of the population, of the means of production, and of property. It has agglomerated population, centralized means of production, and has concentrated property in a few hands. The necessary consequence of this was political centralization. Independent, or but loosely connected provinces, with separate interests, laws, governments and systems of taxation, became lumped together into one nation, with one government, one code of laws, one national class-interest, one frontier and one customs-tariff.

The bourgeoisie, during its rule of scarce one hundred years, has created more massive and more colossal productive forces than have all preceding generations together. Subjection of Nature's forces to man, machinery, application of chemistry to industry and agriculture, steam-navigation, railways, electric telegraphs, clearing of whole continents for cultivation, canalization of rivers, whole populations conjured out of the ground—what earlier century had even a presentiment that such productive forces slumbered in the lap of social labor?

We see then: the means of production and of exchange, on whose foundation the bourgeoisie built itself up, were generated in feudal society. At a certain stage in the development of these means of production and of exchange, the conditions under which feudal society produced and exchanged, the feudal organization of agriculture and manufacturing industry, in one word, the feudal relations of property became no longer compatible with the already developed productive forces; they became so many fetters. They had to be burst asunder; they were burst asunder.

Into their place stepped free competition, accompanied by a social and political constitution adapted to it, and by the economical and political sway of the bourgeois class.

A similar movement is going on before our own eyes. Modern bourgeois society with its relations of production, of exchange and of property, a society that has conjured up such gigantic means of production and of exchange, is like the sorcerer, who is no longer able to control the powers of the nether world whom he has called up by his spells. For many a decade past the history of industry and commerce is but the history of the revolt of modern productive forces against modern conditions of production, against the property relations that are the conditions for the existence of the bourgeoisie and of its rule. It is enough to mention the commercial crises that by their periodical return put on its trial, each time more threateningly, the existence of the entire bourgeois society. In these crises a great part not only of the existing products, but also of the previously created productive forces, are periodically destroyed. In these crises there breaks out an epidemic that, in all earlier epochs, would have seemed an absurdity—the epidemic of over-production. Society suddenly finds itself put back into a state of momentary barbarism; it appears as if a famine, a universal war of devastation had cut off the supply of every means of subsistence; industry and commerce seem to be destroyed; and why? Because there is too much civilization, too much means of subsistence, too much industry, too much commerce. The productive forces at the disposal of society no longer tend to further the development of the conditions of bourgeois property; on the contrary, they have become too powerful for these conditions, by which they are fettered, and as soon as they overcome these fetters, they bring disorder into the whole of bourgeois society, endanger the existence of bourgeois property. The conditions of bourgeois society are too narrow to comprise the wealth created by them. And how does the bourgeoisie get over these crises? On the one hand by enforced destruction of a mass of productive forces; on the other, by the conquest of new markets, and by the more thorough exploitation of the old ones. That is to say, by paving the way for more extensive and more destructive crises, and by diminishing the means whereby crises are prevented.

The weapons with which the bourgeoisie felled feudalism to the ground are now turned against the bourgeoisie itself.

But not only has the bourgeoisie forged the weapons that bring death to itself; it has also called into existence the men who are to wield those weapons—the modern working class—the proletarians.

In proportion as the bourgeoisie, *i.e.*, capital, is developed, in the same proportion is the proletariat, the modern working class, developed—a class of laborers, who live only so long as they find work, and who find work only so long as their labor increases capital. These laborers, who must sell themselves piecemeal, are a commodity, like every other article of commerce, and are consequently exposed to all the vicissitudes of competition, to all the fluctuations of the market.

Owing to the extensive use of machinery and to division of labor, the work of the proletarians has lost all individual character, and consequently, all charm for the workman. He becomes an appendage of the machine, and it is only the most simple, most monotonous, and most easily acquired knack, that is required of him. Hence, the cost of production of a workman is restricted, almost entirely, to the means of subsistence that he requires for his maintenance, and for the propagation of his race. But the price of a commodity, and therefore also of labor, is equal to its cost of production. In proportion, therefore, as the repulsiveness of the work increases, the wage decreases. Nay more, in proportion as the use of machinery and division of labor increases, in the same proportion the burden of toil also increases, whether by prolongation of the working hours, by increase of the work exacted in a given time or by increased speed of the machinery, etc.

Modern industry has converted the little workshop of the patriarchal master into the great factory of the industrial capitalist. Masses of laborers, crowded into the factory, are organized like soldiers. As privates of the industrial army they are placed under the command of a perfect hierarchy of officers and sergeants. Not only are they slaves of the bourgeois class, and of the bourgeois State; they are daily and hourly enslaved by the machine, by the over-looker, and, above all, by the individual bourgeois manufacturer himself. The more openly this despotism proclaims gain to be its end and aim, the more petty, the more hateful and the more embittering it is.

The less the skill and exertion of strength implied in manual labor, in other words, the more modern industry becomes developed, the more is the labor of men superseded by that of women. Differences of age and sex have no longer any distinctive social validity for the working class. All are instruments of labor, more or less expensive to use, according to their age and sex.

No sooner is the exploitation of the laborer by the manufacturer, so far, at an end, that he receives his wages in cash, than he is set upon by the other portions of the bourgeoisie, the landlord, the shopkeeper, the pawnbroker, etc.

The lower strata of the middle class—the small tradespeople, shopkeepers, and retired tradesmen generally, the handicraftsmen and peasants—all these sink gradually into the proletariat, partly because their diminutive capital does not suffice for the scale on which Modern Industry is carried on, and is swamped in the competition with the large capitalists, partly because their specialized skill is rendered worthless by new methods of production. Thus the proletariat is recruited from all classes of the population.

The proletariat goes through various stages of development. With its birth begins its struggle with the bourgeoisie. At first the contest is carried on by individual laborers, then by the workpeople of a factory, then by the operatives of one trade, in one locality, against the individual bourgeois who directly exploits them. They direct their attacks not against the bourgeois conditions of production, but against the instruments of production themselves; they destroy imported wares that compete with their labor, they smash to pieces machinery, they set factories ablaze, they seek to restore by force the vanished status of the workman of the Middle Ages.

At this stage the laborers still form an incoherent mass scattered over the whole country, and broken up by their mutual competition. If anywhere they unite to form more compact bodies, this is not yet the consequence of their own active union, but of the union of the bourgeoisie, which class, in order to attain its own political ends, is compelled to set the whole proletariat in motion, and is moreover yet, for a time, able to do so. At this stage, therefore, the proletarians do not fight their enemies, but the enemies of their enemies, the remnants of absolute monarchy, the landowners, the nonindustrial bourgeois, the petty bourgeoisie. Thus the whole historical movement is concentrated in the hands of the bourgeoisie; every victory so obtained is a victory for the bourgeoisie.

But with the development of industry the proletariat not only increases in number; it becomes concentrated in greater masses, its strength grows, and it feels that strength more. The various interests and conditions of life within the ranks of the proletariat are more and more equalized, in proportion as machinery obliterates all distinctions of labor, and nearly everywhere reduces wages to the same low level. The growing competition among the bourgeois, and the resulting commercial crises, make the wages of the workers ever more fluctuating. The unceasing improvement of machinery, ever more rapidly developing, makes their livelihood more and more precarious; the collisions between individual workmen and individual bourgeois take more and more the character of collisions between two classes. Thereupon the workers begin to form combinations (Trade Unions) against the bourgeois; they club together in order to keep up the rate of wages; they found permanent associations in order to make provision beforehand for these occasional revolts. Here and there the contest breaks out into riots.

Now and then the workers are victorious, but only for a time. The real fruit of their battles lies, not in the immediate result, but in the ever-expanding union of the workers. This union is helped on by the improved means of communication that are created by modern industry and that place the workers of different localities in contact with one another. It was just this contact that was needed to centralize the numerous local struggles, all of the same character, into one national struggle between classes. But every class struggle is a political struggle. And that union, to attain which the burghers of the Middle Ages, with their miserable highways, required centuries, the modern proletarians, thanks to railways, achieve in a few years.

This organization of the proletarians into a class, and consequently into a political party, is continually being upset again by the competition between the workers themselves. But it ever rises up again, stronger, firmer, mightier. It compels legislative recognition of particular interests of the workers, by taking advantage of the divisions among the bourgeoisie itself. Thus the ten-hours' bill [to limit working hours] in England was carried.

Altogether collisions between the classes of the old society further, in many ways, the course of development of the proletariat. The bourgeoisie finds itself involved in a constant battle. At first with the aristocracy; later on, with those portions of the bourgeoisie itself, whose interests have become antagonistic to the progress of industry; at all times, with the bourgeoisie of foreign countries. In all these battles it sees itself compelled to appeal to the proletariat, to ask for its help, and thus, to drag it into the political arena. The bourgeoisie itself, therefore, supplies the proletariat with its own elements of political and general education, in other words, it furnishes the proletariat with weapons for fighting the bourgeoisie.

Further, as we have already seen, entire sections of the ruling classes are, by the advance of industry, precipitated into the proletariat, or are at least threatened in their conditions of existence. These also supply the proletariat with fresh elements of enlightenment and progress.

Finally, in times when the class struggle nears the decisive hour, the process of dissolution going on within the ruling class, in fact within the whole range of society, assumes such a violent, glaring character, that a small section of the ruling class cuts itself adrift, and joins the revolutionary class, the class that holds the future in its hands. Just as, therefore, at an earlier period, a section of the nobility went over to the bourgeoisie, so now a portion of the bourgeoisie goes over to the proletariat, and in particular, a portion of the bourgeois ideologists, who have raised themselves to the level of comprehending theoretically the historical movement as a whole.

Of all the classes that stand face to face with the bourgeoisie today, the proletariat alone is a really revolutionary class. The other classes decay and finally disappear in the face of Modern Industry; the proletariat is its special and essential product.

The lower middle class, the small manufacturer, the shopkeeper, the artisan, the peasant, all these fight against the bourgeoisie, to save from extinction their existence as fractions of the middle class. They are therefore not revolutionary, but conservative. Nay more, they are reactionary, for they try to roll back the wheel of history. If by chance they are revolutionary, they are so only in view of their impending transfer into the proletariat, they thus defend not their present, but their future interests, they desert their own standpoint to place themselves at that of the proletariat.

The *lumpenproletariat*—the "dangerous class," the social scum, that passively rotting mass thrown off by the lowest layers of old society—may, here and there, be swept into the movement by a proletarian revolution; its conditions of life, however, prepare it far more for the part of a bribed tool of reactionary intrigue [e.g., as "scabs" or strikebreakers].

In the conditions of the proletariat, those of old society at large are already virtually swamped. The proletarian is without property; his relation to his wife and children has no longer anything in common with the bourgeois family-relations; modern industrial labor, modern subjection to capital, the same in England as in France, in America as in Germany, has stripped him of every trace of national character. Law, morality, religion, are to him so many bourgeois prejudices, behind which lurk in ambush just as many bourgeois interests.

All the preceding classes that got the upper hand, sought to fortify their already acquired status by subjecting society at large to their conditions of appropriation. The proletarians cannot become masters of the productive forces of society, except by abolishing their own previous mode of appropriation, and thereby also every other previous mode of appropriation. They have nothing of their own to secure and to fortify; their mission is to destroy all previous securities for, and insurances of, individual property.

All previous historical movements were movements of minorities, or in the interests of minorities. The proletarian movement is the self-conscious, independent movement of the immense majority, in the interests of the immense majority. The proletariat, the lowest stratum of our present society, cannot stir, cannot raise itself up, without the whole superincumbent strata of official society being sprung into the air.

Though not in substance, yet in form, the struggle of the proletariat with the bourgeoisie is at first a national struggle. The proletariat of each country must, of course, first of all settle matters with its own bourgeoisie.

In depicting the most general phases of the development of the proletariat, we traced the more or less veiled civil war, raging within existing society, up to the point where that war breaks out into open revolution, and where the violent overthrow of the bourgeoisie lays the foundation for the sway of the proletariat.

Hitherto, every form of society has been based, as we have already seen, on the antagonism of oppressing and oppressed classes. But in order to oppress a class, certain conditions must be assured to it under which it can, at least, continue its slavish existence. The serf, in the period of serfdom, raised himself to membership in the commune, just as the petty bourgeois, under the yoke of feudal absolutism, managed to develop into a bourgeois. The modern laborer, on the contrary, instead of rising with the progress of industry, sinks deeper and deeper below the conditions of existence of his own class. He becomes a pauper, and pauperism develops more rapidly than population and wealth. And here it becomes evident, that the bourgeoisie is unfit any longer to be the ruling class in society, and to impose its conditions of existence upon society as an over-riding law. It is unfit to rule because it is incompetent to assure an existence to its slave within his slavery, because it cannot help letting him sink into such a state, that it has to feed him, instead of being fed by him. Society can no longer live under this bourgeoisie, in other words, its existence is no longer compatible with society.

The essential condition for the existence, and for the sway of the bourgeois class, is the formation and augmentation of capital; the condition for capital is wage-labor. Wage-labor rests exclusively on competition between the laborers. The advance of industry, whose involuntary promoter is the bourgeoisie, replaces the isolation of the laborers, due to competition, by their revolutionary combination, due to association. The development of Modern Industry, therefore, cuts from under its feet the very foundation on which the bourgeoisie produces and appropriates products. What the bourgeoisie, therefore, produces, above all, is its own grave-diggers. Its fall and the victory of the proletariat are equally inevitable [*unvermeidlich*: unavoidable].

II. Proletarians and Communists

In what relation do the Communists stand to the proletarians as a whole?

The Communists do not form a separate party opposed to other working-class parties.

They have no interests separate and apart from those of the proletariat as a whole.

They do not set up any sectarian principles of their own, by which to shape and mould the proletarian movement.

The Communists are distinguished from the other working-class parties by this only: (1) In the national struggles of the proletarians of the different countries, they point out and bring to the front the common interests of the entire proletariat, independently of all nationality. (2) In the various stages of development which the struggle of the working class against the bourgeoisie has to pass through, they always and everywhere represent the interests of the movement as a whole.

The Communists, therefore, are on the one hand, practically, the most advanced and resolute section of the working-class parties of every country, that section which pushes forward all others; on the other hand, theoretically, they have over the great mass of the proletariat the advantage of clearly understanding the line of march, the conditions, and the ultimate general results of the proletarian movement.

The immediate aim of the Communists is the same as that of all the other proletarian parties: formation of the proletariat into a class, overthrow of the bourgeois supremacy, conquest of political power by the proletariat.

The theoretical conclusions of the Communists are in no way based on ideas or principles that have been invented, or discovered, by this or that would-be universal reformer.

They merely express, in general terms, actual relations springing from an existing class struggle, from a historical movement going on under our very eyes. The abolition of existing property relations is not at all a distinctive feature of Communism.

All property relations in the past have continually been subject to historical change consequent upon the change in historical conditions.

The French Revolution, for example, abolished feudal property in favor of bourgeois property.

The distinguishing feature of Communism is not the abolition of property generally, but the abolition of bourgeois property. But modern bourgeois private property is the final and most complete expression of the system of producing and appropriating products, that is based on class antagonisms, on the exploitation of the many by the few.

In this sense, the theory of the Communists may be summed up in the single sentence: Abolition of private property.

We Communists have been reproached with the desire of abolishing the right of personally acquiring property as the fruit of a man's own labor, which property is alleged to be the groundwork of all personal freedom, activity and independence.

Hard-won, self-acquired, self-earned property! Do you mean the property of the petty artisan and of the small peasant, a form of property that preceded the bourgeois form? There is no need to abolish that; the development of industry has to a great extent already destroyed it, and is still destroying it daily.

Or do you mean modern bourgeois private property?

But does wage-labor create any property for the laborer? Not a bit. It creates capital, *i.e.*, that kind of property which exploits wage-labor, and which cannot increase except upon condition of begetting a new supply of wage-labor for fresh exploitation. Property, in its present form, is based on the antagonism of capital and wage-labor. Let us examine both sides of this antagonism.

To be a capitalist, is to have not only a purely personal, but a social *status* in production. Capital is a collective product, and only by the united action of many members, nay, in the last resort, only by the united action of all members of society, can it be set in motion.

Capital is, therefore, not a personal, it is a social power.

When, therefore, capital is converted into common property, into the property of all members of society, personal property is not thereby transformed into social property. It is only the social character of the property that is changed. It loses its class-character. Let us now take wage-labor.

The average price of wage-labor is the minimum wage, *i.e.*, that quantum of the means of subsistence, which is absolutely requisite to keep the laborer in bare existence as a laborer. What, therefore, the wage-laborer appropriates by means of his labor, merely suffices to prolong and reproduce a bare existence. We by no means intend to abolish this personal appropriation of the products of labor, an appropriation that is made for the maintenance and reproduction of human life, and that leaves no surplus wherewith to command the labor of others. All that we want to do away with, is the miserable character of this appropriation, under which the laborer lives merely to increase capital, and is allowed to live only in so far as the interest of the ruling class requires it.

In bourgeois society, living labor is but a means to increase accumulated labor. In Communist society, accumulated labor is but a means to widen, to enrich, to promote the existence of the laborer. In bourgeois society, therefore, the past dominates the present; in Communist society, the present dominates the past. In bourgeois society capital is independent and has individuality, while the living person is dependent and has no individuality.

And the abolition of this state of things is called by the bourgeois, abolition of individuality and freedom! And rightly so. The abolition of bourgeois individuality, bourgeois independence, and bourgeois freedom is undoubtedly aimed at.

By freedom is meant, under the present bourgeois conditions of production, free trade, free selling and buying.

But if selling and buying disappears, free selling and buying disappears also. This talk about free selling and buying, and all the other "brave words" of our bourgeoisie about freedom in general, have a meaning, if any, only in contrast with restricted selling and buying, with the fettered traders of the Middle Ages, but have no meaning when opposed to the Communistic abolition of buying and selling, of the bourgeois conditions of production, and of the bourgeoisie itself.

You are horrified at our intending to do away with private property. But in your existing society, private property is already done away with for nine-tenths of the population; its existence for the few is solely due to its non-existence in the hands of those nine-tenths. You reproach us, therefore, with intending to do away with a form of property, the necessary condition for whose existence is the non-existence of any property for the immense majority of society.

In one word, you reproach us with intending to do away with your property. Precisely so; that is just what we intend.

From the moment when labor can no longer be converted into capital, money, or rent, into a social power capable of being monopolized, *i.e.*, from the moment when individual property can no longer be transformed into bourgeois property, into capital, from that moment, you say, individuality vanishes.

You must, therefore, confess that by "individual" you mean no other person than the bourgeois, than the middle-class owner of property. This person must, indeed, be swept out of the way, and made impossible.

Communism deprives no man of the power to appropriate the products of society; all that it does is to deprive him of the power to subjugate the labor of others by means of such appropriation.

It has been objected that upon the abolition of private property all work will cease, and universal laziness will overtake us.

According to this, bourgeois society ought long ago to have gone to the dogs through sheer idleness; for those of its members who work, acquire nothing, and those who acquire anything, do not work. The whole of this objection is but another expression of the tautology: that there can no longer be any wage-labor when there is no longer any capital.

All objections urged against the Communistic mode of producing and appropriating material products, have, in the same way, been urged against the Communistic modes of producing and appropriating intellectual products. Just as, to the bourgeois, the disappearance of class property is the disappearance of production itself, so the disappearance of class culture is to him identical with the disappearance of all culture.

That culture, the loss of which he laments, is, for the enormous majority, a mere training to act as a machine.

But don't wrangle with us so long as you apply, to our intended abolition of bourgeois property, the standard of your bourgeois notions of freedom, culture, law, etc. Your very ideas are but the out-growth of the conditions of your bourgeois production and bourgeois property, just as your jurisprudence is but the will of your class made into a law for all, a will, whose essential character and direction are determined by the economical conditions of existence of your class.

The selfish misconception that induces you to transform into eternal laws of nature and of reason, the social forms springing from your present mode of production and form of property—historical relations that rise and disappear in the progress of production—this misconception you share with every ruling class that has preceded you. What you see clearly in the case of ancient property, what you admit in the case of feudal property, you are of course forbidden to admit in the case of your own bourgeois form of property.

Abolition of the family! Even the most radical flare up at this infamous proposal of the Communists.

On what foundation is the present family, the bourgeois family, based? On capital, on private gain. In its completely developed form this family exists only among the bourgeoisie. But this state of things finds its complement in the practical absence of the family among the proletarians, and in public prostitution.

The bourgeois family will vanish as a matter of course when its complement vanishes, and both will vanish with the vanishing of capital.

Do you charge us with wanting to stop the exploitation of children by their parents? To this crime we plead guilty.

But, you will say, we destroy the most hallowed of relations, when we replace home education by social.

And your education! Is not that also social, and determined by the social conditions under which you educate, by the intervention, direct or indirect, of society, by means of schools, etc.? The Communists have not invented the intervention of society in education; they do but seek to alter the character of that intervention, and to rescue education from the influence of the ruling class.

The bourgeois clap-trap about the family and education, about the hallowed co-relation of parent and child, becomes all the more disgusting, the more, by the action of Modern Industry, all family ties among the proletarians are torn asunder, and their children transformed into simple articles of commerce and instruments of labor.

But you Communists would introduce community of women, screams the whole bourgeoisie in chorus.

The bourgeois sees in his wife a mere instrument of production. He hears that the instruments of production are to be exploited in common, and, naturally, can come to no other conclusion than that the lot of being common to all will likewise fall to the women.

He has not even a suspicion that the real point aimed at is to do away with the status of women as mere instruments of production.

For the rest, nothing is more ridiculous than the virtuous indignation of our bourgeois at the community of women which, they pretend, is to be openly and officially established by the Communists. The Communists have no need to introduce community of women; it has existed almost from time immemorial.

Our bourgeois, not content with having the wives and daughters of their proletarians at their disposal, not to speak of common prostitutes, take the greatest pleasure in seducing each other's wives.

Bourgeois marriage is in reality a system of wives in common and thus, at the most, what the Communists might possibly be reproached with, is that they desire to introduce, in substitution for a hypocritically concealed, an openly legalized community of women. For the rest, it is self-evident that the abolition of the present system of production must bring with it the abolition of the community of women springing from that system, *i.e.*, of prostitution both public and private.

The Communists are further reproached with desiring to abolish countries and nationality.

The working men have no country. We cannot take from them what they have not got. Since the proletariat must first of all acquire political supremacy, must rise to be the leading class of the nation, must constitute itself *the* nation, it is, so far, itself national, though not in the bourgeois sense of the word.

National differences and antagonisms between peoples are daily more and more vanishing, owing to the development of the bourgeoisie, to freedom of commerce, to the world-market, to uniformity in the mode of production and in the conditions of life corresponding thereto.

The supremacy of the proletariat will cause them to vanish still faster. United action, of the leading civilized countries at least, is one of the first conditions for the emancipation of the proletariat.

In proportion as the exploitation of one individual by another is put an end to, the exploitation of one nation by another will also be put an end to. In proportion as the antagonism between classes within the nation vanishes, the hostility of one nation to another will come to an end.

The charges against Communism made from a religious, a philosophical, and, generally, from an ideological standpoint, are not deserving of serious examination.

Does it require deep intuition to comprehend that man's ideas, views and conceptions, in one word, man's consciousness, changes with every change in the conditions of his material existence, in his social relations and in his social life?

What else does the history of ideas prove, than that intellectual production changes its character in proportion as material production is changed? The ruling ideas of each age have ever been the ideas of its ruling class.

When people speak of ideas that revolutionize society, they do but express the fact, that within the old society, the elements of a new one have been created, and that the dissolution of the old ideas keeps even pace with the dissolution of the old conditions of existence.

When the ancient world was in its last throes, the ancient religions were overcome by Christianity. When Christian ideas succumbed in the 18th century to rationalist ideas, feudal society fought its death battle with the then revolutionary bourgeoisie. The ideas of religious liberty and freedom of conscience merely gave expression to the sway of free competition within the domain of knowledge.

"Undoubtedly," it will be said, "religious, moral, philosophical and juridical ideas have been modified in the course of historical development. But religion, morality, philosophy, political science, and law, constantly survived this change."

"There are, besides, eternal truths, such as Freedom, Justice, etc., that are common to all states of society. But Communism abolishes eternal truths, it abolishes all religion, and all morality, instead of constituting them on a new basis; it therefore acts in contradiction to all past historical experience."

What does this accusation reduce itself to? The history of all past society has consisted in the development of class antagonisms, antagonisms that assumed different forms at different epochs.

But whatever form they may have taken, one fact is common to all past ages, *viz.*, the exploitation of one part of society by the other. No wonder, then, that the social consciousness of past ages, despite all the multiplicity and variety it displays, moves within certain common forms, or general ideas, which cannot completely vanish except with the total disappearance of class antagonisms.

The Communist revolution is the most radical rupture with traditional property relations; no wonder that its development involves the most radical rupture with traditional ideas.

But let us have done with the bourgeois objections to Communism.

We have seen above, that the first step in the revolution by the working class, is to raise the proletariat to the position of ruling class, to win the battle of democracy.

The proletariat will use its political supremacy to wrest, by degrees, all capital from the bourgeoisie, to centralize all instruments of production in the hands of the State, *i.e.*, of the proletariat organized as the ruling class; and to increase the total of productive forces as rapidly as possible.

Of course, in the beginning, this cannot be effected except by means of despotic inroads on the rights of property, and on the conditions of bourgeois production; by means of measures, therefore, which appear economically insufficient and untenable, but which, in the course of the movement, outstrip themselves, necessitate further inroads upon the old social order, and are unavoidable as a means of entirely revolutionizing the mode of production.

These measures will of course be different in different countries.

Nevertheless in the most advanced countries, the following will be pretty generally applicable.

1   Abolition of property in land and application of all rents of land to public purposes.
2   A heavy progressive or graduated income tax.
3   Abolition of all right of inheritance.
4   Confiscation of the property of all emigrants and rebels.
5   Centralization of credit in the hands of the State, by means of a national bank with State capital and an exclusive monopoly.
6   Centralization of the means of communication and transport in the hands of the State.
7   Extension of factories and instruments of production owned by the State; the bringing into cultivation of waste-lands, and the improvement of the soil generally in accordance with a common plan.
8   Equal liability of all to labor. Establishment of industrial armies, especially for agriculture.
9   Combination of agriculture with manufacturing industries; gradual abolition of the distinction between town and country, by a more equable distribution of the population over the country.

10 Free education for all children in public schools. Abolition of children's factory labor in its present form. Combination of education with industrial production, etc., etc.

When, in the course of development, class distinctions have disappeared, and all production has been concentrated in the hands of a vast association of the whole nation, the public power will lose its political character. Political power, properly so called, is merely the organized power of one class for oppressing another. If the proletariat during its contest with the bourgeoisie is compelled, by the force of circumstances, to organize itself as a class, if, by means of a revolution, it makes itself the ruling class, and, as such, sweeps away by force the old conditions of production, then it will, along with these conditions, have swept away the conditions for the existence of class antagonisms and of classes generally, and will thereby have abolished its own supremacy as a class.

In place of the old bourgeois society, with its classes and class antagonisms, we shall have an association, in which the free development of each is the condition for the free development of all ...

In short, the Communists everywhere support every revolutionary movement against the existing social and political order of things.

In all these movements they bring to the front, as the leading question in each, the property question, no matter what its degree of development at the time.

Finally, they labor everywhere for the union and agreement of the democratic parties of all countries.

The Communists disdain to conceal their views and aims. They openly declare that their ends can be attained only by the forcible overthrow of all existing social conditions. Let the ruling classes tremble at a Communistic revolution. The proletarians have nothing to lose but their chains. They have a world to win.

WORKING MEN OF ALL COUNTRIES, UNITE!

NOTE

1   Clemens von Metternich (1773–1859) was foreign minister of the Hapsburg (or Austrian) Empire; Francois P. G. Guizot (1787–1874) was a French statesman.—Eds.

On the Materialist Conception of History

KARL MARX*

The following excerpt from Marx's preface to his *A Contribution to the Critique of Political Economy* (1859) provides a particularly clear and succinct account of what Marx meant by "the materialist conception [or interpretation] of history," which he called "a guiding thread for my studies." Following this historical-materialist thread led Marx to conclude that capitalism is a transitory historical stage that will be superseded and replaced by a less competitive, more cooperative, and truly humane and egalitarian economic and social system.

* *Source*: Karl Marx and Friedrich Engels, *Selected Works in One Volume* (New York: International Publishers, 1968), pp. 181–185. Reprinted by permission.

ON THE MATERIALIST CONCEPTION OF HISTORY

In the year 1842–43, as editor of the *Rheinische Zeitung* [*Rhineland Times*], I experienced for the first time the embarrassment of having to take part in discussions on so-called material interests … [A]t that time when the good will "to go further" greatly outweighed knowledge of the subject, a philosophically weakly tinged echo of French socialism and communism made itself audible in the *Rheinische Zeitung*. I declared myself against this amateurism, but frankly confessed at the same time … that my previous studies did not permit me even to venture any judgment on the content of the French tendencies …

The first work which I undertook for a solution of the doubts which assailed me was a critical review of the Hegelian philosophy of right … My investigation led to the result that legal relations as well as forms of state are to be grasped neither from themselves nor from the so-called general development of the human mind, but rather have their roots in the material conditions of life … The general result at which I arrived and which, once won, served as a guiding thread for my studies, can be briefly formulated as follows: In the social production of their life, men enter into definite relations that are indispensable and independent of their will, relations of production which correspond to a definite stage of development of their material productive forces. The sum total of these relations of production constitutes the economic structure of society, the real foundation, on which rises a legal and political superstructure and to which correspond definite forms of social consciousness. The mode of production of material life conditions [i.e., shapes or influences] the social, political and intellectual life process in general. It is not the consciousness of men that determines their being, but, on the contrary, their social being that determines their consciousness. At a certain stage of their development, the material–productive forces of society come in conflict with the existing relations of production, or—what is but a legal expression for the same thing—with the property relations within which they have been at work hitherto.

From forms of development of the productive forces these relations turn into their fetters. Then begins an epoch of social revolution. With the change of the economic foundation the entire immense superstructure is more or less rapidly transformed. In considering such transformations a distinction should always be made between the material transformation of the economic conditions of production, which can be determined with the precision of natural science, and the legal, political, religious, aesthetic or philosophic—in short, ideological—forms in which men become conscious of this conflict and fight it out. Just as our opinion of an individual is not based on what he thinks of himself, so can we not judge of such a period of transformation by its own consciousness; on the contrary, this consciousness must be explained rather from the contradictions of material life, from the existing conflict between the social productive forces and the relations of production. No social order ever perishes before all the productive forces for which there is room in it have developed; and new, higher relations of production never appear before the material conditions of their existence have matured in the womb of the old society itself. Therefore mankind always sets itself only such tasks as it can solve; since, looking at the matter more closely, it will always be found that the task itself arises only when the material conditions for its solution already exist or are at least in the process of formation. In broad outlines Asiatic, ancient, feudal, and modern bourgeois modes of production can be designated as progressive epochs in the economic formation of society. The bourgeois relations of production are the last antagonistic form of the social process of production—antagonistic not in the sense of individual antagonism, but of one arising from the social conditions of life of the individuals; at the same time the productive forces developing in the womb of bourgeois society create the material conditions for the solution of that antagonism. This social formation brings, therefore, the prehistory of human society to a close.

PART 6

SOCIALISM AND COMMUNISM AFTER MARX

Karl Marx, the most influential of all socialist thinkers, died in 1883, but socialism as an ideology did not die with him. On the contrary, socialism in the late nineteenth and early twentieth centuries was bursting with life—and with lively quarrels about the direction that socialism ought to take. Marx's followers, as we shall see, quarreled among themselves about how best to understand and implement Marx's theory. They also quarreled with the many other socialists— anarchists, Fabians, Christian socialists, and many more—who did not look to Marx's theory for inspiration and guidance. Out of these quarrels two broad tendencies emerged. On one side were those Marxists who held that only the revolutionary overthrow of capitalism could make socialism possible; on the other were those, both Marxists and non-Marxists, who insisted that socialism could and should be achieved gradually by peaceful political means. The revolutionary Marxism of the first group eventually came to be known as *communism*, while the members of the second group called their position *socialism* or, occasionally, *democratic socialism*.

It was not long after Marx's death that various sects calling themselves "Marxist" sprang up in Europe and elsewhere. Each claimed to be the only "true" or "real" Marxists. Each was critical of the others, and all were adamantly opposed to non-Marxian socialists of various stripes. The one thing on which they could all agree was that capitalism was doomed.

One group of Marxists, the "revisionists," held that Marx's theory, in the best scientific spirit, must be subjected to criticism and revision in light of new factual evidence. This was the argument advanced by Eduard Bernstein (1850–1932) in his book *Evolutionary Socialism* (1899). Contrary to Marx's prediction about the ever-increasing "immiseration of the proletariat," the working classes in Europe and North America had actually become better off: Real wages had risen, working conditions had improved, and so had the average worker's standard of living. This was not, Bernstein hastened to add, because the capitalists had become benign or kindly employers but because the working class had developed its political muscles. Laborers had organized trade unions and called strikes to raise their wages and improve their working conditions. And they had organized and supported working-class parties to elect representatives pledged to promote their interests. By these means the proletariat had forced concessions from a reluctant ruling class that was beginning to lose its legitimacy and authority. Thus Bernstein believed that violent revolution was no longer necessary (if indeed it ever had been). Capitalist society was slowly but surely "evolving" into a more egalitarian, just, and humane socialist society. Instead of focusing on a distant utopian end—the creation of a communist society—Marxists and other socialists should devote their energies to day-to-day trade union activities and parliamentary politics.

Bernstein's "revisionist" views were harshly criticized by other Marxists. Rosa Luxemburg (1871–1919), Karl Kautsky (1854–1938), and other prominent German Marxists were highly critical of Bernstein's nonrevolutionary version of Marxism. But the harshest criticisms came from the East. Marxists in Russia—including Georgi Plekhanov (1856–1918) and Vladimir Ilyich Ulyanov (1870–1924), better known as Lenin—condemned Bernstein as a "bourgeois" traitor to Marxism.

The only Marxism worthy of the name, Lenin argued, was radical in its aims and revolutionary in its strategy. The aim was nothing less than the creation of a classless communist society. And this aim, he argued, could be accomplished only with the assistance of a revolutionary "vanguard party" whose leadership was composed of radicalized bourgeois intellectuals like himself. After all, as Lenin often noted, Marx and Engels were not workers but members of the intelligentsia. Left to themselves, the workers would behave just as Bernstein had said they would: that is, workers would organize themselves into trade unions and form working-class political parties in hopes of reforming the capitalist system from within. To cooperate with the capitalist system, said Lenin, was to be corrupted by it. Better to bury it once and for all. Hence the need for a relatively small, tightly knit, highly organized conspiratorial party to raise class consciousness, educate the workers about where their "real" interests lay, and prepare the way for a revolution made in the name of, but not directly by, the proletariat.

Yet Russia in the early twentieth century seemed an odd place for a proletarian revolution, if only because the vast majority of Russian workers were neither factory workers nor wage-laborers but poor and illiterate peasants who tilled the soil. Set in their ways, suspicious of outsiders, and often superstitious, such people seemed the very embodiment of what Marx had called the "idiocy of rural life." They appeared singularly ill-suited to be the agents of radical revolutionary transformation, as Lenin readily acknowledged. But the peasants were discontented, and they were numerous. They could therefore be the clay fit for molding by an elite vanguard party.

Lenin's reinterpretation of Marxism had two novel aspects, neither of which Marx had anticipated: the idea that revolutionary political consciousness had to be brought to the proletariat and the peasantry from outside and the idea that the source of such consciousness was to be an elite vanguard party. It is indeed this version of Marxism—Marxism-Leninism—that proved to be the single most influential and important variant of Marxism throughout the twentieth century. In the Soviet Union, China, Cuba, Vietnam, Eastern Europe, and elsewhere, the Marxist-Leninist model, as adapted and modified by Joseph Stalin (1879–1953),

Mao Zedong (1893–1976), and others, served as an ideology to legitimize an all-powerful party ruling over a highly centralized government and a planned economy managed by government bureaucrats. It is this ideology, and the system it spawned and justified, that in the 1980s and early 1990s came under withering attack from within those countries and even from factions within their respective Communist parties. Communism, as we once knew it, is now nearly extinct.

For more than a century—from Marx's death in 1883 until the collapse of the Soviet Union in 1991—communism was the dominant form of socialism. But it was never the only form. In fact, non-Marxian socialism has been no less varied than its communist counterparts. Anarchists such as Mikhail Bakunin (1814–1876) criticized Marx and the Marxists for the dictatorial implications of their theory and political program. Fabian socialists in England advocated a gradualist, parliamentary path to socialism, as did the American Edward Bellamy (1850–1898) in his utopian novel *Looking Backward*. Christian socialists—including Bellamy's cousin, the American Baptist minister Francis Bellamy (1855–1931), author of the Pledge of Allegiance—looked to Jesus's teachings for inspiration. In the course of the twentieth century, moreover, many socialists advocated a mixture of worker-owned businesses and free-market competition that they called *market socialism*. Whether these and other variants of socialism will flourish as communism falters and fails remains an open question. If socialism does have a future, however, it seems clear that it will be in some form other than Soviet-style communism.

Evolutionary Socialism

*EDUARD BERNSTEIN**

Eduard Bernstein (1850–1932) believed that Marx's theory of social change was generally correct in outline but false or mistaken in several important details. He therefore favored revising Marx's theory to make it consistent with newly emerging facts—including the fact that the predicted "immiseration of the proletariat" had not occurred. Rather than becoming worse off, Bernstein noted, European and North American workers were increasingly prosperous. This had happened, he claimed, because the capitalist system was "evolving" into socialism as it was transformed by trade unions and by working-class or socialist political parties. Bernstein's book *Evolutionary Socialism* (originally published in 1899) provided the classic statement of "revisionist" Marxism.

* *Source*: Eduard Bernstein, *Evolutionary Socialism*, translated by Edith Harvey (New York: B. W. Huebsch, 1909), pp. 203–213, 216–222, 224.

EVOLUTIONARY SOCIALISM

... No socialist capable of thinking, dreams today in England of an imminent victory for socialism by means of a violent revolution—none dreams of a quick conquest of Parliament by a revolutionary proletariat. But they rely more and more on work in the municipalities and other self-governing bodies. The early contempt for the trade union movement has been given up; a closer sympathy has been won for it and, here and there also, for the co-operative movement.

And the ultimate aim? Well, that just remains an ultimate aim. "The working classes have no fixed and perfect Utopias to introduce by means of a vote of the nation. They know that in order to work out their own emancipation—and with it that higher form of life which the present form of society irresistibly makes for by its own economic development—they, the working classes, have to pass through long struggles, a whole series of historical processes, by means of which men and circumstances will be completely transformed. They have no ideals to realize, they have only to set at liberty the elements of the new society which have already been developed in the womb of the collapsing bourgeois society." So writes Marx in *Civil War in France*. I was thinking of this utterance, not in every point but in its fundamental thought in writing down the sentence about the ultimate aim. For after all what does it say but that the movement, the series of processes, is everything, whilst every aim fixed beforehand in its details is immaterial to it. I have declared already that I willingly abandon the form of the sentence about the ultimate aim as far as it admits the interpretation that every general aim of the working class movement formulated as a principle should be declared valueless. But the preconceived theories about the drift of the movement which go beyond such a generally expressed aim, which try to determine the direction of the movement and its character without an ever-vigilant eye upon facts and experience, must necessarily always pass into Utopianism, and at some time or other stand in the way, and hinder the real theoretical and practical progress of the movement.

Whoever knows even but a little of the history of German social democracy also knows that the party has become important by continued action in contravention of such theories and of infringing resolutions founded on them ... A theory or declaration of principle which does not allow attention being paid at every stage of development to the actual interests of the working classes, will always be set aside just as all forswearing of reforming detail work and of the support of neighboring middle class parties has again and again been forgotten; and again and again at the congresses of the party will the complaint be heard that here and there in the electoral contest the ultimate aim of socialism has not been put sufficiently in the foreground.

[Some of my Marxist critics] ... cart me over to the "opponents of scientific socialism."

Unfortunately for "scientific" socialism, the Marxist propositions on the hopelessness of the position of the worker have been upset in a book [by Marx himself] which bears the title, *Capital: A Critique of Political Economy*. There we read of the "physical and moral regeneration" of the textile workers in Lancashire through the [English] Factory Law of 1847, which "struck the feeblest eye." A bourgeois republic was not even necessary to bring about a certain improvement in the situation of a large section of workers! In the same book we read that the society of today is no firm crystal but an organism capable of change and constantly engaged in a process of change, that also in the treatment of economic questions on the part of the official representatives of this society an "improvement was unmistakable." Further that the author had devoted so large a space in his book to the results of the English Factory Laws in order to spur the Continent to imitate them and thus to work so that the process of transforming society may be accomplished in ever more humane forms. All of which signifies not hopelessness but capability of improvement in the condition of the worker. And, as since 1866, when this was written, the legislation depicted has not grown weaker but has been improved, made more general, and has been supplemented by laws and organizations working in the same direction, there can be no more doubt to-day than formerly of the hopefulness of the position of the worker. If to state such facts means following the "immortal Bastiat," then among the first ranks of these followers is—Karl Marx.[1]

Now, it can be asserted against me that Marx certainly recognized those improvements, but that the chapter on the historical tendency of capitalist accumulation at the end of the first volume of *Capital* shows how little these details influenced his fundamental mode of viewing things. To which I answer that as far as that is correct it speaks against that chapter and not against me.

One can interpret this chapter in very different kinds of ways. I believe I was the first to point out, and indeed repeatedly, that it was a summary characterization of the tendency of a development which is found in capitalist accumulation, but which in practice is not carried out completely and which therefore need not be driven to the critical point of the antagonism there depicted. Engels has never expressed himself against this interpretation of mine, never, either verbally or in print, declared it to be wrong. Nor did he say a word against me when I wrote, in 1891: "It is clear that where legislation, this systematic and conscious action of society, interferes in an appropriate way, the working of the tendencies of economic development is thwarted, under some circumstances can even be annihilated. Marx and Engels have not only never denied this, but, on the contrary, have always emphasized it." If one reads the chapter mentioned with this idea, one will also, in a few sentences, silently place the word "tendency" and thus be spared the need of bringing this chapter into accord with reality by distorting arts of interpretation. But then the chapter itself would become of less value the more progress is made in actual evolution. For its theoretic importance does not lie in the argument of the general tendency to capitalistic centralization and accumulation which had been affirmed long before Marx by bourgeois economists and socialists, but in the presentation, peculiar to Marx, of circumstances and forms under which it would work at a more advanced stage of evolution, and of the results to which it would lead. But in this respect actual evolution is really always bringing forth new arrangements, forces, facts, in face of which that presentation seems insufficient and loses to a corresponding extent the capability of serving as a sketch of the coming evolution. That is how I understand it.

One can, however, understand this chapter differently. One can conceive it in this way, that all the improvements mentioned there, and some possibly ensuing, only create temporary remedies against the oppressive tendencies of capitalism, that they signify unimportant modifications which cannot in the long run effect anything substantially against the critical point of antagonisms laid down by Marx, that this will finally appear—if not literally yet substantially— in the manner depicted, and will lead to catastrophic change by violence. This interpretation can be founded on the categoric wording of the last sentences of the chapter, and receives a certain confirmation because at the end reference is again made to the *Communist Manifesto*, whilst Hegel also appeared shortly before with his negation of the negation—the restoration on a new foundation of individual property negated by the capitalist manner of production.

According to my view, it is impossible simply to declare the one conception right and the other absolutely wrong. To me the chapter illustrates a dualism which runs through the whole monumental work of Marx, and which also finds expression in a less pregnant fashion in other passages—a dualism which consists in this, that the work aims at being a scientific inquiry and also at proving a theory laid down long before its drafting; a formula lies at the basis of it in which the result to which the exposition should lead is fixed beforehand. The return to the *Communist Manifesto* points here to a real residue of Utopianism in the Marxist system. Marx had accepted the solution of the Utopians in essentials, but had recognized their means and proofs as inadequate. He therefore undertook a revision of them, and this with the zeal, the critical acuteness, and love of truth of a scientific genius. He suppressed no important fact, he also forbore belittling artificially the importance of these facts as long as the object of the inquiry had no immediate reference to the final aim of the formula to be proved. To that point his work is free of every tendency necessarily interfering with the scientific method.

For the general sympathy with the strivings for emancipation of the working classes does not in itself stand in the way of the scientific method. But, as Marx approaches a point when that final aim enters seriously into the question, he becomes uncertain and unreliable. Such contradictions then appear as were shown in the book under consideration, for instance, in the section on the movement of incomes in modern society. It thus appears that this great scientific spirit was, in the end, a slave to a doctrine. To express it figuratively, he has raised a mighty building within the framework of a scaffolding he found existing, and in its erection he kept strictly to the laws of scientific architecture as long as they did not collide with the conditions which the construction of the scaffolding prescribed, but he neglected or evaded them when the scaffolding did not allow of their observance. Where the scaffolding put limits in the way of the building, instead of destroying the scaffolding, he changed the building itself at the cost of its right proportions and so made it all the more dependent on the scaffolding. Was it the consciousness of this irrational relation which caused him continually to pass from completing his work to amending special parts of it? However that may be, my conviction is that wherever that dualism shows itself the scaffolding must fall if the building is to grow in its right proportions. In the latter, and not in the former, is found what is worthy to live in Marx.

Nothing confirms me more in this conception than the anxiety with which some persons seek to maintain certain statements in *Capital*, which are falsified by facts. It is just some of the more deeply devoted followers of Marx who have not been able to separate themselves from the dialectical form of the work—that is the scaffolding alluded to—who do this. At least, that is only how I can explain the words of a man, otherwise so amenable to facts as Karl Kautsky, who, when I observed in Stuttgart that the number of wealthy people for many years had increased, not decreased, answered: "If that were true then the date of our victory would not only be very long postponed, but we should never attain our goal. If it be capitalists who increase and not those with no possessions, then we are going ever further from our goal the more evolution progresses, then capitalism grows stronger, not socialism."[2]

That the number of the wealthy increases and does not diminish is not an invention of bourgeois "harmony economists," but a fact established by the boards of assessment for taxes, often to the chagrin of those concerned, a fact which can no longer be disputed. But what is the significance of this fact as regards the victory of socialism? Why should the realization of socialism depend on its refutation? Well, simply for this reason: because the dialectical scheme seems so to prescribe it; because a post threatens to fall out of the scaffolding if one admits that the social surplus product is appropriated by an increasing instead of a decreasing number of possessors. But it is only the speculative theory that is affected by this matter; it does not at all affect the actual movement. Neither the struggle of the workers for democracy in politics nor their struggle for democracy in industry is touched by it. The prospects of this struggle do not depend on the theory of concentration of capital in the hands of a diminishing number of magnates, nor on the whole dialectical scaffolding of which this is a plank, but on the growth of social wealth and of the social productive forces, in conjunction with general social progress, and, particularly, in conjunction with the intellectual and moral advance of the working classes themselves.

Suppose the victory of socialism depended on the constant shrinkage in the number of capitalist magnates, social democracy, if it wanted to act logically, either would have to support the heaping up of capital in ever fewer hands, or at least to give no support to anything that would stop this shrinkage. As a matter of fact it often enough does neither the one nor the other. These considerations, for instance, do not govern its votes on questions of taxation. From the standpoint of the catastrophic theory a great part of this practical activity of the working classes is an undoing of work that ought to be allowed to be done. It is not social democracy which is wrong in this respect. The fault lies in the doctrine which assumes that progress depends on the deterioration of social conditions ...

[In earlier] circumstances a reference to politics could appear only to be a turning aside from more pressing duties. Today these conditions have been to some extent removed, and therefore no person capable of reflecting will think of criticizing political action ...

[L]aw, or the path of legislative reform, is the slower way, and revolutionary force the quicker and more radical. But that only is true in a restricted sense. Whether the legislative or the revolutionary method is the more promising depends entirely on the nature of the measures and on their relation to different classes and customs of the people.

In general, one may say here that the revolutionary way (always in the sense of revolution by violence) does quicker work as far as it deals with removal of obstacles which a privileged minority places in the path of social progress: that its strength lies on its negative side.

Constitutional legislation works more slowly in this respect as a rule. Its path is usually that of compromise, not the prohibition, but the buying out of acquired rights. But it is stronger than the revolution scheme where prejudice and the limited horizon of the great mass of the people appear as hindrances to social progress, and it offers greater advantages where it is a question of the creation of permanent economic arrangements capable of lasting; in other words, it is best adapted to positive social-political work.

In legislation, intellect dominates over emotion in quiet times; during a revolution emotion dominates over intellect. But if emotion is often an imperfect leader, the intellect is a slow motive force. Where a revolution sins by over haste, the every-day legislator sins by procrastination. Legislation works as a systematic force, revolution as an elementary force.

As soon as a nation has attained a position where the rights of the propertied minority have ceased to be a serious obstacle to social progress, where the negative tasks of political action are less pressing than the positive, then the appeal to a revolution by force becomes a meaningless phrase. One can overturn a government or a privileged minority, but not a nation. When the working classes do not possess very strong economic organizations of their own, and have not attained, by means of education on self-governing bodies, a high degree of mental independence, the dictatorship of the proletariat means the dictatorship of club orators and writers. I would not wish that those who see in the oppression and tricking of the working men's organizations and in the exclusion of working men from the legislature and government the highest point of the art of political policy should experience their error in practice. Just as little would I desire it for the working class movement itself.

One has not overcome Utopianism if one assumes that there is in the present, or ascribes to the present, what is to be in the future. We have to take working men as they are. And they are neither so universally pauperized [i.e., impoverished] as was set out in the *Communist Manifesto*, nor so free from prejudices and weaknesses as their courtiers wish to make us believe. They have the virtues and failings of the economic and social conditions under which they live. And neither these conditions nor their effects can be put on one side from one day to another.

Have we attained the required degree of development of the productive forces for the abolition of classes? In face of the fantastic figures which were formerly set up in proof of this and which rested on generalizations based on the development of particularly favored industries, socialist writers in modern times have endeavored to reach by carefully detailed calculations, appropriate estimates of the possibilities of production in a socialist society, and their results are very different from those figures. Of a general reduction of hours of labor to five, four, or even three or two hours, such as was formerly accepted, there can be no hope at any time within sight, unless the general standard of life is much reduced. Even under a collective organization of work, labor must begin very young and only cease at a rather advanced age, if it is to be reduced considerably below an eight-hours' day. Those persons ought to understand this first of all who indulge in the most extreme exaggerations regarding the ratio of the number of the nonpropertied classes to that of the propertied. But he who thinks irrationally on one point does so usually on another ...

[H]e who surveys the actual workers' movement will also find that the freedom from those qualities which appeared Philistine to a person born in the bourgeoisie, is very little valued by the workers, that they in no way support the morale of proletarianism, but, on the contrary, tend to make a Philistine out of a proletarian. With the roving proletarian without a family and home, no lasting, firm trade union movement would be possible. It is no bourgeois prejudice, but a conviction gained through decades of labor organization, which has made so many of the English labor leaders—socialists and non-socialists—into zealous adherents of the temperance movement. The working class socialists know the faults of their class, and the most conscientious among them, far from glorifying these faults, seek to overcome them with all their power.

We cannot demand from a class, the great majority of whose members live under crowded conditions, are badly educated, and have an uncertain and insufficient income, the high intellectual and moral standard which the organization and existence of a socialist community presupposes. We will, therefore, not ascribe it to them by way of fiction. Let us rejoice at the great stock of intelligence, renunciation, and energy which the modern working class movement has partly revealed, partly produced; but we must not assign, without discrimination to the masses, the millions, what holds good, say, of hundreds of thousands. I will not repeat the declarations which have been made to me on this point by working men [themselves] … [I]t is not every epoch that produces a Marx, and even for a man of equal genius the working class movement of today is too great to enable him to occupy the position which Marx fills in its history. Today it needs, in addition to the fighting spirit, the coordinating and constructive thinkers who are intellectually enough advanced to be able to separate the chaff from the wheat, who are great enough in their mode of thinking to recognize also the little plant that has grown on another soil than theirs, and who, perhaps, though not kings, are warm-hearted republicans in the domain of socialist thought.

NOTES

1 Claude-Frederic Bastiat (1801–1850) was a French economist and opponent of socialism.—Eds.
2 Karl Kautsky (1854–1938) was a Marxist theorist and a leader of the German Social Democratic Party.—Eds.

Revisionism, Imperialism, and Revolution

*V. I. LENIN**

Marxism-Leninism, as the ideology of the Soviet Union was officially called before the dramatic changes of the late 1980s, was largely the creation of one man. Vladimir Ilyich Ulyanov (1870–1924)—better known by his revolutionary pseudonym, Lenin—was, until his death, the preeminent Russian revolutionary and Marxian theorist. In "adapting" Marxism to Russian conditions, Lenin made several significant changes. For one, he held that a proletarian revolution could occur in Russia, despite the fact that Russia in the early twentieth century had a relatively small proletariat (the overwhelming majority of Russian workers were not wage-laborers but peasants who tilled the soil). For another, he claimed that only a small, highly organized, conspiratorial "vanguard" party could supply the political will (or "consciousness") and leadership required to radically transform such an economically and politically backward country. A fiercely combative critic of other interpretations of Marxism, Lenin claimed that his alone was the "true" interpretation; all others— including the "revisionist" view espoused by Bernstein—were deviations from or distortions of Marx's "scientific" outlook. If revolution had not come to the advanced capitalist countries, as Marx had predicted, that was because the workers in those countries were afflicted with "trade-union consciousness," that is, the mistaken view that they could organize themselves into trade unions and political parties to promote their interests. This strategy was successful, said Lenin, only because the capitalist countries were exploiting the workers of nonindustrial countries. Such exploitation would cease—and revolution would come to capitalist countries themselves—when workers in those underdeveloped countries made their own anticolonial or anti-imperialist revolutions.

* *Source*: V. I. Lenin, *Izbrannye proizvedenii a v dvukh tomakh (Selected Works in Two Volumes)*, (Moscow, 1936), vol. 1, pp. 39–45 and pp. 587–589; vol. 2, pp. 133–146. Translated expressly for this volume by Anna Brailovsky.

MARXISM AND REVISIONISM

A well-known saying proclaims that if geometrical axioms concerned human interests they would most likely be refuted. Theories of natural history that concerned the old prejudices of theology provoked, and still provoke, the most rabid opposition. It is no wonder that the teaching of Marx, which directly serves to enlighten and organize the leading class in contemporary society, indicates the tasks facing this class, and demonstrates the inevitable (by virtue of economic development) replacement of the present system by a new order—it is no wonder that this teaching has had to fight for every step along the path of its life.

There is no point of even speaking of bourgeois science and philosophy, taught in the official manner by official professors in order to befuddle the rising generation of the propertied classes and to "coach" it against enemies external and internal. This science will not even hear of Marxism, declaring it to have been refuted and annihilated. Both young scholars making a career of refuting socialism, and [decrepit] elders, preserving the testaments of all sorts of outworn "systems," attack Marx with equal fervor. The growth of Marxism, and the fact that its ideas are spreading and taking hold among the working class, inevitably provokes greater frequency and intensity of these bourgeois sorties against Marxism, which becomes stronger, more hardened and more vigorous each time it is "annihilated" by official science.

But even among doctrines connected with the struggle of the working class, prevalent mainly among the proletariat, it was very far from immediate that Marxism attained a firm position. In the first half-century of its existence (from the 1840s on) Marxism was engaged in combat with theories fundamentally hostile to it. In the early 1840s Marx and Engels settled accounts with the radical Young Hegelians who subscribed to the viewpoint of philosophical idealism.[1] At the end of the forties a struggle emerges in the field of economic doctrine—against Proudhonism.[2] The fifties mark the culmination of this struggle in criticism of the parties and doctrines that manifested themselves in the stormy year of 1848.[3] In the sixties the struggle shifts from the field of general theory to a field closer to the immediate workers' movement: the ejection of Bakuninism[4] from the International. In the early seventies in Germany, the Proudhonist Mühlberger comes for a brief time to the fore, and in the late seventies it is the positivist Dühring.[5] But the influence of either on the proletariat is already absolutely insignificant. Marxism has already unquestionably conquered all other ideologies of the workers' movement.

By the nineties this victory was, in its main features, complete. Even in the Romance-language countries, where the traditions of Proudhonism held their ground longest of all, the workers' parties in effect built their programs and tactics on Marxist foundations. The revived international organization of the workers' movement—in the form of periodic international congresses—established itself immediately and almost without resistance on Marxist grounds in every essential. But after Marxism had ousted all the more or less self-contained doctrines hostile to it, the tendencies that had been expressed in those doctrines began to seek other pathways. The forms and causes of the struggle changed, but the struggle continued. And the second half-century of the existence of Marxism began (in the nineties) with a struggle of a current hostile to Marxism being waged within Marxism itself.

[Eduard] Bernstein, a one-time orthodox Marxist, gave his name to this current, having come forth with the most noise and the most consistent articulation of corrections to Marx—a re-examination of Marx, revisionism.[6] Even in Russia where—owing to the economic backwardness of the country and the preponderance of a peasant population weighed down by the remnants of serfdom—non-Marxist socialism naturally persisted longest of all; even in Russia, it is plainly, before our very eyes, transforming into revisionism. Both in the agrarian question (the program of the municipalization of all land) and in general questions of program and tactics, our Social-Narodniks[7] are increasingly substituting the "corrections" to Marx for the moribund, obsolescent remnants of the old system, which in its own way was self-contained and fundamentally hostile to Marxism.

Pre-Marxist socialism has been defeated. It now continues the struggle not on its own independent ground, but on the general ground of Marxism, as revisionism. Let us take a look, then, at what the ideological content of revisionism may be.

In the sphere of philosophy revisionism took up the rear of bourgeois professorial "science." The professors went "back to Kant"—and revisionism dragged along after the neo-Kantians.[8] The professors repeated the [banalities] uttered a thousand times by the priests against philosophical materialism—and the revisionists, smiling condescendingly, mumbled ... that materialism had been "refuted" long ago. The professors disparaged Hegel as a "dead dog," and preaching idealism themselves, only an idealism a thousand times more petty and banal than Hegel's, contemptuously shrugged their shoulders at the subject of dialectics—and the revisionists clambered after them into the swamp of the philosophical banalization of science, replacing "clever" (and revolutionary) dialectics with "simple" (and calm) "evolution." The professors earned their official keep by adjusting both their idealist and their "critical" systems to approach the reigning medieval "philosophy" (i.e., to theology)—and the revisionists sidled up to them, trying to make religion a "private affair" not in relation to the modern state, but in relation to the party of the leading class.

There is no need to speak of what significance such "corrections" of Marx had in actual class terms: the matter is self-evident ...

Going on to political economy, it must be noted first of all that in this sphere the "corrections" of the revisionists were much more multifaceted and circumstantial; attempts were made to influence the public with "new data on economic development." It was said that consolidation and the ousting of small-scale production by large-scale production do not occur in agriculture at all, while they occur in the spheres of commerce and industry extremely slowly. It was said that crises had now become rarer and weaker, and that cartels and trusts would probably enable capital to eliminate crises altogether. It was said that the "theory of collapse" toward which capitalism is headed was unfounded, given the tendency of class antagonisms to become milder and less acute. It was said, finally, that it would not be amiss to correct Marx's theory of value, too ...

The struggle against the revisionists on these questions reanimated the theoretical thinking of international socialism as fruitfully as did Engels's controversy with Dühring twenty years earlier. The arguments of the revisionists were examined on hand of facts and figures. It was proven that the revisionists were systematically painting contemporary small-scale production in rosy tones.

The technical and commercial superiority of large-scale *production* over small-scale, not only in industry, but also in agriculture, is proven by irrefutable facts. But in agriculture, commodity production is far less developed, and modern statisticians and economists are usually not particularly capable of singling out the special branches (sometimes even the operations) of agriculture that indicate the progressive involvement of global economic *exchange*. On the ruins of natural economy, small-scale production survives on a continually worsening diet, by chronic starvation, by lengthening the working day, by deterioration in the quality and care of cattle, in a word, by the very same methods with which cottage industry survived in the face of capitalist manufacture. Every advance in science and technology inevitably and implacably undermines the foundations of small-scale production in capitalist society; and the task of socialist political economy is to investigate this process in all its frequently complicated and [convoluted] forms, and to demonstrate to the small-scale producer the impossibility of his holding his own under capitalism, the hopelessness of peasant farming under capitalism, and the necessity for the peasant to adopt the viewpoint of the proletariat. On this question the revisionists sinned in the scientific sense, by superficial generalizations of facts snatched one-sidedly out of the context of the capitalist system as a whole; in the political sense, they sinned in that they inevitably, whether they wanted to or not, invited or urged the peasant to take the point of view of the small proprietor (i.e., the point of view of the bourgeoisie) instead of urging him to take the point of view of the revolutionary proletarian.

With the theory of crises and the theory of collapse, matters stood even worse for revisionism. Only for a very brief time, and only for the most short-sighted people, was it conceivable to think of refashioning the foundations of Marx's theory under the influence of a few years of industrial boom and prosperity. That crises were not a thing of the past was very quickly demonstrated to the revisionists by reality: crisis came after prosperity. The forms, the sequence, the picture of particular crises changed, but crises remained an inevitable component of the capitalist system. Cartels and trusts, while they unify production, at the same time exacerbate for all to see the anarchy of production and the proletariat's lack of financial means, thereby making class antagonisms more acute to an unprecedented extent. It is precisely the most recent gigantic trusts that make especially obvious, to an especially great extent, that capitalism is heading for collapse—in the sense both of isolated political and economic crises and in the sense of the complete collapse of the entire capitalist system. The recent financial crisis in America and the horrible increase of unemployment all over Europe, to say nothing of the impending industrial crisis of which many signs portend—all this has led to the recent "theories" of the revisionists becoming forgotten by everybody, including, it seems, many of the revisionists themselves. Only it would not do well to forget the lessons this instability of the intellectuals has taught the working class.

As to the theory of value, it need only be said that apart from rather vague hints and sighs in the direction of Böhm-Bawerk,[9] here the revisionists have contributed absolutely nothing, and have therefore left no traces whatever in the development of scientific thought.

In the sphere of politics, revisionism did actually try to re-examine the foundation of Marxism, namely, the doctrine of class struggle. Political freedom, democracy and universal suffrage eliminate the ground for class struggle—we were told—and render false the old proposition of the *Communist Manifesto* that laborers have no fatherland. In a democracy, so they would have it, since the "will of the majority" rules, one must neither view the state as an organ of class rule, nor reject alliances with the progressive social-reform bourgeoisie against the reactionaries.

It's indisputable that these revisionist objections amounted to a rather well-constructed system of views: namely, the long familiar liberal-bourgeois views. The liberals have always said that bourgeois parliamentarianism destroys classes and class divisions, since all citizens without distinction have the right to vote and the right to participate in the government of the country. The whole history of Europe in the second half of the nineteenth century, and the whole history of the Russian revolution in the early twentieth, plainly demonstrate how absurd such views are. Economic distinctions are not mitigated but aggravated and intensified under the freedom of "democratic" capitalism. Parliamentarianism does not eliminate, but lays bare the essence of the most democratic bourgeois republics as organs of class oppression. By helping to enlighten and to organize immeasurably wider masses of the population than those which had previously taken an active part in political events, parliamentarianism thus paves the way not for the elimination of crises and political revolutions, but for the maximum intensification of civil war during such revolutions. The events in Paris in the spring of 1871 and in Russia in the winter of 1905 showed clear as day how inevitably this intensification comes about. The French bourgeoisie, without a moment's hesitation, made a deal with the national enemy, with the foreign army which had ruined its fatherland, in order to crush the proletarian movement. Whoever does not understand the inevitable inner dialectics of parliamentarianism and bourgeois democracy—which leads to an even more abrupt resolution of disputes by mass violence than in previous times—will never be able to conduct, on the ground of this parliamentarianism, campaigns of propaganda and agitation consistent in principle, actually preparing the working-class masses for victorious participation in such "disputes." The experience of alliances, agreements and blocs with social-reform liberalism in the West and with the liberal reformists (Cadets) in the Russian revolution has convincingly shown that these agreements only blunt the consciousness of the masses, not strengthening but weakening the actual significance of their struggle, linking fighters with elements that are least capable of fighting and the most unreliable and treacherous. French Millerandism[10]—the largest experiment in applying revisionist political tactics on a wide and truly national scale—has provided a practical appraisal of revisionism that will never be forgotten by the proletariat all over the world.

A natural complement to the economic and political tendencies of revisionism was its attitude to the ultimate aim of the socialist movement. "The ultimate aim is nothing; the movement is everything"—this catch-phrase of Bernstein's expresses the essence of revisionism better than many long deliberations. To determine its conduct on a case to case basis, to adapt itself to the events of the day and to the vagaries of political trifles, to forget the fundamental interests of the proletariat and the basic features of the entire capitalist system, and all of capitalist evolution, to sacrifice these fundamental interests for the real or assumed advantages of the moment—such is the politics of revisionism. And it patently follows from the very nature of this politics that it may assume an infinite variety of forms, and that every more or less "new" issue, every more or less unexpected and unforeseen turn of events, though such a turn may alter the basic course of development only to a minute degree and only for the briefest period, will always inevitably give rise to one or another variety of revisionism.

The inevitability of revisionism is predicated on its class roots in modern society. Revisionism is an international phenomenon. No socialist who is even the least bit informed and capable of thinking could have the slightest doubt that the relation between the orthodox and the Bernsteinians in Germany, the Guesdists and the Jaurèsists (and now particularly the Broussists) in France, the Social Democratic Federation and the Independent Labour Party in Great Britain, Brouckère and Vandervelde in Belgium, the Integralists and the Reformists in Italy, the Bolsheviks and the Mensheviks in Russia,[11] is everywhere essentially of the same kind, notwithstanding the immense variety of national conditions and historical factors in the present circumstances of all these countries. The "division" within contemporary international socialism now runs essentially along the same line in all the different countries of the world, which testifies to a tremendous step forward in comparison to what was happening thirty or forty years ago, when non-uniform tendencies in different countries were struggling within one unified international socialist movement. And even the "revisionism from the left" that has now taken form in the Romance-language countries as "revolutionary syndicalism" is also adapting itself to Marxism, "correcting" it: Labriola in Italy and Lagardelle in France[12] constantly make appeals from Marx-the-improperly-understood to Marx-who-understands-properly.

We cannot stop here to analyze the ideological content of *this* revisionism, which is still far from being as developed as opportunist revisionism: it has not yet become internationalized, has not yet withstood a single large-scale practical clash with a socialist party in even a single country. We confine ourselves therefore to that "revisionism from the right" that was described above.

Wherein lies its inevitability in capitalist society? Why is it more profound than the differences of national particularities and of degrees of capitalist development? Because in every capitalist country, at the side of the proletariat, there are always broad strata of petty bourgeoisie, small proprietors. Capitalism arose and is constantly arising out of small-scale production with numerous "middle strata" that are inevitably generated anew by capitalism (appendages to the factory, cottage industry, small workshops scattered all over the country in the face of the demands of big industries, such as the bicycle and automobile industries, etc.). These new small producers are just as inevitably cast out again into the ranks of the proletariat. It is quite natural that the petty-bourgeois world-view should again and again crop up in the ranks of the broad workers' parties. It is quite natural that this should be so and always will be so, right up to the upheavals of the proletarian revolution. For it would be a profound mistake to think that the "complete" proletarianization of the majority of the population is necessary to carry out such a revolution. What we now frequently experience only in the domain of ideology: disputes over theoretical corrections to Marx; what now crops up in practice only with regard to particular individual issues of the labor movement, in the form of tactical disagreements with the revisionists and divisions on those grounds—is bound to be experienced by the working class on an incomparably larger scale, when the proletarian revolution exacerbates all the disputed questions, concentrates all dissonances on points that are of the most immediate importance in determining the conduct of the masses, and compels in the heat of battle to distinguish enemies from friends, and to cast out bad allies in order to deal decisive blows to the enemy.

The ideological struggle waged by revolutionary Marxism against revisionism at the end of the nineteenth century is but a prelude to the great revolutionary battles of the proletariat, which is marching forward toward the complete victory of its cause despite all the vacillations and weaknesses of the petty bourgeoisie.

IMPERIALISM: THE HIGHEST STAGE OF CAPITALISM

… When nine-tenths of Africa had been seized (by 1900), when the whole world had been divided up, inevitably there arrived the era of monopoly colonial possession and, consequently, of particularly acute struggle for the division and the repartition of the world.

The extent to which monopolistic capitalism has intensified all the contradictions of capitalism is generally known. It suffices to point to the high cost of living and to the tyranny of the cartels. This intensification of contradictions constitutes the most powerful driving force of the transitional period of history that began with the time of the final victory of global finance capital.

Monopolies, oligarchy, the striving for domination rather than the striving for freedom, the exploitation of an increasing number of small or weak nations by a handful of the richest or most powerful nations—all this has given birth to those distinctive features of imperialism that compel us to characterize it as parasitic or decaying capitalism. More and more prominently there emerges, as one of the tendencies of imperialism, the creation of the "rentier state," the usurer state, in which the bourgeoisie lives increasingly on the export of capital and by "clipping coupons." It would be a mistake to believe that this tendency to decay precludes the rapid growth of capitalism. No. In the epoch of imperialism, certain branches of industry, certain strata of the bourgeoisie, certain nations demonstrate now one and now another of these tendencies to a greater or lesser degree. On the whole, capitalism is growing immeasurably faster than ever; but not only is this growth becoming more uneven in general, but this unevenness also manifests itself in part in the decay of countries that are richest in capital (Britain).

In regard to the rapidity of Germany's economic development, [Jakob] Riesser, the author of the study on big German banks, states: "The progress of the preceding period (1848–70), which was not overly slow, relates to the speed of all economic development in Germany, including its banks, during the present period (1870–1905) in approximately the same way that the speed of the mail coach in the good old days relates to the speed of the contemporary automobile, which races so swiftly that it becomes a danger both to the innocent pedestrian, and to the occupants of the car themselves." In its turn, this extraordinarily quickly-growing finance capital—precisely because it has grown so quickly—is not against transitioning to a more "tranquil" possession of colonies that are subject to seizure, and not only by peaceful means, from richer nations. Meanwhile, in the United States, economic development in the last decades proceeded even more rapidly than in Germany, and precisely *thanks* to this fact, the parasitic features of this newest form of American capitalism have emerged with particular prominence. On the other hand, a comparison of, say, the republican American bourgeoisie with the monarchist Japanese or German bourgeoisie demonstrates that the greatest political distinction diminishes to an extreme degree in the epoch of imperialism— not because it is unimportant in general, but because in all these cases we are talking about a bourgeoisie with the specific features of parasitism.

The high level of monopoly profits received by capitalists in one of the many branches of industry, in one of the many countries, etc., makes it economically possible for them to bribe certain segments of the labor force—and for a time, a fairly considerable minority of them—winning them over to the side of the bourgeoisie in a given industry or nation against all the others. And the intensified antagonism between imperialist nations caused by the partitioning of the world intensifies this tendency.

STATE AND REVOLUTION

Ordinary discussions about the state continually make the same mistake against which [Friedrich] Engels cautions here, and which we noted in passing previously. Namely: they continually forget that the elimination of the state also means the elimination of democracy; that the withering away of the state is the withering away of democracy.

At first glance such a claim seems extremely strange and incomprehensible; perhaps some might even become apprehensive that we are expecting the advent of a social order in which the principle of the subordination of the minority to the majority will not be observed—for is not democracy after all the recognition of this principle?

No. Democracy is *not* identical with the subordination of the minority to the majority. Democracy is a *state* that acknowledges the subordination of the minority to the majority; i.e., it is an organization for the systematic use of force by one class against another, one portion of the population against another.

Our ultimate goal is the elimination of the state, i.e. all organized and systematic uses of force, any use of force against people as such. We do not expect the advent of a social order in which the principle of the subordination of the minority to the majority would not be observed. But we are convinced that as we strive for socialism it will begin to evolve into communism, and in conjunction with this any necessity for the use of force against people in general, for the *subordination* of one person to another, one portion of the population to another, will vanish—for people will become *habituated* to observing the fundamental conditions of society *without force* and *without subordination.*

It is in order to underscore this element of habit that Engels speaks of a new *generation*, which has "grown up under new, free social conditions [and] will turn out to be capable of tossing out all that state system rubbish"—any state system, including the democratic republican state system.

To explain this requires examining the question of the economic basis for the withering away of the state.

The Economic Basis of the Withering Away of the State

The most substantial explanation of this question was provided by Marx in his "Critique of the Gotha Program" (letter to Bracke, May 5, 1875, published in *Die Neue Zeit* [*The New Time*], Bd. 1, No. 18, 1890–91). The polemical part of this remarkable work, which consists of a critique of Lassalleanism,[13] has, so to speak, overshadowed its positive part; namely: the analysis of the connection between the development of communism and the withering away of the state.

1. Marx's Statement of the Question

From a superficial comparison of Marx's letter to [Wilhelm] Bracke of May 5, 1875 and our earlier examination of Engels' letter to Bebel of March 28, 1875 it might seem that Marx is far more "pro-state" than Engels, and that the difference between the two authors' views of the state is quite significant.

Engels suggests to [August] Bebel that they quit going on about the state altogether and completely banish the word state from the program, substituting for it the word "community"; Engels even declares that the Commune was no longer a state in the proper sense. Meanwhile Marx even speaks about the "future state system of communist society," i.e., as if he acknowledges the necessity of the state, even under communism.

But such a view would be fundamentally mistaken. A closer examination demonstrates that the views of Marx and Engels regarding the state and its withering away correspond entirely, and the aforementioned statement by Marx refers specifically to the *dying system* of state.

Clearly, it is out of the question to try to determine the moment that the state shall "wither away" in the future, especially since this obviously constitutes a lengthy process. The apparent difference between Marx and Engels is explained by the difference between the tasks that each set for himself and pursued. Engels set himself the task of demonstrating to Bebel—explicitly, bluntly, and in broad strokes—the utter absurdity of the prevailing prejudices regarding the state (which were shared to no small degree by Lasalle). Marx touches upon *this* question only in passing. He is interested in a different theme: the *development* of communist society.

Marx's entire theory is nothing other than the application of the theory of development—in its most consistent, complete, considered, and richly meaningful form—to modern capitalism. It is natural that for Marx the question would arise of the application of this theory also to the *impending* collapse of capitalism and to the *future* development of *future* communism.

But on the basis of what *facts* could one pose the question of the future development of future communism?

On the basis of the fact that it *arises* out of capitalism, develops historically from capitalism, and results from the action of the social force that is *born* of capitalism. In Marx, there is not the shadow of the attempt to construct utopias and vainly guess about what cannot be known. Marx posits the question of communism as a naturalist writer would for instance posit the question of the development of a new biological variety, given that we know that it arose in such and such a way, and is evolving in a certain particular direction.

First of all, Marx sweeps away the confusion introduced by the Gotha Program[14] into the question of the relationship between state and society.

... "Contemporary society"—he writes—"is a capitalist society, which exists in all civilized countries more or less free of an admixture of medievalism, more or less differentiated by the particular historical development of each country, more or less developed." In contrast, "the contemporary state" changes with each state border. It is completely different in the Prussian-German empire from that in Switzerland; completely different in England from that in the United States. "The contemporary state," consequently, is a fiction.

However, despite the colorful variety of their forms, the various states of various civilized countries have this in common between them—that they are standing on the soil of contemporary bourgeois society, in a more or less developed stage of capitalism. They therefore have certain common essential characteristics. In this sense, one can speak of a "contemporary state system" in contrast to that future in which its current root, bourgeois society, will wither away.

Consequently the question presents itself thus: what sort of transformation will the state system undergo in communist society? In other words: what social functions will then remain that are analogous to state functions? This question can only be answered scientifically; and regardless of how many thousands of times the word "people" is combined with the word "state," this will not bring us "the smallest bit closer to its resolution." ...

Having ridiculed any discussion of the "people's state" in this manner, Marx poses the question and cautions, as it were, that in order to answer it scientifically one may bring to bear only well-established scientific facts.

The first thing that is established with complete certainty by the entire theory of development, and all of science as a whole—and which the utopians had forgotten, and which today's opportunists, who are afraid of socialist revolution, are forgetting—is the circumstance that historically there must undoubtedly be a special stage or special phase of *transition* from capitalism to communism.

2. The Transition from Capitalism to Communism

... "Between capitalism and communist society"—Marx continues—"lies a period of revolutionary transformation of one into the other. This period also corresponds with a transitional political period, and the state during this period can be nothing other than the *revolutionary dictatorship of the proletariat*." ...

This conclusion rests for Marx upon the analysis of the role the proletariat plays in contemporary capitalist society, upon the facts concerning the development of this society and irreconcilability of the opposing interests of the proletariat and the bourgeoisie.

Previously the question had been posed this way: in order to secure its emancipation, the proletariat must overthrow the bourgeoisie, win political power, establish its revolutionary dictatorship.

Now the question is posed somewhat differently: the transition from capitalist society, which is evolving toward communism, to communist society is not possible without a "transitional political period," and the state during this period could only be the revolutionary dictatorship of the proletariat.

How then does this dictatorship relate to democracy?

We have seen that the "Communist Manifesto" simply places two concepts side by side: "the transformation of the proletariat into the ruling class" and "the attainment of democracy." On the basis of everything that has been set out above it is possible to determine more precisely how democracy changes in the transition from capitalism to communism.

In capitalist society, provided it develops under the most favorable conditions, we have a more or less complete democracy in a democratic republic. But this democracy is always hemmed in by the narrow frame of capitalist exploitation, and for that reason always remains in essence a democracy for the minority, only for the propertied classes, only for the rich. In capitalist society, freedom always remains approximately the same as it had been in the ancient Greek republics: freedom for the slave owners. Due to the conditions of capitalist exploitation, contemporary slaves for hire remain so crushed by need and poverty that "democracy is their last concern," "politics is their last concern"; that in the ordinary, peaceful course of events, the majority of the population is alienated from participation in public and political life.

The correctness of this assertion is perhaps most clearly confirmed by Germany precisely because in this state, constitutional legality has endured with amazing longevity and stability for almost half a century (1871–1914), and during this time, social democracy has been able to achieve far more than it has in other countries toward the "use of legality" and toward the organization of such a high proportion of workers into a political party; like no where else in the world.

And what is this greatest proportion of politically conscious and active wage slaves out of all those observed in capitalist society? One million members in the [German] Social-Democratic Party—out of 15 million wage workers! Three million in trade organizations—out of 15 million!

Democracy for a paltry minority, democracy for the rich—that is the democracy of capitalist society. If we take a closer look at the mechanism of capitalist democracy, then we will see everywhere and all over, in the "minor"—supposedly minor—details of voting rights (residential requirements, the exclusion of women, etc.), and in the technical aspects of the representative institutions, and in the *de facto* obstacles to the right of assembly (public buildings are not for "paupers!"), and in the purely capitalist organization of the daily press, and so on, and so forth, then we will see restriction after restriction upon democracy. These restrictions, exceptions, obstacles for the poor seem minor, especially in the eyes of one who has never known need and has never come into contact with the oppressed classes in their mass existence (and such are nine-tenths, if not ninety-nine hundredths, of the bourgeois publicists and politicians)—but taken together, these restrictions exclude and push out poverty from politics, from active participation in democracy.

Marx grasped this *essence* of capitalist democracy splendidly when he said in his analysis of the experience of the Commune: the oppressed are allowed once every few years to decide which particular representative of the oppressing class shall represent and repress them in parliament!

But departing from this capitalist democracy—which is inescapably narrow, and stealthily pushes aside the poor, and is therefore hypocritical and deceitful to the core— forward development does not proceed simply, directly, and smoothly "towards greater and greater democracy," as the liberal professors and petty-bourgeois opportunists would have it. No. Forward development, i.e., development towards communism, proceeds through the dictatorship of the proletariat, and cannot proceed otherwise, for it is impossible to *break the resistance* of the capitalist exploiters through any other agency or any other way.

As for the dictatorship of the proletariat—i.e., the organization of the vanguard of the oppressed into a ruling class for the suppression of the oppressors—it cannot result simply in a mere expansion of democracy. *Simultaneously* with an immense expansion of democracy—which becomes *for the first time* democracy for the poor, democracy for the people, and not democracy for the money-bags—the dictatorship of the proletariat imposes a series of restrictions on the freedom of the oppressors, the exploiters, the capitalists. We must suppress them in order to free humanity from wage slavery, their resistance must be crushed by force; it is clear that where there is suppression, where there is force, there is no freedom and no democracy.

Engels expressed this beautifully in his letter to Bebel when he said ... that "the proletariat needs the state, not in the interests of freedom but in the interest of the suppression of its opponents, and when it shall become possible to speak of freedom, there will be no state."

Democracy for the vast majority of the people, and suppression by force, i.e., exclusion from democracy, for the exploiters and oppressors of the people— this is the nature of the transformation of democracy during the *transition* from capitalism to communism.

Only in communist society, when the resistance of the capitalists has been completely broken, when capitalists have disappeared, when there are no classes (i.e., there is no distinction between the members of society with regard to their relation to the social means of production), *only* then does "the state cease to exist and it becomes *possible to speak of freedom.*" Only then will it be possible to realize a democracy that is actually complete, and actually without any exceptions whatsoever. And only then will democracy begin to *wither away*, due to the simple circumstance that, freed from capitalist slavery, from the countless horrors, savageries, absurdities, and infamies of capitalist exploitation, people will gradually become *accustomed* to observing the fundamental rules of community life that have been known for centuries and repeated for thousands of years in all the dictums— and to observe them without force, without coercion, without subordination, *without the special apparatus* for coercion called the state.

The expression "the state withers away" is very well-chosen, for it indicates both the gradual and the spontaneous nature of the process. Only habit can, and undoubtedly will, have such an effect; for we observe all around us millions of times how easily people become accustomed to observing the necessary rules of community life when there is no exploitation, when there is nothing that arouses indignation, protest and revolt, and creates the need for *suppression.*

And so: in capitalist society we have a democracy that is curtailed, impoverished, false, a democracy only for the rich, for the minority. The dictatorship of the proletariat, the period of transition to communism, will for the first time provide democracy for the people, for the majority, along with the necessary suppression of the minority, the exploiters. Communism alone is capable of providing truly complete democracy, and the more complete it is, the sooner it will become unnecessary and wither away of its own accord.

In other words, under capitalism we have the state in the proper sense of the word; a special machine for the suppression of one class by another, and in particular, of majority by the minority. Obviously, the success of an undertaking such as the systematic suppression of the exploited majority by the exploiting minority requires the utmost ferocity and savagery of suppression, it requires seas of blood, through which mankind wades its way in conditions of slavery, serfdom, and wage labor.

Furthermore, in the *transition* from capitalism to communism suppression is *still* necessary, but it is already the suppression of the exploiting minority by the exploited majority. A special apparatus, a special machine for suppression, the "state," is *still* necessary, but it is already a transitional state. It is no longer a state in the proper sense of the word; for the suppression of the exploiting minority by the majority of yesterday's wage slaves is a task so comparatively easy, simple and natural that it will cost far less bloodshed than suppressing the revolt of slaves, serfs, or wage-laborers, and it will come out much cheaper for mankind. And it is compatible with the spread of democracy to such an overwhelming majority of the population that the need for a *special machine* of suppression will begin to disappear. The exploiters, naturally, are unable to suppress the people without the most complex machine for performing such a task, but the *people* can suppress the exploiters even with a very simple "machine," virtually without a "machine," without a special apparatus, by the simple *organization of the armed masses* (such as the Soviets of Workers' and Soldiers' Deputies—we note, getting a bit ahead of ourselves).

Finally, only communism makes the state absolutely unnecessary, for there is *nobody* to be suppressed—"nobody" in the sense of a *class*, of a systematic struggle against a particular section of the population. We are not utopians, and do not in the least deny the possibility and inevitability of excesses on the part of *individual persons*, or the need to suppress *those* excesses. But, in the first place, no special machine, no special apparatus of suppression, is needed for this: this will be done by the armed people themselves, as simply and easily as any crowd of civilized people, even in modern society, breaks apart a fight or prevents the violation of a woman. And, secondly, we know that the root social cause of excesses, which consist in breaking the rules of the community, is the exploitation of the people, their need and their poverty. With the removal of this chief cause, excesses will inevitably begin to "wither away." We do not know how quickly and in what succession, but we do know they will wither away. With their withering away the state will wither away too.

Without veering off into utopias, Marx defined in more detail what can be defined *now* with regard to this future; namely: differentiation between the lower and higher phases (levels, stages) of communist society.

3. The First Phase of Communist Society

In the *Critique of the Gotha Program*, Marx refutes in detail Lassalle's idea that under socialism the worker will receive the "undiminished" or "full product of his labor." Marx shows that it is also necessary to deduct from the total social labor of all society a reserve fund, and a fund for the expansion of production and for the replacement of "worn out" machinery, and so on; and then, from the means of consumption, a fund for the upkeep of government, for schools, hospitals, old people's homes, and so on.

Instead of Lassalle's hazy, unclear, general phrase ("the full product of his labor to the worker"), Marx provides a sober reckoning of how exactly socialist society will have to keep house. Marx attempts a concrete analysis of the conditions of life in a society without capitalism, and says:

> What we are dealing with here [in analyzing the program of the workers' party] is not a communist society that has *developed* on its own foundations, but, on the contrary, one that is just *emerging* precisely from capitalist society, for that reason, in every respect, economically, morally, and intellectually, it still bears the hallmarks of the old society from the depths of which it emerged.

It is this communist society, which has just emerged into the light of day out of the depths of capitalism and which bears in every respect the hallmarks of the old society, that Marx calls the "first," or lowest, phase of communist society.

The means of production have already ceased to be the private property of individuals. The means of production belong to the whole of society. Each member of society, having performed a given portion of the socially necessary work, receives from society an attestation that he has done a such and such an amount of work. And on the basis of this attestation, he receives from the public store of consumer goods a corresponding quantity of products. After deducting the amount of labor that goes to the public fund, every worker, consequently, receives from society as much as he has given to it.

"Equality" seems to reign supreme.

But when Lassalle says, having in mind such a social order (which is usually called socialism, but in Marx goes by the term "the first phase of communism"), that this is "fair distribution," that this is "the equal right of all to an equal product of labor," Lassalle is mistaken and Marx clarifies his mistake.

"Equal right," says Marx, "is actually present here, but it is *still* a right under 'bourgeois law' [translator's note: Russian uses the same word for "law" and "right"] which, like any law, *presupposes inequality*." Any law is an application of the *same* measure to different people who in reality are not the same, are not equal to one another; and that is why "equal right" is a violation of equality and an injustice. In point of fact, everyone, having performed a share of social labor equal to the others, receives an equal share of the social product (after the above-mentioned deductions).

But in the meantime, individual people are not equivalent: one is stronger, another is weaker; one is married, another is not; one has more children, another has fewer, and so on.

"... Given equal labor," Marx concludes, "and hence an equal share in the social consumption fund, one will in fact receive more than another, one will turn out to be richer than another, and so on. To avoid all this, instead of being equal the right must be unequal."

It follows, then, that the first phase of communism is not yet capable of providing justice and equality: differences and unjust differences in wealth will still remain, but the *exploitation* of man by man will have become impossible, for there will be no possibility to seize the *means of production*—the factories, machines, land, and so on—and make them private property. In smashing Lassalle's petty-bourgeois, vague phrase about "equality" and "justice" *in general,* Marx shows the *course of development* of communist society, which is *compelled* at first to eliminate *only* the particular "injustice" that the means of production have been seized by individuals, and which is *unable* simultaneously to also eliminate the further injustice, which consists in the distribution of consumer goods "according to the amount of labor performed" (and not according to needs).

The vulgar economists, including the bourgeois professors, and including "our own" Tugan, constantly reproach the socialists for supposedly forgetting about the inequality of people and "dreaming" of eliminating this inequality. Such a reproach, as we see, only proves the extreme ignorance of the bourgeois ideologists.

Not only does Marx take into account the inevitable inequality of people with the greatest exactitude, but he equally takes into account that simply transforming the means of production into the common property of the entire society (commonly called "socialism") *does not remove* the inadequacies of distribution and the inequality of "bourgeois laws," which *continue to prevail* because products are divided "in accordance with labor."

... "But these inadequacies," Marx continues, "are inevitable in the first phase of communist society in the form in which it emerges, after prolonged birth pangs, from capitalist society. The law can never be above the economic structure of society and the cultural development conditioned by it."

In this way, in the first phase of communist society (usually called socialism) "bourgeois law" is *not* abolished in its entirety, but only in part, only in proportion to the economic revolution already attained, i.e., only with respect to the means of production. "Bourgeois law" recognizes them as the private property of individuals. Socialism makes them *common* property. *To that extent*—and only to that extent alone— "bourgeois law" disappears.

However, it still persists in its other part; it persists in its capacity as regulator (determining factor) of the distribution of products and the distribution of labor among the members of society. "He who does not work should not eat"—this socialist principle is already realized. "An equal quantity of products for an equal quantity of labor"—this socialist principle is already realized too. But this is not yet communism, and it does not yet abolish "bourgeois law," which gives unequal individuals equal quantities of products in exchange for unequal (actually unequal) amounts of labor.

This is an "inadequacy," says Marx, but it is unavoidable in the first phase of communism; for one cannot believe, without falling into utopianism, that having overthrown capitalism people will immediately learn to work for society with *no rules of law whatsoever.* Neither does the abolition of capitalism provide the economic prerequisites for *such* a change immediately.

But aside from "bourgeois law," there *are* no other rules. So therefore, there still remains the need for a state, which, while safeguarding the common ownership of the means of production, would safeguard equality of labor and the equality of product distribution.

The state withers away because there are no more capitalists, no more classes, and therefore it is no longer possible to suppress any class at all.

But the state has not withered away completely yet, because there remains the safeguarding of "bourgeois law," which sanctifies actual inequality. For the state to wither away completely, complete communism is necessary.

4. The Higher Phase of Communist Society

Marx continues:

> ... In the higher phase of communist society, when the enslaving subordination of the individual to the division of labor has disappeared; when the antithesis between mental and physical labor has disappeared with it; when labor has ceased being merely a means to make a living and becomes in itself life's prime want; when the productive forces have grown in tandem with the all-round development of the individual, and all the springs of societal wealth will flow at their fullest capacity—only then will it be possible to completely overstep the narrow horizon of bourgeois law and society shall be able to inscribe on its banners: From each according to his ability, to each according to his needs!

Only now can we fully appreciate the correctness of Engels' remarks in which he mercilessly ridiculed the absurdity of combining the words "freedom" and "state." So long as the state exists there is no freedom. When there is freedom, there will be no state.

The economic basis for the complete withering away of the state consists in communism at that advanced stage of development at which the antithesis between mental and physical labor disappears, and consequently, one of the most significant sources of contemporary social inequality also disappears—a source, moreover, that cannot on any account be removed all at once, solely by the conversion of the means of production into public property, solely by the expropriation of the capitalists.

This expropriation will create the *possibility* for the tremendous development of production capacities. And seeing how even now capitalism is already *retarding* this development incredibly, and how much progress could be made on the basis of contemporary technological achievements, we are entitled to say with complete confidence that the expropriation of the capitalists will inevitably result in an enormous expansion of the production capacities of human society. But how quickly this development progresses, how quickly it will arrive at the break with the division of labor, at the elimination of the antithesis between mental and physical labor, at the transformation of labor into "life's prime want"—this we do not and *cannot* know.

That is why we are entitled to speak only of the inevitable withering away of the state, emphasizing the protracted nature of this process and its dependence upon the speed of the development of the *highest* phase of communism, and leaving completely open the question of the duration or of the concrete forms of this withering away—for the basis on which to resolve such questions *does not exist*.

It will be possible for the state to wither away completely when society effects the rule: "From each according to his ability, to each according to his needs," i.e., when people have become so accustomed to observing the fundamental rules of communal life and their labor has become so productive that they will voluntarily work *according to their ability*. "The narrow horizon of bourgeois law," which compels one to calculate with the coldness of Shylock whether one has worked an extra half hour more than the next person, whether one has not been paid less than the next—this narrow horizon will then be overcome. The distribution of products will then no longer require society to regulate the amount of product that everyone receives; each will freely take "according to his needs."

From the bourgeois point of view, it is easy to declare that such a social order is "sheer utopia" and to sneer at the socialists for promising everyone the right to receive from society, without any control of the individual citizen's labor, any quantity of truffles, cars, pianos, etc. Such sneering is what most bourgeois "learned" people get away with even nowadays, but in this way they only reveal their own ignorance and their mercenary defense of capitalism.

Ignorance—for no socialist would ever think to "promise" that the highest phase of communism will arrive; and the *prediction* of the great socialists that it will arrive also presupposes something *other* than the present-day productivity of labor and the present-day philistines capable, like Pomyalovsky's seminarians, of damaging the stores of communal wealth "for no reason" and demanding the impossible.

Until the "highest" phase of communism arrives, socialists demand the *strictest* control by society and *by the state* over the measure of labor and the measure of consumption; however, this control must *begin* with the expropriation of the capitalists, with control over the capitalists by the workers, and it must be carried out not by a state of bureaucrats, but by a state of *armed* workers.

The mercenary defense of capitalism by the bourgeois ideologists ... consists precisely in the fact that they substitute arguments and discussions about the distant future for the vital and burning question of *present-day* politics: the expropriation of the capitalists, the conversion of *all* citizens into workers in the service of one large "syndicate"—namely, the whole state; and the complete subordination of all the work of this entire syndicate to a state that is truly democratic, *the state of the Soviets of Workers' and Soldiers' Deputies*.

In essence, when a learned professor ... speaks of foolhardy utopias, of the demagogic promises of the Bolsheviks, of the impossibility of "introducing" socialism, what he has in mind is in fact the highest stage or phase of communism, the introduction of which no one has even conceived, much less promised, for it absolutely cannot be "introduced."

And this brings us to the question of the scientific distinction between socialism and communism, which Engels touched upon in his above-quoted argument about the incorrectness of the term "Social-Democrat." Politically, the distinction between the first, or lower, and the higher phase of communism will in time, most likely, be tremendous. But it would be ridiculous to acknowledge it at this point, under capitalism; and it is only isolated anarchists who might have put it at the forefront (if there are still any left among the anarchists who have learned nothing in the wake of the "Plekhanov" conversion of the Kropotkins, Grave, Corneliseen, and other "stars" of anarchism into social-chauvinists or "anarcho-trenchists"—such as Ghe,[15] one of the few anarchists who still maintain a sense of honor and a conscience).

But the scientific difference between socialism and communism is clear. What is usually called socialism is what Marx called the "first," or lower, phase of communist society. To the extent that the means of production become *communal* property, the word "communism" is also applicable here, providing we do not forget that this is *not* complete communism. The great significance of Marx's explications consists in that fact that here, too, he consistently applies materialist dialectics, the theory of development, and regards communism as something which develops *out of* capitalism. Instead of scholastically-invented, "concocted" determinations and fruitless arguments over words (What is socialism? What is communism?), Marx provides an analysis of what might be called the stages of the economic maturity of communism.

In its first phase, or first stage, communism *cannot* as yet be fully economically mature, fully free from the traditions or vestiges of capitalism. That is the source of interesting phenomena such as the retention of "the narrow horizon of *bourgeois* law" under communism in its first phase. Of course, bourgeois law in regard to the distribution of *consumer* goods inevitably presupposes a *bourgeois state* as well, for law is nothing without an apparatus capable of *enforcing* the observance of the rules of law.

It follows that not only does bourgeois law remain for a time under communism, but even the bourgeois state, without the bourgeoisie!

This may seem like a paradox or simply a dialectical mind game, of which Marxism is often accused by people who have not taken the slightest trouble to study its extraordinarily profound content.

But in point of fact, life shows us remnants of the old in the new at every step, both in nature and in society. And Marx did not arbitrarily insert a bit of "bourgeois" law into communism, but rather took what is economically and politically inevitable in a society emerging out of the *bowels* of capitalism.

Democracy has enormous significance in the struggle of the working class against the capitalists for the emancipation of the former. But democracy is by no means an ultimate boundary not to cross; it is merely one of the stages on the path from federalism to capitalism and from capitalism to communism.

Democracy means equality. The great significance of the proletariat's struggle for equality, and of the banner of equality, is clear if it is understood correctly in the sense of the elimination of *classes*. But democracy means only *formal* equality. And as soon as equality is achieved for all members of society *in relation* to ownership of the means of production, i.e., equality of labor and equality of wages, humanity will inevitably be confronted with the question of going further: from formal equality to actual equality, i.e., to the realization of the rule "from each according to his ability, to each according to his needs." By what stages, by way of what practical measures humanity will proceed toward this supreme aim we do not and cannot know. But it is important to realize how infinitely deceitful is the ordinary bourgeois conception that socialism is supposedly something lifeless, rigid, fixed once and for all, when in reality *only* with socialism will there begin a rapid, genuine, truly mass movement forward in all spheres of public and private life, in which the *majority*, and after that the whole, of the population participates.

Democracy is a form of the state, one of its varieties. And consequently, like any state, it represents the organized, systematic use of force against people. On the one hand. But, on the other hand, it signifies the formal recognition of equality between citizens, the equal right of all to determine the structure of the state and its administration. And this, in turn, is bound up with in the fact that, at a certain stage in the development of democracy, it first of all rallies an anti-capitalist revolutionary class, the proletariat, and gives it the opportunity to shatter, smash to bits, wipe off the face of the earth the bourgeois, even the republican-bourgeois, state machine, the standing army, the police and the bureaucracy and to replace them with a *more* democratic—though still a state—machine in the form of a mass of armed workers who transition to universal participation of the people in the militia.

Here "quantity turns into quality": *such* a degree of democracy implies stepping out of the framework of bourgeois society and beginning its socialist reorganization. If *everyone* actually takes part in the administration of the state, capitalism really can't hold on. And the development of capitalism, in turn, creates the *preconditions* for truly "everyone" to *be able* to take part in the administration of the state. These preconditions include: universal literacy, which has already been achieved in a number of the most advanced capitalist countries; then the "training and disciplining" of millions of workers by the large, complex, socialized apparatus of the postal service, railways, big factories, large-scale commerce, banking, etc., etc.

Given these *economic* preconditions, it is quite possible to proceed immediately, overnight, from overthrowing the capitalists and the bureaucrats to replacing them with armed workers, with the universally armed population, in the task of *control* of production and distribution, in the task of *keeping account* of labor and products. (One should not confuse the question of control and accounting with the question of the scientifically trained staff of engineers, agronomists, and so on. These gentlemen are working today in obedience to the wishes of the capitalists and will work even better tomorrow in obedience to the wishes of the armed workers).

Accounting and control—that is *the chief thing* that is required for the "arrangement," the proper functioning, of the *first phase* of communist society. *All* citizens are transformed here into hired employees of the state, which consists of the armed workers. *All* citizens become employees and workers of a *single* nationwide state "syndicate." The important thing is that they should work equally, do their proper share of work, and get equal pay. The accounting and control of this have been *simplified* by capitalism to the utmost and reduced to the extraordinarily simple operations—which any literate person can manage—of observation and recording, knowledge of the four operations of arithmetic, and issuing appropriate receipts.

When the *majority* of the people begin, independently and everywhere, to keep such accounts and exercise such control over the capitalists (now converted into employees) and over the petty little intellectuals who keep their capitalist affectations, then this control will become truly universal, general, and national; and there will be no getting away from it, there will be "nowhere to hide."

The whole of society will have become a single accounting office and a single factory, with equality of labor and equality of pay.

But this "factory" discipline, which—having defeated the capitalists, having overthrown the exploiters—the proletariat will extend to the whole of society, does not in any way represent our ideal, our ultimate goal. Rather, it is only a *step* that is necessary to radically cleanse society of all the vileness and loathsomeness of capitalist exploitation, *and to make further* progress.

From the moment all members of society, or at least the vast majority of them, have learned to manage the state *themselves*, have taken this task into their own hands, have organized control over the insignificant capitalist minority, over the petty gentry who wish to preserve their capitalist affectations and over the workers who have been thoroughly corrupted by capitalism—from this moment the need for government of any kind begins to disappear altogether. The more complete the democracy, the closer the moment when it becomes unnecessary. The more democratic the "state," which consists of the armed workers and is "no longer a state in the proper sense of the word," the quicker *every form* of state begins to wither away.

For when *everyone* learns to govern and will actually manage societal production on their own, and independently maintain account of and control over the parasites, the children of the gentry, the swindlers and other like "guardians of capitalist traditions," then the escape from this national accounting and control will inevitably become so insurmountably difficult, such a rare exception, and will probably be accompanied by such swift and severe punishment (for the armed workers are practical men and not sentimental little intellectuals, and they scarcely allow anyone to trifle with them), that the *necessity* of observing the simple, fundamental rules of any communal living will very soon become a *habit*.

And then the door will be thrown wide open for the transition from the first phase of communist society to its higher phase, and with it to the complete withering away of the state.

Notes

1   The Young or "Left" Hegelians were followers of the German philosopher G. W. F. Hegel (1770–1831), who held that human history is the story of the struggle of "spirit" (*Geist*) to overcome obstacles to its self-realization. The orthodox or "Old Hegelians" argued that Spirit is the Holy Spirit, while the Young Hegelians held that this refers to the human spirit.—Eds.

2   The doctrine advanced by the French economist Pierre-Joseph Proudhon (1809–1865), which he called "mutualism" or "anarchism."—Eds.

3   In 1848 a series of revolutions swept across Europe. Although several—most notably in France—were temporarily successful, they were brutally repressed.—Eds.

4   The doctrine advocated by Mikhail Bakunin (1814–1876), a Russian anarchist or anarcho-communist who was highly critical of Karl Marx and his followers. He predicted, presciently, that Marx's "dictatorship of the proletariat" would quickly become a dictatorship *over* the proletariat. See selection 6.43.—Eds.

5   Eugen Dühring (1833–1921) was a German philosopher and economist who was highly critical of Marx and Marxism.—Eds.

6   Eduard Bernstein (1850–1932) was the leading "revisionist" Marxist. In his *Evolutionary Socialism* (1899) he proposed revising Marxian theory and advocated a gradual, peaceful and parliamentary path to socialism. See selection 6.39.—Eds.

7　The Narodniks were members of a middle-class movement for Russian social and political reform. Among the reforms they advocated was the overthrow—by violence, if necessary—of the Tsarist system of authoritarian rule.—Eds.

8　Immanuel Kant (1724–1804) was a prominent German philosopher and defender of the Enlightenment (see selection 3.17). He held that human beings belonged to "the kingdom of ends"—i.e., they were ends in themselves and should never be treated merely as means to someone else's ends—and thus he categorically condemned slavery. Eduard Bernstein and other "revisionist" Marxists invoked Kant in condemning the revolutionary Marxist (i.e., Leninist) view that people can and should be sacrificed in the present for the sake of future peoples' happiness.—Eds.

9　Eugen Böhm-Bawerk (1851–1914) was an Austrian economist, staunch defender of the capitalist free market system, and ardent critic of Karl Marx and Marxian theory.—Eds.

10　The doctrine defended by the reform-minded French Prime Minister (and later president) Alexandre Millerand (1859–1943), who advocated a peaceful parliamentary path to socialism.—Eds.

11　The Bernsteinians were followers of the revisionist Marxist Eduard Bernstein (see note 6, above). The Guesdists were followers of the French socialist Jules Guesde (1845–1922). The Jaurèsists were followers of the French socialist Jean Jaurès (1859–1914). The Broussists were anti-authoritarian reform-minded French socialists. Charles de Brouckère (1796–1860) was a liberal Belgian politician who advocated Belgium's annexation by France. Emile Vandervelde (1866–1938) was a French socialist and follower of Jules Guesde. Integralists were nationalists who held that a nation is an interdependent organism.—Eds.

12　Antonio Labriola (1843–1904) was an Italian philosopher and Marxist theorist whose ideas influenced the PCI (Italian Communist Party). Hubert Lagardelle (1874–1958) was a French socialist and theorist of Syndicalism.—Eds.

13　Lassalleianists were followers of the German socialist Ferdinand Lassalle (1825–1864), who with his followers advocated a parliamentary, state-centered path to socialism.—Eds.

14　The Gotha Program was a name of the party platform adopted by the German Social Democratic Party at its first party congress, held at the German town of Gotha in 1875. Marx's extensive criticisms of that program are to be found in his *Critique of the Gotha Program* (written in 1875, published in 1891), on which Lenin relies here.—Eds.

15　The Russian thinker Georgi Plekhanov (1856–1918) was a self-identified "Marxist" revolutionary who supported the Bolshevik Revolution of 1917, but immediately thereafter became a political adversary of Lenin. The Russian Peter Kropotkin (1842–1921) and the Frenchman Jean Grave (1854–1939) were prominent anarchists with whom Lenin disagreed. Christiaan Cornelissen (1864–1942) was a Dutch syndicalist, or defender of a brand of socialism that Lenin abhorred. Like Plekhanov, Alexander Ghe (1879–1919) was a Russian anarchist and strong supporter of the 1917 Russian Revolution.—Eds.

The Permanent Revolution

*LEON TROTSKY**

Leon Trotsky was the revolutionary name of Lev Davidovich Bronstein (1879–1940), one of the leading theorists and strategists of the Russian Bolsheviks. In the years before the Bolsheviks (or Communists) seized power in 1917, Trotsky developed the idea of "the permanent revolution" as a way of justifying a socialist regime in a nonindustrial country like Russia. After the Communists gained control and formed the Soviet Union, Trotsky fell out with Joseph Stalin, whose policy of "socialism in one country" was directly opposed to Trotsky's "permanent revolution." Trotsky went into exile in 1929—the year in which he wrote *The Permanent Revolution*—and was living in Mexico when he was murdered in 1940 by one of Stalin's secret agents.

---

* *Source*: Leon Trotsky, *The Permanent Revolution* (New York: Pathfinder Press, 1969). Copyright © 1969 by Pathfinder Press. Reprinted by permission.

WHAT IS THE PERMANENT REVOLUTION?

Basic Postulates

I hope that the reader will not object if, to end this book, I attempt, without fear of repetition, to formulate succinctly my principal conclusions.

1   The theory of the permanent revolution now demands the greatest attention from every Marxist, for the course of the class and ideological struggle has fully and finally raised this question from the realm of reminiscences over old differences of opinion among Russian Marxists, and converted it into a question of the character, the inner connections and methods of the international revolution in general.

2   With regard to countries with a belated bourgeois development, especially the colonial and semi-colonial countries, the theory of the permanent revolution signifies that the complete and genuine solution of their tasks of achieving *democracy and national emancipation* is conceivable only through the dictatorship of the proletariat as the leader of the subjugated nation, above all of its peasant masses.

3   Not only the agrarian, but also the national question assigns to the peasantry— the overwhelming majority of the population in backward countries—an exceptional place in the democratic revolution. Without an alliance of the proletariat with the peasantry the tasks of the democratic revolution cannot be solved, nor even seriously posed. But the alliance of these two classes can be realized in no other way than through an irreconcilable struggle against the influence of the national-liberal bourgeoisie.

4   No matter what the first episodic stages of the revolution may be in the individual countries, the realization of the revolutionary alliance between the proletariat and the peasantry is conceivable only under the political leadership of the proletarian vanguard, organized in the Communist Party. This in turn means that the victory of the democratic revolution is conceivable only through the dictatorship of the proletariat which bases itself upon the alliance with the peasantry and solves first of all the tasks of the democratic revolution.

5   Assessed historically, the old slogan of Bolshevism—"the democratic dictatorship of the proletariat and peasantry"—expressed precisely the above-characterized relationship of the proletariat, the peasantry and the liberal bourgeoisie. This has been confirmed by the experience of October [1917, when the Communists seized power in Russia]. But Lenin's old formula did not settle in advance the problem of what the reciprocal relations would be between the proletariat and the peasantry within the revolutionary bloc. In other words, the formula deliberately retained a certain algebraic quality, which had to make way for more precise arithmetical quantities in the process of historical experience. However, the latter showed, and under circumstances that exclude any kind of misinterpretation, that no matter how great the revolutionary role of the peasantry may be, it nevertheless cannot be an independent role and even less a leading one. The peasant follows either the worker or the bourgeois. This means that the "democratic dictatorship of the

proletariat and peasantry" is only conceivable as a *dictatorship of the proletariat that leads the peasant masses behind it.*

6   A democratic dictatorship of the proletariat and peasantry, as a regime that is distinguished from the dictatorship of the proletariat by its class content, might be realized only in a case where an *independent revolutionary* party could be constituted, expressing the interests of the peasants and in general of petty-bourgeois democracy—a party capable of conquering power with this or that degree of aid from the proletariat, and of determining its revolutionary program. As all modern history attests—especially the Russian experience of the last twenty-five years—an insurmountable obstacle on the road to the creation of a peasants' party is the petty-bourgeoisie's lack of economic and political independence and its deep internal differentiation. By reason of this the upper sections of the petty-bourgeoisie (of the peasantry) go along with the big bourgeoisie in all decisive cases, especially in war and in revolution; the lower sections go along with the proletariat; the intermediate section being thus compelled to choose between the two extreme poles. Between Kerenskyism and the Bolshevik power, between the Kuomintang and the dictatorship of the proletariat, there is not and cannot be any intermediate stage, that is, no democratic dictatorship of the workers and peasants.[1]

7   The Comintern's [i.e., Communist International's] endeavor to foist upon the Eastern countries the slogan of the democratic dictatorship of the proletariat and peasantry, finally and long ago exhausted by history, can have only a reactionary effect. Insofar as this slogan is counterposed to the slogan of the dictatorship of the proletariat, it contributes politically to the dissolution of the proletariat in the petty-bourgeois masses and thus creates the most favorable conditions for the hegemony of the national bourgeoisie and consequently for the collapse of the democratic revolution. The introduction of this slogan into the program of the Comintern is a direct betrayal of Marxism and of the October tradition of Bolshevism.

8   The dictatorship of the proletariat which has risen to power as the leader of the democratic revolution is inevitably and very quickly confronted with tasks, the fulfilment of which is bound up with deep inroads into the rights of bourgeois property. The democratic revolution grows over directly into the socialist revolution and thereby becomes a *permanent* revolution.

9   The conquest of power by the proletariat does not complete the revolution, but only opens it. Socialist construction is conceivable only on the foundation of the class struggle, on a national and international scale. This struggle, under the conditions of an overwhelming predominance of capitalist relationships on the world arena, must inevitably lead to explosions, that is, internally to civil wars and externally to revolutionary wars. Therein lies the permanent character of the socialist revolution as such, regardless of whether it is a backward country that is involved, which only yesterday accomplished its democratic revolution, or an old capitalist country which already has behind it a long epoch of democracy and parliamentarianism.

10   The completion of the socialist revolution within national limits is unthinkable. One of the basic reasons for the crisis in bourgeois society is the fact that the productive forces created by it can no longer be reconciled

with the framework of the national state. From this follow, on the one hand, imperialist wars, on the other, the utopia of a bourgeois United States of Europe. The socialist revolution begins on the national arena, it unfolds on the international arena, and is completed on the world arena. Thus, the socialist revolution becomes a permanent revolution in a newer and broader sense of the word; it attains completion only in the final victory of the new society on our entire planet.

11 The above-outlined sketch of the development of the world revolution eliminates the question of countries that are "mature" or "immature" for socialism in the spirit of that pedantic, lifeless classification given by the present program of the Comintern. Insofar as capitalism has created a world market, a world division of labor and world productive forces, it has also prepared the world economy as a whole for socialist transformation. Different countries will go through this process at different tempos. Backward countries may, under certain conditions, arrive at the dictatorship of the proletariat sooner than advanced countries, but they will come later than the latter to socialism.

A backward colonial or semi-colonial country, the proletariat of which is insufficiently prepared to unite the peasantry and take power, is thereby incapable of bringing the democratic revolution to its conclusion. Contrariwise, in a country where the proletariat has power in its hands as the result of the democratic revolution, the subsequent fate of the dictatorship and socialism depends in the last analysis not only and not so much upon the national productive forces as upon the development of the international socialist revolution.

12 The theory of socialism in one country, which rose on the yeast of the reaction against October, is the only theory that consistently and to the very end opposes the theory of the permanent revolution.

The attempt of the epigones, under the lash of our criticism, to confine the application of the theory of socialism in one country exclusively to Russia, because of its specific characteristics (its vastness and its natural resources), does not improve matters but only makes them worse. The break with the internationalist position always and invariably leads to national *messianism*, that is, to attributing special superiorities and qualities to one's own country, which allegedly permit it to play a role to which other countries cannot attain.

The world division of labor, the dependence of Soviet industry upon foreign technology, the dependence of the productive forces of the advanced countries of Europe upon Asiatic raw materials, etc., make the construction of an independent socialist society in any single country in the world impossible.

13 The theory of [Joseph] Stalin and [Nikolai] Bukharin, running counter to the entire experience of the Russian revolution, not only sets up the democratic revolution mechanically in contrast to the socialist revolution, but also makes a breach between the national revolution and the international revolution.

This theory imposes upon revolutions in backward countries the task of establishing an unrealizable regime of democratic dictatorship, which it counterposes to the dictatorship of the proletariat. Thereby this theory introduces illusions and fictions into politics, paralyses the struggle for power of the proletariat in the East, and hampers the victory of the colonial revolution.

The very seizure of power by the proletariat signifies, from the standpoint of the epigones' theory, the completion of the revolution ("to the extent of nine-tenths," according to Stalin's formula) and the opening of the epoch of national reforms. The theory of the *kulak* [farmer] growing into socialism and the theory of the "neutralization" of the world bourgeoisie are consequently inseparable from the theory of socialism in one country. They stand or fall together.

By the theory of national socialism, the Communist International is down-graded to an auxiliary weapon useful only for the struggle against military intervention. The present policy of the Comintern, its regime and the selection of its leading personnel correspond entirely to the demotion of the Communist International to the role of an auxiliary unit which is not destined to solve independent tasks.

14 The program of the Comintern created by Bukharin is eclectic through and through. It makes the hopeless attempt to reconcile the theory of socialism in one country with Marxist internationalism, which is, however, inseparable from the permanent character of the world revolution. The struggle of the Communist Left Opposition for a correct policy and a healthy regime in the Communist International is inseparably bound up with the struggle for the Marxist program. The question of the program is in turn inseparable from the question of the two mutually exclusive theories: the theory of permanent revolution and the theory of socialism in one country. The problem of the permanent revolution has long ago outgrown the episodic differences of opinion between Lenin and Trotsky, which were completely exhausted by history. The struggle is between the basic ideas of Marx and Lenin on the one side and the eclecticism of the centrists on the other.

NOTE

1   Alexander Kerensky (1881–1970) was a Russian socialist reformer and prime minister of the provisional government that the Bolsheviks overthrew in 1917; the Kuomintang was the Nationalist Party of China.—Eds.

On the People's Democratic Dictatorship

MAO ZEDONG*

The Chinese Communist Revolution, led by Mao Zedong (1893–1976), routed the Kuomintang (Nationalist) forces of Chiang Kai-shek in 1949. In attempting to adapt Marxism-Leninism to Chinese conditions, Mao set even greater store by the peasantry than had Lenin. After the revolution, the "people"—by which Mao meant mainly the peasantry, under the stern guidance of the Chinese Communist Party—were to rule. The "people's democratic dictatorship" meant rule not so much by, as on behalf of, the numerically largest class, namely, the peasantry. This interim "dictatorship" was to be a period of civic "education" for the peasantry and harsh "re-education" for others. Once in power, Mao—like Stalin in the Soviet Union—made himself a larger-than-life object of veneration and worship.

* *Source*: Mao Zedong, *Lun Renmin Minzhu Zhuanzheng* [*On the People's Democratic Dictatorship*] in Mao Zedong, *Xuanji* [Mao Zedong, *Selected Writings*], (Beijing: People's Press, 1991), vol. 4. Translated expressly for this volume by Zhipei Chi.

ON THE PEOPLE'S DEMOCRATIC DICTATORSHIP

In Commemoration of the Twenty-Eighth Anniversary of the Communist Party of China

June 30, 1949

As of July 1st, 1949, the Communist Party of China has reached twenty-eight years of age. Like an individual, [the party also] has its childhood, adolescence, adulthood and old age. The Chinese Communist Party is no longer a child, nor a teenage youth, but an adult. People will die when they get old, and so will the party. When social classes are eliminated, the party and the state, as tools of class struggle, will lose their function and the need for them. Thus they will decline gradually and perish following the end of their historical mission and then [human society] will enter a more advanced stage. We are in direct opposition to the parties of the bourgeoisie. They fear the demise of class, state power and party, whereas we declare publicly that we strive hard to create the conditions facilitating the demise of all of these. The leadership of the communist party and the state power of the people's dictatorship are just such conditions. Without admitting this truth, a person cannot make himself a communist. For those young people who have not studied Marxism-Leninism and just recently become party members, they might not know this truth, but they have to know, or they cannot acquire the correct world view. They have to know that eradicating the class, state power and parties is the same path for all mankind and the only differences are time and conditions. Communists the world over are wiser than the bourgeoisie because they know the law of the existence and development of things and dialectics, and they look farther. The reason why the bourgeoisie do not welcome this truth is that they don't want to be overthrown. Being overthrown, like currently the Kuomintang [Chinese Nationalist] counter-revolutionaries by us and in the past Japanese imperialists by us and people across countries, was unthinkably painful for them. Yet for the working class, working people and the communist party, it is not the matter of being overthrown, but of working hard to create the conditions for the natural demise of class, state power and political parties and bringing human society into the stage of Great Harmony. I mention in passing this vision of human progress in order to clarify the problems we talk about in the following section.

Our party has been around twenty-eight years. As we all know, it has not been a peaceful time, for we underwent difficult situations and we have had to fight enemies from home and abroad. We thank Marx, Engels, Lenin and Stalin for the weapon they gave us. This weapon is not the machine-gun, but Marxism-Leninism.

Lenin, in his 1920 book, *"Left-Wing" Communism, an Infantile Disorder*, described how the Russians found the revolutionary theory.[1] The Russians underwent decades of hardship before they found Marxism. China shared the same or similar experiences as those prior to the October Revolution in Russia [of 1917]. The suppression of feudalism was the same. The backwardness of the economy and the culture was similar. Both were less developed, and China was even worse. It was also the same that in both countries, enlightened people sought to rejuvenate their nation by seeking the truth of revolution while disregarding hardship and struggle.

Since the defeat in the Opium War[2] of 1840, the progressive Chinese, in extreme difficulties, looked for truth from the West. Hong Xiuquan,[3] Kang Youwei,[4] Yan Fu[5] and Sun Yat-sen, represent those who sought truth from the West before the birth of the Chinese Communist Party. At that time, Chinese seeking progress, would read any books containing new theories from the West. The number of Chinese students sent to Japan, Britain, the United States, France and Germany reached an astonishing level. Domestically, imperial examinations were abolished and new schools[6] sprang up like bamboo shoots after a spring rain, as people wanted to learn from the West. In my youth, I studied and learned these things too. They represented Western bourgeoisie democratic culture, i.e. the so called "New Learning," including the social theories and natural science of that time, in contrast to the "Old Learning" of Chinese feudal culture. People who learned these new theories, for a long time, believed such theories could save China. These theories were rarely doubted by the school of the New Learning, except by some from the Old Learning. [The New Learning School believed that] in order to save China, we had to modernize, and to modernize we had to learn from foreign countries. Among foreign countries, only the Western ones were advanced, as only they had successfully established capitalist modern states. Japan effectively emulated the West, so those Chinese also tried to learn from Japan. From the point of view of the Chinese of that time, Russia was a backward country, and few wanted to learn from it. This was how the Chinese attempted to learn from other countries from the 1840s to the early twentieth century.

The invasion by the imperialist countries shattered the dream of China emulating the West. Oddly enough, why was it that teachers always invaded the pupil? The Chinese learned many things from the West, but they could not make a go of it, and the dream was never realized. Numerous struggles, including the nationwide Xinhai Revolution [Revolution of 1911],[7] all failed. The situation of the country became worse and worse, and people barely survived in this environment. Skepticism arose, increased and deepened. The First World War shook the world. The Russians carried out the October Revolution, and established the first socialist state in the world. Under Lenin and Stalin, the great revolutionary power of the Russian proletariat and working people, which used to be hidden deep and was invisible to foreigners, erupted like a volcano and let Chinese and all humankind view them in a new light. Then, and only then, the Chinese thinking and life began a new era. The Chinese had found the universal truth, Marxism-Leninism, and things started to change.

Marxism was introduced to China by the Russians. Before the Bolshevik Revolution, the Chinese knew neither Lenin and Stalin nor even Marx and Engels. The gunshots of the October Revolution brought us Marxism-Leninism. The Russian revolution helped the world and at the same time enabled China's progressives to contemplate anew the fate of their own country and reconsider their problems from the proletarian world-view. Follow Russia's path—this was the conclusion they reached. In 1919, the May Fourth Movement[8] broke out in China. In 1921, the Chinese Communist Party was formed. In his despair Sun Yat-sen encountered the October Revolution and the Chinese Communist Party. He welcomed the Bolshevik Revolution, the help from Russia, and the cooperation of the Chinese Communist Party. Following the death of Sun Yat-sen, Chiang

Kai-shek rose to power. In his twenty-two year rule, Chiang Kai-shek brought the country to an impasse. During this period, the anti-fascist Second World War, in which the Soviet Union was the backbone of resistance, three big imperialist states were brought down, and two were weakened. There was only one big imperialist state, the U.S., which remained uninjured. However, the domestic crisis in the U.S. was severe. It wanted to enslave the whole world, and arm Chiang's army to kill millions of Chinese. After beating back the Japanese imperialists and the following three years of the people's war of liberation, the Chinese people under the leadership of the Chinese Communist Party have basically achieved victory.

This is how Western bourgeoisie civilization, democracy and the scheme for a bourgeois republic have all gone bankrupt in the minds of the Chinese people. Bourgeoisie democracy has given way to the people's democracy led by the proletariat, and the bourgeois republic to the people's republic. This creates the possibility that through the people's republic we can reach socialism and communism, eradicate classes, and achieve the Great Harmony of the world. Kang You-wei wrote *The Book of Great Harmony*, but he did not and never could find a way to the Great Harmony. Foreign nations can build bourgeois republics, but China cannot, because China is under the oppression of the imperialist countries. The only way is through the people's republic under the leadership of the working class.

We have tried every other way, but all have failed. Some of those who used to linger on other paths have fallen, some are awakened, and some are transforming their minds. Things change so fast that some people feel shocked and feel that they need to learn anew. Such a mood is understandable, and we welcome such a desire for new study.

The vanguard of Chinese proletariat learned Marxism-Leninism after the October Revolution and established the Chinese Communist Party. Then followed the political struggle and after twenty-eight years of passing those tortuous paths, we finally achieved basic victory. The twenty-eight years' experience arrives at the same conclusion that Sun Yat-sen drew in his testament based on forty years' experience; that is, believing deeply that in order to attain victory, "[we] must awaken the public, and unite together with all nations in the world that treats us as equals." Sun Yat-sen had a different world-view from us, and observed and grappled with problems from [a] different class standpoint. Yet in the 1920s in the question of how to fight imperialism, we reached an almost identical conclusion.

Sun Yat-sen passed away twenty-four years ago. [Since his death], the theory and practice of the Chinese revolution under the leadership of the Chinese Communist Party has made big advances in both theory and practice and fundamentally changed the situation of China. So far the major and basic experience the Chinese people have learned is two-fold: first, domestically, [we] mobilize people. This means to unite the proletariat, the peasantry, the urban petty bourgeoisie and the national bourgeoisie to form a domestic united front led by the working class, and develop such a united front into a state which is a people's democratic dictatorship led by the proletariat and founded on an alliance of workers and peasants. Secondly, internationally, we unite all nations and people who treat us equally to move forward together. That is, ally ourselves with the Soviet Union, all people's democracies, and the proletariat and masses in all other countries to form an international united front.

"You lean to one side." Exactly. Leaning to one side is what Sun Yat-sen's forty years' and the communist party's twenty-eight years' experience has taught us. In order to achieve victory and hold it, we must lean to one side. Based on forty years' and twenty-eight years' experience, all Chinese without exception must lean either to the imperialist or the socialist side. There is no alternative. Sitting on the fence will not do and the third road[9] does not even exist. We stand against Chiang Kai-shek's counter-revolutionaries who side with the imperialists, and also against those fantasies about the third road.

"You are so provocative." We are talking about how to deal with internal and external counter-revolutionaries, i.e. imperialists and their running dogs, not anyone else. For these people, it has nothing to do with provocation. Whether you are provocative or not, they remain the same, since they are counter-revolutionaries. [We should] draw a clear line between revolutionaries and counter-revolutionaries, reveal the conspiracies and plots of the counter-revolutionaries, alert the revolutionaries and make them vigilant and attentive, boost our morale and willingness to fight and crush the enemy's arrogance, only then can we isolate the counter-revolutionaries and defeat them or take over their power. [We] should not have even a bit of cowardice in front of a wild beast. We should learn [what] Wu Song[10] [did] on the Chingyang Ridge. For Wu Song, it did not matter whether he provoked the tiger in the Chingyang Ridge or not. The tiger was the same either way, it always wanted to eat people. You either slay the tiger, or be eaten by the tiger, it's one or the other.

"We need to do business." Perfectly correct. Business always needs to be done. We only fight against those domestic and international counter-revolutionaries who hinder our business and no one else. Everybody should know, it is the imperialists and their running dogs, the Chiang Kai-shek counter-revolutionaries, who stand in our way and hinder our business with foreign countries and prevent us from establishing diplomatic relations with other countries. [If] we can unite all internal and external forces to smash the domestic and international counter-revolutionaries, we can then do business and establish diplomatic relation[s] with all foreign countries based on equality, reciprocity and mutual respect for territorial integrity and sovereignty.

"We can win a victory without international assistance." This is a wrong idea. In the era of imperialism, it is impossible for a real people's revolution in any country to gain victory on its own and without various forms of assistance from international revolutionary forces. Even if the revolution succeeds, it is impossible to consolidate it without such assistance. This was how the great October Revolution succeeded and was consolidated, as Lenin and Stalin have already told us. It was how the Second World War brought down three imperialist countries and established people's democracies. The present and future of China should be the same. Let's think about it: If there were no Soviet Union, without victory in the anti-fascism Second World War, without the defeat of Japanese imperialists, without the establishment of peoples' democracies, without the continuing struggle of oppressed nations in the East, without the internal struggle by the masses of the people against their counter-revolutionary rulers in capitalist states such as America, Britain, France, Germany, Italy, Japan and so on, if not for all of these factors combined, then the power of the international counter-revolutionaries repressing us would be several times larger than it is now. Under such circumstance, could we have won a victory? Of course not. And even if we succeeded, there could be no consolidation of our power. The Chinese people have had more than enough of such experience. The testament of Sun Yat-sen on his death bed long ago reflected on the necessity of uniting with international revolutionary forces.

"We need assistance from Britain and America." At the present time, this is a naive idea. The rulers of Britain and America are still imperialists, so why would they aid a people's republic? Why do these countries do business with us, assuming that they might be willing to lend money to us in the future based on mutual interest? It is because capitalists in these countries want to make money, and their bankers want to earn interest in order to solve their own crises, not for aiding the Chinese people at all. The Communist parties and progressive parties in these countries are pushing their government to do business with us and even build diplomatic relations. Such behavior is out of kindness, and this is true aid, totally different from what the bourgeoisie in these countries do. Throughout Sun Yat-sen's life, he tried countless times to call for aid from these capitalist countries but in vain and faced endless rejections. He only got international assistance once in his entire life and it was from the Soviet Union. Let readers take a look at Sun Yat-sen's testament. He advised us earnestly not to look for assistance from imperialist countries, but to "unite with those nations treating us as equals." Mr. Sun had learned his lesson, he had suffered losses and been duped. We should remember his words and never be duped again. Internationally we belong to the side of the anti-imperialist front headed by the Soviet Union, and genuine assistance can only be found from this side rather than from the imperialist side.

"You are dictators." Kind gentlemen, you are right, yes, we are dictators. Every lesson we learn from the past several decades forces us to implement people's democratic dictatorship, or people's democratic despotism. Whatever names, it refers to the same regime that deprives the right of speech to the counter-revolutionaries and grants it only to the people.

Who are the people? In China currently, the people are the working class, the peasants, the urban petty bourgeoisie and the national bourgeoisie. Under the leadership of the working class and the Chinese Communist Party, these classes unite together to build our own country, elect our own government, and coerce the imperialists' running dogs—that is, the landlord class, the bureaucrat bourgeoisie, and their representatives the Kuomintang counter-revolutionaries and their accomplices. We impose dictatorship on them and repress them. They are only allowed to comply with our rule and not allowed to speak and act freely. If they speak and act in an unruly fashion, we would suppress them immediately and punish them. In contrast, for the people, we have democracy. The people have the right of free speech, assembly and association and so on. The right to vote is granted to the people, not to the counter-revolutionaries. These two aspects, i.e. democracy for the people and dictatorship for counter-revolutionaries, should be combined, and this is the people's democratic dictatorship.

Why should we act like this? Everybody knows clearly. If we did not act like this, the revolution would fail, people would suffer and the nation would perish.

"Don't you want to eliminate state power?" We do want this, but not right now, we cannot do it yet. Why? It is because imperialism still exists, domestic counter-revolutionaries still exist, and classes still exist. Our mission is to consolidate the people's state apparatus, including mainly the people's army, the people's police and the people's courts, in order to beef up national defense and protect the people's interests. Based on these steps, China can have the chance to advance under the leadership of the proletariat and the Communist Party of China [can progress] from an agricultural country to an industrialized country, from a new democratic society to a socialist and communist society, eliminate classes and achieve Great Harmony. The state apparatus, including the army, policy, courts, etc., are instruments of class repression. They are the tools for the repression of the enemy class and know nothing of "benevolence."

"You are not benevolent." Quite so. We never implement a policy of benevolence upon counter-revolutionaries and their reactionary behavior. Benevolent policy is only for the people, not for counter-revolutionaries and their reactionary behavior.

The people's state exists to protect the people. Only in such a state can the people educate and remold themselves through democratic means on a nationwide scale, to avoid being influenced by domestic and foreign counter-revolutionaries (such influence is still significant, will last for a long time, and cannot be eradicated anytime soon), transform their bad habits and ideas inherited from the old society, shun the wrong path suggested by the counter-revolutionaries, and move toward the direction of a socialist and communist society.

Here we use the democratic method that is, to persuade rather than to compel. When the people break the law, they also need to be punished, put in jail and even given the death penalty, but only under rare conditions. It is totally different from the dictatorship forced upon the counter-revolutionaries as a class.

As for the counter-revolutionary class and individuals within it, when their regime has been overthrown, they can still be granted lands and jobs in order to survive, as long as they don't rebel, sabotage [the society] or make trouble. Let them transform themselves through labor into new people. [However], if they don't want to work, then the people's state will need to force them to labor. Besides, propaganda and educational work will be done on them in a patient and thorough way, just like what we used to do to on captive army officers in the past. This might also be called a "policy of benevolence," if you like, but the educational work on the enemy classes is a far cry from the self-education we carry on inside the ranks of the revolutionary people.

The remolding of the counter-revolutionaries can be possible only by a state of the people's democratic dictatorship state led by the communist party. If we do it well, the major exploitive classes in China—the landlord class and the bureaucrat (monopoly) bourgeoisie—would be gone for good. The national bourgeoisie remain. We can now educate many of them. When in the future we realize socialism; that is, nationalize private enterprise, we can educate and transform them further. The people have a powerful state apparatus in their hands, so that [we are not afraid that] the national bourgeoisie would rebel.

The serious problem is how to educate the peasants. The peasant economy is scattered, and judging by the Soviet experience, it takes lengthy and painstaking work to socialize agriculture. Without socializing agriculture, there can't be complete and consolidated socialism. The process of socializing agriculture has to be matched by the development of industry in which the state enterprise holds a major role. The state of the people's democratic dictatorship should solve the problem of national industrialization in a systematic manner. As my concern here is not the economic problem, I won't dwell on that further here.

In 1924, in the first national congress of the Kuomintang, led by Sun Yat-sen himself and attended by some Chinese Communist Party members, they passed a famous declaration. The declaration said, "Contemporary democratic institutions around the world are often controlled by the capitalist class, and are used to oppress the common people. However, the democracy advocated by the Kuomintang, is owned by the common people, and not privately owned by a small group of people." Except for the issue of who leads whom, the principle of democracy in the declaration corresponds as a general political program to what we call People's Democracy or New Democracy. A state shared only by common people and not privately held by the bourgeoisie—if we add the leadership of the proletariat, it becomes the state of the people's democratic dictatorship.

Chiang Kai-shek betrayed Sun Yat-sen in that he used the dictatorship of the bureaucrat bourgeoisie and landlord class to suppress the common people in China. This counter-revolutionary dictatorship lasted for twenty-two years, and has been overthrown only recently by the common people led by the Chinese Communist Party.

Those foreign counter-revolutionaries who condemn us as exercising "dictatorship" or resorting to "totalitarianism" are in reality those who exercise it. These people are exactly those to whom Sun Yat-sen referred when he mentioned the contemporary capitalist class in every country who repress the common people. It is from these scoundrels that Chiang Kai-Shek learned his counter-revolutionary dictatorship.

Philosopher Zhu Xi of the Song Dynasty wrote many books and had many sayings that people forget. However, one saying people never forget, and that is, "deal with a man in the way he deals with you."[11] This is just what we do. We deal with the imperialists and their running dogs, Chiang Kai-shek's counter-revolutionaries, as they deal with us. That is exactly what we do, nothing else!

Revolutionary and counter-revolutionary dictatorships are in direct opposition, but the former learns from the latter. Such learning is very important. If the revolutionary people cannot acquire this method of dealing with the counter-revolutionary class, they cannot sustain their regime and would be overthrown by domestic and foreign [forces] who would restore their rule, and revolutionary people would suffer disaster.

The foundation of the people's democratic dictatorship is the alliance between the working class, the peasantry and the urban petty bourgeoisie, and especially the alliance between the working class and the peasantry, as these two classes account for eighty to ninety percent of the Chinese population. The power to overthrow foreign imperialists and the Kuomintang counter-revolutionaries comes mainly from these two classes. In the transition from New Democracy to socialism, [we have to] mainly rely on the alliance of these two classes.

The people's democratic dictatorship requires the leadership of the working class. The reason is that only the proletariat is the most farsighted, most selfless, and most thoroughly revolutionary. The whole history of revolution demonstrates that without the leadership of the proletariat, revolution fails, whereas once we have the proletariat to lead, the revolution succeeds. In the age of imperialism, no other class in any country can lead a genuine revolution towards victory. The fact that the Chinese petty bourgeoisie and national bourgeoisie have tried several times to lead the revolution but have failed to do so is clear evidence of this.

The national bourgeoisie at this current time is still of great significance. We still have foreign imperialists in our midst, and this enemy is evil and powerful. Modern industry only occupies a tiny portion of the Chinese national economy. We don't have reliable statistics now, but according to some estimates, before the war against Japan modern industry only accounted for about ten percent of our gross domestic product. In order to counter imperialist oppression and advance the status of our backward national economy, China should mobilize any factors contributing to our economy and our people's welfare, and unite with the national bourgeoisie in common struggle. Our current policy is to regulate capitalism rather than extinguish it. However, the national bourgeoisie cannot be the leader of the revolution, nor can they occupy major roles in the state. The reason is that their socio-economic status determines their weakness: they lack broad vision and sufficient courage, and many of them fear the masses.

Sun Yat-sen called for "awakening the people," or "assisting peasants and workers." But who is to "awaken" and "assist" them? He meant the petty bourgeoisie and national bourgeoisie. However, they cannot do so. Sun Yat-sen's forty years' revolution failed, and for what reason? Because in the age of imperialism, the petty bourgeoisie and the national bourgeoisie are incapable of leading any real revolution to victory. This is the reason.

Our twenty-eight year-old revolution is totally different. We have had a number of valuable experiences. [We have a party] which is well-disciplined, armed with the theory of Marxism-Leninism, self-critical, and closely connected to the people; an army led by such a party; and a united front under the leadership of such a party bringing together all of the different revolutionary classes and parties. These three are the major weapons we use to win over our enemies. These three weapons are what make us different from our predecessors. Relying on them, we have achieved basic victory. We have gone along tortuous paths. We have fought against intra-party opportunistic tendencies, either from the "left" or "right" wing. Every time we made grave mistakes in these three areas, the revolution faltered. Mistakes and adversity have taught us lessons, and we have become wiser and learned to do things better. Every party, every individual, cannot avoid making mistakes, but we need to make fewer. When we make mistakes, we should correct them immediately. The faster and more thoroughly we correct our wrongs, the better.

Summarizing our experience into one point: the people's democratic dictatorship under the leadership of the proletariat (through the Communist Party) should be founded on the alliance of workers and peasants. Such a dictatorship should unite and cooperate with international revolutionary forces. This is our formula, our main experience, and our main guiding principle.

The Party's twenty-eight years are a long time, but we only accomplished one thing—we have achieved basic victory in the revolutionary struggle. It deserves celebration, as this is the victory of the people, and victory in such a big country as China. However, we need to do more. To take the example of walking, our past work is like finishing the first step in the Long March. Enemies remain that still need to be extinguished. The burdensome task of economic buildup is ahead of us. Things we are familiar with are going to be useless, and things we are not familiar with are going to be forced upon us. This is the difficulty. The imperialists predict that we cannot handle economic problems, and wait on the sidelines to watch our failure.

We must overcome difficulties, and we must learn what we do not yet know. We must turn to every experienced person (no matter who they are) to learn economics. We must make them our teachers, and learn humbly and in earnest. We must admit what we know and what we don't know, and never pretend to know what we actually don't know. Don't behave like bureaucrats. Immerse ourselves in learning for a several months, for one or two years, or even for three or five years, and eventually we can learn it. At the beginning, some Soviet Communist members did not know how to develop their economy, and imperialists also waited for their failure. However, the Soviet Communist Party finally achieved victory. Under the leadership of Lenin and Stalin, they not only knew how to make a revolution, but also how to engage in construction. They have already built a great and shining socialist country. The Soviet Communist Party is our best teacher, and we must learn from it. The domestic and international situation is favorable to us, and we can rely on the weapon of the people's democratic dictatorship and unite everybody except the counter-revolutionaries in our country to steadily move toward our destination.

NOTES

1 See V. I. Lenin, *"Left-Wing" Communism, an Infantile Disorder*, Chapter 2. Lenin said, "For about half a century—approximately from the forties to the nineties of the last century—progressive thought in Russia, oppressed by a most brutal and reactionary tsarism, sought eagerly for a correct revolutionary theory, and followed with the utmost diligence and thoroughness each and every 'last word' in this sphere in Europe and America. Russia achieved Marxism—the only correct revolutionary theory—through the agony she experienced in the course of half a century of unparalleled torment and sacrifice, of unparalleled revolutionary heroism, incredible energy, devoted, searching, study, practical trial, disappointment, verification, and comparison with European experience."

2 From 1840 to 1842, due to the Chinese people's opposition to the opium trade, Britain sent its troops to invade China under the pretext of protecting commerce. Lin Zexu led resistant forces against the British invaders and inflicted significant loss on them. People in Fujian, Zhejiang and Jiangsu also fought anti-British battles. In 1842, the British forces invaded the Yangtze River valley and compelled the Qing Dynasty to sign the first unequal and humiliating treaty in modern Chinese history, i.e. the Treaty of Nanjing. The main content of the treaty included the cession of Hong Kong, large amounts of reparations, the opening of five ports for trade, including, Xiamen, Fuzhou, Ningbo, and Shanghai, and fixed tariffs on British goods to be agreed upon between the British and the Qing governments.

3 Hong Xiuquan (1814–1864), of Huaxian, Guangdong, was the leader of the Taiping peasant revolution in 19th century. He realized the corruption of the Qing Dynasty and the grave situation of the nation facing foreign invasion, so he absorbed the idea of equality from Christians and promoted his "God Worshippers." In 1851, [he,] together with Yang Xiuqing and some other leaders started a rebellion in Jintian, Guangxi and named their regime the Tianping Heavenly Kingdom. In 1859, he approved and

implemented policies recommended in the *New Essay on Economics and Politics* written by Hong Renxuan.

4 Kang Youwei (1858–1927), was born in Nanhai, Guangdong. In 1895, after the defeat of China in the First Sino-Japanese War, more than 1300 civil examination candidates led by Kang Youwei signed a 10,000-word petition to the Emperor and called for "reform" from the autocratic system to constitutional monarchy. In 1898, the Emperor Guangxu assigned positions in the political hierarchy to Kang Youwei, Liang Qichao and Tan Shitong and others and tried to reform and modernize China. Later, the conservatives represented by Empress Dowager Cixi seized power again and the reform thus failed. Kang and Liang fled oversea[s], and organized the Protect the Emperor Society, opposing the bourgeois and petty bourgeois revolutionaries, who were represented by Sun Yat-sen. Kang and his followers thus turned into counter-revolutionaries. Kang's works include *A Study of the 'New Text' Forgeries, A Study of the Reforms of Confucius, Da Tongshu* or *The Book of Great Harmony,* and so on.

5 Yan Fu (1854–1921), of Minhou, Fujian, studied at a naval academy in Britain. After China's defeat by Japan in the Sino-Japanese war of 1894, he advocated constitutional monarchy and reform in China. He translated Thomas Huxley's *Evolution and Ethics,* Adam Smith's *Wealth of Nations,* John Stuart Mill's *System of Logic* and Montesquieu's *De l'esprit des lois,* and helped spread out thought of the European bourgeoisie in China.

6 "The school" was a system copying western educational institutions. "The Imperial examination" was the part of the feudal Chinese exam system. In the late nineteenth century, the reform-minded Chinese intellectuals called for the abolition of the imperial exam, and for the building of schools. However, the diehard conservatives strongly opposed it.

7 The Xinhai Revolution [Revolution of 1911] was led by the United Allegiance Society, a bourgeoisie revolutionary group directed by Sun Yat-sen. The revolution overthrew the corrupted rule of the Qing Dynasty. On October 10, 1911, the revolutionaries mobilized the New Army to revolt in Wuchang, Hubei, and this was followed by uprisings in other provinces. The counter-revolutionary Qing government, propped up by international imperialism, soon collapsed. In January 1912, the interim government of the Republic of China was established in Nanjing and Sun Yat-sen was elected to be the provisional president. The monarchical system which dominated China for two thousand years thus perished and the idea of democratic republic thereafter pervaded the hearts and minds of Chinese people. However, the power of the bourgeois revolutionaries was too weak and they had the tendency to compromise, so they were unable to unite the majority to launch a thorough revolution against feudalism and imperialism. The fruit of the Xinhai Revolution was soon seized by Yuan Shikai, one of the Beiyang Army warlords, and China became mired in the situation of semi-feudalism and semi-colonialism and thus the revolution failed.

8 The May Fourth Movement broke out on May 4, 1919. It was a patriotic movement against feudalism and imperialism. At that time, the First World War had just ended, and the victorious states, including Britain, America, France, Italy, etc., held a peace conference in Paris to deal with Germany. The meeting decided to award the rights of Germany in Shandong to Japan. China was among the victors, but the Beijing government nevertheless planned to accept the decision. On May 4, students marched and protested against the unreasonable decision and the compromise of the Beijing government. The movement soon resonated with people all around the country, and after June 3, it developed into a patriotic movement against feudalism and imperialism writ large, and was joined by the working class, the petty bourgeois, and the national bourgeois. The May Fourth Movement was also known as the counter-feudal New Culture Movement, which started with the debut of *Youth Magazine* (later *The New Youth*) in 1915. It erected the two flags of "science" and "democracy," opposing the old and advocating the new ethics, and opposing the old and calling for the new literature. The progressive participants of the May Fourth Movement accepted Marxism, and developed the New Culture Movement into the Marxist Movement. They also were

dedicated to combining Marxism and the Chinese labor movement, and prepared the theory and cadres for the establishment of the Chinese Communist Party.

9   In the early stages of the people's liberation war, some democrats held the illusion of seeking a third road, an alternative to the dictatorship of the big landlords and the big bourgeoisie, led by the Kuomintang and the people's democratic dictatorship under the leadership of the Communist Party. Such a third road did not exist. In essence, it was the road to the Anglo-Saxon style bourgeois dictatorship.

10   Wu Song is a hero in the Chinese novel *Shuihu Zhuan [Heroes of the Marshes]*, who killed a tiger in Chingyang Ridge barehanded. The story was popular among the common people.

11   The quotation is from Zhu Xi's commentary on *The Confucian Doctrine of the Mean*, Chapter 13.

Anarcho-Communism vs. Marxism

*MIKHAIL BAKUNIN**

Among Marx's earliest critics were the "anarcho-communists," including Mikhail Bakunin (1814–1876). A Russian anarchist (from the Greek *an archos*, meaning "no rule" or "no government"), Bakunin disputed Marx's claim that communism would lead to "the withering away of the state." Instead, Bakunin predicted, the supposedly temporary interim state that Marx called "the dictatorship of the proletariat" would prove to be a permanent dictatorship *over* the proletariat by state officials who would jealously guard their own power and privilege. Bakunin insisted that state power must be smashed once and for all by a proletarian revolution. Only in a voluntary anarchist society, he claimed, could people combine and associate as free and equal producers and comrades.

* *Source*: Michel Bakounine [Mikhail Bakunin], "Lettre à la Liberté," *Oeuvres* (Paris: P.-V. Stock, 1910), vol. 4, pp. 341–350, 378. Translated from the French by Terence Ball.

LETTER TO *LA LIBERTÉ* (BRUSSELS)

5 October 1872, Zurich

Gentlemen:

The victory of Mr. Karl Marx and his disciples is now complete ... The Marxists have now removed their masks and, as is all-too-typical of power-loving men, always in the name of that "sovereignty of the people" which from now on will be the platform from which all who aspire to control the masses will operate, they have boldly begun to enslave the people of the Socialist International.

If the International were less vital and vigorous—if it were based, as they believe, only on the organized command centers, rather than on the real solidarity of the objective interests and aims of the workers of every civilized country ... —the declarations of that wretched Hague Congress, the ever-malleable representative of Marxist theory and practice, would have killed it ...

A state, a government, a universal dictatorship! The dream of [such would-be despots as Pope] Gregory VIII, Pope Boniface, King Charles V or the Emperor Napoleon, now reproduced in a new form but still with the same aims, this time in the camp of the democratic socialists! Can one conceive of anything more ridiculous, or more revolting?

To pretend that a group of men—even the brightest and best-intentioned among them—could become the mind, soul, and shaping and unifying will of the revolutionary movement and economic organization of the proletariat of all countries is such a massive affront to common sense and historical experience that one is astonished that a brilliant man like Mr. Marx could have conceived of it.

At least the Popes could excuse themselves by resorting to the Absolute Truth which they claimed the Holy Spirit had given to them, and which they had no choice but to believe. Mr. Marx has no such excuse, and I shall not insult him by saying that he fancies himself to have scientifically discovered some sort of absolute truth. But accepting that the absolute does not exist, no infallible dogma is available to the International and thus no authoritative political or economic theory. Our assemblies and councils should never try to be like the ecumenical councils, decreeing compulsory principles for the faithful to believe.

Only one law unites all members, individuals, sections and federations of the International, and constitutes its only true foundation. That law is THE INTERNATIONAL SOLIDARITY OF ALL WORKERS IN ALL COUNTRIES IN THEIR ECONOMIC STRUGGLE AGAINST THE EXPLOITERS OF LABOR. The actual organization of that solidarity through the free action of the proletariat ... constitutes the real and living unity of the International.

Who can doubt that from this ever broader organization of militant proletarian solidarity against bourgeois exploitation that the political struggle of the proletariat must intensify? We anarcho-communists agree with the Marxists about that. But we must now confront the question that separates us so profoundly from the Marxists.

We hold that the necessarily revolutionary policy of the proletariat must have as its one and only objective the smashing of the State. We cannot conceive of talking about international solidarity while, at the same time, attempting to preserve states—except perhaps in some dream about a universal state, i.e., universal slavery, as dreamed by powerful emperors and popes—because by its very nature the state subverts solidarity and is a permanent cause of war. We cannot conceive of talking about the liberty or the emancipation of the proletariat within or by means of the state. To speak of the state is to speak of domination. And all domination entails the subjugation of the people and thus their exploitation by some governing minority.

We do not accept, even in the course of revolutionary transition, either national conventions, or constituent assemblies, or "revolutionary dictatorships"; because we are convinced that a sincere, real and honest revolution can only be made by the masses. When [the revolution] is directed by a small number of ruling individuals it inevitably and immediately turns reactionary. Such is our belief, though this is not the time to explain it in detail.

The Marxists profess very different ideas. Like good Germans, they worship at the shrine of State power ... The only kind of emancipation the Marxists recognize is what comes out of their so-called "People's State" (*Volkstaat*). Far from being opponents of "patriotism," they all too often fly the flag of Pan-Germanism. There may well be a noticeable difference between German Chancellor Otto von Bismarck's policies and Marx's; but between the Marxists and ourselves there is a deep divide. They favor government, while we do not: we are anarchists.

These are the two political tendencies that today divide the International into two camps. On the one side is Germany, all but alone; on the other, to one or another degree, are Italy, Spain, the Swiss Jura, much of France, Belgium, Holland, and, shortly, the Slavs. These two tendencies locked horns at the Hague Congress and, thanks to the cleverness of Mr. Marx and the completely artificial organization of that Congress, the German tendency emerged victorious.

Was the crucial question then resolved? No. It was not even properly discussed. The majority voted like a well-trained regiment, trampling all discussion under its vote. The contradiction is thus livelier and more menacing than ever, and Mr. Marx himself, despite being drunk with victory, can hardly imagine otherwise. And even if he had for an instant held such a vain hope, the combined protest of the Swiss, Spanish, Belgian and Dutch delegations (not to mention Italy, which did not send delegates to such an obviously rigged Congress)—so moderate in form but all the more powerful for that—must soon have disabused him.

That protest, in itself, is merely a mild harbinger of the storm of opposition which will rage in every country penetrated by the principles and passion of social revolution. And the entire storm will have been stirred up by the Marxists' unhappy preoccupation with making the political question a basis and a binding principle of the International.

Between these two tendencies no conciliation or compromise is possible. Only the practice of social revolution, great new historical experiments, and the logic of events might one day direct them toward a shared solution. And, as we are persuaded of the worth of our own principle, we hope that the Germans themselves—the workers of Germany, that is, not their leaders—will finally join us in destroying those people's prisons which some call states, and to condemn politics, which is merely the art of dominating and deceiving the masses.

... I can see how despots, crowned or uncrowned, could have dreamed of ruling the world. But what can we say when a friend of the proletariat, a revolutionary who says he sincerely supports the emancipation of the masses, then sets himself up as director and ultimate judge of every revolutionary movement which might emerge in every country, and boldly dreams of subjecting them to a singular thought that he has hatched in his own head!

I think that Mr. Marx is a very serious if not always very honest revolutionary, and that he is truly in favor of the elevation of the masses; and so I marvel at how he manages to ignore the fact that the establishment of a universal dictatorship (whether individual or collective) which would require some sort of engineer-in-chief of world revolution, to rule and direct the insurrectionary movement of the masses throughout the world, in much the same way as a machine is operated—that the establishment of such a supreme dictatorship would be sufficient to stifle revolution and distort and paralyze all popular movements ...

The political state in every country, he says, is always the product and faithful expression of its economic situation; in order to change the former it is necessary to change the latter. The entire secret of historical evolutions, according to Marx, is this. He pays no attention to other factors in history, such as the consequence (utterly clear though it is) of political, legal and religious institutions on the economic conditions. He says: "Misery produces political slavery, the state"; but he does not recognize the converse: "Political slavery, the state, reproduces and maintains misery, as a condition of its existence; thus in order to destroy misery, the state must be destroyed."

Anarchism:
What It Really Stands For

EMMA GOLDMAN*

In the late nineteenth and early twentieth centuries, Emma Goldman (1869–1940) was widely known as "Red Emma" because of her activity on behalf of radical causes. Born in Russia, she moved to the United States when she was seventeen and remained there for most of her life. Her outspoken advocacy of anarchism, socialism, and women's rights led to prison sentences for, among other things, openly promoting birth control and opposing the draft during World War I. She was deported to Russia in 1919, where she became an outspoken critic of the newly established communist regime. In the following essay, Goldman defends anarcho-communism by clarifying its aims and responding to common criticisms—and, in her view, misconceptions—of anarchism.

* *Source*: Emma Goldman, *Anarchism and Other Essays* (New York: Mother Earth Association Publishers, 1910), pp. 47–67.

ANARCHISM: WHAT IT REALLY STANDS FOR

The history of human growth and development is at the same time the history of the terrible struggle of every new idea heralding the approach of a brighter dawn. In its tenacious hold on tradition, the Old has never hesitated to make use of the foulest and cruelest means to stay the advent of the New, in whatever form or period the latter may have asserted itself. Nor need we retrace our steps into the distant past to realize the enormity of opposition, difficulties, and hardships placed in the path of every progressive idea. The rack, the thumbscrew, and the knout [whip] are still with us; so are the convict's garb and the social wrath, all conspiring against the spirit that is serenely marching on.

Anarchism could not hope to escape the fate of all other ideas of innovation. Indeed, as the most revolutionary and uncompromising innovator, Anarchism must needs meet with the combined ignorance and venom of the world it aims to reconstruct.

To deal even remotely with all that is being said and done against Anarchism would necessitate the writing of a whole volume. I shall therefore meet only two of the principal objections. In so doing, I shall attempt to elucidate what Anarchism really stands for.

The strange phenomenon of the opposition to Anarchism is that it brings to light the relation between so-called intelligence and ignorance. And yet this is not so very strange when we consider the relativity of all things. The ignorant mass has in its favor that it makes no pretense of knowledge or tolerance. Acting, as it always does, by mere impulse, its reasons are like those of a child. "Why?" "Because." Yet the opposition of the uneducated to Anarchism deserves the same consideration as that of the intelligent man.

What, then, are the objections? First, Anarchism is impractical, though a beautiful ideal. Second, Anarchism stands for violence and destruction, hence it must be repudiated as vile and dangerous. Both the intelligent man and the ignorant mass judge not from a thorough knowledge of the subject, but either from hearsay or false interpretation.

A practical scheme, says Oscar Wilde,[1] is either one already in existence, or a scheme that could be carried out under the existing conditions; but it is exactly the existing conditions that one objects to, and any scheme that could accept these conditions is wrong and foolish. The true criterion of the practical, therefore, is not whether the latter can keep intact the wrong or foolish; rather is it whether the scheme has vitality enough to leave the stagnant waters of the old, and build, as well as sustain, new life. In the light of this conception, Anarchism is indeed practical. More than any other idea, it is helping to do away with the wrong and foolish; more than any other idea, it is building and sustaining new life.

The emotions of the ignorant man are continuously kept at a pitch by the most bloodcurdling stories about Anarchism. Not a thing is too outrageous to be employed against this philosophy and its exponents. Therefore Anarchism represents to the unthinking what the proverbial bad man does to the child—a black monster bent on swallowing everything; in short, destruction and violence.

Destruction and violence! How is the ordinary man to know that the most violent element in society is ignorance; that its power of destruction is the very thing Anarchism is combating? Nor is he aware that Anarchism, whose roots, as it were, are part of nature's forces, destroys, not healthful tissue, but parasitic growths that feed on the life's essence of society. It is merely clearing the soil from weeds and sagebrush, that it may eventually bear healthy fruit.

Someone has said that it requires less mental effort to condemn than to think. The widespread mental indolence, so prevalent in society, proves this to be only too true. Rather than to go to the bottom of any given idea, to examine into its origin and meaning, most people will either condemn it altogether, or rely on some superficial or prejudicial definition of non-essentials.

Anarchism urges man to think, to investigate, to analyze every proposition; but that the brain capacity of the average reader be not taxed too much, I also shall begin with a definition, and then elaborate on the latter.

> ANARCHISM:—The philosophy of a new social order based on liberty unrestricted by man-made law; the theory that all forms of government rest on violence, and are therefore wrong and harmful, as well as unnecessary.

The new social order rests, of course, on the materialistic basis of life; but while all Anarchists agree that the main evil today is an economic one, they maintain that the solution of that evil can be brought about only through the consideration of *every phase* of life—individual, as well as the collective; the internal, as well as the external phases.

A thorough perusal of the history of human development will disclose two elements in bitter conflict with each other; elements that are only now beginning to be understood, not as foreign to each other, but as closely related and truly harmonious, if only placed in proper environment: the individual and social instincts. The individual and society have waged a relentless and bloody battle for ages, each striving for supremacy, because each was blind to the value and importance of the other. The individual and social instincts—the one a most potent factor for individual endeavor, for growth, aspiration, self-realization; the other an equally potent factor for mutual helpfulness and social well-being.

The explanation of the storm raging within the individual, and between him and his surroundings, is not far to seek. The primitive man, unable to understand his being, much less the unity of all life, felt himself absolutely dependent on blind, hidden forces ever ready to mock and taunt him. Out of that attitude grew the religious concepts of man as a mere speck of dust dependent on superior powers on high, who can only be appeased by complete surrender. All the early sagas rest on that idea, which continues to be the *leit-motif* of the biblical tales dealing with the relation of man to God, to the State, to society. Again and again the same motif, *man is nothing, the powers are everything.* Thus Jehovah would only endure man on condition of complete surrender. Man can have all the glories of the earth, but he must not become conscious of himself. The State, society, and moral laws all sing the same refrain: Man can have all the glories of the earth, but he must not become conscious of himself.

Anarchism is the only philosophy which brings to man the consciousness of himself; which maintains that God, the State, and society are non-existent, that their promises are null and void, since they can be fulfilled only through man's subordination. Anarchism is therefore the teacher of the unity of life; not merely in nature, but in man. There is no conflict between the individual and the social instincts, any more than there is between the heart and the lungs: the one the receptacle of a precious life essence, the other the repository of the element that keeps the essence pure and strong. The individual is the heart of society, conserving the essence of social life; society is the lungs which are distributing the element to keep the life essence—that is, the individual—pure and strong.

"The one thing of value in the world," says Emerson,[2] "is the active soul; this every man contains within him. The active soul sees absolute truth and utters truth and creates." In other words, the individual instinct is the thing of value in the world. It is the true soul that sees and creates the truth alive, out of which is to come a still greater truth, the reborn social soul.

Anarchism is the great liberator of man from the phantoms that have held him captive; it is the arbiter and pacifier of the two forces for individual and social harmony. To accomplish that unity, Anarchism has declared war on the pernicious influences which have so far prevented the harmonious blending of individual and social instincts, the individual and society.

Religion, the dominion of the human mind; Property, the dominion of human needs; and Government, the dominion of human conduct, represent the stronghold of man's enslavement and all the horrors it entails. Religion! How it dominates man's mind, how it humiliates and degrades his soul. God is everything, man is nothing, says religion. But out of that nothing God has created a kingdom so despotic, so tyrannical, so cruel, so terribly exacting that naught but gloom and tears and blood have ruled the world since gods began. Anarchism rouses man to rebellion against this black monster. Break your mental fetters, says Anarchism to man, for not until you think and judge for yourself will you get rid of the dominion of darkness, the greatest obstacle to all progress.

Property, the dominion of man's needs, the denial of the right to satisfy his needs. Time was when property claimed a divine right, when it came to man with the same refrain, even as religion, "Sacrifice! Abnegate! Submit!" The spirit of Anarchism has lifted man from his prostrate position. He now stands erect, with his face toward the light. He has learned to see the insatiable, devouring, devastating nature of property, and he is preparing to strike the monster dead.

"Property is robbery," said the great French Anarchist, Proudhon.[3] Yes, but without risk and danger to the robber. Monopolizing the accumulated efforts of man, property has robbed him of his birth-right, and has turned him loose a pauper and an outcast. Property has not even the time-worn excuse that man does not create enough to satisfy all needs. The A B C student of economics knows that the productivity of labor within the last few decades far exceeds normal demand a hundredfold. But what are normal demands to an abnormal institution? The only demand that property recognizes is its own gluttonous appetite for greater wealth, because wealth means power: the power to subdue, to crush, to exploit, the power to enslave, to outrage, to degrade. America is particularly boastful of her great power, her enormous national wealth. Poor America, of what avail is all her wealth, if the individuals comprising the nation are wretchedly poor? If they live in squalor, in filth, in crime, with hope and joy gone, a homeless, soilless army of human prey.

It is generally conceded that unless the returns of any business venture exceed the cost, bankruptcy is inevitable. But those engaged in the business of producing wealth have not yet learned even this simple lesson. Every year the cost of production in human life is growing larger (50,000 killed, 100,000 wounded in America last year); the returns to the masses, who help to create wealth, are ever getting smaller. Yet America continues to be blind to the inevitable bankruptcy of our business of production. Nor is this the only crime of the latter. Still more fatal is the crime of turning the producer into a mere particle of a machine, with less will and decision than his master of steel and iron. Man is being robbed not merely of the products of his labor, but of the power of free initiative, of originality, and the interest in, or desire for, the things he is making.

Real wealth consists in things of utility and beauty, in things that help to create strong, beautiful bodies and surroundings inspiring to live in. But if man is doomed to wind cotton around a spool, or dig coal, or build roads for thirty years of his life, there can be no talk of wealth. What he gives to the world is only gray and hideous things, reflecting a dull and hideous existence—too weak to live, too cowardly to die. Strange to say, there are people who extol this deadening method of centralized production as the proudest achievement of our age. They fail utterly to realize that if we are to continue in machine subserviency, our slavery is more complete than was our bondage to the King. They do not want to know that centralization is not only the death knell of liberty, but also of health and beauty, of art and science, all these being impossible in a clock-like, mechanical atmosphere.

Anarchism cannot but repudiate such a method of production: its goal is the freest possible expression of all the latent powers of the individual. Oscar Wilde defines a perfect personality as "one who develops under perfect conditions, who is not wounded, maimed, or in danger." A perfect personality, then, is only possible in a state of society where man is free to choose the mode of work, the conditions of work, and the freedom to work. One to whom the making of a table, the building of a house, or the tilling of the soil, is what the painting is to the artist and the discovery to the scientist—the result of inspiration, of intense longing, and deep interest in work as a creative force. That being the ideal of Anarchism, its economic arrangements must consist of voluntary productive and distributive associations, gradually developing into free communism, as the best means of producing with the least waste of human energy. Anarchism, however, also recognizes the right of the individual, or numbers of individuals, to arrange at all times for other forms of work, in harmony with their tastes and desires.

Such free display of human energy being possible only under complete individual and social freedom, Anarchism directs its forces against the third and greatest foe of all social equality; namely, the State, organized authority, or statutory law—the dominion of human conduct.

Just as religion has fettered the human mind, and as property, or the monopoly of things, has subdued and stifled man's needs, so has the State enslaved his spirit, dictating every phase of conduct. "All government in essence," says Emerson, "is tyranny." It matters not whether it is government by divine right or majority rule. In every instance its aim is the absolute subordination of the individual.

Referring to the American government, the greatest American Anarchist, David Thoreau,[4] said: "Government, what is it but a tradition, though a recent one, endeavoring to transmit itself unimpaired to posterity, but each instance losing its integrity; it has not the vitality and force of a single living man. Law never made man a whit more just; and by means of their respect for it, even the well disposed are daily made agents of injustice."

Indeed, the keynote of government is injustice. With the arrogance and self-sufficiency of the King who could do no wrong, governments ordain, judge, condemn, and punish the most insignificant offenses, while maintaining themselves by the greatest of all offenses, the annihilation of individual liberty. Thus Ouida[5] is right when she maintains that "the State only aims at instilling those qualities in its public by which its demands are obeyed, and its exchequer is filled. Its highest attainment is the reduction of mankind to clockwork. In its atmosphere all those finer and more delicate liberties, which require treatment and spacious expansion, inevitably dry up and perish. The State requires a taxpaying machine in which there is no hitch, an exchequer in which there is never a deficit, and a public, monotonous, obedient, colorless, spiritless, moving humbly like a flock of sheep along a straight high road between two walls."

Yet even a flock of sheep would resist the chicanery of the State, if it were not for the corruptive, tyrannical, and oppressive methods it employs to serve its purposes. Therefore Bakunin[6] repudiates the State as synonymous with the surrender of the liberty of the individual or small minorities—the destruction of social relationship, the curtailment, or complete denial even, of life itself, for its own aggrandizement. The State is the altar of political freedom and, like the religious altar, it is maintained for the purpose of human sacrifice.

In fact, there is hardly a modern thinker who does not agree that government, organized authority, or the State, is necessary *only* to maintain or protect property and monopoly. It has proven efficient in that function only.

Even George Bernard Shaw, who hopes for the miraculous from the State under Fabianism,[7] nevertheless admits that "it is at present a huge machine for robbing and slave-driving of the poor by brute force." This being the case, it is hard to see why the clever prefacer wishes to uphold the State after poverty shall have ceased to exist.

Unfortunately there are still a number of people who continue in the fatal belief that government rests on natural laws, that it maintains social order and harmony, that it diminishes crime, and that it prevents the lazy man from fleecing his fellows. I shall therefore examine these contentions.

A natural law is that factor in man which asserts itself freely and spontaneously without any external force, in harmony with the requirements of nature. For instance, the demand for nutrition, for sex gratification, for light, air, and exercise, is a natural law. But its expression needs not the machinery of government, needs not the club, the gun, the handcuff, or the prison. To obey such laws, if we may call it obedience, requires only spontaneity and free opportunity. That governments do not maintain themselves through such harmonious factors is proven by the terrible array of violence, force, and coercion all governments use in order to live. Thus Blackstone[8] is right when he says, "Human laws are invalid, because they are contrary to the laws of nature."

Unless it be the order of Warsaw after the slaughter of thousands of people, it is difficult to ascribe to governments any capacity for order or social harmony.

Order derived through submission and maintained by terror is not much of a safe guaranty; yet that is the only "order" that governments have ever maintained. True social harmony grows naturally out of solidarity of interests. In a society where those who always work never have anything, while those who never work enjoy everything, solidarity of interests is non-existent; hence social harmony is but a myth. The only way organized authority meets this grave situation is by extending still greater privileges to those who have already monopolized the earth, and by still further enslaving the disinherited masses. Thus the entire arsenal of government—laws, police, soldiers, the courts, legislatures, prisons—is strenuously engaged in "harmonizing" the most antagonistic elements in society.

The most absurd apology for authority and law is that they serve to diminish crime. Aside from the fact that the State is itself the greatest criminal, breaking every written and natural law, stealing in the form of taxes, killing in the form of war and capital punishment, it has come to an absolute standstill in coping with crime. It has failed utterly to destroy or even minimize the horrible scourge of its own creation.

Crime is naught but misdirected energy. So long as every institution of today, economic, political, social, and moral, conspires to misdirect human energy into wrong channels; so long as most people are out of place doing the things they hate to do, living a life they loathe to live, crime will be inevitable, and all the laws on the statutes can only increase, but never do away with, crime. What does society, as it exists today, know of the process of despair, the poverty, the horrors, the fearful struggle the human soul must pass on its way to crime and degradation. Who that knows this terrible process can fail to see the truth in these words of Peter Kropotkin:[9]

> Those who will hold the balance between the benefits thus attributed to law and punishment and the degrading effect of the latter on humanity; those who will estimate the torrent of depravity poured abroad in human society by the informer, favored by the Judge even, and paid for in clinking cash by governments, under the pretext of aiding to unmask crime; those who will go within prison walls and there see what human beings become when deprived of liberty, when subjected to the care of brutal keepers, to coarse, cruel words, to a thousand stinging, piercing humiliations, will agree with us that the entire apparatus of prison and punishment is an abomination which ought to be brought to an end.

The deterrent influence of law on the lazy man is too absurd to merit consideration. If society were only relieved of the waste and expense of keeping a lazy class, and the equally great expense of the paraphernalia of protection this lazy class requires, the social tables would contain an abundance for all, including even the occasional lazy individual. Besides, it is well to consider that laziness results either from special privileges, or physical and mental abnormalities. Our present insane system of production fosters both, and the most astounding phenomenon is that people should want to work at all now. Anarchism aims to strip labor of its deadening, dulling aspect, of its gloom and compulsion. It aims to make work an instrument of joy, of strength, of color, of real harmony, so that the poorest sort of a man should find in work both recreation and hope.

To achieve such an arrangement of life, government, with its unjust, arbitrary, repressive measures, must be done away with. At best it has but imposed one single mode of life upon all, without regard to individual and social variations and needs. In destroying government and statutory laws, Anarchism proposes to rescue the self-respect and independence of the individual from all restraint and invasion by authority. Only in freedom can man grow to his full stature. Only in freedom will he learn to think and move, and give the very best in him. Only in freedom will he realize the true force of the social bonds which knit men together, and which are the true foundation of a normal social life.

But what about human nature? Can it be changed? And if not, will it endure under Anarchism?

Poor human nature, what horrible crimes have been committed in thy name! Every fool, from king to policeman, from the flatheaded parson to the visionless dabbler in science, presumes to speak authoritatively of human nature. The greater the mental charlatan, the more definite his insistence on the wickedness and weaknesses of human nature. Yet, how can any one speak of it today, with every soul in a prison, with every heart fettered, wounded, and maimed?

John Burroughs[10] has stated that experimental study of animals in captivity is absolutely useless. Their character, their habits, their appetites undergo a complete transformation when torn from their soil in field and forest. With human nature caged in a narrow space, whipped daily into submission, how can we speak of its potentialities?

Freedom, expansion, opportunity, and, above all, peace and repose, alone can teach us the real dominant factors of human nature and all its wonderful possibilities.

Anarchism, then, really stands for the liberation of the human mind from the dominion of religion; the liberation of the human body from the dominion of property; liberation from the shackles and restraint of government. Anarchism stands for a social order based on the free grouping of individuals for the purpose of producing real social wealth; an order that will guarantee to every human being free access to the earth and full enjoyment of the necessities of life, according to individual desires, tastes, and inclinations.

This is not a wild fancy or an aberration of the mind. It is the conclusion arrived at by hosts of intellectual men and women the world over; a conclusion resulting from the close and studious observation of the tendencies of modern society: individual liberty and economic equality, the twin forces for the birth of what is fine and true in man.

As to methods, Anarchism is not, as some may suppose, a theory of the future to be realized through divine inspiration. It is a living force in the affairs of our life, constantly creating new conditions. The methods of Anarchism therefore do not comprise an iron-clad program to be carried out under all circumstances. Methods must grow out of the economic needs of each place and clime, and of the intellectual and temperamental requirements of the individual. The serene, calm character of a Tolstoy[11] will wish different methods for social reconstruction than the intense, overflowing personality of a Michael Bakunin or a Peter Kropotkin. Equally so it must be apparent that the economic and political needs of Russia will dictate more drastic measures than would England or America. Anarchism does not stand for military drill and uniformity; it does, however, stand for the spirit of revolt, in whatever form, against everything that hinders human growth.

All Anarchists agree in that, as they also agree in their opposition to the political machinery as a means of bringing about the great social change.

"All voting," says Thoreau, "is a sort of gaming, like checkers, or backgammon, a playing with right and wrong; its obligation never exceeds that of expediency. Even voting for the right thing is doing nothing for it. A wise man will not leave the right to the mercy of chance, nor wish it to prevail through the power of the majority." A close examination of the machinery of politics and its achievements will bear out the logic of Thoreau.

What does the history of parliamentarism show? Nothing but failure and defeat, not even a single reform to ameliorate the economic and social stress of the people. Laws have been passed and enactments made for the improvement and protection of labor. Thus it was proven only last year that Illinois, with the most rigid laws for mine protection, had the greatest mine disasters. In States where child labor laws prevail, child exploitation is at its highest, and though with us the workers enjoy full political opportunities, capitalism has reached the most brazen zenith.

Even were the workers able to have their own representatives, for which our good Socialist politicians are clamoring, what chances are there for their honesty and good faith? One has but to bear in mind the process of politics to realize that its path of good intentions is full of pitfalls: wire-pulling, intriguing, flattering, lying, cheating; in fact, chicanery of every description, whereby the political aspirant can achieve success. Added to that is a complete demoralization of character and conviction, until nothing is left that would make one hope for anything from such a human derelict. Time and time again the people were foolish enough to trust, believe, and support with their last farthing aspiring politicians, only to find themselves betrayed and cheated.

It may be claimed that men of integrity would not become corrupt in the political grinding mill. Perhaps not; but such men would be absolutely helpless to exert the slightest influence in behalf of labor, as indeed has been shown in numerous instances. The State is the economic master of its servants. Good men, if such there be, would either remain true to their political faith and lose their economic support, or they would cling to their economic master and be utterly unable to do the slightest good. The political arena leaves one no alternative, one must either be a dunce or a rogue.

The political superstition is still holding sway over the hearts and minds of the masses, but the true lovers of liberty will have no more to do with it. Instead, they believe with Stirner[12] that man has as much liberty as he is willing to take. Anarchism therefore stands for direct action, the open defiance of, and resistance to, all laws and restrictions, economic, social, and moral. But defiance and resistance are illegal. Therein lies the salvation of man. Everything illegal necessitates integrity, self-reliance, and courage. In short, it calls for free, independent spirits, for "men who are men, and who have a bone in their backs which you cannot pass your hand through."

Universal suffrage itself owes its existence to direct action. If not for the spirit of rebellion, of the defiance on the part of the American revolutionary fathers, their posterity would still wear the King's coat. If not for the direct action of a John Brown[13] and his comrades, America would still trade in the flesh of the black man. True, the trade in white flesh is still going on; but that, too, will have to be abolished by direct action. Trade unionism, the economic arena of the modern gladiator, owes its existence to direct action. It is but recently that law and government have attempted to crush the trade union movement, and condemned the exponents of man's right to organize to prison as conspirators. Had they sought to assert their cause through begging, pleading, and compromise, trade unionism would today be a negligible quantity. In France, in Spain, in Italy, in Russia, nay even in England (witness the growing rebellion of English labor unions) direct, revolutionary, economic action has become so strong a force in the battle for industrial liberty as to make the world realize the tremendous importance of labor's power. The General Strike, the supreme expression of the economic consciousness of the workers, was ridiculed in America but a short time ago. Today every great strike, in order to win, must realize the importance of the solidaric general protest.

Direct action, having proved effective along economic lines, is equally potent in the environment of the individual. There a hundred forces encroach upon his being, and only persistent resistance to them will finally set him free. Direct action against the authority in the shop, direct action against the authority of the law, direct action against the invasive, meddlesome authority of our moral code, is the logical, consistent method of Anarchism.

Will it not lead to a revolution? Indeed, it will. No real social change has ever come about without a revolution. People are either not familiar with their history, or they have not yet learned that revolution is but thought carried into action.

Anarchism, the great leaven of thought, is today permeating every phase of human endeavor. Science, art, literature, the drama, the effort for economic betterment, in fact every individual and social opposition to the existing disorder of things, is illumined by the spiritual light of Anarchism. It is the philosophy of the sovereignty of the individual. It is the theory of social harmony. It is the great, surging, living truth that is reconstructing the world, and that will usher in the Dawn.

NOTES

1   The Irish playwright Oscar Wilde (1854–1900).—Eds.
2   The American essayist Ralph Waldo Emerson (1803–1882).—Eds.
3   The French anarcho-socialist Pierre-Joseph Proudhon (1809–1865), who held that "[private] property is theft."—Eds.
4   The American author Henry David Thoreau (1817–1862). Here and elsewhere Goldman quotes from Thoreau's "Civil Disobedience" (1849). Her assertion that Thoreau was an anarchist, however, is open to doubt. In "Civil Disobedience" he writes that "unlike those who call themselves no-government men [i.e., anarchists], I ask for, not at once no government, but at once a better government." Far from wishing to smash the state, Thoreau concludes his famous essay by envisioning "a still more perfect and glorious State, which also I have imagined, but not yet anywhere seen."—Eds.
5   Ouida was the pseudonym of the English novelist Marie Louise de la Ramie (1839–1908).—Eds.
6   The Russian anarchist Mikhail Bakunin (1814–1876). See selection 6.43 in this volume.—Eds.
7   The Irish dramatist and essayist George Bernard Shaw (1856–1950), who was also a Fabian socialist.—Eds.

8   The English jurist Sir William Blackstone (1723–1780), author of *Commentaries on the Laws of England* (1769).—Eds.

9   The Russian anarchist and nobleman Peter Kropotkin (1842–1921).—Eds.

10   The American naturalist and author John Burroughs (1837–1921).—Eds.

11   Count Leo Tolstoy (1828–1910), Russian pacifist and author of *War and Peace* (1869) and *Anna Karenina* (1877).—Eds.

12   Max Stirner was the pseudonym of Johann Casper Schmidt (1806–1856), author of *The Ego and His Own* (1844).—Eds.

13   The American abolitionist John Brown (1800–1859), who led the ill-fated raid on the U.S. arsenal at Harpers Ferry in Virginia.—Eds.

Looking Backward

EDWARD BELLAMY*

Like Eduard Bernstein and some anarcho-communists, the American socialist Edward Bellamy (1850–1898) thought that the process of evolution was leading inevitably to a cooperative socialist society. Unlike the anarchists, however, Bellamy believed that the state would continue to have a role under socialism, albeit a very different one. Bellamy put these ideas into his best-selling novel *Looking Backward* (1888). There Bellamy's late nineteenth-century hero, Julian West, falls into a deep trance-like sleep, awakening (or so it seems) in the year 2000 to find that a socialist evolution had occurred in the interim. In the following excerpts from *Looking Backward*, West's host, Dr. Leete, and the minister, Mr. Barton, lament the evils of the old capitalist system and explain the advantages of the new, and more just, socialist society.

---

* *Source*: Edward Bellamy, *Looking Backward* (Boston: Ticknor, 1888).

LOOKING BACKWARD

By way of attempting to give the reader some general impression of the way people lived together in those days, and especially of the relations of the rich and poor to one another, perhaps I cannot do better than to compare society as it then was to a prodigious [stage]coach which the masses of humanity were harnessed to and dragged toilsomely along a very hilly and sandy road. The driver was hunger, and permitted no lagging, though the pace was necessarily very slow. Despite the difficulty of drawing the coach at all along so hard a road, the top was covered with passengers who never got down, even at the steepest ascents. These seats on top were very breezy and comfortable. Well up out of the dust, their occupants could enjoy the scenery at their leisure, or critically discuss the merits of the straining team. Naturally such places were in great demand and the competition for them was keen, every one seeking as the first end in life to secure a seat on the coach for himself and to leave it to his child after him. By the rule of the coach a man could leave his seat to whom he wished, but on the other hand there were many accidents by which it might at any time be wholly lost. For all that they were so easy, the seats were very insecure, and at every sudden jolt of the coach persons were slipping out of them and falling to the ground, where they were instantly compelled to take hold of the rope and help to drag the coach on which they had before ridden so pleasantly. It was naturally regarded as a terrible misfortune to lose one's seat, and the apprehension that this might happen to them or their friends was a constant cloud upon the happiness of those who rode.

But did they think only of themselves? you ask. Was not their very luxury rendered intolerable to them by comparison with the lot of their brothers and sisters in the harness, and the knowledge that their own weight added to their toil? Had they no compassion for fellow beings from whom fortune only distinguished them? Oh, yes; commiseration was frequently expressed by those who rode for those who had to pull the coach, especially when the vehicle came to a bad place in the road, as it was constantly doing, or to a particular steep hill. At such times, the desperate straining of the team, their agonized leaping and plunging under the pitiless lashing of hunger, the many who fainted at the rope and were trampled in the mire, made a very distressing spectacle which often called forth highly creditable displays of feeling on the top of the coach. At such times the passengers would call down encouragingly to the toilers of the rope, exhorting them to patience, and holding out hopes of possible compensation in another world for the hardness of their lot, while others contributed to buy salves and liniments for the crippled and injured. It was agreed that it was a great pity that the coach should be so hard to pull, and there was a sense of general relief when the specially bad piece of road was gotten over. This relief was not, indeed, wholly on account of the team, for there was always some danger at these bad places of a general overturn in which all would lose their seats.

It must in truth be admitted that the main effect of the spectacle of the misery of the toilers at the rope was to enhance the passengers' sense of the value of their seats upon the coach, and to cause them to hold on to them more desperately than before. If the passengers could only have felt assured that neither they nor their friends would ever fall from the top, it is probable that, beyond contributing to the funds for liniments and bandages, they would have troubled themselves extremely little about those who dragged the coach.

I am well aware that this will appear to the men and women of the twentieth century as incredible inhumanity, but there are two facts, both very curious, which partly explain it. In the first place, it was firmly and sincerely believed that there was no other way in which Society could get along, except the many pulled at the rope and the few rode, and not only this, but that no very radical improvement even was possible, either in the harness, the coach, the roadway, or the distribution of the toil. It had always been as it was, and it always would be so. It was a pity, but it could not be helped, and philosophy forbade wasting compassion on what was beyond remedy.

The other fact is yet more curious, consisting in a singular hallucination which those on the top of the coach generally shared, that they were not exactly like their brothers and sisters who pulled at the rope, but of finer clay, in some way belonging to a higher order of beings who might justly expect to be drawn. This seems unaccountable, but, as I once rode on this very coach and shared that very hallucination, I ought to be believed. The strangest thing about the hallucination was that those who had but just climbed up from the ground, before they had outgrown the marks of the rope upon their hands, began to fall under its influence. As for those whose parents and grandparents before them had been so fortunate as to keep their seats on the top, the conviction they cherished of the essential difference between their sort of humanity and the common article was absolute ...

Production and Distribution

[T]he warehouse ... [provided a] remarkable illustration ... of the prodigiously multiplied efficiency which perfect organization can give to labor. It is like a gigantic mill, into the hopper of which goods are being constantly poured by the train-load and ship-load, to issue at the other end in packages of pounds and ounces, yards and inches, pints and gallons, corresponding to the infinitely complex personal needs of half a million people. Dr. Leete, with the assistance of data furnished by me as to the way goods were sold in my day, figured out some astounding results in the way of the economies effected by the modern system.

As we set out homeward, I said: "After what I have seen today, together with what you have told me, and what I learned under Miss Leete's tutelage at the sample store, I have a tolerably clear idea of your system of distribution, and how it enables you to dispense with a circulating medium. But I should like very much to know something more about your system of production. You have told me in general how your industrial army is levied and organized, but who directs its efforts? What supreme authority determines what shall be done in every department, so that enough of everything is produced and yet no labor wasted? It seems to me that this must be a wonderfully complex and difficult function, requiring very unusual endowments."

"Does it indeed seem so to you?" responded Dr. Leete. "I assure you that it is nothing of the kind, but on the other hand so simple, and depending on principles so obvious and easily applied, that the functionaries at Washington to whom it is trusted require to be nothing more than men of fair abilities to discharge it to the entire satisfaction of the nation. The machine which they direct is indeed a vast one, but so logical in its principles and direct and simple in its workings, that it all but runs itself; and nobody but a fool could derange it, as I think you will agree after a few words of explanation. Since you already have a pretty good idea of the working of the distributive system, let us begin at that end. Even in your day statisticians were able to tell you the number of yards of cotton, velvet, woolen, the number of barrels of flour, potatoes, butter, number of pairs of shoes, hats, and umbrellas annually consumed by the nation. Owing to the fact that production was in private hands, and that there was no way of getting statistics of actual distribution, these figures were not exact, but they were nearly so. Now that every pin which is given out from a national warehouse is recorded, of course the figures of consumption for any week, month, or year, in the possession of the department of distribution at the end of that period, are precise. On these figures, allowing for tendencies to increase or decrease and for any special causes likely to affect demand, the estimates, say for a year ahead, are based. These estimates, with a proper margin for security, having been accepted by the general administration, the responsibility of the distributive department ceases until the goods are delivered to it. I speak of the estimates being furnished for an entire year ahead, but in reality they cover that much time only in case of the great staples for which the demand can be calculated on as steady. In the great majority of smaller industries for the product of which popular taste fluctuates, and novelty is frequently required, production is kept barely ahead of consumption, the distributive department furnishing frequent estimates based on the weekly state of demand.

"Now the entire field of productive and constructive industry is divided into ten great departments, each representing a group of allied industries, each particular industry being in turn represented by a subordinate bureau, which has a complete record of the plant and force under its control, of the present product, and means of increasing it. The estimates of the distributive department, after adoption by the administration, are sent as mandates to the ten great departments, which allot them to the subordinate bureaus representing the particular industries, and these set the men at work. Each bureau is responsible for the task given it, and this responsibility is enforced by departmental oversight and that of the administration; nor does the distributive department accept the product without its own inspection; while even if in the hands of the consumer an article turns out unfit, the system enables the fault to be traced back to the original work-man. The production of the commodities for actual public consumption does not, of course, require by any means all the national force of workers. After the necessary contingents have been detailed for the various industries, the amount of labor left for other employment is expended in creating fixed capital, such as buildings, machinery, engineering works, and so forth."

"One point occurs to me," I said, "on which I should think there might be dissatisfaction. Where there is no opportunity for private enterprise, how is there any assurance that the claims of small minorities of the people to have articles produced, for which there is no wide demand, will be respected? An official decree at any moment may deprive them of the means of gratifying some special taste, merely because the majority does not share it."

"That would be tyranny indeed," replied Dr. Leete, "and you may be very sure that it does not happen with us, to whom liberty is as dear as equality or fraternity. As you come to know our system better, you will see that our officials are in fact, and not merely in name, the agents and servants of the people. The administration has no power to stop the production of any commodity for which there continues to be a demand. Suppose the demand for any article declines to such a point that its production becomes very costly. The price has to be raised in proportion, of course, but as long as the consumer cares to pay it, the production goes on. Again, suppose an article not before produced is demanded. If the administration doubts the reality of the demand, a popular petition guaranteeing a certain basis of consumption compels it to produce the desired article. A government, or a majority, which should undertake to tell the people, or a minority, what they were to eat, drink, or wear, as I believe governments in America did in your day, would be regarded as a curious anachronism indeed. Possibly you had reasons for tolerating these infringements of personal independence, but we should not think them endurable. I am glad you raised this point, for it has given me a chance to show you how much more direct and efficient is the control over production exercised by the individual citizen now than it was in your day, when what you called private initiative prevailed, though it should have been called capitalist initiative, for the average private citizen had little enough share in it."

"You speak of raising the price of costly articles," I said, "How can prices be regulated in a country where there is no competition between buyers or sellers?"

"Just as they were with you," replied Dr. Leete. "You think that needs explaining," he added, as I looked incredulous, "but the explanation need not be long; the cost of the labor which produced it was recognized as the legitimate basis of the price of an article in your day, and so it is in ours. In your day, it was the difference in wages that made the difference in the cost of labor; now it is the relative number of hours constituting a day's work in different trades, the maintenance of the worker being equal in all cases. The cost of a man's work in a trade so difficult that in order to attract volunteers the hours have to be fixed at four a day is twice as great as that in a trade where the men work eight hours. The result as to the cost of labor, you see, is just the same as if the man working four hours were paid, under your system, twice the wages the other gets. This calculation applied to the labor employed in the various processes of a manufactured article gives its price relatively to other articles. Besides the cost of production and transportation, the factor of scarcity affects the prices of some commodities. As regards the great staples of life, of which an abundance can always be secured, scarcity is eliminated as a factor. There is always a large surplus kept on hand from which any fluctuations of demand or supply can be corrected, even in most cases of bad crops. The prices of the staples grow less year by year, but rarely, if ever, rise. There are, however, certain classes of articles permanently, and others temporarily, unequal to the demand, as, for example, fresh fish or dairy products in the latter category, and the products of high skill and rare materials in the other. All that can be done here is to equalize the inconvenience of the scarcity. This is done by temporarily raising the price if the scarcity be temporary, or fixing it high if it be permanent. High prices in your day meant restriction of the articles affected to the rich, but nowadays, when the means of all are the same, the effect is only that those to whom the articles seem most desirable are the ones who purchase them. Of course the nation, as any other caterer for the public needs must be, is frequently left with small lots of goods on its hands by changes in taste, unseasonable weather, and various other causes. These it has to dispose of at a sacrifice just as merchants often did in your day, charging up the loss to the expenses of the business. Owing, however, to the vast body of consumers to which such lots can be simultaneously offered, there is rarely any difficulty in getting rid of them at trifling loss. I have given you now some general notion of our system of production, as well as distribution. Do you find it as complex as you expected?"

I admitted that nothing could be much simpler.

"I am sure," said Dr. Leete, "that it is within the truth to say that the head of one of the myriad private businesses of your day, who had to maintain sleepless vigilance against the fluctuations of the market, the machinations of his rivals, and the failure of his debtors, had a far more trying task than the group of men at Washington who nowadays direct the industries of the entire nation. All this merely shows, my dear fellow, how much easier it is to do things the right way than the wrong. It is easier for a general up in a balloon, with perfect survey of the field, to maneuver a million men to victory than for a sergeant to manage a platoon in a thicket."

"The general of this army, including the flower of the manhood of the nation, must be the foremost man in the country, really greater even than the President of the United States," I said.

"He is the President of the United States," replied Dr. Leete, "or rather the most important function of the presidency is the headship of the industrial army."

"How is he chosen?" I asked.

"I explained to you before," replied Dr. Leete, "when I was describing the force of the motive of emulation among all grades of the industrial army, that the line of promotion for the meritorious lies through three grades to the officer's grade, and thence up through the lieutenancies to the captaincy or foremanship, and superintendency or colonel's rank. Next, with an intervening grade in some of the larger trades, come the general of the guild, under whose immediate control all the operations of the trade are conducted. This officer is at the head of the national bureau representing his trade, and is responsible for its work to the administration. The general of his guild holds a splendid position, and one which amply satisfies the ambition of most men, but above his rank, which may be compared—to follow the military analogies familiar to you—to that of a general of division or major-general, is that of the chiefs of the ten great departments, or groups of allied trades. The chiefs of these ten grand divisions of the industrial army may be compared to your commanders of army corps, or lieutenant-generals, each having from a dozen to a score of generals of separate guilds reporting to him. Above these ten great officers, who form his council, is the general-in-chief, who is the President of the United States.

"The general-in-chief of the industrial army must have passed through all the grades below him, from the common laborers up. Let us see how he rises. As I have told you, it is simply by the excellence of his record as a worker that one rises through the grades of the privates and becomes a candidate for a lieutenancy. Through the lieutenancies he rises to the colonelcy, or superintendent's position, by appointment from above, strictly limited to the candidates of the best records. The general of the guild appoints to the ranks under him, but he himself is not appointed, but chosen by suffrage."

"By suffrage!" I exclaimed. "Is not that ruinous to the discipline of the guild, by tempting the candidates to intrigue for the support of the workers under them?"

"So it would be, no doubt," replied Dr. Leete, "if the workers had any suffrage to exercise, or anything to say about the choice. But they have nothing. Just here comes in a peculiarity of our system. The general of the guild is chosen from among the superintendents by vote of the honorary members of the guild, that is, of those who have served their time in the guild and received their discharge. As you know, at the age of forty-five we are mustered out of the army of industry, and have the residue of life for the pursuit of our own improvement or recreation. Of course, however, the associations of our active lifetime retain a powerful hold on us. The companionships we formed then remain our companionships till the end of life. We always continue honorary members of our former guilds, and retain the keenest and most jealous interest in their welfare and repute in the hands of the following generation. In the clubs maintained by the honorary members of the several guilds, in which we meet socially, there are no topics of conversation so commonly as those which relate to these matters, and the young aspirants for guild leadership who can pass the criticism of us old fellows are likely to be pretty well equipped. Recognizing this fact, the nation entrusts to the honorary members of each guild the election of its general, and I venture to claim that no previous form of society could have developed a body of electors so ideally adapted to their office, as regards absolute impartiality, knowledge of the special qualifications and record of candidates, solicitude for the best result, and complete absence of self-interest.

"Each of the ten lieutenant-generals or heads of departments is himself elected from among the generals of the guilds grouped as a department, by vote of the honorary members of the guilds thus grouped. Of course there is a tendency on the part of each guild to vote for its own general, but no guild of any group has nearly enough votes to elect a man not supported by most of the others. I assure you that these elections are exceedingly lively."

"The President, I suppose, is selected from among the ten heads of the great departments," I suggested.

"Precisely, but the heads of departments are not eligible to the presidency till they have been a certain number of years out of office. It is rarely that a man passes through all the grades to the headship of a department much before he is forty, and at the end of a five years' term he is usually forty-five. If more, he still serves through his term, and if less, he is nevertheless discharged from the industrial army at its termination. It would not do for him to return to the ranks. The interval before he is a candidate for the presidency is intended to give time for him to recognize fully that he has returned into the general mass of the nation, and is identified with it rather than with the industrial army. Moreover, it is expected that he will employ this period in studying the general condition of the army, instead of that of the special group of guilds of which he was the head. From among the former heads of departments who may be eligible at the time, the President is elected by vote of all the men of the nation who are not connected with the industrial army."

"The army is not allowed to vote for President?"

"Certainly not. That would be perilous to its discipline, which it is the business of the President to maintain as the representative of the nation at large. His right hand for this purpose is the inspectorate, a highly important department of our system; to the inspectorate come all complaints or information as to defects in goods, insolence or inefficiency of officials, or dereliction of any sort in the public service. The inspectorate, however, does not wait for complaints. Not only is it on the alert to catch and sift every rumor of a fault in the service, but it is its business, by systematic and constant oversight and inspection of every branch of the army, to find out what is going wrong before anybody else does. The President is usually not far from fifty when elected, and serves five years, forming an honorable exception to the rule of retirement at forty-five. At the end of his term of office, a national Congress is called to receive his report and approve or condemn it. If it is approved, Congress usually elects him to represent the nation for five years more in the international council. Congress, I should also say, passes on the reports of the outgoing heads of departments, and a disapproval renders any one of them ineligible for President. But it is rare, indeed, that the nation has occasion for other sentiments than those of gratitude toward its high officers. As to their ability, to have risen from the ranks, by tests so various and severe, to their positions, is proof in itself of extraordinary qualities, while as to faithfulness, our social system leaves them absolutely without any other motive than that of winning the esteem of their fellow citizens. Corruption is impossible in a society where there is neither poverty to be bribed nor wealth to bribe, while as to demagoguery or intrigue for office, the conditions of promotion render them out of the question."

"One point I do not quite understand," I said. "Are the members of the liberal professions eligible to the presidency? and if so, how are they ranked with those who pursue the industries proper?"

"They have no ranking with them," replied Dr. Leete. "The members of the technical professions, such as engineers and architects, have a ranking with the constructive guilds; but the members of the liberal professions, the doctors and teachers, as well as the artists and men of letters who obtain remissions of industrial service, do not belong to the industrial army. On this ground they vote for the President, but are not eligible to his office. One of its main duties being the control and discipline of the industrial army, it is essential that the President should have passed through all its grades to understand his business."

"That is reasonable," I said; "but if the doctors and teachers do not know enough of industry to be President, neither, I should think, can the President know enough of medicine and education to control those departments."

"No more does he," was the reply. "Except in the general way that he is responsible for the enforcement of the laws as to all classes, the President has nothing to do with the faculties of medicine and education, which are controlled by boards of regents of their own, in which the President is ex-officio chairman, and has the casting vote. These regents, who, of course, are responsible to Congress, are chosen by the honorary members of the guilds of education and medicine, the retired teachers and doctors of the country."

"Do you know," I said, "the method of electing officials by votes of the retired members of the guilds is nothing more than the application on a national scale of the plan of government by alumni, which we used to a slight extent occasionally in the management of our higher educational institutions."

"Did you, indeed?" exclaimed Dr. Leete, with animation. "That is quite new to me, and I fancy will be to most of us, and of much interest as well. There has been great discussion as to the germ of the idea, and we fancied that there was for once something new under the sun. Well! well! In your higher educational institutions! that is interesting indeed. You must tell me more of that."

"Truly, there is very little more to tell than I have told already," I replied. "If we had the germ of your idea, it was but as a germ …"

[Later Julian West attends a church service and hears the following sermon.—Eds.]

Mr. Barton's Sermon

"We have had among us, during the past week, a critic from the nineteenth century, a living representative of the epoch of our great-grandparents. It would be strange if a fact so extraordinary had not somewhat strongly affected our imaginations. Perhaps most of us have been stimulated to some effort to realize the society of a century ago, and figure to ourselves what it must have been like to live then. In inviting you now to consider certain reflections upon this subject which have occurred to me, I presume that I shall rather follow than divert the course of your own thoughts …

"Although the idea of the vital unity of the family of mankind, the reality of human brotherhood, was very far from being apprehended by them as the moral axiom it seems to us, yet it is a mistake to suppose that there was no feeling at all corresponding to it. I could read you passages of great beauty from some of their writers which show that the conception was clearly attained by a few, and no doubt vaguely by many more. Moreover, it must not be forgotten that the nineteenth century was in name Christian, and the fact that the entire commercial and industrial frame of society was the embodiment of the anti-Christian spirit must have had some weight, though I admit it was strangely little, with the nominal followers of Jesus Christ.

"When we inquire why it did not have more, why, in general, long after a vast majority of men had agreed as to the crying abuses of the existing social arrangement, they still tolerated it, or contented themselves with talking of petty reforms in it, we come upon an extraordinary fact. It was the sincere belief of even the best of men at that epoch that the only stable elements in human nature, on which a social system could be safely founded were its worst propensities. They had been taught and believed that greed and self-seeking were all that held mankind together, and that all human associations would fall to pieces if anything were done to blunt the edge of these motives or curb their operation. In a word, they believed—even those who longed to believe otherwise—the exact reverse of what seems to us self-evident; they believed, that is, that the anti-social qualities of men, and not their social qualities, were what furnished the cohesive force of society. It seemed reasonable to them that men lived together solely for the purpose of overreaching and oppressing one another, and of being overreached and oppressed, and that while a society that gave full scope to these propensities could stand, there would be little chance for one based on the idea of co-operation for the benefit of all. It seems absurd to expect any one to believe that convictions like these were ever seriously entertained by men; but that they were not only entertained by our great-grandfathers, but were responsible for the long delay in doing away with the ancient order, after a conviction of its intolerable abuses had become general, is as well established as any fact in history can be. Just here you will find the explanation of the profound pessimism of the literature of the last quarter of the nineteenth century, the note of melancholy in its poetry, and the cynicism of its humor.

"Feeling that the condition of the race was unendurable, they had no clear hope of anything better. They believed that the evolution of humanity had resulted in leading it into a *cul de sac*, and that there was no way of getting forward. The frame of men's minds at this time is strikingly illustrated by treatises which have come down to us, and may even now be consulted in our libraries by the curious, in which laborious arguments are pursued to prove that despite the evil plight of men, life was still, by some slight preponderance of considerations, probably better worth living than leaving. Despising themselves, they despised their Creator. There was a general decay of religious belief. Pale and watery gleams, from skies thickly veiled by doubt and dread, alone lighted up the chaos of earth. That men should doubt Him whose breath is in their nostrils, or dread the hands that moulded them, seems to us indeed a pitiable insanity; but we must remember that children who are brave by day have sometimes foolish fears at night. The dawn has come since then. It is very easy to believe in the fatherhood of God in the twentieth century ...

"You know the story of that last, greatest, and most bloodless of revolutions. In the time of one generation men laid aside the social traditions and practices of barbarians, and assumed a social order worthy of rational and human beings. Ceasing to be predatory in their habits, they became co-workers, and found in fraternity, at once, the science of wealth and happiness. 'What shall I eat and drink, and wherewithal shall I be clothed?' stated as a problem beginning and ending in self, had been an anxious and an endless one. But when once it was conceived, not from the individual, but the fraternal standpoint, 'What shall we eat and drink, and wherewithal shall we be clothed?'—its difficulties vanished.

"Poverty with servitude had been the result, for the mass of humanity, of attempting to solve the problem of maintenance from the individual standpoint, but no sooner had the nation become the sole capitalist and employer than not alone did plenty replace poverty, but the last vestige of the serfdom of man to man disappeared from earth. Human slavery, so often vainly scotched, at last was killed. The means of subsistence no longer doled out by men to women, by employer to employed, by rich to poor, was distributed from a common stock as among children at the father's table. It was impossible for a man any longer to use his fellowmen as tools for his own profit. His esteem was the only sort of gain he could thenceforth make out of him. There was no more either arrogance or servility in the relations of human beings to one another. For the first time since the creation every man stood up straight before God. The fear of want and the lust of gain became extinct motives when abundance was assured to all and immoderate possessions were made impossible of attainment. There were no more beggars nor almoners. Equity left charity without an occupation. The Ten Commandments became well-nigh obsolete in a world where there was no temptation to theft, no occasion to lie either for fear or favor, no room for envy where all were equal, and little provocation to violence where men were disarmed of power to injure one another. Humanity's ancient dream of liberty, equality, fraternity, mocked by so many ages, at last was realized.

"As in the old society the generous, the just, the tender-hearted had been placed at a disadvantage by the possession of those qualities, so in the new society the cold-hearted, the greedy, and self-seeking found themselves out of joint with the world. Now that the conditions of life for the first time ceased to operate as a forcing process to develop the brutal qualities of human nature, and the premium which had heretofore encouraged selfishness was not only removed, but placed upon unselfishness, it was for the first time possible to see what unperverted human nature really was like. The depraved tendencies, which had previously overgrown and obscured the better to so large an extent, now withered like cellar fungi in the open air, and the nobler qualities showed a sudden luxuriance which turned cynics into panegyrists and for the first time in human history tempted mankind to fall in love with itself. Soon was fully revealed, what the divines and philosophers of the old world never would have believed, that human nature in its essential qualities is good, not bad, that men by their natural intention and structure are generous, not selfish, pitiful, not cruel, sympathetic, not arrogant, godlike in aspiration, instinct with divinest impulses of tenderness and self-sacrifice, images of God indeed, not the travesties upon Him they had seemed. The constant pressure, through numberless generations, of conditions of life which might have perverted angels, had not been able to essentially alter the natural nobility of the stock, and these conditions once removed, like a bent tree, it had sprung back to its normal uprightness ...

"But how is it with us who stand on this height which they gazed up to? Already we have well-nigh forgotten, except when it is especially called to our minds by some occasion like the present, that it was not always with men as it is now. It is a strain on our imaginations to conceive the social arrangements of our immediate ancestors. We find them grotesque. The solution of the problem of physical maintenance so as to banish care and crime, so far from seeming to us an ultimate attainment, appears but as a preliminary to anything like real human progress. We have but relieved ourselves of an impertinent and needless harassment which hindered our ancestors from undertaking the real ends of existence. We are merely stripped for the race; no more. We are like a child which has just learned to stand upright and to walk. It is a great event, from the child's point of view, when he first walks. Perhaps he fancies that there can be little beyond that achievement, but a year later he has forgotten that he could not always walk. His horizon did but widen when he rose, and enlarge as he moved. A great event indeed, in one sense, was his first step, but only as a beginning, not as the end. His true career was but then first entered on. The enfranchisement of humanity in the last century, from mental and physical absorption in working and scheming for the mere bodily necessities, may be regarded as a species of second birth of the race, without which its first birth to an existence that was but a burden would forever have remained unjustified, but whereby it is now abundantly vindicated. Since then, humanity has entered on a new phase of spiritual development, an evolution of higher faculties, the very existence of which in human nature our ancestors scarcely suspected. In place of the dreary hopelessness of the nineteenth century, its profound pessimism as to the future of humanity, the animating idea of the present age is an enthusiastic conception of the opportunities of our earthly existence, and the unbounded possibilities of human nature. The betterment of mankind from generation to generation, physically, mentally, morally, is recognized as the one great object supremely worthy of effort and of sacrifice. We believe the race for the first time to have entered on the realization of God's ideal of it, and each generation must now be a step upward.

"Do you ask what we look for when unnumbered generations shall have passed away? I answer, the way stretches far before us, but the end is lost in light. For twofold is the return of man to God 'who is our home,' the return of the individual by the way of death, and the return of the race by the fulfilment of the evolution, when the divine secret hidden in the germ shall be perfectly unfolded. With a tear for the dark past, turn we then to the dazzling future, and, veiling our eyes, press forward. The long and weary winter of the race is ended. Its summer has begun. Humanity has burst the chrysalis. The heavens are before it."

On Democratic Socialism in the United States

BERNIE SANDERS*

Bernie Sanders is a United States senator from Vermont, a 2016 presidential candidate, and a self-described "democratic socialist." For this, Sanders (1941–) has taken a good deal of criticism from those who regard socialism as, at best, an exotic European import, or at worst as an ideological offshoot of the old Soviet Union or China—but, in either case, as deeply un-American. In this speech, Sanders clarifies his beliefs and attempts to show how many of the fundamental government programs and policies that most Americans view as essential today were once derided as "socialist." These include President Roosevelt's "New Deal," initiatives such as Social Security, and the creation of minimum wage laws, unemployment benefits, the forty-hour work week, and many others. Similarly, President Johnson's later "Great Society" programs, such as Medicare and Medicaid, which guarantee minimum basic levels of health care to the elderly and poor, were likewise vilified as "socialist" at their inception. Unlike some socialists, Sanders says that he is not in favor of the government owning the means of production. Likewise, many of the historical policies he favors are actually much more closely akin to welfare liberalism. Nevertheless, Sanders insists that in an era of great and growing economic inequality, a shrinking middle class, increasing poverty, rampant unemployment and underemployment, and a still-broken health care system, today's federal government must take new proactive steps to address the ills associated with unfettered capitalism. Sanders argues that such state action is firmly in line with Roosevelt's earlier insistence on the centrality of economic rights for achieving real freedom. Some of the measures Sanders advocates—such as a single-payer universal health care system, tuition-free education at public colleges, and a guaranteed "living wage"—will no doubt strike some Americans as "socialist." Sanders might respond that in the future these policies will be as much taken for granted as earlier initiatives that were once condemned as "socialist."

---

* *Source*: https://berniesanders.com/democratic-socialism-in-the-united-states/

ON DEMOCRATIC SOCIALISM IN THE UNITED STATES

In his inaugural remarks in January 1937, in the midst of the Great Depression, President Franklin Delano Roosevelt looked out at the nation and this is what he saw.

He saw tens of millions of its citizens denied the basic necessities of life.

He saw millions of families trying to live on incomes so meager that the pall of family disaster hung over them day by day.

He saw millions denied education, recreation, and the opportunity to better their lot and the lot of their children.

He saw millions lacking the means to buy the products they needed and by their poverty and lack of disposable income denying employment to many other millions.

He saw one-third of a nation ill-housed, ill-clad, ill-nourished.

And he acted. Against the ferocious opposition of the ruling class of his day, people he called economic royalists, Roosevelt implemented a series of programs that put millions of people back to work, took them out of poverty and restored their faith in government. He redefined the relationship of the federal government to the people of our country. He combatted cynicism, fear and despair. He reinvigorated democracy. He transformed the country.

And that is what we have to do today.

And, by the way, almost everything he proposed was called "socialist." Social Security, which transformed life for the elderly in this country was "socialist." The concept of the "minimum wage" was seen as a radical intrusion into the marketplace and was described as "socialist." Unemployment insurance, abolishing child labor, the 40-hour work week, collective bargaining, strong banking regulations, deposit insurance, and job programs that put millions of people to work were all described, in one way or another, as "socialist." Yet, these programs have become the fabric of our nation and the foundation of the middle class.

Thirty years later, in the 1960s, President Johnson passed Medicare and Medicaid to provide health care to millions of senior citizens and families with children, persons with disabilities and some of the most vulnerable people in this county. Once again these vitally important programs were derided by the right wing as socialist programs that were a threat to our American way of life.

That was then. Now is now.

Today, in 2015, despite the Wall Street crash of 2008, which drove this country into the worst economic downturn since the Depression, the American people are clearly better off economically than we were in 1937.

But, here is a very hard truth that we must acknowledge and address. Despite a huge increase in technology and productivity, despite major growth in the U.S. and global economy, tens of millions of American families continue to lack the basic necessities of life, while millions more struggle every day to provide a minimal standard of living for their families. The reality is that for the last 40 years the great middle class of this country has been in decline and faith in our political system is now extremely low.

The rich get much richer. Almost everyone else gets poorer. Super PACs funded by billionaires buy elections. Ordinary people don't vote. We have an economic and political crisis in this country and the same old, same old establishment politics and economics will not effectively address it.

If we are serious about transforming our country, if we are serious about rebuilding the middle class, if we are serious about reinvigorating our democracy, we need to develop a political movement which, once again, is prepared to take on and defeat a ruling class whose greed is destroying our nation. The billionaire class cannot have it all. Our government belongs to all of us, and not just the one percent.

We need to create a culture which, as Pope Francis reminds us, cannot just be based on the worship of money. We must not accept a nation in which billionaires compete as to the size of their super-yachts, while children in America go hungry and veterans sleep out on the streets.

Today, in America, we are the wealthiest nation in the history of the world, but few Americans know that because so much of the new income and wealth goes to the people on top. In fact, over the last 30 years, there has been a massive transfer of wealth – trillions of wealth – going from the middle class to the top one-tenth of 1 percent – a handful of people who have seen a doubling of the percentage of the wealth they own over that period.

Unbelievably, and grotesquely, the top one-tenth of 1 percent owns nearly as much wealth as the bottom 90 percent.

Today, in America, millions of our people are working two or three jobs just to survive. In fact, Americans work longer hours than do the people of any industrialized country. Despite the incredibly hard work and long hours of the American middle class, 58 percent of all new income generated today is going to the top one percent.

Today, in America, as the middle class continues to disappear, median family income, is $4,100 less than it was in 1999. The median male worker made over $700 less than he did 42 years ago, after adjusting for inflation. Last year, the median female worker earned more than $1,000 less than she did in 2007.

Today, in America, the wealthiest country in the history of the world, more than half of older workers have no retirement savings – zero – while millions of elderly and people with disabilities are trying to survive on $12,000 or $13,000 a year. From Vermont to California, older workers are scared to death. "How will I retire with dignity?," they ask?

Today, in America, nearly 47 million Americans are living in poverty and over 20 percent of our children, including 36 percent of African American children, are living in poverty — the highest rate of childhood poverty of nearly any major country on earth.

Today, in America, 29 million Americans have no health insurance and even more are underinsured with outrageously high co-payments and deductibles. Further, with the United States paying the highest prices in the world for prescription drugs, 1 out of 5 patients cannot afford to fill the prescriptions their doctors write.

Today, in America, youth unemployment and underemployment is over 35 percent. Meanwhile, we have more people in jail than any other country and countless lives are being destroyed as we spend $80 billion a year locking up fellow Americans.

The bottom line is that today in America we not only have massive wealth and income inequality, but a power structure which protects that inequality. A handful of super-wealthy campaign contributors have enormous influence over the political process, while their lobbyists determine much of what goes on in Congress.

In 1944, in his State of the Union speech, President Roosevelt outlined what he called a second Bill of Rights. This is one of the most important speeches ever made by a president but, unfortunately, it has not gotten the attention that it deserves.

In that remarkable speech this is what Roosevelt stated, and I quote: "We have come to a clear realization of the fact that true individual freedom cannot exist without economic security and independence. Necessitous men are not free men." End of quote. In other words, real freedom must include economic security. That was Roosevelt's vision 70 years ago. It is my vision today. It is a vision that we have not yet achieved. It is time that we did.

In that speech, Roosevelt described the economic rights that he believed every American was entitled to: The right to a decent job at decent pay, the right to adequate food, clothing, and time off from work, the right for every business, large and small, to function in an atmosphere free from unfair competition and domination by monopolies. The right of all Americans to have a decent home and decent health care.

What Roosevelt was stating in 1944, what Martin Luther King, Jr. stated in similar terms 20 years later and what I believe today, is that true freedom does not occur without economic security.

People are not truly free when they are unable to feed their family. People are not truly free when they are unable to retire with dignity. People are not truly free when they are unemployed or underpaid or when they are exhausted by working long hours. People are not truly free when they have no health care.

So let me define for you, simply and straightforwardly, what democratic socialism means to me. It builds on what Franklin Delano Roosevelt said when he fought for guaranteed economic rights for all Americans. And it builds on what Martin Luther King, Jr. said in 1968 when he stated that; "This country has socialism for the rich, and rugged individualism for the poor." It builds on the success of many other countries around the world that have done a far better job than we have in protecting the needs of their working families, the elderly, the children, the sick and the poor.

Democratic socialism means that we must create an economy that works for all, not just the very wealthy.

Democratic socialism means that we must reform a political system in America today which is not only grossly unfair but, in many respects, corrupt.

It is a system, for example, which during the 1990s allowed Wall Street to spend $5 billion in lobbying and campaign contributions to get deregulated. Then, ten years later, after the greed, recklessness, and illegal behavior of Wall Street led to their collapse, it is a system which provided trillions in government aid to bail them out. Wall Street used their wealth and power to get Congress to do their bidding for deregulation and then, when their greed caused their collapse, they used their wealth and power to get Congress to bail them out. Quite a system!

And, then, to add insult to injury, we were told that not only were the banks too big to fail, the bankers were too big to jail. Kids who get caught possessing marijuana get police records. Wall Street CEOs who help destroy the economy get raises in their salaries. This is what Martin Luther King, Jr. meant by socialism for the rich and rugged individualism for everyone else.

In my view, it's time we had democratic socialism for working families, not just Wall Street, billionaires and large corporations. It means that we should not be providing welfare for corporations, huge tax breaks for the very rich, or trade policies which boost corporate profits as workers lose their jobs. It means that we create a government that works for works for all of us, not just powerful special interests. It means that economic rights must be an essential part of what America stands for.

It means that health care should be a right of all people, not a privilege. This is not a radical idea. It exists in every other major country on earth. Not just Denmark, Sweden or Finland. It exists in Canada, France, Germany and Taiwan. That is why I believe in a Medicare-for-all single payer health care system. Yes. The Affordable Care Act, which I helped write and voted for, is a step forward for this country. But we must build on it and go further.

Medicare for all would not only guarantee health care for all people, not only save middle class families and our entire nation significant sums of money, it would radically improve the lives of all Americans and bring about significant improvements in our economy.

People who get sick will not have to worry about paying a deductible or making a co-payment. They could go to the doctor when they should, and not end up in the emergency room. Business owners will not have to spend enormous amounts of time worrying about how they are going to provide health care for their employees. Workers will not have to be trapped in jobs they do not like simply because their employers are offering them decent health insurance plans. Instead, they will be able to pursue the jobs and work they love, which could be an enormous boon for the economy. And by the way, moving to a Medicare for all program will end the disgrace of Americans paying, by far, the highest prices in the world for prescription drugs.

Democratic socialism means that, in the year 2015, a college degree is equivalent to what a high school degree was 50 years ago – and that public education must allow every person in this country, who has the ability, the qualifications and the desire, the right to go to a public colleges or university tuition free. This is also not a radical idea. It exists today in many countries around the world. In fact, it used to exist in the United States.

Democratic socialism means that our government does everything it can to create a full employment economy. It makes far more sense to put millions of people back to work rebuilding our crumbling infrastructure, than to have a real unemployment rate of almost 10%. It is far smarter to invest in jobs and educational opportunities for unemployed young people, than to lock them up and spend $80 billion a year through mass incarceration.

Democratic socialism means that if someone works forty hours a week, that person should not be living in poverty: that we must raise the minimum wage to a living wage – $15 an hour over the next few years. It means that we join the rest of the world and pass the very strong Paid Family and Medical Leave legislation now in Congress. How can it possibly be that the United States, today, is virtually the only nation on earth, large or small, which does not guarantee that a working class woman can stay home for a reasonable period of time with her new-born baby? How absurd is that?

Democratic socialism means that we have government policy which does not allow the greed and profiteering of the fossil fuel industry to destroy our environment and our planet, and that we have a moral responsibility to combat climate change and leave this planet healthy and habitable for our kids and grandchildren.

Democratic socialism means, that in a democratic, civilized society the wealthiest people and the largest corporations must pay their fair share of taxes. Yes. Innovation, entrepreneurship and business success should be rewarded. But greed for the sake of greed is not something that public policy should support. It is not acceptable that in a rigged economy in the last two years the wealthiest 15 Americans saw their wealth increase by $170 billion, more wealth than is owned by the bottom 130 million Americans. Let us not forget what Pope Francis has so elegantly stated; "We have created new idols. The worship of the golden calf of old has found a new and heartless image in the cult of money and the dictatorship of an economy which is faceless and lacking any truly humane goal."

It is not acceptable that major corporations stash their profits in the Cayman Islands and other offshore tax havens to avoid paying $100 billion in taxes each and every year. It is not acceptable that hedge fund managers pay a lower effective tax rate than nurses or truck drivers. It is not acceptable that billionaire families are able to leave virtually all of their wealth to their families without paying a reasonable estate tax. It is not acceptable that Wall Street speculators are able to gamble trillions of dollars in the derivatives market without paying a nickel in taxes on those transactions.

Democratic socialism, to me, does not just mean that we must create a nation of economic and social justice. It also means that we must create a vibrant democracy based on the principle of one person one vote. It is extremely sad that the United States, one of the oldest democracies on earth, has one of the lowest voter turnouts of any major country, and that millions of young and working class people have given up on our political system entirely. Every American should be embarrassed that in our last national election 63% of the American people, and 80% of young people, did not vote. Clearly, despite the efforts of many Republican governors to suppress the vote, we must make it easier for people to participate in the political process, not harder. It is not too much to demand that everyone 18 years of age is registered to vote – end of discussion.

Further, it is unacceptable that we have a corrupt campaign finance system which allows millionaires, billionaires and large corporations to contribute as much as they want to Super Pacs to elect candidates who will represent their special interests. We must overturn Citizens United and move to public funding of elections.

So the next time you hear me attacked as a socialist, remember this:

I don't believe government should own the means of production, but I do believe that the middle class and the working families who produce the wealth of America deserve a fair deal.

I believe in private companies that thrive and invest and grow in America instead of shipping jobs and profits overseas.

I believe that most Americans can pay lower taxes – if hedge fund managers who make billions manipulating the marketplace finally pay the taxes they should.

I don't believe in special treatment for the top 1%, but I do believe in equal treatment for African-Americans who are right to proclaim the moral principle that Black Lives Matter.

I despise appeals to nativism and prejudice, and I do believe in immigration reform that gives Hispanics and others a pathway to citizenship and a better life.

I don't believe in some foreign "ism", but I believe deeply in American idealism.

I'm not running for president because it's my turn, but because it's the turn of all of us to live in a nation of hope and opportunity not for some, not for the few, but for all …

PART 7

FASCISM

Fascism emerged after World War I as a reaction against the two leading ideologies of the time, liberalism and socialism. Fascists complained that liberalism and socialism divide the members of society against one another—liberals by emphasizing individualism, socialists by stressing the conflict between social classes. In contrast, fascism presents a picture of individuals and classes merely as cells in a much larger, all-embracing organism—the society or state—which can be strong only when all the parts unite behind a single party and a supreme leader.

This was the core of the fascist ideology as it developed in Italy under Benito Mussolini (1883–1945) and in Germany under Adolf Hitler (1889–1945). Mussolini's Fascist Party took its name from the Italian word *fasciare*, "to fasten or bind," and its derivative *fasci*, meaning "group." Fascism was the force that would lead Italy to a new empire as glorious as the Roman Empire of ancient times. Everything and everyone would have to be dedicated to the service of the state, which was the legal and institutional embodiment of the power, unity, and majesty of the Italian people or nation. As Mussolini and his followers repeated over and over again, "Everything in the state, nothing outside the state, nothing against the state."

As this slogan suggests, fascism in its pure form is a totalitarian ideology. In fact, the Italian fascists coined the word "totalitarian" to define their antidemocratic aims and to distinguish their ideology from liberalism and socialism, which they saw as advocating democracy. Democracy requires equality of some sort, whether it be in the liberals' insistence on equality before the law and equal opportunity for individuals or in the socialists' insistence on equal power for all in a classless society. But Mussolini and his followers had no use for either democracy or equality. Democracy is all talk and no action; equality merely restrains the strong in order to protect the weak. The fascists did appeal to the masses for support, to be sure, but in their view the common people were to exercise power not by thinking or speaking for themselves but by blindly following their leaders to victory. As another of Mussolini's many slogans proclaimed, "Believe, obey, fight!"

Hitler and his National Socialists (or "Nazis" for short) adopted a similar position in Germany in the 1920s and 1930s. With Hitler as supreme leader, the Nazi Party was to unify all German-speaking peoples into a single state that would go on to become a great new empire (or *Reich*). Hence the Nazi slogan, *Ein Volk, ein Reich, ein Führer*—"one people, one empire, one supreme leader."

The chief difference between German Nazism and Italian fascism was the racial element in Nazi theory. For Nazis, race is the fundamental fact of human life. There is no such thing as a single or universal human nature, for human beings belong to different races, and each race has its own unique characteristics and its own destiny. One race, the Aryan, is naturally stronger, more intelligent, and more creative than all of the others, and the destiny of this "master race" is to subjugate or eliminate all other races.

Aside from this important difference, fascism and Nazism are essentially similar. Both emerged from a combination of forces that developed during the nineteenth century—the Counter-Enlightenment, elitism, irrationalism, racism, and nationalism. The Counter-Enlightenment included a number of thinkers, such as Joseph de Maistre (see Part 4), who rejected the key elements of eighteenth-century Enlightenment thought (for a classic exposition of Enlightenment thought, see Immanuel Kant's essay "What Is Enlightenment?" in Part 3). The Counter-Enlightenment thinkers denied that reason alone can bring about great progress and improvement in human life. Counter-Enlightenment theorists and various elitist theories of the late 1800s were also alike in denying that the common people are capable of ruling themselves. In this way both contributed to the antidemocratic character of fascism. This was also true of such "irrationalists" as Georges Sorel (1847–1922), who maintained that "myths" and emotions play a greater part than reason in motivating the masses.

Finally, and perhaps most significantly, fascists are intensely nationalistic. Nationalism is the belief that the world is naturally divided into distinct nations, or peoples, each of which ought to be united in its own political unit, or nation-state. Although nationalistic tendencies have been evident in many parts of the world throughout history, they became especially powerful in the latter half of the nineteenth century, particularly in Italy and Germany—two countries that were not forged into distinct nation-states until the 1860s and 1870s. The desire to preserve and strengthen this unity played a large part in the rise of Italian fascism and German Nazism.

Mussolini and Hitler both died in 1945, the former killed by antifascist Italian guerrillas, the latter a suicide in his Berlin bunker. Their defeat in World War II dealt a crushing, if not fatal, blow to the fascists and Nazis. We should not forget that fascism was not confined to Italy and Germany, nor has it altogether disappeared—as the activities of various fascists and neo-Nazis in Europe, South Africa, the Middle East, and the Americas clearly remind us. The neo-Nazi elements of the "militia" movement in the United States have attracted Americans opposed to racial integration and the idea of a "color-blind" constitution. They hold that the "white" race should dominate blacks, Jews, and other "inferior" races. Their numbers may not be large, but they provide evidence that the legacy of Mussolini and Hitler is still a powerful political force.

Civilization and Race

JOSEPH-ARTHUR DE GOBINEAU*

Why do great empires and civilizations rise to power and glory, only to decay and disappear? In the nineteenth century, the French diplomat Joseph-Arthur de Gobineau (1816–1882) thought he had found a simple but compelling answer to this question: *race*. In his *Essay on the Inequality of Human Races* (1853–1855), from which the following selection is taken, Gobineau argued that the mingling of races has always led, and must continue to lead, to the downfall of great civilizations.

---

* *Source*: Joseph-Arthur de Gobineau, *The Inequality of Human Races*, translated by Adrian Collins (New York: G.P. Putnam's Sons, 1915), pp. 1–2, 25, 150–151, 154–155, 178–179, 205–211.

THE INEQUALITY OF HUMAN RACES: INTRODUCTION

... The racial question overshadows all other problems of history, it holds the key to them all, and the inequality of the races from whose fusion a people is formed is enough to explain the whole course of its destiny. Every one must have had some inkling of this colossal truth, for every one must have seen how certain agglomerations of men have descended on some country, and utterly transformed its way of life; how they have shown themselves able to strike out a new vein of activity where, before their coming, all had been sunk in torpor. Thus, to take an example, a new era of power was opened for Great Britain by the Anglo-Saxon invasion, thanks to a decree of Providence, which by sending to this island some of the peoples governed by the sword of your Majesty's illustrious ancestors, was to bring two branches of the same nation under the scepter of a single house—a house that can trace its glorious title to the dim sources of the heroic nation itself.

Recognizing that both strong and weak races exist, I preferred to examine the former, to analyze their qualities, and especially to follow them back to their origins. By this method I convinced myself at last that everything great, noble, and fruitful in the works of man on this earth, in science, art, and civilization, derives from a single starting-point, is the development of a single germ and the result of a single thought; it belongs to one family alone, the different branches of which have reigned in all the civilized countries of the universe ...

Chapter I: The Mortal Disease of Civilizations and Societies
Proceeds from General Causes Common to Them All

The fall of civilizations is the most striking, and, at the same time, the most obscure, of all the phenomena of history. It is a calamity that strikes fear into the soul, and yet has always something so mysterious and so vast in reserve, that the thinker is never weary of looking at it, of studying it, of groping for its secrets. No doubt the birth and growth of peoples offer a very remarkable subject for the observer; the successive development of societies, their gains, their conquests, their triumphs, have something that vividly takes the imagination and holds it captive. But all these events, however great one may think them, seem to be easy of explanation; one accepts them as the mere outcome of the intellectual gifts of man. Once we recognize these gifts, we are not astonished at their results; they explain, by the bare fact of their existence, the great stream of being whose source they are. So, on this score, there need be no difficulty or hesitation. But when we see that after a time of strength and glory all human societies come to their decline and fall—all, I say, not this or that; when we see in what awful silence the earth shows us, scattered on its surface, the wrecks of the civilizations that have preceded our own—not merely the famous civilizations, but also many others, of which we know nothing but the names, and some, that lie as skeletons of stone, deep in world-old forests, and have not left us even this shadow of a memory; when the mind returns to our modern States, reflects on their extreme youth, and confesses that they are a growth of yesterday, and that some of them are already toppling to their fall: then at last we recognize, not without a certain philosophic shudder, that the words of the prophets on the instability of mortal things apply with the same rigor to civilizations as to peoples, to people as to States, to States as to individuals; and we are forced to affirm that every assemblage of men, however ingenious the network of social relations that protects it, acquires on the very day of its birth, hidden among the elements of its life, the seed of an inevitable death.

But what is this seed, this principle of death? Is it uniform, as its results are, and do all civilizations perish from the same cause?

At first sight we are tempted to answer in the negative; for we have seen the fall of many empires, Assyria, Egypt, Greece, Rome, amid the clash of events that had no likeness one to the other. Yet, if we pierce below the surface, we soon find that this very necessity of coming to an end, that weighs imperiously on all societies without exception, presupposes such a general cause, which, though hidden, cannot be explained away. When we start from this fixed principle of natural death—a principle unaffected by all the cases of violent death—we see that all civilizations, after they have lasted some time, betray to the observer some little symptoms of uneasiness, which are difficult to define, but not less difficult to deny; these are of a like nature in all times and all places. We may admit one obvious point of difference between the fall of States and that of civilizations, when we see the same kind of culture sometimes persisting in a country under foreign rule and weathering every storm of calamity, at other times being destroyed or changed by the slightest breath of a contrary wind; but we are, in the end, more and more driven to the idea that the principle of death which can be seen at the base of all societies is not only inherent in their life, but also uniform and the same for all.

… How and why is a nation's vigor lost? How does it degenerate? These are the questions which we must try to answer. Up to the present, men have been content with finding the word, without unveiling the reality that lies behind. This further step I shall now attempt to take.

The word *degenerate*, when applied to a people, means (as it ought to mean) that the people has no longer the same intrinsic value as it had before, because it has no longer the same blood in its veins, continual adulterations having gradually affected the quality of that blood. In other words, though the nation bears the name given by its founders, the name no longer connotes the same race; in fact, the man of a decadent time, the *degenerate* man properly so called, is a different being, from the racial point of view from the heroes of the great ages. I agree that he still keeps something of their essence; but the more he degenerates the more attenuated does this "something" become. The heterogeneous elements that henceforth prevail in him give him quite a different nationality—a very original one, no doubt, but such originality is not to be envied. He is only a very distant kinsman of those he still calls his ancestors. He, and his civilization with him, will certainly die on the day when the primordial race-unit is so broken up and swamped by the influx of foreign elements, that its effective qualities have no longer a sufficient freedom of action. It will not, of course, absolutely disappear, but it will in practice be so beaten down and enfeebled, that its power will be felt less and less as time goes on. It is at this point that all the results of degeneration will appear, and the process may be considered complete.

Chapter XIII: The Human Races Are Intellectually Unequal; Mankind Is Not Capable of Infinite Progress

In order to appreciate the intellectual differences between races, we ought first to ascertain the degree of stupidity to which mankind can descend. We know already the highest point that it can reach, namely civilization.

Most scientific observers up to now have been very prone to make out the lowest types as worse than they really are.

Nearly all the early accounts of a savage tribe paint it in hideous colors, far more hideous than the reality. They give it so little power of reason and understanding, that it seems to be on a level with the monkey and below the elephant. It is true that we find the contrary opinion. If a captain is well received in an island, if he meets, as he believes, with a kind and hospitable welcome, and succeeds in making a few natives do a small amount of work with his sailors, then praises are showered on the happy people. They are declared to be fit for anything and capable of everything; and sometimes the enthusiasm bursts all bounds, and swears it has found among them some higher intelligences.

We must appeal from both judgments—harsh and favorable alike. The fact that certain Tahitians have helped to repair a whaler does not make their nation capable of civilization. Because a man of Tonga-Tabu shows goodwill to strangers, he is not necessarily open to ideas of progress. Similarly, we are not entitled to degrade a native of a hitherto unknown coast to the level of the brute, just because he receives his first visitors with a flight of arrows, or because he is found eating raw lizards and mud pies. Such a banquet does not certainly connote a very high intelligence or very cultivated manners. But even in the most hideous cannibal there is a spark of the divine fire, and to some extent the flame of understanding can always be kindled in him. There are no tribes so low that they do not pass some judgments, true or false, just or unjust, on the things around them; the mere existence of such judgments is enough to show that in every branch of mankind some ray of intelligence is kept alive. It is this that makes the most degraded savages accessible to the teachings of religion and distinguishes them in a special manner, of which they are themselves conscious, from even the most intelligent beasts.

Are however these moral possibilities, which lie at the back of every man's consciousness, capable of infinite extension? Do all men possess in an equal degree an unlimited power of intellectual development? In other words, has every human race the capacity for becoming equal to every other? The question is ultimately concerned with the infinite capacity for improvement possessed by the species as a whole, and with the equality of races. I deny both points.

The idea of an infinite progress is very seductive to many modern philosophers, and they support it by declaring that our civilization has many merits and advantages which our differently trained ancestors did not possess. They bring forward all the phenomena that distinguished our modern societies. I have spoken of these already; but I am glad to be able to go through them again.

We are told that our scientific opinions are truer than they were; that our manners are, as a rule, kindly, and our morals better than those of the Greeks and Romans. Especially with regard to political liberty, they say, have we ideas and feelings, beliefs and tolerances, that prove our superiority. There are even some hopeful theorists who maintain that our institutions should lead us straight to that garden of the Hesperides which was sought so long, and with such ill-success, since the time when the ancient navigators reported that it was not in the Canaries ...[1]

A little more serious consideration of history will show what truth there is in these high claims ...

Chapter XVI: Recapitulation; the Respective Characteristics of the Three Great Races; the Superiority of the White Type, and, Within This Type, of the Aryan Family

I have shown the unique place in the organic world occupied by the human species, the profound physical, as well as moral, differences separating it from all other kinds of living creatures. Considering it by itself, I have been able to distinguish, on physiological grounds alone, three great and clearly marked types, the black, the yellow, and the white. However uncertain the aims of physiology may be, however meagre its resources, however defective its methods, it can proceed thus far with absolute certainty.

The negroid [black] variety is the lowest, and stands at the foot of the ladder. The animal character, that appears in the shape of the pelvis, is stamped on the negro from birth, and foreshadows his destiny. His intellect will always move within a very narrow circle. He is not however a mere brute, for behind his low receding brow, in the middle of his skull, we can see signs of a powerful energy, however crude its objects. If his mental faculties are dull or even non-existent, he often has an intensity of desire, and so of will, which may be called terrible. Many of his senses, especially taste and smell, are developed to an extent unknown to the other two races.

The very strength of his sensations is the most striking proof of his inferiority. All food is good in his eyes, nothing disgusts or repels him. What he desires is to eat, to eat furiously, and to excess; no carrion is too revolting to be swallowed by him. It is the same with odors; his inordinate desires are satisfied with all, however coarse or even horrible. To these qualities may be added an instability and capriciousness of feeling, that cannot be tied down to any single object, and which, so far as he is concerned, do away with all distinctions of good and evil. We might even say that the violence with which he pursues the object that has aroused his senses and inflamed his desires is a guarantee of the desires being soon satisfied and the object forgotten. Finally, he is equally careless of his own life and that of others: he kills willingly, for the sake of killing; and this human machine, in whom it is so easy to arouse emotion, shows, in face of suffering, either a monstrous indifference or a cowardice that seeks a voluntary refuge in death.

The yellow race is the exact opposite of this type. The skull points forward, not backward. The forehead is wide and bony, often high and projecting. The shape of the face is triangular, the nose and chin showing none of the coarse protuberances that mark the negro. There is further a general proneness to obesity, which, though not confined to the yellow type, is found there more frequently than in the others. The yellow man has little physical energy, and is inclined to apathy; he commits none of the strange excesses so common among negroes. His desires are feeble, his willpower rather obstinate than violent; his longing for material pleasures, though constant, is kept within bounds. A rare glutton by nature, he shows far more discrimination in his choice of food. He tends to mediocrity in everything; he understands easily enough anything not too deep or sublime. He has a love of utility and a respect for order, and knows the value of a certain amount of freedom. He is practical, in the narrowest sense of the word. He does not dream or theorize; he invents little, but can appreciate and take over what is useful to him. His whole desire is to live in the easiest and most comfortable way possible. The yellow races are thus clearly superior to the black. Every founder of a civilization would wish the backbone of this society, his middle class, to consist of such men. But no civilized society could be created by them; they could not supply its nerve-force, or set in motion the springs of beauty and action.

We come now to the white peoples. These are gifted with reflective energy, or rather with an energetic intelligence. They have a feeling for utility, but in a sense far wider and higher, more courageous and ideal, than the yellow races; a perseverance that takes account of obstacles and ultimately finds a means of overcoming them; a greater physical power, an extraordinary instinct for order, not merely as a guarantee of peace and tranquility, but as an indispensable means of self-preservation. At the same time, they have a remarkable, and even extreme, love of liberty, and are openly hostile to the formalism under which the Chinese are glad to vegetate, as well as to the strict despotism which is the only way of governing the negro.

The white races are, further, distinguished by an extraordinary attachment to life. They know better how to use it, and so, as it would seem, set a greater price on it; both in their own persons and those of others, they are more sparing of life. When they are cruel, they are conscious of their cruelty; it is very doubtful whether such a consciousness exists in the negro. At the same time, they have discovered reasons why they should surrender this busy life of theirs, that is so precious to them. The principal motive is honor, which under various names has played an enormous part in the ideas of the race from the beginning. I need hardly add that the word honor, together with all the civilizing influences connoted by it, is unknown to both the yellow and the black man.

On the other hand, the immense superiority of the white peoples in the whole field of the intellect is balanced by an inferiority in the intensity of their sensations. In the world of the senses, the white man is far less gifted than the others, and so is less tempted and less absorbed by considerations of the body, although in physical structure he is far the most vigorous.

Such are the three constituent elements of the human race. I call them secondary types, as I think myself obliged to omit all discussion of the Adamite [i.e., original] man. From the combination, by intermarriage, of the varieties of these types come the tertiary groups. The quaternary formations are produced by the union of one of these tertiary types, or of a pure-blooded tribe, with another group taken from one of the two foreign species.

Below these categories others have appeared—and still appear. Some of these are very strongly characterized, and form new and distinct points of departure, coming as they do from races that have been completely fused. Others are incomplete, and ill-ordered, and, one might even say, anti-social, since their elements, being too numerous, too disparate, or too barbarous, have had neither the time nor the opportunity for combining to any fruitful purpose. No limits, except the horror excited by the possibility of infinite intermixture, can be assigned to the number of these hybrid and checkered races that make up the whole of mankind.

It would be unjust to assert that every mixture is bad and harmful. If the three great types had remained strictly separate, the supremacy would no doubt have always been in the hands of the finest of the white races, and the yellow and black varieties would have crawled forever at the feet of the lowest of the whites. Such a state is so far ideal, since it has never been beheld in history; and we can imagine it only by recognizing the undisputed superiority of those groups of the white races which have remained the purest.

It would not have been all gain. The superiority of the white race would have been clearly shown, but it would have been bought at the price of certain advantages which have followed the mixture of blood. Although these are far from counter-balancing the defects they have brought in their train, yet they are sometimes to be commended. Artistic genius, which is equally foreign to each of the three great types, arose only after the intermarriage of white and black. Again, in the Malayan variety, a human family was produced from the yellow and black races that had more intelligence than either of its ancestors. Finally, from the union of white and yellow, certain intermediary peoples have sprung, who are superior to the purely Finnish tribes as well as to the negroes.

I do not deny that these are good results. The world of art and great literature that comes from the mixture of blood, the improvement and ennoblement of inferior races—all these are wonders for which we must need be thankful. The small have been raised. Unfortunately, the great have been lowered by the same process; and this is an evil that nothing can balance or repair. Since I am putting together the advantages of racial mixtures, I will also add that to them is due the refinement of manners and beliefs, and especially the tempering of passion and desire. But these are merely transitory benefits, and if I recognize that the mulatto, who may become a lawyer, a doctor, or a businessman, is worth more than his negro grandfather, who was absolutely savage, and fit for nothing, I must also confess that the Brahmans of primitive India, the heroes of the Iliad [of Homer] and the Shahnameh [the Persian Book of Kings], the warriors of Scandinavia—the glorious shades of noble races that have disappeared—give us a higher and more brilliant idea of humanity, and were more active, intelligent, and trusty instruments of civilization and grandeur than the peoples, hybrid a hundred times over, of the present day. And the blood even of these was no longer pure.

However it has come about, the human races, as we find them in history, are complex; and one of the chief consequences has been to throw into disorder most of the primitive characteristics of each type. The good as well as the bad qualities are seen to diminish in intensity with repeated intermixture of blood; but they also scatter and separate off from each other, and are often mutually opposed. The white race originally possessed the monopoly of beauty, intelligence, and strength. By its union with other varieties, hybrids were created, which were beautiful without strength, strong without intelligence, or, if intelligent, both weak and ugly. Further, when the quantity of white blood was increased to an indefinite amount of successive infusions, and not by a single admixture, it no longer carried with it its natural advantages, and often merely increased the confusion already existing in the racial elements. Its strength, in fact, seemed to be its only remaining quality, and even its strength served only to promote disorder. The apparent anomaly is easily explained. Each stage of a perfect mixture produces a new type from diverse elements, and develops special faculties. As soon as further elements are added, the vast difficulty of harmonizing the whole creates a state of anarchy. The more this increases, the more do even the best and richest of the new contributions diminish in value, and by their mere presence add fuel to an evil which they cannot abate. If mixtures of blood are, to a certain extent, beneficial to the mass of mankind, if they raise and ennoble it, this is merely at the expense of mankind itself, which is stunted, abased, enervated, and humiliated in the persons of its noblest sons. Even if we admit that it is better to turn a myriad of degraded beings into mediocre men than to preserve the race of princes whose blood is adulterated and impoverished by being made to suffer this dishonorable change, yet there is still the unfortunate fact that the change does not stop here; for when the mediocre men are once created at the expense of the greater, they combine with other mediocrities, and from such unions, which grow ever more and more degraded, is born a confusion which, like that of Babel, ends in utter impotence, and leads societies down to the abyss of nothingness whence no power on earth can rescue them.

Such is the lesson of history. It shows us that all civilizations derive from the white race, that none can exist without its help, and that a society is great and brilliant only so far as it preserves the blood of the noble group that created it, provided that this group itself belongs to the most illustrious branch of our species.

Of the multitude of peoples which live or have lived on the earth, ten alone have risen to the position of complete societies. The remainder have gravitated round these more or less independently, like planets round their suns. If there is any element of life in these ten civilizations that is not due to the impulse of the white races, any seed of death that does not come from the inferior stocks that mingled with them, then the whole theory on which this book rests is false. On the other hand, if the facts are as I say, then we have an irrefragable proof of the nobility of our own species. Only the actual details can set the final seal of truth on my system, and they alone can show with sufficient exactness the full implications of my main thesis, that peoples degenerate only in consequence of the various admixtures of blood which they undergo; that their degeneration corresponds exactly to the quantity and quality of the new blood, and that the rudest possible shock to the vitality of a civilization is given when the ruling elements in a society and those developed by racial change have become so numerous that they are clearly moving away from the homogeneity necessary to their life, and it therefore becomes impossible for them to be brought into harmony and so acquire the common instincts and interests, the common logic of existence, which is the sole justification for any social bond whatever. There is no greater curse than such disorder, for however bad it may have made the present state of things, it promises still worse for the future.

NOTE

1   In classical mythology the Hesperides were nymphs who guarded a garden where golden apples grew—a garden once thought to be in the Canary Islands off the northwest coast of Africa.—Eds.

The Doctrine of Fascism

BENITO MUSSOLINI*

As founder and leader of the Fascist Party of Italy, Benito Mussolini (1883–1945) brought together the various elements that make fascism a distinctive ideology. As a young man Mussolini considered himself a Marxian socialist, but World War I convinced him that nations, not social classes, are the primary forces in history and politics. After seizing control of the Italian government in 1922, Mussolini set out to convert Italy into a modern industrial and military power in order to create a new Italian empire. The following article, published under Mussolini's name but written by scholars sympathetic to fascism, appeared in the *Enciclopedia Italiana* in 1932.

* *Source*: Benito Mussolini, *The Doctrine of Fascism*, in *The Social and Political Doctrines of Contemporary Europe*, edited by Michael Oakeshott, pp. 164–179. (Cambridge University Press, 1939). © 1947 Cambridge University Press. Reprinted by permission of Cambridge University Press.

FUNDAMENTAL IDEAS

1   Like every sound political conception, Fascism is both practice and thought; action in which a doctrine is immanent, and a doctrine which, arising out of a given system of historical forces, remains embedded in them and works there from within. Hence it has a form correlative to the contingencies of place and time, but it has also a content of thought which raises it to a formula of truth in the higher level of the history of thought. In the world one does not act spiritually as a human will dominating other wills without a conception of the transient and particular reality under which it is necessary to act, and of the permanent and universal reality in which the first has its being and its life. In order to know men it is necessary to know man; and in order to know man it is necessary to know reality and its laws. There is no concept of the State which is not fundamentally a concept of life: philosophy or intuition, a system of ideas which develops logically or is gathered up into a vision or into a faith, but which is always, at least virtually, an organic conception of the world.

2   Thus Fascism could not be understood in many of its practical manifestations as a party organization, as a system of education, as a discipline, if it were not always looked at in the light of its whole way of conceiving life, a spiritualized way. The world seen through Fascism is not this material world which appears on the surface, in which man is an individual separated from all others and standing by himself, and in which he is governed by a natural law that makes him instinctively live a life of selfish and momentary pleasure. The man of Fascism is an individual who is nation and fatherland, which is a moral law, binding together individuals and the generations into a tradition and a mission, suppressing the instinct for a life enclosed within the brief round of pleasure in order to restore within duty a higher life free from the limits of time and space: a life in which the individual, through the denial of himself, through the sacrifice of his own private interests, through death itself, realizes that completely spiritual existence in which his value as a man lies.

3   Therefore it is a spiritualized conception, itself the result of the general reaction of modern times against the flabby materialistic positivism of the nineteenth century. Anti-positivistic, but positive: not skeptical, nor agnostic, nor pessimistic, nor passively optimistic, as are, in general, the doctrines (all negative) that put the centre of life outside man, who with his free will can and must create his own world. Fascism desires an active man, one engaged in activity with all his energies: it desires a man virilely conscious of the difficulties that exist in action and ready to face them. It conceives of life as a struggle, considering that it behooves man to conquer for himself that life truly worthy of him, creating first of all in himself the instrument (physical, moral, intellectual) in order to construct it. Thus for the single individual, thus for the nation, thus for humanity. Hence the high value of culture in all its forms (art, religion, science), and the enormous importance of education. Hence also the essential value of work, with which man conquers nature and creates the human world (economic, political, moral, intellectual).

4   This positive conception of life is clearly an ethical conception. It covers the whole of reality, not merely the human activity which controls it. No action

can be divorced from moral judgement; there is nothing in the world which can be deprived of the value which belongs to everything in its relation to moral ends. Life, therefore, as conceived by the Fascist, is serious, austere, religious: the whole of it is poised in a world supported by the moral and responsible forces of the spirit. The Fascist disdains the "comfortable" life.

5   Fascism is a religious conception in which man is seen in his immanent relationship with a superior law and with an objective Will that transcends the particular individual and raises him to conscious membership of a spiritual society. Whoever has seen in the religious politics of the Fascist regime nothing but mere opportunism has not understood that Fascism besides being a system of government is also, and above all, a system of thought.

6   Fascism is an historical conception, in which man is what he is only in so far as he works with the spiritual process in which he finds himself, in the family or social group, in the nation and in the history in which all nations collaborate. From this follows the great value of tradition, in memories, in language, in customs, in the standards of social life. Outside history man is nothing. Consequently Fascism is opposed to all the individualistic abstractions of a materialistic nature like those of the eighteenth century; and it is opposed to all Jacobin utopias and innovations.[1] It does not consider that "happiness" is possible upon earth, as it appeared to be in the desire of the economic literature of the eighteenth century, and hence it rejects all teleological theories according to which mankind would reach a definitive stabilized condition at a certain period in history. This implies putting oneself outside history and life, which is a continual change and coming to be. Politically, Fascism wishes to be a realistic doctrine; practically, it aspires to solve only the problems which arise historically of themselves and that of themselves find or suggest their own solution. To act among men, as to act in the natural world, it is necessary to enter into the process of reality and to master the already operating forces.

7   Against individualism, the Fascist conception is for the State; and it is for the individual in so far as he coincides with the State, which is the conscience and universal will of man in his historical existence. It is opposed to classical Liberalism, which arose from the necessity of reacting against absolutism, and which brought its historical purpose to an end when the State was transformed into the conscience and will of the people. Liberalism denied the State in the interests of the particular individual; Fascism reaffirms the State as the true reality of the individual. And if liberty is to be the attribute of the real man, and not of that abstract puppet envisaged by individualistic Liberalism, Fascism is for liberty. And for the only liberty which can be a real thing, the liberty of the State and of the individual within the State. Therefore, for the Fascist, everything is in the State, and nothing human or spiritual exists, much less has value, outside the State. In this sense Fascism is totalitarian, and the Fascist State, the synthesis and unity of all values, interprets, develops and gives strength to the whole life of the people.

8   Outside the State there can be neither individuals nor groups (political parties, associations, syndicates, classes). Therefore Fascism is opposed to Socialism, which confines the movement of history within the class struggle and ignores the unity of classes established in one economic and moral reality in the State;

and analogously it is opposed to class syndicalism. Fascism recognizes the real exigencies for which the socialist and syndicalist movement arose, but while recognizing them wishes to bring them under the control of the State and give them a purpose within the corporative system of interests reconciled within the unity of the State.

9   Individuals form classes according to the similarity of their interests, they form syndicates according to differentiated economic activities within these interests; but they form first, and above all, the State, which is not to be thought of numerically as the sum-total of individuals forming the majority of a nation. And consequently Fascism is opposed to Democracy, which equates the nation to the majority, lowering it to the level of that majority; nevertheless it is the purest form of democracy if the nation is conceived, as it should be, qualitatively and not quantitatively, as the most powerful idea (most powerful because most moral, most coherent, most true) which acts within the nation as the conscience and the will of a few, even of One, which ideal tends to become active within the conscience and the will of all—that is to say, of all those who rightly constitute a nation by reason of nature, history or race, and have set out upon the same line of development and spiritual formation as one conscience and one sole will. Not a race,[2] nor a geographically determined region, but as a community historically perpetuating itself, a multitude unified by a single idea, which is the will to existence and to power: consciousness of itself, personality.

10   This higher personality is truly the nation in so far as it is the State. It is not the nation that generates the State, as according to the old naturalistic concept which served as the basis of the political theories of the national States of the nineteenth century. Rather the nation is created by the State, which gives to the people, conscious of its own moral unity, a will and therefore an effective existence. The right of a nation to independence derives not from a literary and ideal consciousness of its own being, still less from a more or less unconscious and inert acceptance of a *de facto* situation, but from an active consciousness, from a political will in action and ready to demonstrate its own rights: that is to say, from a state already coming into being. The State, in fact, as the universal ethical will, is the creator of right.

11   The nation as the State is an ethical reality which exists and lives in so far as it develops. To arrest its development is to kill it. Therefore the State is not only the authority which governs and gives the form of laws and the value of spiritual life to the wills of individuals, but it is also a power that makes its will felt abroad, making it known and respected, in other words, demonstrating the fact of its universality in all the necessary directions of its development. It is consequently organization and expansion, at least virtually. Thus it can be likened to the human will which knows no limits to its development and realizes itself in testing its own limitlessness.

12   The Fascist State, the highest and most powerful form of personality, is a force, but a spiritual force, which takes over all the forms of the moral and intellectual life of man. It cannot therefore confine itself simply to the functions of order and supervision as Liberalism desired. It is not simply a mechanism which limits the sphere of the supposed liberties of the individual. It is the form,

the inner standard and the discipline of the whole person; it saturates the will as well as the intelligence. Its principle, the central inspiration of the human personality living in the civil community, pierces into the depths and makes its home in the heart of the man of action as well as of the thinker, of the artist as well as of the scientist: it is the soul of the soul.

13 Fascism, in short, is not only the giver of laws and the founder of institutions, but the educator and promoter of spiritual life. It wants to remake, not the forms of human life, but its content, man, character, faith. And to this end it requires discipline and authority that can enter into the spirits of men and there govern unopposed. Its sign, therefore, is the Lictors' rods, the symbol of unity, of strength and justice ...[3]

POLITICAL AND SOCIAL DOCTRINE

3   Above all, Fascism, in so far as it considers and observes the future and the development of humanity quite apart from the political considerations of the moment, believes neither in the possibility nor in the utility of perpetual peace. It thus repudiates the doctrine of Pacifism—born of a renunciation of the struggle and an act of cowardice in the face of sacrifice. War alone brings up to their highest tension all human energies and puts the stamp of nobility upon the peoples who have the courage to meet it. All other trials are substitutes, which never really put a man in front of himself in the alternative of life and death. A doctrine, therefore, which begins with a prejudice in favor of peace is foreign to Fascism; as are foreign to the spirit of Fascism, even though acceptable by reason of the utility which they might have in given political situations, all internationalistic and socialistic systems which, as history proves, can be blown to the winds when emotional, idealistic and practical movements storm the hearts of peoples. Fascism carries over this anti-pacifist spirit even into the lives of individuals. The proud motto of the *Squadrista* [Italian Fascist "Blackshirt"], "Me ne frego" ["I don't give a damn"], written on the bandages of a wound is an act of philosophy which is not only stoical, it is the epitome of a doctrine that is not only political: it is education for combat, the acceptance of the risks which it brings; it is a new way of life for Italy. Thus the Fascist accepts and loves life, he knows nothing of suicide and despises it; he looks on life as duty, ascent, conquest: life which must be noble and full: lived for oneself, but above all for those others near and far away, present and future.

4   The "demographic" policy of the regime follows from these premises. Even the Fascist does in fact love his neighbor, but this "neighbor" is not for him a vague and ill-defined concept; love for one's neighbor does not exclude necessary educational severities, and still less differentiations and distances. Fascism rejects universal concord, and, since it lives in the community of civilized peoples, it keeps them vigilantly and suspiciously before its eyes, it follows their states of mind and the changes in their interests and it does not let itself be deceived by temporary and fallacious appearances.

5   Such a conception of life makes Fascism the precise negation of that doctrine which formed the basis of the so-called Scientific or Marxian Socialism: the doctrine of historical Materialism, according to which the history of

human civilizations can be explained only as the struggle of interest between the different social groups and as arising out of change in the means and instruments of production. That economic improvements—discoveries of raw materials, new methods of work, scientific inventions—should have an importance of their own, no one denies, but that they should suffice to explain human history to the exclusion of all other factors is absurd: Fascism believes, now and always, in holiness and in heroism, that is in acts in which no economic motive—remote or immediate—plays a part. With this negation of historical materialism, according to which men would be only by-products of history, who appear and disappear on the surface of the waves while in the depths the real directive forces are at work, there is also denied the immutable and irreparable "class struggle" which is the natural product of this economic conception of history, and above all it is denied that the class struggle can be the primary agent of social changes. Socialism, being thus wounded in these two primary tenets of its doctrine, nothing of it is left save the sentimental aspiration—old as humanity—towards a social order in which the sufferings and the pains of the humblest folk could be alleviated. But here Fascism rejects the concept of an economic "happiness" which would be realized socialistically and almost automatically at a given moment of economic evolution by assuring to all a maximum prosperity. Fascism denies the possibility of the materialistic conception of "happiness" and leaves it to the economists of the first half of the eighteenth century; it denies, that is, the equation of prosperity with happiness, which would transform men into animals with one sole preoccupation: that of being well-fed and fat, degraded in consequence to a merely physical existence.

6   After Socialism, Fascism attacks the whole complex of democratic ideologies and rejects them both in their theoretical premises and in their applications or practical manifestations. Fascism denies that the majority, through the mere fact of being a majority, can rule human societies; it denies that this majority can govern by means of a periodical consultation; it affirms the irremediable, fruitful and beneficent inequality of men, who cannot be levelled by such a mechanical and extrinsic fact as universal suffrage. By democratic regimes we mean those in which from time to time the people is given the illusion of being sovereign, while true effective sovereignty lies in other, perhaps irresponsible and secret, forces. Democracy is a regime without a king, but with very many kings, perhaps more exclusive, tyrannical and violent than one king even though a tyrant ...

7   ... Fascism rejects in democracy the absurd conventional lie of political equalitarianism clothed in the dress of collective irresponsibility and the myth of happiness and indefinite progress. But if democracy can be understood in other ways, that is, if democracy means not to relegate the people to the periphery of the State, then Fascism could be defined as an "organized, centralized, authoritarian democracy."

8   In face of Liberal doctrines, Fascism takes up an attitude of absolute opposition both in the field of politics and in that of economics. It is not necessary to exaggerate—merely for the purpose of present controversies—the importance of Liberalism in the past century, and to make of that which was one of the

numerous doctrines sketched in that century a religion of humanity for all times, present and future ... The "Liberal" century, after having accumulated an infinity of Gordian knots,[4] tried to untie them by the hecatomb [i.e., mass slaughter] of the [First] World War. Never before has any religion imposed such a cruel sacrifice. Were the gods of Liberalism thirsty for blood? Now Liberalism is about to close the doors of its deserted temples because the peoples feel that its agnosticism in economics, its indifferentism in politics and in morals, would lead, as they have led, the States to certain ruin. In this way one can understand why all the political experiences of the contemporary world are anti-Liberal, and it is supremely ridiculous to wish on that account to class them outside of history; as if history were a hunting ground reserved to Liberalism and its professors, as if Liberalism were the definitive and no longer surpassable message of civilization.

9   But the Fascist repudiations of Socialism, Democracy, Liberalism must not make one think that Fascism wishes to make the world return to what it was before 1789, the year which has been indicated as the year of the beginning of the liberal-democratic age. One does not go backwards. The Fascist doctrine has not chosen De Maistre as its prophet.[5] Monarchial absolutism is a thing of the past and so also is every theocracy. So also feudal privileges and division into impenetrable and isolated castes have had their day. The theory of Fascist authority has nothing to do with the police State. A party that governs a nation in a totalitarian way is a new fact in history. References and comparisons are not possible. Fascism takes over from the ruins of Liberal Socialistic democratic doctrines those elements which still have a living value. It preserves those that can be called the established facts of history, it rejects all the rest, that is to say the idea of a doctrine which holds good for all times and all peoples. If it is admitted that the nineteenth century has been the century of Socialism, Liberalism and Democracy, it does not follow that the twentieth must also be the century of Liberalism, Socialism and Democracy. Political doctrines pass; peoples remain. It is to be expected that this century may be that of authority, a century of the "Right," a Fascist century. If the nineteenth was the century of the individual (Liberalism means individualism) it may be expected that this one may be the century of "collectivism" and therefore the century of the State. That a new doctrine should use the still vital elements of other doctrines is perfectly logical. No doctrine is born quite new, shining, never before seen. No doctrine can boast of an absolute "originality." It is bound, even if only historically, to other doctrines that have been, and to develop into other doctrines that will be. Thus the scientific socialism of Marx is bound to the Utopian Socialism of the Fouriers, the Owens and the Saint-Simons;[6] thus the Liberalism of the nineteenth century is connected with the whole "Enlightenment" of the eighteenth century. Thus the doctrines of democracy are bound to the *Encyclopédie*.[7] Every doctrine tends to direct the activity of men towards a determined objective; but the activity of man reacts upon the doctrine, transforms it, adapts it to new necessities or transcends it. The doctrine itself, therefore, must be, not words, but an act of life. Hence, the pragmatic veins in Fascism, its will to power, its will to be, its attitude in the face of the fact of "violence" and of its own courage.

10   The keystone of Fascist doctrine is the conception of the State, of its essence, of its tasks, of its ends. For Fascism the State is an absolute before which individuals and groups are relative. Individuals and groups are "thinkable" in so far as they are within the State. The Liberal State does not direct the interplay and the material and spiritual development of the groups, but limits itself to registering the results; the Fascist State has a consciousness of its own, a will of its own, on this account it is called an "ethical" State ...

11   From 1929 up to the present day these doctrinal positions have been strengthened by the whole economic-political evolution of the world. It is the State alone that grows in size, in power. It is the State alone that can solve the dramatic contradictions of capitalism. What is called the crisis cannot be overcome except by the State, within the State ... But when one says liberalism, one says the individual; when one says Fascism, one says the State. But the Fascist State is unique; it is an original creation. It is not reactionary, but revolutionary in that it anticipates the solutions of certain universal problems. These problems are no longer seen in the same light: in the sphere of politics they are removed from party rivalries, from the supreme power of parliament, from the irresponsibility of assemblies; in the sphere of economics they are removed from the sphere of the syndicates' activities—activities that were ever widening their scope and increasing their power both on the workers' side and on the employers'—removed from their struggles and their designs; in the moral sphere they are divorced from ideas of the need for order, discipline and obedience, and lifted into the plane of the moral commandments of the fatherland. Fascism desires the State to be strong, organic and at the same time founded on a wide popular basis. The Fascist State has also claimed for itself the field of economics and, through the corporative, social and educational institutions which it has created, the meaning of the State reaches out to and includes the farthest offshoots; and within the State, framed in their respective organizations, there revolve all the political, economic and spiritual forces of the nation. A State founded on millions of individuals who recognize it, feel it, are ready to serve it, is not the tyrannical State of the medieval lord. It has nothing in common with the absolutist States that existed either before or after 1789. In the Fascist State the individual is not suppressed, but rather multiplied, just as in a regiment a soldier is not weakened but multiplied by the number of his comrades. The Fascist State organizes the nation, but it leaves sufficient scope to individuals; it has limited useless or harmful liberties and has preserved those that are essential. It cannot be the individual who decides in this matter, but only the State.

12   The Fascist State does not remain indifferent to the fact of religion in general and to that particular positive religion which is Italian Catholicism. The State has no theology, but it has an ethic. In the Fascist State religion is looked upon as one of the deepest manifestations of the spirit; it is, therefore, not only respected, but defended and protected. The Fascist State does not create a "God" of its own, as Robespierre once, at the height of the Convention's foolishness, wished to do; nor does it vainly seek, like Bolshevism, to expel religion from the minds of men; Fascism respects the God of the ascetics, of

the saints, of the heroes, and also God as seen and prayed to by the simple and primitive heart of the people.

13 The Fascist State is a will to power and to government. In it the tradition of Rome is an idea that has force. In the doctrine of Fascism Empire is not only a territorial, military or mercantile expression, but spiritual or moral. One can think of an empire, that is to say a nation that directly or indirectly leads other nations, without needing to conquer a single square kilometer of territory. For Fascism the tendency to Empire, that is to say, to the expansion of nations, is a manifestation of vitality; its opposite, staying at home, is a sign of decadence: peoples who rise or re-rise are imperialist, peoples who die are renunciatory. Fascism is the doctrine that is most fitted to represent the aims, the states of mind, of a people, like the Italian people, rising again after many centuries of abandonment or slavery to foreigners. But Empire calls for discipline, co-ordination of forces, duty and sacrifice; this explains many aspects of the practical working of the regime and the direction of many of the forces of the State and the necessary severity shown to those who would wish to oppose this spontaneous and destined impulse of the Italy of the twentieth century, to oppose it in the name of the superseded ideologies of the nineteenth, repudiated wherever great experiments of political and social transformation have been courageously attempted: especially where, as now, peoples thirst for authority, for leadership, for order. If every age has its own doctrine, it is apparent from a thousand signs that the doctrine of the present age is Fascism. That it is a doctrine of life is shown by the fact that it has resuscitated a faith. That this faith has conquered minds is proved by the fact that Fascism has had its dead and its martyrs.

Fascism henceforward has in the world the universality of all those doctrines which, by fulfilling themselves, have significance in the history of the human spirit.

NOTES

1 The Jacobins were a utopian-radical sect in the French Revolution.—Eds.
2 "Race; it is an emotion, not a reality; ninety-five percent of it is emotion."—Mussolini.
3 Lictors were ancient Roman civil servants who served as bodyguards for those who held high political office. Their symbol was the *fasces*, or tightly bound bundle of rods, from which the term "fascism" is derived.—Eds.
4 According to ancient legend, the knot tied by the peasant-turned-king Gordius was so complex that no one could untie it, although many had tried. The Gordian knot was finally "untied" by Alexander the Great, who cut it with his sword.—Eds.
5 The monarchist and reactionary critic of the French Revolution, Joseph de Maistre (1753–1821). See selection 4.29 in this volume.—Eds.
6 Charles Fourier (1772–1837), Robert Owen (1771–1858), and Count Claude-Henri de Saint-Simon (1760–1825) were early nineteenth-century socialists whom Marx and Engels scorned as "utopian" rather than "scientific" thinkers.—Eds.
7 The massive eighteenth-century French encyclopedia that attempted to classify and communicate all human knowledge in a comprehensive and systematic way. It was both an achievement and a symbol of the European Enlightenment.—Eds.

The Political Theory
of Fascism

ALFREDO ROCCO*

As we saw in selection 7.48, the Italian fascists took pains to distinguish their political ideology from liberalism and socialism. By stressing their differences with liberalism and socialism—and by rejecting democracy— they tried to define a coherent and distinctive fascist ideology. This task fell to intellectuals such as Alfredo Rocco (1875–1935), the author of the following selection. Rocco was a professor of law and a theorist for the Italian National Association, which was a precursor of the Italian Fascist Party. He subsequently joined the Fascist Party and served as minister of justice in Mussolini's government.

* *Source*: Alfredo Rocco, *The Political Doctrine of Fascism*, translated by Dante Bigongiari (International Conciliation, no. 223, Carnegie Endowment for International Peace, 1926). © Carnegie Endowment for International Peace. Reprinted by permission.

THE POLITICAL THEORY OF FASCISM

It is true that Fascism is, above all, action and sentiment and that such it must continue to be. Were it otherwise, it could not keep up that immense driving force, that renovating power which it now possesses and would merely be the solitary meditation of a chosen few. Only because it is feeling and sentiment, only because it is the unconscious reawakening of our profound racial instinct, has it the force to stir the soul of the people, and to set free an irresistible current of national will. Only because it is action, and as such actualizes itself in a vast organization and in a huge movement, has it the conditions for determining the historical course of contemporary Italy.

But Fascism is thought as well and it has a theory, which is an essential part of this historical phenomenon, and which is responsible in a great measure for the successes that have been achieved. To the existence of this ideal content of Fascism, to the truth of this Fascist logic we ascribe the fact that though we commit many errors of detail, we very seldom go astray on fundamentals, whereas all the parties of the opposition, deprived as they are of an informing, animating principle, of a unique directing concept, do very often wage their war faultlessly in minor tactics, better trained as they are in parliamentary and journalistic maneuvers but they constantly break down on the important issues. Fascism, moreover, considered as action, is a typically Italian phenomenon and acquires a universal validity because of the existence of this coherent and organic doctrine. The originality of Fascism is due in great part to the autonomy of its theoretical principles. For even when, in its external behavior and in its conclusions, it seems identical with other political creeds, in reality it possesses an inner originality due to the new spirit which animates it and to an entirely different theoretical approach.

Common Origins and Common Background of Modern Political Doctrines: From Liberalism to Socialism

Modern political thought remained, until recently, both in Italy and outside of Italy under the absolute control of those doctrines which, proceeding from the Protestant Reformation and developed by the adepts of natural law in the XVII and XVIII centuries, were firmly grounded in the institutions and customs of the English, of the American, and of the French Revolutions. Under different and sometimes clashing forms these doctrines have left a determining imprint upon all theories and actions both social and political, of the XIX and XX centuries down to the rise of Fascism. The common basis of all these doctrines ... is a social and state concept which I shall call mechanical or atomistic.

Society, according to this concept, is merely a sum total of individuals, a plurality which breaks up into its single components. Therefore the ends of a society, so considered, are nothing more than the ends of the individuals which compose it and for whose sake it exists. An atomistic view of this kind is also necessarily anti-historical, inasmuch as it considers society in its spatial attributes and not in its temporal ones; and because it reduces social life to the existence of a single generation. Society becomes thus a sum of determined individuals, viz., the generation living at a given moment. This doctrine which I call atomistic and which appears to be anti-historical, reveals from under a concealing cloak a strongly materialistic nature. For in its endeavors to isolate the present from the past and the future, it rejects the spiritual inheritance of ideas and sentiments which each generation receives from those preceding and hands down to the following generation, thus destroying the unity and the spiritual life itself of human society.

This common basis shows the close logical connection existing between all political doctrines; the substantial solidarity, which unites all the political movements, from Liberalism to Socialism, that until recently have dominated Europe. For these political schools differ from one another in their methods, but all agree as to the ends to be achieved. All of them consider the welfare and happiness of individuals to be the goal of society, itself considered as composed of individuals of the present generation. All of them see in society and in its juridical organization, the state, the mere instrument and means whereby individuals can attain their ends. They differ only in that the methods pursued for the attainment of these ends vary considerably one from the other ...

Thus Liberalism, Democracy, and Socialism, appear to be, as they are in reality, not only the offspring of one and the same theory of government, but also logical derivations one of the other. Logically developed, Liberalism leads to Democracy; the logical development of Democracy issues into Socialism. It is true that for many years, and with some justification, Socialism was looked upon as antithetical to Liberalism. But the antithesis is purely relative and breaks down as we approach the common origin and foundation of the two doctrines, for we find that the opposition is one of method, not of purpose. The end is the same for both, viz., the welfare of the individual members of society. The difference lies in the fact that Liberalism would be guided to its goal by liberty, whereas Socialism strives to attain it by the collective organization of production. There is therefore no antithesis nor even a divergence as to the nature and scope of the state and the relation of individuals to society. There is only a difference of evaluation of the means for bringing about these ends and establishing these relations, which difference depends entirely on the different economic conditions which prevailed at the time when the various doctrines were formulated. Liberalism arose and began to thrive in the period of small industry; Socialism grew with the rise of industrialism and of world-wide capitalism. The dissension therefore between these two points of view, or the antithesis, if we wish so to call it, is limited to the economic field. Socialism is at odds with Liberalism only on the question of the organization of production and of the division of wealth. In religious, intellectual, and moral matters it is liberal, as it is liberal and democratic in its politics. Even the anti-liberalism and anti-democracy of Bolshevism are in themselves purely contingent.[1] For Bolshevism is opposed to Liberalism only in so far as the former is revolutionary, not in its socialistic aspect. For if the opposition of the Bolshevik to liberal and democratic doctrines were to continue, as now seems more and more probable, the result might be a complete break between Bolshevism and Socialism notwithstanding the fact that the ultimate aims of both are identical.

Fascism as an Integral Doctrine of Sociality Antithetical to the Atomism of Liberal, Democratic, and Socialistic Theories

The true antithesis, not to this or that manifestation of the liberal-democratic-socialistic conception of the state but to the concept itself, is to be found in the doctrine of Fascism. For while the disagreement between Liberalism and Democracy, and between Liberalism and Socialism lies in a difference of method, as we have said, the rift between Socialism, Democracy, and Liberalism on one side and Fascism on the other is caused by a difference in concept. As a matter of fact, Fascism never raises the question of methods, using in its political *praxis* now liberal ways, now democratic means and at times even socialistic devices. This indifference to method often exposes Fascism to the charge of incoherence on the part of superficial observers, who do not see that what counts with us is the end and that therefore even when we employ the same means we act with a radically different spiritual attitude and strive for entirely different results. The Fascist concept then of the nation, of the scope of the state, and of the relations obtaining between society and its individual components, rejects entirely the doctrine which I said proceeded from the theories of natural law developed in the course of the 16th, 17th, and 18th centuries and which form the basis of the liberal, democratic, and socialistic ideology …

Fascism replaces therefore the old atomistic and mechanical state theory which was at the basis of the liberal and democratic doctrines with an organic and historic concept. When I say "organic" I do not wish to convey the impression that I consider society as an organism after the manner of the so-called "organic theories of the state"; but rather to indicate that the social groups as fractions of the species receive thereby a life and scope which transcend the scope and life of the individuals identifying themselves with the history and finalities of the uninterrupted series of generations. It is irrelevant in this connection to determine whether social groups, considered as fractions of the species, constitute organisms. The important thing is to ascertain that this organic concept of the state gives to society a continuous life over and beyond the existence of the several individuals.

The relations therefore between state and citizens are completely reversed by the Fascist doctrine. Instead of the liberal-democratic formula, "society for the individual," we have, "individuals for society," with this difference, however: that while the liberal doctrines eliminated society, Fascism does not submerge the individual in the social group. It subordinates him, but does not eliminate him; the individual as a part of his generation ever remaining an element of society however transient and insignificant he may be. Moreover the development of individuals in each generation, when coordinated and harmonized, conditions the development and prosperity of the entire social unit.

At this juncture the antithesis between the two theories must appear complete and absolute. Liberalism, Democracy, and Socialism look upon social groups as aggregates of living individuals; for Fascism they are the recapitulating unity of the indefinite series of generations. For Liberalism, society has no purposes other than those of the members living at a given moment. For Fascism, society has historical and immanent ends of preservation, expansion, improvement, quite distinct from those of the individuals which at a given moment compose it; so distinct in fact that they may even be in opposition. Hence the necessity, for which the older doctrines make little allowance, of sacrifice, even up to the total immolation of individuals, in behalf of society; hence the true explanation of war, eternal law of mankind, interpreted by the liberal-democratic doctrines as a degenerate absurdity or as a maddened monstrosity.

For Liberalism, society has no life distinct from the life of the individuals ... For Fascism, the life of society overlaps the existence of individuals and projects itself into the succeeding generations through centuries and millennia. Individuals come into being, grow, and die, followed by others, unceasingly; social unity remains always identical to itself. For Liberalism, the individual is the end and society the means; nor is it conceivable that the individual, considered in the dignity of an ultimate finality, be lowered to mere instrumentality. For Fascism, society is the end, individuals the means, and its whole life consists in using individuals as instruments for its social ends. The state therefore guards and protects the welfare and development of individuals not for their exclusive interest, but because of the identity of the needs of individuals with those of society as a whole. We can thus accept and explain institutions and practices, which like the death penalty, are condemned by Liberalism in the name of the preeminence of individualism.

The fundamental problem of society in the old doctrines is the question of the rights of individuals. It may be the right to [individual] freedom as the Liberals would have it; or the right to the government of the commonwealth as the Democrats claim it, or the right to economic justice as the Socialists contend; but in every case it is the right of individuals, or groups of individuals (classes). Fascism on the other hand faces squarely the problem of the right of the state and of the duty of individuals. Individual rights are only recognized in so far as they are implied in the rights of the state. In this preeminence of duty we find the highest ethical value of Fascism.

The Problems of Liberty, of Government, and of Social Justice in the Political Doctrine of Fascism

This, however, does not mean that the problems raised by the other schools are ignored by Fascism. It means simply that it faces them and solves them differently, as, for example, the problem of liberty.

There is a Liberal theory of freedom, and there is a Fascist concept of liberty. For we, too, maintain the necessity of safeguarding the conditions that make for the free development of the individual; we, too, believe that the oppression of individual personality can find no place in the modern state. We do not, however, accept a bill of rights which tends to make the individual superior to the state and to empower him to act in opposition to society. Our concept of liberty is that the individual must be allowed to develop his personality in behalf of the state, for these ephemeral and infinitesimal elements of the complex and permanent life of society determine by their normal growth the development of the state. But this individual growth must be normal. A huge and disproportionate development of the individual of classes, would prove as fatal to society as abnormal growths are to living organisms. Freedom therefore is due to the citizen and to classes on condition that they exercise it in the interest of society as a whole and within the limits set by social exigencies, liberty being, like any other individual right, a concession of the state. What I say concerning civil liberties applies to economic freedom as well. Fascism does not look upon the doctrine of economic liberty as an absolute dogma. It does not refer economic problems to individual needs, to individual interest, to individual solutions. On the contrary it considers the economic development, and especially the production of wealth, as an eminently social concern, wealth being for society an essential element of power and prosperity. But Fascism maintains that in the ordinary run of events economic liberty serves the social purposes best; that it is profitable to entrust to individual initiative the task of economic development both as to production and as to distribution; that in the economic world individual ambition is the most effective means for obtaining the best social results with the least effort. Therefore, on the question also of economic liberty the Fascists differ fundamentally from the Liberals; the latter see in liberty a principle, the Fascists accept it as a method. By the Liberals, freedom is recognized in the interest of the citizens; the Fascists grant it in the interest of society. In other terms, Fascists make of the individual an economic instrument for the advancement of society, an instrument which they use so long as it functions and which they subordinate when no longer serviceable. In this guise Fascism solves the eternal problem of economic freedom and of state interference, considering both as mere methods which may or may not be employed in accordance with the social needs of the moment.

What I have said concerning political and economic Liberalism applies also to Democracy. The latter envisages fundamentally the problem of sovereignty; Fascism does also, but in an entirely different manner. Democracy vests sovereignty in the people, that is to say, in the mass of human beings. Fascism discovers sovereignty to be inherent in society when it is juridically [legally] organized as a state. Democracy therefore turns over the government of the state to the multitude of living men that they may use it to further their own interests; Fascism insists that the government be entrusted to men capable of rising above their own private interests and of realizing the aspirations of the social collectivity, considered in its unity and in its relation to the past and future. Fascism therefore not only rejects the dogma of popular sovereignty and substitutes for it that of state sovereignty, but it also proclaims that the great mass of citizens is not a suitable advocate of social interests for the reason that the capacity to ignore individual private interests in favor of the higher demands of society and of history is a very rare gift and the privilege of the chosen few. Natural intelligence and cultural preparation are of great service in such tasks. Still more valuable perhaps is the intuitiveness of rare great minds, their traditionalism and their inherited qualities. This must not however be construed to mean that the masses are not to be allowed to exercise any influence on the life of the state. On the contrary, among peoples with a great history and with noble traditions, even the lowest elements of society possess an instinctive discernment of what is necessary for the welfare of the race, which in moments of great historical crises reveals itself to be almost infallible. It is therefore as wise to afford to this instinct the means of declaring itself as it is judicious to entrust the normal control of the commonwealth to a selected elite.

As for Socialism, the Fascist doctrine frankly recognizes that the problem raised by it as to the relations between capital and labor is a very serious one, perhaps the central one of modern life. What Fascism does not countenance is the collectivistic solution proposed by the Socialists. The chief defect of the socialistic method has been clearly demonstrated by the experience of the last few years. It does not take into account human nature, it is therefore outside of reality, in that it will not recognize that the most powerful spring of human activities lies in individual self-interest and that therefore the elimination from the economic field of this interest results in complete paralysis. The suppression of private ownership of capital carries with it the suppression of capital itself, for capital is formed by savings and no one will want to save, but will rather consume all he makes if he knows he cannot keep and hand down to his heirs the results of his labors. The dispersion of capital means the end of production since capital, no matter who owns it, is always an indispensable tool of production. Collective organization of production is followed therefore by the paralysis of production since, by eliminating from the productive mechanism the incentive of individual interest, the product becomes rarer and more costly. Socialism then, as experience has shown, leads to increase in consumption, to the dispersion of capital and therefore to poverty. Of what avail is it, then, to build a social machine which will more justly distribute wealth if this very wealth is destroyed by the construction of this machine? Socialism committed an irreparable error when it made of private property a matter of justice while in truth it is a problem of social utility. The recognition of individual property rights, then, is a part of the Fascist doctrine not because of its individual bearing but because of its social utility.

We must reject, therefore, the socialistic solution but we cannot allow the problem raised by the Socialists to remain unsolved, not only because justice demands a solution but also because the persistence of this problem in liberal and democratic regimes has been a menace to public order and to the authority of the state. Unlimited and unrestrained class self-defense, evinced by strikes and lockouts, by boycotts and sabotage, leads inevitably to anarchy. The Fascist doctrine, enacting justice among the classes in compliance with a fundamental necessity of modern life, does away with class self-defense, which, like individual self-defense in the days of barbarism, is a source of disorder and of civil war.

Having reduced the problem of these terms, only one solution is possible, the realization of justice among the classes by and through the state. Centuries ago the state, as the specific organ of justice, abolished personal self-defense in individual controversies and substituted for it state justice. The time has now come when class self-defense also must be replaced by state justice. To facilitate the change Fascism has created its own syndicalism.[2] The suppression of class self-defense does not mean the suppression of class defense which is an inalienable necessity of modern economic life. Class organization is a fact which cannot be ignored but it must be controlled, disciplined, and subordinated by the state. The syndicate, instead of being, as formerly, an organ of extra-legal defense, must be turned into an organ of legal defense which will become judicial defense as soon as labor conflicts become a matter of judicial settlement. Fascism therefore has transformed the syndicate, that old revolutionary instrument of syndicalistic socialists, into an instrument of legal defense of the classes both within and without the law courts. This solution may encounter obstacles in its development; the obstacles of malevolence, of suspicion of the untried, of erroneous calculation, etc., but it is destined to triumph even though it must advance through progressive stages.

NOTES

1   Bolshevism refers to the Bolshevik or Leninist variant of Marxist theory and practice.—Eds.

2   Syndicalism, from the French *syndicat* or trade union, was a socialist theory that called for direct action, such as workers' strikes, by trade unions and other working-class organizations.—Eds.

Nation and Race

ADOLF HITLER*

Although Adolf Hitler (1889–1945) was neither an original nor a consistent thinker, his blend of fascism and racism proved to be one of the most potent ideological forces in human history. The following selections are from Hitler's autobiography, *Mein Kampf* ("My Battle"), which he wrote in 1924 while imprisoned for leading an attempt to overthrow the government of the German province of Bavaria. The selections reveal Hitler's racial ideas, his anti-Semitism, his hatred of socialism and liberalism, and other ideas that he and the National Socialists (or Nazis, for short) put into practice once they gained power in Germany in 1933.

---

* *Source*: Adolf Hitler, *Mein Kampf* (Munich: Eher Verlag, 1925); translated by Terence Ball. (*Translator's note*: Portions of this translation are more free-form than literal, inasmuch as Hitler's prose is often prolix and almost impossible to translate word-for-word. A literal translation of some passages—particularly the longer ones—would make no sense in English.)

MEIN KAMPF

Much more than any theoretical treatise, my daily reading of the Social Democratic [i.e., democratic socialist] newspapers enabled me to analyze the internal working of their thinking.

I saw a vast difference between the shining sentiments about freedom, beauty, and dignity in the theoretical literature, the misleading barrage of words allegedly emphasizing the deepest and most belabored "wisdom," the wretched "humanitarian" morality all of which is written with the utter temerity that attends self-righteous certitude. And the verbally violent daily newspapers, resisting no villainy, use every available means of slander, lying with a skill that would bend steel girders, all in the name of this religion of a new "humanity." The first is aimed at the simpletons of the middle, not to mention the upper, "educated," classes, the second to ordinary workers.

My immersion in and reaction to the theoretical works and the newspapers of Social Democracy led me back to my own people [*volk*].

What had seemed to me a wide and uncross-able chasm became for me the fount of a greater love for my people than I had ever experienced.

Only an idiot can look upon the work of this mind-poisoning culprit and still blame the victim. The more free-thinking I made myself in the following years, the clearer my outlook became, and the greater my insight into the inner secret of the Social Democratic successes. I came to understand the importance of the violent demands that I encountered only in Red newspapers, heard at Red rallies, and read only in Red books. I saw with great clarity the unavoidable result of their intolerant doctrine.

The mind of the masses is not open to any doctrine that advocates half-measures or is in any way weak or vacillating.

Just as a woman, whose mental state is not as much influenced by abstract reason as by an inexpressible emotional desire for a force which will round out and complete her nature, and who, as result, would prefer to prostrate herself before strong man than to rule over a weakling—so also the masses love a forceful leader more than a pleading "moderate" and feel much more satisfied by an intolerant doctrine that tolerates no other doctrines, than they are by the granting of liberal "freedom"… which leaves them feeling abandoned and alone. They are no less unaware of the way in which their spirits have been shamelessly terrorized and their human freedom basely abused, for they naively neglect to be suspicious of the utter craziness of the entire Social Democratic doctrine. The masses see only the ruthless brutality and the calculated violence of its manifestos, before which they will always bow.

If Social Democracy were to be opposed by any doctrine of more profound truth, but employing equally brutal methods, the latter[i.e., National Socialism] will triumph, though this will surely demand the most bitter of struggles.

Within a mere two years, both the theory and the technical methods of Social Democracy became completely clear to me.

I understood the malicious mental terror which the Social Democratic movement exerts, especially among the bourgeoisie, which is neither morally nor mentally up to such assaults on their privileges. At some given signal it lets fly a barrage of lies and slanders against whatever foe seems most threatening, until the nerves of the attacked persons give way and, simply to enjoy peace once more, the bourgeoisie sacrifice the despised individual in their midst.

Yet, fools that they are, they gain no peace.

The game begins again and is played repeatedly until fear of the rabid dog results in crippling paralysis.

Since the Social Democrats know from experience the value of force, they attack most violently those in whose nature they detect any of this very rare substance. Conversely, they heap praise upon every coward from the opposition party. On some occasions they do so cautiously, on other occasions boldly, according to the real or imagined quality of his intellect.

They fear a vapid, cowardly genius less than a forceful man of middling intelligence. Yet it is with the greatest enthusiasm that they commend mental and physical weaklings.

Social Democrats know how to create the illusion that theirs is the only way to keep the peace, while simultaneously, slyly but surely, they conquer position after position, sometimes by threatening blackmail, sometimes by outright thievery—always at times when most people are concerned with different other issues, and either don't wish to be disturbed or believe the issue too insignificant to concern them …

Their tactic is based on an exact calculation of every human frailty, and its outcome will produce success with near-mathematical precision—unless the opposing side learns to fight their poisonous gas with more potent poisonous gas of its own.

Our solemn duty is to inform all weaklings that the question before us is: "To be or not to be?"

For myself, I acquired a balanced recognition of the significance of physically terrorizing both the individual and the masses.

Once again the psychic effects can be precisely calculated.

Terror at the workplace, inside the factory, within the meeting hall, and at mass demonstrations will always succeed—unless opposed by equal terror.

You can be sure that the opposition party will cry foul. Although it has long despised all state authority, it will demand that the state come to its aid. And in the ensuing confusion it will find some foolish or gullible officer of the state who, in the idiotic hope of ingratiating himself with the adversarial party for his own future advancement, will help this plague-like party break the back of the opposing party.

The impact of such underhanded victories on the minds of the masses—both supporters and opponents alike—can be gauged only by those who have intimate knowledge of the soul of a people [*volk*], a knowledge acquired not from books, but from life. Although among their supporters the victory appears to signal the just character of their cause, the defeated adversary typically regards any further resistance as futile …

Some truths are so obvious that they are not recognized by most people. These truth-blind people are astounded when someone suddenly discovers what all ought to know. Columbus's eggs abound in their hundreds of thousands, even though Columbuses are rarely encountered.

Almost without exception men wander in the garden of Nature, thinking that they know everything there is to know. Most men blithely ignore one of Nature's most obvious principles: the segregation of all species living on this earth.

As even the hastiest observation shows, Nature's restrictions on the propagation and multiplication of species are strong and severe, amounting to a strict basic law that applies to all species. Each and every animal mates exclusively with a member of its own species. The titmouse mates with the titmouse, the finch with the finch, the stork with the stork, the field-mouse with the field-mouse, the dormouse with the dormouse, the wolf with the she-wolf, and so on, for every species.

Only the strangest and most unusual circumstances can alter this, mainly the compulsion that comes with captivity or any other abnormal circumstance that renders mating within the same species physically impossible. Even then Nature resists this by all available means. Nature's most obvious objection can be seen in her refusing any further capacity for producing offspring to illegitimate issue [i.e., bastards] or in severely limiting the fertility of future generations; in most instances, however, Nature allows these offspring to die of disease or succumb to attacks by predators.

This is plainly and simply natural.

The cross-breeding of any two creatures which are not at exactly the same level produces a qualitative average between the levels of the two parents. Thus the offspring will on average stand higher than the racially inferior parent, but not as high as the higher parent. As a consequence this offspring will sooner or later succumb in its struggle with those at the higher level. Matings of this sort run contrary to Nature's plan that all life tends toward an ever-higher level. This will not happen if inferior associates with superior; but only if the latter wins a complete victory. The stronger must dominate the weaker and not simply blend with him, thereby sacrificing his own superiority. Contrary to what the mentally and physically weaker man claims, this is not cruel; it is merely the law of Nature.

The result of such racial purity, which Nature deems universally valid, is visible not only in the sharply defined external delineation of the various races [skin color, facial features, etc.] but the similarities within races themselves. The fox always remains a fox, the goose remains a goose, the tiger remains a tiger, etc. The only differences within a species reside in varying degrees of ferocity, strength, intelligence, agility, endurance, etc., of the individual members. You will never discover a fox who might, for instance, have humanitarian sympathies for geese, or a cat with a friendly attitude toward mice.

So, here, also the struggle within species arises not from some inner animosity but from love and hunger. In both instances, Nature watches calmly and with deep satisfaction. In the daily struggle for food, creatures which are weak and sickly or less determined to survive succumb, while the competition among males for the female awards the privilege or right to propagate only to the healthiest members of the species. Intra-species competition is Nature's way of improving a species' health and is thus a major factor in raising it to ever-higher levels of development.

If Nature employed different means, all greater and higher development would end and species would degenerate to ever-lower levels. Because the inferior is "superior" only in the numerical sense, the inferior would propagate so much more quickly that the superior would finally be driven to extinction, unless some sort of corrective action were taken. Nature accomplishes exactly that by exposing the inferior to such severe life-conditions that by themselves will limit the number who survive by besting the weakest among them. The number who survive is severely limited, and those who do, and thus live to reproduce, do so by being stronger and healthier than the rest.

Nature does not desire that the weaker members of a species mate with the stronger; nor does she desire the mixing of a higher with a lower race, because otherwise her eons-long work of ever-higher breeding, over hundreds and perhaps even thousands of years, might be smashed with a single blow.

The long experience of history offers numerous proofs of this profound truth. It exhibits with alarming certainty that every mixing of Aryan blood with the blood of inferior races resulted in the destruction of the more cultured race. North America's present population is made up of the greatest portion of people of Germanic descent, who hardly ever mingled their blood with that of the inferior colored peoples. Thus North America exhibits an entirely different humanity and culture from Central America and South America, where the predominantly Hispanic immigrants promiscuously mingled with the natives on a massive scale. This single example shows all too clearly the results of racial mixture. The Germanic inhabitants of the North American continent, who have remained racially pure and unmixed, rose to be masters of the continent; and they will remain masters as long as they do not defile their blood by mixing it with that of inferior races.

Briefly, the result of all racial mixing is therefore always and forever the following:

a   The sure but steady lowering of the level of the superior race;
b   The physical and mental deterioration and thus the start of a slowly but certainly increasing illness within that race.

To aid in bringing about such a state of affairs is therefore nothing less than to defy the divine command of the eternal creator.

And this sinful act is rewarded.

Whenever human beings attempt to defy the immutable laws of Nature, they defy the very principles to which they owe their existence as human beings. Such defiance leads inevitably to their own demise.

At this point we encounter the objections of modern pacifists, as genuinely Jewish in their unbounded pride as they are ignorant! "Man's purpose," they proclaim proudly, "is to overcome Nature!"

Without thinking, untold millions stupidly repeat such Jewish nonsense and conclude by ignorantly imagining themselves the "conquerors of Nature." Although they possess no other weapon than an "idea"—and a wretched one at that—which, if it were valid, the world as it actually exists would not be conceivable.

But, forgetting for the moment the fact that human beings have never in *any* sense "conquered" Nature, but have at most merely temporarily captured some small part of her vast and immense empire of eternal riddles and secrets, they have never actually invented anything at all but have at most only discovered the few things that she allows. And so, far from "conquering" or "dominating" Nature, man's knowledge has increased only insofar as he has learned and followed Nature's laws. This alone has allowed him to be master over other creatures who are without this knowledge. All this aside, an abstract "idea" cannot supersede Nature's own requirements for the evolutionary development of humanity, since that false idea depends entirely on human ingenuity. Without human beings there are no human ideas. Thus ideas are always made possible by the presence of human beings and therefore of all the laws which created the possibility of their very existence.

Not only that, though! Particular ideas are attributable to particular men. This applies especially to those ideas which originate, not in any precise scientific truth, but in the realm of the emotions, or—as it has recently been so beautifully and clearly stated today—which conveys and articulates an "inner experience."

Every one of these ideas—none of which has anything to do with icy logic, but represent only expressions of emotion, ethical views, and the like—are tightly bound to the very existence of men, to whose intelligence, imagination and creativity they owe their existence. In this instance the survival and perpetuation of well-defined races is a necessary condition for the existence of these racially specific ideas. Thus, for example, anyone who truly sought with all his heart the triumph of the idea of pacifism would have to struggle with all his might for Germany's conquest of the world. But if Germany were to be defeated, the sole remaining pacifist would disappear along with the last German. This is because no one else has ever sunk so low as some Germans have in falling for this pacifist nonsense, which runs counter to Nature and to reason. For, strange as it might seem, we would have to make war in order to achieve peace. Nothing short of this was what [U.S. President Woodrow] Wilson, America's so-called "savior of the world," aimed to achieve—or so said some of Germany's self-styled pacifist "prophets"— and Germany's surrender [to the Allies in 1918] became a self-fulfilling prophecy.

As a matter of fact the idea of humanitarian pacifism is legitimate, but only after the highest racial type has already conquered and subjugated the world over which he then rules alone and supreme. Only then will the pacifist idea produce good instead of evil. Let us fight, then, and see what we can achieve. Without such struggle, humanity will have passed the apogee of its development and begin to decline into chaos and barbarity. If you are tempted to laugh, remember that for most of its history our earth traveled through the skies without any human inhabitants—and it can do so again, if we forget that we owe our very existence not to ideas expounded by a handful of insane ideologues but to our knowledge and relentless application of the implacable and irrevocable laws of Nature.

All that we now admire—science, art, technology, and inventions—is the creative outcome of only a small number of peoples and originally perhaps of *a single* race. On them alone rests the survival and continuation of our culture. If these creative individuals were to die, the beauty of the world will die with them.

Although the land, for example, can influence human beings, the outcome of the influence will inevitably differ, depending on which race plants and tills it. The subnormal fertility of a particular piece of land can goad one race to the greatest achievements; but if another inferior race were to occupy the same plot of land they would impoverish and destroy it, bringing about poverty, malnutrition, and starvation. The inner essence of different races inevitably determines the ways in which external conditions will prove decisive. The same external conditions that lead one race to starve inspires the other to triumph and prevail.

The greatest cultures of earlier centuries died out solely because their creative races mixed their blood with uncreative ones.

The final determinant of their decline and death was that they forgot that every culture depends on men, and not the other way around. Thus in order to preserve a particular culture, the man who created it must survive intact and unimpaired. The preservation of both is determined by the strict law of necessity and the right to triumph of the best and strongest race and its individual members.

Anyone who wishes to survive must struggle, and anyone who wants to avoid struggle does not deserve to survive. Although this is difficult, it is unavoidably the way of the world. The worst fate is reserved for the man who believes he can "conquer" Nature; and in acting on that belief he becomes a pitiful laughingstock. Nature rewards him with misery, misfortune, and disease.

Anyone who misjudges and ignores Nature's racial laws in reality surrenders the joy that he seems to be entitled. In so doing he circumvents the victory march of the master race, and, although human, he remains within the restrictive sub-human kingdom of miserable debility.

There is no use arguing about which race or races were the first instigators of culture and were thus the actual originators of everything we summarize under the word *humanity*. Surely it is easier to ask this question solely about today; if we do so we arrive at a clear and concise answer. Everything that counts as the highest human culture [*Kultur*], which encompasses art, science, and technology, have almost without exception, been created by the Aryan. This singular fact allows us to infer that the Aryan alone was the originator of all that counts as culture and humanity. The Aryan is the very model of "man" or "humanity." The Aryan is the Prometheus[1] of humankind from whose brilliant forehead has always sprung the god-like spark of genius. It is this spark that kindles the fire of human knowledge; and that fire illuminates the night that would otherwise puzzle, mystify, surround and envelope us. Being in possession of this fire enables human beings to be masters of lesser creatures. If the Aryan is excluded, darkness will once again envelop the earth, human culture will disappear, and gardens will turn into deserts.

Were we to classify humankind into three categories—culture originators, culture carriers, and culture destroyers—the Aryan alone would fall into the first category. For it is from the Aryan that the foundations and walls of every human invention originates, and only the external appearance and hue are influenced by the changing character traits of the various peoples. The Aryan provides the most magnificent building stones and blueprints for all human progress and only the actual building reveals the real nature of the various races. For example, within mere decades all of eastern Asia will have a culture whose ultimate foundation will be Greek in spirit and German in technology, just as in much of Europe. Only the *outward* appearance will exhibit characteristically Asiatic features. Contrary to what some people believe—that the Japanese merely add European technology to their culture—European science and technology are decorated with Japanese qualities. The foundation of their real life is not any longer their unique Japanese culture, although that culture continues to determine the shape and color of life in Japan. And this is because externally, as a result of its internal differences, it is more noticeable to European visitors. The enormous scientific and technological achievements of Europe and America have been brought about by the Aryans.

Only because of Aryan intelligence, ingenuity and invention can the East follow the general progress of humanity. The Aryans supply the foundation of their competition for daily bread, create weaponry and technical means for it, and only the outward appearance is slowly but surely grafted onto the Japanese character.

If all of a sudden all Aryan influence on Japan were to cease … Japan's current ascendancy in science and technology might continue briefly; but within a short time the well would run dry, the unique Japanese character would be ever more evident, but the current culture would ossify and return to the torpor from which it was saved seventy years ago by the mighty current of Aryan culture. Thus contemporary Japanese development owes its existence to Aryan origin … Hence, if a people gets the most essential elements of its culture from foreign sources, and then adopts and adapts these elements, then that race can be called "*culture-bearing*," but not "*culture-creating*." A study of the various peoples from this perspective proves that none of them were at any point *culture-founding*, but merely *culture-bearing*.

Here is a rough approximation of the way in which Aryans have always operated to change the cultures of other peoples:

Although surprisingly small in number, Aryan races conquer foreign peoples, and then, rising to the challenge by the life-conditions of the new country—climate, fecundity of the soil, and so on—and using the labor of lesser races, raise up all the intellectual and organizational capabilities latent inside them. Sometimes in several millennia or perhaps in a shorter time they create new and vibrant cultures … But when in the course of time these culture-creating Aryans begin to mingle their blood with that of the culture-carrying lower race they violate Nature's law against blood-pollution. For this violation they pay a heavy price and, like Adam and Eve, bring about their expulsion from paradise …

The Aryans have always been the carriers of cultural uplift. Whenever Destiny places them in particular situations, their dormant talent soon begins to assert itself in creative ways. The cultures of the conquered peoples had been molded exclusively by the regnant soil, climatic conditions, and of course the mentality of the conquered people themselves. This final factor is nearly always decisive. The more backward the technological bases of cultural activities, the greater the need for human laborers to take the place of machinery. Absent the opportunity of using the labor of the lower races, Aryans would not have been able to create their own superior culture. This is analogous to the ways in which human beings have tamed beasts to carry their burdens; and now technological advancement is enabling humans to dispense with these beasts, by using machines instead … For example, the automobile is making the horse unnecessary; even though humans have relied on horses for millennia, they no longer need them. But without the horse mankind would not be where it is in modern times.

Therefore a necessary precondition for the creation of superior cultures was the existence of inferior creatures, both animal and human. It is a fact that the first human culture depended less on tamed animals than on the use of inferior human beings.

It was only after conquered human beings were enslaved that animals were tamed and put to work. At first it was the slave who pulled the plow, and only later the horse. Only sentimental morons will view this as an indication of human iniquity because they overlook the fact that this had to happen so that superior human beings could create a culture in which these air-heads could spout their pacifistic nonsense.

Human progress can be compared to the species' climb up a ladder of infinite length—one cannot climb higher without beginning at the lower rungs. And so Aryans had to climb the ladder of reality, not some ideal ladder imagined by contemporary pacifists. Although that road is arduous and burdensome, it points ultimately to the place the pacifist wants us to be, but only in his unrealistic imagination.

Thus it is not by chance that the earliest cultures originated in locales in which Aryans, in their confrontations with inferior peoples, conquered and enslaved them. These slaves in turn served as tools in the development of a higher culture.

Quite clearly, then, the path on which Aryans traveled was well-marked. As conquerors they subjugated inferior peoples and bent them to their iron will for their own purposes. Yet in channeling them into practical but difficult activities, Aryans did not merely spare the lives of their slaves but let them enjoy a life of dependency that was more valuable than their earlier "freedom." Insofar as Aryans remained ruthless masters they preserved and raised human culture. And that is because culture rested solely on their talents and abilities, and thus on the Aryans' own survival. Once the enslaved peoples were raised up and perhaps approximated their conquerors in linguistic ability, the deep division between masters and servants narrowed and disappeared. This resulted in the loss of the Aryans' blood-purity and thus his place in the heaven on earth that they had created for themselves. They became increasingly mongrelized, losing their ability to create culture, and finally began to look, think, and act more like the enslaved inferior race than like their racially pure predecessors. For a little while they could coast along on the culture they had created; but ultimately they were doomed to extinction.

It is in this way that a higher culture and even an entire empire collapse to pave the way for a new one to come.

The commingling of blood and the resulting lowering of the racial level is the one and only cause of the decline and death of old cultures; superior men die less because of losing wars, than by losing the purity of blood that gives them the strength to resist temptation.

Everyone who does not belong to the superior race is worthless. And every event in the history of the world is merely a manifestation of the racially based instinct to survive, for well or ill.

… Aryans are not necessarily superior in their mental abilities per se, but in the degree to which they are willing to devote all of their talents and abilities to promote the good of the community [*gemeinschaft*]. We see in them the highest manifestation of the instinct for individual and communal survival. The pure-blooded Aryan readily sacrifices his individual interests to the interests of the community, even if that means sacrificing his own life.

The Aryans' talent for creating and developing culture does not reside in his gifted intellect alone. If they had only this, they could only destroy, not build; nor could they act together, since the deepest essence of any organization is its individual members' willingness to subordinate their personal views and interests, sacrificing both for the sake of the community. It is only in this way that the individual members serve their real interests. No longer serving himself, he identifies his interests with those of the community of which he is a member; it is only by serving the community that he serves himself. The most marvelous clarification of this outlook is supplied by the word "work" [*arbeit*] which, as the Aryan uses it, does not designate a means of merely sustaining his own life but of sustaining and enriching the larger collective life of the entire community …

This Aryan outlook, which renders self-interest subservient to the interest of the larger community, is truly the starting-point for every genuinely human culture. Only from this can there arise the greatest works of humankind. For these the originator receives small recompense, except for the thanks of posterity. Only by such frugality, poverty, and self-sacrifice is it possible for earlier generations to lay the groundwork for the good life of later ones. All workers, peasants, inventors, etc., who labor without reward in their lifetimes represent this noble conception, even if they are unaware of it.

Whatever can be said of labor as the source of humanity's subsistence and progress can also be said even more strongly about the development and upholding of culture. By sacrificing their own lives for that of the community they earn the thanks of their descendants. This is all that stands in the way of a descent into barbarism, brought about by human beings or by Nature.

The German language has a wonderful word for denoting this type of behavior— *Pflichterfüllung* (fulfilling one's duty)—which means not to be self-interested but to serve the interests of the community.

The essential outlook that gives rise to duty-fulfillment is called "idealism." Idealism is sharply distinguished from self-interestedness and self-love. It is this that makes the individual capable of making sacrifices for the sake of his community and for that of his fellows.

We must understand that idealism is not equivalent to some superficial emotional expression; rather, it has in actuality always has been and forever will be, the precondition for what we call human culture, which is in turn the precondition for the creature we call the human being. Aryans owe their exalted place in the world to this mental outlook and the world in turn owes humanity. The Aryans alone have this purity of spirit which allows them to be unique in joining the clenched fist to the brilliant intellect, the union of which brought into being the wonders of modern culture.

Lacking the Aryans' idealistic outlook, even the most brilliant intellectual abilities would be empty and could count for nothing at all, and most assuredly nothing creative and original.

Because genuine idealism amounts to nothing less than surrendering the interests and the life of the individual to the community, we find here the necessary condition for creating every kind of organization. Thus in making human organization possible idealism serves Nature's own higher purposes. Only idealism motivates men to recognize the right conferred by power; they become the tiny particles of dust that Nature shapes to serve its own ends …

The only powerful force that threatens the Aryans are the Jews. No other race has a more highly developed sense of self-preservation than the Jews, who have the temerity to call themselves "God's chosen people." This race's very survival shows how strong is their sense of self-preservation. What other race in the last two millennia has so slightly changed its outlook, character, and the like? Who else but the Jews have undergone more momentous disasters without being changed one iota? This fact alone bespeaks their unbending will to survive.

The Jews' intellectual abilities have been honed over millennia. They have always prided themselves on their supposed "intelligence." Yet they have not developed their own intellects but have acquired them from foreign peoples. No human mind can ascend to the summit of culture and intellect without assistance from the past; and in acquiring such assistance the Jews excel all others. Every thought derives from a mere fraction of one's own knowledge, and much more extensively on knowledge inherited from the past. The average level of culture gives to individuals, typically without their even being aware of it, a huge store of previously acquired knowledge which they then add to and build upon. For instance, a boy in the modern world comes of age amid an incredible number of relatively recent technological developments which he accepts without question and which enable him to solve difficult and important problems that could not have been solved by even the greatest geniuses of a century earlier. Were a genius of a hundred years ago to arise from the dead, he would be less able to navigate today's world than a typical fifteen-year-old boy of today. And that is because that genius would be without the knowledge developed in the interim which the teenager has imbibed unawares as he grew up.

Because Jews have never had a culture of their own, the bases of their mental development were always built by other people. Their mental abilities have in every epoch been nurtured by the culture that enveloped them. It has never been the other way around.

The Jews' sense of self-love is greater than that of any other race, and their mental abilities superficially impressive; but they are utterly lacking in the one thing that is a necessary condition for a cultured race—an idealistic outlook.

Among Jews the willingness to sacrifice themselves does not transcend any individual Jew's raw sense of self-preservation. To all outward appearances their sense of tribal solidarity rests on an animal instinct that we see in nonhuman animals. Remarkably, this instinct comes into play only when Jews find it useful in facing a common foe. But this soon dissolves and disappears, just as a hungry wolf pack turn on each other once they have killed and begun to devour their prey. So it is with a herd of wild horses, which will band together to scare off an attacker only to separate after they have done so.

So it is with Jews. Their instinct of self-sacrifice is merely superficial, and more apparent than real. With them, the individual is supreme. After the enemy is defeated, the common danger avoided, and the loot hidden away, the illusory harmony within the tribe comes to an end, once more enabling individual Jews to pursue their own narrow self-interest. Jews bond among themselves only when an enemy forces them to, or the prospect of loot arouses their shared greed. Without these enticements the basest selfishness sets in and in an instant the supposedly unified race becomes a rat-horde engaged in a bloody war of mutual extermination.

If by chance world Jewry were the only race on the planet, they would suffocate in dirt and feces, trying desperately to succeed in a hateful struggle to the death, each against the other. Cowards lacking any sense of self-denial, they would turn their struggle into a laughable farce. Thus it would be a grave mistake to suppose that Jews are not thieving allies in struggle in their antagonism toward their fellow human beings. As always, they are motivated only by individual selfishness. So it is that the "Jewish state" is not really a state—an organic community devoted to racial preservation and improvement—but is world-wide, occupying no limited territory at all. Without territorial limitation, there can be no idealism or idealistic outlook within this so-called "state," especially as regards the idea of "work." Exactly insofar as this outlook is missing any hope of creating or conserving a geographically limited state is a non-starter. Therefore, the foundation on which a genuine culture can come into being is precluded.

Insofar as this outlook is absent, any hope of founding and preserving a spatially restricted state is baseless. And since such a state is the foundation of culture, no true culture can come into being.

Thus the Jewish people, in spite of their alleged "intellects," have no genuine culture they can call their own. Such culture as they have is borrowed—or stolen—from other nations. And, once in possession of another peoples' culture, the Jews degrade and destroy it.

To arrive at a judgment of the Jews' conception of culture, the most important factor to consider is that there is no such thing as "Jewish art," and there never will be. The twin monarchs of the arts—music and architecture—have received nothing new or original from the Jews. Anything they achieve in art is either a pastiche or outright theft. Hence, the Jews are utterly lacking in the gifts which differentiate the various races which are endowed with true creativity.

To the degree that Jews come to possess another people's culture, parroting it or perhaps, more often, wrecking it, is observable from a singular fact: the only "art" in which Jews excel is purely imitative—acting. Actors are really only ape-like imitators, lacking any genuine talent for greatness ... Instead of being artists, actors are merely pathetic comedians.

In reality, Jews have no cultural creativity at all, because they lack idealism of any sort. Their intellects are never constructive, only destructive; and although they can be superficially stimulating, they are shallow ... Mankind progresses despite, not because of, the Jew.

Knowing no territorial boundaries and no culture of their own, the Jews are among the world's nomadic peoples—so some people claim. But this is a hugely dangerous delusion. Normal nomadic peoples have a definitely defined, if wide-ranging, territory; this is made necessary because of the limited fertility of the soil and the scarcity of the grasses on which they graze their herds. Even more important is the sharp divide between their primitive stage of technological development and the lack of fecundity of their living-space [*lebensraum*]; the former limits their ability to take full advantage of the latter.

This stands in stark contrast with the Aryans, whose technology—slow but sure in its development—enables them to reside within a limited territory and to fertilize and till the soil to make it satisfy their needs. Without such technology they would either never have settled in these areas or, like the nomad, would be forced to wander endlessly from place to place, never knowing the joy of residing in a single settled territory.

We should remember that, as the North American continent was being explored and settled, many Aryans struggled for a living as hunters, fur traders, and the like, and they often traveled in large groups with wives and children, effectively making them nomads. However, with their numbers increasing and their technology improving (plows, hoes, etc.), they were able to till the soil more effectively and to be victorious against the savage inhabitants of North America. Soon settlements were established in ever greater numbers, all across the vast continent.

Although initially a nomad, the Aryan was never like the Jew, who was never nomadic at all, since he had no conception of work which would lay the foundation for his later intellectual and cultural development.

Although much-diluted, the essential idealistic viewpoint is evident in the nomad, making him seem strange to the Aryan but attractive and recognizable nonetheless. But in the Jew this viewpoint is nowhere to be found, since he was never nomadic, but existed only as a tapeworm within the intestine of some host people. The mere fact that he has left his earlier living-space is irrelevant to his aims but is an outcome of his having been expelled by the people whose hospitality he abused. The Jew's dispersion across the globe is all too typical; he always looks for a new host to which to attach himself and from which he sucks out the life-blood.

This fact, though, is not a feature of all nomads. Only the Jews never consider emigrating from an area in which they have settled; they stay where they are, and so adamantly that they cannot be forced out. Their expansion into new nations happens when particular preconditions exist; lacking these, they would not go there. The Jews are always parasitic—a repulsive bacterium which multiplies and spreads whenever a suitable breeding-ground becomes available. And like a deadly bacterium, the Jews sooner or later kill their host. Jews have always resided within other peoples' nations, within which they organize their own state under the guise of a separate "religious community." Here they hide their true nature. Yet whenever they feel that their power is great enough, they discard the disguise and quickly become the feared figure—the Jew—that always lurked within.

The Jews' existence as bloodsuckers living inside the bodies of foreign states and nations is the feature that led Schopenhauer to call him the "master liar."[2] Their very existence forces Jews to lie constantly and often, in much the same way that the cold climate forces northerners to wear warm clothing.

Their existence inside the bodies of foreign nations lasts only as long as their hosts believe that they are not a people in their own right but are instead a "religious community."

And this is only the first of many huge lies.

That lie is told to allow them to continue existing as bloodsuckers living off of other people, without revealing their true nature. The smarter the individual Jew, the greater his success in deceiving others. This deception allows them to pass as French or English, Germans or Italians, who somehow simply have a different "faith." Gullible government officials are most easily deceived on this score ...

Far from being merely co-religionists, the Jews have forever remained a particular *people* [*volk*] with distinct racial features ... Because of their own inner nature the Jews do not actually have any kind of religious community since they have no sense of idealism, and thus no belief in an afterlife. A religion in the true Aryan meaning of the term has a belief in the afterlife as its central tenet. The Talmud does not prepare Jews for life after death, but only for making worldly profit.[3]

The doctrines of the Jewish religion consist mainly of rules for ensuring the blood-purity of Jews and for governing Jew-to-Jew relations and their relations with gentiles.

This raises not only or merely moral issues but quite limited economic issues as well. As to the moral worth of Jewish religious instruction, ... that can be seen in the character of the Jews themselves. Their lives are exclusively worldly and their inner spirit is as foreign to real Christianity as it is to [Jesus's generous spirit]. Jesus did not hide his contempt for the Jews, and even picked up the lash to drive the money-changers from the House of God—Jews who regard religion as a means of making money. For his trouble Christ was crucified. And now so-called Christian politicians beg for Jewish votes, making crooked deals with atheistic Jewish factions, and conspire with them to undermine Germany's national interests.

To uphold the lie that the Jews are a religion and not a race, ever more lies are told. These include the lie about the Jewish language [i.e., Hebrew]. Instead of using language to convey ideas, they use it to conceal them. Even as they speak French, they think Jewish; and when Jewish poets write German verse, they inwardly reveal their racial allegiance. Until Jews become the rulers of other peoples they must speak those peoples' languages even if they dislike doing so; but once they become the Jews' slaves they will have to give up their own languages and speak a universal language—Esperanto, for instance!—so that the Jews can more readily rule over them.

The degree to which the entire existence of the Jewish race is revealed beyond any doubt by *The Protocols of the Learned Elders of Zion*, so deeply despised by the Jews.[4] "*The Protocols* are counterfeit," shouts the *Frankfurter Zeitung* [*Frankfurt Times*] each week—a protest that proves the *Protocols'* authenticity. What this shows, significantly, is that Jewish "truth-telling" is exposed for the lie that it is. They thereby reveal the real nature of their thinking and acting. Reality itself is the critic they fear most. Anyone who studies the history of the last one-hundred years from the perspective of [*Mein Kampf*] will immediately comprehend the maniacal shouting of the Jewish media. When my book becomes the shared possession of our people [*volk*], the Jewish threat will no longer exist ...

With devilish delight the dark-haired Jewish man lies in wait for the trusting young woman whose blood he then defiles by mixing it with his, thereby estranging her from her *volk*. Using everything at his disposal he attempts to destroy the racial basis of the people he has vowed to conquer. Systematically he defiles girls and young women, not hesitating to transgress the blood-borders that separate his people from theirs. Never forget that it was the Jews who imported Blacks to the Rhineland, with the aim of destroying the despised white race by race-mixing, thereby becoming the master of both.

A racially pure *volk* whose members are attuned to their blood-purity cannot ever be conquered by Jews and made their slaves. Jews can only be masters of mixed-blood bastards. That is why they attempt always to reduce the level of blood-purity by mixing and poisoning the blood of particular individuals. And in the political arena the Jews seek to replace the concept of democracy—rule by the *volk* at large—with that of "the dictatorship of the proletariat."

The Jew has discovered in the proletarian masses the tool with which he can ignore democracy and instead enables him to conquer and rule peoples in a brutally dictatorial manner. Working energetically for revolution in a double sense—political and economic—the Jews provide to people who violently resist their rule an entire network of enemies, national and international, who support the idea of "revolution."

In the financial arena, the Jew subverts the state until publicly owned businesses that fail to return a profit are privatized and fall under Jewish bankers' control.

And in the political arena the Jew starves the state of its economic means of preservation, national defense, trust in its leaders, ridicules the nation's history, and drags into the sewer everything that is great about the nation.

In the cultural arena, the Jew infects all of literature, art, and the theater, mocking all natural feelings that these inspire, and lowers all others down to his degraded level.

And in the arena of religion and morality, both are represented as ridiculous and obsolete, until the last remaining pillars of a nation have been destroyed, and the nation is no more.

This marks the beginning of the greatest and final revolution. When they secure political power the Jews discard the clothing that had concealed the truth about them. The allegedly popular-democratic Jew is revealed at last as the bloodily tyrannical Jew. Within a short period he will attempt to kill off the intellectual elite of the nation and—by depriving the people of that elite's leadership—he makes the people fit for eternal enslavement.

We see the most alarming instance of this phenomenon in Russia, where the Jew savagely and maliciously murdered or starved to death some 30 million Russians just to allow a cabal of Jewish writers and stock broker-bandits to rule over a once-great nation. The result is not merely the extinction of the liberty of the Jew's victims but of the extinction of the Jew himself. After his victim dies the bloodsucking leech dies also …

In the first volume [of *Mein Kampf*] I wrote about the word "folkish" [*volkische*], inasmuch as this word has never been satisfactorily defined. But if we are to establish a unified community of struggle we must define that term. The cover-all term "folkish" seems to be on everyone's lips without anyone knowing what it means. And so, before I take up a discussion of the goals and work of the National Socialist German Workers Party [*Nationalsozialistische Deutsche Arbeiterpartei*], I want to clarify the meaning of that ill-defined term and its place in our political movement …

The idea of "folkish" appears to be imprecisely defined, and admits of numerous interpretations, as does, for example, the term "religious." Like "religious," it is difficult to think of something that is a completely clear definition of "folkish." This lack of clarity has dire implications both for theory and for practice …

As with the word "religious," so too with the concept "folkish": each requires a more precise definition than it currently has. It is only when they become essential elements of a political movement that they acquire a clear meaning. *To achieve our philosophical aims and the political ultimatums that accompany them does not come about through people's innermost feelings, any more than the simple desire for freedom will itself free a people from their bondage. Far from it. Only when an abstract longing for freedom is accompanied by organized struggle and actual weapons will that desire be actualized in the most wonderful way.*

No matter how valid it is, a life-philosophy will remain impotent in the actual forging of a people's way of life unless its tenets are inscribed on the flag of an assertive movement and accompanied by an organized and disciplined political party. Its conquest becomes complete when its ideas take the form of organizational principles and are embodied in a people's community [volksgemeinschaft].

However, without a transcendent idea to undergird the possibility of its advancement, there can be no clear way forward. Only when a unified people share clear convictions can they fight and win. It is on the basis of abstract ideas that a people can forge a political program in which they believe and for which they will fight, using every means at their disposal. Any idealistic principle, which the theorist must espouse, must take concrete form if it is to be implemented in actual political practice. Thus an everlasting ideal is a polar star by means of which weak and fallible men navigate boundless seas. Taking human weakness into account and taking measures to check it, allows fallible humans to reach the farther shore safely and alive. Deriving from the kingdom of eternal ideals and truths, men, using their minds together and as a people, discover what is possible and desirable.

Such a transition from abstract philosophical ideas of ultimate truth to a unified, disciplined and fighting state-community is mankind's most important accomplishment. But the masses of mankind cannot achieve this on their own. They must be inspired and led by a lone commander who alone articulates and embodies the stone-solid principles that guarantee victory in an uncertain world ...

If we wish to extract the essential meaning of the concept "folkish," we reach these conclusions:

In Germany our current political outlook rests generally on the belief that the creation of culture rests with the government, and has no basis in race but is instead the product of economic factors and the thirst for political power. This basic outlook, if allowed to continue, will give rise to a misunderstanding of the role of race, both at the individual and the collective level. The presumption of racial equality is the gravest mistake ever made, and becomes the erroneous foundation for individual and collective misjudgments. This nonsense is the political dogma espoused by Marxism which was created by the Jew Karl Marx. His dogma would never have caught on if the seeds of liberal tolerance had not been planted and produced plants bearing such poisonous fruit. In reality, of course, Karl Marx was the lone individual who, having the vision of a prophet, took notice of the toxins available and distilled them into a deadly compound. Like a magician he made possible the rapid destruction of the world's independent nations. He did this only to further the foul interests of his fellow Jews.

Marx's dogma is merely an extraction of the spirit of a life-philosophy that is now widespread. To contend, as Marx does, that the "bourgeoisie" is powerless against this dogma, is clearly false, since the minds of the bourgeoisie are themselves poisoned by these same ideas, and with some few exceptions, they lead lives that differ only slightly from those of self-styled Marxists. The world of the bourgeoisie is already essentially Marxist inasmuch as it believes that the rule of a certain class— their own—is right; in this they differ from the Marxists who believe in world-domination by the working class but, in reality, by the Jews.

Opposed to this is our folkish philosophy, which classifies humankind according to essential racial characteristics. We view and value the nation-state not as an end in itself, but merely as a means to racial preservation. Therefore we do not believe in racial equality but in racial *inequality* and hierarchy. The best and strongest race must engage in struggle and emerge victorious to conquer and enslave weaker and inferior races. That is all according to the unchanging requirements of nature and nature's law. In acting according to this law we bow to its basically elitist character. Nature takes note of the different worth of different races and of the individuals who belong to them. Contrasting sharply with Marxism and its disordering effect, our folkish philosophy arranges the socio-political world in an orderly way. It subscribes to the view, "each to his own race," not to the race-mixing mongrelization advocated by Marxists. It believes in moral ideas but not if they endanger the existence of the superior race. In an illegitimate and Africanized world all the ideas of beauty and sublimity would be in danger of destruction. These ideas depend upon the existence of the Aryan; if he perishes, a new and permanent Dark Age will settle upon the earth.

Any threat to the survival of human culture by threatening its carriers is, according to our folkish philosophy, the worst crime imaginable. Any threat to the Aryan is an affront to our Divine Creator, in whose image we are made, and amounts to our being expelled from Eden for a second time.

Thus the folkish life-philosophy is connected with nature's inner intentions insofar as it leads to ever-higher breeding within the superior race. Ultimately this will result in Aryan dominion over the earth.

Everyone knows that future generations of humankind will face global problems of such complexity that they can be solved only by a superior race ...

It is all too obvious that this brief description of our folkish philosophy is open to multiple misinterpretations. Several of our more recent political movements base themselves in some respects on this outlook [world-picture or *Weltanschauung*]. As one among many outlooks, it reveals its own uniqueness when contrasted with them. By contrast, the Marxist outlook, presided over by a rigidly hierarchical party, finds opposition in a welter of inchoate and unimpressive perspectives and ideas that cannot hope to rival ours. Such a poor ideological arsenal will not secure for them the victory they seek! Only when Marxism's cosmopolitan outlook is challenged by the folkish outlook, backed by unified leadership, will the latter, armed with nature's eternal truths, win out over the former.

A life-philosophy can be translated into an effective organization only when that philosophy's principles are incorporated into a newly formed political party.

Thus a means must be discovered for making the folkish outlook able to fight the cosmopolitan communist party and their allies and fellow-travelers.

This is the aim of the National Socialist German Workers Party. Our party's aim is to articulate and announce the folkish life-philosophy, made real by being backed by the organization necessary for its success. Even those who are opposed to the idea of an organized party [as opposed to a broad "movement"] must admit this. These are the ones who never tire of saying that the folkish life-philosophy is not an inheritance belonging to any individual, but sleeps and lives in the hearts of untold multitudes. They thereby show that the widespread sharing of folkish ideas was not able to stop in their tracks those partisans who hold opposing views. Were this not the case, the Germans would be destined to achieve a huge victory [over the communists] instead of looking down into a deep chasm. What has so far brought success to the communists' cosmopolitan outlook is their outlook being backed by storm troopers. Conversely, what has brought defeat to proponents of the folkish philosophy is their lack of such a united party and the people who can throw a punch. It is not limitless liberty to articulate their folkish outlook, but the limiting force of a political party that can put fighters in the field to oppose the party's enemies and emerge victorious.

Thus I see my vocation to be pulling those key ideas from the massive and formless body of a large world-view and then remaking these ideas into a fairly hard-edged form to give men something to which they can pledge their unswerving loyalty.

Stated differently: *Drawing upon the essential ideas to be found in the larger folkish world-view, the National Socialist German Workers Party assimilates the most important characteristic features of this world-view and creates a practical political doctrine which it then turns into a weapon of public persuasion and power in the coming struggle for the victory of the folkish world-view.*

NOTES

1   In Greek mythology Prometheus stole fire from the gods to give to mankind. For this transgression he was chained to a mountain peak and daily suffered the torture of having vultures tear open his skin and devour his liver, which grew back overnight. The next day the vultures returned to repeat the torment.—Eds.

2   The German philosopher Arthur Schopenhauer (1788–1860), author of *The World as Will and Idea*.—Eds.

3   The Talmud is a collection of Jewish religious and civil laws as well as ethical instruction in the form of commentaries on and interpretations and applications of the Pentateuch (the first five books of the Old Testament).—Eds.

4   *The Protocols of the Learned Elders of Zion* was a nineteenth-century document purporting to lay out Jewish plans for world domination. Although shown to be a forgery, *The Protocols* continues to be a powerful propaganda weapon in the anti-Semitic arsenal. Hitler was merely one of the more prominent anti-Semites to make use of this forged document.—Eds.

The Turner Diaries

ANDREW MACDONALD
(WILLIAM L. PIERCE)*

The Turner Diaries is a work of fiction that imagines how a world ruled by neo-Nazis might come about and what it would look like once it had arrived. Its author, Andrew Macdonald—a pseudonym for William L. Pierce (1933–2002), a leading American neo-Nazi—sets the novel in 2099, one hundred years after a neo-Nazi movement calling itself The Organization defeated its multi-racial and multi-cultural archenemy, The System, in The Great Revolution of the 1990s, which ended in 1999 in victory for The Organization. The bulk of the book consists of recently discovered diaries written by one Earl Turner, a hero of The Great Revolution who blew up the Pentagon in a suicide bombing raid. The following excerpt from *The Turner Diaries* begins with the final entry from Turner's diaries, followed by the Epilog that ends the novel.

* *Source*: Andrew Macdonald (a.k.a. William L. Pierce), *The Turner Diaries*, 2nd ed. (Hillsboro, WV: National Vanguard Books, 1980). Reprinted by permission.

THE TURNER DIARIES

November 9, 1993. It's still three hours until first light, and all systems are "go." I'll use the time to write a few pages—my last diary entry. Then it's a one-way trip to the Pentagon for me. The warhead is strapped into the front seat of the old Stearman[1] and rigged to detonate either on impact or when I flip a switch in the back seat. Hopefully, I'll be able to manage a low-level air burst directly over the center of the Pentagon. Failing that, I'll at least try to fly as close as I can before I'm shot down.

It's been more than four years since I've flown, but I've thoroughly familiarized myself with the Stearman cockpit and been briefed on the plane's peculiarities: I don't anticipate any piloting problems. The barn-hangar here is only eight miles from the Pentagon. We'll thoroughly warm up the engine in the barn, and when the door is opened I'll go like a bat out of hell, straight for the Pentagon, at an altitude of about 50 feet.

By the time I hit the defensive perimeter I should be making about 150 miles an hour, and it'll take me just under another 70 seconds to reach the target. Two-thirds of the troops around the Pentagon are niggers, which should greatly boost my chances of getting through.

The sky should still be heavily overcast, and there'll be just enough light for me to make out my landmarks. We've painted the plane to be as nearly invisible as possible under the anticipated flying conditions, and I'll be too low for radar-controlled fire. Considering everything, I believe my chances are excellent.

I regret that I won't be around to participate in the final success of our revolution, but I am happy that I have been allowed to do as much as I have. It is a comforting thought in these last hours of my physical existence that, of all the billions of men and women of my race who have ever lived, I will have been able to play a more vital role than all but a handful of them in determining the ultimate destiny of mankind. What I will do today will be of more weight in the annals of the race than all the conquests of Caesar and Napoleon—if I succeed!

And succeed I must, or the entire revolution will be in the gravest danger. Revolutionary Command estimates that the System will launch its invasion against California within the next 48 hours. Once the order is issued from the Pentagon, we will be unable to halt the invasion. And if my mission today fails, there'll not be enough time for us to try something else.

Monday night, after we had made the final decision on this mission, I underwent the rite of Union. Actually, I have been undergoing the rite for the past 30 hours, and it will not be complete for another three; only in the moment of my death will I achieve full membership in the Order.

To many that may seem a gloomy prospect, I suppose, but not to me. I have known what was ahead of me since my trial last March, and I am grateful that my probationary period has been cut short by five months, partly because of the present crisis and partly because my performance since March has been considered exemplary.

The ceremony Monday was more moving and beautiful than I could have imagined it would be. More than 200 of us assembled in the cellar of the Georgetown gift shop, from which the partitions and stacked crates had been removed to make room for us. Thirty new probationary members were sworn into the Order, and 18 others, including me, participated in the rite of Union. I alone, however, was singled out, because of my unique status.

When Major Williams summoned me, I stepped forward and then turned to face the silent sea of robed figures. What a contrast with the tiny gathering only two years earlier, when seven of us met upstairs for my initiation! The Order, even with its extraordinary standards, is growing with astonishing rapidity.

Knowing fully what was demanded in character and commitment of each man who stood before me, my chest swelled with pride. These were no soft-bellied, conservative businessmen assembled for some Masonic mumbo-jumbo; no loudmouthed, beery red-necks letting off a little ritualized steam about "the goddam niggers"; no pious, frightened churchgoers whining for the guidance or protection of an anthropomorphic deity. These were *real men, White* men, men who were now *one* with me in spirit and consciousness as well as in blood.

As the torchlight flickered over the coarse, gray robes of the motionless throng, I thought to myself: These men are the best my race has produced in this generation—and they are as good as have been produced in any generation. In them are combined fiery passion and icy discipline, deep intelligence and instant readiness for action, a strong sense of self-worth and a total commitment to our common cause. On them hang the hopes of everything that will ever be. They are the vanguard of the coming New Era, the pioneers who will lead our race out of its present depths and toward the unexplored heights above. And I am *one* with them!

Then I made my brief declaration: "Brothers! Two years ago, when I entered your ranks for the first time, I consecrated my life to our Order and to the purpose for which it exists. But then I faltered in the fulfillment of my obligation to you. Now I am ready to meet my obligation fully. I offer you my life. Do you accept it?"

In a rumbling unison their reply came back: "Brother! We accept your life. In return we offer you everlasting life in us. Your deed shall not be in vain, nor shall it be forgotten, until the end of time. To this commitment we pledge our lives."

I know, as certainly as it is possible for a man to know anything, that the Order will not fail me if I do not fail it. The Order has a life which is more than the sum of the lives of its members. When it speaks collectively, as it did Monday, something deeper and older and wiser than any of us speaks—something which cannot die. Of that deeper life I am now about to partake.

Of course, I would have liked to have children by Katherine, so that I could also have immortality of another sort, but that is not to be. I am satisfied.

They've been warming up the engine for about 10 minutes now, and Bill is signaling to me that it's time to go. The rest of the crew has already taken cover in the blast shelter we dug under the barn floor. I will now entrust my diary to Bill, and he will later put it in the hiding place with the other volumes.

Epilog

Thus end Earl Turner's diaries, as unpretentiously as they began.

His final mission was successful, of course, as we all are reminded each year on November 9—our traditional Day of the Martyrs.

With the System's principal military nerve center destroyed, the System's forces poised outside the Organization's California enclave continued to wait for orders which never came. Declining morale, soaring desertions, growing Black indiscipline, and finally, the inability of the System to maintain the integrity of its supply line to its California troops resulted in the gradual erosion of the threat of invasion. Eventually the System began regrouping its forces elsewhere, to meet new challenges in other parts of the country.

And then, just as the Jews had feared, the flow of Organization activists turned exactly 180 degrees from what it had been in the weeks and months immediately prior to July 4, 1993. From scores of training camps in the liberated zone, first hundreds, then thousands of highly motivated guerrilla fighters began slipping through the System's diminishing ring of troops and moving eastward. With these guerrilla forces the Organization followed the example of its Baltimore members and rapidly established dozens of new enclaves, primarily in the nuclear-devastated areas, where System authority was weakest.

The Detroit enclave was initially the most important of these. Bloody anarchy had reigned among the survivors in the Detroit area for several weeks after the nuclear blasts of September 8. Eventually, a semblance of order had been restored, with System troops loosely sharing power with the leaders of a number of Black gangs in the area. Although there were a few isolated White strongholds which kept the roving mobs of Black plunderers and rapists at bay, most of the disorganized and demoralized White survivors in and around Detroit offered no effective resistance to the Blacks, and, just as in other heavily Black areas of the country, they suffered terribly.

Then, in mid-December, the Organization seized the initiative. A number of synchronized lightning raids on the System's military strong-points in the Detroit area resulted in an easy victory.

The Organization then established certain patterns in Detroit which were soon followed elsewhere. All captured White troops, as soon as they had laid down their weapons, were offered a chance to fight with the Organization against the System. Those who immediately volunteered were taken aside for preliminary screening and then sent to camps for indoctrination and special training. The others were machine-gunned on the spot, without further ado.

The same degree of ruthlessness was used in dealing with the White civilian population. When the Organization's cadres moved into the White strongholds in the Detroit suburbs, the first thing they found it necessary to do was to liquidate most of the local White leaders, in order to establish the unquestioned authority of the Organization. There was no time or patience for trying to reason with shortsighted Whites who insisted that they weren't "racists" or "revolutionaries" and didn't need the help of any "outside agitators" in dealing with their problems, or who had some other conservative or parochial fixation.

The Whites of Detroit and the other new enclaves were organized more along the lines described by Earl Turner for Baltimore than for California, but even more rapidly and roughly. In most areas of the country there was no opportunity for an orderly, large-scale separation of non-Whites, as in California, and consequently a bloody race war raged for months, taking a terrible toll of those Whites who were not in one of the Organization's tightly controlled, all-White enclaves.

Food became critically scarce everywhere during the winter of 1993–1994. The Blacks lapsed into cannibalism, just as they had in California, while hundreds of thousands of starving Whites, who earlier had ignored the Organization's call for a rising against the System, began appearing at the borders of the various liberated zones begging for food. The Organization was only able to feed the White populations already under its control by imposing the severest rationing, and it was necessary to turn many of the latecomers away.

Those who were admitted—and that meant only children, women of child-bearing age, and able-bodied men willing to fight in the Organization's ranks—were subjected to much more severe racial screening than had been used to separate Whites from non-Whites in California. It was no longer sufficient to be merely White; in order to eat one had to be judged the bearer of especially valuable genes.

In Detroit the practice was first established (and it was later adopted elsewhere) of providing any able-bodied White male who sought admittance to the Organization's enclave with one hot meal and a bayonet or other edged weapon. His forehead was then marked with an indelible dye, and he was turned out and could be readmitted permanently only by bringing back the head of a freshly killed Black or other non-White. This practice assured that precious food would not be wasted on those who would not or could not add to the Organization's fighting strength, but it took a terrible toll of the weaker and more decadent White elements.

Tens of millions perished during the first half of 1994, and the total White population of the country reached a low point of approximately 50 million by August of that year. By then, however, nearly half the remaining Whites were in Organization enclaves, and food production and distribution in the enclaves had grown until it was barely sufficient to prevent further losses from starvation.

Although a central government of sorts still existed, the System's military and police forces were, for all practical purposes, reduced to a number of essentially autonomous local commands, whose principal activity became looting for food, liquor, gasoline, and women. Both the Organization and the System avoided large-scale encounters with each other, the Organization confining itself to short, intense raids on System troop concentrations and other facilities, and the System's forces confining themselves to guarding their sources of supply and, in some areas, to attempting to limit the further expansion of the Organization's enclaves.

But the Organization's enclaves continued to expand, nevertheless, both in size and number, all through the five Dark Years preceding the New Era. At one time there were nearly 2,000 separate Organization enclaves in North America. Outside these zones of order and security, the anarchy and savagery grew steadily worse, with the only real authority wielded by marauding bands which preyed on each other and on the unorganized and defenseless masses.

Many of these bands were composed of Blacks, Puerto Ricans, Chicanos, and half-White mongrels. In growing numbers, however, Whites also formed bands along racial lines, even without Organization guidance. As the war of extermination wore on, millions of soft, city-bred, brainwashed Whites gradually began regaining their manhood. The rest died.

The Organization's growing success was not without its setbacks, of course. One of the most notable of these was the terrible Pittsburgh Massacre, of June

1994. The Organization had established an enclave there in May of that year, forcing the retreat of local System forces, but it did not act swiftly enough in identifying and liquidating the local Jewish element.

A number of Jews, in collaboration with White conservatives and liberals, had time to work out a plan of subversion. The consequence was that System troops, aided by their fifth column inside the enclave, recaptured Pittsburgh. The Jews and Blacks then went on a wild rampage of mass murder, reminiscent of the worst excesses of the Jew-instigated Bolshevik Revolution in Russia, 75 years earlier. By the time the blood-orgy ended, virtually every White in the area had either been butchered or forced to flee. The surviving staff members of the Organization's Pittsburgh Field Command, whose hesitation in dealing with the Jews had brought on the catastrophe, were rounded up and shot by a special disciplinary squad acting on orders from Revolutionary Command.

The only time, after November 9, 1993, the Organization was forced to detonate a nuclear weapon on the North American continent was a year later, in Toronto. Hundreds of thousands of Jews had fled the United States to that Canadian city during 1993 and 1994, making almost a second New York of it and using it as their command center for the war raging to the south. So far as both the Jews and the Organization were concerned, the U.S.–Canadian border had no real significance during the later stages of the Great Revolution, and by mid-1994 conditions were only slightly less chaotic north of the border than south of it.

Throughout the Dark Years neither the Organization nor the System could hope for a completely decisive advantage over the other, so long as they both retained the capability for nuclear warfare. During the first part of this period, when the System's conventional military strength greatly exceeded the Organization's, only the Organization's threat of retaliation with its more than 100 nuclear warheads hidden inside the major population centers still under System control kept the System, in most cases, from moving against the Organization's liberated zones.

Later, when Organizational gains, together with growing attrition of the System's forces through desertions, tilted the balance of conventional strength toward the Organization, the System retained control over a number of military units armed with nuclear weapons and, by threatening to use these, forced the Organization to leave certain System strongholds inviolate.

Even the System's elite, pampered nuclear troops were not immune to the processes of attrition which sapped the System's conventional strength, however, and they could postpone the inevitable only temporarily. On January 30, 1999, in the momentous Truce of Omaha, the last group of System generals surrendered their commands to the Organization, in return for a pledge that they and their immediate families would be allowed to live out the remainders of their lives unmolested. The Organization kept its pledge, and a special reservation on an island off the California coast was set aside for the generals.

Then, of course, came the mopping-up period, when the last of the non-White bands were hunted down and exterminated, followed by the final purge of undesirable racial elements among the remaining White population.

From the liberation of North America until the beginning of the New Era for our whole planet, there elapsed the remarkably short time of just under 11 months.

Professor Anderson has recorded and analyzed the events of this climactic period in detail in his *History of the Great Revolution*. Here it is sufficient to note that, with the principal centers of world Jewish power annihilated and the nuclear threat of the Soviet Union neutralized, the most important obstacles to the Organization's worldwide victory were out of the way.

From as early as 1993 the Organization had had active cells in Western Europe, and they grew with extraordinary rapidity in the six years preceding the victory in North America. Liberalism had taken its toll in Europe, just as in America, and the old order in most places was a rotted-out shell with only a surface semblance of strength. The disastrous economic collapse in Europe in the spring of 1999, following the demise of the System in North America, greatly helped in preparing the European masses morally for the Organization's final takeover.

That takeover came in a great, Europe-wide rush in the summer and fall of 1999, as a cleansing hurricane of change swept over the continent, clearing away in a few months the refuse of a millennium or more of alien ideology and a century or more of profound moral and material decadence. The blood flowed ankle-deep in the streets of many of Europe's great cities momentarily, as the race traitors, the offspring of generations of dysgenic breeding, and hordes of *Gastarbeiter*[2] met a common fate. Then the great dawn of the New Era broke over the Western world.

The single remaining power center on earth not under Organizational control by early December 1999 was China. The Organization was willing to postpone the solution of the Chinese problem for several years, but the Chinese themselves forced the Organization to take immediate and drastic action. The Chinese, of course, had invaded the Asiatic regions of the Soviet Union immediately after the nuclear strike of September 8, 1993, but until the fall of 1999 they had remained east of the Urals, consolidating the vast, new, conquered territory.

When, during the summer and early fall of 1999, one European nation after another was liberated by the Organization, the Chinese decided to make a grab for European Russia. The Organization countered this move massively, using nuclear missiles to knock out the still-primitive Chinese missile and strategic-bomber capabilities, as well as hitting a number of new Chinese troop concentrations west of the Urals. Unfortunately, this action did not stem the Yellow tide flowing north and west from China.

The Organization still required time to reorganize and reorient the European populations newly under its control before it could hope to deal in a conventional manner with the enormous numbers of Chinese infantry pouring across the Urals into Europe; all its dependable troops at that time were hardly sufficient even for garrison duty in the newly liberated and still not entirely pacified areas of eastern and southern Europe.

Therefore, the Organization resorted to a combination of chemical, biological, and radiological means, on an enormous scale, to deal with the problem. Over a period of four years some 16 million square miles of the earth's surface, from the Ural Mountains to the Pacific and from the Arctic Ocean to the Indian Ocean, were effectively sterilized. Thus was the Great Eastern Waste created.

Only in the last decade have certain areas of the Waste been declared safe for colonization. Even so, they are "safe" only in the sense that the poisons sowed there a century ago have abated to the point that they are no longer a hazard to life. As everyone is aware, the bands of mutants which roam the Waste remain a real threat, and it may be another century before the last of them has been eliminated and White colonization has once again established a human presence throughout this vast area.

But it was in the year 1999, according to the chronology of the Old Era—just 110 years after the birth of the Great One[3]—that the dream of a White world finally became a certainty. And it was the sacrifice of the lives of uncounted thousands of brave men and women of the Organization during the preceding years which had kept that dream alive until its realization could no longer be denied.

Among those uncounted thousands Earl Turner played no small part. He gained immortality for himself on that dark November day 106 years ago when he faithfully fulfilled his obligation to his race, to the Organization, and to the holy Order which had accepted him into its ranks. And in so doing he helped greatly to assure that his race would survive and prosper, that the Organization would achieve its worldwide political and military goals, and that the Order would spread its wise and benevolent rule over the earth for all time to come.

NOTES

1   The Stearman 75 is a two-seater biplane built by Boeing Aircraft Company and used to train pilots before and during World War II.—Eds.
2   *Gastarbeiter* is the German word for foreign-born "guest workers" in Europe.—Eds.
3   "The Great One" is a thinly veiled reference to Adolf Hitler (1889–1945).—Eds.

PART 8

LIBERATION IDEOLOGIES AND THE POLITICS OF IDENTITY

The latter half of the twentieth century witnessed the emergence of several "liberation" ideologies. These include women's liberation, black liberation, gay liberation, native peoples' (or aboriginal) liberation, liberation theology, and even animal liberation. In one respect, these are vastly different ideologies in that each addresses different groups—women, native and black people, gays, and others. But these groups need not be opposed or antithetical in their aims. Indeed, one liberation movement's membership may, and often does, overlap with another's. For that matter, there would be no contradiction in a black, lesbian liberation theologian dedicating herself to the defense of aboriginal rights. But by and large we can view these various liberation ideologies as separate members of a diverse and extended ideological family.

This family shares several common characteristics. First, each liberation ideology addresses itself to a particular group, sex, race, class, species, and so on. Second, this group is in some sense oppressed by another (blacks oppressed by whites, women by men, gays by "straights," indigenous people by colonizers, the poor by the rich, animals by humans). Third, the ideology aims to liberate the oppressed group from its oppressors not only by removing external obstacles (for example, laws that discriminate against African Americans) but by exposing, criticizing, and overcoming *internal* barriers—or in the poet William Blake's phrase, the "mind-forged manacles"—to their self-emancipation. These internal obstacles might include, for example, self-loathing, low self-esteem, feelings of inferiority, incompetence, stupidity, and so on. A fourth feature common to all liberation ideologies is their attempt to "raise the consciousness" of the oppressed, thereby enabling them to free themselves from their own internalized fetters. (This feature, as we shall see, does not apply in the case of animal liberation.) Fifth and finally, liberation ideologies are also addressed to the oppressors, who, as the philosophers G. W. F. Hegel and Jean-Jacques Rousseau both noted, are enslaved by their own sense of superiority. "The one who thinks himself the master of others," Rousseau wrote in his *Social Contract* (1762), "is as much a slave as they."

The ideology of black liberation is addressed to people of African ancestry, particularly those whose feelings of inferiority have been intensified by their having accepted uncritically the dominant "white" standards of talent, intelligence, beauty, "normal" behavior, musical tastes, and so on. Black liberationists have tried to raise the consciousness of blacks by affirming the integrity and worth of African cultures, promoting black pride and identity through "black is beautiful" campaigns, and encouraging black history's recovery and remembrance of black people's contributions to Western history and culture. In these and many other ways, the ideology of black liberation helps blacks to discover, criticize, and break their own mind-forged manacles. But it also leads white people to examine their own deep-seated attitudes and prejudices as a prelude to overcoming them.

Much the same is true of the ideology of women's liberation, or feminism. That ideology is addressed to women of all races, on the assumption that women of every color and creed and class face problems that are unique to them as women. In addition to overt discrimination—legal and economic barriers and sexual harassment in the workplace and elsewhere—women face the covert or hidden obstacles of sexist attitudes and beliefs. Such attitudes include, for example, views about what is and is not "women's work," women as sex objects, and many others as well. The women's liberation movement has tried to raise women's consciousness by exposing and criticizing sexist attitudes in the classroom, the workplace, the family, the media—and in women's own minds as well. Many women have internalized and accepted sexist stereotypes about women's limitations and shortcomings. By exposing and criticizing these false beliefs, feminism helps women break down and overcome these internalized barriers. But the ideology of women's liberation is also addressed to men, encouraging them to examine their own hidden or half-conscious sexist stereotypes and attitudes toward women. Thus feminism attempts to liberate both women and men from the mutually stifling confines of sexual prejudice.

The ideology of gay liberation—or, more recently, LGBT (Lesbian, Gay, Bisexual, and Transgender)—is of relatively recent vintage. Gay men and lesbians, along with bisexual and transgendered people, face numerous obstacles, particularly if their sexual orientation or identity is publicly known. Many gays and lesbians prefer to keep their same-sex attraction a secret, fearing that they will lose their jobs, housing, health insurance, and other benefits that heterosexuals take for granted. In addition to such overt discrimination, many gays and lesbians experience more subtle oppression, which comes from internalizing straight or homophobic beliefs about and attitudes toward so-called sexual deviants or perverts. Such people sometimes suffer from feelings of shame, worthlessness, and self-loathing. Some contemplate suicide; others engage in other kinds of self-destructive actions and practices. The ideology of the gay liberation movement attempts to counter these tendencies by exposing and criticizing homophobic beliefs and attitudes, by instilling a sense of gay pride and identity, and by encouraging gays to "come out of the closet" and openly proclaim their sexual orientation. This ideology is also addressed to straights, inviting them to examine and overcome their own homophobic beliefs and attitudes.

Similar concerns are at work in the native peoples' liberation movement. The ideology of this movement is addressed to aboriginal or indigenous people in several parts of the world, including Australia, New Zealand, and North America. It aims to reclaim and celebrate customs, traditions, and identities that were eclipsed by European settlers and missionaries. These newly arrived immigrants typically dismissed native beliefs and practices as "primitive," "savage," and "uncivilized," and set out—sometimes by fraud and by force—to "civilize" the original inhabitants of the lands they were settling. Once-proud peoples were made ashamed of their traditions and customs. Now the advocates of aboriginal liberation seek to restore this pride and revive the sense of their people's identity. This they do in various ways: by publicizing their people's history and accomplishments; by working for the recovery of tribal lands and self-government; and by restoring ancient customs, languages, and religious beliefs, among others. Like other liberation ideologies, however, the basic aim is to overcome demeaning stereotypes and prejudices—inscribed, for instance, in the names of sports teams (such as the Washington Redskins, among others)—thereby freeing both oppressed and oppressor.

The primary audience of liberation theology is poor people, particularly peasants in Latin America and blacks in North America, Africa, and elsewhere. The former not only face overt oppression from wealthy landlords and perhaps military death squads; the latter live in the shadow of a long legacy of racism and oppression. Both have internalized the "culture of silence." This phrase refers to deep-seated beliefs about one's powerlessness and helplessness—the belief that one's views and voice will not and cannot make any difference in one's condition. One is, in short, doomed to suffer in silence, to accept one's unhappy lot in life as fate, the will of God, or of other forces beyond one's control. Liberation theology in Latin America and Black Liberation Theology (BLT) in North America and Africa attempts to expose and criticize these attitudes in order to help poor peasants overcome them. It does so by offering a radical reading or interpretation of the Bible that views Jesus as a liberator and a champion of the poor and downtrodden. Rightly understood, Jesus's teachings can help the poor find their voices and liberate themselves from the forces that oppress them. In addition to being addressed to the poor and oppressed, liberation theology also speaks to their affluent oppressors, inviting them to examine their own consciences and exercise their "preferential option for the poor" by supporting the peasants' struggles against poverty and oppression.

The ideology of animal liberation is likewise intended to liberate an oppressed group, in this case nonhuman animals, from their human oppressors. According to the proponents of animal liberation, many, perhaps most, humans harbor prejudiced or "speciesist" views about the innate inferiority of animals and the superiority of humans. We humans therefore feel free to confine them in tiny cages, to kill them and eat their flesh or wear their fur, and to perform painful experiments on them. It is precisely this prejudice that the animal liberation movement aims to expose and overcome. One qualification is necessary, of course, in the case of animal liberation. Since one presumably cannot reason with or raise the consciousness of nonhuman animals, the addressee must therefore be their oppressors, namely, humans who participate in, or benefit from, the suffering and deaths of animals. The ideology of animal liberation thus aims to raise the consciousness of humans, thereby helping them to challenge their speciesist attitudes and alter their actions accordingly.

Different as they are, the various liberation ideologies constitute a continuing challenge to conventional beliefs and outlooks.

What to the Slave Is the Fourth of July?

FREDERICK DOUGLASS*

Frederick Douglass (1818–1895) was born into slavery. While still a slave he taught himself—illegally—to read and write. At age twenty he escaped from his master—another illegal act—and made his way to freedom in the North. He became a prolific author and eloquent orator, turning his talents to the abolitionist (anti-slavery) cause. Douglass was also outspoken in advocating women's rights, including the right to vote. He broadcast his views on these and other issues in books, in speeches, and in his newspaper, *The North Star*—so named because escaped slaves, traveling only by night, used the North (or Polar) Star to guide them to freedom. In the following selection Douglass asks his white audience to imagine, as they celebrate the Fourth of July and the Declaration of Independence, how a slave must feel on that day. To a slave the ideals celebrated on that day—freedom and independence—ring hollow. Not until slaves gain full freedom will July 4th be a meaningful holiday for every American.

---

*   *Source*: Frederick Douglass, "What to the Slave is the Fourth of July?" *The North Star*, July 5, 1852.

WHAT TO THE SLAVE IS THE FOURTH OF JULY?

Fellow Citizens, I am not wanting [lacking] in respect for the fathers of this republic. The signers of the Declaration of Independence were brave men. They were great men, too great enough to give frame to a great age. It does not often happen to a nation to raise, at one time, such a number of truly great men. The point from which I am compelled to view them is not, certainly, the most favorable; and yet I cannot contemplate their great deeds with less than admiration. They were statesmen, patriots and heroes, and for the good they did, and the principles they contended for, I will unite with you to honor their memory …

… Fellow-citizens, pardon me, allow me to ask, why am I called upon to speak here today? What have I, or those I represent, to do with your national independence? Are the great principles of political freedom and of natural justice, embodied in that Declaration of Independence, extended to us? and am I, therefore, called upon to bring our humble offering to the national altar, and to confess the benefits and express devout gratitude for the blessings resulting from your independence to us?

Would to God, both for your sakes and ours, that an affirmative answer could be truthfully returned to these questions! Then would my task be light, and my burden easy and delightful. For who is there so cold, that a nation's sympathy could not warm him? Who so obdurate and dead to the claims of gratitude, that would not thankfully acknowledge such priceless benefits? Who so stolid and selfish, that would not give his voice to swell the hallelujahs of a nation's jubilee, when the chains of servitude had been torn from his limbs? I am not that man. In a case like that, the dumb might eloquently speak, and the "lame man leap as an hart [deer]."

But such is not the state of the case. I say it with a sad sense of the disparity between us I am not included within the pale of glorious anniversary! Your high independence only reveals the immeasurable distance between us. The blessings in which you, this day, rejoice, are not enjoyed in common. The rich inheritance of justice, liberty, prosperity and independence, bequeathed by your fathers, is shared by you, not by me. The sunlight that brought light and healing to you, has brought stripes and death to me. This Fourth July is yours, not mine. You may rejoice, I must mourn. To drag a man in fetters into the grand illuminated temple of liberty, and call upon him to join you in joyous anthems, were inhuman mockery and sacrilegious irony. Do you mean, citizens, to mock me, by asking me to speak to-day? If so, there is a parallel to your conduct. And let me warn you that it is dangerous to copy the example of a nation whose crimes, towering up to heaven, were thrown down by the breath of the Almighty, burying that nation in irrevocable ruin! I can to-day take up the plaintive lament of a peeled and woe-smitten people!

> By the rivers of Babylon, there we sat down. Yea! we wept when we remembered Zion. We hanged our harps upon the willows in the midst thereof. For there, they that carried us away captive, required of us a song; and they who wasted us required of us mirth, saying, Sing us one of the songs of Zion. How can we sing the Lord's song in a strange land? If I forget thee, O Jerusalem, let my right hand forget her cunning. If I do not remember thee, let my tongue cleave to the roof of my mouth.

Fellow-citizens, above your national, tumultuous joy, I hear the mournful wail of millions! whose chains, heavy and grievous yesterday, are, to-day, rendered more intolerable by the jubilee shouts that reach them. If I do forget, if I do not faithfully remember those bleeding children of sorrow this day, "may my right hand forget her cunning, and may my tongue cleave to the roof of my mouth!" To forget them, to pass lightly over their wrongs, and to chime in with the popular theme, would be treason most scandalous and shocking, and would make me a reproach before God and the world. My subject, then, fellow-citizens, is American slavery. I shall see this day and its popular characteristics from the slave's point of view. Standing there identified with the American bondman, making his wrongs mine, I do not hesitate to declare, with all my soul, that the character and conduct of this nation never looked blacker to me than on this 4th of July! Whether we turn to the declarations of the past, or to the professions of the present, the conduct of the nation seems equally hideous and revolting. America is false to the past, false to the present, and solemnly binds herself to be false to the future. Standing with God and the crushed and bleeding slave on this occasion, I will, in the name of humanity which is outraged, in the name of liberty which is fettered, in the name of the constitution and the Bible which are disregarded and trampled upon, dare to call in question and to denounce, with all the emphasis I can command, everything that serves to perpetuate slavery the great sin and shame of America! "I will not equivocate; I will not excuse"; I will use the severest language I can command; and yet not one word shall escape me that any man, whose judgment is not blinded by prejudice, or who is not at heart a slaveholder, shall not confess to be right and just.

But I fancy I hear some one of my audience say, "It is just in this circumstance that you and your brother abolitionists fail to make a favorable impression on the public mind. Would you argue more, and denounce less; would you persuade more, and rebuke less; your cause would be much more likely to succeed." But, I submit, where all is plain there is nothing to be argued. What point in the anti-slavery creed would you have me argue? On what branch of the subject do the people of this country need light? Must I undertake to prove that the slave is a man? That point is conceded already. Nobody doubts it. The slaveholders themselves acknowledge it in the enactment of laws for their government. They acknowledge it when they punish disobedience on the part of the slave. There are seventy-two crimes in the State of Virginia which, if committed by a black man (no matter how ignorant he be), subject him to the punishment of death; while only two of the same crimes will subject a white man to the like punishment. What is this but the acknowledgment that the slave is a moral, intellectual, and responsible being? The manhood of the slave is conceded. It is admitted in the fact that Southern statute books are covered with enactments forbidding, under severe fines and penalties, the teaching of the slave to read or to write. When you can point to any such laws in reference to the beasts of the field, then I may consent to argue the manhood of the slave. When the dogs in your streets, when the fowls of the air, when the cattle on your hills, when the fish of the sea, and the reptiles that crawl, shall be unable to distinguish the slave from a brute, then will I argue with you that the slave is a man!

For the present, it is enough to affirm the equal manhood of the Negro race. Is it not astonishing that, while we are ploughing, planting, and reaping, using all kinds of mechanical tools, erecting houses, constructing bridges, building ships, working in metals of brass, iron, copper, silver and gold; that, while we are reading, writing and ciphering, acting as clerks, merchants and secretaries, having among us lawyers, doctors, ministers, poets, authors, editors, orators and teachers; that, while we are engaged in all manner of enterprises common to other men, digging gold in California, capturing the whale in the Pacific, feeding sheep and cattle on the hill-side, living, moving, acting, thinking, planning, living in families as husbands, wives and children, and, above all, confessing and worshipping the Christian's God, and looking hopefully for life and immortality beyond the grave, we are called upon to prove that we are men!

Would you have me argue that man is entitled to liberty? that he is the rightful owner of his own body? You have already declared it. Must I argue the wrongfulness of slavery? Is that a question for Republicans? Is it to be settled by the rules of logic and argumentation, as a matter beset with great difficulty, involving a doubtful application of the principle of justice, hard to be understood? How should I look to-day, in the presence of Americans, dividing, and subdividing a discourse, to show that men have a natural right to freedom? speaking of it relatively and positively, negatively and affirmatively. To do so, would be to make myself ridiculous, and to offer an insult to your understanding. There is not a man beneath the canopy of heaven that does not know that slavery is wrong for him.

What, am I to argue that it is wrong to make men brutes, to rob them of their liberty, to work them without wages, to keep them ignorant of their relations to their fellow men, to beat them with sticks, to flay their flesh with the lash, to load their limbs with irons, to hunt them with dogs, to sell them at auction, to sunder their families, to knock out their teeth, to burn their flesh, to starve them into obedience and submission to their masters? Must I argue that a system thus marked with blood, and stained with pollution, is wrong? No! I will not. I have better employment for my time and strength than such arguments would imply.

What, then, remains to be argued? Is it that slavery is not divine; that God did not establish it; that our doctors of divinity are mistaken? There is blasphemy in the thought. That which is inhuman, cannot be divine! Who can reason on such a proposition? They that can, may; I cannot. The time for such argument is passed.

At a time like this, scorching irony, not convincing argument, is needed. O! had I the ability, and could reach the nation's ear, I would, today, pour out a fiery stream of biting ridicule, blasting reproach, withering sarcasm, and stern rebuke. For it is not light that is needed, but fire; it is not the gentle shower, but thunder. We need the storm, the whirlwind, and the earthquake. The feeling of the nation must be quickened; the conscience of the nation must be roused; the propriety of the nation must be startled; the hypocrisy of the nation must be exposed; and its crimes against God and man must be proclaimed and denounced.

What, to the American slave, is your 4th of July? I answer; a day that reveals to him, more than all other days in the year, the gross injustice and cruelty to which he is the constant victim. To him, your celebration is a sham; your boasted liberty, an unholy license; your national greatness, swelling vanity; your sounds of rejoicing are empty and heartless; your denunciation of tyrants, brass fronted impudence; your shouts of liberty and equality, hollow mockery; your prayers and hymns, your sermons and thanksgivings, with all your religious parade and solemnity, are, to Him, mere bombast, fraud, deception, impiety, and hypocrisy—a thin veil to cover up crimes which would disgrace a nation of savages. There is not a nation on the earth guilty of practices more shocking and bloody than are the people of the United States, at this very hour.

Go where you may, search where you will, roam through all the monarchies and despotisms of the Old World, travel through South America, search out every abuse, and when you have found the last, lay your facts by the side of the everyday practices of this nation, and you will say with me, that, for revolting barbarity and shameless hypocrisy, America reigns without a rival ...

... Allow me to say, in conclusion, notwithstanding the dark picture I have this day presented, of the state of the nation, I do not despair of this country. There are forces in operation which must inevitably work [i.e., bring about] the downfall of slavery. "The arm of the Lord is not shortened," and the doom of slavery is certain. I, therefore, leave off where I began, with hope. While drawing encouragement from "the Declaration of Independence," the great principles it contains, and the genius of American Institutions, my spirit is also cheered by the obvious tendencies of the age. Nations do not now stand in the same relation to each other that they did ages ago. No nation can now shut itself up from the surrounding world and trot round in the same old path of its fathers without interference. The time was when such could be done. Long established customs of hurtful character could formerly fence themselves in, and do their evil work with social impunity. Knowledge was then confined and enjoyed by the privileged few, and the multitude walked on in mental darkness. But a change has now come over the affairs of mankind. Walled cities and empires have become unfashionable. The arm of commerce has borne away the gates of the strong city. Intelligence is penetrating the darkest corners of the globe. It makes its pathway over and under the sea, as well as on the earth. Wind, steam, and lightning are its chartered agents. Oceans no longer divide, but link nations together. From Boston to London is now a holiday excursion. Space is comparatively annihilated. Thoughts expressed on one side of the Atlantic are distinctly heard on the other.

The far off and almost fabulous [i.e., fabled] Pacific rolls in grandeur at our feet. The Celestial Empire, the mystery of ages, is being solved. The fiat of the Almighty, "Let there be Light," has not yet spent its force. No abuse, no outrage whether in taste, sport or avarice, can now hide itself from the all-pervading light. The iron shoe, and crippled foot of China must be seen in contrast with nature. Africa must rise and put on her yet unwoven garment. "Ethiopia shall stretch out her hand unto God." In the fervent aspirations of William Lloyd Garrison, I say, and let every heart join in saying it:

> God speed the year of jubilee
> The wide world o'er!
> When from their galling chains set free,
> Th' oppress'd shall vilely bend the knee,
> And wear the yoke of tyranny
> Like brutes no more.
> That year will come, and freedom's reign,
> To man his plundered rights again
> Restore.

God speed the day when human blood
Shall cease to flow!
In every clime be understood,
The claims of human brotherhood,
And each return for evil, good,
Not blow for blow;
That day will come all feuds to end,
And change into a faithful friend
Each foe.

God speed the hour, the glorious hour,
When none on earth
Shall exercise a lordly power,
Nor in a tyrant's presence cower;
But to all manhood's stature tower,
By equal birth!
That hour will come, to each, to all,
And from his Prison-house, to thrall
Go forth.

Until that year, day, hour, arrive,
With head, and heart, and hand I'll strive,
To break the rod, and rend the gyve [shackle],
The spoiler of his prey deprive—
So witness Heaven!
And never from my chosen post,
Whate'er the peril or the cost,
Be driven.

Race Matters

CORNEL WEST*

Cornel West (1953–) is one of America's leading public intellectuals. He holds a Ph.D. in philosophy from Princeton University, where he taught until becoming Professor of Philosophy and Christian Practice at Union Theological Seminary. He is the author of nineteen books and editor of thirteen others. However, West has always been interested in influencing civic life beyond the academy and to that end has been a regular guest on a wide range of television and radio programs, appeared in numerous films and documentaries, and even released three spoken-word albums. In 1994 West published his classic book, *Race Matters*, which focused on the state of race relations in America at the end of the twentieth century. The book appeared in the immediate aftermath of civil upheaval in Los Angeles following the acquittal of five white police officers in the beating of African-American motorist Rodney King. Rejecting what he saw as simplistic solutions from both the political right and left, West argued instead that issues of race in America had to be contemplated against the backdrop of a much broader set of failings in American society. These included *de facto* segregation, massive economic inequality and its consequences, spiritual impoverishment, and political corruption and scapegoating, as well as police brutality toward racial minorities. With the election of the first African-American president of the United States in the intervening years, some commentators have argued that the country has become a "post-racial" society. Others, including West, argue that many of the problems that contributed to racial tensions in American society at the end of the twentieth century persist today, and that in fact many of them have actually been exacerbated in the generation since the civil unrest in Los Angeles.

* *Source*: Cornel West, *Race Matters* (New York: Vintage Books, 2001), pp. 6–11. Reprinted by permission.

RACE MATTERS

To engage in a serious discussion of race in America, we must begin not with the problems of black people but with the flaws of American society—flaws rooted in historic inequalities and longstanding cultural stereotypes. How we set up the terms for discussing racial issues shapes our perception and response to these issues. As long as black people are viewed as a "them," the burden falls on blacks to do all the "cultural" and "moral" work necessary for healthy race relations. The implication is that only certain Americans can define what it means to be American—and the rest must simply "fit in."

The emergence of strong black-nationalist sentiments among blacks, especially among young people, is a revolt against this sense of having to "fit in." The variety of black-nationalist ideologies, from the moderate views of Supreme Court Justice Clarence Thomas in his youth to those of Louis Farrakhan today, rest upon a fundamental truth: white America has been historically weak-willed in ensuring racial justice and has continued to resist fully accepting the humanity of blacks. As long as double standards and differential treatment abound as long as the rap performer Ice-T is harshly condemned while former Los Angeles Police Chief Daryl F. Gates's antiblack comments are received in polite silence, as long as Dr. Leonard Jeffries's anti-Semitic statements are met with vitriolic outrage while presidential candidate Patrick J. Buchanan's anti-Semitism receives a genteel response—black nationalisms will thrive.

Afrocentrism, a contemporary species of black nationalism, is a gallant yet misguided attempt to define an African identity in a white society perceived to be hostile. It is gallant because it puts black doings and sufferings, not white anxieties and fears, at the center of discussion. It is misguided because—out of fear of cultural hybridization and through silence on the issue of class, retrograde views on black women, gay men, and lesbians, and a reluctance to link race to the common good—it reinforces the narrow discussions about race.

To establish a new framework, we need to begin with a frank acknowledgment of the basic humanness and Americanness of each of us. And we must acknowledge that as a people—*E Pluribus Unum*—we are on a slippery slope toward economic strife, social turmoil, and cultural chaos. If we go down, we go down together. The Los Angeles upheaval forced us to see not only that we are not connected in ways we would like to be but also, in a more profound sense, that this failure to connect binds us even more tightly together. The paradox of race in America is that our common destiny is more pronounced and imperiled precisely when our divisions are deeper. The Civil War and its legacy speak loudly here. And our divisions are growing deeper. Today, 86 percent of white suburban Americans live in neighborhoods that are less than 1 percent black, meaning that the prospects for the country depend largely on how its cities fare in the hands of a suburban electorate. There is no escape from our interracial interdependence, yet enforced racial hierarchy dooms us as a nation to collective paranoia and hysteria—the unmaking of any democratic order.

The verdict in the Rodney King case, which sparked the incidents in Los Angeles, was perceived to be wrong by the vast majority of Americans. But whites have often failed to acknowledge the widespread mistreatment of black people, especially black men, by law enforcement agencies, which helped ignite the spark. The verdict was merely the occasion for deep-seated rage to come to the surface. This rage is fed by the "silent" depression ravaging the country—in which real weekly wages of all American workers since 1973 have declined nearly 20 percent, while at the same time wealth has been upwardly distributed.

The exodus of stable industrial jobs from urban centers to cheaper labor markets here and abroad, housing policies that have created "chocolate cities and vanilla suburbs" (to use the popular musical artist George Clinton's memorable phrase), white fear of black crime, and the urban influx of poor Spanish-speaking and Asian immigrants—all have helped erode the tax base of American cities just as the federal government has cut its support and programs. The result is unemployment, hunger, homelessness, and sickness for millions.

And a pervasive spiritual impoverishment grows. The collapse of meaning in life—the eclipse of hope and absence of love of self and others, the breakdown of family and neighborhood bonds—leads to the social deracination and cultural denudement of urban dwellers, especially children. We have created rootless, dangling people with little link to the supportive networks—family, friends, school—that sustain some sense of purpose in life. We have witnessed the collapse of the spiritual communities that in the past helped Americans face despair, disease, and death and that transmit through the generations dignity and decency, excellence and elegance.

The result is lives of what we might call "random nows," of fortuitous and fleeting moments preoccupied with "getting over"—with acquiring pleasure, property, and power by any means necessary. (This is not what Malcolm X meant by this famous phrase.) Post-modern culture is more and more a market culture dominated by gangster mentalities and self-destructive wantonness. This culture engulfs all of us—yet its impact on the disadvantaged is devastating, resulting in extreme violence in everyday life. Sexual violence against women and homicidal assaults by young black men on one another are only the most obvious signs of this empty quest for pleasure, property, and power.

Last, this rage is fueled by a political atmosphere in which images, not ideas, dominate, where politicians spend more time raising money than debating issues. The functions of parties have been displaced by public polls, and politicians behave less as thermostats that determine the climate of opinion than as thermometers registering the public mood. American politics has been rocked by an unleashing of greed among opportunistic public officials—who have followed the lead of their counterparts in the private sphere, where, as of 1989, 1 percent of the population owned 37 percent of the wealth and 10 percent of the population owned 86 percent of the wealth—leading to a profound cynicism and pessimism among the citizenry.

And given the way in which the Republican Party since 1968 has appealed to popular xenophobic images—playing the black, female, and homophobic cards to realign the electorate along race, sex, and sexual-orientation lines—it is no surprise that the notion that we are all part of one garment of destiny is discredited. Appeals to special interests rather than to public interests reinforce this polarization. The Los Angeles upheaval was an expression of utter fragmentation by a powerless citizenry that includes not just the poor but all of us.

WHAT IS TO BE DONE? How do we capture a new spirit and vision to meet the challenges of the post-industrial city, post-modern culture, and post-party politics?

First, we must admit that the most valuable sources for help, hope, and power consist of ourselves and our common history. As in the ages of Lincoln, Roosevelt, and King, we must look to new frameworks and languages to understand our multilayered crisis and overcome our deep malaise.

Second, we must focus our attention on the public square—the common good that undergirds our national and global destinies. The vitality of any public square ultimately depends on how much we *care* about the quality of our lives together. The neglect of our public infrastructure, for example—our water and sewage systems, bridges, tunnels, highways, subways, and streets—reflects not only our myopic economic policies, which impede productivity, but also the low priority we place on our common life.

The tragic plight of our children clearly reveals our deep disregard for public wellbeing. About one out of every five children in this country lives in poverty, including one out of every two black children and two out of every five Hispanic children. Most of our children—neglected by overburdened parents and bombarded by the market values of profit-hungry corporations—are ill-equipped to live lives of spiritual and cultural quality. Faced with these facts, how do we expect ever to constitute a vibrant society?

One essential step is some form of large-scale public intervention to ensure access to basic social goods—housing, food, health care, education, child care, and jobs. We must invigorate the common good with a mixture of government, business, and labor that does not follow any existing blueprint. After a period in which the private sphere has been sacralized and the public square gutted, the temptation is to make a fetish of the public square. We need to resist such dogmatic swings.

Last, the major challenge is to meet the need to generate new leadership. The paucity of courageous leaders—so apparent in the response to the events in Los Angeles—requires that we look beyond the same elites and voices that recycle the older frameworks. We need leaders—neither saints nor sparkling television personalities—who can situate themselves within a larger historical narrative of this country and our world, who can grasp the complex dynamics of our peoplehood and imagine a future grounded in the best of our past, yet who are attuned to the frightening obstacles that now perplex us. Our ideals of freedom, democracy, and equality must be invoked to invigorate all of us, especially the landless, propertyless, and luckless. Only a visionary leadership that can motivate "the better angels of our nature," as Lincoln said, and activate possibilities for a freer, more efficient, and stable America—only that leadership deserves cultivation and support.

This new leadership must be grounded in grassroots organizing that highlights democratic accountability. Whoever *our* leaders will be as we approach the twenty-first century, their challenge will be to help Americans determine whether a genuine multiracial democracy can be created and sustained in an era of global economy and a moment of xenophobic frenzy.

Let us hope and pray that the vast intelligence, imagination, humor, and courage of Americans will not fail us. Either we learn a new language of empathy and compassion, or the fire this time will consume us all.

A Vindication of the Rights of Woman

MARY WOLLSTONECRAFT*

Mary Wollstonecraft (1759–1797) was an English novelist and political writer. In *A Vindication of the Rights of Men* (1790), she defended the French Revolution against Edmund Burke's attack (see selection 4.28 for excerpts from Burke's *Reflections on the Revolution in France*). In her longer and more famous book, *A Vindication of the Rights of Woman* (1792), Wollstonecraft argued that "the rights of man" must extend to the other half of the human race, namely, women. In this second *Vindication*, from which the following selection is taken, Wollstonecraft places particular stress upon the importance of education. Education is vital to men and women alike, she believed, for it enables them to acquire knowledge and to develop reason and virtue. Indeed, her claim is that women, "in common with men, are placed on this earth to unfold their faculties"—that is, their talents and abilities.

* *Source*: Mary Wollstonecraft, *A Vindication of the Rights of Woman* (Philadelphia: Matthew Carey, 1794), pp. 87–109.

A VINDICATION OF THE RIGHTS OF WOMAN

That woman is naturally weak, or degraded by a concurrence of circumstances, is, I think, clear. But this position I shall simply contrast with a conclusion, which I have frequently heard fall from sensible men in favor of an aristocracy; that the mass of mankind cannot be anything, or the obsequious slaves, who patiently allow themselves to be driven forward, would feel their own consequence, and spurn their chains. Men, they further observe, submit everywhere to oppression, when they have only to lift up their heads to throw off the yoke; yet, instead of asserting their birthright, they quietly lick the dust, and say, "Let us eat and drink, for tomorrow we die." Women, I argue from analogy, are degraded by the same propensity to enjoy the present moment, and at last despise the freedom which they have not sufficient virtue to struggle to attain. But I must be more explicit.

With respect to the culture of the heart, it is unanimously allowed that sex is out of the question; but the line of subordination in the mental powers is never to be passed over. Only "absolute in loveliness," the portion of rationality granted to woman is, indeed, very scanty; for denying her genius and judgment, it is scarcely possible to divine what remains to characterize intellect.

The stamen of immortality, if I may be allowed the phrase, is the perfectibility of human reason; for, were man created perfect, or did a flood of knowledge break upon him, when he arrived at maturity, that precluded error, I should doubt whether his existence would be continued after the dissolution of the body. But, in the present state of things, every difficulty in morals that escapes from human discussion, and equally baffles the investigation of profound thinking, and the lightning glance of genius, is an argument on which I build my belief of the immortality of the soul. Reason is, consequently, the simple power of improvement; or, more properly speaking, of discerning truth. Every individual is in this respect a world in itself. More or less may be conspicuous in one being than another; but the nature of reason must be the same in all, if it be an emanation of divinity, the tie that connects the creature with the Creator; for, can that soul be stamped with the heavenly image, that is not perfected by the exercise of its own reason? Yet outwardly ornamented with elaborate care, and so adorned to delight man, "that with honor he may love," the soul of woman is not allowed to have this distinction, and man, ever placed between her and reason, she is always represented as only created to see through a gross medium, and to take things on trust. But dismissing these fanciful theories, and considering woman as a whole, let it be what it will, instead of a part of man, the inquiry is whether she have reason or not. If she have ... she was not created merely to be the solace of man ...

The power of generalizing ideas, of drawing comprehensive conclusions from individual observations, is the only acquirement, for an immortal being, that really deserves the name of knowledge. Merely to observe, without endeavoring to account for anything, may (in a very incomplete manner) serve as the common sense of life; but where is the store laid up that is to clothe the soul when it leaves the body?

This power has not only been denied to women; but writers have insisted that it is inconsistent, with a few exceptions, with their sexual character. Let men prove this, and I shall grant that woman only exists for man. I must, however, previously remark, that the power of generalizing ideas, to any great extent, is not very common amongst men or women. But this exercise is the true cultivation of the understanding; and everything conspires to render the cultivation of the understanding more difficult in the female than the male world.

I am naturally led by the assertion to the main subject of the present chapter, and shall now attempt to point out some of the causes that degrade the sex, and prevent women from generalizing their observations.

I shall not go back to the remote annals of antiquity to trace the history of woman; it is sufficient to allow that she has always been either a slave or a despot, and to remark that each of these situations equally retards the progress of reason. The grand source of female folly and vice has ever appeared to me to arise from narrowness of mind; and the very constitution of civil governments has put almost insuperable obstacles in the way to prevent the cultivation of the female understanding; yet virtue can be built on no other foundation. The same obstacles are thrown in the way of the rich, and the same consequences ensue.

Necessity has been proverbially termed the mother of invention; the aphorism may be extended to virtue. It is an acquirement, and an acquirement to which pleasure must be sacrificed; and who sacrifices pleasure when it is within the grasp, whose mind has not been opened and strengthened by adversity, or the pursuit of knowledge goaded on by necessity? Happy is it when people have the cares of life to struggle with, for these struggles prevent their becoming a prey to enervating vices, merely from idleness. But if from their birth men and women be placed in a torrid zone, with the meridian sun of pleasure darting directly upon them, how can they sufficiently brace their minds to discharge the duties of life, or even to relish the affections that carry them out of themselves?

Pleasure is the business of woman's life, according to the present modification of society; and while it continues to be so, little can be expected from such weak beings. Inheriting in a lineal descent from the first fair defect in nature—the sovereignty of beauty—they have, to maintain their power, resigned the natural rights which the exercise of reason might have procured them, and chosen rather to be short-lived queens than labor to obtain the sober pleasures that arise from equality. Exalted by their inferiority (this sounds like a contradiction), they constantly demand homage as women, though experience should teach them that men who pride themselves upon paying this arbitrary insolent respect to the sex, with the most scrupulous exactness, are most inclined to tyrannize over, and despise the very weakness they cherish ...

Ah! why do women—I write with affectionate solicitude—condescend to receive a degree of attention and respect from strangers different from that reciprocation of civility which the dictates of humanity and the politeness of civilization authorize between man and man? And why do they not discover, when "in the noon of beauty's power," that they are treated like queens only to be deluded by hollow respect, till they are led to resign, or not assume, their natural prerogatives? Confined, then, in cages like the feathered race [i.e., birds], they have nothing to do but to plume themselves, and stalk with mock majesty from perch to perch. It is true they are provided with food and raiment, for which they neither toil nor spin; but health, liberty, and virtue are given in exchange. But where, amongst mankind, has been found sufficient strength of mind to enable a being to resign these adventitious prerogatives—one who, rising with the calm dignity of reason above opinion, dared to be proud of the privileges inherent in man? And it is vain to expect it whilst hereditary power chokes the affections, and nips reason in the bud ...

Mankind, including every description, wish to be loved and respected by *something*, and the common herd will always take the nearest road to the completion of their wishes. The respect paid to wealth and beauty is the most certain and unequivocal, and, of course, will always attract the vulgar eye of common minds. Abilities and virtues are absolutely necessary to raise men from the middle rank of life into notice, and the natural consequence is notorious—the middle rank contains most virtue and abilities. Men have thus, in one station at least, an opportunity of exerting themselves with dignity, and of rising by the exertions which really improve a rational creature; but the whole female sex are, till their character is formed, in the same condition as the rich, for they are born—I now speak of a state of civilization—with certain sexual privileges; and whilst they are gratuitously granted them, few will ever think of works of supererogation to obtain the esteem of a small number of superior people.

When do we hear of women who, starting out of obscurity, boldly claim respect on account of their great abilities or daring virtues? Where are they to be found? "To be observed, to be attended to, to be taken notice of with sympathy, complacency, and approbation, are all the advantages which they seek." True! my male readers will probably exclaim; but let them, before they draw any conclusion, recollect that this was not written originally as descriptive of women, but of the rich. In Dr. [Adam] Smith's *Theory of Moral Sentiments* I have found a general character of people of rank and fortune, that, in my opinion, might with the greatest propriety be applied to the female sex. I refer the sagacious reader to the whole comparison, but must be allowed to quote a passage to enforce an argument that I mean to insist on, as the one most conclusive against a sexual character. For if, excepting warriors, no great men of any denomination have ever appeared amongst the nobility, may it not be fairly inferred that their local situation swallowed up the man, and produced a character similar to that of women, who are *localized*—if I may be allowed the word—by the rank they are placed in by *courtesy*? Women, commonly called ladies, are not to be contradicted in company, are not allowed to exert any manual strength; and from them the negative virtues only are expected, when any virtues are expected—patience, docility, good humor, and flexibility— virtues incompatible with any vigorous exertion of intellect. Besides, by living more with each other, and being seldom absolutely alone, they are more under the influence of sentiments than passions. Solitude and reflection are necessary to give to wishes the force of passions, and to enable the imagination to enlarge the object, and make it the most desirable. The same may be said of the ideas, collected by impassioned thinking or calm investigation, to acquire that strength of character on which great resolves are built ...

In the middle rank of life, to continue the comparison, men, in their youth, are prepared for professions, and marriage is not considered as the grand feature in their lives; whilst women, on the contrary, have no other scheme to sharpen their faculties. It is not business, extensive plans, or any of the excursive flights of ambition, that engross their attention; no, their thoughts are not employed in rearing such noble structures. To rise in the world, and have the liberty of running from pleasure to pleasure, they must marry advantageously, and to this object their time is sacrificed, and their persons often legally prostituted. A man when he enters any profession has his eye steadily fixed on some future advantage (and the mind gains great strength by having all its efforts directed to one point), and, full of his business, pleasure is considered as mere relaxation; whilst women seek for pleasure as the main purpose of existence. In fact, from the education, which they receive from society, the love of pleasure may be said to govern them all; but does this prove that there is a sex in souls? It would be just as rational to declare that the courtiers in France, when a destructive system of despotism had formed their character, were not men, because liberty, virtue, and humanity, were sacrificed to pleasure and vanity. Fatal passions, which have ever domineered over the *whole* race!

The same love of pleasure, fostered by the whole tendency of their education, gives a trifling turn to the conduct of women in most circumstances; for instance, they are ever anxious about secondary things; and on the watch for adventures instead of being occupied by duties ...

In short, women, in general, as well as the rich of both sexes have acquired all the follies and vices of civilization, and missed the useful fruit. It is not necessary for me always to premise that I speak of the condition of the whole sex, leaving exceptions out of the question. Their senses are inflamed, and their understandings neglected, consequently they become the prey of their sense, delicately termed sensibility, and are blown about by every momentary gust of feeling. Civilized women are, therefore, so weakened by false refinement, that, respecting morals, their condition is much below what it would be were they left in a state nearer to nature. Ever restless and anxious, their over-exercised sensibility not only renders them uncomfortable themselves, but troublesome, to use a soft phrase, to others. All their thoughts turn on things calculated to excite emotion and feeling, when they should reason, their conduct is unstable, and their opinions are wavering—not the wavering produced by deliberation or progressive views, but by contradictory emotions. By fits and starts they are warm in many pursuits; yet this warmth, never concentrated into perseverance, soon exhausts itself; exhaled by its own heat, or meeting with some other fleeting passion, to which reason has never given any specific gravity, neutrality ensues. Miserable, indeed, must be that being whose cultivation of mind has only tended to inflame its passions! A distinction should be made between inflaming and strengthening them. The passions thus pampered, whilst the judgment is left unformed, what can be expected to ensue? Undoubtedly, a mixture of madness and folly! ...

And will moralists pretend to assert that this is the condition in which one-half of the human race should be encouraged to remain with listless inactivity and stupid acquiescence? Kind instructors! what were we created for? To remain, it may be said, innocent; they mean in a state of childhood. We might as well never have been born, unless it were necessary that we should be created to enable man to acquire the noble privilege of reason, the power of discerning good from evil, whilst we lie down in the dust from whence we were taken, never to rise again ...

I come round to my old argument; if woman be allowed to have an immortal soul, she must have, as the employment of life, an understanding to improve. And when, to render the present state more complete, though everything proves it to be but a fraction of a mighty sum, she is incited by present gratification to forget her grand destination, nature is counteracted, or she was born only to procreate and rot. Or, granting brutes of every description a soul, though not a reasonable one, the exercise of instinct and sensibility may be the step which they are to take, in this life, towards the attainment of reason in the next; so that through all eternity they will lag behind man, who, why we cannot tell, had the power given him of attaining reason in his first mode of existence.

When I treat of the peculiar duties of women, as I should treat of the peculiar duties of a citizen or father, it will be found that I do not mean to insinuate that they should be taken out of their families, speaking of the majority. "He that hath wife and children," says Lord [Francis] Bacon, "hath given hostages to fortune; for they are impediments to great enterprises, either of virtue or mischief. Certainly the best works, and of greatest merit for the public, have proceeded from the unmarried or childless men." I say the same of women. But the welfare of society is not built on extraordinary exertions; and were it more reasonably organized, there would be still less need of great abilities, or heroic virtues.

In the regulation of a family, in the education of children, understanding, in an unsophisticated sense, is particularly required—strength both of body and mind; yet the men who, by their writings, have most earnestly labored to domesticate women, have endeavored, by arguments dictated by a gross appetite, which satiety had rendered fastidious, to weaken their bodies and cramp their minds. But, if even by these sinister methods they really *persuaded* women, by working on their feelings, to stay at home, and fulfill the duties of a mother and a mistress of a family, I should cautiously oppose opinions that led women to right conduct, by prevailing on them to make the discharge of such important duties the main business of life, though reason were insulted. Yet, and I appeal to experience, if by neglecting the understanding they be as much, nay, more detached from these domestic employments than they could by the most serious intellectual pursuit, though it may be observed, that the mass of mankind will never vigorously pursue an intellectual object, I may be allowed to infer that reason is absolutely necessary to enable a woman to perform any duty properly, and I must again repeat, that sensibility is not reason.

The comparison with the rich still occurs to me; for, when men neglect the duties of humanity, women will follow their example; a common stream hurries them both along with thoughtless celerity. Riches and honors prevent a man from enlarging his understanding, and enervate all his powers by reversing the order of nature, which has ever made true pleasure the reward of labor. Pleasure—enervating pleasure—is, likewise, within women's reach without earning it. But, till hereditary possessions are spread abroad, how can we expect men to be proud of virtue? And, till they are, women will govern them by the most direct means, neglecting their dull domestic duties to catch the pleasure that sits lightly on the wing of time.

Declaration of the Rights of Woman and the Female Citizen

OLYMPE DE GOUGES*

Olympe de Gouges was the pen name of Marie Gouze (1748–1793), an early feminist, playwright, anti-slavery activist, and political pamphleteer during the French Revolution. She thought it outrageous and unjust that the 1789 Declaration of the Rights of Man and of Citizens (see selection 3.15) did not recognize women as citizens with political and civil rights. In 1791 de Gouges wrote the following counter-declaration, to which she appended a model marriage contract that took the form of an egalitarian "social contract" between a man and a woman. One of the noteworthy features of her Declaration is the way in which it connects political rights with responsibilities and legal liabilities, as when she proclaims: "Woman has the right to mount the gallows; she should equally have the right to mount the rostrum" to express her opinions publicly. Although her advocacy of sexual equality was considered radical at the time, de Gouges associated with the moderate Girondist faction during the French Revolution and opposed the execution of King Louis XVI. Her criticism of Robespierre and other radical revolutionaries during the Reign of Terror led to her arrest and execution in 1793.

---

* Source: *Declaration des droits de la femme et de la citoyenne* (Olympe de Gouges collection, Bibliothèque Nationale, Paris, 1791). Translated by Sharilyn Geistfeld and Terence Ball.

DECLARATION OF THE RIGHTS OF WOMAN
Preamble

Mothers, daughters, sisters—the female representatives of the nation—demand to be constituted as a national assembly. Considering that ignorance, neglect or scorn for the rights of woman are the sole cause of public miseries and governmental corruption, they have resolved to affirm in a solemn declaration the natural, unchangeable and sacred rights of woman. This declaration, being constantly present to all members of the social body, will always remind them of their rights and duties. It will enable women's acts of power, and those of powerful men, to be judged at all times against the aim of all political institutions and, accordingly, to gain greater respect. By being founded on simple and incontestable principles, female citizens' demands will henceforth tend always to maintain the constitution, good morals, and the happiness of all.

Consequently, the sex that is as superior in beauty as it is in courage during the ordeal of child-birth, recognizes and declares in the presence and under the auspices of the Supreme Being, the following Rights of Woman and of Female Citizens.

1 Woman is born free and remains equal to man in rights. Social distinctions may be based only on common utility.
2 The aim of all political associations is the preservation of the natural and imprescriptible rights of woman and man. These rights are liberty, property, security, and especially resistance to oppression.
3 The principle of all sovereignty resides essentially in the nation, which is nothing but the rejoining of woman and man. No body, nor any individual, may exercise authority which does not emanate expressly from the nation.
4 Liberty and justice consist of restoring all that belongs to others. Hence only man's perpetual tyranny imposes limits on the exercise of women's natural rights. These limits are to be lifted by the laws of nature and reason.
5 The laws of nature and reason forbid all acts that harm society. All acts which are not forbidden by these wise and divine laws may not be prevented, and no one can be forced to do what these laws do not require.
6 Law must be the expression of the general will. All male and female citizens must contribute to its formation either in person or through their representatives. The law should be the same for all: female and male citizens, being equal in the eyes of the law, must be equally eligible for all public honors, positions, and forms of employment according to their ability and without any distinctions other than their virtues and their talents.
7 No woman is exempted. She is to be accused, arrested and detained in cases determined by law. Women, like men, obey this rigorous law.
8 The law should establish only punishments that are strictly and evidently necessary, and no one can be punished except by means of a law established and publicized prior to commission of the crime, and legally applicable to women.
9 Once a woman is found guilty, the law is to be applied rigorously.

10 No one should be disturbed for expressing even his most basic opinions. Woman has the right to mount the gallows; she should equally have the right to mount the rostrum, if what she says does not disturb the public order as established by law.

11 The free communication of thoughts and opinions is one of the most precious rights of woman, since this liberty assures the legitimacy of children to their fathers. Every female citizen may thus say freely, I am the mother of a child who belongs to you, without being forced to conceal the truth due to a barbarous prejudice [against having a child out of wedlock], as long as responsibility is taken for any abuse of this liberty in cases determined by law [i.e., women are not allowed to lie about the identity of the father].

12 Guaranteeing the rights of woman and citizen requires the guarantee's general utility. This guarantee should be instituted for the advantage of all and not for the particular benefit of individuals entrusted with it.

13 For the support of public authority and paying the expenses of administration, men and women should be taxed equally. Since woman must share all duties and other painful tasks, she should also share the benefits that come from holding offices, honors and jobs.

14 Female and male citizens have the right to verify, either personally or through their representatives, the necessity of public taxes. Female citizens can agree to pay taxes only if they receive an equal share, not only of wealth, but also of public administration, and have a hand in determining the apportionment, assessment, collection and duration of taxes.

15 The mass of women, joined together with men in having to pay taxes, has the right to demand an accounting for his administration from every public agent.

16 Any society in which the guarantee of rights is not assured, or the separation of powers is uncertain, has no constitution. The constitution is null if the majority of people comprising the nation have not cooperated in writing it.

17 Property belongs to both sexes whether united or separated. For each sex this is an inviolable and sacred right. No one can be deprived of property, since it is the true patrimony of nature, except when public necessity, legally certified, obviously requires it. Even then, owners of property confiscated for public purposes must be compensated in advance of its seizure.

Seneca Falls Declaration of Sentiments and Resolutions*

In 1840 a group of American women delegates were excluded from the World Anti-Slavery Convention in London because of their sex. One member of the delegation, Lucretia Mott (1793–1880), later joined Elizabeth Cady Stanton (1815–1902) in organizing the Seneca Falls (New York) Convention of 1848 to protest the various forms of discrimination to which women were subjected. The Convention adopted the following Declaration of Sentiments and Resolutions, with its intentionally ironic echoes of the U.S. Declaration of Independence.

---

* *Source*: Elizabeth Cady Stanton, Susan B. Anthony, and Matilda Joslyn Gage, eds., *History of Woman Suffrage*, 2 vols. (New York, 1881), vol. 1, pp. 70–73.

1. DECLARATION OF SENTIMENTS

When, in the course of human events, it becomes necessary for one portion of the family of man to assume among the people of the earth a position different from that which they have hitherto occupied, but one to which the laws of nature and of nature's God entitle them, a decent respect to the opinions of mankind requires that they should declare the causes that impel them to such a course.

We hold these truths to be self-evident: that all men and women are created equal; that they are endowed by their Creator with certain inalienable rights; that among these are life, liberty, and the pursuit of happiness; that to secure these rights governments are instituted, deriving their just powers from the consent of the governed. Whenever any form of government becomes destructive of these ends, it is the right of those who suffer from it to refuse allegiance to it, and to insist upon the institution of a new government, laying its foundation on such principles, and organizing its powers in such form, as to them shall seem most likely to effect their safety and happiness. Prudence, indeed, will dictate that governments long established should not be changed for light and transient causes; and accordingly all experience hath shown that mankind are more disposed to suffer while evils are sufferable, than to right themselves by abolishing the forms to which they are accustomed. But when a long train of abuses and usurpations, pursuing invariably the same object, evinces a design to reduce them under absolute despotism, it is their duty to throw off such government, and to provide new guards for their future security. Such has been the patient sufferance of the women under this government, and such is now the necessity which constrains them to demand the equal station to which they are entitled.

The history of mankind is a history of repeated injuries and usurpations on the part of man toward woman, having in direct object the establishment of an absolute tyranny over her. To prove this, let facts be submitted to a candid world.

He has never permitted her to exercise her inalienable right to the elective franchise.

He has compelled her to submit to laws, in the formation of which she had no voice.

He has withheld from her rights which are given to the most ignorant and degraded men—both natives and foreigners.

Having deprived her of this first right of a citizen, the elective franchise, thereby leaving her without representation in the halls of legislation, he has oppressed her on all sides.

He has made her, if married, in the eye of the law, civilly dead.

He has taken from her all right in property, even to the wages she earns.

He has made her, morally, an irresponsible being, as she can commit many crimes with impunity, provided they be done in the presence of her husband. In the covenant of marriage, she is compelled to promise obedience to her husband, he becoming, to all intents and purposes, her master—the law giving him power to deprive her of her liberty, and to administer chastisement.

He has so framed the laws of divorce, as to what shall be the proper causes, and in case of separation, to whom the guardianship of the children shall be given, as to be wholly regardless of the happiness of women—the law, in all cases, going upon a false supposition of the supremacy of man, and giving all power into his hands.

After depriving her of all rights as a married woman, if single, and the owner of property, he has taxed her to support a government which recognizes her only when her property can be made profitable to it.

He has monopolized nearly all the profitable employments, and from those she is permitted to follow, she receives but a scanty remuneration. He closes against her all the avenues to wealth and distinction which he considers most honorable to himself. As a teacher of theology, medicine, or law, she is not known.

He has denied her the facilities for obtaining a thorough education, all colleges being closed against her.

He allows her in Church, as well as State, but a subordinate position, claiming Apostolic authority for her exclusion from the ministry, and, with some exceptions, from any public participation in the affairs of the Church.

He has created a false public sentiment by giving to the world a different code of morals for men and women, by which moral delinquencies which exclude women from society, are not only tolerated, but deemed of little account in man.

He has usurped the prerogative of Jehovah himself, claiming it as his right to assign for her a sphere of action, when that belongs to her conscience and to her God.

He has endeavored, in every way that he could, to destroy her confidence in her own powers, to lessen her self-respect and to make her willing to lead a dependent and abject life.

Now, in view of this entire disfranchisement of one-half the people of this country, their social and religious degradation—in view of the unjust laws above mentioned, and because women do feel themselves aggrieved, oppressed, and fraudulently deprived of their most sacred rights, we insist that they have immediate admission to all the rights and privileges which belong to them as citizens of the United States.

In entering upon the great work before us, we anticipate no small amount of misconception, misrepresentation, and ridicule; but we shall use every instrumentality within our power to effect our object. We shall employ agents, circulate tracts, petition the State and National legislatures, and endeavor to enlist the pulpit and the press in our behalf. We hope this Convention will be followed by a series of Conventions embracing every part of the country.

2. RESOLUTIONS

WHEREAS, The great precept of nature is conceded to be, that "man shall pursue his own true and substantial happiness." [The English jurist Sir William] Blackstone in his *Commentaries* remarks, that this law of Nature being coeval with mankind, and dictated by God himself, is of course superior in obligation to any other. It is binding over all the globe, in all countries and at all times; no human laws are of any validity if contrary to this, and such of them as are valid, derive all their force, and all their validity, and all their authority, mediately and immediately, from this original; therefore,

Resolved, That all laws which prevent woman from occupying such a station in society as her conscience shall dictate, or which place her in a position inferior to that of man, are contrary to the great precept of nature, and therefore of no force or authority.

Resolved, That woman is man's equal—was intended to be so by the Creator, and the highest good of the race demands that she should be recognized as such.

Resolved, That the women of this country ought to be enlightened in regard to the laws under which they live, that they may no longer publish their degradation by declaring themselves satisfied with their present position, nor their ignorance, by asserting that they have all the rights they want.

Resolved, That inasmuch as man, while claiming for himself intellectual superiority, does accord to woman moral superiority, it is pre-eminently his duty to encourage her to speak and teach, as she has an opportunity, in all religious assemblies.

Resolved, That the same amount of virtue, delicacy, and refinement of behavior that is required of woman in the social state, should also be required of man, and the same transgressions should be visited with equal severity on both man and woman.

Resolved, That the objection of indelicacy and impropriety, which is so often brought against woman when she addresses a public audience, comes with a very ill-grace from those who encourage, by their attendance, her appearance on the stage, in the concert, or in feats of the circus.

Resolved, That woman has too long rested satisfied in the circumscribed limits which corrupt customs and a perverted application of the Scriptures have marked out for her, and that it is time she should move in the enlarged sphere which her great Creator has assigned her.

Resolved, That it is the duty of the women of this country to secure to themselves their sacred right to the elective franchise.

Resolved, That the equality of human rights results necessarily from the fact of the identity of the race in capabilities and responsibilities.

Resolved, That the speedy success of our cause depends upon the zealous and untiring efforts of both men and women, for the overthrow of the monopoly of the pulpit, and for the securing to women an equal participation with men in the various trades, professions, and commerce.

Resolved, therefore, That, being invested by the Creator with the same capabilities, and the same consciousness of responsibility for their exercise, it is demonstrably the right and duty of woman, equally with man, to promote every righteous cause by every righteous means; and especially in regard to the great subjects of morals and religion, it is self-evidently her right to participate with her brother in teaching them, both in private and in public, by writing and by speaking, by any instrumentalities proper to be used, and in any assemblies proper to be held; and this being a self-evident truth growing out of the divinely implanted principles of human nature, any custom or authority adverse to it, whether modern or wearing the hoary sanction of antiquity, is to be regarded as a self-evident falsehood, and at war with mankind.

Oppression

*MARILYN FRYE**

Oppression takes many forms, including those subtle forms that are half-hidden in our language and habits of thought. So argues the feminist author and activist Marilyn Frye (1941–), who until her recent retirement taught philosophy at Michigan State University. Frye is the author of several books, including *The Politics of Reality*, from which the following essay is taken, and other essays in feminism and philosophy.

* *Source*: Marilyn Frye, *Politics of Reality: Essays in Feminist Theory* (1983), pp. 1–16. © 1983 by Marilyn Frye. Reprinted by permission of Crossing Press, an imprint of the Crown Publishing Group, a division of Penguin Random Hous LLC.

OPPRESSION

It is a fundamental claim of feminism that women are oppressed. The word "oppression" is a strong word. It repels and attracts. It is dangerous and dangerously fashionable and endangered. It is much misused, and sometimes not innocently.

The statement that women are oppressed is frequently met with the claim that men are oppressed too. We hear that oppressing is oppressive to those who oppress as well as to those they oppress. Some men cite as evidence of their oppression their much-advertised inability to cry. It is tough, we are told, to be masculine. When the stresses and frustrations of being a man are cited as evidence that oppressors are oppressed by their oppressing, the word "oppression" is being stretched to meaninglessness; it is treated as though its scope includes any and all human experience of limitation of suffering no matter the cause, degree or consequence. Once such usage has been put over on us, then if ever we deny that any person or group is oppressed, we seem to imply that we think they never suffer and have no feelings. We are accused of insensitivity; even of bigotry. For women, such accusation is particularly intimidating, since sensitivity is one of the few virtues that has been assigned to us. If we are found insensitive, we may fear we have no redeeming traits at all and perhaps are not real women. Thus are we silenced before we begin: the name of our situation drained of meaning and our guilt mechanisms tripped.

But this is nonsense. Human beings can be miserable without being oppressed, and it is perfectly consistent to deny that a person or group is oppressed without denying that they have feelings or that they suffer.

We need to think clearly about oppression, and there is much that mitigates against this. I do not want to undertake to prove that women are oppressed (or that men are not), but I want to make clear what is being said when we say it. We need this word, this concept, and we need it to be sharp and sure.

I

The root of the word "oppression" is the element "press." *The press of the crowd; pressed into military service; to press a pair of pants; printing press; press the button.* Presses are used to mold things or flatten them or reduce them in bulk, sometimes to reduce them by squeezing out the gases or liquids in them. Something pressed is something caught between or among forces and barriers which are so related to each other that jointly they restrain, restrict or prevent the thing's motion or mobility. Mold. Immobilize. Reduce.

The mundane experience of the oppressed provides another clue. One of the most characteristic and ubiquitous features of the world as experienced by oppressed people is the double bind—situations in which options are reduced to a very few and all of them expose one to penalty, censure or deprivation. For example, it is often a requirement upon oppressed people that we smile and be cheerful. If we comply, we signal our docility and our acquiescence in our situation. We need not, then, be taken note of. We acquiesce in being made invisible, in our occupying no space. We participate in our own erasure. On the other hand, anything but the sunniest countenance exposes us to being perceived as mean, bitter, angry or dangerous. This means, at the least, that we may be found "difficult" or unpleasant to work with, which is enough to cost one one's livelihood; at worst, being seen as mean, bitter, angry or dangerous has been known to result in rape, arrest, beating and murder. One can only choose to risk one's preferred form and rate of annihilation.

Another example: It is common in the United States that women, especially younger women, are in a bind where neither sexual activity nor sexual inactivity is all right. If she is heterosexually active, a woman is open to censure and punishment for being loose, unprincipled or a whore. The "punishment" comes in the form of criticism, snide and embarrassing remarks, being treated as an easy lay by men, scorn from her more restrained female friends. She may have to lie and hide her behavior from her parents. She must juggle the risks of unwanted pregnancy and dangerous contraceptives. On the other hand, if she refrains from heterosexual activity, she is fairly constantly harassed by men who try to persuade her into it and pressure her to "relax" and "let her hair down"; she is threatened with labels like "frigid," "uptight," "manhater," "bitch" and "cocktease." The same parents who would be disapproving of her sexual activity may be worried by her inactivity because it suggests she is not or will not be popular, or is not sexually normal. She may be charged with lesbianism. If a woman is raped, then if she has been heterosexually active she is subject to the presumption that she liked it (since her activity is presumed to show that she likes sex), and if she has not been heterosexually active, she is subject to the presumption that she liked it (since she is supposedly "repressed and frustrated"). Both heterosexual activity and heterosexual nonactivity are likely to be taken as proof that you wanted to be raped, and hence, of course, weren't *really* raped at all. You can't win. You are caught in a bind, caught between systematically related pressures.

Women are caught like this, too, by networks of forces and barriers that expose one to penalty, loss or contempt whether one works outside the home or not, is on welfare or not, bears children or not, raises children or not, marries or not, stays married or not, is heterosexual, lesbian, both or neither. Economic necessity; confinement to racial and/or sexual job ghettos; sexual harassment; sex discrimination; pressures of competing expectations and judgments about *women*, *wives* and *mothers* (in the society at large, in racial and ethnic subcultures and in one's own mind); dependence (full or partial) on husbands, parents or the state; commitment to political ideas; loyalties to racial or ethnic or other "minority" groups; the demands of self-respect and responsibilities to others. Each of these factors exists in complex tension with every other, penalizing or prohibiting all of the apparently available options. And nipping at one's heels, always, is the endless pack of little things. If one dresses one way, one is subject to the assumption that one is advertising one's sexual availability; if one dresses another way, one appears to "not care about oneself" or to be "unfeminine." If one uses "strong language," one invites categorization as a whore or slut; if one does not, one invites categorization as a "lady"—one too delicately constituted to cope with robust speech or the realities to which it presumably refers.

The experience of oppressed people is that the living of one's life is confined and shaped by forces and barriers which are not accidental or occasional and hence avoidable, but are systematically related to each other in such a way as to catch one between and among them and restrict or penalize motion in any direction. It is the experience of being caged in: all avenues, in every direction, are blocked or booby trapped.

Cages. Consider a birdcage. If you look very closely at just one wire in the cage, you cannot see the other wires. If your conception of what is before you is determined by this myopic focus, you could look at that one wire, up and down the length of it, and be unable to see why a bird would not just fly around the wire any time it wanted to go somewhere. Furthermore, even if, one day at a time, you myopically inspected each wire, you still could not see why a bird would have trouble going past the wires to get anywhere. There is no physical property of any one wire, *nothing* that the closest scrutiny could discover, that will reveal how a bird could be inhibited or harmed by it except in the most accidental way. It is only when you step back, stop looking at the wires one by one, microscopically, and take a macroscopic view of the whole cage, that you can see why the bird does not go anywhere; and then you will see it in a moment. It will require no great subtlety of mental powers. It is perfectly *obvious* that the bird is surrounded by a network of systematically related barriers, no one of which would be the least hindrance to its flight, but which, by their relations to each other, are as confining as the solid walls of a dungeon.

It is now possible to grasp one of the reasons why oppression can be hard to see and recognize: one can study the elements of an oppressive structure with great care and some good will without seeing the structure as a whole, and hence without seeing or being able to understand that one is looking at a cage and that there are people there who are caged, whose motion and mobility are restricted, whose lives are shaped and reduced.

The arresting of vision at a microscopic level yields such common confusion as that about the male door-opening ritual. This ritual, which is remarkably widespread across classes and races, puzzles many people, some of whom do and some of whom do not find it offensive. Look at the scene of the two people approaching a door. The male steps slightly ahead and opens the door. The male holds the door open while the female glides through. Then the male goes through. The door closes after them. "Now how," one innocently asks, "can those crazy women's libbers say that is oppressive? The guy *removed* a barrier to the lady's smooth and unruffled progress." But each repetition of this ritual has a place in a pattern, in fact in several patterns. One has to shift the level of one's perception in order to see the whole picture.

The door-opening pretends to be a helpful service, but the helpfulness is false. This can be seen by noting that it will be done whether or not it makes any practical sense. Infirm men and men burdened with packages will open doors for able-bodied women who are free of physical burdens. Men will impose themselves awkwardly and jostle everyone in order to get to the door first. The act is not determined by convenience or grace. Furthermore, these very numerous acts of unneeded or even noisome "help" occur in counterpoint to a pattern of men not being helpful in many practical ways in which women might welcome help. What *women* experience is a world in which gallant princes charming commonly make a fuss about being helpful and providing small services when help and services are of little or no use, but in which there are rarely ingenious and adroit princes at hand when substantial assistance is really wanted either in mundane affairs or in situations of threat, assault or terror. There is no help with the (his) laundry; no help typing a report at 4:00 A.M.; no help in mediating disputes among relatives or children. There is nothing but advice that women should stay indoors after dark, be chaperoned by a man, or when it comes down to it, "lie back and enjoy it."

The gallant gestures have no practical meaning. Their meaning is symbolic. The door-opening and similar services provided are services which really are needed by people who are for one reason or another incapacitated—unwell, burdened with parcels, etc. So the message is that women are incapable. The detachment of the acts from the concrete realities of what women need and do not need is a vehicle for the message that women's actual needs and interests are unimportant or irrelevant. Finally, these gestures imitate the behavior of servants toward masters and thus mock women, who are in most respects the servants and caretakers of men. The message of the false helpfulness of male gallantry is female dependence, the invisibility or insignificance of women, and contempt for women.

One cannot see the meanings of these rituals if one's focus is riveted upon the individual event in all its particularity, including the particularity of the individual man's present conscious intentions and motives and the individual woman's conscious perception of the event in the moment. It seems sometimes that people take a deliberately myopic view and fill their eyes with things seen microscopically in order not to see macroscopically. At any rate, whether it is deliberate or not, people can and do fail to see the oppression of women because they fail to see macroscopically and hence fail to see the various elements of the situation as systematically related in larger schemes.

As the cageness of the birdcage is a macroscopic phenomenon, the oppressiveness of the situations in which women live our various and different lives is a macroscopic phenomenon. Neither can be *seen* from a microscopic perspective. But when you look macroscopically you can see it—a network of forces and barriers which are systematically related and which conspire to the immobilization, reduction and molding of women and the lives we live.

II

The image of the cage helps convey one aspect of the systematic nature of oppression. Another is the selection of occupants of the cages, and analysis of this aspect also helps account for the invisibility of the oppression of women.

It is as a woman (or as a Chicano or as a Black or Asian or lesbian) that one is entrapped.

"Why can't I go to the park; you let Jimmy go!"

"Because it's not safe for girls."

"I want to be a secretary, not a seamstress; I don't want to learn to make dresses."

"There's no work for negroes in that line; learn a skill where you can earn your living."

When you question why you are being blocked, why this barrier is in your path, the answer has not to do with individual talent or merit, handicap or failure; it has to do with your membership in some category understood as a "natural" or "physical" category. The "inhabitant" of the "cage" is not an individual but a group, all those of a certain category. If an individual is oppressed, it is in virtue of being a member of a group or category of people that is systematically reduced, molded, immobilized. Thus, to recognize a person as oppressed, one has to see that individual as belonging to a group of a certain sort.

There are many things which can encourage or inhibit perception of someone's membership in the sort of group or category in question here. In particular, it seems reasonable to suppose that if one of the devices of restriction and definition of the group is that of physical confinement or segregation, the confinement and separation would encourage recognition of the group as a group. This in turn would encourage the macroscopic focus which enables one to recognize oppression and encourages the individual's identification and solidarity with other individuals of the group or category. But physical confinement and segregation of the group is not common to all oppressive structures, and when an oppressed group is geographically and demographically dispersed the perception of it as a group is inhibited. There may be little or nothing in the situation of the individuals encouraging the macroscopic focus which would reveal the unity of the structure bearing down on all members of that group.

A great many people, female and male and of every race and class, simply do not believe that *woman* is a category of oppressed people, and I think that this is in part because they have been fooled by the dispersal and assimilation of women throughout and into the systems of the class and race which organize men. Our simply being dispersed makes it difficult for women to have knowledge of each other and hence difficult to recognize the shape of our common cage. The dispersal and assimilation of women throughout economic classes and races also divides us against each other practically and economically and thus attaches *interest* to the inability to see: for some, jealousy of their benefits, and for some, resentment of the others' advantages.

To get past this, it helps to notice that in fact women of all races and classes *are* together in a ghetto of sorts. There is a women's place, a sector, which is inhabited by women of all classes and races, and it is not defined by geographical boundaries but by function. The function is the service of men and men's interests as men define them, which includes the bearing and rearing of children. The details of the service and the working conditions vary by race and class, for men of different races and classes have different interests, perceive their interests differently, and express their needs and demands in different rhetorics, dialects and languages. But there are also some constants.

Whether in lower-, middle- or upper-class home or work situations, women's service always includes personal service (the work of maids, butlers, cooks, personal secretaries), sexual service (including provision for his genital sexual needs and bearing his children, but also including "being nice," "being attractive for him," etc.), and ego service (encouragement, support, praise, attention). Women's service work also is characterized everywhere by the fatal combination of responsibility and powerlessness: we are held responsible and we hold ourselves responsible for good outcomes for men and children in almost every respect though we have in almost no case power adequate to that project. The details of the subjective experience of this servitude are local. They vary with economic class and race and ethnic tradition as well as the personalities of the men in question. So also are the details of the forces which coerce our tolerance of this servitude particular to the different situations in which different women live and work.

All this is not to say that women do not have, assert and manage sometimes to satisfy our own interests, nor to deny that in some cases and in some respects women's independent interests do overlap with men's. But at every race/class level and even across race/class lines men do not serve women as women serve men. "Women's sphere" may be understood as the "service sector," taking the latter expression much more widely and deeply than is usual in discussions of the economy.

III

It seems to be the human condition that in one degree or another we all suffer frustration and limitation, all encounter unwelcome barriers, and all are damaged and hurt in various ways. Since we are a social species, almost all of our behavior and activities are structured by more than individual inclination and the conditions of the planet and its atmosphere. No human is free of social structures, nor (perhaps) would happiness consist in such freedom. Structure consists of boundaries, limits and barriers; in a structured whole, some motions and changes are possible, and others are not. If one is looking for an excuse to dilute the word "oppression," one can use the fact of social structure as an excuse and say that everyone is oppressed. But if one would rather get clear about what oppression is and is not, one needs to sort out the sufferings, harms and limitations and figure out which are elements of oppression and which are not.

From what I have already said here, it is clear that if one wants to determine whether a particular suffering, harm or limitation is part of someone's being oppressed, one has to look at it *in context* in order to tell whether it is an element in an oppressive structure: one has to see if it is part of an enclosing structure of forces and barriers which tends to the immobilization and reduction of a group or category of people. One has to look at how the barrier or force fits with others and to whose benefit or detriment it works. As soon as one looks at examples, it becomes obvious that not everything which frustrates or limits a person is oppressive, and not every harm or damage is due to or contributes to oppression.

If a rich white playboy who lives off income from his investments in South African diamond mines should break a leg in a skiing accident at Aspen and wait in pain in a blizzard for hours before he is rescued, we may assume that in that period he suffers. But the suffering comes to an end; his leg is repaired by the best surgeon money can buy and he is soon recuperating in a lavish suite, sipping Chivas Regal [upscale Scotch whisky]. Nothing in this picture suggests a structure of barriers and forces. He is a member of several oppressor groups and does not suddenly become oppressed because he is injured and in pain. Even if the accident was caused by someone's malicious negligence, and hence someone can be blamed for it and morally faulted, that person still has not been an agent of oppression.

Consider also the restriction of having to drive one's vehicle on a certain side of the road. There is no doubt that this restriction is almost unbearably frustrating at times, when one's lane is not moving and the other lane is clear. There are surely times, even, when abiding by this regulation would have harmful consequences. But the restriction is obviously wholesome for most of us most of the time. The restraint is imposed for our benefit, and does benefit us; its operation tends to encourage our *continued* motion, not to immobilize us. The limits imposed by traffic regulations are limits most of us would cheerfully impose on ourselves given that we knew others would follow them too. They are part of a structure which shapes our behavior, not to our reduction and immobilization, but rather to the protection of our continued ability to move and act as we will.

Another example: The boundaries of a racial ghetto in an American city serve to some extent to keep white people from going in, as well as to keep ghetto dwellers from going out. A particular white citizen may be frustrated or feel deprived because s/he cannot stroll around there and enjoy the "exotic" aura of a "foreign" culture, or shop for bargains in the ghetto swap shops. In fact, the existence of the ghetto, of racial segregation, does deprive the white person of knowledge and harm her/his character by nurturing unwarranted feelings of superiority. But this does not make the white person in this situation a member of an oppressed race or a person oppressed because of her/his race. One must look at the barrier. It limits the activities and the access of those on both sides of it (though to different degrees). But it is a product of the intention, planning and action of whites for the benefit of whites, to secure and maintain privileges that are available to whites generally, as members of the dominant and privileged group. Though the existence of the barrier has some bad consequences for whites, the barrier does not exist in a systematic relationship with other barriers and forces forming a structure oppressive to whites; quite the contrary. It is part of a structure which oppresses the ghetto dwellers and thereby (and by white intention) protects and furthers white interests as dominant white culture understands them. This barrier is not oppressive to whites, even though it is a barrier to whites.

Barriers have different meanings to those on opposite sides of them, even though they are barriers to both. The physical walls of a prison no more dissolve to let an outsider in than to let an insider out, but for the insider they are confining and limiting while to the outsider they may mean protection from what s/he takes to be threats posed by insiders—freedom from harm or anxiety. A set of social and economic barriers and forces separating two groups may be felt, even painfully, by members of both groups and yet may mean confinement to one and liberty and enlargement of opportunity to the other.

The service sector of the wives/mommas/assistants/girls is almost exclusively a woman-only sector; its boundaries not only enclose women but to a very great extent keep men out. Some men sometimes encounter this barrier and experience it as a restriction on this movement, their activities, their control of their choices of "lifestyle." Thinking they might like the simple nurturant life (which they may imagine to be quite free of stress, alienation and hard work), and feeling deprived since it seems closed to them, they thereupon announce the discovery that they are oppressed, too, by "sex roles." But that barrier is erected and maintained by men, for the benefit of men. It consists of cultural and economic forces and pressures in a culture and economy controlled by men in which, at every economic level and in all racial and ethnic subcultures, economy, tradition—and even ideologies of liberation—work to keep at least local culture and economy in male control.

The boundary that sets apart women's sphere is maintained and promoted by men generally for the benefit of men generally, and men do benefit from its existence, even the man who bumps into it and complains of the inconvenience. That barrier is protecting his classification and status as a male, as superior, as having a right to sexual access to a female or females. It protects a kind of citizenship which is superior to that of females of his class and race, his access to a wider range of better paying and higher status work, and his right to prefer unemployment to the degradation of doing lower status or "women's" work.

If a person's life or activity is affected by some force or barrier that person encounters, one may not conclude that the person is oppressed simply because the person encounters that barrier or force; not simply because the encounter is unpleasant, frustrating or painful to that person at that time; nor simply because the existence of the barrier or force, or the processes which maintain or apply it, serve to deprive that person of something of value. One must look at the barrier or force and answer certain questions about it. Who constructs and maintains it? Whose interests are served by its existence? Is it part of a structure which tends to confine, reduce, and immobilize some group? Is the individual a member of the confined group? Various forces, barriers and limitations a person may encounter or live with may be part of an oppressive structure or not, and if they are, that person may be on either the oppressed or the oppressor side of it. One cannot tell which by how loudly or how little the person complains.

IV

Many of the restrictions and limitations we live with are more or less internalized and self-monitored, and are part of our adaptations to the requirements and expectations imposed by the needs and tastes and tyrannies of others. I have in mind such things as women's cramped postures and attenuated strides and men's restraint of emotional self-expression (except for anger). Who gets what out of the practice of those disciplines, and who imposes what penalties for improper relaxations of them? What are the rewards of this self-discipline?

Can men cry? Yes, in the company of women. If a man cannot cry, it is in the company of men that he cannot cry. It is men, not women, who require this restraint; and men not only require it, they reward it. The man who maintains a steely or tough or laid-back demeanor (all are forms which suggest invulnerability) marks himself as a member of the male community and is esteemed by other men. Consequently, the maintenance of that demeanor contributes to the man's self-esteem. It is felt as good, and he can feel good about himself. The way this restriction fits into the structures of men's lives is as one of the socially required behaviors which, if carried off, contribute to their acceptance and respect by significant others and to their own self-esteem. It is to their benefit to practice this discipline.

Consider, by comparison, the discipline of women's cramped physical postures and attenuated stride. This discipline can be relaxed in the company of women; it generally is at its most strenuous in the company of men. Like men's emotional restraint, women's physical restraint is required by men. But unlike the case of men's emotional restraint, women's physical restraint is not rewarded. What do we get for it? Respect and esteem and acceptance? No. They mock us and parody our mincing steps. We look silly, incompetent, weak and generally contemptible. Our exercise of this discipline tends to low esteem and low self-esteem. It does not benefit us. It fits in a network of behaviors through which we constantly announce to others our membership in a lower caste and our unwillingness and/or inability to defend our bodily or moral integrity. It is degrading and part of a pattern of degradation.

Acceptable behavior for both groups, men and women, involves a required restraint that seems in itself silly and perhaps damaging. But the social effect is drastically different. The woman's restraint is part of a structure oppressive to women; the man's restraint is part of a structure oppressive to women.

V

One is marked for application of oppressive pressures by one's membership in some group or category. Much of one's suffering and frustration befalls one partly or largely because one is a member of that category. In the case at hand, it is the category, *woman*. Being a woman is a major factor in my not having a better job than I do; being a woman selects me as a likely victim of sexual assault or harassment; it is my being a woman that reduces the power of my anger to a proof of my insanity. If a woman has little or no economic or political power, or achieves little of what she wants to achieve, a major causal factor in this is that she is a woman. For any woman of any race or economic class, being a woman is significantly attached to whatever disadvantages and deprivations she suffers, be they great or small.

None of this is the case with respect to a person's being a man. Simply being a man is not what stands between him and a better job; whatever assaults and harassments he is subject to, being male is not what selects him for victimization; being male is not a factor which would make his anger impotent—quite the opposite. If a man has little or no material or political power, or achieves little of what he wants to achieve, his being male is no part of the explanation. Being male is something he has going *for* him, even if race or class or age or disability is going against him.

Women are oppressed, *as women*. Members of certain racial and/or economic groups and classes, both the males and the females, are oppressed *as* members of those races and/or classes. But men are not oppressed *as men* … and isn't it strange that any of us should have been confused and mystified about such a simple thing?

Feminism is for Everybody

BELL HOOKS*

The woman born Gloria Watkins but better known by her pen name, bell hooks (1952–), describes herself as a writer, feminist theorist, and cultural critic. She has done as much as any recent thinker to bring the particular issues central to African-American women's experience to the forefront of feminist debates. In this selection, however, hooks's aim is the still broader one of responding to simplistic caricatures of feminism as anti-male. She does so by defining feminism as "a movement to end sexism, sexist exploitation, and oppression." As such, hooks argues, feminism is not born of hatred for or opposition to men, *per se*. Instead, feminists (both women and men) oppose a system of ideas, social practices, and institutions affecting both sexes, a system that hooks describes as deeply pernicious. While the effects of sexism interact in complex ways inflected by differences in race, class, and gender, hooks nevertheless insists that some commitments—such as defending women's reproductive rights— are definitional of the feminist movement.

* *Source*: bell hooks, *Feminism is for Everybody: Passionate Politics* (New York: Routledge, 2015 [2000]), pp. xi–6. Reprinted by permission.

INTRODUCTION: Come Closer to Feminism

Everywhere I go I proudly tell folks who want to know who I am and what I do that I am a writer, a feminist theorist, a cultural critic. I tell them I write about movies and popular culture, analyzing the message in the medium. Most people find this exciting and want to know more. Everyone goes to movies, watches television, glances through magazines, and everyone has thoughts about the messages they receive, about the images they look at. It is easy for the diverse public I encounter to understand what I do as a cultural critic, to understand my passion for writing (lots of folks want to write, and do). But feminist theory — that's the place where the questions stop. Instead I tend to hear all about the evil of feminism and the bad feminists: how "they" hate men; how "they" want to go against nature and god; how "they" are all lesbians; how "they" are taking all the jobs and making the world hard for white men, who do not stand a chance.

When I ask these same folks about the feminist books or magazines they read, when I ask them about the feminist talks they have heard, about the feminist activists they know, they respond by letting me know that everything they know about feminism has come into their lives third-hand, that they really have not come close enough to feminist movement to know what really happens, what it's really about. Mostly they think feminism is a bunch of angry women who want to be like men. They do not even think about feminism as being about rights — about women gaining equal rights. When I talk about the feminism I know — up close and personal — they willingly listen, although when our conversations end, they are quick to tell me I am different, not like the "real" feminists who hate men, who are angry. I assure them I am as a real and as radical a feminist as one can be, and if they dare to come closer to feminism they will see it is not how they have imagined it.

Each time I leave one of these encounters, I want to have in my hand a little book so that I can say, read this book, and it will tell you what feminism is, what the movement is about. I want to be holding in my hand a concise, fairly easy to read and understand book; not a long book, not a book thick with hard to understand jargon and academic language, but a straightforward, clear book — easy to read without being simplistic. From the moment feminist thinking, politics, and practice changed my life, I have wanted this book. I have wanted to give it to the folk I love so that they can understand better this cause, this feminist politics I believe in so deeply, that is the foundation of my political life.

I have wanted them to have an answer to the question "what is feminism?" that is rooted neither in fear nor fantasy. I have wanted them to have this simple definition to read again and again so they know: "Feminism is a movement to end sexism, sexist exploitation, and oppression." I love this definition, which I first offered more than 10 years ago in my book *Feminist Theory: From Margin to Center*. I love it because it so clearly states that the movement is not about being anti-male. It makes it clear that the problem is sexism. And that clarity helps us remember that all of us, female and male, have been socialized from birth on to accept sexist thought and action. As a consequence, females can be just as sexist as men. And while that does not excuse or justify male domination, it does mean that it would be naive and wrongminded for feminist thinkers to see the movement as simplistically being for women against men. To end patriarchy (another way of naming the institutionalized sexism) we need to be clear that we are all participants in perpetuating sexism until we change our minds and hearts, until we let go of sexist thought and action and replace it with feminist thought and action.

Males as a group have and do benefit the most from patriarchy, from the assumption that they are superior to females and should rule over us. But those benefits have come with a price. In return for all the goodies men receive from patriarchy, they are required to dominate women, to exploit and oppress us, using violence if they must to keep patriarchy intact. Most men find it difficult to be patriarchs. Most men are disturbed by hatred and fear of women, by male violence against women, even the men who perpetuate this violence. But they fear letting go of the benefits. They are not certain what will happen to the world they know most intimately if patriarchy changes. So they find it easier to passively support male domination even when they know in their minds and hearts that it is wrong. Again and again men tell me they have no idea what it is feminists want. I believe them. I believe in their capacity to change and grow. And I believe that if they knew more about feminism they would no longer fear it, for they would find in feminist movement the hope of their own release from the bondage of patriarchy.

It is for these men, young and old, and for all of us, that I have written this short handbook, the book I have spent more than 20 years longing for. I had to write it because I kept waiting for it to appear, and it did not. And without it there was no way to address the hordes of people in this nation who are daily bombarded with anti-feminist backlash, who are being told to hate and resist a movement that they know very little about. There should be so many little feminist primers, easy to read pamphlets and books telling us all about feminism, that this book would be just another passionate voice speaking out on behalf of feminist politics. There should be billboards; ads in magazines; ads on buses, subways, trains; television commercials spreading the word, letting the world know more about feminism. We are not there yet. But this is what we must do to share feminism, to let the movement into everyone's mind and heart. Feminist change has already touched all our lives in a positive way. And yet we lose sight of the positive when all we hear about feminism is negative.

When I began to resist male domination, to rebel against patriarchal thinking (and to oppose the strongest patriarchal voice in my life — my mother's voice), I was still a teenager, suicidal, depressed, uncertain about how I would find meaning in my life and a place for myself. I needed feminism to give me a foundation of equality and justice to stand on. Mama has come around to feminist thinking. She sees me and all her daughters (we are six) living better lives because of feminist politics. She sees the promise and hope in feminist movement. It is that promise and hope that I want to share with you in this book, with everybody.

Imagine living in a world where there is no domination, where females and males are not alike or even always equal, but where a vision of mutuality is the ethos shaping our interaction. Imagine living in a world where we can all be who we are, a world of peace and possibility. Feminist revolution alone will not create such a world; we need to end racism, class elitism, imperialism. But it will make it possible for us to be fully self-actualized females and males able to create beloved community, to live together, realizing our dreams of freedom and justice, living the truth that we are all "created equal." Come closer. See how feminism can touch and change your life and all our lives. Come closer and know firsthand what feminist movement is all about. Come closer and you will see: feminism is for everybody.

FEMINIST POLITICS: Where We Stand

Simply put, feminism is a movement to end sexism, sexist exploitation, and oppression. This was a definition of feminism I offered in *Feminist Theory: From Margin to Center* more than 10 years ago. It was my hope at the time that it would become a common definition everyone would use. I liked this definition because it did not imply that men were the enemy. By naming sexism as the problem it went directly to the heart of the matter. Practically, it is a definition which implies that all sexist thinking and action is the problem, whether those who perpetuate it are female or male, child or adult. It is also broad enough to include an understanding of systemic institutionalized sexism. As a definition it is open-ended. To understand feminism it implies one has to necessarily understand sexism.

As all advocates of feminist politics know, most people do not understand sexism, or if they do, they think it is not a problem. Masses of people think that feminism is always and only about women seeking to be equal to men. And a huge majority of these folks think feminism is anti-male. Their misunderstanding of feminist politics reflects the reality that most folks learn about feminism from patriarchal mass media. The feminism they hear about the most is portrayed by women who are primarily committed to gender equality — equal pay for equal work, and sometimes women and men sharing household chores and parenting. They see that these women are usually white and materially privileged. They know from mass media that women's liberation focuses on the freedom to have abortions, to be lesbians, to challenge rape and domestic violence. Among these issues, masses of people agree with the idea of gender equity in the workplace — equal pay for equal work.

Since our society continues to be primarily a "Christian" culture, masses of people continue to believe that god has ordained that women be subordinate to men in the domestic household. Even though masses of women have entered the workforce, even though many families are headed by women who are the sole breadwinners, the vision of domestic life which continues to dominate the nation's imagination is one in which the logic of male domination is intact, whether men are present in the home or not. The wrongminded notion of feminist movement which implied it was anti-male carried with it the wrongminded assumption that all female space would necessarily be an environment where patriarchy and sexist thinking would be absent. Many women, even those involved in feminist politics, chose to believe this as well.

There was indeed a great deal of anti-male sentiment among early feminist activists who were responding to male domination with anger. It was that anger at injustice that was the impetus for creating a women's liberation movement. Early on most feminist activists (a majority of whom were white) had their consciousness raised about the nature of male domination when they were working in anti-classist and anti-racist settings with men who were telling the world about the importance of freedom while subordinating the women in their ranks. Whether it was white women working on behalf of socialism, black women working on behalf of civil rights and black liberation, or Native American women working for indigenous rights, it was clear that men wanted to lead, and they wanted women to follow. Participating in these radical freedom struggles awakened the spirit of rebellion and resistance in progressive females and led them towards contemporary women's liberation.

As contemporary feminism progressed, as women realized that males were not the only group in our society who supported sexist thinking and behavior — that females could be sexist as well anti-male sentiment no longer shaped the movement's consciousness. The focus shifted to an all-out effort to create gender justice. But women could not band together to further feminism without confronting our sexist thinking. Sisterhood could not be powerful as long as women were competitively at war with one another. Utopian visions of sisterhood based solely on the awareness of the reality that all women were in some way victimized by male domination were disrupted by discussions of class and race. Discussions of class differences occurred early on in contemporary feminism, preceding discussions of race. Diana Press published revolutionary insights about class divisions between women as early as the mid-'70s in their collection of essays *Class and Feminism*. These discussions did not trivialize the feminist insistence that "sisterhood is powerful," they simply emphasized that we could only become sisters in struggle by confronting the ways women — through sex, class, and race — dominated and exploited other women, and created a political platform that would address these differences.

Even though individual black women were active in contemporary feminist movement from its inception, they were not the individuals who became the "stars" of the movement, who attracted the attention of mass media. Often individual black women active in feminist movement were revolutionary feminists (like many white lesbians). They were already at odds with reformist feminists who resolutely wanted to project a vision of the movement as being solely about women gaining equality with men in the existing system. Even before race became a talked about issue in feminist circles it was clear to black women (and to their revolutionary allies in struggle) that they were never going to have equality within the existing white supremacist capitalist patriarchy.

From its earliest inception feminist movement was polarized. Reformist thinkers chose to emphasize gender equality. Revolutionary thinkers did not want simply to alter the existing system so that women would have more rights. We wanted to transform that system, to bring an end to patriarchy and sexism. Since patriarchal mass media was not interested in the more revolutionary vision, it never received attention in mainstream press. The vision of "women's liberation" which captured and still holds the public imagination was the one representing women as wanting what men had. And this was the vision that was easier to realize. Changes in our nation's economy, economic depression, the loss of jobs, etc., made the climate ripe for our nation's citizens to accept the notion of gender equality in the workforce.

Given the reality of racism, it made sense that white men were more willing to consider women's rights when the granting of those rights could serve the interests of maintaining white supremacy. We can never forget that white women began to assert their need for freedom after civil rights, just at the point when racial discrimination was ending and black people, especially black males, might have attained equality in the workforce with white men. Reformist feminist thinking focusing primarily on equality with men in the workforce overshadowed the original radical foundations of contemporary feminism which called for reform as well as overall restructuring of society so that our nation would be fundamentally anti-sexist.

Most women, especially privileged white women, ceased even to consider revolutionary feminist visions, once they began to gain economic power within the existing social structure. Ironically, revolutionary feminist thinking was most accepted and embraced in academic circles. In those circles the production of revolutionary feminist theory progressed, but more often than not that theory was not made available to the public. It became and remains a privileged discourse available to those among us who are highly literate, well-educated, and usually materially privileged. Works like *Feminist Theory: From Margin to Center* that offer a liberatory vision of feminist transformation never receive mainstream attention. Masses of people have not heard of this book. They have not rejected its message; they do not know what the message is.

While it was in the interest of mainstream white supremacist capitalist patriarchy to suppress visionary feminist thinking which was not anti-male or concerned with getting women the right to be like men, reformist feminists were also eager to silence these forces. Reformist feminism became their route to class mobility. They could break free of male domination in the workforce and be more self-determining in their lifestyles. While sexism did not end, they could maximize their freedom within the existing system. And they could count on there being a lower class of exploited subordinated women to do the dirty work they were refusing to do. By accepting and indeed colluding with the subordination of working-class and poor women, they not only ally themselves with the existing patriarchy and its concomitant sexism, they give themselves the right to lead a double life, one where they are the equals of men in the workforce and at home when they want to be. If they choose lesbianism they have the privilege of being equals with men in the workforce while using class power to create domestic lifestyles where they can choose to have little or no contact with men.

Lifestyle feminism ushered in the notion that there could be as many versions of feminism as there were women. Suddenly the politics was being slowly removed from feminism. And the assumption prevailed that no matter what a woman's politics, be she conservative or liberal, she too could fit feminism into her existing lifestyle. Obviously this way of thinking has made feminism more acceptable because its underlying assumption is that women can be feminists without fundamentally challenging and changing themselves or the culture. For example, let's take the issue of abortion. If feminism is a movement to end sexist oppression, and depriving females of reproductive rights is a form of sexist oppression, then one cannot be anti-choice and be feminist. A woman can insist she would never choose to have an abortion while affirming her support of the right of women to choose and still be an advocate of feminist politics. She cannot be anti-abortion and an advocate of feminism. Concurrently there can be no such thing as "power feminism" if the vision of power evoked is power gained through the exploitation and oppression of others.

Feminist politics is losing momentum because feminist movement has lost clear definitions. We have those definitions. Let's reclaim them. Let's share them. Let's start over. Let's have T-shirts and bumper stickers and postcards and hip-hop music, television and radio commercials, ads everywhere and billboards, and all manner of printed material that tells the world about feminism. We can share the simple yet powerful message that feminism is a movement to end sexist oppression. Let's start there. Let the movement begin again.

Homosexuality: The Nature and Harm Arguments

JOHN CORVINO*

One of the aims of the Gay Liberation movement is to enable gays and lesbians to be happy, healthy, contributing members of a society that recognizes and accepts differences in sexual orientation among its members. This requires educating or "raising the consciousness" not only of gay people but of their heterosexual or "straight" neighbors and coworkers as well. In the following essay, the philosopher John Corvino (1969–) confronts and criticizes two mainstays of anti-gay attitudes: the assertions that homosexuality is unnatural and harmful. Like other advocates of Gay Liberation, Corvino believes that confronting their own homophobia—that is, their fear of homosexuals and homosexuality—can lead "gays" and "straights" alike to overcome homophobia's stunting and stifling effects.

* *Source*: John Corvino, "Homosexuality: The Nature and Harm Arguments," in Alan Soble, ed., *The Philosophy of Sex: Contemporary Readings*, (Lanham, MD: Rowman & Littlefield, 1997), pp. 137–148. Reprinted by permission of the publisher.

HOMOSEXUALITY: THE NATURE AND HARM ARGUMENTS

Tommy and Jim are a homosexual couple I know. Tommy is an accountant; Jim is a botany professor. They are in their early forties and have been together fourteen years, the last five of which they've lived in a Victorian house that they've lovingly restored. Though their relationship has had its challenges, each has made sacrifices for the sake of the other's happiness and the relationship's long-term success.

I assume that Tommy and Jim have sex with each other (although I've never bothered to ask). Furthermore, I suspect that they probably *should* have sex with each other. For one thing, sex is pleasurable. But it is also much more than that: a sexual relationship can unite two people in a way that virtually nothing else can. It can be an avenue of growth, communication, and lasting interpersonal fulfillment. These are reasons most heterosexual couples have sex even if they don't want children, don't want children yet, or don't want additional children. And if these reasons are good enough for most heterosexual couples, then they should be good enough for Tommy and Jim.

Of course, having a reason to do something does not preclude there being an even better reason for not doing it. Tommy might have a good reason for drinking orange juice (it's tasty and nutritious) but an even better reason for not doing so (he's allergic). The point is that one would need a pretty good reason for denying a sexual relationship to Tommy and Jim, given the intense benefits widely associated with such relationships. The question I shall consider in this paper is thus quite simple: Why shouldn't Tommy and Jim have sex?[1]

I. Homosexuality Is Unnatural

Many contend that homosexual sex is "unnatural." But what does that mean? Many things that people value—clothing, houses, medicine, and government, for example—are unnatural in some sense. On the other hand, many things that people detest—disease, suffering, and death, for example—are natural in some sense (after all, they occur "in nature"). If the unnaturalness charge is to be more than empty rhetorical flourish, those who levy it must specify what they mean. Borrowing from Burton Leiser, I will examine several possibilities.[2]

1   *What is unusual or abnormal is unnatural.* One meaning of "unnatural" refers to that which deviates from the norm, that is, from what most people do. Obviously, most people engage in heterosexual relationships. But does it follow that it is wrong to engage in homosexual relationships? Relatively few people read Sanskrit, pilot ships, play the mandolin, breed goats, or write with both hands, yet none of these activities is immoral simply because it is unusual. As the Ramsey Colloquium, a group of Jewish and Christian scholars who oppose homosexuality, write, "The statistical frequency of an act does not determine its moral status."[3] So while homosexuality might be "unnatural" in the sense of being unusual, that fact is morally irrelevant.

2   *What is not practiced by other animals is unnatural.* Some people argue, "Even animals know better than to behave homosexually; homosexuality

must be wrong." This argument is doubly flawed. First, it rests on a false premise. Numerous studies— including Anne Perkins's study of "gay" sheep and George and Molly Hunt's study of "lesbian" seagulls—have shown that some animals do form homosexual pairbonds.[4] Second, even if that premise were true, it would not prove that homosexuality is immoral. After all, animals don't cook their food, brush their teeth, attend college, or drive cars; human beings do all these things without moral censure. Indeed, the idea that animals could provide us with our standards, especially our sexual standards, is simply amusing.

3 *What does not proceed from innate desires is unnatural.* Recent studies suggesting a biological basis for homosexuality have resulted in two popular positions. One side says, "Homosexual people are born that way; therefore it's natural (and thus good) for them to form homosexual relationships." The other side retorts, "No, homosexuality is a lifestyle choice, therefore it's unnatural (and thus wrong)." Both sides seem to assume a connection between the cause or origin of homosexual orientation, on the one hand, and the moral value of homosexual activity, on the other. And insofar as they share that assumption, both sides are wrong.

Consider first the pro-homosexual side: "They are born that way; therefore it's natural and good." This inference assumes that all innate desires are good ones (that is, that they should be acted upon). But that assumption is clearly false. Research suggests that some people are born with a predisposition towards violence, but such people have no more right to strangle their neighbors than anyone else. So while some people may be born with homosexual tendencies, it doesn't follow that they ought to act on them.

Nor does it follow that they ought *not* to act on them, even if the tendencies are not innate. I probably do not have any innate tendency to write with my left hand (since I, like everyone else in my family, have always been right-handed), but it doesn't follow that it would be immoral for me to do so. So simply asserting that homosexuality is a "lifestyle choice" will not show that it is an immoral lifestyle choice.

Do people "choose" to be homosexual? People certainly don't seem to choose their sexual *feelings*, at least not in any direct or obvious way. (Do you? Think about it.) Rather, they find certain people attractive and certain activities arousing, whether they "decide" to or not. Indeed, most people at some point in their lives wish that they could control their feelings more (for example, in situations of unrequited love) and find it frustrating that they cannot. What they *can* control to a considerable degree is how and when they act upon those feelings. In that sense, both homosexuality and heterosexuality involve "lifestyle choices." But in either case, determining the cause or origin of the feelings will not determine whether it is moral to act upon them.

4 *What violates an organ's principal purpose is unnatural.* Perhaps when people claim that homosexual sex is unnatural they mean that it cannot result in procreation. The idea behind the argument is that human organs have various "natural" purposes: eyes are for seeing, ears are for hearing,

genitals are for procreating. According to this argument, it is immoral to use an organ in a way that violates its particular purpose.

Many of our organs, however, have multiple purposes. Tommy can use his mouth for talking, eating, breathing, licking stamps, chewing gum, kissing Jim, and it seems rather arbitrary to claim that all but the last use are "natural."[5] (And if we say that some of the other uses are "unnatural, but not immoral," we have failed to specify a morally relevant sense of the term "natural.")

Just because people can and do use their sexual organs to procreate, it does not follow that they should not use them for other purposes. Sexual organs seem very well suited for expressing love, for giving and receiving pleasure, and for celebrating, replenishing, and enhancing a relationship, even when procreation is not a factor. Unless opponents of homosexuality are prepared to condemn heterosexual couples who use contraception or individuals who masturbate, they must abandon this version of the unnaturalness argument. Indeed, even the Roman Catholic Church, which forbids contraception and masturbation, approves of sex for sterile couples and of sex during pregnancy, neither of which can lead to procreation. The Church concedes here that intimacy and pleasure are morally legitimate purposes for sex, even in cases where procreation is impossible. But since homosexual sex can achieve these purposes as well, it is inconsistent for the Church to condemn it on the grounds that it is not procreative.

One might object that sterile heterosexual couples do not *intentionally* turn away from procreation, whereas homosexual couples do. But this distinction doesn't hold. It is no more possible for Tommy to procreate with a woman whose uterus has been removed than it is for him to procreate with Jim. By having sex with either one, he is intentionally engaging in a nonprocreative sexual act.

Yet one might press the objection further: Tommy and the woman *could* produce children if the woman were fertile. Whereas homosexual relationships are essentially infertile, heterosexual relationships are only incidentally so. But what does that prove? Granted, it might require less of a miracle for a woman without a uterus to become pregnant than for Jim to become pregnant, but it would require a miracle nonetheless. Thus it seems that the real difference here is not that one couple is fertile and the other not, or that one couple "could" be fertile (with the help of a miracle) and the other not, but rather that one couple is male-female and the other male-male. In other words, sex between Tommy and Jim is wrong because it's male-male—that is, because it's homosexual. But that, of course, is no argument at all.[6]

5   *What is disgusting or offensive is unnatural.* It often seems that when people call homosexuality "unnatural" they really just mean that it's disgusting. But plenty of morally neutral activities—handling snakes, eating snails, performing autopsies, cleaning toilets, and so on—disgust people. Indeed, for centuries most people found interracial relationships disgusting, yet that feeling, which has by no means disappeared, hardly proves that

such relationships are wrong. In sum, the charge that homosexuality is unnatural, at least in its most common forms, is longer on rhetorical flourish than on philosophical cogency.

II. Homosexuality Is Harmful

One might argue, instead, that homosexuality is harmful. The Ramsey Colloquium, for instance, argues that homosexuality leads to the breakdown of the family and, ultimately, of human society, and points to the "alarming rates of sexual promiscuity, depression, and suicide and the ominous presence of AIDS within the homosexual subculture."[7] Thomas Schmidt marshals copious statistics to show that homosexual activity undermines physical and psychological health.[8] Such charges, if correct, would seem to provide strong evidence against homosexuality. But are the charges correct? And do they prove what they purport to prove?

One obvious (and obviously problematic) way to answer the first question is to ask people like Tommy and Jim. It would appear that no one is in a better position to judge the homosexual "lifestyle" than those who live it. Yet it is unlikely that critics would trust their testimony. Indeed, the more that homosexual people try to explain their lives, the more critics accuse them of deceitfully promoting an agenda. (It's like trying to prove that you're not crazy. The more you object, the more people think, "That's exactly what a crazy person would say.")

One might instead turn to statistics. An obvious problem with this tack is that both sides of the debate bring forth extensive statistics and "expert" testimony, leaving the average observer confused. There is a more subtle problem as well. Because of widespread antigay sentiment, many homosexual people will not acknowledge their feelings to themselves, much less to researchers.[9] I have known a number of gay men who did not "come out" until their 40s and 50s, and no amount of professional competence on the part of interviewers would have been likely to open their closets sooner. Such problems compound the usual difficulties of finding representative population samples for statistical study.

Yet even if the statistical claims of gay-rights opponents were true, would they prove what they purport to prove? I think not, for the following reasons. First, as any good statistician realizes, correlation does not equal cause. Even if homosexual people were more likely to commit suicide, be promiscuous, or contract AIDS than the general population, it would not follow that their homosexuality causes them to do these things. An alternative and very plausible explanation is that these phenomena, like the disproportionately high crime rates among blacks, are at least partly a function of society's treatment of the group in question. Suppose you were told from a very early age that the romantic feelings that you experienced were sick, unnatural, and disgusting. Suppose further that expressing these feelings put you at risk of social ostracism or, worse yet, physical violence. Is it not plausible that you would, for instance, be more inclined to depression than you would be without such obstacles? And that such depression could, in its extreme forms, lead to suicide or other self-destructive behaviors? (It is indeed remarkable that in the face of such obstacles couples like Tommy and Jim continue to flourish.)

A similar explanation can be given for the alleged promiscuity of homosexuals.[10] The denial of legal marriage, the pressure to remain in the closet, and the overt hostility toward homosexual relationships are all more conducive to transient, clandestine encounters than they are to long-term unions. As a result, that which is challenging enough for heterosexual couples—settling down and building a life together—becomes far more challenging for homosexual couples.

Indeed, there is an interesting tension in the critics' position here. Opponents of homosexuality commonly claim that "marriage and the family … are fragile institutions in need of careful and continuing support."[11] And they point to the increasing prevalence of divorce and premarital sex among heterosexuals as evidence that such support is declining. Yet they refuse to concede that the complete absence of similar support for homosexual relationships might explain many of the alleged problems of homosexuals. The critics can't have it both ways: If heterosexual marriages are in trouble despite the various social, economic, and legal incentives for keeping them together, society should be little surprised that homosexual relationships—which not only lack such supports but face overt attack—are difficult to maintain.

One might object that if social ostracism were the main cause of homosexual people's problems, then homosexual people in more "tolerant" cities like New York and San Francisco should exhibit fewer such problems than their small-town counterparts; yet statistics do not seem to bear this out. This objection underestimates the extent of antigay sentiments in our society. By the time many gay and lesbian people move to urban centers, much damage has already been done to their psyches. Moreover, the visibility of homosexuality in urban centers makes homosexual people there more vulnerable to attack (and thus more likely to exhibit certain difficulties). Finally, note that urbanites *in general* (not just homosexual urbanites) tend to exhibit higher rates of promiscuity, depression, and sexually transmitted disease than the rest of the population.

But what about AIDS? Opponents of homosexuality sometimes claim that even if homosexual sex is not, strictly speaking, immoral, it is still a bad idea, since it puts people at risk for AIDS and other sexually transmitted diseases. But that claim is misleading. Note that it is infinitely more risky for Tommy to have sex with a woman who is HIV-positive than with Jim, who is HIV-negative. The reason is simple: It's not homosexuality that's harmful, it's the virus, and the virus may be carried by both heterosexual and homosexual people.

Now it may be the case that in a given population a homosexual male is statistically more likely to carry the virus than a heterosexual female, and thus, from a purely statistical standpoint, male homosexual sex is more risky than heterosexual sex (in cases where the partner's HIV status is unknown). But surely opponents of homosexuality need something stronger than this statistical claim. For if it is wrong for men to have sex with men because their doing so puts them at a higher AIDS risk than heterosexual sex, then it is also wrong for women to have sex with men because their doing so puts them at a higher AIDS risk than homosexual sex (lesbians as a group have the lowest incidence of AIDS). Purely from the standpoint of AIDS risk, women ought to prefer lesbian sex.

If this response seems silly, it is because there is obviously more to choosing a romantic or sexual partner than determining AIDS risk. And a major part of the decision, one that opponents of homosexuality consistently overlook, is considering whether one can have a mutually fulfilling relationship with the partner. For many people like Tommy and Jim, such fulfillment, which most heterosexuals recognize to be an important component of human flourishing, is only possible with members of the same sex.

Of course, the foregoing argument hinges on the claim that homosexual sex can only cause harm indirectly. Some would object that there are certain activities (anal sex, for instance) that for anatomical reasons are intrinsically harmful. But an argument against anal intercourse is by no means tantamount to an argument against homosexuality: neither all nor only homosexuals engage in anal sex. There are plenty of other things for both gay men and lesbians to do in bed. Indeed, for women, it appears that the most common forms of homosexual activity may be *less* risky than penile-vaginal intercourse, since the latter has been linked to cervical cancer.[12]

In sum, there is nothing *inherently* risky about sex between persons of the same gender. It is only risky under certain conditions: for instance, if they exchange diseased bodily fluids or if they engage in certain "rough" forms of sex that could cause tearing of delicate tissue. Heterosexual sex is equally risky under such conditions. Thus, even if statistical claims like those of Schmidt and the Ramsey Colloquium were true, they would not prove that homosexuality is immoral. At best they would prove that homosexual people, like everyone else, ought to take great care when deciding to become sexually active.

Of course, there's more to a flourishing life than avoiding harm. One might argue that even if Tommy and Jim are not harming each other by their relationship, they are still failing to achieve the higher level of fulfillment possible in a heterosexual relationship, which is rooted in the complementarity of male and female. But this argument just ignores the facts. Tommy and Jim are homosexual *precisely because* they find relationships with men (and in particular, with each other) more fulfilling than relationships with women. Even evangelicals (who have long advocated "faith healing" for homosexuals) are beginning to acknowledge that the choice for most homosexual people is not between homosexual relationships and heterosexual relationships, but rather between homosexual relationships and celibacy.[13] What the critics need to show, therefore, is that no matter how loving, committed, mutual, generous, and fulfilling the relationship may be, Tommy and Jim would flourish more if they were celibate. This is a formidable (indeed, probably impossible) task.

Thus far I have focused on the allegation that homosexuality harms those who engage in it. But what about the allegation that homosexuality harms other, nonconsenting parties? Here I will briefly consider two claims: that homosexuality threatens children and that it threatens society.

Those who argue that homosexuality threatens children may mean one of two things. First, they may mean that homosexual people are child molesters. Statistically, the vast majority of reported cases of child sexual abuse involve young girls and their fathers, stepfathers, or other familiar (and presumably heterosexual) adult males.[14] But opponents of homosexuality argue that when one adjusts for relative percentages in the population, homosexual males appear more likely than heterosexual males to be child molesters. As I argued above, the problems with obtaining reliable statistics on homosexuality render such calculations difficult. Fortunately, they are also unnecessary.

Child abuse is a terrible thing. But when a heterosexual male molests a child (or rapes a woman, or commits assault), the act does not reflect upon all heterosexuals. Similarly, when a homosexual male molests a child, there is no reason why that act should reflect upon all homosexuals. Sex with adults of the same sex is one thing; sex with *children* of the same sex is quite another. Conflating the two not only slanders innocent people, it also misdirects resources intended to protect children. Furthermore, many men convicted of molesting young boys are sexually attracted to adult women and report no attraction to adult men.[15] To call such men "homosexual" or even "bisexual" is probably to stretch such terms too far.[16]

Alternatively, those who charge that homosexuality threatens children might mean that the increasing visibility of homosexual relationships makes children more likely to become homosexual. The argument for this view is patently circular. One cannot prove that doing *X* is bad by arguing that it causes people to do *X*, which is bad. One must first establish independently that *X* is bad. That said, there is not a shred of evidence to demonstrate that exposure to homosexuality leads children to become homosexual.

But doesn't homosexuality threaten society? A Roman Catholic priest once put the argument to me as follows: "Of course homosexuality is bad for society. If everyone were homosexual, there would be no society."

Perhaps it is true that if everyone were homosexual, there would be no society. But if everyone were a celibate priest, society would collapse just as surely, and my priest-friend didn't seem to think that he was doing anything wrong simply by failing to procreate. Jeremy Bentham made the point somewhat more acerbically roughly two hundred years ago: "If then merely out of regard to population it were right that [homosexuals] should be burnt alive, monks ought to be roasted alive by a slow fire."[17]

From the fact that the continuation of society requires procreation, it does not follow that *everyone* must procreate. Moreover, even if such an obligation existed, it would not preclude homosexuality. At best it would preclude *exclusive* homosexuality: Homosexual people who occasionally have heterosexual sex can procreate just fine. And given artificial insemination, even those who are exclusively homosexual can procreate. In short, the priest's claim—if everyone were homosexual, there would be no society—is false, and even if it were true, it would not establish that homosexuality is immoral.

The Ramsey Colloquium commits a similar fallacy.[18] Noting (correctly) that heterosexual marriage promotes the continuation of human life, they then infer that homosexuality is immoral because it fails to accomplish the same.[19] But from the fact that procreation is good it does not follow that childlessness is bad, a point that the members of the Colloquium, several of whom are Roman Catholic priests, should readily concede.

I have argued that Tommy and Jim's sexual relationship harms neither them nor society. On the contrary, it benefits both. It benefits them because it makes them happier, not merely in a short-term, hedonistic sense, but in a long-term, "big picture" sort of way. And in turn it benefits society, since it makes Tommy and Jim more stable, more productive, and more generous than they would otherwise be. In short, their relationship, including its sexual component, provides the same kinds of benefits that infertile, heterosexual relationships provide (and perhaps other benefits as well). Nor should we fear that accepting their relationship and others like it will cause people to flee in droves from the institution of heterosexual marriage. After all, as Thomas Williams points out, the usual response to a gay person is not "How come he gets to be gay and I don't?"[20]

Conclusion

As a last resort, opponents of homosexuality typically change the subject: "But what about incest, polygamy, and bestiality? If we accept Tommy and Jim's sexual relationship, why shouldn't we accept those as well?" Opponents of interracial marriage used a similar slippery-slope argument thirty years ago when the Supreme Court struck down anti-miscegenation laws.[21] It was a bad argument then and it is a bad argument now.

Just because there are no good reasons to oppose interracial or homosexual relationships, it does not follow that there are no good reasons to oppose incestuous, polygamous, or bestial relationships. One might argue, for instance, that incestuous relationships threaten delicate familial bonds, that polygamous relationships result in unhealthy jealousies (and sexism), or that bestial relationships (do I need to say it?) aren't really "relationships" at all, at least not in the sense we've been discussing. Perhaps even better arguments could be offered (given much more space than I have here). The point is that there is no logical connection between homosexuality, on the one hand, and incest, polygamy, and bestiality, on the other.

Why, then, do critics continue to push this objection? Perhaps it's because accepting homosexuality requires them to give up one of their favorite arguments: "It's wrong because we've always been taught that it's wrong." This argument—call it the argument from tradition—has an obvious appeal: People reasonably favor "tried and true" ideas over unfamiliar ones, and they recognize the foolishness of trying to invent morality from scratch. But the argument from tradition is also a dangerous argument, as any honest look at history will reveal.

To recognize Tommy and Jim's relationship as good is to admit that our moral traditions are imperfect. Condemning people out of habit is easy. Overcoming deep-seated prejudice takes courage.[22]

NOTES

1   Although my central example in the paper is a gay male couple, much of what I say will apply *mutatis mutandis* to lesbians as well, since many of the same arguments are used against them. This is not to say that gay male sexuality and lesbian sexuality are largely similar or that discussions of the former will cover all that needs to be said about the latter. Furthermore, the fact that I focus on a long-term couple should not be taken to imply any judgment about homosexual activity outside of such unions. If the argument of this paper is successful, then the evaluation of homosexual activity outside of committed unions should be largely (if not entirely) similar to the evaluation of heterosexual activity outside of committed unions.

2   Burton, M. Leiser, *Liberty, Justice, and Morals: Contemporary Value Conflicts* (New York: Macmillan, 1986), pp. 51–57.

3   The Ramsey Colloquium, "The Homosexual Movement," *First Things*, March 1994, pp. 15–20.

4   For an overview of some of these studies, see Simon LeVay's *Queer Science* (Cambridge, Mass: M.I.T. Press, 1996), Chap. 10.

5   I have borrowed some items in this list from Richard Mohr's pioneering work, *Gays/ Justice* (New York: Columbia University Press, 1988), p. 36.

6   For a fuller explanation of this type of natural law argument, see John Finnis, "Law, Morality, and 'Sexual Orientation," *Notre Dame Law Review* 69:5 (1994): 1049–76; revised, shortened, and reprinted in John Corvino, ed., *Same Sex: Debating the Ethics, Science, and Culture of Homosexuality* (Lanham, Md.: Rowman and Littlefield, 1997). For a cogent and well-developed response, see Andrew Koppelman, "A Reply to the New Natural Lawyers," in the same volume.

7   The Ramsey Colloquium, p. 19.

8   Thomas Schmidt, *Straight and Narrow? Compassion and Clarity in the Homosexuality Debate* (Downer's Grove, Ill.: InterVarsity Press, 1995), Chap. 6, "The Price of Love."

9   Both the American Psychological Association and the American Public Health Association have conceded this point. "Reliable data on the incidence of homosexual orientation are difficult to obtain due to the criminal penalties and social stigma attached to homosexual behavior and the consequent difficulty of obtaining representative samples of people to study." See *Amici Curiae* brief in *Bowers v. Hardwick*, Supreme Court Nos. 85–140 (October Term 1985).

10   It is worth noting that allegations of promiscuity are probably exaggerated. Note that the study most commonly cited to prove homosexual male promiscuity, the Bell and Weinberg study, took place in 1978, in an urban center (San Francisco), at the height of the sexual revolution—hardly a broad sample. (See Alan P. Bell and Martin S. Weinberg, *Homosexualities* [New York: Simon and Schuster, 1978].) The far more recent and extensive University of Chicago study agreed that homosexual and bisexual people "have higher average numbers of partners than the rest of the sexually active people in the study," but concluded that the differences in the mean number of partners "do not appear very large" (Edward O. Laumann, et al., *The Social Organization of Sexuality: Sexual Practices in the United States* [Chicago: University of Chicago Press, 1994], pp. 314, 316). I am grateful to Andrew Koppelman for drawing my attention to the Chicago study.

11   The Ramsey Colloquium, p. 19.

12   See S. R. Johnson, E. M. Smith, and S. M. Guenther, "Comparison of Gynecological Health Care Problems Between Lesbian and Bisexual Women," *Journal of Reproductive Medicine* 32 (1987), pp. 805–11.

13   See, for example, Stanton L. Jones, "The Loving Opposition," *Christianity Today*, 37:8 (July 19, 1993).

14   See Danya Glaser and Stephen Frosh, *Child Sexual Abuse*, 2nd ed. (Houndmills, Eng.: Macmillan, 1993), pp. 13–17, and Kathleen Coulbourn Faller, *Understanding Child Sexual Maltreatment* (Newbury Park, Calif.: Sage, 1990), pp. 16–20.

15   See Frank G. Bolton, Jr., Larry A. Morris, and Ann E. MacEachron, *Males at Risk: The Other Side of Child Sexual Abuse* (Newbury Park, Calif.: Sage, 1989), p. 61.

16   Part of the problem here arises from the grossly simplistic categorization of people into two or, at best, three sexual orientations: heterosexual, homosexual, and bisexual. Clearly, there is great variety within (and beyond) these categories. See Frederick Suppe, "Explaining Homosexuality: Philosophical Issues, and Who Cares Anyhow?" in Timothy F. Murphy, ed., *Gay Ethics: Controversies in Outing, Civil Rights, and Sexual Science* (New York: Haworth Press, 1994), especially pp. 234–38.

17   [Jeremy Bentham], "An Essay on 'Paederasty,'" in Robert Baker and Frederick Elliston, eds., *The Philosophy of Sex* (Buffalo, N.Y.: Prometheus, 1984), pp. 360–61. Bentham uses the word "paederast" where we would use the term "homosexual"; the latter term was not coined until 1869, and the term "heterosexual" was coined a few years after that. Today, "pederasty" refers to sex between men and boys, a different phenomenon from the one Bentham was addressing.

18   The Ramsey Colloquium, pp. 17–18.

19   The argument is a classic example of the fallacy of denying the antecedent: If *X* promotes procreation, then *X* is good; *X* does not promote procreation; therefore, *X* is not good. Compare: If *X* is president, then *X* lives in the White House; Chelsea Clinton is not president; therefore Chelsea Clinton does not live in the White House.

20   Actually, Williams makes the point with regard to celibacy, while making an analogy between celibacy and homosexuality. See Thomas Williams, "A Reply to the Ramsey Colloquium," in *Same Sex*.

21   Loving *v*. Virginia, 1967.

22   This paper grew out of a lecture, "What's (Morally) Wrong with Homosexuality?" which I first delivered at the University of Texas in 1992 and have since delivered at numerous other universities around the country. I am grateful to countless audience members, students, colleagues, and friends for helpful dialogue over the years. I would especially like to thank the following individuals for detailed comments on recent drafts of the paper: Edwin B. Allaire, Daniel Bonevac, David Bradshaw, David Cleaves, Mary Beth Mader, Richard D. Mohr, Jonathan Rauch, Robert Schuessler, Alan Soble, James P. Sterba, and Thomas Williams. I dedicate this paper to my partner, Carlos Casillas.

On Liberation

VINE DELORIA, JR.*

Vine Deloria (1933–2005) was a Native American activist and author who taught at the University of Colorado as well as the University of Arizona, where he established the first master's degree program in American Indian Studies in the United States. In this essay, Deloria rejects "liberation theology" as an inappropriate framework for achieving indigenous peoples' freedom. Deloria maintains that liberation theology (see selection 8.61) was born of a Western theological, philosophical, and scientific framework that is insufficiently inclusive of non-European worldviews, and therefore has only a very limited conception of what native or indigenous people believe real freedom entails. On his view, true liberation will be achieved only when we realize that Western approaches to understanding are not universally valid; rather, he argues, all knowledge is relative to the type of questions that we human beings formulate. Insisting that knowledge is more a matter of cultural preference than the depiction of some underlying reality about the world, Deloria argues for altering human thinking from a Western focus on narrow "ideas" to an indigenous focus on holistic "visions," a path that he believes will liberate not only native peoples, but all people.

* *Source*: Vine Deloria, Jr., *For This Land: Writings on Religion in America* (New York: Routledge, 1999), pp. 100–107. Reprinted by permission.

On Liberation

Liberation theology assumes that the common experience of oppression is sufficient to create the desire for a new coalition of dissident minorities. Adherents of this movement indiscriminately classify all minorities—racial, ethnic, and sexual—in a single category of people seeking liberation. Such classification is an easy way to eliminate specific complaints of specific groups and a clever way to turn aside efforts of dissenting groups to get their particular goals fulfilled. For instead of listening to their complaints, observers—and particularly liberal observers who pose as sympathetic fellow-travelers—can tie up the conversation endlessly by eliciting questions, framed within the liberation ideology, that require standard and nonsensical answers. Liberation theology, then, was an absolute necessity if the establishment was going to continue to control the minds of minorities. If a person of a minority group had not invented it, the liberal establishment most certainly would have created it.

The immediate response to such an accusation is one of horrified refusal to believe that there could be any racial or sexual minority that does not consider itself to be under oppression. This is followed by the perennial suggestion that if dissident minorities "got organized" instead of remaining separate they would be able to get things done. Those who reject that concept of oppression merely prove that they are so completely the victims of oppression that they do not even recognize it. The circular logic closes neatly in upon them, making them victims indeed. Liberation theology is simply the latest gimmick to keep minority groups circling the wagons with the vain hope that they can eliminate the oppression that surrounds them. It does not seek to destroy the roots of oppression, but merely to change the manner in which oppression manifests itself. No winner, no matter how sincere, willingly surrenders his power over others. He may devise clever ways to appear to share such power, but he always keeps a couple of aces up his sleeve in case things get out of control.

If there were any serious concern about liberation we would see thousands of people simply walk away from the vast economic, political, and intellectual machine we call Western civilization and refuse to be enticed to participate in it any longer. Liberation is not a difficult task when one no longer finds value in a set of institutions or beliefs. We are liberated from the burden of Santa Claus and the moral demand to be "good" when, as maturing adolescents, we reject the concept of Santa Claus. Thereafter we have no sense of guilt in late November that we have not behaved properly during the year, and no fear that a lump of coal rather than a gift will await us Christmas morning. In the same manner, we are freed and liberated once we realize the insanity and fantasy of the present manner of interpreting our experiences in the world. Liberation, in its most fundamental sense, requires a rejection of everything we have been taught and its replacement by only those things we have experienced as having values.

But this replacement only begins the task of liberation. For the history of Western thinking in the past eight centuries has been one of replacement of ideas within a framework that has remained basically unchanged for nearly two millenia. Challenging this framework of interpretation means a rearrangement of our manner of perceiving the world, and it involves a reexamination of the body of human knowledge and its structural reconstruction into a new format. Such a task appears to be far from the struggles of the present. It seems abstract and meaningless in the face of contemporary suffering. And it suggests that people can be made to change their oppressive activity by intellectual reorientation alone.

All these questions arise, however, because of the fundamental orientation of Western peoples toward the world. We assume that we know the structure of reality and must only make certain minor adjustments in the machinery that operates it in order to bring our institutions into line. Immediate suffering is thus placed in juxtaposition with abstract metaphysical conceptions of the world and, because we can see immediate suffering, we feel impelled to change conditions quickly to relieve tensions, never coming to understand how the basic attitude toward life and its derivative attitudes toward minority groups continues to dominate the goals and activities that appear designed to create reforms.

Numerous examples can be cited to show that our efforts to bring justice into the world have been short-circuited by the passage of events, and that those efforts are unsuccessful because we have failed to consider the basic framework within which we pose questions, analyze alternatives, and suggest solutions. Consider the examples from our immediate past. In the early sixties college application forms included a blank line on which all prospective students were required to indicate their race. Such information was used to discriminate against those of a minority background, and so reformers demanded that the question be dropped. By the time all colleges had been forced to eliminate questions concerning the race of applicants, the Civil Rights Movement had so sensitized those involved in higher education that scholarships were made available in great numbers to people of minority races. There was no way, however, to allocate such scholarships because college officials could no longer determine the racial background of students on the basis of their applications for admission.

Much of the impetus for low-cost housing in the cities was based upon the premise that in the twentieth century people should not have to live in hovels but that adequate housing should be constructed for them. Yet in the course of tearing down slums and building new housing projects, low-income housing areas were eliminated. The construction cost of the new projects made it necessary to charge higher rentals. Former residents of the low-income areas could not afford to live in the new housing, so they moved to other parts of the city and created exactly the same conditions that had originally provoked the demand for low-rent housing.

Government schools had a very difficult time teaching American Indian children the English language. (One reason was the assumption of teachers that all languages had Latin roots, and their inability to adapt the programs when they discovered that Indian languages were not so derived.) Hence programs in bilingual teaching methods were authorized that would use the native language to teach the children English, an underhanded way of eliminating the native language. Between the time that bilingual programs were conceived and the time that they were finally funded, other programs that concentrated on adequate housing had an unexpected effect on the educational process. Hundreds of new houses were built in agency towns, and Indians moved from remote areas of the different reservations into those towns where they could get good housing. Since they were primarily younger couples with young children, the housing development meant that most Indian children were now growing up in the agency communities and were learning English as a first language. Thus, the bilingual programs, which began as a means of teaching English as a second language, became the method designed to preserve the native vernacular by teaching it as a second language to students who had grown up speaking English.

Example after example could be cited, each testifying to the devastating effect of a general attitude toward the world that underlies the Western approach to human knowledge. The basis of this attitude is the assumption that the world operates in certain predetermined ways, that it operates continuously under certain natural laws, and that the nature of every species is homogeneous, with few real deviations. One can trace this attitude back into the Western past. Religious concepts, which have since been transformed into scientific and political beliefs, remain objects of belief as securely as if they had never been severed from their theological moorings.

Let us trace a few examples. Originally the continuity of the world was conceived as a demonstration of the divine plan and God, conceived as a lawgiver in the moral sense, became a law-giver in the scientific sense also. Scientific data was classified in certain ways that in the eyes of Western peoples became a part of the structure of nature. Phenomena that did not fit into the structure that had been created were said to "violate" the laws of nature and hence to be untrue in the religious sense and unimportant in the scientific sense. When evolution replaced the concept of creation in the book of Genesis, it became an inviolable law in the eyes of Western people in much the same way that the literal interpretation of the biblical story had been accepted by Western people in former centuries.

The world was originally conceived in terms of the Near East as the center of reality. As awareness extended to other peoples, this world gradually expanded until by the Middle Ages it encompassed those regions that were in commercial contact with Western Europe. The discovery of the Western hemisphere created a certain degree of trauma, for suddenly there was an awareness of lands and peoples of which Western Europeans had no previous knowledge. The only way that these people could be accounted for was by reference to the Scriptures. So it was hypothesized that the aboriginal peoples in North and South America must have been the Ten Lost Tribes of Israel who had crossed into the New World over a land bridge somewhere in northern Asia. The basic assumption of this theory was the creation of the human species as a single act, performed by the Christian God, with its subsequent history one of populating the planet.

The rise of social science, and the downgrading of theological answers to what were considered scientific questions concerning the nature and history of human societies, meant that social science had to provide answers to questions formulated within the theological context. With virtually no reconsideration of the basic question of the creation (or origination in scientific terms) of our species as the product of a single act, anthropologists promptly adopted the old theological explanation of the peopling of the Western Hemisphere, developing the Bering Strait theory of migration to account for the phenomenon. Whether secular or sacred, the classification of American natives as a derivative, inferior group of Asian-European peoples, albeit far removed from those roots by the postulation of many millenia of wandering, became a status from which American Indians have been unable to escape.

The emphasis on objective knowledge by Western peoples has meant the development of an attitude that sees reality as basically physical, the knowledge thereof basically mental or verbal, and the elimination of any middle ground between extremes. Thus religion has become a matter of the proper exposition of doctrines, and non-Western religions have been judged on their development of a systematic moral and ethical code rather than the manner in which they conducted themselves. When a religion is conceived as a code of verbal importance rather than a way of life, loopholes in the code become more important than the code itself since, by eliminating or escaping the direct violation of the code by a redefinition of the code or a relaxation of its intended effect, one can maintain two types of behavior, easily discerned in a practical way, as if they were identical and consistent with a particular picture of reality.

In recent decades Western science had made an important discovery, important at least for Western peoples who had formerly confused themselves with their own belief system. Western science was premised upon the proposition that God had made the world according to certain laws. These laws were capable of discovery by human reason, and the task of science was to discover as many of these laws as possible. So human knowledge was misconceived as the only description of physical reality, a tendency Alfred North Whitehead called the principle of "misplaced concreteness." With the articulation of theories of indeterminancy in modern physics, this naive attitude toward human knowledge radically shifted and became an acknowledgement that what we had formerly called nature was simply our knowledge of nature based upon the types of questions we had decided to use to organize the measurements we were making of the physical world.

The shift in emphasis meant that all knowledge became a relative knowledge, valid only for the types of questions we were capable of formulating. Depending upon the types of information sought, we could measure and observe certain patterns of phenomena, but these patterns existed in our heads rather than in nature itself. Knowledge thus became a matter of cultural preference rather than an indication of the ultimate structure of reality. Presumably if one culture asked a certain type of question while another asked another type of question, the two different answers could form two valid perspectives on the world. Whether these two perspectives could be reconciled in one theory of knowledge depended upon the broader pattern of interpretation that thinkers brought into play with respect to the data. When this new factor of interpretation is applied specifically to different cultures and traditions, we can see that what have been called primitive superstitions have the potential of being regarded as sophisticated insights into the nature of things, at least on an equal basis with Western knowledge. The traditional manner in which Western peoples think is now only one of the possible ways of describing a natural process. It may not, in fact, even be as accurate, insofar as it can relate specific facts without perverting them, as non-Western ways of correlating knowledge.

This uncertainty is liberating in a much more fundamental way than any other development in the history of Western civilization. It means that religious, political, economic, and historical analyses of human activities that have been derived from the Western tradition do not have an absolute claim upon us. We are free to seek a new synthesis that draws information from every culture, and every period of human history has as a boundary only the requirement that it make more sense of more data than any other synthesis. Even the initial premises of such a synthesis can be different from what we have previously used to begin our formulation of a picture of reality.

When we apply this new freedom to some of the examples cited above, we see that the proper question we should have asked with respect to housing did not concern housing at all, but covered the more general question of the nature of a community. We discover that the college applications and the bilingual programs should have been transcended by questions concerning the nature of knowledge, how it is transmitted, and how it can be expanded, rather than how specific predetermined courses of action can be implemented. Once we reject the absolute nature of Western conceptions of problems, we are able to see different types of questions inherent in our immediate problem areas. The immediacy we feel when observing conditions under which people live should enable us to raise new issues that contain within themselves new ways of conceiving solutions. An old Indian saying captures the radical difference between Indians and Western peoples quite adequately. The white man, the Indians maintain, has ideas; Indians have visions. Ideas have a single dimension and require a chain of connected ideas to make sense. The connections that are made between ideas can lead to great insights on the nature of things, or they can lead to the inexorable logic of Catch-22 in which the logic inevitably leads to the polar opposite of the original proposition. The vision, on the other hand, presents a whole picture of experience and has a central meaning that stands on its own feet as an independent revelation. It is said that Albert Einstein could not conceive of his problems in physics in conceptual terms but instead had visions of a whole event. He then spent his time attempting to translate elements of that event that could be separated into mathematical and verbal descriptions that could be communicated to others. It is this difference, the change from inductive and deductive logic to transformation of perceived realities, that becomes the liberating factor, not additional information or continual replacement of data and concepts within the traditional framework of interpretation.

Let us return, then, to our discussion of the manner in which racial minorities have been perceived by the white community, particularly by the liberal establishment, in the past decade and a half. Minority groups, conceived to be different from the white majority, are perceived to be lacking some critical element of humanity that, once received, would bring them to some form of equality with the white majority. The trick has been in identifying that missing element, and each new articulation of goals is immediately attributed to every minority group and appears to answer the question that has been posed by the sincere but unreflective liberal community.

Liberation is simply the manner in which this missing element is presently conceived by people interested in reform. It will become another social movement fad and eventually fade away to be replaced with yet another instant analysis of the situation. Until fundamental questions regarding the assumptions that form the basis for Western civilization are raised and new articulations of reality are discovered, the impulse to grab quickly and apparently easy answers will continue. Social conditions will continue to be described in a cause-and-effect logic that has dominated Western thinking for its entire intellectual lifetime. Programs will be designed that fail to account for the change in conditions that occurs continually in human societies. Ideas will continue to dominate our concerns and visions will not come.

If we are then to talk seriously about the necessity of liberation, we are talking about the destruction of the whole complex of Western theories of knowledge and the construction of a new and more comprehensive synthesis of human knowledge and experience. This is no easy task and it cannot be accomplished by people who are encompassed within the traditional Western logic and the resulting analyses such logic provides. If we change the very way that Western peoples think, the way they collect data, which data they gather, and how they arrange that information, then we are speaking truly of liberation. For it is the manner in which people conceive reality that motivates them to behave in certain ways, that provides them with a system of values, and that enables them to justify their activities. A new picture of reality, a reality conceived as a vision and not as a series of related or connected ideas, can accomplish over a longer period of time many changes we have been unable to effect while conceiving solutions as short-term remedies.

More important for our discussion is the recognition that all parts of human experience are related and the proposed solution to any particular problem overlooks the changes that will occur in related activities because of their relationship. Fundamental changes initiated by a new picture of reality will create a transformation, and will avoid the traditional replacement of words with new words. In summary we now challenge the basic assumptions of Western man. To wit:

1   that time is uniform and continuous;
2   that our species originated from a single source;
3   that our descriptions of nature are absolute knowledge;
4   that the world can be divided into subjective and objective;
5   that our understanding of our species is homogeneous;
6   that ultimate reality, including divinity, is homogeneous;
7   that by projection of present conditions we can understand human history, planetary history, or the universe;
8   that inductive and deductive reasoning are the primary tools for gaining knowledge.

As we create a new set of propositions that transcend these theses we will achieve liberation in a fundamental sense and the synthesis that emerges will be a theology. But it will transform present feelings of sympathy to shared experiences, it will transform tolerance to understanding, and it will transform appreciation of separate cultural traditions into a new universal cultural expression. And everyone will become liberated.

(1977)

Liberation Theology

GUSTAVO GUTIERREZ*

An influential movement within Christianity, especially the Roman Catholic Church, the "theology of liberation" views Jesus Christ as the champion and liberator of poor and oppressed people. Christ's teachings, as interpreted by liberation theologians such as Father Gustavo Gutierrez (1928–) of Peru, are aimed as much at social justice in this world as salvation in the next. Far from being "normal" or "natural" features of human life, poverty and oppression are the products of sin—of greed and lust for power—among the affluent. Liberation theology aims at raising the consciousness not only of the poor but also of affluent people, who are asked to confront and overcome their own sin by exercising the "option for the poor." Since 2001, Gutierrez has been a professor of theology at the University of Notre Dame in Indiana. In 2013, shortly after his election, Pope Francis—who, unlike his predecessors, has a favorable view of liberation theology—summoned Father Gutierrez to the Vatican for discussions about alleviating poverty and oppression.

* *Source*: Gustavo Gutierrez, *A Theology of Liberation*, 2nd ed., translated by Sister Caridad Inda and John Eagleson (Maryknoll, NY: Orbis Books, 1988), pp. 29–33. Reprinted by permission of Orbis Books.

LIBERATION AND DEVELOPMENT
From the Critique of Developmentalism to Social Revolution

The term *development* has synthesized the aspirations of poor peoples during the last few decades. Recently, however, it has become the object of severe criticism due both to the deficiencies of the development policies proposed to the poor countries to lead them out of their underdevelopment and also to the lack of concrete achievements of the interested governments. This is the reason why *developmentalism (desarrollismo)*, a term derived from *development (desarrollo)*, is now used in a pejorative sense, especially in Latin America.

Much has been said in recent times about development. Poor countries competed for the help of the rich countries. There were even attempts to create a certain development mystique. Support for development was intense in Latin America in the 1950s, producing high expectations. But since the supporters of development did not attack the roots of the evil, they failed and caused instead confusion and frustration.

One of the most important reasons for this turn of events is that development—approached from an economic and modernizing point of view—has been frequently promoted by international organizations closely linked to groups and governments which control the world economy. The changes encouraged were to be achieved within the formal structure of the existing institutions without challenging them. Great care was exercised, therefore, not to attack the interests of large international economic powers nor those of their natural allies, the ruling domestic interest groups. Furthermore, the so-called changes were often nothing more than new and underhanded ways of increasing the power of strong economic groups.

Developmentalism thus came to be synonymous with *reformism* and modernization, that is to say, synonymous with timid measures, really ineffective in the long run and counterproductive to achieving a real transformation. The poor countries are becoming ever more clearly aware that their underdevelopment is only the by-product of the development of other countries, because of the kind of relationship which exists between the rich and the poor countries. Moreover, they are realizing that their own development will come about only with a struggle to break the domination of the rich countries.

This perception sees the conflict implicit in the process. Development must attack the root causes of the problems and among them the deepest is economic, social, political, and cultural dependence of some countries upon others—an expression of the domination of some social classes over others. Attempts to bring about changes within the existing order have proven futile. This analysis of the situation is at the level of scientific rationality. Only a radical break from the status quo, that is, a profound transformation of the private property system, access to power of the exploited class, and a social revolution that would break this dependence would allow for the change to a new society, a socialist society—or at least allow that such a society might be possible.

In this light, to speak about the process of *liberation* begins to appear more appropriate and richer in human content. Liberation in fact expresses the inescapable moment of radical change which is foreign to the ordinary use of the term *development*. Only in the context of such a process can a policy of development be effectively implemented, have any real meaning, and avoid misleading formulations.

Man, the Master of His Own Destiny

To characterize the situation of the poor countries as dominated and oppressed leads one to speak of economic, social, and political liberation. But we are dealing here with a much more integral and profound understanding of human existence and its historical future.

A broad and deep aspiration for liberation inflames the history of mankind in our day, liberation from all that limits or keeps man from self-fulfillment, liberation from all impediments to the exercise of his freedom. Proof of this is the awareness of new and subtle forms of oppression in the heart of advanced industrial societies, which often offer themselves as models to the underdeveloped countries. In them subversion does not appear as a protest against poverty, but rather against wealth. The context in the rich countries, however, is quite different from that of the poor countries: we must beware of all kinds of imitations as well as new forms of imperialism—revolutionary this time—of the rich countries, which consider themselves central to the history of mankind. Such mimicry would only lead the revolutionary groups of the Third World to a new deception regarding their own reality. They would be led to fight against windmills.

But, having acknowledged this danger, it is important to remember also that the poor countries would err in not following these events closely, since their future depends at least partially upon what happens on the domestic scene in the dominant countries. Their own efforts at liberation cannot be indifferent to that proclaimed by growing minorities in rich nations. There are, moreover, valuable lessons to be learned by the revolutionaries of the countries on the periphery, who could in turn use them as corrective measures in the difficult task of building a new society.

What is at stake in the South as well as in the North, in the West as well as the East, on the periphery and in the center is the possibility of enjoying a truly human existence, a free life, a dynamic liberty which is related to history as a conquest. We have today an ever-clearer vision of this dynamism and this conquest, but their roots stretch into the past …

[The German philosopher G. W. F.] Hegel followed this approach, introducing with vitality and urgency the theme of history. To a great extent his philosophy is a reflection on the French Revolution. This historical event had vast repercussions, for it proclaimed the right of every man to participate in the direction of the society to which he belongs. For Hegel man is aware of himself "only by being acknowledged or 'recognized'" by another consciousness. But this being recognized by another presupposes an initial conflict, "a life-and-death struggle," because it is "solely by risking life that freedom is obtained."[1]

Through the lord-bondsman dialectic (resulting from this original confrontation), the historical process will then appear as the genesis of consciousness and therefore of the gradual liberation of man. Through the dialectical process man constructs himself and attains a real awareness of his own being; he liberates himself in the acquisition of genuine freedom which through work transforms the world and educates man. For Hegel "world history is the progression of the awareness of freedom." Moreover, the driving force of history is the difficult conquest of freedom, hardly perceptible in its initial stages. It is the passage from awareness of freedom to real freedom. "It is Freedom in itself that comprises within itself the infinite necessity of bringing itself to consciousness and thereby, since knowledge about itself is its very nature, to reality." Thus man gradually takes hold of the reins of his own destiny. He looks ahead and turns towards a society in which he will be free of all alienation and servitude. This focus will initiate a new dimension in philosophy: social criticism.

[Karl] Marx deepened and renewed this line of thought in his unique way ... The new attitude was expressed clearly in the famous *Theses on Feuerbach*, in which Marx presented concisely but penetratingly the essential elements of his approach. In them, especially in the First Thesis, Marx situated himself equidistant between the old materialism and idealism; more precisely, he presented his position as the dialectical transcendence of both. Of the first he retained the affirmation of the objectivity of the external world; of the second he kept man's transforming capacity. For Marx, to know was something indissolubly linked to the transformation of the world through work. Basing his thought on these first intuitions, he went on to construct a scientific understanding of historical reality. He analyzed capitalistic society, in which were found concrete instances of the exploitation of man by his fellows and of one social class by another. Pointing the way towards an era in history when man can live humanly, Marx created categories which allowed for the elaboration of a science of history.

The door was opened for science to help man take one more step on the road to critical thinking. It made him more aware of the socioeconomic determinants of his ideological creations and therefore freer and more lucid in relation to them. But at the same time these new insights enabled man to have greater control and rational grasp of his historical initiatives. (This interpretation is valid unless of course one holds a dogmatic and mechanistic interpretation of history.) These initiatives ought to assure the change from the capitalistic mode of production to the socialistic mode, that is to say, to one oriented towards a society in which man can begin to live freely and humanly. He will have controlled nature, created the conditions for a socialized production of wealth, done away with private acquisition of excessive wealth, and established socialism.

But modern man's aspirations include not only liberation from *exterior* pressures which prevent his fulfillment as a member of a certain social class, country, or society. He seeks likewise an *interior* liberation, in an individual and intimate dimension; he seeks liberation not only on a social plane but also on a psychological. He seeks an interior freedom understood however not as an ideological evasion from social confrontation or as the internalization of a situation of dependency. Rather it must be in relation to the real world of the human psyche as understood since [Sigmund] Freud.

A new frontier was in effect opened up when Freud highlighted the unconscious determinants of human behavior, with repression as the central element of man's psychic makeup. Repression is the result of the conflict between instinctive drives and the cultural and ethical demands of the social environment. For Freud, unconscious motivations exercise a tyrannical power and can produce aberrant behavior. This behavior is controllable only if the subject becomes aware of these motivations through an accurate reading of the new language of meanings created by the unconscious. Since Hegel we have seen *conflict* used as a germinal explanatory category and *awareness* as a step in the conquest of freedom. In Freud however they appear in a psychological process which ought also to lead to a fuller liberation of man.

The scope of liberation on the collective and historical level does not always and satisfactorily include psychological liberation. Psychological liberation includes dimensions which do not exist in or are not sufficiently integrated with collective, historical liberation. We are not speaking here, however, of facilely separating them or putting them in opposition to another ...

Alienation and exploitation as well as the very struggle for liberation from them have ramifications on the personal and psychological planes which it would be dangerous to overlook in the process of constructing a new society and a new man. These personal aspects—considered not as excessively privatized, but rather as encompassing all human dimensions—are also under consideration in the contemporary debate concerning greater participation of all in political activity. This is so even in a socialist society ...

To conceive of history as a process of the liberation of man is to consider freedom as a historical conquest; it is to understand that the step from an abstract to a real freedom is not taken without a struggle against all the forces that oppress man, a struggle full of pitfalls, detours, and temptations to run away. The goal is not only better living conditions, a radical change of structures, a social revolution; it is much more: the continuous creation, never ending, of a new way to be a man, a *permanent cultural revolution*.

In other words, what is at stake above all is a dynamic and historical conception of man, oriented definitively and creatively toward his future, acting in the present for the sake of tomorrow. Teilhard de Chardin has remarked that man has taken hold of the reins of evolution.[2] History, contrary to essentialist and static thinking, is not the development of potentialities preexistent in man; it is rather the conquest of new, qualitatively different ways of being a man in order to achieve an ever more total and complete fulfillment of the individual in solidarity with all mankind.

The Concept of Liberation Theologically Considered

Although we will consider liberation from a theological perspective more extensively later, it is important at this time to attempt an initial treatment in the light of what we have just discussed.

The term *development* is relatively new in the texts of the ecclesiastical magisterium. Except for a brief reference by Pius XII, the subject is broached for the first time by John XXIII in the encyclical letter *Mater et Magistra*.[3] *Pacem in terris*[4] gives the term special attention. *Gaudium et spes*[5] dedicates a whole section to it, though the treatment is not original. All these documents stress the urgency of eliminating the existing injustices and the need for an economic development geared to the service of man. Finally, *Populorum progressio*[6] discusses development as its central theme. Here the language and ideas are clearer; the adjective *integral* is added to development, putting things in a different context and opening new perspectives ...

The theme of liberation appears more completely discussed in the message from eighteen bishops of the Third World, published as a specific response to the call made by *Populorum progressio*. It is also treated frequently—almost to the point of being a synthesis of its message—in the conclusions of the Second General Conference of Latin American Bishops held in Medellín, Colombia, in 1968, which have more doctrinal authority than the eighteen bishops' message. In both these documents the focus has changed. The situation is not judged from the point of view of the countries at the center, but rather of those on the periphery, providing insiders' experience of their anguish and aspirations.

The product of a profound historical movement, this aspiration to liberation is beginning to be accepted by the Christian community as a sign of the times, as a call to commitment and interpretation. The Biblical message, which presents the work of Christ as a liberation, provides the framework for this interpretation. Theology seems to have avoided for a long time reflecting on the conflictual character of human history, the confrontations among men, social classes, and countries. St. Paul continuously reminds us, however, of the paschal core of Christian existence and of all of human life: the passage from the old man to the new, from sin to grace, from slavery to freedom.

"For freedom Christ has set us free" (Galatians, 5:1), St. Paul tells us. He refers here to liberation from sin insofar as it represents a selfish turning in upon oneself. To sin is to refuse to love one's neighbors and, therefore, the Lord himself. Sin—a breach of friendship with God and others—is according to the Bible the ultimate cause of poverty, injustice, and the oppression in which men live. In describing sin as the ultimate cause we do not in any way negate the structural reasons and the objective determinants leading to these situations. It does, however, emphasize the fact that things do not happen by chance and that behind an unjust structure there is a personal or collective will responsible—a willingness to reject God and neighbor. It suggests, likewise, that a social transformation, no matter how radical it may be, does not automatically achieve the suppression of all evils.

But St. Paul asserts not only that Christ liberated us; he also tells us that he did it in order that we might be free. Free for what? Free to love. "In the language of the Bible," writes [German theologian Dietrich] Bonhoeffer, "freedom is not something man has for himself but something he has for others ... It is not a possession, a presence, an object ... but a relationship and nothing else. In truth, freedom is a relationship between two persons. Being free means 'being free for the other,' because the other has bound me to him. Only in relationship with the other am I free."[7] The freedom to which we are called presupposes the going out of oneself, the breaking down of our selfishness and of all the structures that support our selfishness; the foundation of this freedom is openness to others. The fullness of liberation—a free gift from Christ—is communion with God and with other men.

Conclusion

Summarizing what has been said above, we can distinguish three reciprocally interpenetrating levels of meaning of the term *liberation*, or in other words, three approaches to the process of liberation.

In the first place, *liberation* expresses the aspirations of oppressed peoples and social classes, emphasizing the conflictual aspect of the economic, social, and political process which puts them at odds with wealthy nations and oppressive classes. In contrast, the word *development*, and above all the policies characterized as developmentalist [*desarrollista*], appear somewhat aseptic, giving a false picture of a tragic and conflictual reality. The issue of development does in fact find its true place in the more universal, profound, and radical perspective of liberation. It is only within this framework that *development* finds its true meaning and possibilities of accomplishing something worthwhile.

At a deeper level, *liberation* can be applied to an understanding of history. Man is seen as assuming conscious responsibility for his own destiny. This understanding provides a dynamic context and broadens the horizons of the desired social changes. In this perspective the unfolding of all the man's dimensions is demanded—a man who makes himself throughout his life and throughout history. The gradual conquest of true freedom leads to the creation of a new man and a qualitatively different society. This vision provides, therefore, a better understanding of what in fact is at stake in our times.

Finally, the word *development* to a certain extent limits and obscures the theological problems implied in the process designated by this term. On the contrary the word *liberation* allows for another approach leading to the Biblical sources which inspire the presence and action of man in history. In the Bible, Christ is presented as the one who brings us liberation. Christ the Savior liberates man from sin, which is the ultimate root of all disruption of friendship and of all injustice and oppression. Christ makes man truly free, that is to say, he enables man to live in communion with him; and this is the basis for all human brotherhood.

NOTES

1   G.W.F. Hegel, *The Phenomenology of Mind*, trans. J. B. Baillie (New York: Humanities Press, Inc., 1964), pp. 229, 232–233.
2   Pierre Teilhard de Chardin (1881–1955), French Catholic priest and theologian.—Eds.
3   *Mother and Teacher*; English title, *Christianity and Social Progress.*
4   *Peace on Earth.*
5   *Joy and Hope*; English title, *The Church and the Modern World.*
6   *Development of Peoples.*
7   *Creation and Fall, Temptation* (New York: Macmillan Company, 1966), p. 37.

All Animals Are Equal

PETER SINGER*

Just as oppressed people suffer from discriminatory beliefs and attitudes—
women from sexism, people of color from racism, gays from homophobia—
so too, says the Australian philosopher Peter Singer (1946–), do animals
suffer from "speciesism." Speciesism is the belief that one particular
animal species—the human species—is innately superior to all others. This
supposed superiority leads humans to engage in the morally unjustifiable
oppression, exploitation, and slaughter of other species. According to
Singer, who now is a professor at Princeton University, the aim of the
animal liberation movement is to expose, criticize, and overcome these
widely shared speciesist attitudes.

---

* *Source*: Peter Singer, "All Animals are Equal," *Philosophic Exchange* 1, Summer 1974. © Peter Singer 1974.
Reprinted by permission of Peter Singer.

ALL ANIMALS ARE EQUAL

In recent years a number of oppressed groups have campaigned vigorously for equality. The classic instance is the Black Liberation movement, which demands an end to the prejudice and discrimination that has made blacks second-class citizens. The immediate appeal of the black liberation movement and its initial, if limited, success made it a model for other oppressed groups to follow. We became familiar with liberation movements for Spanish-Americans, gay people, and a variety of other minorities. When a majority group—women—began their campaign, some thought we had come to the end of the road. Discrimination on the basis of sex, it has been said, is the last universally accepted form of discrimination, practiced without secrecy or pretense even in those liberal circles that have long prided themselves on their freedom from prejudice against racial minorities.

One should always be wary of talking of "the last remaining form of discrimination." If we have learnt anything from liberation movements, we should have learnt how difficult it is to be aware of latent prejudice in our attitudes to particular groups until this prejudice is forcefully pointed out.

A liberation movement demands an expansion of our moral horizons and an extension or reinterpretation of the basic moral principle of equality. Practices that were previously regarded as natural and inevitable come to be seen as the result of an unjustifiable prejudice. Who can say with confidence that all his or her attitudes and practices are beyond criticism? If we wish to avoid being numbered amongst the oppressors, we must be prepared to re-think even our most fundamental attitudes. We need to consider them from the point of view of those most disadvantaged by our attitudes, and the practices that follow from these attitudes. If we can make this unaccustomed mental switch we may discover a pattern in our attitudes and practices that consistently operates so as to benefit one group—usually the one to which we ourselves belong—at the expense of another. In this way we may come to see that there is a case for a new liberation movement. My aim is to advocate that we make this mental switch in respect of our attitudes and practices towards a very large group of beings: members of species other than our own—or, as we popularly though misleadingly call them, animals. In other words, I am urging that we extend to other species the basic principle of equality that most of us recognize should be extended to all members of our own species.

All this may sound a little far-fetched, more like a parody of other liberation movements than a serious objective. In fact, in the past the idea of "The Rights of Animals" really has been used to parody the case for women's rights. When Mary Wollstonecraft, a forerunner of later feminists, published her *Vindication of the Rights of Woman* in 1792, her ideas were widely regarded as absurd, and they were satirized in an anonymous publication entitled *A Vindication of the Rights of Brutes*. The author of this satire (actually Thomas Taylor, a distinguished Cambridge philosopher) tried to refute Wollstonecraft's reasonings by showing that they could be carried one stage further. If sound when applied to women, why should the arguments not be applied to dogs, cats, and horses? They seemed to hold equally well for these "brutes"; yet to hold that brutes had rights was manifestly absurd; therefore the reasoning by which this conclusion had been reached must be unsound, and if unsound when applied to brutes, it must also be unsound when applied to women, since the very same arguments had been used in each case.

One way in which we might reply to this argument is by saying that the case for equality between men and women cannot validly be extended to nonhuman animals. Women have a right to vote, for instance, because they are just as capable of making rational decisions as men are; dogs, on the other hand, are incapable of understanding the significance of voting, so they cannot have the right to vote. There are many other obvious ways in which men and women resemble each other closely, while humans and other animals differ greatly. So, it might be said, men and women are similar beings, and should have equal rights, while humans and nonhumans are different and should not have equal rights.

The thought behind this reply to Taylor's analogy is correct up to a point, but it does not go far enough. There *are* important differences between humans and other animals, and these differences must give rise to *some* differences in the rights that each have. Recognizing this obvious fact, however, is no barrier to the case for extending the basic principle of equality to nonhuman animals. The differences that exist between men and women are equally undeniable, and the supporters of Women's Liberation are aware that these differences may give rise to different rights. Many feminists hold that women have the right to an abortion on request. It does not follow that since these same people are campaigning for equality between men and women they must support the right of men to have abortions too. Since a man cannot have an abortion, it is meaningless to talk of his right to have one. Since a pig can't vote, it is meaningless to talk of his right to vote. There is no reason why either Women's Liberation or Animal Liberation should get involved in such nonsense. The extension of the basic principle of equality from one group to another does not imply that we must treat both groups in exactly the same way, or grant exactly the same rights to both groups. Whether we should do so will depend on the nature of the members of the two groups. The basic principle of equality, I shall argue, is equality of consideration; and equal consideration for different beings may lead to different treatment and different rights.

So there is a different way of replying to Taylor's attempt to parody Wollstonecraft's arguments, a way which does not deny the differences between humans and nonhumans, but goes more deeply into the question of equality, and concludes by finding nothing absurd in the idea that the basic principle of equality applies to so-called "brutes." I believe that we reach this conclusion if we examine the basis on which our opposition to discrimination on grounds of race or sex ultimately rests. We will then see that we would be on shaky ground if we were to demand equality for blacks, women, and other groups of oppressed humans while denying equal consideration to nonhumans.

When we say that all human beings, whatever their race, creed, or sex, are equal, what is it that we are asserting? Those who wish to defend a hierarchical, inegalitarian society have often pointed out that by whatever test we choose, it simply is not true that all humans are equal. Like it or not, we must face the fact that humans come in different shapes and sizes; they come with differing moral capacities, differing intellectual abilities, differing amounts of benevolent feeling and sensitivity to the needs of others, differing abilities to communicate effectively, and differing capacities to experience pleasure and pain. In short, if the demand for equality were based on the actual equality of all human beings, we would have to stop demanding equality. It would be an unjustifiable demand.

Still, one might cling to the view that the demand for equality among human beings is based on the actual equality of the different races and sexes. Although humans differ as individuals in various ways, there are no differences between the races and sexes *as such*. From the mere fact that a person is black, or a woman, we cannot infer anything else about that person. This, it may be said, is what is wrong with racism and sexism. The white racist claims that whites are superior to blacks, but this is false—although there are differences between individuals, some blacks are superior to some whites in all of the capacities and abilities that could conceivably be relevant. The opponent of sexism would say the same: a person's sex is no guide to his or her abilities, and this is why it is unjustifiable to discriminate on the basis of sex.

This is a possible line of objection to racial and sexual discrimination. It is not, however, the way that someone really concerned about equality would choose, because taking this line could, in some circumstances, force one to accept a most inegalitarian society. The fact that humans differ as individuals, rather than as races or sexes, is a valid reply to someone who defends a hierarchical society like, say, South Africa, in which all whites are superior in status to all blacks. The existence of individual variations that cut across the lines of race or sex, however, provides us with no defence at all against a more sophisticated opponent of equality, one who proposes that, say, the interests of those with I.Q. ratings above 100 be preferred to the interests of those with I.Q.s below 100. Would a hierarchical society of this sort really be so much better than one based on race or sex? I think not. But if we tie the moral principle of equality to the factual equality of the different races or sexes, taken as a whole, our opposition to racism and sexism does not provide us with any basis for objecting to this kind of inegalitarianism.

There is a second important reason why we ought not to base our opposition to racism and sexism on any kind of factual equality, even the limited kind which asserts that variations in capacities and abilities are spread evenly between the different races and sexes: we can have no absolute guarantee that these abilities and capacities really are distributed evenly, without regard to race or sex, among human beings. So far as actual abilities are concerned, there do seem to be certain measurable differences between both races and sexes. These differences do not, of course, appear in each case, but only when averages are taken. More important still, we do not yet know how much of these differences is really due to the different genetic endowments of the various races and sexes, and how much is due to environmental differences that are the result of past and continuing discrimination. Perhaps all of the important differences will eventually prove to be environmental rather than genetic. Anyone opposed to racism and sexism will certainly hope that this will be so, for it will make the task of ending discrimination a lot easier; nevertheless it would be dangerous to rest the case against racism and sexism on the belief that all significant differences are environmental in origin. The opponent of, say, racism who takes this line will be unable to avoid conceding that if differences in ability did after all prove to have some genetic connection with race, racism would in some way be defensible.

It would be folly for the opponent of racism to stake his whole case on a dogmatic commitment to one particular outcome of a difficult scientific issue which is still a long way from being settled. While attempts to prove that differences in certain selected abilities between races and sexes are primarily genetic in origin have certainly not been conclusive, the same must be said of attempts to prove that these differences are largely the result of environment. At this stage of the investigation we cannot be certain which view is correct, however much we may hope it is the latter.

Fortunately, there is no need to pin the case for equality to one particular outcome of this scientific investigation. The appropriate response to those who claim to have found evidence of genetically-based differences in ability between the races or sexes is not to stick to the belief that the genetic explanation must be wrong, whatever evidence to the contrary may turn up: instead we should make it quite clear that the claim to equality does not depend on intelligence, moral capacity, physical strength, or similar matters of fact. Equality is a moral ideal, not a simple assertion of fact. There is no logically compelling reason for assuming that a factual difference in ability between two people justifies any difference in the amount of consideration we give to satisfying their needs and interests. The principle of the equality of human beings is not a description of an alleged actual equality among humans: it is a prescription of how we should treat humans.

Jeremy Bentham incorporated the essential basis of moral equality into his utilitarian system of ethics in the formula: "Each to count for one and none for more than one." In other words, the interests of every being affected by an action are to be taken into account and given the same weight as the like interests of any other being. A later utilitarian, Henry Sidgwick, put the point in this way: "The good of any one individual is of no more importance, from the point of view (if I may say so) of the Universe, than the good of any other."[1] More recently, the leading figures in contemporary moral philosophy have shown a great deal of agreement in specifying as a fundamental presupposition of their moral   eories some similar requirement which operates so as to give everyone's interest. equal consideration—although they cannot agree on how this requirement is best formulated.[2]

It is an implication of this principle of equality that our concern for others ought not to depend on what they are like, or what abilities they possess— although precisely what this concern requires us to do may vary according to the characteristics of those affected by what we do. It is on this basis that the case against racism and the case against sexism must both ultimately rest; and it is in accordance with this principle that speciesism is also to be condemned. If possessing a higher degree of intelligence does not entitle one human to use another for his own ends, how can it entitle humans to exploit nonhumans?

Many philosophers have proposed the principle of equal consideration of interests, in some form or other, as a basic moral principle; but, as we shall see in more detail shortly, not many of them have recognised that this principle applies to members of other species as well as to our own. Bentham was one of the few who did realize this. In a forward-looking passage, written at a time when black slaves in the British dominions were still being treated much as we now treat nonhuman animals, Bentham wrote:

The day *may* come when the rest of the animal creation may acquire those rights which never could have been witholden [i.e., withheld] from them but by the hand of tyranny. The French have already discovered that the blackness of the skin is no reason why a human being should be abandoned without redress to the caprice of a tormentor. It may one day come to be recognized that the number of the legs, the villosity [hairiness] of the skin, or the termination of the *os sacrum*, are reasons equally insufficient for abandoning a sensitive being to the same fate. What else is it that should trace the insuperable line? Is it the faculty of reason, or perhaps the faculty of discourse? But a full-grown horse or dog is beyond comparison a more rational, as well as a more conversable animal, than an infant of a day, or a week, or even a month, old. But suppose they were otherwise, what would it avail? The question is not, Can they reason? nor Can they *talk*? but, *Can they suffer?*[3]

In this passage Bentham points to the capacity for suffering as the vital characteristic that gives a being the right to equal consideration. The capacity for suffering—or more strictly, for suffering and/or enjoyment or happiness—is not just another characteristic like the capacity for language, or for higher mathematics. Bentham is not saying that those who try to mark "the insuperable line" that determines whether the interests of a being should be considered happen to have selected the wrong characteristic. The capacity for suffering and enjoying things is a prerequisite for having interests at all, a condition that must be satisfied before we can speak of interests in any meaningful way. It would be nonsense to say that it was not in the interests of a stone to be kicked along the road by a schoolboy. A stone does not have interests because it cannot suffer. Nothing that we can do to it could possibly make any difference to its welfare. A mouse, on the other hand, does have an interest in not being tormented, because it will suffer if it is.

If a being suffers, there can be no moral justification for refusing to take that suffering into consideration. No matter what the nature of the being, the principle of equality requires that its suffering be counted equally with the like suffering—insofar as rough comparisons can be made—of any other being. If a being is not capable of suffering, or of experiencing enjoyment or happiness, there is nothing to be taken into account. This is why the limit of sentience (using the term as a convenient, if not strictly accurate, shorthand for the capacity to suffer or experience enjoyment or happiness) is the only defensible boundary of concern for the interests of others. To mark this boundary by some characteristic like intelligence or rationality would be to mark it in an arbitrary way. Why not choose some other characteristic, like skin color?

The racist violates the principle of equality by giving greater weight to the interests of members of his own race, when there is a clash between their interests and the interests of those of another race. Similarly the speciesist allows the interests of his own species to override the greater interests of members of other species.[4] The pattern is the same in each case. Most human beings are speciesists. I shall now very briefly describe some of the practices that show this.

For the great majority of human beings, especially in urban, industrialized societies, the most direct form of contact with members of other species is at meal times: we eat them. In doing so we treat them purely as means to our ends. We regard their life and well-being as subordinate to our taste for a particular kind of dish. I say "taste" deliberately; this is purely a matter of pleasing our palate. There can be no defence of eating flesh in terms of satisfying nutritional needs, since it has been established beyond doubt that we could satisfy our need for protein and other essential nutrients far more efficiently with a diet that replaced animal flesh by soy beans, or products derived from soy beans, and other high-protein vegetable products.[5]

It is not merely the act of killing that indicates what we are ready to do to other species in order to gratify our tastes. The suffering we inflict on the animals while they are alive is perhaps an even clearer indication of our speciesism than the fact that we are prepared to kill them.[6] In order to have meat on the table at a price that people can afford, our society tolerates methods of meat production that confine sentient animals in cramped, unsuitable conditions for the entire durations of their lives. Animals are treated like machines that convert fodder into flesh, and any innovation that results in a higher "conversion ratio" is liable to be adopted. As one authority on the subject has said, "cruelty is acknowledged only when profitability ceases ..."[7]

Since, as I have said, none of these practices cater for anything more than our pleasures of taste, our practice of rearing and killing other animals in order to eat them is a clear instance of the sacrifice of the most important interests of other beings in order to satisfy trivial interests of our own. To avoid speciesism we must stop this practice, and each of us has a moral obligation to cease supporting the practice. Our custom is all the support that the meat industry needs. The decision to cease giving it that support may be difficult, but it is no more difficult than it would have been for a white Southerner to go against the traditions of his society and free his slaves: if we do not change our dietary habits, how can we censure those slaveholders who would not change their own way of living?

The same form of discrimination may be observed in the widespread practice of experimenting on other species in order to see if certain substances are safe for human beings, or to test some psychological theory about the effect of severe punishment on learning, or to try out various new compounds just in case something turns up ...

In the past, argument about vivisection has often missed this point, because it has been put in absolutist terms: Would the abolitionist be prepared to let thousands die if they could be saved by experimenting on a single animal? The way to reply to this purely hypothetical question is to pose another: Would the experimenter be prepared to perform his experiment on an orphaned human infant, if that were the only way to save many lives? (I say "orphan" to avoid the complication of parental feelings, although in doing so I am being overfair to the experimenter, since the nonhuman subjects of experiments are not orphans.) If the experimenter is not prepared to use an orphaned human infant, then his readiness to use nonhumans is simple discrimination, since adult apes, cats, mice and other mammals are more aware of what is happening to them, more self-directing and, so far as we can tell, at least as sensitive to pain, as any human infant. There seems to be no relevant characteristic that human infants possess that adult mammals do not have to the same or a higher degree. (Someone might try to argue that what makes it wrong to experiment on a human infant is that the infant will, in time and if left alone, develop into more than the nonhuman, but one would then, to be consistent, have to oppose abortion, since the fetus has the same potential as the infant—

indeed, even contraception and abstinence might be wrong on this ground, since the egg and sperm, considered jointly, also have the same potential. In any case, this argument still gives us no reason for selecting a nonhuman, rather than a human with severe and irreversible brain damage, as the subject for our experiments.)

The experimenter, then, shows a bias in favor of his own species whenever he carries out an experiment on a nonhuman for a purpose that he would not think justified him in using a human being at an equal or lower level of sentience, awareness, ability to be self-directing, etc. No one familiar with the kinds of results yielded by most experiments on animals can have the slightest doubt that if this bias were eliminated the number of experiments performed would be a minute fraction of the number performed today.

Experimenting on animals, and eating their flesh, are perhaps the two major forms of speciesism in our society. By comparison, the third and last form of speciesism is so minor as to be insignificant, but it is perhaps of some special interest to those for whom this article was written. I am referring to speciesism in contemporary philosophy.

Philosophy ought to question the basic assumptions of the age. Thinking through, critically and carefully, what most people take for granted is, I believe, the chief task of philosophy, and it is this task that makes philosophy a worthwhile activity. Regrettably, philosophy does not always live up to its historic role. Philosophers are human beings and they are subject to all the preconceptions of the society to which they belong. Sometimes they succeed in breaking free of the prevailing ideology: more often they become its most sophisticated defenders. So, in this case, philosophy as practiced in the universities today does not challenge anyone's preconceptions about our relations with other species. By their writings, those philosophers who tackle problems that touch upon the issue reveal that they make the same unquestioned assumptions as most other humans, and what they say tends to confirm the reader in his or her comfortable speciesist habits.

I could illustrate this claim by referring to the writings of philosophers in various fields—for instance, the attempts that have been made by those interested in rights to draw the boundary of the sphere of rights so that it runs parallel to the biological boundaries of the species *homo sapiens*, including infants and even mental defectives, but excluding those other beings of equal or greater capacity who are so useful to us at mealtimes and in our laboratories. I think it would be a more appropriate conclusion to this article, however, if I concentrated on the problem with which we have been centrally concerned, the problem of equality.

It is significant that the problem of equality, in moral and political philosophy, is invariably formulated in terms of human equality. The effect of this is that the question of the equality of other animals does not confront the philosopher, or student, as an issue itself—and this is already an indication of the failure of philosophy to challenge accepted beliefs. Still, philosophers have found it difficult to discuss the issue of human equality without raising, in a paragraph or two, the question of the status of other animals. The reason for this, which should be apparent from what I have said already, is that if humans are to be regarded as equal to one another, we need some sense of "equal" that does not require any actual, descriptive equality of capacities, talents, or other qualities. If equality is to be related to any actual characteristics of humans, these characteristics must be some lowest common denominator, pitched so low that no human lacks them—but then the philosopher comes up against the catch that any such set of characteristics which covers *all* humans will not be possessed *only by humans*. In other words, it turns out that in the only sense in which we can truly say, as an assertion of fact, that all humans are equal, at least some members of other species are also equal—equal, that is, to each other and to humans. If, on the other hand, we regard the statement "All humans are equal" in some nonfactual way, perhaps as a prescription, then, as I have already argued, it is even more difficult to exclude nonhumans from the sphere of equality.

This result is not what the egalitarian philosopher originally intended to assert. Instead of accepting the radical outcome to which their own reasonings naturally point, however, most philosophers try to reconcile their beliefs in human equality and animal inequality by arguments that can only be described as devious.

As a first example, I take William Frankena's well-known article "The Concept of Social Justice." Frankena opposes the idea of basing justice on merit, because he sees that this could lead to highly inegalitarian results. Instead he proposes the principle that

> all men are to be treated as equals, not because they are equal, in any respect, but simply because they are human. They are human because they have emotions and desires, and are able to think, and hence are capable of enjoying a good life in a sense in which other animals are not.[8]

But what is this capacity to enjoy the good life which all humans have, but no other animals? Other animals have emotions and desires, and appear to be capable of enjoying a good life. We may doubt that they can think—although the behavior of some apes, dolphins and even dogs suggests that some of them can—but what is the relevance of thinking? Frankena goes on to admit that by "the good life" he means "not so much the morally good life as the happy or satisfactory life," so thought would appear to be unnecessary for enjoying the good life; in fact to emphasize the need for thought would make difficulties for the egalitarian since only some people are capable of leading intellectually satisfying lives, or morally good lives. This makes it difficult to see what Frankena's principle of equality has to do with simply being *human*. Surely every sentient being is capable of leading a life that is happier or less miserable than some alternative life, and hence has a claim to be taken into account. In this respect the distinction between humans and nonhumans is not a sharp division, but rather a continuum along which we move gradually, and with overlaps between the species, from simple capacities for enjoyment and satisfaction, or pain and suffering, to more complex ones.

Faced with a situation in which they see a need for some basis for the moral gulf that is commonly thought to separate humans and animals but can find no concrete difference that will do the job without undermining the equality of humans, philosophers tend to waffle. They resort to high-sounding phrases like "the intrinsic dignity of the human individual."[9] They talk of the "intrinsic worth of all men" as if men (humans?) had some worth that other beings did not.[10] Or they say that humans, and only humans, are "ends in themselves," while "everything other than a person can only have value for a person."[11]

This idea of a distinctive human dignity and worth has a long history; it can be traced back directly to the Renaissance humanists, for instance, to Pico della Mirandola's *Oration on the Dignity of Man*. Pico and other humanists based their estimate of human dignity on the idea that man possessed the central, pivotal position in the "Great Chain of Being" that led from the lowliest forms of matter to God himself; this view of the universe, in turn, goes back to both classical and Judeo-Christian doctrines. Contemporary philosophers have cast off these metaphysical and religious shackles and freely invoke the dignity of mankind without needing to justify the idea at all. Why should we not attribute "intrinsic dignity" or "intrinsic worth" to ourselves? Fellow humans are unlikely to reject the accolades we so generously bestow on them, and those to whom we deny the honor are unable to object. Indeed, when one thinks only of humans, it can be very liberal, very progressive, to talk of the dignity of all human beings. In so doing, we implicitly condemn slavery, racism, and other violations of human rights. We admit that we ourselves are in some fundamental sense on a par with the poorest, most ignorant members of our own species. It is only when we think of humans as no more than a small subgroup of all the beings that inhabit our planet that we may realize that in elevating our own species we are at the same time lowering the relative status of all other species.

The truth is that the appeal to the intrinsic dignity of human beings appears to solve the egalitarian's problems only as long as it goes unchallenged. Once we ask *why* it should be that all humans—including infants, mental defectives, psychopaths, Hitler, Stalin and the rest—have some kind of dignity or worth that no elephant, pig, or chimpanzee can ever achieve, we see that this question is as difficult to answer as our original request for some relevant fact that justifies the inequality of humans and other animals. In fact, these two questions are really one: talk of intrinsic dignity or moral worth only takes the problem back one step, because any satisfactory defence of the claim that all and only humans have intrinsic dignity would need to refer to some relevant capacities or characteristics that all and only humans possess. Philosophers frequently introduce ideas of dignity, respect and worth at the point at which other reasons appear to be lacking, but this is hardly good enough. Fine phrases are the last resource of those who have run out of arguments.

In case there are those who still think it may be possible to find some relevant characteristic that distinguishes all humans from all members of other species, I shall refer again, before I conclude, to the existence of some humans who quite clearly are below the level of awareness, self-consciousness, intelligence, and sentience, of many nonhumans. I am thinking of humans with severe and irreparable brain damage, and also of infant humans. To avoid the complication of the relevance of a being's potential, however, I shall henceforth concentrate on permanently retarded humans.

Philosophers who set out to find a characteristic that will distinguish humans from other animals rarely take the course of abandoning these groups of humans by lumping them in and with the other animals. It is easy to see why they do not. To take this line without rethinking our attitudes to other animals would entail that we have the right to perform painful experiments on retarded humans for trivial reasons; similarly it would follow that we had the right to rear and kill these humans for food. To most philosophers these consequences are as unacceptable as the view that we should stop treating nonhumans in this way.

Of course, when discussing the problem of equality it is possible to ignore the problem of mental defectives, or brush it aside as if somehow insignificant.[12] This is the easiest way out. What else remains? My final example of speciesism in contemporary philosophy has been selected to show what happens when a writer is prepared to face the question of human equality and animal inequality without ignoring the existence of mental defectives, and without resorting to obscurantist mumbo jumbo. Stanley Benn's clear and honest article "Egalitarianism and Equal Consideration of Interests"[13] fits this description.

Benn, after noting the usual "evident human inequalities" argues, correctly I think, for equality of consideration as the only possible basis for egalitarianism. Yet Benn, like other writers, is thinking only of "equal consideration of human interests." Benn is quite open in his defence of this restriction of equal consideration:

Not to possess human shape is a disqualifying condition. However faithful or intelligent a dog may be, it would be a monstrous sentimentality to attribute to him interests that could be weighed in an equal balance with those of human beings ... if, for instance, one had to decide between feeding a hungry baby or a hungry dog, anyone who chose the dog would generally be reckoned morally defective, unable to recognize a fundamental inequality of claims.

    This is what distinguishes our attitude to animals from our attitude to imbeciles. It would be odd to say that we ought to respect equally the dignity or personality of the imbecile and of the rational man ... but there is nothing odd about saying that we should respect their interests equally, that is, that we should give to the interests of each the same serious consideration as claims to considerations necessary for some standard of well-being that we can recognize and endorse.

Benn's statement of the basis of the consideration we should have for imbeciles seems to me correct, but why should there be any fundamental inequality of claims between a dog and a human imbecile? Benn sees that if equal consideration depended on rationality, no reason could be given against using imbeciles for research purposes, as we now use dogs and guinea pigs. This will not do: "But of course we do distinguish imbeciles from animals in this regard," he says. That the common distinction is justifiable is something Benn does not question; his problem is how it is to be justified. The answer he gives is this:

We respect the interests of men and give them priority over dogs not *insofar* as they are rational, but because rationality is the human norm. We say it is *unfair* to exploit the deficiencies of the imbecile who falls short of the norm, just as it would be unfair, and not just ordinarily dishonest, to steal from a blind man. If we do not think in this way about dogs, it is because we do not see the irrationality of the dog as a deficiency or a handicap, but as normal for the species. The characteristics, therefore, that distinguish the normal man from the normal dog make it intelligible for us to talk of other men having interests and capacities, and therefore claims, of precisely the same kind as we make on our own behalf. But although these characteristics may provide the point of the distinction between men and other species, they are not in fact the qualifying conditions for membership, or the distinguishing criteria of the class of morally considerable persons; and this is precisely because a man does not become a member of a different species, with its own standards of normality, by reason of not possessing these characteristics.

The final sentence of this passage gives the argument away. An imbecile, Benn concedes, may have no characteristics superior to those of a dog; nevertheless this does not make the imbecile a member of "a different species" as the dog is. *Therefore* it would be "unfair" to use the imbecile for medical research as we use the dog. But why? That the imbecile is not rational is just the way things have worked out, and the same is true of the dog—neither is any more responsible for their mental level. If it is unfair to take advantage of an isolated defect, why is it fair to take advantage of a more general limitation? I find it hard to see anything in this argument except a defence of preferring the interests of members of our own species because they are members of our own species. To those who think there might be more to it, I suggest the following mental exercise. Assume that it has been proven that there is a difference in the average, or normal, intelligence quotient for two different races, say whites and blacks. Then substitute the term "white" for every occurrence of "men" and "black" for every occurrence of "dog" in the passage quoted; and substitute "high I.Q." for "rationality" and when Benn talks of "imbeciles" replace this term by "dumb whites"—that is, whites who fall well below the normal white I.Q. score. Finally, change "species" to "race." Now reread the passage. It has become a defence of a rigid, no-exceptions division between whites and blacks, based on I.Q. scores, *notwithstanding an admitted overlap* between whites and blacks in this respect. The revised passage is, of course, outrageous, and this is not only because we have made fictitious assumptions in our substitutions. The point is that in the original passage Benn was defending a rigid division in the amount of consideration due to members of different species, despite admitted cases of overlap. If the original did not, at first reading, strike us as being as outrageous as the revised version does, this is largely because although we are not racists ourselves, most of us are speciesists. Like the other articles, Benn's stands as a warning of the ease with which the best minds can fall victim to a prevailing ideology.

NOTES

1   *The Methods of Ethics* (7th ed.), p. 382.
2   For example, R. M. Hare, *Freedom and Reason* (Oxford, 1963) and J. Rawls, *A Theory of Justice* (Harvard, 1972); for a brief account of the essential agreement on this issue between these and other positions, see R. M. Hare, "Rules of War and Moral Reasoning," *Philosophy and Public Affairs*, vol. 1, no. 2 (1972).
3   *Introduction to the Principles of Morals and Legislation*, chap. 17.
4   I owe the term "speciesism" to Richard Ryder.
5   In order to produce 1 lb. of protein in the form of beef or veal, we must feed 21 lbs. of protein to the animal. Other forms of livestock are slightly less inefficient, but the average ratio in the U.S. is still 1:8. It has been estimated that the amount of protein lost to humans in this way is equivalent to 90% of the annual world protein deficit. For a brief account, see Frances Moore Lappé, *Diet for a Small Planet* (Friends of the Earth/Ballantine, New York, 1971), pp. 4–11.
6   Although one might think that killing a being is obviously the ultimate wrong one can do, I think that the infliction of suffering is a clearer indication of speciesism because it might be argued that at least part of what is wrong with killing a human is that

most humans are conscious of their existence over time, and have desires and purposes that extend into the future—see, for instance, M. Tooley, "Abortion and Infanticide," *Philosophy and Public Affairs*, vol. 2, no. 1 (1972). Of course, if one took this view one would have to hold—as Tooley does—that killing a human infant or mental defective is not in itself wrong, and is less serious than killing certain higher mammals that probably do have a sense of their own existence over time.

7   Ruth Harrison, *Animal Machines* (Stuart, London, 1964).

8   In R. Brandt (ed.), *Social Justice* (Prentice Hall, Englewood Cliffs, 1962), p. 19.

9   Frankena, *op. cit.*, p. 23.

10   H. A. Bedau, "Egalitarianism and the Idea of Equality," in *Nomos IX: Equality*, J. R. Pennock and J. W. Chapman, ed. New York, 1967.

11   G. Vlastos, "Justice and Equality," in Brandt, *Social Justice*, p. 48.

12   For example, Bernard Williams, "The Idea of Equality," in *Philosophy, Politics and Society* (second series), P. Laslett and W. Runciman, ed. (Blackwell, Oxford, 1962), p. 118; J. Rawls, *A Theory of Justice*, pp. 509–510.

13   *Nomos IX: Equality*, the passages quoted are on pp. 62ff.

PART 9

GREEN POLITICS:
ECOLOGY AS IDEOLOGY

More than a decade ago, the world entered the third millennium CE. At first sight, the time scale—some 3000 years of "civilization"—seems so vast as to defy comprehension. And yet such measures of human time are minuscule when compared to biological and geological time scales, in which 3000 years is but the blink of an eye.

We live, Greens say, at a pivotal time, not only in human history but in the biological history of the Earth's myriad species and the ecosystems that sustain them. What we human beings do—how we think and therefore act—will, for better or worse, affect future humans and animals and other forms of life for many generations. We are at a crisis point and a watershed. We need to learn to think in the longer term, and with a wider vision. And such thinking begins with a clear recognition and account of the crisis that we humans have helped to bring about.

There is by now little doubt that the world of the early twenty-first century is beset by an ecological crisis of unprecedented proportions. Global warming; the killing of forests and lakes by acid rain; the depletion of the earth's protective ozone layer; the pollution of our air and water; radioactive waste from nuclear power plants; the destruction of tropical rain forests; the death of birds, fish, and mammals from oil spills, pesticides, and acidifying and warming oceans; the rapid extinction of hundreds of species; the loss of polar ice and glaciers resulting in rising sea levels—these and many other events are all part of the interconnected series of crises that is often spoken of as a single environmental crisis. This crisis can be traced, in large part, to the population explosion and the rise and rapid proliferation of particular technologies such as the internal combustion engine and the nuclear reactor. But the environmental crisis can also be traced to *ideologies*—that is, to widely shared and still-prevalent ideas, beliefs, and attitudes about our relation to nature and to other species.

The ecological or green movement is a relatively recent arrival on the political scene. And, like other political movements, it has its own ideology—or, as many Greens prefer to say, an "ethic." Although not yet fully formed, this ideology or ethic is critical of other mainstream ideologies, right, left, and center. Liberalism,

Marxism, and modern conservatism are alike, the Greens say, in picturing human beings as "masters" or "conquerors" of nature, which is viewed in turn as a "resource-base" without intrinsic value or worth. An alternative Green ideology invites us to see ourselves as members of a species that exists in and because of nature. Nature nurtures us and all our fellow species. We are all part of a marvelously intricate and complex web of life. To the degree that we are greedy and selfish, to the extent that we are ignorant and heedless of our proper place in nature, we endanger this delicate web. Yet this is precisely what we humans have done and continue to do. And, unless we change our ways—and some of our heretofore unexamined basic beliefs—very soon, we and our children and grandchildren will pay a heavy price.

Clearly the green movement and its ideology raise deep and difficult questions about what it means to be a human being and how humans are related to nature, to other species, and to future generations. Difficult as they are, however, we will have to attempt to answer them aright if our species and others are to survive and flourish. But where might the answers be found? Some Greens say that the answers are to be found in the life sciences, such as biology and ecology. Others say that the answers are in philosophy or religion—in the meditations of Dr. Albert Schweitzer and Mahatma Gandhi, for example—or perhaps in the ideas and practices of supposedly primitive peoples such as Native Americans and Australian Aborigines. Still others claim that we must invent an entirely new religion or perhaps a "planetary ethic" with a respect for the Earth and all life at its core. But whatever the source, say the Greens, the answers cannot be found in older ideologies, for they do not even pose the right questions in the first place. Hence, the need for an alternative ideology or ethic.

Exactly what such an ideology or ethic might look like remains a matter of dispute. There are at present two rival visions. One is the "garden" vision, which sees humans as caretakers and cultivators of the Earth. According to this view, humans are to be responsible managers and conscientious stewards of the natural environment and not its exploiters or conquerors. Human beings are part of nature, but not reducible to it, and are responsible for its care and cultivation. Its model is the fertile and well-tended garden.

The alternative, or "wilderness" vision, sees human beings as a danger to themselves and especially to other species and their natural habitats. The human desire to dominate nature, to "develop" various natural resources for human enjoyment or benefit, is itself the problem to be overcome. Humans should resist the temptation to dominate, develop, and cultivate nature and learn to love wilderness and wild creatures by leaving them alone. Its model is an untamed and uncultivated wilderness.

These two visions or models are, of course, ideal types—simplified sketches of the complex relationship among human beings and other species, and of the ecosystems that sustain all life on Earth. And yet each captures some sense of the difference between two fundamentally different, but recognizably green, outlooks. The thinking of most Greens incorporates elements of both the garden and wilderness visions. Each will no doubt figure, in some form or other, into a more fully worked-out environmental or green ideology.

Although it is too early to say precisely what form such a green ideology would take, several fundamental features are already quite clear. First and most important is the view that all things are connected. Every species, including our own, lives in interdependent relations with other species and with the environment that sustains all creatures. From this a second feature follows: all life, and the environment that sustains it, is intrinsically valuable and therefore deserves recognition, respect, and protection. A third feature is the recognition that all human actions, however small or seemingly insignificant, have consequences for the biosphere. Fourth, these consequences can and typically do stretch into the indefinite future, affecting human beings, animals, and ecosystems for generations to come. We must therefore extend our time horizon to take into account the health and well-being of future generations. A fifth feature of the emerging green ideology is its emphasis on individual or personal, as well as political or collective, responsibility. The slogan "Think globally, act locally" succinctly summarizes this view. From this there follows a sixth feature—a green conception of democracy as a decentralized, grassroots form of self-rule that maximizes the opportunity for individual participation and personal responsibility at the local level.

Most Greens would probably agree that these six features form the core of their environmental ethic or ideology. But, despite a fairly widespread agreement about fundamental principles and ends, Greens disagree among themselves about the best means for achieving these ends. Some say that the green movement should act as an interest group within the present political system; others say that the system itself is in need of a fundamental transformation. Some Greens favor low-key, subtle strategies for educating and informing the public; others opt for highly visible campaigns of protest and acts of civil disobedience; and some radical environmentalists favor acts of "ecotage" or "monkey wrenching" to deter or punish polluters, developers, dumpers of toxic wastes, and others from despoiling the environment. In recent years there has even been an attempt to forge a link between environmentalism and Christian evangelism. According to a number of prominent evangelists, Christians have a responsibility to engage in "creation care." God commands the faithful to be good stewards of His creation, they say, and this requires that the faithful do what they can to oppose global warming and other threats to all of God's creations, human and nonhuman alike. Not all evangelists are environmentalists, to be sure, nor are all environmentalists evangelists. But the existence of Christian evangelical environmentalism is testimony to the diversity of the green movement.

Despite their differences in strategy, tactics, and background, in sum, most Greens are in broad agreement regarding ends. Theirs is a voice—or a chorus of voices—that we shall hear more often, and more loudly, as the new century unfolds.

Sustainability in the Age of Ecology

LESLIE PAUL THIELE*

Leslie Paul Thiele is Distinguished Professor in the Department of Political Science at the University of Florida and served as the founding director of its Sustainability Studies Program. His central concerns are the responsibilities of citizenship and the opportunities for leadership in a world of rapid technological, social, and ecological change. His books include *Indra's Net and the Midas Touch: Living Sustainably in a Connected World* (2011) and *Sustainability* (2013), as well as several others. In this essay, Thiele begins by providing a brief history of the concept of sustainability and its practice. He then turns to Aldo Leopold, the father of modern ecological thinking, and describes the fundamental lessons Leopold taught about the complex web of interdependence between human beings and the natural world, and the dangers of unintended consequences in the wake of human behavior. Taking seriously Leopold's injunction to "think like a mountain," Thiele concludes with a set of meditations on what he takes to be the contemporary requirements for living sustainably in an interconnected world where our actions have not only local consequences, but global ones as well.

---

* *Source*: Written expressly for this volume and used by permission of the author.

SUSTAINABILITY IN THE AGE OF ECOLOGY

The trail led through a dark-green forest, fording ice-cold streams and skirting moss-covered boulders. Here and there tree trunks once vertical lay half sunk into the forest floor, a feast of recycling for fungi and scores of stealthier organisms. The prone trees, adorned more diversely in death than in life, appeared to be patiently observing their own rebirth. A community of life was at work. Walking through these sun-dappled shoreline woods, rich in the scent of cedar and pine, I sensed the ineffable worth of the natural world. It is not only a resource of great value, but a source of inspiration.

To be sure, nature provides scores of resources to satisfy our material needs. But it offers priceless aesthetic and spiritual goods as well. And perhaps most crucially today, nature provides an education in sustainable living. It teaches. How can we safeguard such gifts, I asked myself, for our own benefit and for future generations? This question, conceived during a summer hike with my sons in the Kootenay region of British Columbia, Canada, brought to mind the writings of Aldo Leopold, another avid hiker. Leopold's seminal work expresses the crucial need to preserve the integrity, stability, and beauty of the natural world, and explores how this might be achieved sustainably by grounding social and economic life upon ecological principles.

Sustainability Past and Present

Before examining how Leopold set the stage for sustainability, it is important briefly to review its history as a concept and practice. The word *sustainability* entered common parlance only in the last several decades. Over this short span of time, the advocates of sustainability have altered the ways of life of countless individuals across the globe, initiated widespread changes in civil society, transformed the business world, and prompted historic policies for organizations and governments at all levels, from the local to the national to the global. Today sustainability is one of a very few ideals—along with democracy and human rights—that has gained near universal endorsement.

But what does sustainability really mean? Perhaps the term is most easily defined by saying what it is not. A practice or institution is *not* sustainable if it undermines the conditions of its own viability. It is not sustainable, for example, to extract water from lakes, rivers, or aquifers faster than they are recharged naturally by rain and snow. The rate and scale of the current practice, in this instance, proves its eventual undoing, as the lakes, rivers, or aquifers will in time become too depleted to provide their crucial resource. Likewise, eroding cropland through intensive agriculture faster than topsoil is naturally regenerated is unsustainable. Eventually, the decreasing fertility of the land will preclude viable farming. And running a shop or service by means of ever increasing debt where revenues never exceed expenses is an unsustainable practice. It will produce a bankruptcy rather than a business.

Sustainability is most commonly defined as meeting current needs in a way that does not undermine future wellbeing. The wellbeing in question may be limited to the participants of a particular practice or institution. By and large, however, when people use the word *sustainability* they are also concerned with the wellbeing of future generations. In this sense, it is unsustainable to exploit a resource faster than it naturally regenerates even if those who will suffer from its depletion are yet to be born. The ethic of sustainability is nicely captured by a popular saying: "We have not inherited the earth from our parents, we have borrowed it from our children."[1] The natural world is not ours to dispose, only to hold in trust.

If current trends continue, future inhabitants of our planet will endure a hotter and more disruptive climate, rising and more acidic oceans, greatly diminished biodiversity, and crucial natural resources—such as fresh water and arable land—in dangerously short supply. Sustainability expands our time horizons, making the reversal of these alarming trends an obligation.

The motivation for and practices of sustainability date back to ancient times. For millennia, our species has cultivated the knowledge, skills, habits, and virtues that fostered sustainable living. Before the development of agriculture some 10,000 years ago, humans lived in small, hunter-gatherer tribes, foraging fruits, seeds, and roots and hunting wildlife. When they depleted food resources around their encampment, they would move further up river or across the savannah. Knowing hunger all too well, they would frown upon any squandering of resources. Waste not, want not.

With the advent of agriculture, human populations grew in size and became less migratory. But the avoidance of waste remained a common concern. In turn, agricultural societies had to plan for the future. Seeds from harvested crops required collecting and storing over fall and winter, to be planted again in the spring. The prime edict of sustainability for early agricultural peoples was "Never eat your seed corn!" If all harvested seeds were consumed, there would be nothing to plant come spring. To care only for today's appetites with no thought of tomorrow's needs is a recipe for disaster.

Early practices of sustainability were not limited to frugality and foresight regarding food and crops. In the ancient city of Athens, young men attended the Ephebic College to gain the status of citizen. Graduates of the college pledged to revere the laws of the city, maintain its ideals, and cultivate civic virtues. The Ephebic Oath concluded with the words: "Thus in all these ways we will transmit this City, not only not less, but greater and more beautiful than it was transmitted to us." The Ephebic Oath is a 2500-year-old declaration of civic sustainability. Then, as today, the ideal of sustainability entails more than satisfying the most basic needs. It concerns living, preserving, and passing on the good life.

To sustain the good life requires the exercise of prudence or practical wisdom, according to the ancient Roman orator and statesman Marcus Tullius Cicero. Cicero stated that "Precaution is better than cure." His praise of prudence as a form of wise reasoning and foresighted caution was echoed in many ancient societies. The *Analects* of Confucius dictate that "He who gives no thought to difficulties in the future is sure to be beset by worries much closer at hand."[2] Likewise, the indigenous peoples of what are now eastern Canada and the United States, known as the Iroquois nation, developed the *Great Law of Peace*. It stipulated that Iroquois leaders should "Look and listen for the welfare of the whole people and have always in view not only the present but also the coming generations, even those whose faces are yet beneath the surface of the ground—the unborn of the future Nation."[3] The Iroquois, it is said, looked to the welfare of seven generations of progeny before taking any action. This "Seventh Generation Principle" grew from practical wisdom, a moral virtue that allowed indigenous societies to sustain their world and themselves.

Ancient peoples were not always successful in these efforts. Many societies of the distant past killed off wildlife, decimated forests, and eroded or waterlogged their croplands. The downfall of the ancient Sumerians of Mesopotamia, the Anasazi of southwestern North America, and the Mayan civilization of Central America were likely the result of such unsustainable practices regarding farmlands and forests.

Concern for the degradation or depletion of farmlands, forests, and other natural resources sparked conservation efforts in the United States in the late 1800s and early 1900s. Gifford Pinchot, Chief of the United States Forest Service, wrote: "The central thing for which Conservation stands is to make this country the best possible place to live in, both for us and for our descendants. It stands against the waste of natural resources which cannot be renewed, such as coal and iron; it stands for the perpetuation of the resources which can be renewed, such as the food-producing soils and the forests; and most of all its stands for an equal opportunity for every American citizen to get his fair share of benefit from these resources, both now and hereafter."[4] Pinchot's definition of conservation, now over a hundred years old, still captures much of what sustainability means today.

Pinchot was known as the "father of conservation." His friend, John Muir, was also conservation minded. But Muir developed a different orientation to the natural world. An avid outdoorsman and the founder of the Sierra Club, Muir pushed Pinchot and his contemporaries to look beyond the prudent exploitation of natural resources to satisfy basic human needs. He focused on the aesthetic qualities of nature, and the spiritual renewal it fostered. Muir believed that nature had intrinsic worth, beyond its material and economic value. And he believed that human beings, as part of nature, were participants in a vast web of interdependent relationships. "When you try to pick out any thing by itself," Muir observed, "you find it hitched to everything else in the universe." Muir's declaration of interdependence set the stage for the nature preservation movement, an effort to move beyond conservation understood as the "wise use" of natural resources. Preserving nature in a pristine state through the establishment of parks and wilderness areas bore witness to a deeper connection to the natural world and its inherent value.

Aldo Leopold and the Age of Ecology

Aldo Leopold (1887–1948) worked under Pinchot's direction in the U.S. Forest Service. Like Pinchot, Leopold advocated the scientific management of natural resources to ensure long-term human benefits. At the time, that meant participating in a federal program of killing wolves on public lands. The aim was to increase deer populations for hunters while also minimizing losses of ranch livestock. "I was young then, and full of trigger-itch," Leopold said. "I thought that because fewer wolves meant more deer, that no wolves would mean hunters' paradise."[5] The extermination program was a huge success in terms of the number of predators killed. Wolves were virtually eliminated in the contiguous United States by 1935. But there were unintended consequences.

Leopold witnessed first hand growing herds of deer that, in the absence of natural predators, overshot the carrying capacity of their habitats. He wrote:

> I have watched the face of many a newly wolfless mountain, and seen the south-facing slopes wrinkle with a maze of new deer trails. I have seen every edible bush and seedling browsed, first to anemic desuetude, and then to death. I have seen every edible tree defoliated to the height of a saddle horn. Such a mountain looks as if someone had given God a new pruning shears, and forbidden Him all other exercise. In the end the starved bones of the hoped-for deer herd, dead of its own too-much, bleach with the bones of the dead sage, or molder under the high-lined junipers.[6]

The delicate balance in nature between predator and prey had been upset, leaving growing herds of deer to destroy the land, and in short order, their own prospects of survival. The federal program aimed at increasing the availability of natural resources for humans was carried out with insufficient understanding of nature's interdependencies. Everything is hitched. Severing one strand of nature's web—in this case the wolves—weakened the whole fabric of life.

Faced with a disaster that he participated in making, Leopold had a Muirian epiphany. He developed a "land ethic" that aimed to transform our relationship to the natural world, shifting us from "conqueror of the land-community to plain member and citizen of it."[7] This new vision of our species—as one thread of a complex, interconnected, ecological web of relations—was published in Leopold's most famous work, *A Sand County Almanac*, a year after his death.

A central precept of Leopold's land ethic is that "A thing is right when it tends to preserve the integrity, stability, and beauty of the biotic community. It is wrong when it tends otherwise."[8] The goal is to see the biotic community or ecosystem as a whole, as an intricate and dynamic network of relationships, and then to act to preserve its integrity, stability, and beauty. The human need for natural resources is acknowledged. But such economic needs—and their limits—are placed within a broader ecological framework of understanding. Implementing the land ethic entailed "thinking like a mountain," that is, thinking from the perspective of a living geography that endures in time. Leopold's was the seminal contribution to the now thriving field of ecological ethics. As one environmental historian observed, Leopold's book "signaled the arrival of the Age of Ecology."[9]

To a great extent, sustainability in the age of ecology might be thought of as a revival of indigenous beliefs about nature as a web of interdependencies whose beauty and bounty allow the good life. Today, however, sustainability is greatly informed by the natural and social sciences. It is guided by our knowledge of the intricate relationships of flora and fauna that define ecosystems, of geologic and atmospheric relationships, and of the equally if not more complex cultural, technological, and economic relationships that define social systems. It is not enough to hold the conviction that everything is connected. To successfully engage in conservation and preservation, we must know *how* the parts are connected, and the consequences of tampering with them.

To think like a mountain is to think about both the intended and unintended consequences of actions. Everything we do has effects *and* side effects. The latter are generally unanticipated and unpredictable. The "first law of human ecology" is that "We can never do merely one thing."[10] When we act into a web of relations, especially if we sever a strand of this web, the impact of our action reverberates far and wide, with unknown repercussions. The law of unintended consequences, Lester Milbrath observes, is a "central axiom of environmentalism." It follows that "We must learn to ask, for every action, And then what?"[11]

Consider climate change in this light. The thickening blanket of greenhouse gases encircling the earth is largely the product of humans' burning coal and petroleum and burning or harvesting forests (since trees absorb carbon dioxide). Our species did not set out to heat its planet to dangerous levels. Climate change is a side effect of our exploitation of fossil fuels and forests. Many worry that this unintended consequence of human industry may, in the end, destroy human civilization. Yet when we use paper, plastic, or wood products, switch on the lights or start our cars, few of us ask ourselves the most pressing question: And then what?

Virtually all the environmental threats that we face today are the unintended consequences of human actions designed for other purposes. Wendell Berry observes that we have "never known what we are doing because we have never known what we have been undoing."[12] The web of nature harbors such complexity that no amount of investigation can fully reveal its intricacies or the eventual consequences of our plucking its strands. Ecological understanding cautions us about altering or severing linkages in this network of interdependence—whether those between wolves and deer or carbon dioxide emissions and solar radiation.

Deep complexity forbids control, and guarantees side effects.

Sustainability in the age of ecology has advanced beyond its early variants among ancient and indigenous peoples. As always, it entails trying to satisfy current needs without sacrificing long-term wellbeing. But our technological capacities have made the unintended effects of our actions more powerful and pervasive. In turn, the needs and wellbeing in question now cross geographical as well as generational boundaries. Greenhouse gases in the atmosphere do not respect national borders. Other environmental problems are also global in their causes, effects, and potential solutions. For these reasons, contemporary sustainability expands our moral and practical concerns in time *and* in space, bringing the welfare of others—those living across frontiers and in the future—into consideration.

Leopold's book was titled *A Sand County Almanac* because it focused on issues of conservation specific to the sandy-soiled land communities near his farm in Wisconsin. While it also addressed concerns of other geographic areas, including those in the southwest U.S., Canada, and Mexico, Leopold did not focus on global ecological relationships, such as those brought to fore today by climate change. In the first half of the 20th century, when *A Sand County Almanac* was conceived, such issues remained largely undiscovered. Leopold wrote that "All ethics so far evolved rest upon a single premise: that the individual is a member of a community of interdependent parts."[13] What Leopold and earlier conservation-minded peoples could not have appreciated is that the community of interdependent parts that sustains us today has become planetary. Today, *global* ecology defines our most crucial problems and prospects.

Society, Environment, and Economy

Our lives are sustained by biological, geological, and atmospheric relationships that span the globe. Our lives are also sustained by economic, technological, and social networks, as well as political and legal conventions, laws, alliances, and organizations that are global in scope. In such an interdependent world, the consequences of our actions (both intended and unintended) inevitably cross borders and generations, spanning frontiers and casting long shadows into the future. The carbon dioxide emitted from our car's tailpipes will have its greatest impact on people yet to be born, and likely on people we will never meet, who live on the other side of the planet. In turn, the quality of our lives, and the lives of our children and grandchildren, will greatly depend on how people from other nations and cultures choose to act in the face of climate change and other environmental threats. Ethics, Leopold suggested, entails our sustaining the community that sustains us. Increasingly, that community is planetary in scope.

Oftentimes *sustainability* is equated with *environmental protection*. To be sustainable, however, a practice or institution must do much more than directly preserve nature. In a globally interdependent world—our world—environmental protection stands or falls with our ability to meet the social and economic needs of local and global communities. That is because it is difficult if not impossible to protect the environment when people's basic needs remain unsatisfied.

You are not running a sustainable business, no matter how "green" your products or services, if you cannot pay your employees for lack of revenues. A viable economy matters. In turn, until peoples' most basic needs are met, they are unlikely to engage in environmental caretaking with great foresight. Dire poverty often forces people to hunt endangered species for food, or slash and burn rain forests to grow crops for subsistence or export. "To care about the environment," the anthropologist and conservationist Richard Leakey has observed, "requires at least one square meal a day."[14] Leakey's point is that short-term survival needs typically trump long-term environmental conservation. But poverty is not the only obstacle to conservation. Wealth brings its own environmental threats. Over the last century, the planet's resources have been depleted and its lands, waters, and skies polluted with greenhouse gases and other industrial wastes much more by the wealthy of the world than by the poor, despite the much smaller numbers of the former.

Environmentalists—at least those devoted to wilderness preservation such as Dave Foreman and the organization he founded, Earth First!—are often perceived as protecting nature without concern for human welfare. Agrarian author and poet Wendell Berry has pointed out that nature lives not only in untouched wilderness but also in our farms and gardens, and that protecting fertile, unpolluted land to grow healthy food should be a top priority for environmentalists.[15] Like Berry, advocates of sustainability deny that we have to choose between wilderness *or* gardens. They insist that sustaining healthy, fertile lands that meet human needs is a crucial means to sustaining the wilderness lying beyond our farms and gardens.

Environmental protection depends upon education and empowerment. The way society is organized—equitably or inequitably, informed or ignorant, empowered or disempowered—greatly affects the state of the environment, not to mention the health, welfare, and happiness of people.[16] With this in mind, sustainability is said to rest on the three pillars of *Society*, *Environment*, and *Economy*, sometimes labeled *People*, *Planet*, and *Profit*. To practice sustainability we have to balance the pursuit of three interdependent values: 1) environmental protection; 2) economic viability and opportunity; and 3) social education, equity, and empowerment.

Sustainability requires us, as individuals, to do our share to protect the natural world and conserve resources. This obligation is often summarized by the mandate to *Reduce, Reuse, and Recycle*. But individual responsibility on our part as consumers, though necessary, is insufficient. As Lester Brown writes, "Saving civilization is not a spectator sport;" it cannot be accomplished by individuals engaged solely in "lifestyle changes."[17] Political participation is also required, as the pursuit of sustainability depends on collective action at local, national, and global levels. We cannot safeguard people, planet, and profit without politics. We must act not only as responsible *consumers*, but as responsible *citizens*.

Whether an individual or collective undertaking, sustainability is an aspiration not an achievement. Leopold wrote that "We shall never achieve harmony with land, any more than we shall achieve absolute justice or liberty for people. In these higher aspirations the important thing is not to achieve, but to strive."[18] Sustainability is not a destination to be reached. It is a series of trails to be blazed, fueled by the hard-won virtues of hope and courage. In turn, Leopold realized that the balanced pursuit of social, environmental, and economic values is a dynamic process. It changes with time, as local and global environments, technological capabilities, and cultural norms and resources evolve. And it changes with place: it means and entails different things for a Nepalese yak herder and a New York hairstylist.

Ecology teaches us that healthy biotic communities respond well to change. They become resilient by adapting.[19] When the rate and scale of change that organisms face is moderate, successful responses are possible. When the rate and scale of change is too drastic, however, biotic communities cannot adapt in time. In such circumstances, ecosystems may collapse and species go extinct.

In planet earth's 4.5 billion year history, there have been at least five extinction crises. These were drastic events such as meteor impacts or large-scale volcanic disruptions that decimated life across the globe. Today we are in the midst of a sixth extinction crisis. This one is of our own doing, largely a product of humans having usurped natural habitat, hunted, gathered, or fished excessively, and polluted environments. The most dangerous form of pollution today—that of our atmosphere with greenhouse gases—is occurring at such an accelerated rate that countless species are likely to be pushed into extinction as their habitats rapidly become hotter, drier, or wetter. The rate and scale of change is simply too great for these species to adapt. In such conditions, efforts to preserve biodiversity become much more challenging. We can no longer simply establish protected parks and wilderness areas, as Muir suggested. In a world of disruptive climate change, many species of endangered flora and fauna may have to migrate to new habitats—to higher latitudes or elevations—in order to survive.

With this in mind, sustainability might best be defined as managing the rate and scale of change in society, the environment, and the economy so as to preserve their core values and relationships. It is no small thing to determine what core values and relationships need to be preserved, and what can and must change in order to ensure this preservation. Sustainability requires good stewardship of the earth: we must manage the rate and scale of our harvesting, manufacturing, and discarding with knowledge and care. It also requires safeguarding the rich diversity and profound mystery of nature by leaving much wilderness be, lest our doings produce too many undoings.

Frequently, what most needs managing is our penchant for control. Sustainability often requires a hands-off approach, allowing nature to evolve in its own time. In his essay "Walking," Henry David Thoreau wrote "In wildness is the preservation of the world." The wildness of nature invites a relationship to that which is beyond our comprehension, and beyond our control. In this respect, it offers spiritual renewal.

Technology and the Future of Sustainability

Some environmentalists, known as ecological modernists, advocate the full embrace of technological control as a means of preserving biodiversity and other core ecological values. "The prophets of ecological modernism," one commentator writes, "believe technology is the solution and not the problem. They say that harnessing innovation and entrepreneurship can save the planet … The modernists wear their environmentalism with pride, but are pro-nuclear, pro-genetically modified crops, pro-megadams, pro-urbanization and pro-geoengineering of the planet to stave off climate change. They say they embrace these technologies not to conquer nature, like old-style 20th century modernists, but to give nature room. If we can do our business in a smaller part of the planet—through smarter, greener and more efficient technologies—then nature can have the rest."[20] Despite such good intentions, it is not at all clear that deploying the aforementioned technologies will save more of the planet for nature. Of one thing we can be sure, however: these technologies will have unintended consequences. And given their proposed scale—such as planetary geoengineering efforts to reverse climate change or the genetic modification of plants and animals—the unintended consequences may be massive and irreversible.

Consider the prospect of geoengineering. One prominent proposal for slowing down global warming is the introduction of massive amounts of sulfur dioxide into the upper atmosphere to reflect solar radiation back into space. Atmospheric geoengineering does nothing to reverse, or even slow down, the production of greenhouse gases or the acidification of the oceans these gases cause. It simply offsets their heat-trapping tendencies temporarily by deflecting more sunlight. In this respect, geoengineering the atmosphere to combat climate change has been likened to fighting obesity with a corset and a diet of doughnuts.[21] We may gain the illusion of control temporarily, but the long-term prognosis is grim.

For these and other reasons, many advocates of sustainability reject the technological optimism of the ecological modernists. They advocate cultural transformation instead. Rather than treating symptoms with technological quick fixes, they suggest that we cure the disease by changing human values and practices. The needed cultural transformation includes *reducing* consumption, *reusing* materials, *recycling* what we cannot reuse, and, as importantly, *reconnecting* with nature and small-scale, empowered communities.

Doug Tompkins, co-founder of the retail brands *North Face* and *Esprit*, does not believe that technology can save us, or the planet. Indeed, he believes technology enslaves us and destroys the earth. Tompkins states:

> The computer is a mechanism for acceleration, it accelerates economic activity and this is eating up the world ... That's what the computer's real work does and it does that 24/7, 365 days a year, non-stop just to satisfy our own narrow needs ... If you just hold your cell phone for 30 seconds and think backwards through its production you have the entire techno-industrial culture wrapped up there. You can't have that device without everything that goes with it ... and it's that techno-industrial culture that's destroying the world.[22]

Whenever we employ a technological device, Tompkins prompts us to ask: And then what? Yet today much of what we need to know in order to sustain ecosystems, geologic and atmospheric relationships, and social networks is made possible by computers and other technologies of learning. Ironically, Tompkins himself uses a laptop computer to organize his extensive efforts of nature preservation and to communicate his sustainability values. "I did not want to compromise my engagement," he observes, "so I was forced to use the very technology that is undoing the world." Not all of us can devote hundreds of millions of dollars to nature preservation, as Tompkins does. But all of us are caught in the same dilemma that he faces. We participate in economies and technologies that have the potential for great harm and good.

The idea for this essay was born on a walk through a pristine forest, but I could not trust memory to retain my thoughts. Lacking paper and pen, I resorted to texting myself on a smartphone, which was along for the hike because it doubles as my camera. It felt odd stopping mid-hike, amidst all the glorious and inspiring beauty of the mountain forest, to thumb an electronic message on a tiny keyboard deploying the latest technology. I wondered about the bargain being struck at that moment along the scented shoreline woods. And I realized that the pursuit of sustainability confronts us with an endless stream of such dilemmas.

Each day the choices we make affect the sustainability of our communities and the planet. Each day we must ask, And then what? *before* we act. Clear answers to this question remain elusive, and are often in dispute by experts. In grappling with these conundrums, we will undoubtedly make mistakes. And even our most celebrated successes will yield unintended consequences.

With this in mind, the goal is not to devise fail-safe solutions to the daunting social and environmental problems that we face. Any technology big enough to serve as a panacea is also big enough, and likely, to produce unintended consequences of potentially catastrophic dimensions. So we must think like a mountain, determine our core values and relationships, and act with both practical wisdom and imagination. We have to restrain our consumption, connect with our communities, and promote "safe to fail" experimentation that blazes cultural and technological pathways to sustainable living.

Leopold understood this imperative. He suggested that we model human societies on the dynamic adaptability of ecological communities. Ethics, including the ecological ethics he played such a large part in developing, were considered the "tentative" products of "social evolution." They are and must be tentative, Leopold stipulated, "because evolution never stops."[23] Nature does not make permanent solutions. Rather, it evolves organisms and ecosystems that function well in particular circumstances. Once evolution stops, life stops. A sustainable society models itself on nature in this regard. There are no permanent solutions to the challenge of satisfying human needs and wants in a finite world because these needs and wants change with time and place, as does the natural environment that allows their satisfaction. To be sustainable, a network defined by relationships of interdependence—whether biological or social—must evolve.

By ushering in the age of ecology, Leopold effectively scribed a preamble to the challenge of sustainability. How this challenge will be met carries with it the fate of civilization. This story, yet to be written, will be the product of the hands, hearts, and minds of today's youth, a generation inheriting a world of unprecedented threat and opportunity.

NOTES

1   International Union for the Conservation of Nature and Natural Resources, *World Conservation Strategy*, section 1 "Introduction: living resource conservation for sustainable development." Accessed at *data.iucn.org /dbtw-wpd/edocs/WCS-004.pdf.*
2   Confucius, *The Analects* (New York: Penguin, 1979), p. 134.
3   See http://www.ratical.org/many_worlds/6Nations/EoL/index.html#ToC; http://www.indigenouspeople.net/iroqcon.htm
4   Gifford Pinchot, *The Fight for Conservation* (New York: Doubleday, Page and Company, 1910), p. 79.
5   Aldo Leopold, *A Sand County Almanac* (New York: Ballantine Books, 1966), p. 138.
6   Ibid, pp. 139–40.
7   Ibid, p. 240.
8   Ibid, p. 262.
9   Donald Worster, *Nature's Economy* (Cambridge: Cambridge University Press, 1994), p. 284.
10   Garrett Hardin, "The cybernetics of competition: A Biologist's View of Society," *Perspectives in Biology and Medicine* 7 (1963):58–84. Reprinted in Garrett Hardin, *Stalking the Wild Taboo*, (Los Altos: William Kaufmann, 1978).
11   Lester Milbrath, "Environmental Understanding: A New Concern for Political Socialization," in Orit Ichilov, ed., *Political Socialization: Citizenship, Education and Democracy* (New York: Teachers College Press, 1990), p. 292.
12   Quoted in Wes Jackson, "Toward an Ignorance-Based Worldview" (21–36) in Bill Vitek and Wes Jackson, eds. *The Virtues of Ignorance: Complexity, Sustainability, and the Limits of Knowledge* (Lexington: University of Kentucky Press, 2008), p. 26.
13   Leopold, *A Sand County Almanac*, p. 239.
14   Quoted in Stephan Schmidheiny, *Changing Course: A Global Business Perspective on Development and the Environment* (Cambridge: MIT Press, 1992), p. 135.
15   See Michael Pollen, "Wendell Berry's Wisdom," *The Nation*, September 2, 2009; accessed at http://michaelpollan.com/articles-archive/the-nation-magazine-wendell-berrys-wisdom/
16   Richard Wilkinson and Kate Pickett, *The Spirit Level: Why Greater Equality Makes Societies Stronger* (New York: Bloomsbury Press, 2009. Mariano Torras and James Boyce, "Income, inequality, and pollution: a reassessment of the environmental Kuznets Curve," *Ecological Economics* 25 (1998): 147–60; J. Boyce, A. Klemer, P. Templet and C. Willis, "Power distribution, the environment, and public health: a

state-level analysis," *Ecological Economics* 29 (1999):127–40. Julian Agyeman, Robert Bullard and Bob Evans, "Towards Just Sustainabilities: Perspectives and Possibilities," in *Just Sustainabilities: Development in an Unequal World,* ed. Julian Agyeman, Robert Bullard and Bob Evans (Cambridge: MIT Press, 2003), p. 325.

17 Lester Brown, *World on the Edge*: *How to Prevent Environmental and Economic Collapse* (New York: Earth Policy Institute, 2011), pp. 200–02.

18 Leopold, *A Sand County Almanac*, p. 210.

19 C.S. Holling and Lance H. Gunderson, "Resilience and Adaptive Cycles" (pp. 25–62) in Lance H. Gunderson and C.S. Holling, eds., *Panarchy: Understanding Transformations in Human and Natural Systems* (Washington: Island Press, 2002), p. 31.

20 Fred Pierce, "New Green Vision: Technology As Our Planet's Last Best Hope," *Environment 360,* July 15, 2013. http://e360.yale.edu/feature/new_green_vision_technology_as_our_planets_last_best_hope/2671/

21 Graeme Wood, "Moving Heaven and Earth," *The Atlantic,* July 2009 (70–76), p. 73.

22 Jo Confino, "How technology has stopped evolution and is destroying the world," *The Guardian,* July 11, 2013, http://www.guardian.co.uk/sustainable-business/technology-stopped-evolution-destroying-world?CMP=&et_cid=41623&et_rid=6984265&Linkid=How+technology+has+stopped+evolution+and+is+destroying+the+world+

23 Leopold, *A Sand County Almanac*, p. 263.

Getting Along with Nature

*WENDELL BERRY**

Wendell Berry (1934–) is a Kentucky farmer, poet, novelist, essayist, and conservationist. A longtime champion of the family farm and sustainable agriculture, Berry offers an eloquent defense of the "garden" view against advocates of the "wilderness" vision. Human beings are not a species set apart from nature and from nonhuman animals. They are natural creatures whose "nature" is to cultivate the earth. Such intervention does, of course, affect nature, but it need not always or necessarily do so for the worse. To cultivate the earth in ways that respect and protect its fertility and diversity is not contrary to nature but is to "get along with nature."

* *Source*: Wendell Berry, "Getting Along with Nature" in Berry, *Home Economics: Fourteen Essays* (San Francisco: North Point Press, 1987). © 2009 by Wendell Berry. Reprinted by permission of Counterpoint.

GETTING ALONG WITH NATURE

The defenders of nature and wilderness—like their enemies the defenders of the industrial economy—sometimes sound as if the natural and the human were two separate estates, radically different and radically divided. The defenders of nature and wilderness sometimes seem to feel that they must oppose any human encroachment whatsoever, just as the industrialists often apparently feel that they must make the human encroachment absolute or, as they say, "complete the conquest of nature." But there is danger in this opposition, and it can be best dealt with by realizing that these pure and separate categories are pure ideas and do not otherwise exist.

Pure nature, anyhow, is not good for humans to live in, and humans do not want to live in it—or not for very long. Any exposure to the elements that lasts more than a few hours will remind us of the desirability of the basic human amenities: clothing, shelter, cooked food, the company of kinfolk and friends—perhaps even of hot baths and music and books.

It is equally true that a condition that is *purely* human is not good for people to live in, and people do not want to live for very long in it. Obviously, the more artificial a human environment becomes, the more the word "natural" becomes a term of value. It can be argued, indeed, that the conservation movement, as we know it today, is largely a product of the industrial revolution. The people who want clean air, clear streams, and wild forests, prairies, and deserts are the people who no longer have them.

People cannot live apart from nature; that is the first principle of the conservationists. And yet, people cannot live in nature without changing it. But this is true of *all* creatures; they depend upon nature, and they change it. What we call nature is, in a sense, the sum of the changes made by the various creatures and natural forces in their intricate actions and influences upon each other and upon their places. Because of the woodpeckers, nature is different from what it would be without them. It is different also because of the borers and ants that live in tree trunks, and because of the bacteria that live in the soil under the trees. The making of these differences is the making of the world.

Some of the changes made by wild creatures we would call beneficent: beavers are famous for making ponds that turn into fertile meadows; trees and prairie grasses build soil. But sometimes, too, we would call natural changes destructive. According to early witnesses, for instance, large areas around Kentucky salt licks were severely trampled and eroded by the great herds of hoofed animals that gathered there. The buffalo "streets" through hilly country were so hollowed out by hoof-wear and erosion that they remain visible almost two centuries after the disappearance of the buffalo. And so it can hardly be expected that humans would not change nature. Humans, like all other creatures, must make a difference; otherwise, they cannot live. But unlike other creatures, humans must make a choice as to the kind and scale of the difference they make. If they choose to make too small a difference, they diminish their humanity. If they choose to make too great a difference, they diminish nature, and narrow their subsequent choices; ultimately, they diminish or destroy themselves. Nature, then, is not only our source but also our limit and measure. Or, as the poet Edmund Spenser put it almost four hundred years ago, Nature, who is the "greatest goddesse," acts as a sort of earthly lieutenant of God, and Spenser represents her as both a mother and judge. Her jurisdiction is over the relations between the creatures; she deals "Right to all ... indifferently," for she is "the equall mother" of all "[a]nd knittest each to each, as brother unto brother." Thus, in Spenser, the natural principles of fecundity and order are pointedly linked with the principle of justice, which we may be a little surprised to see that he attributes also to nature. And yet in his insistence on an "indifferent" natural justice, resting on the "brotherhood" of *all* creatures, not just of humans, Spenser would now be said to be on sound ecological footing.

In nature we know that wild creatures sometimes exhaust their vital sources and suffer the natural remedy: drastic population reductions. If lynxes eat too many snowshoe rabbits—which they are said to do repeatedly—then the lynxes starve down to the carrying capacity of their habitat. It is the carrying capacity of the lynx's habitat, not the carrying capacity of the lynx's stomach, that determines the prosperity of lynxes. Similarly, if humans use up too much soil—which they have often done and are doing—then they will starve down to the carrying capacity of *their* habitat. This is nature's "indifferent" justice. As Spenser saw in the sixteenth century, and as we must learn to see now, there is no appeal from this justice. In the hereafter, the Lord may forgive our wrongs against nature, but on earth, so far as we know, He does not overturn her decisions.

One of the differences between humans and lynxes is that humans can see that the principle of balance operates between lynxes and snowshoe rabbits, as between humans and topsoil; another difference, we hope, is that humans have the sense to act on their understanding. We can see, too, that a stable balance is preferable to a balance that tilts back and forth like a seesaw, dumping a surplus of creatures alternately from either end. To say this is to renew the question of whether or not the human relationship with nature is necessarily an adversary relationship, and it is to suggest that the answer is not simple.

But in dealing with this question and in trying to do justice to the presumed complexity of the answer, we are up against an American convention of simple opposition to nature that is deeply established both in our minds and in our ways. We have opposed the primeval forests of the East and the primeval prairies and deserts of the West, we have opposed man-eating beasts and crop-eating insects, sheep-eating coyotes, and chicken-eating hawks. In our lawns and gardens and fields, we oppose what we call weeds. And yet more and more of us are beginning to see that this opposition is ultimately destructive even of ourselves, that it does not explain many things that need explaining—in short, that it is untrue.

If our proper relation to nature is not opposition, then what is it? This question becomes complicated and difficult for us because none of us, as I have said, wants to live in a "pure" primeval forest or in a "pure" primeval prairie; we do not want to be eaten by grizzly bears; if we are gardeners, we have a legitimate quarrel with weeds; if, in Kentucky, we are trying to improve our pastures, we are likely to be enemies of the nodding thistle. But, do what we will, we remain under the spell of the primeval forests and prairies that we have cut down and broken; we turn repeatedly and with love to the thought of them and to their surviving remnants. We find ourselves attracted to the grizzly bears, too, and know that they and other great, dangerous animals remain alive in our imaginations as they have been all through human time. Though we cut down the nodding thistles, we acknowledge their beauty and are glad to think that there must be some place where they belong. (They may, in fact, not always be out of place in pastures; if, as seems evident, overgrazing makes an ideal seedbed for these plants, then we must understand them as a part of nature's strategy to protect the ground against abuse by animals.) Even the ugliest garden weeds earn affection from us when we consider how faithfully they perform an indispensable duty in covering the bare ground and in building humus. The weeds, too, are involved in the business of fertility.

We know, then, that the conflict between the human and the natural estates really exists and that it is to some extent necessary. But we are learning, or relearning, something else, too, that frightens us: namely, that this conflict often occurs at the expense of *both* estates. It is not only possible but altogether probable that by diminishing nature we diminish ourselves, and vice versa.

The conflict comes to light most suggestively, perhaps, when advocates for the two sides throw themselves into absolute conflict where no absolute difference can exist. An example of this is the battle between defenders of coyotes and defenders of sheep, in which the coyote-defenders may find it easy to forget that the sheep ranchers are human beings with some authentic complaints against coyotes, and the sheep-defenders find it easy to sound as if they advocate the total eradication of both coyotes and conservationists. Such conflicts—like the old one between hawk-defenders and chicken-defenders—tend to occur between people who use nature indirectly and people who use it directly. It is a dangerous mistake, I think, for either side to pursue such a quarrel on the assumption that victory would be a desirable result.

The fact is that people need both coyotes and sheep, need a world in which both kinds of life are possible. Outside the heat of conflict, conservationists probably know that a sheep is one of the best devices for making coarse foliage humanly edible and that wool is ecologically better than the synthetic fibers, just as most shepherds will be aware that wild nature is of value to them and not lacking in interest and pleasure.

The usefulness of coyotes is, of course, much harder to define than the usefulness of sheep. Coyote fur is not a likely substitute for wool, and, except as a last resort, most people don't want to eat coyotes. The difficulty lies in the difference between what is ours and what is nature's: What is ours is ours because it is directly useful. Coyotes are useful *indirectly*, as part of the health of nature, from which we and our sheep alike must live and take our health. The fact, moreover, may be that sheep and coyotes need each other, at least in the sense that neither would prosper in a place totally unfit for the other.

This sort of conflict, then, does not suggest the possibility of victory so much as it suggests the possibility of a compromise—some kind of peace, even an alliance, between the domestic and the wild. We know that such an alliance is necessary. Most conservationists now take for granted that humans thrive best in ecological health and that the test or sign of this health is the survival of a diversity of wild creatures. We know, too, that we cannot imagine ourselves apart from those necessary survivals of our own wildness that we call our instincts. And we know that we cannot have a healthy agriculture apart from the teeming wilderness in the topsoil, in which worms, bacteria, and other wild creatures are carrying on the fundamental work of decomposition, humus making, water storage, and drainage. "In wildness is the preservation of the world," as Thoreau said, may be a spiritual truth, but it is also a practical fact.

On the other hand, we must not fail to consider the opposite proposition—that, so long at least as humans are in the world, in human culture is the preservation of wildness—which is equally, and more demandingly, true. If wildness is to survive, then *we* must preserve it. We must preserve it by public act, by law, by institutionalizing wildernesses in some places. But such preservation is probably not enough. I have heard Wes Jackson of the Land Institute say, rightly I think, that if we cannot preserve our farmland, we cannot preserve the wilderness. That said, it becomes obvious that if we cannot preserve our cities, we cannot preserve the wilderness. This can be demonstrated practically by saying that the same attitudes that destroy wildness in the topsoil will finally destroy it everywhere; or by saying that if *everyone* has to go to a designated public wilderness for the necessary contact with wildness, then our parks will be no more natural than our cities.

But I am trying to say something more fundamental than that. What I am aiming at—because a lot of evidence seems to point this way—is the probability that nature and human culture, wildness and domesticity, are not opposed but are interdependent. Authentic experience of either will reveal the need of one for the other. In fact, examples from both past and present prove that a human economy and wildness can exist together not only in compatibility but to their mutual benefit.

One of the best examples I have come upon recently is the story of two Sonora Desert oases in Gary Nabhan's book, *The Desert Smells Like Rain*. The first of these oases, A'al Waipia, in Arizona, is dying because the park service, intending to preserve the natural integrity of the place as a bird sanctuary for tourists, removed the Papago Indians who had lived and farmed there. The place was naturally purer after the Indians were gone, but the oasis also began to shrink as the irrigation ditches silted up. As Mr. Nabhan puts it, "an odd thing is happening to their 'natural' bird sanctuary. They are losing the heterogeneity of the habitat, and with it, the birds. The old trees are dying … These riparian trees are essential for the breeding habitat of certain birds. Summer annual seed plants are conspicuously absent … Without the soil disturbance associated with plowing and flood irrigation, these natural foods for birds and rodents no longer germinate."

The other oasis, Ki:towak, in old Mexico, still thrives because a Papago village is still there, still farming. The village's oldest man, Luis Nolia, is the caretaker of the oasis, cleaning the springs and ditches, farming, planting trees: "Luis … blesses the oasis," Mr. Nabhan says, "for his work keeps it healthy." An ornithologist who accompanied Mr. Nabhan found twice as many species of birds at the farmed oasis as he found at the bird sanctuary, a fact that Mr. Nabhan's Papago friend, Remedio, explained in this way: "That's because those birds, they come where the people are. When the people live and work in a place, and plant their seeds and water their trees, the birds go live with them. They like those places, there's plenty to eat and that's when we are friends to them."

Another example, from my own experience, is suggestive in a somewhat different way. At the end of July 1981, while I was using a team of horses to mow a small triangular hillside pasture that is bordered on two sides by trees, I was suddenly aware of wings close below me. It was a young red-tailed hawk, who flew up into a walnut tree. I mowed on to the turn and stopped the team. The hawk then glided to the ground not twenty feet away. I got off the mower, stood and watched, even spoke, and the hawk showed no fear. I could see every feather distinctly, claw and beak and eye, the creamy down of the breast. Only when I took a step toward him, separating myself from the team and mower, did he fly. While I mowed three or four rounds, he stayed near, perched in trees or standing erect and watchful on the ground. Once, when I stopped to watch him, he was clearly watching me, stooping to see under the leaves that screened me from him. Again, when I could not find him, I stooped, saying to myself, "This is what he did to look at me," and as I did so I saw him looking at me.

Why had he come? To catch mice? Had he seen me scare one out of the grass? Or was it curiosity?

A human, of course, cannot speak with authority of the motives of hawks. I am aware of the possibility of explaining the episode merely by the hawk's youth and inexperience. And yet it does not happen often or dependably that one is approached so closely by a hawk of any age. I feel safe in making a couple of assumptions. The first is that the hawk came because of the conjunction of the small pasture and its wooded borders, of open hunting ground and the security of trees. This is the phenomenon of edge or margin that we know to be one of the powerful attractions of a diversified landscape, both to wildlife and to humans. The human eye itself seems drawn to such margins, hungering for the difference made in the countryside by a hedgy fencerow, a stream, or a grove of trees. And we know that these margins are biologically rich, the meeting of two kinds of habitat. But another difference also is important here: the difference between a large pasture and a small one, or, to use Wes Jackson's terms, the difference between a field and a patch. The pasture I was mowing was a patch—small, intimate, nowhere distant from its edges.

My second assumption is that the hawk was emboldened to come so near because, though he obviously recognized me as a man, I was there with the team of horses, with whom he familiarly and confidently shared the world.

I am saying, in other words, that this little visit between the hawk and me happened because the kind and scale of my farm, my way of farming, and my technology *allowed* it to happen. If I had been driving a tractor in a hundred-acre cornfield, it would not have happened.

In some circles I would certainly be asked if one can or should be serious about such an encounter, if it has any value. And though I cannot produce any hard evidence, I would unhesitatingly answer yes. Such encounters involve another margin—the one between domesticity and wildness—that attracts us irresistibly; they are among the best rewards of outdoor work and among the reasons for loving to farm. When the scale of farming grows so great and obtrusive as to forbid them, the *life* of farming is impoverished.

But perhaps we do find hard evidence of a sort when we consider that *all* of us—the hawk, the horses, and I—were there for our benefit and, to some extent, for our *mutual* benefit: The horses live from the pasture and maintain it with their work, grazing, and manure; the team and I together furnish hunting ground to the hawk; the hawk serves us by controlling the field mouse population.

These meetings of the human and the natural estates, the domestic and the wild, occur invisibly, of course, in any well-farmed field. The wilderness of a healthy soil, too complex for human comprehension, can yet be husbanded, can benefit from human care, and can deliver incalculable benefits in return. Mutuality of interest and reward is a possibility that can reach to any city backyard, garden, and park, but in any place under human dominance—which is, now, virtually everyplace—it is a possibility that is *both* natural and cultural. If humans want wildness to be possible, then they have to make it possible. If balance is the ruling principle and a stable balance the goal, then, for humans, attaining this goal requires a consciously chosen and deliberately made partnership with nature.

In other words, we can be true to nature only by being true to human nature—to our animal nature as well as to cultural patterns and restraints that keep us from acting like animals. When humans act like animals, they become the most dangerous of animals to themselves and other humans, and this is because of another critical difference between humans and animals: Whereas animals are usually restrained by the limits of physical appetites, humans have mental appetites that can be far more gross and capacious than physical ones. Only humans squander and hoard, murder and pillage because of notions.

The work by which good human and natural possibilities are preserved is complex and difficult, and it probably cannot be accomplished by raw intelligence and information. It requires knowledge, skills, and restraints, some of which must come from our past. In the hurry of technological progress, we have replaced some tools and methods that worked with some that do not work. But we also need culture-borne instructions about who or what humans are and how and on what assumptions they should act. The Chain of Being, for instance—which gave humans a place between animals and angels in the order of Creation—is an old idea that has not been replaced by any adequate new one. It was simply rejected, and the lack of it leaves us without a definition.

Lacking the ancient definition, or any such definition, we do not know at what point to restrain or deny ourselves. We do not know how ambitious to be, what or how much we may safely desire, when or where to stop. I knew a barber once who refused to give a discount to a bald client, explaining that his artistry consisted, not in the cutting off, but in the knowing when to stop. He spoke, I think, as a true artist and a true human. The lack of such knowledge is extremely dangerous in and to an individual. But ignorance of when to stop is a modern epidemic; it is the basis of "industrial progress" and "economic growth." The most obvious practical result of this ignorance is a critical disproportion of scale between the scale of human enterprises and their sources in nature.

The scale of the energy industry, for example, is too big, as is the scale of the transportation industry. The scale of agriculture, from a technological or economic point of view, is too big, but from a demographic point of view, the scale is too small. When there are enough people on the land to use it but not enough to husband it, then the wildness of the soil that we call fertility begins to diminish, and the soil itself begins to flee from us in water and wind.

If the human economy is to be fitted into the natural economy in such a way that both may thrive, the human economy must be built to proper scale. It is possible to talk at great length about the difference between proper and improper scale. It may be enough to say here that that difference is *suggested* by the difference between amplified and unamplified music in the countryside, or the difference between the sound of a motorboat and the sound of oarlocks. A proper human sound, we may say, is one that allows other sounds to be heard. A properly scaled human economy or technology allows a diversity of other creatures to thrive.

"The proper scale," a friend wrote to me, "confers freedom and simplicity … and doubtless leads to long life and health." I think that it also confers joy. The renewal of our partnership with nature, the rejoining of our works to their proper places in the natural order, reshaped to their proper scale, implies the reenjoyment both of nature and of human domesticity. Though our task will be difficult, we will greatly mistake its nature if we see it as grim, or if we suppose that it must always be necessary to suffer at work in order to enjoy ourselves in places specializing in "recreation."

Once we grant the possibility of a proper human scale, we see that we have made a radical change of assumptions and values. We realize that we are less interested in technological "breakthroughs" than in technological elegance. Of a new tool or method we will no longer ask: Is it fast? Is it powerful? Is it a labor saver? How many workers will it replace? We will ask instead: Can we (and our children) afford it? Is it fitting to our real needs? Is it becoming to us? Is it unhealthy or ugly? And though we may keep a certain interest in innovation and in what we may become, we will renew our interest in what we have been, realizing that conservationists must necessarily conserve *both* inheritances, the natural and the cultural.

To argue the necessity of wildness to, and in, the human economy is by no means to argue against the necessity of wilderness. The survival of wilderness—of places that we do not change, where we allow the existence even of creatures we perceive as dangerous—is necessary. Our sanity probably requires it. Whether we go to those places or not, we need to know that they exist. And I would argue that we do not need just the great public wildernesses, but millions of small private or semiprivate ones. Every farm should have one; wildernesses can occupy corners of factory grounds and city lots—places where nature is given a free hand, where no human work is done, where people go only as guests. These places function, I think, whether we intend them to or not, as sacred groves—places we respect and leave alone, not because we understand well what goes on there, but because we do not.

We go to wilderness places to be restored, to be instructed in the natural economies of fertility and healing, to admire what we cannot make. Sometimes, as we find to our surprise, we go to be chastened or corrected. And we go in order to return with renewed knowledge by which to judge the health of our human economy and our dwelling places. As we return from our visits to the wilderness, it is sometimes possible to imagine a series of fitting and decent transitions from wild nature to the human community and its supports: from forest to woodlot to the "two-story agriculture" of tree crops and pasture to orchard to meadow to grain field to garden to household to neighborhood to village to city—so that even when we reached the city we would not be entirely beyond the influence of the nature of that place.

What I have been implying is that I think there is a bad reason to go to the wilderness. We must not go there to escape the ugliness and the dangers of the present human economy. We must not let ourselves feel that to go there is to escape. In the first place, such an escape is now illusory. In the second place, if, even as conservationists, we see the human and the natural economies as necessarily opposite or opposed, we subscribe to the very opposition that threatens to destroy them both. The wild and the domestic now often seem isolated values, estranged from one another. And yet these are not exclusive polarities like good and evil. There can be continuity between them, and there must be.

What we find, if we weight the balance too much in favor of the domestic, is that we involve ourselves in dangers both personal and public. Not the least of these dangers is dependence on distant sources of money and materials. Farmers are in deep trouble now because they have become too dependent on corporations and banks. They have been using methods and species that enforce this dependence. But such a dependence is not safe, either for farmers or for agriculture. It is not safe for urban consumers. Ultimately, as we are beginning to see, it is not safe for banks and corporations—which, though they have evidently not thought so, are dependent upon farmers. Our farms are endangered because—like the interstate highways or modern hospitals or modern universities—they cannot be inexpensively used. To be usable at all they require great expense.

When the human estate becomes so precarious, our only recourse is to move it back toward the estate of nature. We undoubtedly need better plant and animal species than nature provided us. But we are beginning to see that they can be too much better—too dependent on us and on "the economy," too expensive. In farm animals, for instance, we want good commercial quality, but we can see that the ability to produce meat or milk can actually be a threat to the farmer and to the animal if not accompanied by qualities we would call natural: thriftiness, hardiness, physical vigor, resistance to disease and parasites, ability to breed and give birth without assistance, strong mothering instincts. These natural qualities decrease care, work, and worry; they also decrease the cost of production. They save feed and time; they make diseases and cures exceptional rather than routine.

We need crop and forage species of high productive ability also, but we do not need species that will not produce at all without expensive fertilizers and chemicals. Contrary to the premise of agribusiness advertisements and of most expert advice, farmers do not thrive by production or by "skimming" a large "cash flow." They cannot solve their problems merely by increasing production or income. They thrive, like all other creatures, according to the difference between their income and their expenses.

One of the strangest characteristics of the industrial economy is the ability to increase production again and again without ever noticing—or without acknowledging—the *costs* of production. That one Holstein cow should produce 50,000 pounds of milk in a year may appear to be marvelous—a miracle of modern science. But what if her productivity is dependent upon the consumption of a huge amount of grain (about a bushel a day), and therefore upon the availability of cheap petroleum? What if she is too valuable (and too delicate) to be allowed outdoors in the rain? What if the proliferation of her kind will again drastically reduce the number of dairy farms and farmers? Or, to use a more obvious example, can we afford a bushel of grain at a cost of five to twenty bushels of topsoil lost to erosion?

"It is good to have Nature working for you," said Henry Besuden, the dean of American Southdown breeders. "She works for a minimum wage." That is true. She works at times for almost nothing, requiring only that we respect her work and give her a chance, as when she maintains—indeed, improves—the fertility and productivity of a pasture by the natural succession of clover and grass or when she improves a clay soil for us by means of the roots of a grass sod. She works for us by preserving health or wholeness, which for all our ingenuity we cannot make. If we fail to respect her health, she deals out her justice by withdrawing her protection against disease—which we *can* make, and do.

To make this continuity between the natural and the human, we have only two sources of instruction: nature herself and our cultural tradition. If we listen only to the apologists for the industrial economy, who respect neither nature nor culture, we get the idea that it is somehow our goodness that makes us so destructive: The air is unfit to breathe, the water is unfit to drink, the soil is washing away, the cities are violent and the countryside neglected, all because we are intelligent, enterprising, industrious, and generous, concerned only to feed the hungry and to "make a better future for our children." Respect for nature causes us to doubt this, and our cultural tradition confirms and illuminates our doubt: No good thing is destroyed by goodness; good things are destroyed by wickedness. We may identify that insight as Biblical, but it is taken for granted by both the Greek and the Biblical lineages of our culture, from Homer and Moses to William Blake. Since the start of the industrial revolution, there have been voices urging that this inheritance may be safely replaced by intelligence, information, energy, and money. No idea, I believe, could be more dangerous.

Feminism and the Mastery of Nature

VAL PLUMWOOD*

Val Plumwood (1939–2008) was an Australian ecofeminist philosopher deeply critical of the "androcentric," or male-centered, viewpoint she identified at the heart of what she called the "standpoint of mastery." Plumwood argues in this essay that such a view is built on a false dichotomy that strictly separates reason (associated with males) from non-reason or feeling (associated with females). By extension, this distinction also splits culture (seen as the sole creation of men) from nature (seen as the province of women; hence, "Mother Nature"). Because this is so, Plumwood and other ecofeminists argue, men have seen the natural world like the world of women, as ripe for plunder, subordination, and exploitation. However, unlike some ecofeminists, Plumwood was wary of simply appropriating those terms like "empathy" and "nurturing" that are conventionally associated with "Mother Earth," or the Greek goddess Gaia. She believed it a mistake to see only "good" phenomena at work in the natural world or to associate them exclusively with women while rejecting rationality as solely male and a "bad" trait underpinning universal patriarchy, or rule by men. To the contrary, Plumwood rejected such "essentialist" notions (or the idea of male and female "essences") as well as the belief that patriarchy is a universal phenomenon. Rather, she argues that the real problem is a particular Western view of "anthropocentrism" (or human centeredness) based on a partial or one-sided view of "rationality" that defines concepts like "progress" and "civilization" in a too-narrow fashion that rules out other ways of life, while simultaneously wreaking ecological devastation.

---

* *Source*: Val Plumwood, *Feminism and the Mastery of Nature* (New York: Routledge, 2003 [1993]), pp. 7–14. Reprinted by permission.

THE VISION OF ECOLOGICAL FEMINISM: PROBLEMS AND QUESTIONS

The story of a land where women live at peace with themselves and with the natural world is a recurrent theme of feminist utopias. This is a land where there is no hierarchy, among humans or between humans and animals, where people care for one another and for nature, where the earth and the forest retain their mystery, power and wholeness, where the power of technology and of military and economic force does not rule the earth, or at least that part of it controlled by women. For usually this state is seen as a beleaguered one, surviving against the hostile intent of men, who control a world of power and inequality, of military and technological might and screaming poverty, where power is the game and power means domination of both nature and people. Feminist vision often draws the contrasts starkly—it is life versus death, [the earth goddess] Gaia versus Mars [the god of war], mysterious forest versus technological desert, women versus men.

It is hard to deny the power of that vision, or its ability to harness the hope and the sorrow the present world holds for those who can bear to confront its current course. We do live in a world increasingly and distressingly like the feminist dystopias, where technological mastery extinguishes both nature and less technologically 'rational' cultures, where we face the imminent prospect of loss of the world's forests along with the bulk of its species diversity and human cultural diversity, where already many cultures have had the whole basis of ancient survival patterns destroyed by a species of development and 'progress' which produces inequality as inexorably as it produces pollution and waste, and where the dominance of 'rational' man threatens ultimately to produce the most irrational of results, the extinction of our species along with many others. Ecological feminism tells us that it is no accident that this world is dominated by men.

If we are women, we have as a group an interest in escaping our ancient domination. We women also have an interest, which we share with all other living creatures, and among them with men, in a sound and healthy planet, in sound, healthy and balanced ecosystems and in a sustainable and satisfying way of living on the earth. But according to ecological feminism [ecofeminism] there is more to it than that, and more to the connection of the movements than this accidental one, of women who happen to be green. Gender is at least a major part of the problem, and there is a way of relating to the other that is especially associated with women, which contains the seeds of a different human relationship to the earth and perhaps too of human survival on it and with it.

But as it is often stated the ecofeminist vision, so sane and so attractive, seems to raise many problems and questions. Is ecofeminism giving us a version of the story that the goodness of women will save us? Is it only women (and perhaps only certain properly womanly women) who can know the mysterious forest, or is that knowledge, and that love, in principle, accessible to us all? Do we have to renounce the achievements of culture and technology to come to inhabit the enchanted forest? Can we affirm women's special qualities without endorsing their traditional role and confinement to a 'woman's sphere'? Can a reign of women possibly be the answer to the earth's destruction and to all the other related problems? Is ecofeminism giving us another version of the story that all problems will cease when the powerless take over power? Is ecofeminism inevitably based in gynocentric essentialism?

I come from a background in both environmental philosophy and activism, and feminist philosophy and activism, yet my initial reaction to the position asserting such a link, like that of many people, was one of mistrust. It seemed to combine a romantic conception of both women and nature, the idea that women have special powers and capacities of nurturance, empathy and 'closeness to nature', which are unsharable by men and which justify their special treatment, which of course nearly always turns out to be inferior treatment. It seemed to be the antithesis of feminism, giving positive value to the 'barefoot and pregnant' image of women and validating their exclusion from the world of culture and relegation to that of nature, a position which is perhaps best represented in modern times by the masculinist writer D. H. Lawrence. It appeared to provide a green version of the 'good woman' argument of the suffragettes, in which good and moral women, who are nurturant, empathic and life-orientated, confront and reclaim the world from bad men, who are immersed in power, hierarchy and a culture of death. Later reading showed me the diversity of the position and that, while an element of this is present in some accounts, by no means all of them conform to this romantic picture, nor is it a necessary part of a position which takes seriously the idea of a non-accidental connection between the liberation movements.

One essential feature of all ecological feminist positions is that they give positive value to a connection of women with nature which was previously, in the west, given negative cultural value and which was the main ground of women's devaluation and oppression. Ecological feminists are involved in a great cultural revaluation of the status of women, the feminine and the natural, a revaluation which must recognize the way in which their historical connection in western culture has influenced the construction of feminine identity and, as I shall try to show, of both masculine and human identity. Beyond that there is a great deal of diversity; ecological feminists differ on how and even whether women are connected to nature, on whether such connection is in principle sharable by men, on how to treat the exclusion of women from culture, and on how the revaluing of the connection with nature connects with the revaluing of traditional feminine characteristics generally, to mention a few areas. There is enormous variation in ecological feminist literature on all these areas.[1]

Like any other diverse position, ecological feminism is amenable to careful and less careful statements, and some versions of ecofeminism do provide a version of the argument that it is the goodness of women which will save us. This is an argument, with its Christian overtones of fall and feminine redemption, which appeared in Victorian times as the view that women's moral goodness, their purity, patience, self-sacrifice, spirituality and maternal instinct, meant either that they would redeem fallen political life (if given the vote), or, on the alternate version, that they were too good for fallen political life and so should not have the vote. The first version ignores the way in which these sterling qualities are formed by powerlessness and will fail to survive translation to a context of power; the second covertly acknowledges this, but insists that in order to maintain these qualities for the benefit of men, women must remain powerless.

A popular contemporary green version attributes to women a range of different but related virtues, those of empathy, nurturance, cooperativeness and connectedness to others and to nature, and usually finds the basis for these also in women's reproductive capacity. It replaces the 'angel in the house' version of women by the 'angel in the ecosystem' version. The myth of this angel is, like the Victorian version, of dubious value for women; unlike the more usual misogynist accounts which western culture provides of women, it recognizes strengths in women's way of being, but it does so in an unsatisfactory and unrealistic way, and again fails to recognize the dynamic of power.

Simplistic versions of this story attribute these qualities to women directly and universally. But it is only plausible to do this if one practices a denial of the reality of women's lives, and not least a denial of the divisions between women themselves, both within the women's movement and in the wider society. Not all women are empathic, nurturant and co-operative. And while many of these virtues have been real, they have been restricted to a small circle of close others. Women do not necessarily treat other women as sisters or the earth as a mother; women are capable of conflict, of domination and even, in the right circumstances, of violence. Western women may not have been in the forefront of the attack on nature, driving the bulldozers and operating the chainsaws, but many of them have been support troops, or have been participants, often unwitting but still enthusiastic, in a modern consumer culture of which they are the main symbols, and which assaults nature in myriad direct and indirect ways daily. And of course women have also played a major role, largely unacknowledged, in a male-led and male dominated environment movement, in resisting and organizing against the assault on nature. The invisible, undervalued alternative economy which has for so long framed their identity is less strongly based on disregard for the earth than the masculine-centered official economy of the developed world. As we shall see, the western mapping of a gender hierarchy on to the nature/culture distinction has been a major culprit in the destruction of the biosphere. But if we think that the fact of being female guarantees that we are automatically provided with an ecological consciousness and can do no wrong to nature or to one another, we are going to be badly disappointed.

The 'angel in the ecosystem' is a simplistic version of the affirmation of feminine qualities, both individual and cultural, which has been such a marked feature of this century's second wave of feminism, especially that which has stressed difference. The link is not nearly as simple as the 'angel' version of women's character takes it to be—in fact the 'angel' argument involves a classic sex/gender confusion, since to say that there are connections, for instance, between phallocentrism and anthropocentrism, is not to say anything at all about women in general being 'close to nature'. Nevertheless, there is an important point in the linkage of women to many of these qualities which our culture needs now to affirm, and a vitally important critique in the addition of the critical dimension of gender to the story of human, and especially western, relations to nature. Clarifying and refining what it is that is liberatory and defensible about this affirmation of the feminine, and clarifying just how these qualities are connected to women, has been the major task of the search for a feminist identity and for feminist theory and scholarship in the last twenty years, and this task continues to challenge our political and philosophical understandings and frontiers.

The need to clarify and refine the statement and meaning of this affirmation for the case of ecological feminism is one of the major themes in the next two chapters. An ecological feminist analysis of these problems may help in turn to advance our understanding of some of these questions, which have been difficult and often divisive for feminist theory. Clarification and development of an ecofeminist position in a way that is both strategically useful (for the social movements involved) and theoretically rigorous is one of the central intellectual endeavors of our time. Ecological feminism is essentially a response to a set of key problems thrown up by the two great social currents of the later part of this century—feminism and the environment movement—and addresses a number of shared problems. There is the problem of how to reintegrate nature and culture across the great western division between them and of how to give a positive value to what has been traditionally devalued and excluded as nature without simply reversing values and rejecting the sphere of culture. There is the problem of how (and whether) to try to reconcile the movements and their associated theoretical critiques (of phallocentrism and anthropocentrism), which have many areas of conflict as well as some common ground. These are central problems for the theories, strategies and alliances of both movements.

GREEN CRITIQUES AND CULTURAL UNIVERSALISM

There is also the need to rid both critiques of the arrogant ethnocentrism which has been such a marked feature of western worldviews. Accounts of a generalized 'patriarchy' as the villain behind the ecological crisis implicitly assume that western culture is human culture. But the gendered character of nature/culture dualism, and of the whole web of other dualisms interconnected with it, is not a feature of human thought or culture per se, and does not relate the universal man to the universal woman; it is specifically a feature of western thought. It is important that a critical ecological feminist analysis recognizes this, and some have failed to do so clearly. Women in certain New Guinea cultures, for example, are seen as aligned with the domestic or cultivated sphere, men with the forest and with wild land (McCormack and Strathern 1980). We cannot therefore see the alignment of women to nature as the entire basis and source of women's oppression, as some accounts have done, since women often stand in relatively powerless positions even in cultures which have not made the connection of women to nature or which have a different set of genderized dichotomies. Nevertheless the association of women with nature and men with culture or reason can still be seen as providing much of the basis of the cultural elaboration of women's oppression in the west, of the particular form that it takes in the western context, and that is still of considerable explanatory value. Once cultural universalism is rejected, we can draw on these features to explain much that is especially western in our ways of relating to each other and to nature. That is how I have tried to use them here.

The concepts of humanity and nature have been used in a similarly universalized fashion in the critique of anthropocentrism. Critics have rightly complained that the use of the blanket category 'human' obscures highly relevant cultural and other differences between human groups, and differences in responsibility for and benefits from the exploitation of nature (Bookchin 1988; 1989).[2] The Penan who defend the forest at the risk of their lives are not to be held responsible, as 'humans', for its destruction in the way that the agents of westernized development are. A universalized concept of 'humanity' can be used also to deflect political critique and to obscure the fact that the forces directing the destruction of nature and the wealth produced from it are owned and controlled overwhelmingly by an unaccountable, mainly white, mainly male elite. This criticism applies to those ways of developing the critique which hold that it is simply humanity as a species which is the problem and which use the blanket concept 'human' to cover over vitally important social, political and gender-based analyses of the problem. These problematic formulations of the critique of anthropocentrism tend to assume some sort of underlying species selfishness, perhaps as part of 'human nature', and to focus on a general reduction in human numbers as the solution.

But this approach should not be confused with the critique of the way human identity has been treated in particular influential cultures such as western culture. According to the way of understanding the critique developed here, it is the development in certain cultures, especially and originally western culture, of a particular concept and practice of human identity and relationship to nature which is the problem, not the state of being human as such. The difference might be compared to the difference between ways of understanding patriarchal domination which see males (biology) as the problem, and accounts of the problem in terms of particular understandings and practices of masculine identity in particular social and cultural contexts (gender). There has been much confusion on this point, which has led to charges that critiques which question human domination are 'anti-human', treat being human as a disease; and so on (Bookchin 1988). The critique of human domination must be part of the familiar and healthy practice of self-critical reflection, not an acultural and ahistorical expression of self-hatred and collective human-species guilt.

Similarly, although the critique must involve some recognition of the human species as a whole as more limited in its claims on the earth and in its relation to other species, this does not translate into any simple claim about the need for blanket reductions in human numbers, or into the view that different human groupings have equal responsibility for and benefit equally from the destruction of nature. The human colonization of the earth is human-centred in the competitive, chauvinistic sense that it benefits certain humans in the short term (although not in evolutionary terms) at the expense of other species. But it is not human-centered in any good sense, since not all humans share in or benefit from this process or from its ideology of rational imperialism. Indeed as in the case of other empires, many humans—including women as well as those identified as less fully human— are the victims of its rational hierarchy, just as many humans are the victims rather than the beneficiaries of the assault on nature.

Thus understood, the critique of human domination is in no way incompatible with older critiques which reject human hierarchy. In fact it complements and makes more complete our understanding of this hierarchy. But just as the exploitation of women cannot be justified by more equal parceling out of the spoils between males in the way the pre-feminist critiques invoking equality and fraternity assumed, so the destruction of nature cannot be justified by a more equal distribution of the results among human groups, as the pre-ecological critiques often suggested.

Human domination of nature wears a garment cut from the same cloth as intra-human domination, but one which, like each of the others, has a specific form and shape of its own. Human relations to nature are not only ethical, but also political.

ECOLOGICAL FEMINISM AND GREEN THEORY

What might loosely be called 'green theory' includes several sub-critiques and positions whose relationship has recently been the subject of vigorous and often bitter debate, and which have some common ground but apparently a number of major divergences.[3] The debate seems to have revealed that the green movement still lacks a coherent liberatory theory, and raises the question of whether it is and must remain no more than a political alliance of convenience between different interest groups affected differently by the assault on nature.

Yet such a perspective connecting human and non-human forms of domination does seem both possible and essential to do justice to the concerns which the movement has articulated in the last two decades. Key aspects of environmental critiques are centered on the way that control over and exploitation of nature contributes to, or is even more strongly linked to, control over and exploitation of human beings. As numerous studies have shown, high technology agriculture and forestry in the third world which are ecologically insensitive also strengthen the control of elites and social inequality, increasing, for example, men's control over the economy at the expense of women, and they do these things not just as a matter of accident. People suffer because the environment is damaged, and also from the process which damages it, because the process has disregard for needs other than those of an elite built into it. We die of the product (the destruction of nature) and also of the process (technological brutality alias technological rationality serving the end of commodification). As the free water we drink from common streams, and the free air we breathe in common, become increasingly unfit to sustain life, the biospheric means for a healthy life will increasingly be privatized and become the privilege of those who can afford to pay for them. The losers will be (and in many places already are) those, human and non-human, without market power, and environmental issues and issues of justice must increasingly converge.

It seems that unless we are to treat these two sorts of domination as in only temporary and accidental alliance (which would abandon the most important insights of the green movement), an adequate green philosophy will have to cater for both sorts of concerns, those concerned with human social systems and those concerned with nature, and give an important place to their connection and accommodation. What is at stake in the internal debate on this issue of political ecology (which has involved social ecology, deep ecology and ecofeminism) is also the question of liberatory coherence and of the relationship between the radical movements and critiques of oppression each of these internal green positions is aligned with. The quest for coherence is not the demand that each form of oppression submerges its hard-won identity in a single, amorphous, oceanic movement. Rather it asks that each form of oppression develop sensitivity to other forms, both at the level of practice and that of theory.[4]

NOTES

1 To consider just one area of diversity: those versions of ecological feminism (mostly characteristic of the 1970s and the first half of the 1980s) close to cultural feminism often take women's oppression to be the key form of oppression which explains all others. For these positions, as Charlene Spretnak writes, 'identifying the dynamics— largely fear and resentment— behind the dominance of male over female is the key to comprehending every expression of patriarchal culture with its hierarchical, militaristic, mechanistic, industrialist forms' (Spretnak 1990). Social ecological feminists join black feminists in seeing women's oppression as one among a number of forms of oppression (hooks 1981; 1984; 1989; Combahee 1978). Social ecological feminism draws especially on black and anti-colonial feminism and socialist feminism (Ruether 1975; Haraway 1989; 1991; Hartsock 1985; Mies 1986; Warren 1987; 1990; King 1989; 1990; Shiva 1989; 1992; Spelman 1988). But unlike those forms which are concerned exclusively with race, class and gender (Wajcman 1991; Walby 1992), it integrates a concern with nature into its investigation of multiple grounds of exploitation and shows how all these types of exploitation mutually determine and support one another. Karen Warren writes that such a feminism 'would build on these insights [of socialist and black feminism] to develop a more expansive and complete feminism, one which ties the liberation of women to the liberation of all systems of oppression' (1987:133). Such a feminism can aim to use understandings and insights from feminist thought to enrich understandings of the destruction of nature, without attempting to reduce one to the other. This form of ecological feminism is not committed to the thesis that women's struggle is identical with the struggle for nature, or that fixing one problem would automatically fix the other, which is a causal fallacy for most linked phenomena. See Plumwood (1991a).

2 Murray Bookchin writes of deep ecology: '"Humanity" surfaces in a vague and unearthly form to embrace everyone in a realm of universal guilt ... we ... lose sight of the social and of the differences that fragment "Humanity" into a host of human beings—men, women, ethnic groups, oppressors and oppressed' (1988:6A).

3 On the ecopolitics debate between social ecology, ecofeminism and deep ecology see especially Biehl (1987; 1988; 1991); Bookchin (1988; 1989; 1991); Bradford (1989); Chase (1991); Cheney (1987); Eckersley (1989); Fox (1989); Plumwood (1991a). A useful contribution is Tokar (1989).

4 Many postmodernist writers on the topic of movement connection object strenuously to absorption or 'totalization', but are unable to envisage interaction in any more positive terms than mutual disruption, disintegration, or destabilization (Quinby 1990). This is indeed 'a philosophical insurance policy' (Brennan 1991b) against effective opposition to the master.

Whose Earth Is It, Anyway?

JAMES H. CONE*

James H. Cone (1938–), a leading theorist of Black Liberation Theology (BLT), is currently the Charles A. Briggs Distinguished Professor of Systematic Theology at Union Theological Seminary and an ordained minister in the African Methodist Episcopal Church. He is also the author of many books, including *Black Theology and Black Power* (1997). In the following essay, Dr. Cone makes a case for black liberationists allying themselves with (mostly white) environmentalists to fight for social and environmental justice. According to Cone, social justice and environmental justice are two sides of the same coin. And that is because people of color are disproportionately exposed to environmental hazards from pollution, the siting of toxic waste dumps, and dangerous chemicals. Like Martin Luther King, Jr., and Malcolm X, Dr. Cone contends that achieving social justice requires the exercise of political power, and that black liberationists and environmentalists should not shy away from acquiring and using such power.

* *Source*: James H. Cone, "Whose Earth Is It, Anyway?" in Cone, *Risks of Faith: The Emergence of a Black Theology of Liberation, 1968–1998* (Boston: Beacon Press, 1999), pp. 138–145. Reprinted by permission of the author.

WHOSE EARTH IS IT, ANYWAY?

Connecting racism with the degradation of the earth is a necessity for the African American community.

> The earth is the Lord's and all that is in it,
> The world, and those who live in it.
>
> —Psalm 24:1 (NRSV)

> We say the earth is our mother —
> we cannot own her; she owns us.[1]
>
> —Pacific peoples

The logic that led to slavery and segregation in the Americas, colonization and Apartheid in Africa, and the rule of white supremacy throughout the world is the same one that leads to the exploitation of animals and the ravaging of nature. It is a mechanistic and instrumental logic that defines everything and everybody in terms of their contribution to the development and defense of white world supremacy. People who fight against white racism but fail to connect it to the degradation of the earth are anti-ecological—whether they know it or not. People who struggle against environmental degradation but do not incorporate in it a disciplined and sustained fight against white supremacy are racists whether they acknowledge it or not. The fight for justice cannot be segregated but must be integrated with the fight for life in all its forms.

Until recently, the ecological crisis has not been a major theme in the liberation movements in the African American community. "Blacks don't care about the environment" is a typical comment by white ecologists. Racial and economic justice has been at best only a marginal concern in the mainstream environmental movement. "White people care more about the endangered whale and the spotted owl than they do about the survival of young blacks in our nation's cities" is a well-founded belief in the African American community. Justice fighters for blacks and the defenders of the earth have tended to ignore each other in their public discourse and practice. Their separation from each other is unfortunate because they are fighting the same enemy—human beings' domination of each other and nature.

The leaders in the mainstream environmental movement are mostly middle- and upper-class whites who are unprepared culturally and intellectually to dialogue with angry blacks. The leaders in the African American community are leery of talking about anything with whites that will distract from the menacing reality of racism. What both groups fail to realize is how much they need each other in the struggle for "justice, peace and the integrity of creation."[2]

In this essay, I want to challenge the black freedom movement to take a critical look at itself through the lens of the ecological movement and also challenge the ecological movement to critique itself through a radical and ongoing engagement of racism in American history and culture. Hopefully, we can break the silence and promote genuine solidarity between the two groups and thereby enhance the quality of life for the whole inhabited earth—humankind and otherkind.

Expanding the Race Critique

No threat has been more deadly and persistent for black and Indigenous peoples than the rule of white supremacy in the modern world. For over five hundred years, through the wedding of science and technology, white people have been exploiting nature and killing people of color in every nook and cranny of the planet in the name of God and democracy. According to the English historian Basil Davidson, the Atlantic slave trade "cost Africa fifty million souls."[3] Author Eduardo Galeano claims that 150 years of Spanish and Portuguese colonization in Central and South America reduced the Indigenous population from 90 million to 3.5 million.[4] During the twenty-three-year reign of terror of King Leopold II of Belgium in the Congo (1885–1908), scholarly estimates suggest that approximately 10 million Congolese met unnatural deaths—"fully half the territory's population."[5] The tentacles of white supremacy have stretched around the globe. No people of color have been able to escape its cultural, political and economic domination.

Blacks in the U.S. have been the most visible and articulate opponents of white racism. From Frederick Douglas and Sojourner Truth to Martin Luther King, Jr., Malcolm X, and Fannie Lou Hamer, African Americans have waged a persistent fight against white racism in all its overt and covert manifestations. White racism denied the humanity of black people, with even theologians debating whether blacks had souls. Some said blacks were subhuman "beasts."[6] Other more progressive theologians, like Union Seminary's Reinhold Niebuhr, hoped that the inferiority of the Negro was not "biological" but was due instead to "cultural backwardness," which could gradually with education be overcome.[7]

Enslaved for 244 years, lynched and segregated another 100, blacks, with militant words and action, fought back in every way they could—defending their humanity against all who had the nerve to question it. Malcolm X, perhaps the most fierce and uncompromising public defender of black humanity, expressed the raw feelings of most blacks: "We declare our right on this earth … to be a human being, to be respected as a human being, to be given the rights of a human being in this society, on this earth, in this day, which we intend to bring into existence by any means necessary."[8]

Whites bristled when they heard Malcolm talk like that. They not only knew Malcolm meant what he said but feared that most blacks agreed with him—though they seldom said so publicly. Whites also knew that if they were black, they too would say a resounding "amen!" to Malcolm's blunt truth. "If you want to know what I'll do," Malcolm told whites, "figure out what you'll do."[9]

White theologians thanked God for being "truly longsuffering, 'slow to anger and plenteous in mercy' (Ps. 103:8)," as Reinhold Niebuhr put it, quoting the Hebrew Scriptures. Niebuhr knew that white people did not have a leg to stand on before the bar of God's justice regarding their treatment of people of color. "If," Niebuhr wrote, "the white man were to expiate his sins committed against the darker races, few would have the right to live."[10]

Black liberation theology is a product of a fighting spirituality derived from nearly four hundred years of black resistance. As one who encountered racism first as a child in Bearden, Arkansas, no day in my life has passed in which I did not have to deal with the open and hidden violence of white supremacy. Whether in the society or the churches, at Adrian College or Union Seminary, racism was always there—often smiling and sometimes angry. Since writing my first essay on racism in the white church and its theology thirty years ago, I decided that I would never be silent about white supremacy and would oppose it with my whole being.

While white racism must be opposed at all cost, our opposition will not be effective unless we expand our vision. Racism is profoundly interrelated with other evils, including the degradation of the earth. It is important for black people, therefore, to make the connection between the struggle against racism and other struggles for life. A few black leaders recognized this need and joined the nineteenth century abolitionist movement with the Suffragist movement and the 1960s civil rights movement with the second wave of the women's movement. Similar links were made with the justice struggles of other U.S. minorities, gay rights struggles, and poor peoples' fight for freedom around the world. Martin Luther King, Jr.'s idea of the "beloved community" is a potent symbol for people struggling to build one world community where life in all its forms is respected. "All life is interrelated," King said. "Whatever affects one directly affects all indirectly ... There is an interrelated structure of reality."

Connecting racism with the degradation of the earth is a much-needed work in the African American community, especially in black liberation theology and the black churches. Womanist theologians have already begun this important intellectual work. Delores Williams explores a "parallel between defilement of black women's bodies" and the exploitation of nature. Emilie Townes views "toxic waste landfills in African American communities" as "contemporary versions of lynching a whole people." Karen Baker-Fletcher, using prose and poetry, appropriates the biblical and literary metaphors of dust and spirit to speak about the embodiment of God in creation. "Our task," she writes, "is to grow large hearts, large minds, reconnecting with earth, Spirit, and one another. Black religion must grow ever deeper in the heart."[11]

The leadership of African American churches turned its much-needed attention toward ecological issues in the early 1990s. The catalyst, as usual in the African American community, was a group of black churchwomen in Warren County, North Carolina, who in 1982 lay their bodies down on a road before dump trucks carrying soil contaminated with highly toxic PCBs (polychlorinated biphenyl) to block their progress. In two weeks, more than four hundred protesters were arrested, "the first time anyone in the United States had been jailed trying to halt a toxic waste landfill."[12] Although local residents were not successful in stopping the landfill construction, that incident sparked the attention of civil rights and black church leaders and initiated the national environmental justice movement. In 1987 the United Church of Christ Commission of Racial Justice issued its groundbreaking "Report on Race and Toxic Wastes in the United States." This study found that "among a variety of indicators race was the best predictor of the location of hazardous waste facilities in the U.S."[13] Forty percent of the nation's commercial hazardous waste landfill capacity was in three predominately African American and Hispanic communities. The largest landfill in the nation is found in Sumter County, Alabama, where nearly 70 percent of its seventeen thousand residents are black and 96 percent are poor.

In October 1991 the First National People of Color Environmental Leadership Summit was convened in Washington, D.C. More than 650 grassroots and national leaders from fifty states, the District of Columbia, Mexico, Puerto Rico, and the Marshall Islands participated. They represented more than three hundred environmental groups of color. They all agreed that "If this nation is to achieve environmental justice, the environment in urban ghettoes, barrios, reservations, and rural poverty pockets must be given the same protection as that provided to the suburbs."[14]

The knowledge that people of color are disproportionately affected by environmental pollution angered the black church community and fired up its leadership to take a more active role in fighting against "environmental racism," a phrase that was coined by Benjamin Chavis who was then the Director of the UCC Commission on Racial Justice.[15] Bunyan Bryant, a professor in the School of Natural Resources and Environment at the University of Michigan and a participant in the environmental justice movement, defines environmental racism as "an extension of racism."

It refers to those institutional rules, regulations, and policies or government or corporate decisions that deliberately target certain communities for least desirable land uses, resulting in the disproportionate exposure of toxic and hazardous waste on communities based upon certain prescribed biological characteristics. Environmental racism is the unequal protection against toxic and hazardous waste exposure and the systematic exclusion of people of color from environmental decisions affecting their communities.[16]

The more blacks found out about the racist policies of the government and corporations the more determined they became in their opposition to environmental injustice. In December 1993, under the sponsorship of the National Council of Churches, leaders of mainline black churches held a historic two-day summit meeting on the environment in Washington, D.C. They linked environmental issues with civil rights and economic justice. They did not talk much about the ozone layer, global warming, the endangered whale, or the spotted owl. They focused primarily on the urgent concerns of their communities: toxic and hazardous wastes, lead poisoning, landfills and incinerators. "We have been living next to the train tracks, trash dumps, coal plants and insect-infested swamps for many decades," Bishop Frederick C. James of the A.M.E. Church said. "We in the Black community have been disproportionately affected by toxic dumping, disproportionately affected by lead paint at home, disproportionately affected by dangerous chemicals in the workplace." Black clergy also linked local problems with global issues. "If toxic waste is not safe enough to be dumped in the United States, it is not safe enough to be dumped in Ghana, Liberia, Somalia nor anywhere else in the world," proclaimed Charles G. Adams, pastor of Hartford Memorial Baptist Church in Detroit. "If hazardous materials are not fit to be disposed in the suburbs, they are certainly not fit to be disposed of in the cities."[17]

Like black church leaders, African American politicians also are connecting social justice issues with ecology. According to the League of Conservation Voters, the Congressional Black Caucus has "the best environmental record of any voting bloc in Congress."[18] "Working for clean air, clean water, and a clean planet," declared Rep. John Lewis of Georgia, "is just as important, if not more important, than anything I have ever worked on, including civil rights."[19]

Black and other poor people in all racial groups receive much less than their fair share of everything good in the world and a disproportionate amount of the bad. Middle class and elite white environmentalists have been very effective in implementing the slogan "Not In My Backyard" (NIMBY). As a result, corporations and the government merely turned to the backyards of the poor to deposit their toxic waste. The poor live in the least desirable areas of our cities and rural communities. They work in the most polluted and physically dangerous workplaces. Decent health care hardly exists. With fewer resources to cope with the dire consequences of pollution, the poor bear an unequal burden for technological development while the rich reap most of the benefits. This makes racism and poverty ecological issues. If blacks and other hard-hit communities do not raise these ethical and political problems, they will continue to die a slow and silent death on the planet.

Ecology touches every sphere of human existence. It is not just an elitist or a white middle class issue. A clean safe environment is a human and civil rights issue that impacts the lives of poor blacks and other marginal groups. We therefore must not let the fear of distracting from racism blind us to the urgency of the ecological crisis. What good is it to eliminate racism if we are not around to enjoy a racist free environment?

The survival of the earth, therefore, is a moral issue for everybody. If we do not save the earth from destructive human behavior, no one will survive. That fact alone ought to be enough to inspire people of all colors to join hands in the fight for a just and sustainable planet.

Expanding the Ecological Critique. We are indebted to ecologists in all fields and areas of human endeavor for sounding the alarm about the earth's distress. They have been so effective in raising ecological awareness that few people deny that our planet is in deep trouble. For the first time in history, humankind has the knowledge and power to destroy all life—either with a nuclear bang or a gradual poisoning of the land, air, and sea.

Scientists have warned us of the dire consequences of what human beings are doing to the environment. Theologians and ethicists have raised the moral and religious issues. Grassroots activists in many communities are organizing to stop the killing of nature and its creatures. Politicians are paying attention to people's concern for a clean, safe environment. "It is not so much a question of whether the lion will one day lie down with the lamb," writes Alice Walker, "but whether human beings will ever be able to lie down with any creature or being at all."[20]

What is absent from much of the talk about the environment in First World countries is a truly radical critique of the culture most responsible for the ecological crisis. This is especially true among white ethicists and theologians in the U.S. In most of the essays and books I have read, there is hardly a hint that perhaps whites could learn something of how we got into this ecological mess from those who have been the victims of white world supremacy. White ethicists and theologians sometimes refer to the disproportionate impact of hazardous waste on blacks and other people of color in the U.S. and Third World and even cite an author or two, here and there throughout the development of their discourse on ecology. They often include a token black or Indian in anthologies on ecotheology, ecojustice, and ecofeminism. It is "politically correct" to demonstrate a knowledge of and concern for people of color in progressive theological circles. But people of color are not treated *seriously*, that is, as if they have something *essential* to contribute to the conversation. Environmental justice concerns of poor people of color hardly ever merit serious attention, not to mention organized resistance. How can we create a genuinely mutual ecological dialogue between whites and people of color if one party acts as if they have all the power and knowledge?

Since [the first] Earth Day in 1970, the environmental movement has grown into a formidable force in American society and ecological reflections on the earth have become a dominant voice in religion, influencing all disciplines. It is important to ask, however, whose problems define the priorities of the environmental movement? Whose suffering claims its attention? "Do environmentalists care about poor people?"[21] Environmentalists usually respond something like Rafe Pomerance puts it: "A substantial element of our agenda has related to improving the environment for everybody."[22] Others tell a different story. Former Assistant Secretary of Interior James Joseph says that "environmentalists tend to focus on those issues that provide recreative outlets instead of issues that focus on equity." Black activist Cliff Boxley speaks even more bluntly, labeling the priorities of environmentalists as "green bigotry." "Conservationists are more interested in saving the habitats of birds than in the construction of low-income housing."[23]

Do we have any reason to believe that the culture most responsible for the ecological crisis will also provide the moral and intellectual resources for the earth's liberation? White ethicists and theologians apparently think so, since so much of their discourse about theology and the earth is just talk among themselves. But I have a deep suspicion about the theological and ethical values of white culture and religion. For five hundred years whites have acted as if they owned the world's resources and have forced people of color to accept their scientific and ethical values. People of color have studied dominant theologies and ethics because our physical and spiritual survival partly depended on it. Now that humanity has reached the possibility of extinction, one would think that a critical assessment of how we got to where we are would be the next step for sensitive and caring theologians of the earth. While there is some radical questioning along these lines, it has not been persistent or challenging enough to compel whites to look outside of their dominating culture for ethical and cultural resources for the earth's salvation. One can still earn a doctorate degree in ethics and theology at American seminaries, even at Union Seminary in New York, and not seriously engage racism in this society and the world. If we save the planet and have a society of inequality, we wouldn't have saved much.

According to Audre Lorde, "the master's tools will never dismantle the master's house."[24] They are too narrow and thus assume that people of color have nothing to say about race, gender, sexuality, and the earth—all of which are interconnected. We need theologians and ethicists who are interested in mutual dialogue, honest conversation about justice for the earth and all of its inhabitants. We need whites who are eager to know something about the communities of people of color—our values, hopes, and dreams. Whites know so little about our churches and communities that it is often too frustrating to even talk to them about anything that matters. Dialogue requires respect and knowledge of the other—their history, culture and religion. No one racial or national group has all the answers but all groups have something to contribute to the earth's healing.

Many ecologists speak often of the need for humility and mutual dialogue. They tell us that we are all interrelated and interdependent, including human and otherkind. The earth is not a machine. It is an organism in which all things are a part of each other. "Every entity in the universe," writes Catherine Keller, "can be described as a process of interconnection with every other being."[25] If white ecologists really believe that, why do most still live in segregated communities? Why are their essays and books about the endangered earth so monological—that is, a conversation of a dominant group talking to itself? Why is there so much talk of love, humility, interrelatedness, and interdependence, and yet so little of these values reflected in white people's dealings with people of color?

Blacks and other minorities are often asked why they are not involved in the mainstream ecological movement. To white theologians and ethicists I ask, why are you not involved in the dialogue on race? I am not referring primarily to President Clinton's failed initiative, but to the initiative started by the Civil Rights and Black Power movements and black liberation theology more than forty years ago. How do we account for the conspicuous white silence on racism, not only in the society and world but especially in theology, ethics, and ecology? I have yet to read a white theologian or ethicist who has incorporated a sustained, radical critique of white supremacy in their theological discourse similar to their engagement of Anti-Semitism, class contradictions, and patriarchy.

To be sure, a few concerned white theologians have written about their opposition to white racism but not because race critique was essential to their theological identity. It is usually just a gesture of support for people of color when solidarity across differences is in vogue. As soon as it is not longer socially and intellectually acceptable to talk about race, white theologians revert back to their silence. But as Elie Wiesel said in his Nobel Peace Prize Acceptance Speech, "we must always take sides. Neutrality helps the oppressor, never the victim. Silence encourages the tormentor, never the tormented."[26] Only when white theologians realize that a fight against racism is a fight for their humanity will we be able to create a coalition of blacks, whites and other people of color in the struggle to save the earth.

Today ecology is in vogue and many people are talking about our endangered planet. I want to urge us to deepen our conversation by linking the earth's crisis with the crisis in the human family. If it is important to save the habitats of birds and other species, then it is at least equally important to save black lives in the ghettoes and prisons of America. As Gandhi said, "the earth is sufficient for everyone's need but not for everyone's greed."[27]

NOTES

1   Cited in Samuel Rayan, "The Earth is the Lord's," in *Ecotheology: Voices from South and North,* ed. David G. Hallman (Geneva: WCC Publications, 1994), p. 142.

2   See *Justice, Peace and the Integrity of Creation,* papers and Bible studies ed. James W. van Hoeven for the World Alliance of Reformed Churches Assembly, Seoul, Korea,

August 1989; and Preman Niles, *Resisting the Threats to Life: Covenanting for Justice, Peace and the Integrity of Creation* (Geneva: WCC Publications, 1989).

3   Basil Davidson, *The African Slave Trade: Precolonial History 1450–1850* (Boston: Little, Brown, 1961), p. 80.

4   Eduardo Galeano, *Open Veins of Latin America: Five Centuries of the Pillage of a Continent* (London: Monthly Review Press, 1973), p. 50.

5   See Adam Hochschild, "Hearts of Darkness: Adventures in the Slave Trade," *San Francisco Examiner Magazine*, August 16, 1998, 13. This essay is an excerpt from his book, *King Leopold's Ghosts: A Story of Greed, Terror and Heroism in Colonial Africa* (New York: Houghton Mifflin, 1998). Louis Turner suggests that five to eight million were killed in the Congo. See his *Multinational Companies and the Third World* (New York: Hill and Wang, 1973), p. 27.

6   See Chas. Carroll, *The Negro a Beast* (St. Louis: American Book and Bible House, 1900).

7   See Reinhold Niebuhr, "Justice to the American Negro from State, Community and Church" in his *Pious and Secular America* (New York: Charles Scribner's Sons, 1958), p. 81.

8   Malcolm X, *By Any Means Necessary* (New York: Pathfinder Press, 1970), p. 56.

9   *Malcolm X Speaks,* ed. George Breitman (New York: Grove Press, 1965), pp. 197–98.

10 Reinhold Niebuhr, "The Assurance of Grace" in *The Essential Reinhold Niebuhr: Selected Essays and Addresses,* ed. and introduced by Robert M. Brown (New Haven: Yale University Press, 1986), p. 65.

11 See Delores Williams, "A Womanist Perspective on Sin" in *A Troubling in My Soul: Womanist Perspectives on Evil and Suffering,* ed. Emilie M. Townes (Maryknoll, N.Y.: Orbis, 1993), pp. 145–47; and her "Sin, Nature, and Black Women's Bodies," in *Ecofeminism and the Sacred,* ed. Carol J. Adams (New York: Continuum, 1993), pp. 24–29; Emilie Townes, *In a Blaze of Glory: Womanist Spirituality as Social Witness* (Nashville: Abingdon, 1995), p. 55; and Karen Baker-Fletcher, *Sisters of Dust, Sisters of Spirit: Womanist Wordings on God and Creation* (Minneapolis: Fortress, 1998), p. 93.

12 Robert Bullard, *Dumping in Dixie: Race, Class, and Environmental Quality* (Boulder, Colo.: Westview Press, 1990), p. 31.

13 Cited in Bunyan Bryant and Paul Mohai, eds., *Race and the Incidence of Environmental Hazards: A Time for Discourse* (Boulder, Colo.: Westview Press, 1992), p. 2. See also "African American Denominational Leaders Pledge Their Support to the Struggle against Environmental Racism," *The A.M.E. Christian Recorder*, May 18, 1998, pp. 8, 11.

14 Cited in Robert D. Bullard, ed., *Unequal Protection: Environmental Justice and Communities of Color* (San Francisco: Sierra Club Books, 1994), p. 20.

15 Benjamin Chavis is now known as Benjamin Chavis Muhammad and is currently serving as the National Minister in Louis Farrakhan's Nation of Islam.

16 Bunyan Bryant, "Introduction" in his edited work, *Environmental Justice: Issues, Policies, and Solutions* (Washington, D.C.: Island Press, 1995), p. 5. Benjamin Chavis defined environmental racism as "racial discrimination in environmental policymaking. It is racial discrimination in the enforcement of regulations and laws. It is racial discrimination in the deliberate targeting of communities of color for toxic waste disposal and the siting of polluting industries. It is racial discrimination in the official sanctioning of the life-threatening presence of poisons and pollutants in communities of color. And, it is racial discrimination in the history of excluding people of color from the mainstream environmental groups, decisionmaking boards, commissions, and regulatory bodies" ("Foreword" in Robert Bullard, ed., *Confronting Environmental Racism: Voices from the Grassroots* [Boston: South End Press, 1993], p. 3.)

17 *National Black Church Environmental and Economic Justice Summit*, Washington, D.C., December 1 and 2, 1993, The National Council of Churches of Christ in the U.S.A., Prophetic Justice Unit. This is a booklet with all the speeches of the meeting, including the one by Vice President Gore.

18 See Ronald A. Taylor, "Do Environmentalists Care about Poor People?" *U.S. News and World Report,* April 2, 1984, p. 51.

19 John Lewis's quotation is cited in Deeohn and David Hahn-Baker, "Environmentalists and Environmental Justice Policy" in Bunyan Bryant, ed., *Environmental Justice,* p. 68.

20 Alice Walker, *Living by the Word: Selected Writings 1973–1987* (San Diego: Harcourt Brace Jovanovich, 1988), p. 173.

21 See Ronald A. Taylor, "Do Environmentalists Care about Poor People?"

22 Ibid., p. 51.

23 Ibid.

24 Audre Lorde, *Sister Outsider* (Trumansburg, N.Y.: Crossing Press, 1984), p. 110.

25 Catherine Keller, *From a Broken Web: Separation, Sexism, Self* (Boston: Beacon, 1986), p. 5.

26 See Eli Wiesel, "Nobel Peace Prize Acceptance Speech," December 10, 1986.

27 Cited in Leonado Boff, *Cry of the Earth, Cry of the Poor* (Maryknoll, N.Y.: Orbis, 1997), p. 2.

Laudato Si': On Care for our Common Home

POPE FRANCIS*

Like his predecessors Pope Benedict XVI and John Paul II, Pope Francis is concerned with what some evangelical Christians call "creation care." The following encyclical, or teaching document, is to date the most extensive and systematic statement of Catholic teaching on the natural environment. Here Pope Francis expresses his grave concern about the adverse effects of climate change on the earth's ecosystems and on human beings, particularly poor people residing in the Third World. Addressing and attempting to mitigate these adverse effects is not only a scientific issue, Francis contends, but a *moral* matter.

---

* *Source*: *Laudato si': On Care for our Common Home* (The Vatican, 2015). Available at http://w2.vatican.va/content/francesco/en/encyclicals/documents/papa-francesco_20150524_enciclica-laudato-si.html. © Libreria Editrice Vaticana. Reprinted by permission.

LAUDATO SI': ON CARE FOR OUR COMMON HOME

1. *"LAUDATO SI', mi' Signore"* – *"Praise be to you, my Lord"*. In the words of this beautiful canticle, Saint Francis of Assisi reminds us that our common home is like a sister with whom we share our life and a beautiful mother who opens her arms to embrace us. "Praise be to you, my Lord, through our Sister, Mother Earth, who sustains and governs us, and who produces various fruit with colored flowers and herbs".[1] …

MY APPEAL

13. The urgent challenge to protect our common home includes a concern to bring the whole human family together to seek a sustainable and integral development, for we know that things can change. The Creator does not abandon us; he never forsakes his loving plan or repents of having created us. Humanity still has the ability to work together in building our common home. Here I want to recognize, encourage and thank all those striving in countless ways to guarantee the protection of the home which we share. Particular appreciation is owed to those who tirelessly seek to resolve the tragic effects of environmental degradation on the lives of the world's poorest. Young people demand change. They wonder how anyone can claim to be building a better future without thinking of the environmental crisis and the sufferings of the excluded.

14. I urgently appeal, then, for a new dialogue about how we are shaping the future of our planet. We need a conversation which includes everyone, since the environmental challenge we are undergoing, and its human roots, concern and affect us all. The worldwide ecological movement has already made considerable progress and led to the establishment of numerous organizations committed to raising awareness of these challenges. Regrettably, many efforts to seek concrete solutions to the environmental crisis have proved ineffective, not only because of powerful opposition but also because of a more general lack of interest. Obstructionist attitudes, even on the part of believers, can range from denial of the problem to indifference, nonchalant resignation or blind confidence in technical solutions. We require a new and universal solidarity. As the bishops of Southern Africa have stated: "Everyone's talents and involvement are needed to redress the damage caused by human abuse of God's creation".[2] All of us can cooperate as instruments of God for the care of creation, each according to his or her own culture, experience, involvements and talents …

V. GLOBAL INEQUALITY

48. The human environment and the natural environment deteriorate together; we cannot adequately combat environmental degradation unless we attend to causes related to human and social degradation. In fact, the deterioration of the environment and of society affects the most vulnerable people on the planet: "Both everyday experience and scientific research show that the gravest effects of all attacks on the environment are suffered by the poorest".[3] For example, the depletion of fishing reserves especially hurts small fishing communities without

the means to replace those resources; water pollution particularly affects the poor who cannot buy bottled water; and rises in the sea level mainly affect impoverished coastal populations who have nowhere else to go. The impact of present imbalances is also seen in the premature death of many of the poor, in conflicts sparked by the shortage of resources, and in any number of other problems which are insufficiently represented on global agendas.[4]

49. It needs to be said that, generally speaking, there is little in the way of clear awareness of problems which especially affect the excluded. Yet they are the majority of the planet's population, billions of people. These days, they are mentioned in international political and economic discussions, but one often has the impression that their problems are brought up as an afterthought, a question which gets added almost out of duty or in a tangential way, if not treated merely as collateral damage. Indeed, when all is said and done, they frequently remain at the bottom of the pile. This is due partly to the fact that many professionals, opinion makers, communications media and centers of power, being located in affluent urban areas, are far removed from the poor, with little direct contact with their problems. They live and reason from the comfortable position of a high level of development and a quality of life well beyond the reach of the majority of the world's population. This lack of physical contact and encounter, encouraged at times by the disintegration of our cities, can lead to a numbing of conscience and to tendentious analyses which neglect parts of reality. At times this attitude exists side by side with a "green" rhetoric. Today, however, we have to realize that a true ecological approach *always* becomes a social approach; it must integrate questions of justice in debates on the environment, so as to hear *both the cry of the earth and the cry of the poor.*

50. Instead of resolving the problems of the poor and thinking of how the world can be different, some can only propose a reduction in the birth rate. At times, developing countries face forms of international pressure which make economic assistance contingent on certain policies of "reproductive health". Yet "while it is true that an unequal distribution of the population and of available resources creates obstacles to development and a sustainable use of the environment, it must nonetheless be recognized that demographic growth is fully compatible with an integral and shared development".[5] To blame population growth instead of extreme and selective consumerism on the part of some, is one way of refusing to face the issues. It is an attempt to legitimize the present model of distribution, where a minority believes that it has the right to consume in a way which can never be universalized, since the planet could not even contain the waste products of such consumption. Besides, we know that approximately a third of all food produced is discarded, and "whenever food is thrown out it is as if it were stolen from the table of the poor".[6] Still, attention needs to be paid to imbalances in population density, on both national and global levels, since a rise in consumption would lead to complex regional situations, as a result of the interplay between problems linked to environmental pollution, transport, waste treatment, loss of resources and quality of life.

51. Inequity affects not only individuals but entire countries; it compels us to consider an ethics of international relations. A true "ecological debt" exists, particularly between the global north and south, connected to commercial

imbalances with effects on the environment, and the disproportionate use of natural resources by certain countries over long periods of time. The export of raw materials to satisfy markets in the industrialized north has caused harm locally, as for example in mercury pollution in gold mining or sulfur dioxide pollution in copper mining. There is a pressing need to calculate the use of environmental space throughout the world for depositing gas residues which have been accumulating for two centuries and have created a situation which currently affects all the countries of the world. The warming caused by huge consumption on the part of some rich countries has repercussions on the poorest areas of the world, especially Africa, where a rise in temperature, together with drought, has proved devastating for farming. There is also the damage caused by the export of solid waste and toxic liquids to developing countries, and by the pollution produced by companies which operate in less developed countries in ways they could never do at home, in the countries in which they raise their capital: "We note that often the businesses which operate this way are multinationals. They do here what they would never do in developed countries or the so-called first world. Generally, after ceasing their activity and withdrawing, they leave behind great human and environmental liabilities such as unemployment, abandoned towns, the depletion of natural reserves, deforestation, the impoverishment of agriculture and local stock breeding, open pits, riven hills, polluted rivers and a handful of social works which are no longer sustainable".[7]

52. The foreign debt of poor countries has become a way of controlling them, yet this is not the case where ecological debt is concerned. In different ways, developing countries, where the most important reserves of the biosphere are found, continue to fuel the development of richer countries at the cost of their own present and future. The land of the southern poor is rich and mostly unpolluted, yet access to ownership of goods and resources for meeting vital needs is inhibited by a system of commercial relations and ownership which is structurally perverse. The developed countries ought to help pay this debt by significantly limiting their consumption of non-renewable energy and by assisting poorer countries to support policies and programs of sustainable development. The poorest areas and countries are less capable of adopting new models for reducing environmental impact because they lack the wherewithal to develop the necessary processes and to cover their costs. We must continue to be aware that, regarding climate change, there are *differentiated responsibilities*. As the United States bishops have said, greater attention must be given to "the needs of the poor, the weak and the vulnerable, in a debate often dominated by more powerful interests".[8] We need to strengthen the conviction that we are one single human family. There are no frontiers or barriers, political or social, behind which we can hide, still less is there room for the globalization of indifference.

VI. WEAK RESPONSES

53. These situations have caused sister earth, along with all the abandoned of our world, to cry out, pleading that we take another course. Never have we so hurt and mistreated our common home as we have in the last two hundred years. Yet we are called to be instruments of God our Father, so that our planet might be what he desired when he created it and correspond with his plan for peace, beauty and

fullness. The problem is that we still lack the culture needed to confront this crisis. We lack leadership capable of striking out on new paths and meeting the needs of the present with concern for all and without prejudice towards coming generations. The establishment of a legal framework which can set clear boundaries and ensure the protection of ecosystems has become indispensable; otherwise, the new power structures based on the techno-economic paradigm may overwhelm not only our politics but also freedom and justice.

54. It is remarkable how weak international political responses have been. The failure of global summits on the environment make it plain that our politics are subject to technology and finance. There are too many special interests, and economic interests easily end up trumping the common good and manipulating information so that their own plans will not be affected. The *Aparecida Document* urges that "the interests of economic groups which irrationally demolish sources of life should not prevail in dealing with natural resources".[9] The alliance between the economy and technology ends up sidelining anything unrelated to its immediate interests. Consequently the most one can expect is superficial rhetoric, sporadic acts of philanthropy and perfunctory expressions of concern for the environment, whereas any genuine attempt by groups within society to introduce change is viewed as a nuisance based on romantic illusions or an obstacle to be circumvented.

55. Some countries are gradually making significant progress, developing more effective controls and working to combat corruption. People may well have a growing ecological sensitivity but it has not succeeded in changing their harmful habits of consumption which, rather than decreasing, appear to be growing all the more. A simple example is the increasing use and power of air-conditioning. The markets, which immediately benefit from sales, stimulate ever greater demand. An outsider looking at our world would be amazed at such behavior, which at times appears self-destructive.

56. In the meantime, economic powers continue to justify the current global system where priority tends to be given to speculation and the pursuit of financial gain, which fail to take the context into account, let alone the effects on human dignity and the natural environment. Here we see how environmental deterioration and human and ethical degradation are closely linked. Many people will deny doing anything wrong because distractions constantly dull our consciousness of just how limited and finite our world really is. As a result, "whatever is fragile, like the environment, is defenseless before the interests of a deified market, which become the only rule".[10]

57. It is foreseeable that, once certain resources have been depleted, the scene will be set for new wars, albeit under the guise of noble claims. War always does grave harm to the environment and to the cultural riches of peoples, risks which are magnified when one considers nuclear arms and biological weapons. "Despite the international agreements which prohibit chemical, bacteriological and biological warfare, the fact is that laboratory research continues to develop new offensive weapons capable of altering the balance of nature".[11] Politics must pay greater attention to foreseeing new conflicts and addressing the causes which can lead to them. But powerful financial interests prove most resistant to this effort, and political planning tends to lack breadth of vision. What would induce anyone, at

this stage, to hold on to power only to be remembered for their inability to take action when it was urgent and necessary to do so?

58. In some countries, there are positive examples of environmental improvement: rivers, polluted for decades, have been cleaned up; native woodlands have been restored; landscapes have been beautified thanks to environmental renewal projects; beautiful buildings have been erected; advances have been made in the production of non-polluting energy and in the improvement of public transportation. These achievements do not solve global problems, but they do show that men and women are still capable of intervening positively. For all our limitations, gestures of generosity, solidarity and care cannot but well up within us, since we were made for love.

59. At the same time we can note the rise of a false or superficial ecology which bolsters complacency and a cheerful recklessness. As often occurs in periods of deep crisis which require bold decisions, we are tempted to think that what is happening is not entirely clear. Superficially, apart from a few obvious signs of pollution and deterioration, things do not look that serious, and the planet could continue as it is for some time. Such evasiveness serves as a license to carrying on with our present lifestyles and models of production and consumption. This is the way human beings contrive to feed their self-destructive vices: trying not to see them, trying not to acknowledge them, delaying the important decisions and pretending that nothing will happen ...

IV. POLITICS AND ECONOMY IN DIALOGUE FOR HUMAN FULFILMENT

189. Politics must not be subject to the economy, nor should the economy be subject to the dictates of an efficiency-driven paradigm of technocracy. Today, in view of the common good, there is urgent need for politics and economics to enter into a frank dialogue in the service of life, especially human life. Saving banks at any cost, making the public pay the price, foregoing a firm commitment to reviewing and reforming the entire system, only reaffirms the absolute power of a financial system, a power which has no future and will only give rise to new crises after a slow, costly and only apparent recovery. The financial crisis of 2007-08 provided an opportunity to develop a new economy, more attentive to ethical principles, and new ways of regulating speculative financial practices and virtual wealth. But the response to the crisis did not include rethinking the outdated criteria which continue to rule the world. Production is not always rational, and is usually tied to economic variables which assign to products a value that does not necessarily correspond to their real worth. This frequently leads to an overproduction of some commodities, with unnecessary impact on the environment and with negative results on regional economies.[12] The financial bubble also tends to be a productive bubble. The problem of the real economy is not confronted with vigor, yet it is the real economy which makes diversification and improvement in production possible, helps companies to function well, and enables small and medium businesses to develop and create employment.

190. Here too, it should always be kept in mind that "environmental protection cannot be assured solely on the basis of financial calculations of costs and benefits. The environment is one of those goods that cannot be adequately safeguarded or promoted by market forces".[13] Once more, we need to reject a magical conception of the market, which would suggest that problems can be solved simply by an increase in the profits of companies or individuals. Is it realistic to hope that those who are obsessed with maximizing profits will stop to reflect on the environmental damage which they will leave behind for future generations? Where profits alone count, there can be no thinking about the rhythms of nature, its phases of decay and regeneration, or the complexity of ecosystems which may be gravely upset by human intervention. Moreover, biodiversity is considered at most a deposit of economic resources available for exploitation, with no serious thought for the real value of things, their significance for persons and cultures, or the concerns and needs of the poor.

191. Whenever these questions are raised, some react by accusing others of irrationally attempting to stand in the way of progress and human development. But we need to grow in the conviction that a decrease in the pace of production and consumption can at times give rise to another form of progress and development. Efforts to promote a sustainable use of natural resources are not a waste of money, but rather an investment capable of providing other economic benefits in the medium term. If we look at the larger picture, we can see that more diversified and innovative forms of production which impact less on the environment can prove very profitable. It is a matter of openness to different possibilities which do not involve stifling human creativity and its ideals of progress, but rather directing that energy along new channels.

192. For example, a path of productive development, which is more creative and better directed, could correct the present disparity between excessive technological investment in consumption and insufficient investment in resolving urgent problems facing the human family. It could generate intelligent and profitable ways of reusing, revamping and recycling, and it could also improve the energy efficiency of cities. Productive diversification offers the fullest possibilities to human ingenuity to create and innovate, while at the same time protecting the environment and creating more sources of employment. Such creativity would be a worthy expression of our most noble human qualities, for we would be striving intelligently, boldly and responsibly to promote a sustainable and equitable development within the context of a broader concept of quality of life. On the other hand, to find ever new ways of despoiling nature, purely for the sake of new consumer items and quick profit, would be, in human terms, less worthy and creative, and more superficial.

193. In any event, if in some cases sustainable development were to involve new forms of growth, then in other cases, given the insatiable and irresponsible growth produced over many decades, we need also to think of containing growth by setting some reasonable limits and even retracing our steps before it is too late. We know how unsustainable is the behavior of those who constantly consume and destroy, while others are not yet able to live in a way worthy of their human dignity. That is why the time has come to accept decreased growth in some parts of the world, in order to provide resources for other places to experience healthy growth.

Benedict XVI has said that "technologically advanced societies must be prepared to encourage more sober lifestyles, while reducing their energy consumption and improving its efficiency".[14]

194. For new models of progress to arise, there is a need to change "models of global development";[15] this will entail a responsible reflection on "the meaning of the economy and its goals with an eye to correcting its malfunctions and misapplications".[16] It is not enough to balance, in the medium term, the protection of nature with financial gain, or the preservation of the environment with progress. Halfway measures simply delay the inevitable disaster. Put simply, it is a matter of redefining our notion of progress. A technological and economic development which does not leave in its wake a better world and an integrally higher quality of life cannot be considered progress. Frequently, in fact, people's quality of life actually diminishes – by the deterioration of the environment, the low quality of food or the depletion of resources – in the midst of economic growth. In this context, talk of sustainable growth usually becomes a way of distracting attention and offering excuses. It absorbs the language and values of ecology into the categories of finance and technocracy, and the social and environmental responsibility of businesses often gets reduced to a series of marketing and image-enhancing measures.

195. The principle of the maximization of profits, frequently isolated from other considerations, reflects a misunderstanding of the very concept of the economy. As long as production is increased, little concern is given to whether it is at the cost of future resources or the health of the environment; as long as the clearing of a forest increases production, no one calculates the losses entailed in the desertification of the land, the harm done to biodiversity or the increased pollution. In a word, businesses profit by calculating and paying only a fraction of the costs involved. Yet only when "the economic and social costs of using up shared environmental resources are recognized with transparency and fully borne by those who incur them, not by other peoples or future generations",[17] can those actions be considered ethical. An instrumental way of reasoning, which provides a purely static analysis of realities in the service of present needs, is at work whether resources are allocated by the market or by state central planning.

196. What happens with politics? Let us keep in mind the principle of subsidiarity, which grants freedom to develop the capabilities present at every level of society, while also demanding a greater sense of responsibility for the common good from those who wield greater power. Today, it is the case that some economic sectors exercise more power than states themselves. But economics without politics cannot be justified, since this would make it impossible to favor other ways of handling the various aspects of the present crisis. The mindset which leaves no room for sincere concern for the environment is the same mindset which lacks concern for the inclusion of the most vulnerable members of society. For "the current model, with its emphasis on success and self-reliance, does not appear to favour an investment in efforts to help the slow, the weak or the less talented to find opportunities in life".[18]

197. What is needed is a politics which is far-sighted and capable of a new, integral and interdisciplinary approach to handling the different aspects of the crisis. Often, politics itself is responsible for the disrepute in which it is held, on account

of corruption and the failure to enact sound public policies. If in a given region the state does not carry out its responsibilities, some business groups can come forward in the guise of benefactors, wield real power, and consider themselves exempt from certain rules, to the point of tolerating different forms of organized crime, human trafficking, the drug trade and violence, all of which become very difficult to eradicate. If politics shows itself incapable of breaking such a perverse logic, and remains caught up in inconsequential discussions, we will continue to avoid facing the major problems of humanity. A strategy for real change calls for rethinking processes in their entirety, for it is not enough to include a few superficial ecological considerations while failing to question the logic which underlies present-day culture. A healthy politics needs to be able to take up this challenge.

198. Politics and the economy tend to blame each other when it comes to poverty and environmental degradation. It is to be hoped that they can acknowledge their own mistakes and find forms of interaction directed to the common good. While some are concerned only with financial gain, and others with holding on to or increasing their power, what we are left with are conflicts or spurious agreements where the last thing either party is concerned about is caring for the environment and protecting those who are most vulnerable. Here too, we see how true it is that "unity is greater than conflict".[19]

NOTES

1 *Canticle of the Creatures*, in *Francis of Assisi: Early Documents*, vol. 1, New York-London-Manila, 1999, pp. 113–114.
2 Southern African Catholic Bishops' Conference, *Pastoral Statement on the Environmental Crisis* (5 September 1999).
3 Bolivian Bishops' Conference, Pastoral Letter on the Environment and Human Development in Bolivia *El universo, don de Dios para la vida* (23 March 2012), p. 17.
4 Cf. German Bishops' Conference, Commission for Social Issues, *Der Klimawandel: Brennpunkt globaler, intergenerationeller und ökologischer Gerechtigkeit* (September 2006), pp. 28–30.
5 Pontifical Council for Justice and Peace, *Compendium of the Social Doctrine of the Church*, p. 483.
6 *Catechesis* (5 June 2013): Insegnamenti 1/1 (2013), p. 280.
7 Bishops of the Patagonia-Comahue Region (Argentina), *Christmas Message* (December 2009), p. 2.
8 United States Conference of Catholic Bishops, *Global Climate Change: A Plea for Dialogue, Prudence and the Common Good* (15 June 2001).
9 Fifth General Conference of the Latin American and Caribbean Bishops, *Aparecida Document* (29 June 2007), p. 471.
10 Apostolic Exhortation *Evangelii Gaudium* (24 November 2013), 56: AAS 105 (2013), p. 1043.
11 John Paul II, *Message for the 1990 World Day of Peace*, 12: AAS 82 (1990), p. 154.
12 Cf. Mexican Bishops' Conference, Episcopal Commission for Pastoral and Social Concerns, *Jesucristo, vida y esperanza de los indígenas e campesinos* (14 January 2008).
13 Pontifical Council for Justice and Peace, *Compendium of the Social Doctrine of the Church*, p. 470.
14 *Message for the 2010 World Day of Peace*, 9: AAS 102 (2010), p. 46.
15 Ibid.
16 Ibid., 5: p. 43.
17 Benedict XVI, Encyclical Letter *Caritas in Veritate* (29 June 2009), 50: AAS 101 (2009), p. 686.

18 Apostolic Exhortation *Evangelii Gaudium* (24 November 2013), 209: AAS 105 (2013), p. 1107.
19 Ibid., 228: AAS 105 (2013), p. 1113.

PART 10

RADICAL ISLAMISM

In 1993 terrorists tried to destroy the World Trade Center in New York; in 2001, using hijacked airplanes rather than bombs, they succeeded. These and other horrific events—including the 2013 Boston Marathon bombings, the 2015 terrorist attacks in Paris, and shootings in San Bernardino and elsewhere—have awakened people in the Western world to a new threat to their peace and security. This threat takes the form of an ideology that is variously called political Islamism, radical Islamism, Islamic fundamentalism, or—more controversially—Islamofascism. As all of its various names indicate, this new ideology is an outgrowth and an extreme form of the Islamic religion.

Islam takes its name from the Arabic word *islam*, which means "submission." It is not submission in general that Islam requires, however, but submission to Allah, or God. For it is only through submission to God's will that the individual can find peace in this life and paradise in the next. That is the central belief of Muslims, people of the Islamic faith. Muslims are of many different nationalities and inhabit almost every part of the globe, but their numbers are concentrated in North Africa, the Middle and Near East, and Indonesia. Islam has dominated most of this territory virtually since the religion began around 620 CE, when the prophet Mohammed announced in Arabia that he had received a revelation from the angel Gabriel. The report of this and subsequent revelations make up the *Qur'an* (Koran), the holy book of Islam that Muslims take to be the divine word of Allah. Together with Mohammed's own words and deeds (or Sunna), which Muslims are supposed to emulate, the *Qur'an* forms the basis of the Islamic faith—a monotheistic faith, like Judaism and Christianity, that worships one all-knowing, all-powerful, and merciful God.

For Muslims, Islam is more than a religion in the narrower Western sense of the term. It is a complete way of life, with rules governing everything from manners to morals, marriage, diet, dress, prayer, personal finance, and family life. On this much Muslims are agreed. It would be a mistake, however, to view Islam as a unified monolith. Islam is in fact a religion deeply divided within itself—

between Sunnis and Shi'ites, liberal modernizers and conservative traditionalists, tolerant moderates and radical extremists.

In the Middle East and North Africa, Muslims have long felt themselves and their faith threatened by external enemies. Radical Islamism differs from mainstream Islam largely because the radicals see the threat as greater and the danger more imminent. To put the point simply, these threats have come in four waves. The first wave comprised the Christian Crusades (roughly 1100–1300 CE), or military expeditions to retake the Holy Land for Christendom, to convert or kill "infidels" (that is, non-Christians), and, not least, to gain territory and wealth for Europeans. A second threatening wave came with European imperial expansion into North Africa and the Middle East in the nineteenth and early twentieth centuries. France governed much of North Africa, and Britain controlled most of the territory from Egypt through India, including Palestine, Arabia, and Persia (now Iran). The British were also instrumental in paving the way for what many Muslims saw as a third threat: the establishment of the state of Israel in Palestine after World War II. To them, a Jewish state in a predominantly Muslim region was both injury and insult. More recently, a fourth wave of threat has appeared in the form of influential Western ideas—liberalism, secularism, materialism, religious toleration, and sexual equality, for example—that fall under the general heading of "modernity" or "modernism." These "modern" ideas can be deeply disturbing to conservative Muslim sensibilities, especially as they are often communicated through satellite television, the Internet, videotapes, and other media that depict a world in which women are on socially equal terms with men and almost everyone is more concerned with sex and wealth than with God and religion.

Many Muslims also complain that the United States has added military insult to moral injury by using covert operations and military force to topple regimes believed to be unfriendly to American political and business interests. The United States has also supported pro-Western but undemocratic governments headed by hereditary monarchs in Saudi Arabia, Kuwait, and elsewhere. The monarchs have returned the favor by keeping the oil flowing to the United States and other nations. Following the Persian Gulf War of 1991, moreover, Saudi rulers allowed the United States to station troops inside Saudi Arabia, the home of Mecca and Medina, the two most sacred sites in Islam. To many Muslims, including a Saudi named Osama bin Laden, this was tantamount to an American invasion and occupation of Muslim holy lands, and thus a grave threat to Islam itself. Many Muslims have also been alarmed by the United States' strong and long-standing support of Israel, which in their view illegally occupies the land of Palestine and threatens its Arab neighbors.

Besides external threats from the United States and Israel, radical Islamists contend that Muslim countries face internal threats from Middle Eastern regimes that pay lip service to Islam but cooperate with foreign "infidels." This explains the hostility of al-Qaeda and other radical Islamists to the royal family of Saudi Arabia, which in their view rules ruthlessly and corruptly, and which for a time even allowed American bases and troops on the sacred soil of Islam. Before Iraq was invaded by the United States and its allies in 2003, moreover, radical Islamists were at odds with Saddam Hussein, who ruled over a secular state that allowed a measure of religious toleration, sexual equality, the selling of alcohol, and other abominations.

What is to be done in response to this situation, or to the general threat posed to Islam by the West or by modernity? On these points there is much disagreement among Muslims. To the radical Islamist, however, there is a one-word response: *jihad.*

The Islamic faith calls all Muslims to *jihad,* which is the Arabic word for "struggle." To many Muslims—perhaps most of them—this means primarily that they are called to struggle against their own selfish and sinful tendencies. The radical Islamists, by contrast, take *jihad* to be first and foremost an outward struggle against the enemies of Islam; that is to say, against those who espouse any and all ideas that are inimical to or threaten the beliefs of Islam, such as liberalism and secularism. To protect the Islamic religion and way of life is a sacred duty. To that end radical Islamists believe that any means are permissible, including violence. Terrorism is a weapon of the weak against the strong. To moderate Muslims who say that the *Qur'an* forbids suicide and the shedding of innocent blood, radical Islamists say that they are following the *Qur'an* in giving like for like: Israelis have shed the blood of innocent Palestinian women and children; the Palestinian "martyrs" are therefore justified in shedding their own and the blood of supposedly "innocent" Israeli women and children. And, as in Israel, so too elsewhere: Whoever threatens Muslims and their Islamic faith should be opposed by any and all means possible. In a sacred struggle to defend the faith, any and all means are morally permissible. Moreover, *jihad* is to be waged not only against the West—against the United States and its European and Israeli allies—but against corrupt and secular governments or regimes in supposedly Muslim countries.

For their part, moderate or mainstream Muslims reject radical Islamism—and especially its ready recourse to terrorism—as a perversion of the Prophet's teachings in the *Qur'an* and Sunna. These include a prohibition on the killing of innocent noncombatants. Radical Islamism flourishes among a minority of Muslims, however, as it appeals to those who see their world filled with real or imagined threats, of conspiracies and cabals, against Islam and its faithful adherents. It is a response to a real or perceived crisis—the crisis brought about by the clash of West and (Middle) East, of secular modernity and religious tradition. Radical Islamism is thus a *reactionary* ideology, inasmuch as it represents a reaction against perceived threats posed by the pressures of modernization and secularization.

Signposts Along the Road

*SAYYID QUTB**

While there is no single theorist to whom one can point as a source or fountainhead of radical Islamism, there is one especially influential thinker in this movement, Sayyid Qutb (1906–1966), an Egyptian theorist and author of numerous books, including *Islam and Social Justice* (1949), *The Battle Between Islam and Capitalism* (1950), *In the Shade of the Qur'an* (eight volumes, 1952–1982), and most notably, *Signposts Along the Road* (1964). In the following excerpt from *Signposts*, Qutb (pronounced "cootub") contends that Western liberalism and secularism must be resisted by Muslims who are resolute in their faith and prepared to engage in *jihad* (struggle). Qutb is highly critical of Muslims who seek to "modernize" and "reform" Arabic societies—and indeed, Islam itself— by introducing Western and secular ideas of religious toleration, freedom, and justice. That many Muslims find these changes attractive only indicates the pervasive influence of the West, which is mired in *jahiliyya* ("darkness" or "ignorance") and threatens to drag Muslim societies into that darkness. Muslim "modernizers" and "reformers" in the Middle East are attempting nothing less than the importation of the "new *jahiliyya*" into Muslim societies, thereby subverting and corrupting Islam itself. Islam can only be saved by a small band of exceptionally devout Muslims (*jama'a*) who will wage holy war or *jihad* against everything that the West stands for— modernity, capitalism, religious toleration, sexual equality, and the like— and be prepared to give their lives in this sacred cause. Muslims must go on the offensive against the "aggressors" who import these ideas into Muslim society. This is the ideological basis of radical Islamism.

* *Source*: Sayyid Qutb, *Ma'alim fi-tariq* [*Signposts Along the Road*] (Cairo, Egypt: Dar El Shuruk Publishers, 1973), pp. 3–7. Translated expressly for this volume by Lina Benabdallah and used by permission.

INTRODUCTION

Humanity, today, is standing on the edge of an abyss. It is so not because of the pending threat of complete annihilation—since this is a symptom of the disease rather than the disease itself—but because it is devoid of those values which guide human life toward development and progress. This is especially obvious and clearest in the Western world, which has nothing more to offer to humanity in terms of "values." Even worse, it is a world which is unable to satisfy its own conscience and to justify its own existence.

Democracy in the Western world has proven so unsuccessful, to the point of sterility, that it is ironically turning—even if slowly—to Eastern bloc-type economic systems under the umbrella of socialism. However, the Eastern bloc has not fared any better. Its social theories, with Marxism in the lead, have attracted large flocks of followers in both the East and West. But Marxism has been defeated at the level of thought, to the extent that it is now almost exclusively theoretical and its practical merits have been lost. Marxism as a theory failed because it conflicts with human nature and with human needs, and it only prospers in conditions of total despair and destruction, or in societies that have become accustomed to dictatorships for long periods of time. However, even such environments have started to show the weakness of Marxism's material and economic systems, which are at the core of this system's foundation. Russia, for instance, which represents the ultimate example of a communist system, is witnessing a sharp decline in its wealth when it was in surplus during the rule of the Tsars. It, in fact, sells what gold reserves it owns in order to obtain food as a consequence of the failures of collective farming, as well as the failures of a system which clashes with human nature.

Therefore, mankind is in need of a new kind of leadership!

The leadership of Western man is almost at its end, not because Western civilization has become materially poor or because its military or economic might has weakened. Rather, the Western system's supremacy is coming to an end because it does not offer any more life-changing values that allow it to carry a leadership role.

There is a need for a kind of leadership that allows for two kinds of things to occur simultaneously. On the one hand, this new leadership needs to preserve and develop the material status achieved by mankind thanks to European genius and its material creativity. And, on the other hand, there is a need for this leadership to feed humanity with new values, ideals, and a way of life which does not conflict with human nature and with human needs—a new and original as well as a positive and practicable way forward at the same time.

Islam, alone, has the capacity to provide such a path and such values.

The scientific revolution has fulfilled its purpose and come to an end. This purpose came to the fore during the Renaissance in the sixteenth century and reached its peak during the eighteenth and nineteenth centuries but now is bereft of any new life.

Moreover, all ideologies based on nationalism, chauvinism, and regional blocs also served their purposes during these centuries and are now, too, devoid of vital energy. In short, at the end of the day, all traditional man-made individualist as well as collective theories and systems have been doomed to fail.

Islam's significance has come at a critical and crucial time; the turn of Islam and the Islamic nation to take the lead has come—precisely the kind of Islam which does not oppose material invention since it is considered to be a natural human function (at least) and a form of worship of God as well as a purpose of man's creation (at its best).

> And when Your Sustainer said to the angels, I am going to make My representative on earth. (Qur'an 2:30)

> And I have not created jinns [demons] and men except that they worship ME. (2:143)

Therefore the time has come for the Muslim society to fulfill the task as bestowed upon it by God.

> You are the best community raised for the good of mankind. You enjoin what is good and forbid what is wrong, and you believe in God. (3:110)

> Thus We have made you a middle community, so that you be witnesses for mankind as the Messenger is a witness for you. (2:143)

However, Islam can only function within a society, or rather within a nation because people, especially nowadays, do not give credit to abstract doctrines that have not materialized in a concrete living example. Accordingly, one may say that the very "existence" of an Islamic nation has been extinct for several centuries, because this Islamic nation does not refer to the name of a land wherein Islam resides, nor is it a people whose ancestors lived under an Islamic system at some earlier epoch in history. Rather, the Islamic nation is a group of people whose every aspect of life, perceptions, values, systems, regulations, and principles is inspired by and derived from the Islamic way of life. And a nation with such characteristics became extinct ever since governing though sharia law (laws of God) was suspended in favor of other ruling ways.

There is a need to bring back this sort of Muslim nation and revive this original form of community if Islam is to assume its leadership role in guiding mankind.

It is, hence, necessary to revive that Muslim nation and bring it back from under the trash-heap of the traditional man-made theories of several generations, and from under the crushing weight of those false laws and systems which are not even remotely linked to the Islamic way of life and teachings, even though they might claim to be still standing on ground in what is called "the Islamic World"!

I am well aware that there is a huge distance between "the attempt at renaissance" and "the achievement of leadership," because the Muslim nation has gone astray for a long while. Meanwhile, humans have been led by other ideologies, other nations, other perceptions, and other principles for all this time. During this period, European ingenuity has contributed a great deal to science, culture, law, and material production, which in turn led to ever-higher levels of prosperity, creativity, and material comfort. Naturally, giving up on such comfort or on its representatives and inventors is not an easy task, especially when the alternative— the "Islamic World"—is practically devoid of such inventions.

Nevertheless, despite all such considerations, there is a need for an Islamic revival no matter how great the distance between the attempt at revival and actual leadership, because the first step must not be skipped for our goal to be reached. If we are to perform our task carefully and with wisdom, we first ought to understand clearly the nature of the criteria which are the foundation on which the Islamic community can fulfill its obligation as the supreme leader of mankind. This is essential so that we may not commit any blunders at the very first stage of the revival.

This Islamic community today does not have and is not required to present to mankind an extraordinary achievement in material invention that would impose it as world leader from this standpoint. Indeed, the European genius has outperformed and far surpassed it in this race and it is not to be expected—at least not for several centuries—that the Islamic world can compete against the modern/European world and be victorious in doing so.

Therefore, there must be another quality or characteristic of the Muslim community, something that this modern civilization is lacking. This does not mean that we should neglect material innovation, as it is our duty to give it our full attention and try our best at it. However, we do not engage in material creativity as a prerequisite for world leadership, but rather because it is a necessary component of our existence, and also a duty that Islam imposes on us by virtue of elevating men to the position of representing God on Earth. As stated before, under certain conditions, material creativity is considered a form of worship of God and a purpose of man's creation.

Therefore, it is necessary to come up with a different qualifying and competitive capacity for leadership other than material creativity. And this can only be "faith" and a way of life which allows humanity to preserve the benefits of the successes of material genius on the one hand, while fulfilling basic human needs on the same level of excellence as technology has achieved in terms of material comfort. This faith and way of life would then have to materialize in a human society, which is to say in a Muslim society.

The world today is in a state of *Jahiliyya* (ignorance of God's guidance) as regards the sources of modern ways of living. This state of *Jahiliyya* (darkness or ignorance) is not alleviated or made any better by any number of these elevated material comforts and inventions achieved by material genius. This *Jahiliyya* is characterized by an assault on God's authority and on a specific property of the Divine governance on earth. *Jahiliyya* grants sovereignty to man and makes some men rule over others. It is not cast in the primitive, naïve image of that ancient *Jahiliyya,* but one that claims that God's prescribed way of life does not have to dictate or inspire the right of creating values, legislating rules of collective behavior, and choosing any way of life, but that this rests with men only, without God. The consequence of such an assault on God's authority is an assault on His creatures. Therefore we can attribute the humiliation of human beings under communist systems, and the exploitation of individuals as well as nations under the greedy system of capitalism, to the effects of the assault upon and violation of God's authority and denial of the dignity given to men by God.

In this regard, Islam's way of life is unique in that it is the only path that frees people from worshipping one another in some form or other. Only in the Islamic way of life can all people be freed from worshipping one another by devoting themselves to worshiping God only, accepting guidance from Him only, and submitting only to Him.

This is where the roads go in different directions, and this is the new vision we propose to offer to humanity. This vision and all its practical consequences for human life is the crucial message of which humanity is unaware since it is not a product of Western civilization, nor of Europe's genius, neither Eastern nor Western.

Therefore, we certainly possess something innovative, something unknown to humanity and impossible to be produced by it. However, as previously stated, this innovation needs to manifest itself in a concrete practical manner if it is to be appreciated. It necessitates a society ordering its affairs according to an Islamic system in order to show the innovative potential of such a system to the world. For this to happen, an Islamic revival movement must be initiated in some Muslim country which will eventually be followed by achieving world leadership. So how does this Islamic renaissance come about?

There needs to be a vanguard which sets out with the determination for such a revival, and which is to carry on pursuing the path and plowing through this vast ocean of *Jahiliyya* which has spread throughout all corners of the Earth. This vanguard is to proceed by remaining isolated from this all-encompassing *Jahiliyya* in certain conditions, while simultaneously maintaining some ties with its *Jahiliyya* in others.

As such, this vanguard needs "signposts along the road," milestones which help indicate to the vanguard its starting point, the nature of its role, the responsibility of its function, and the ultimate purpose of its long journey. These signposts are also supposed to indicate the vanguard's stand vis-à-vis this *Jahiliyya* which has spread throughout all the corners of the Earth: Where people converge and can cooperate and where they diverge and must separate; what its characteristics are and what *Jahiliyya*'s characteristics are; how the people of *Jahiliyya* are to be talked to and taught in the language of Islam, and what topics need to be addressed; and where to obtain guidance on all these issues.

These signposts need to be derived from the light of the first source of this faith, the Holy Qur'an, and from its essential teachings, as well as the visions which it inspired in some of its first group of leaders, those whom God raised to fulfill His will through changing the course of history to meet God's prescribed way of life.

I have written *Signposts* for this vanguard that is waiting to be actualized. The book contains four chapters ["The Nature of the Qur'anic Method," "Islamic Concept and Culture," "Jihad in the Cause of God," and "Revival of the Muslim Community and its Characteristics"] extracted from my commentary "Fi Jilal al-Qur'an" [*In the Shade of the Qur'an*] with some changes that are appropriate for the themes of this book. It also contains eight chapters, outside of this introduction, written at different times. The chapters reveal some deep thoughts and truths which I grasped during my meditations over the way of life presented in the Holy Qur'an. These thoughts may appear random and unsystematic, but one thing that is common to all of them is that they are signposts on the road. In sum, they form the first installment of these "signposts" which I hope to follow with further installments every time I have the opportunity of being guided by God to such "signposts." And the guidance is from God.

The Necessity for Islamic Government

AYATOLLAH RUHOLLAH KHOMEINI*

The following selection consists of excerpts from the writings of Ruhollah
Khomeini, a Shi'ite Muslim who was often called *imam* ("leader" or
"model") and *ayatollah* (major religious leader). Khomeini was born
in Iran at the beginning of the twentieth century—some sources say in
1900, others 1902—and by the early 1960s he was acclaimed the "grand
ayatollah." His opposition to the pro-Western government of the Shah
of Iran, Reza Pahlavi, led to Khomeini's forcible exile in 1964. Khomeini
settled in neighboring Iraq, where he continued to denounce the Shah's
regime as ruthless, corrupt, and contrary to the true teachings of Islam.
In 1978 the new leader of Iraq, Saddam Hussein, forced Khomeini into
exile again. This time he settled in a suburb of Paris. From this location
Khomeini continued his campaign against the Shah's government until
massive street demonstrations in Iran's capital persuaded the Shah to flee
to the United States. Khomeini returned to Iran in triumph in February
1979. That December a referendum declared Iran to be an Islamic republic
with Khomeini as its political and religious leader for life—a position he
held until his death in 1989. The following selection, written before the
revolution that brought Khomeini to power, gives a clear indication both
of his objection to "corrupt" regimes, such as that of the Shah, and of
what he thought an Islamic government should do. The explanatory notes
were written by the translator, Hamid Algar.

---

* *Source*: Islam and Revolution: Writings and Declarations of Imam Khomeini, translated by Hamid Algar
(Berkeley, CA: Mizan Press, 1981). Reprinted by permission of Hamid Algar.

THE NECESSITY FOR ISLAMIC GOVERNMENT

A body of laws alone is not sufficient for a society to be reformed. In order for law to ensure the reform and happiness of man, there must be an executive power and an executor. For this reason, God Almighty, in addition to revealing a body of law (i.e., the ordinances of the *shari'a*), has laid down a particular form of government together with executive and administrative institutions.

The Most Noble Messenger [Mohammed] (peace and blessings be upon him) headed the executive and administrative institutions of Muslim society. In addition to conveying the revelation and expounding and interpreting the articles of faith and the ordinances and institutions of Islam, he undertook the implementation of law and the establishment of the ordinances of Islam, thereby bringing into being the Islamic state. He did not content himself with the promulgation of law; rather, he implemented it at the same time, cutting off hands and administering lashings and stonings. After the Most Noble Messenger, his successor had the same duty and function. When the Prophet appointed a successor, it was not for the purpose of expounding articles of faith and law; it was for the implementation of law and the execution of God's ordinances. It was this function—the execution of law and the establishment of Islamic institutions—that made the appointment of a successor such an important matter that the Prophet would have failed to fulfill his mission if he had neglected it. For after the Prophet, the Muslims still needed someone to execute laws and establish the institutions of Islam in society, so that they might attain happiness in this world and the hereafter ...

It is self-evident that the necessity for enactment of the law, which necessitated the formation of a government by the Prophet (upon whom be peace), was not confined or restricted to his time, but continues after his departure from this world. According to one of the noble verses of the Qur'an, the ordinances of Islam are not limited with respect to time or place; they are permanent and must be enacted until the end of time. They were not revealed merely for the time of the Prophet, only to be abandoned thereafter, with retribution and the penal code of Islam no longer to be enacted, or the taxes prescribed by Islam no longer collected, and the defense of the lands and people of Islam suspended. The claim that the laws of Islam may remain in abeyance or are restricted to a particular time or place is contrary to the essential credal bases of Islam. Since the enactment of laws, then, is necessary after the departure of the Prophet from this world, and indeed, will remain so until the end of time, the formation of a government and the establishment of executive and administrative organs are also necessary. Without the formation of a government and the establishment of such organs to ensure that through enactment of the law, all activities of the individual take place in the framework of a just system, chaos and anarchy will prevail and social, intellectual, and moral corruption will arise. The only way to prevent the emergence of anarchy and disorder and to protect society from corruption is to form a government and thus impart order to all the affairs of the country ...

The nature and character of Islamic law and the divine ordinances of the *shari'a* furnish additional proof of the necessity for establishing government, for they indicate that the laws were laid down for the purpose of creating a state and administering the political, economic, and cultural affairs of society.

First, the laws of the *shari'a* embrace a diverse body of laws and regulations, which amounts to a complete social system. In this system of laws, all the needs of man have been met: his dealings with his neighbors, fellow citizens, and clan, as well as children and relatives; the concerns of private and marital life; regulations concerning war and peace and intercourse with other nations; penal and commercial law; and regulations pertaining to trade and agriculture. Islamic law contains provisions relating to the preliminaries of marriage and the form in which it should be contracted, and others relating to the development of the embryo in the womb and what food the parents should eat at the time of conception. It further stipulates the duties that are incumbent upon them while the infant is being suckled, and specifies how the child should be reared, and how the husband and the wife should relate to each other and to their children. Islam provides laws and instructions for all of these matters, aiming, as it does, to produce integrated and virtuous human beings who are walking embodiments of the law, or to put it differently, the law's voluntary and instinctive executors. It is obvious, then, how much care Islam devotes to government and the political and economic relations of society, with the goal of creating conditions conducive to the production of morally upright and virtuous human beings.

The Glorious Qur'an and the Sunna [teachings of Mohammed] contain all the laws and ordinances man needs in order to attain happiness and the perfection of his state ...

Second, if we examine closely the nature and character of the provisions of the law, we realize that their execution and implementation depend upon the formation of a government, and that it is impossible to fulfill the duty of executing God's commands without there being established properly comprehensive administrative and executive organs. Let us now mention certain types of provision in order to illustrate this point; the others you can examine yourselves.

The taxes Islam levies and the form of budget it has established are not merely for the sake of providing subsistence to the poor or feeding the indigent among the descendants of the Prophet (peace and blessings be upon him); they are also intended to make possible the establishment of a great government and to assure its essential expenditures.

For example, *khums* is a huge source of income that accrues to the treasury and represents one item in the budget. According to our Shi'i school of thought, *khums* is to be levied in an equitable manner on all agricultural and commercial profits and all natural resources whether above or below the ground—in short, on all forms of wealth and income. It applies equally to the greengrocer with his stall outside this mosque and to the shipping or mining magnate. They must all pay one-fifth of their surplus income, after customary expenses are deducted, to the Islamic ruler so that it enters the treasury. It is obvious that such a huge income serves the purpose of administering the Islamic state and meeting all its financial needs. If we were to calculate one-fifth of the surplus income of all the Muslim countries (or of the whole world, should it enter the fold of Islam), it would become fully apparent that the purpose for the imposition of such a tax is not merely the upkeep of the *sayyids*[1] or the religious scholars, but on the contrary, something far more significant—namely, meeting the financial needs of the great organs and institutions of government ...

How could the *sayyids* ever need so vast a budget? The *khums* of the bazaar of Baghdad would be enough for the needs of the *sayyids* and the upkeep of the religious teaching institution, as well as all the poor of the Islamic world, quite apart from the *khums* of the bazaars of Tehran, Istanbul, Cairo, and other cities. The provision of such a huge budget must obviously be for the purpose of forming a government and administering the Islamic lands. It was established with the aim of providing for the needs of the people, for public services relating to health, education, defense, and economic development. Further, in accordance with the procedures laid down by Islam for the collection, preservation, and expenditure of this income, all forms of usurpation and embezzlement of public wealth have been forbidden, so that the head of state and all those entrusted with responsibility for conducting public affairs (i.e., members of the government) have no privileges over the ordinary citizen in benefiting from the public income and wealth; all have an equal share ...

Thus, you see that the fiscal provisions of Islam also point to the necessity for establishing a government, for they cannot be fulfilled without the establishment of the appropriate Islamic institutions.

The ordinances pertaining to preservation of the Islamic order and defense of the territorial integrity and the independence of the Islamic *umma*[2] also demanded the formation of a government. An example is the command: "Prepare against them whatever force you can muster and horses tethered" (Qur'an, 8:60), which enjoins the preparation of as much armed defensive force as possible and orders the Muslims to be always on the alert and at the ready, even in time of peace.

If the Muslims had acted in accordance with this command and, after forming a government, made the necessary extensive preparations to be in a state of full readiness for war, a handful of Jews would never have dared to occupy our lands, and to burn and destroy the Masjid al-Aqsa[3] without the people's being capable of making an immediate response. All this has resulted from the failure of the Muslims to fulfill their duty of executing God's law and setting up a righteous and respectable government. If the rulers of the Muslim countries truly represented the believers and enacted God's ordinances, they would set aside their petty differences, abandon their subversive and divisive activities, and join together like the fingers of one hand. Then a handful of wretched Jews (the agents of America, Britain, and other foreign powers) would never have been able to accomplish what they have, no matter how much support they enjoyed from America and Britain. All this has happened because of the incompetence of those who rule over the Muslims.

The verse: "Prepare against them whatever force you can muster" commands you to be as strong and well-prepared as possible, so that your enemies will be unable to oppress you and transgress against you. It is because we have been lacking in unity, strength, and preparedness that we suffer oppression and are at the mercy of foreign aggressors.

There are numerous provisions of the law that cannot be implemented without the establishment of a governmental apparatus; for example, blood money, which must be exacted and delivered to those deserving it, or the corporeal penalties imposed by the law, which must be carried out under the supervision of the Islamic ruler. All of these laws refer back to the institutions of government, for it is governmental power alone that is capable of fulfilling this function.

After the death of the Most Noble Messenger (peace and blessings be upon him), the obstinate enemies of the faith, the Umayyads[4] (God's curses be upon them) did not permit the Islamic state to attain stability with the rule of 'Ali ibn Abi Talib (upon whom be peace). They did not allow a form of government to exist that was pleasing to God, Exalted and Almighty, and to his Most Noble Messenger. They transformed the entire basis of government, and their policies were, for the most part, contradictory to Islam. The form of government of the Umayyads and the Abbasids,[5] and the political and administrative policies they pursued, were anti-Islamic. The form of government was thoroughly perverted by being transformed into a monarchy, like those of the kings of Iran, the emperors of Rome, and the pharaohs of Egypt. For the most part, this non-Islamic form of government has persisted to the present day, as we can see.

Both law and reason require that we not permit governments to retain this non-Islamic or anti-Islamic character. The proofs are clear. First, the existence of a non-Islamic political order necessarily results in the non-implementation of the Islamic political order. Then, all non-Islamic systems of government are the systems of *kufr*,[6] since the ruler in each case is an instance of *taghut*,[7] and it is our duty to remove from the life of Muslim society all traces of *kufr* and destroy them. It is also our duty to create a favorable social environment for the education of believing and virtuous individuals, an environment that is in total contradiction with that produced by the rule of *taghut* and illegitimate power. The social environment created by *taghut* and *shirk*[8] invariably brings about corruption such as you can now observe in Iran, the corruption termed "corruption on earth."[9] This corruption must be swept away, and its instigators punished for their deeds. It is the same corruption that the Pharaoh generated in Egypt with his policies, so that the Qur'an says of him, "Truly he was among the corruptors" (28:4). A believing, pious, just individual cannot possibly exist in a socio-political environment of this nature and still maintain his faith and righteous conduct. He is faced with two choices: either he commits acts that amount to *kufr* and contradict righteousness, or in order not to commit such acts and not to submit to the orders and commands of the *taghut*, the just individual opposes him and struggles against him in order to destroy the environment of corruption. We have in reality, then, no choice but to destroy those systems of government that are corrupt in themselves and also entail the corruption of others, and to overthrow all treacherous, corrupt, oppressive, and criminal regimes.

This is a duty that all Muslims must fulfill, in every one of the Muslim countries, in order to achieve the triumphant political revolution of Islam.

We see, too, that together, the imperialists and the tyrannical self-seeking rulers have divided the Islamic homeland. They have separated the various segments of the Islamic *umma* from each other and artificially created separate nations. There once existed the great Ottoman State, and that, too, the imperialists divided. Russia, Britain, Austria, and other imperialist powers united, and through wars against the Ottomans, each came to occupy or absorb into its sphere of influence part of the Ottoman realm. It is true that most of the Ottoman rulers were incompetent, that some of them were corrupt, and that they followed a monarchical system. Nonetheless, the existence of the Ottoman State represented a threat to the imperialists. It was always possible that righteous individuals might rise up among the people and, with their assistance, seize control of the state, thus putting an end to imperialism by mobilizing the unified resources of the nation. Therefore, after numerous prior wars, the imperialists at the end of World War I divided the Ottoman State, creating in its territories about ten or fifteen petty states.[10] Then each of these was entrusted to one of their servants or a group of their servants, although certain countries were later able to escape the grasp of the agents of imperialism.

In order to assure the unity of the Islamic *umma*, in order to liberate the Islamic homeland from occupation and penetration by the imperialists and their puppet governments, it is imperative that we establish a government. In order to attain the unity and freedom of the Muslim peoples, we must overthrow the oppressive governments installed by the imperialists and bring into existence an Islamic government of justice that will be in the service of the people. The formation of such a government will serve to preserve the disciplined unity of the Muslims; just as Fatimat az-Zahra[11] (upon whom be peace) said in her address: "The Imamate exists for the sake of preserving order among the Muslims and replacing their disunity with unity."

Through the political agents they have placed in power over the people, the imperialists have also imposed on us an unjust economic order, and thereby divided our people into two groups: oppressors and oppressed. Hundreds of millions of Muslims are hungry and deprived of all forms of health care and education, while minorities comprised of the wealthy and powerful live a life of indulgence, licentiousness, and corruption. The hungry and deprived have constantly struggled to free themselves from the oppression of their plundering overlords, and their struggle continues to this day. But their way is blocked by the ruling minorities and the oppressive governmental structures they head. It is our duty to save the oppressed and deprived. It is our duty to be a helper to the oppressed and an enemy to the oppressor …

How can we stay silent and idle today when we see that a band of traitors and usurpers, the agents of foreign powers, have appropriated the wealth and the fruits of labor of hundreds of millions of Muslims—thanks to the support of their masters and through the power of the bayonet—granting the Muslims not the least right to prosperity? It is the duty of Islamic scholars and all Muslims to put an end to this system of oppression and, for the sake of the well-being of hundreds of millions of human beings, to overthrow these oppressive governments and form an Islamic government …

If someone should ask you, "Why has God, the All-Wise, appointed holders of authority and commanded you to obey them?" you should answer him as follows: "He has done so for various causes and reasons. One is that men have been set upon a certain well-defined path and commanded not to stray from it, not to transgress against the established limits and norms, for if they were to stray, they would fall prey to corruption. Now men would not be able to keep to their ordained path and to enact God's laws unless a trustworthy and protective individual (or power) were appointed over them with responsibility for this matter, to prevent them from stepping outside the sphere of the licit and transgressing against the rights of others. If no such restraining individual or power were appointed, nobody would voluntarily abandon any pleasure or interest of his own that might result in harm or corruption to others; everybody would engage in oppressing and harming others for the sake of their own pleasures and interests.

"Another reason and cause is this: we do not see a single group, nation, or religious community that has ever been able to exist without an individual entrusted with the maintenance of its laws and institutions—in short, a head or a leader; for such a person is essential for fulfilling the affairs of religion and the world. It is not permissible, therefore, according to divine wisdom, that God should leave men, His creatures, without a leader and guide, for He knows well that they depend on the existence of such a person for their own survival and perpetuation. It is under his leadership that they fight against their enemies, divide the public income among themselves, perform Friday and congregational prayer, and foreshorten the arms of the transgressors who would encroach on the rights of the oppressed.

"Another proof and cause is this: were God not to appoint an Imam over men to maintain law and order, to serve the people faithfully as a vigilant trustee, religion would fall victim to obsolescence and decay. Its rites and institutions would vanish; the customs and ordinances of Islam would be transformed or even deformed. Heretical innovators would add things to religion and atheists and unbelievers would subtract things from it, presenting it to the Muslims in an inaccurate manner. For we see that men are prey to defects; they are not perfect and must needs strive after perfection. Moreover, they disagree with each other, having varying inclinations and discordant states. If God, therefore, had not appointed over men one who would maintain order and law and protect the revelation brought by the Prophet, in the manner we have described, men would fall prey to corruption; the institutions, laws, customs, and ordinances of Islam would be transformed; and faith and its content would be completely changed, resulting in the corruption of all humanity."

As you can deduce ... there are numerous proofs and causes that necessitate formation of a government and establishment of an authority. These proofs, causes, and arguments are not temporary in their validity or limited to a particular time, and the necessity for the formation of a government, therefore, is perpetual. For example, it will always happen that men overstep the limits laid down by Islam and transgress against the rights of others for the sake of their personal pleasure and benefit ... The wisdom of the Creator has decreed that men should live in accordance with justice and act within the limits set by divine law. This wisdom is eternal and immutable, and constitutes one of the norms of God Almighty. Today and always, therefore, the existence of a holder of authority, a ruler who acts as trustee and maintains the institutions and laws of Islam, is a necessity—a ruler who prevents cruelty, oppression, and violation of the rights of others; who is a trustworthy and vigilant guardian of God's creatures; who guides men to the teachings, doctrines, laws, and institutions of Islam; and who prevents the undesirable changes that atheists and the enemies of religion wish to introduce in the laws and institutions of Islam ...

If the ordinances of Islam are to remain in effect, then, if encroachment by oppressive ruling classes on the rights of the weak is to be prevented, if ruling minorities are not to be permitted to plunder and corrupt the people for the sake of pleasure and material interest, if the Islamic order is to be preserved and all individuals are to pursue the just path of Islam without any deviation, if innovation and the approval of anti-Islamic laws by sham parliaments[12] are to be prevented, if the influence of foreign powers in the Islamic lands is to be destroyed—government is necessary. None of these aims can be achieved without government and the organs of the state. It is a righteous government, of course, that is needed, one presided over by a ruler who will be a trustworthy and righteous trustee. Those who presently govern us are of no use at all for they are tyrannical, corrupt, and highly incompetent.

In the past we did not act in concert and unanimity in order to establish proper government and overthrow treacherous and corrupt rulers. Some people were apathetic and reluctant even to discuss the theory of Islamic government, and some went so far as to praise oppressive rulers. It is for this reason that we find ourselves in the present state. The influence and sovereignty of Islam in society have declined; the nation of Islam has fallen victim to division and weakness; the laws of Islam have remained in abeyance and been subjected to change and modification; and the imperialists have propagated foreign laws and alien culture among the Muslims through their agents for the sake of their evil purposes, causing people to be infatuated with the West. It was our lack of a leader, a guardian, and our lack of institutions of leadership that made all this possible. We need righteous and proper organs of government; that much is self-evident.

NOTES

1   *Sayyids*: the descendants of the Prophet through his daughter Fatima and son-in-law 'Ali, the first of the Twelve Imams.
2   *Umma*: the entire Islamic community, without territorial or ethnic distinction.
3   Masjid al-Aqsa: the site in Jerusalem where the Prophet ascended to heaven in the eleventh year of his mission (Qur'an, 17:1), also the complex of mosques and buildings erected on the site. The chief of these was extensively damaged by arson in 1969, two years after the Zionist usurpation of Jerusalem.
4   Umayyads: members of the dynasty that ruled at Damascus from 41/682 until 132/750 and transformed the caliphate into a hereditary institution. Mu'awiya, frequently mentioned in these pages, was the first of the Umayyad line.
5   Abbasids: the dynasty that replaced the Umayyads and established a new caliphal capital in Baghdad. With the rise of various local rulers, generally of military origin, the power of the Abbasids began to decline from the fourth/tenth century and it was brought to an end by the Mongol conquest in 656/1258.
6   *Kufr*: the rejection of divine guidance; the antithesis of Islam.
7   *Taghut*: one who surpasses all bounds in his despotism and tyranny and claims the prerogatives of divinity for himself, whether explicitly or implicitly.
8   *Shirk*: the assignment of partners to God, either by believing in a multiplicity of gods, or by assigning divine attributes and prerogatives to other-than-God.
9   "Corruption on earth": a broad term including not only moral corruption, but also subversion of the public good, embezzlement and usurpation of public wealth, conspiring with the enemies of the community against its security, and working in general for the overthrow of the Islamic order. See the commentary on Qur'an, 5:33 in Tabataba'i, *al-Mizan*, V, 330–332.
10 It may be apposite to quote here the following passage from a secret report drawn up in January 1916 by T. E. Lawrence, the British organizer of the so-called Arab revolt led by Sharif Husayn of Mecca: "Husayn's activity seems beneficial to us, because it matches with our immediate aims, the breakup of the Islamic bloc and the defeat and disruption of the Ottoman Empire ... The Arabs are even less stable than the Turks. If properly handled they would remain in a state of political mosaic, a tissue of small

jealous principalities incapable of political cohesion." See Philip Knightley and Colin Simpson, *The Secret Lives of Lawrence of Arabia* (New York, 1971), p. 55.

11 Fatimat az-Zahra: Fatima, the daughter of the Prophet and wife of Imam 'Ali.

12 Here the allusion may be in particular to the so-called Family Protection Law of 1967, which Imam Khomeini denounced as contrary to Islam in an important ruling. See Imam Khomeini, *Tauzih al-Masa'il*, n.p., n.d., pp. 462–463, par. 2836, and p. 441.

Jihad Against Jews and Crusaders
World Islamic Front Statement

OSAMA BIN LADEN AND OTHERS*

In February of 1998—three years before the terrorist attacks of September 11, 2001, and five years before the U.S. invasion of Iraq—Osama bin Laden (or Usamah Bin-Ladin) and four other radical Islamist leaders issued the statement reprinted on the following pages. This statement purports to be a *fatwa*, a pronouncement of Islamic law by Islamic scholars, that makes the killing of "Americans and their allies—civilians and military—[a] duty for every Muslim who can do it in any country in which it is possible to do it ... " As the two preceding selections indicate, the roots of radical Islamism are quite deep. In this *fatwa*, however, bin Laden and the other leaders of the "World Islamic Front" concentrate on more immediate grievances that stemmed from the Persian Gulf War of 1991. Bin Laden was killed by a team of U.S. Navy SEALs in 2011 and buried at sea.

* *Source:* Translation by the Federation of American Scientists (http://fas.org/irp/world/para/docs/980223-fatwa.htm). Reprinted by permission of the Federation of American Scientists.

JIHAD AGAINST JEWS AND CRUSADERS

23 February 1998

...

Shaykh Usamah Bin-Muhammad Bin-Ladin Ayman al-Zawahiri, amir of the Jihad Group in Egypt

Abu-Yasir Rifa'i Ahmad Taha, Egyptian Islamic Group

Shaykh Mir Hamzah, secretary of the Jamiat-ul-Ulema-e-Pakistan

Fazlur Rahman, amir of the Jihad Movement in Bangladesh

Praise be to Allah, who revealed the Book [*Qur'an*], controls the clouds, defeats factionalism, and says in His Book: "But when the forbidden months are past, then fight and slay the pagans wherever ye find them, seize them, beleaguer them, and lie in wait for them in every stratagem (of war)"; and peace be upon our Prophet, Muhammad Bin-'Abdallah, who said: I have been sent with the sword between my hands to ensure that no one but Allah is worshipped, Allah who put my livelihood under the shadow of my spear and who inflicts humiliation and scorn on those who disobey my orders.

The Arabian Peninsula has never—since Allah made it flat, created its desert, and encircled it with seas—been stormed by any forces like the crusader armies spreading in it like locusts, eating its riches and wiping out its plantations. All this is happening at a time in which nations are attacking Muslims like people fighting over a plate of food. In the light of the grave situation and the lack of support, we and you are obliged to discuss current events, and we should all agree on how to settle the matter.

No one argues today about three facts that are known to everyone; we will list them, in order to remind everyone:

First, for over seven years [from the 1991 Gulf War to 1998, when this statement was written] the United States has been occupying the lands of Islam in the holiest of places, the Arabian Peninsula, plundering its riches, dictating to its rulers, humiliating its people, terrorizing its neighbors, and turning its bases in the Peninsula into a spearhead through which to fight the neighboring Muslim peoples.

If some people have in the past argued about the fact of the occupation, all the people of the Peninsula have now acknowledged it. The best proof of this is the Americans' continuing aggression against the Iraqi people, using the Peninsula as a staging post, even though all its rulers are against their territories being used to that end, but they are helpless.

Second, despite the great devastation inflicted on the Iraqi people by the crusader-Zionist alliance, and despite the huge number of those killed, which has exceeded 1 million ... despite all this, the Americans are once again trying to repeat the horrific massacres, as though they are not content with the protracted blockade imposed after the ferocious war or the fragmentation and devastation.

So here they come to annihilate what is left of this people and to humiliate their Muslim neighbors.

Third, if the Americans' aims behind these wars are religious and economic, the aim is also to serve the Jews' petty state [Israel] and divert attention from its occupation of Jerusalem and murder of Muslims there. The best proof of this is their eagerness to destroy Iraq, the strongest neighboring Arab state, and their endeavor to fragment all the states of the region such as Iraq, Saudi Arabia, Egypt, and Sudan into paper statelets and through their disunion and weakness to guarantee Israel's survival and the continuation of the brutal crusade occupation of the Peninsula.

All these crimes and sins committed by the Americans are a clear declaration of war on Allah, his messenger, and Muslims. And *ulema* [Muslim scholars] have throughout Islamic history unanimously agreed that the jihad is an individual duty if the enemy destroys the Muslim countries. This was revealed by Imam Bin-Qadamah in "Al-Mughni," Imam al-Kisa'i in "Al-Bada'i," al-Qurtubi in his interpretation, and the shaykh of al-Islam in his books, where he said: "As for the fighting to repulse [an enemy], it is aimed at defending sanctity and religion, and it is a duty as agreed [by the ulema]. Nothing is more sacred than belief except repulsing an enemy who is attacking religion and life."

On that basis, and in compliance with Allah's order, we issue the following fatwa to all Muslims:

The ruling to kill the Americans and their allies—civilians and military—is an individual duty for every Muslim who can do it in any country in which it is possible to do it, in order to liberate the al-Aqsa Mosque in Jerusalem and the holy mosque [Mecca] from their grip, and in order for their armies to move out of all the lands of Islam, defeated and unable to threaten any Muslim. This is in accordance with the words of Almighty Allah, "and fight the pagans all together as they fight you all together," and "fight them until there is no more tumult or oppression, and there prevail justice and faith in Allah."

This is in addition to the words of Almighty Allah: "And why should ye not fight in the cause of Allah and of those who, being weak, are ill-treated (and oppressed)?—women and children, whose cry is: 'Our Lord, rescue us from this town, whose people are oppressors; and raise for us from thee one who will help!' "

We—with Allah's help—call on every Muslim who believes in Allah and wishes to be rewarded to comply with Allah's order to kill the Americans and plunder their money wherever and whenever they find it. We also call on Muslim ulema, leaders, youths, and soldiers to launch the raid on Satan's U.S. troops and the devil's supporters allying with them, and to displace those who are behind them so that they may learn a lesson.

Almighty Allah said: "O ye who believe, give your response to Allah and His Apostle, when He calleth you to that which will give you life. And know that Allah cometh between a man and his heart, and that it is He to whom ye shall all be gathered."

Almighty Allah also says: "O ye who believe, what is the matter with you, that when ye are asked to go forth in the cause of Allah, ye cling so heavily to the earth! Do ye prefer the life of this world to the hereafter? But little is the comfort of this life, as compared with the hereafter. Unless ye go forth, He will punish you with a grievous penalty, and put others in your place; but Him ye would not harm in the least. For Allah hath power over all things."

Almighty Allah also says: "So lose no heart, nor fall into despair. For ye must gain mastery if ye are true in faith."

Declaration of a Caliphate

ABU BAKR AL-BAGHDADI (ISIS)*

In the wake of the 2003 American invasion of Iraq and the chaos that ensued, a new variant of radical Islamism emerged. Beginning as a branch of al-Qaeda in Iraq, this group—now commonly referred to as ISIS (Islamic State of Iraq and Syria)—has opportunistically used the civil war in Syria to conquer large swathes of territory bridging both nations. In 2014, the leader of ISIS, the radical Sunni cleric Abu Bakr al-Baghdadi, declared this land to be a new *caliphate*, or geographical center for the transnational community of Muslim believers, known as the *umma*. In this speech, Baghdadi calls on all "true" Muslims to migrate to the caliphate in order to serve as *mujahideen* (or holy warriors) in a *jihad* (or violent struggle) against their enemies, which include other Muslims as well as the West. ISIS believes that those who fight and die in the service of their new state will become martyrs and enjoy life everlasting, thus achieving true happiness. The willingness of Baghdadi's followers to heed this call by engaging in spectacles of mass terror—acts which ISIS regards as a just response to Western imperialism and other global assaults on Islam—has shocked the world.

* *Source*: Available at http://www.gatestoneinstitute.org/4387/baghdadi-isis-caliphate.

DECLARATION OF A CALIPHATE

Truly all praise belongs to Allah. We praise Him, and seek His help and His forgiveness. We seek refuge with Allah from the evils of our souls and from the consequences of our deeds. Whomever Allah guides can never be led astray, and whomever Allah leads astray can never be guided.

I testify that there is no god except Allah – alone without any partners – and I testify that Muhammad (peace and blessings be upon him) is His slave and Messenger ...

And there is no deed in this virtuous month or in any other month better than jihad in the path of Allah, so take advantage of this opportunity and walk the path of you righteous predecessors. Support the religion of Allah through jihad in the path of Allah. Go forth, O mujahidin in the path of Allah. Terrify the enemies of Allah and seek death in the places where you expect to find it, for the dunyā (worldly life) will come to an end, and the hereafter will last forever.

{So do not weaken and call for peace while you are superior; and Allah is with you and will never deprive you of [the reward of] your deeds. This worldly life is only amusement and diversion} [Muhammad: 35-36].

{And this worldly life is not but diversion and amusement. And indeed, the home of the Hereafter – that is the [eternal] life, if only they knew} [Al-'Ankabūt: 64].

{But the enduring good deeds are better to your Lord for reward and better for [one's] hope} [AlKahf: 46].

And blessed is the one who parts with his dunyā in Ramadan and meets his Lord on a day from amongst the days of forgiveness.

O mujahidin in the path of Allah, be monks during the night and be knights during the day. Bring joy to the hearts of a believing people, and show the tawāghīt (rulers who claim Allah's rights) what they are wary of.

O mujahidin in the path of Allah, truly the matter is that of Allah's religion and His commodity. You only have one soul, and an appointed time of death that will neither be hastened nor delayed. It is a matter of Paradise and Hellfire, happiness and misery. As for the religion of Allah, then it will be victorious. Allah has promised to bring victory to the religion. And as for Allah's commodity, then it is precious and valuable. Indeed His commodity is costly. Indeed His commodity is Paradise. As for the soul, then what a lowly, miserable, wretched soul it is if it does not seek what is with Allah and does not support the religion of Allah.

By Allah, we will never be mujahidin as long as we are stingy with our lives and our wealth. By Allah, we will never be truthful as long as we do not sacrifice our lives and wealth in order to raise high the word of Allah and bring victory to the religion of Allah.

{Indeed, Allah has purchased from the believers their lives and their properties [in exchange] for that they will have Paradise. They fight in the cause of Allah, so they kill and are killed. [It is] a true promise [binding] upon Him in the Torah and the Gospel and the Qur'an. And who is truer to his covenant than Allah? So rejoice in your transaction which you have contracted. And it is that which is the great triumph} [At-Tawbah: 111}.

So take up arms, take up arms, O soldiers of the Islamic State! And fight, fight!

Beware of becoming deluded and losing strength. Beware, for the dunyā has come to you reluctantly, so kick it down, trample it, and leave it behind you. Indeed, what is with Allah is better and more lasting.

Indeed, the ummah of Islam is watching your jihad with eyes of hope, and indeed you have brothers in many parts of the world being inflicted with the worst kinds of torture. Their honor is being violated. Their blood is being spilled. Prisoners are moaning and crying for help. Orphans and widows are complaining of their plight. Women who have lost their children are weeping. Masājid (plural of masjid) are desecrated and sanctities are violated. Muslims' rights are forcibly seized in China, India, Palestine, Somalia, the Arabian Peninsula, the Caucasus, Shām (the Levant), Egypt, Iraq, Indonesia, Afghanistan, the Philippines, Ahvaz, Iran [by the rāfidah (shia)], Pakistan, Tunisia, Libya, Algeria and Morocco, in the East and in the West.

So raise your ambitions, O soldiers of the Islamic State! For your brothers all over the world are waiting for your rescue, and are anticipating your brigades. It is enough for you to just look at the scenes that have reached you from Central Africa, and from Burma before that. What is hidden from us is far worse.

So by Allah, we will take revenge! By Allah, we will take revenge! Even if it takes a while, we will take revenge, and every amount of harm against the ummah will be responded to with multitudes more against the perpetrator.

{And those who, when tyranny strikes them, they defend themselves} [Ash-Shūrā: 39].

And the one who commences is the more oppressive.

Soon, by Allah's permission, a day will come when the Muslim will walk everywhere as a master, having honor, being revered, with his head raised high and his dignity preserved. Anyone who dares to offend him will be disciplined, and any hand that reaches out to harm him will be cut off.

So let the world know that we are living today in a new era. Whoever was heedless must now be alert. Whoever was sleeping must now awaken. Whoever was shocked and amazed must comprehend. The Muslims today have a loud, thundering statement, and possess heavy boots. They have a statement that will cause the world to hear and understand the meaning of terrorism, and boots that will trample the idol of nationalism, destroy the idol of democracy and uncover its deviant nature.

So listen, O ummah of Islam. Listen and comprehend. Stand up and rise. For the time has come for you to free yourself from the shackles of weakness, and stand in the face of tyranny, against the treacherous rulers – the agents of the crusaders and the atheists, and the guards of the jews.

O ummah of Islam, indeed the world today has been divided into two camps and two trenches, with no third camp present: The camp of Islam and faith, and the camp of kufr (disbelief) and hypocrisy – the camp of the Muslims and the mujahidin everywhere, and the camp of the jews, the crusaders, their allies, and with them the rest of the nations and religions of kufr, all being led by America and Russia, and being mobilized by the jews.

Indeed the Muslims were defeated after the fall of their khilāfah (caliphate). Then their state ceased to exist, so the disbelievers were able to weaken and humiliate the Muslims, dominate them in every region, plunder their wealth and resources, and rob them of their rights. They accomplished this by attacking and occupying their lands, placing their treacherous agents in power to rule the Muslims with an iron fist, and spreading dazzling and deceptive slogans such as: civilization, peace, co-existence, freedom, democracy, secularism, baathism, nationalism, and patriotism, among other false slogans.

Those rulers continue striving to enslave the Muslims, pulling them away from their religion with those slogans. So either the Muslim pulls away from his religion, disbelieves in Allah, and disgracefully submits to the manmade shirk (polytheistic) laws of the east and west, living despicably and disgracefully as a follower, by repeating those slogans without will and honor, or he lives persecuted, targeted, and expelled, to end up being killed, imprisoned, or terribly tortured, on the accusation of terrorism. Because terrorism is to disbelieve in those slogans and to believe in Allah. Terrorism is to refer to Allah's law for judgment. Terrorism is to worship Allah as He ordered you. Terrorism is to refuse humiliation, subjugation, and subordination [to the kuffār – infidels]. Terrorism is for the Muslim to live as a Muslim, honorably with might and freedom. Terrorism is to insist upon your rights and not give them up.

But terrorism does not include the killing of Muslims in Burma and the burning of their homes. Terrorism does not include the dismembering and disemboweling of the Muslims in the Philippines, Indonesia, and Kashmir. Terrorism does not include the killing of Muslims in the Caucasus and expelling them from their lands. Terrorism does not include making mass graves for the Muslims in Bosnia and Herzegovina, and the slaughtering of their children. Terrorism does not include the destruction of Muslims' homes in Palestine, the seizing of their lands, and the violation and desecration of their sanctuaries and families. Terrorism does not include the burning of masājid in Egypt, the destruction of the Muslims' homes there, the rape of their chaste women, and the oppression of the mujahidin in the Sinai Peninsula and elsewhere.

Terrorism does not include the extreme torture and degradation of Muslims in East Turkistan and Iran [by the rāfidah], as well as preventing them from receiving their most basic rights. Terrorism does not include the filling of prisons everywhere with Muslim captives. Terrorism does not include the waging of war against chastity and hijab (Muslim women's clothing) in France and Tunis. It does not include the propagation of betrayal, prostitution, and adultery.

Terrorism does not include the insulting of the Lord of Mightiness, the cursing of the religion, and the mockery of our Prophet (peace be upon him). Terrorism does not include the slaughtering of Muslims in Central Africa like sheep, while no one weeps for them and denounces their slaughter.

All this is not terrorism. Rather it is freedom, democracy, peace, security, and tolerance! Sufficient for us is Allah, and He is the best Disposer of affairs.

{And they resented them not except because they believed in Allah, the Exalted in Might, the Praiseworthy} [Al-Burūj: 8].

O Muslims everywhere, glad tidings to you and expect good. Raise your head high, for today – by Allah's grace – you have a state and khilāfah, which will return your dignity, might, rights, and leadership. It is a state where the Arab and non-Arab, the white man and black man, the easterner and westerner are all brothers. It is a khilāfah that gathered the Caucasian, Indian, Chinese, Shāmī, Iraqi, Yemeni, Egyptian, Maghribī (North African), American, French, German, and Australian. Allah brought their hearts together, and thus, they became brothers by His grace, loving each other for the sake of Allah, standing in a single trench, defending and guarding each other, and sacrificing themselves for one another. Their blood mixed and became one, under a single flag and goal, in one pavilion, enjoying this blessing, the blessing of faithful brotherhood. If kings were to taste this blessing, they would abandon their kingdoms and fight over this grace. So all praise and thanks are due to Allah.

Therefore, rush O Muslims to your state. Yes, it is your state. Rush, because Syria is not for the Syrians, and Iraq is not for the Iraqis. The earth is Allah's. {Indeed, the earth belongs to Allah. He causes to inherit it whom He wills of His servants. And the [best] outcome is for the righteous} [Al-A'rāf: 128]. The State is a state for all Muslims. The land is for the Muslims, all the Muslims.

O Muslims everywhere, whoever is capable of performing hijrah (emigration) to the Islamic State, then let him do so, because hijrah to the land of Islam is obligatory.

Allah (the Exalted) said, {Indeed, those whom the angels take [in death] while wronging themselves – [the angels] will say, "In what [condition] were you?" They will say, "We were oppressed in the land." The angels will say, "Was not the earth of Allah spacious [enough] for you to emigrate therein?" For those, their refuge is Hell – and evil it is as a destination} [An-Nisā': 97].

So rush, O Muslims, with your religion to Allah as muhājirīn (emigrants). {And whoever emigrates for the cause of Allah will find on the earth many [alternative] locations and abundance. And whoever leaves his home as an emigrant to Allah and His Messenger and then death overtakes him – his reward has already become incumbent upon Allah. And Allah is ever Forgiving and Merciful} [AnNisā': 100].

We make a special call to the scholars, fuqahā' (experts in Islamic jurisprudence), and callers, especially the judges, as well as people with military, administrative, and service expertise, and medical doctors and engineers of all different specializations and fields. We call them and remind them to fear Allah, for their emigration is wājib 'aynī (an individual obligation), so that they can answer the dire need of the Muslims for them. People are ignorant of their religion and they thirst for those who can teach them and help them understand it. So fear Allah, O slaves of Allah.

O soldiers of the Islamic State, do not be awestruck by the great numbers of your enemy, for Allah is with you. I do not fear for you the numbers of your opponents, nor do I fear your neediness and poverty, for Allah (the Exalted) has promised your Prophet (peace be upon him) that you will not be wiped out by famine, and your enemy will not himself conquer you and violate your land. Allah placed your provision under the shades of your spears. Rather, I fear for you your own sins. Accept each other and do not dispute. Come together and do not argue. Fear Allah in private and public, openly and secretly. Stay away from sins. Expel from your ranks those who openly commit sin. Be wary of pride, haughtiness, and arrogance. Do not become proud on account of gaining some victories. Humble yourselves before Allah. Do not be arrogant towards Allah's slaves. Do not underestimate your enemy regardless of how much strength you gain and how much your numbers grow.

I also remind you to attend to the Muslims and the tribes of Ahlus-Sunnah (the Sunnis) with goodness. Stay awake guarding them so they can be safe and at rest. Be their support. Respond with kindness if they do you wrong. Be gentle with them, giving them as much pardon as you can. Persevere, endure, and remain stationed. Know that today you are the defenders of the religion and the guards of the land of Islam. You will face tribulation and malāhim (fierce battles). Verily, the best place for your blood to be spilled is on the path to liberate the Muslim prisoners imprisoned behind the walls of the tawāghīt. So prepare your arms, and supply yourselves with piety. Persevere in reciting the Qur'an with comprehension of its meanings and practice of its teachings.

This is my advice to you. If you hold to it, you will conquer Rome [i.e., the West] and own the world, if Allah wills.

{Our Lord, we have believed in what You revealed and have followed the Messenger, so register us among the witnesses [to truth]} [Āl 'Imrān: 53].

{Our Lord, do not impose blame upon us if we have forgotten or erred. Our Lord, and lay not upon us a burden like that which You laid upon those before us. Our Lord, and burden us not with that which we have no ability to bear. And pardon us; and forgive us; and have mercy upon us. You are our protector, so give us victory over the disbelieving people} [Al-Baqarah: 286].